D0022556

DATE DUE

Unless Recalled Earlier		
OCT - 4 1994		
MAR 2 2 1995		
JUN 5 1997 NOV 2 1 1997		
OCT 2 8 1999		

DEMCO 38-297

The Geometry of Computer Graphics

The Wadsworth & Brooks/Cole Mathematics Series

Series Editors
Raoul H. Bott, Harvard University
David Eisenbud, Brandeis University
Hugh L. Montgomery, University of Michigan
Paul J. Sally, University of Chicago
Barry Simon, California Institute of Technology
Richard P. Stanley, Massachusetts Institute of Technology

M. Adams, V. Guillemin, *Measure Theory and Probability*

W. Beckner, A. Calderón, R. Fefferman, P. Jones, *Conference on Harmonic Analysis in Honor of Antoni Zygmund*

G. Chartrand, L. Lesniak, *Graphs & Digraphs, Second Edition*

W. Derrick, *Complex Analysis and Applications, Second Edition*

J. Dieudonné, *History of Algebraic Geometry*

R. Dudley, *Real Analysis and Probability*

R. Durrett, *Brownian Motion and Martingales in Analysis*

D. Eisenbud, J. Harris, *Schemes: The Language of Modern Algebraic Geometry*

R. Epstein, W. Carnielli, *Computability: Computable Functions, Logic, and the Foundations of Mathematics*

S. Fisher, *Complex Variables, Second Edition*

G. Folland, *Fourier Analysis and Its Applications*

A. Garsia, *Topics in Almost Everywhere Convergence*

P. Garrett, *Holomorphic Hilbert Modular Forms*

R. Gunning, *Introduction to Holomorphic Functions of Several Variables*
Volume I: Function Theory
Volume II: Local Theory
Volume III: Homological Theory

H. Helson, *Harmonic Analysis*

J. Kevorkian, *Partial Differential Equations: Analytical Solution Techniques*

S. Krantz, *Function Theory of Several Complex Variables, Second Edition*

R. McKenzie, G. McNulty, W. Taylor, *Algebras, Lattices, Varieties, Volume I*

E. Mendelson, *Introduction to Mathematical Logic, Third Edition*

D. Passman, *A Course in Ring Theory*

B. Sagan, *The Symmetric Group: Representations, Combinatorial Algorithms, and Symmetric Functions*

R. Salem, *Algebraic Numbers and Fourier Analysis* and L. Carleson, *Selected Problems on Exceptional Sets*

R. Stanley, *Enumerative Combinatorics, Volume I*

J. Strikwerda, *Finite Difference Schemes and Partial Differential Equations*

K. Stromberg, *An Introduction to Classical Real Analysis*

W. Taylor, *The Geometry of Computer Graphics*

The Geometry of Computer Graphics

Walter F. Taylor
University of Colorado

Wadsworth & Brooks/Cole Advanced Books & Software
Pacific Grove, California

RECEIVED

AUG - 3 1993

MSU - LIBRARY

T
385
. T39
1992

Wadsworth & Brooks/Cole Advanced Books & Software
A Division of Wadsworth, Inc.

© 1992 by Wadsworth, Inc., Belmont, California 94002. All rights reserved. No part of this book may be reproduced, stored in a retrieval system, or transcribed, in any form or by any means—electronic, mechanical, photocopying, recording or otherwise—without the prior written permission of the publisher, Brooks/Cole Publishing Company, Pacific Grove, California 93950–5098, a division of Wadsworth, Inc.

Printed in the United States of America

10 9 8 7 6 5 4 3 2 1

Library of Congress Cataloging-in-Publication Data
Taylor, W. (Walter), [date]–
  The geometry of computer graphics / Walter Taylor.
    p.   cm. — (The Wadsworth & Brooks/Cole mathematics series)

  Includes index.
  ISBN 0-534-17100-1
  1. Computer graphics.   I. Title.   II. Series.
T385.T39 1991   91-26236
006.6—dc20   CIP

PostScript is a registered trademark of Adobe Systems, Inc.; **UNIX** is a registered trademark of AT&T; **Derive** is a registered trademark of Soft Warehouse, Inc.; **Macsyma** is a trademark of Symbolics Inc.; **Maple** is a registered trademark of Waterloo Maple Software; **Mathematica** is a registered trademark of Wolfram Research, Inc. **Tektronix** is a trademark of Tektronix, Inc. The **Yale Bright Star Catalog** is copyright by the Yale University Astronomy Department. All other product names herein are mentioned for educational purposes and are trademarks or registered trademarks of their respective owners.

Sponsoring Editor: *John Kimmel*
Editorial Assistant: *Nancy Miaoulis*
Production Coordinator: *Marlene Thom*
Manuscript Editors: *Phyllis Cairns* and *Harriet Foster*
Interior Design: *Vernon T. Boes*
Cover Design: *Lisa Thompson*
Cover Illustration: *Walter Taylor*
Figure 6.52: *Paul R. Hovda*
Art Coordinator: *Cloyce J. Wall*
Interior Illustration: *Lotus Art* and *Roger Knox*
Cover Printing: *Phoenix Color Corporation*
Printing and Binding: *Arcata Graphics/Fairfield*

Preface

This book is a direct presentation of elementary analytic and projective geometry, as modeled by vectors and matrices and as applied to computer graphics. It shows the reader how to translate these notions of geometry into computer code that will generate pictures representing the relevant concepts. This approach of matrices and computer programming permits one to model a wide variety of geometrical situations from scratch. The diligent student will be able to reproduce all of the book's figures on a personal computer. Along the way, I have included illustrative material on many short topics (spirals, helices, wakes, Bézier curves and splines, tilings, functions of two variables, astronomy, stereo pairs, etc.) to give students an overview of geometry.

PREREQUISITES

The book is written as a course of study for advanced undergraduates. The ideal student will have had two or three semesters of calculus, a semester (or quarter) of linear algebra, and some experience in a structured programming language such as Pascal or C. Students are expected to come both from pure and applied mathematics, and from computer science and various branches of engineering. Moreover, I hope that the book will suffice for readers who wish to explore this material on their own.

A student with the above-mentioned calculus experience will be accustomed to thinking in terms of coordinate geometry (for example, the defining of a curve in the x, y-plane) and will have the mathematical maturity needed to study pure mathematics without immediate feedback. Except in one section, the reader will need calculus more for these intangible benefits than for its subject matter of differentiation, integration and series. The exception is §3.4, which contains a number of geometric topics from calculus and which can be skipped without loss of continuity. Thus, the calculus prerequisite could be relaxed if other circumstances were auspicious.

The most important prerequisite is that of linear algebra, which is the theoretical basis for analytic and projective geometry and for the matrices that represent motions and projections of these geometries. Chapter 1 is a self-contained treatment of the linear algebra that we will need, which is included to establish notation and as a basis for later applications. What one does with this material depends very much on the situation. One extreme would be to include all of Chapter 1 in a course on applied linear algebra for students who begin with no knowledge in this subject. At the other extreme, one could relax the linear algebra prerequisite to a knowledge of matrix theory and begin a review of matrices in §4.5–§4.7 and §5.3, thereby skipping Chapter 1 altogether.

The prerequisite of computing experience is very flexible. Experience on any language or machine is valuable, and so one cannot demand any specific background. This book contains enough examples in the C language to give the reader a rudimentary passive knowledge of that language. An active knowledge of some computer language is needed, but this could probably be acquired as one goes along, at the expense of going slower. In a class setting, some prerequisites are useful for keeping the class together and for reassuring students at the beginning of the semester that they will be able to keep up.

The teaching of this material is accessible to any professional mathematician with some experience in computing or computer scientist with a flair for geometry. To teach this material successfully one should prepare by making a clear assessment of how best to implement the methods of Chapter 2 using available systems, and by working a large number of the examples in advance. The ideas of Chapter 2 are intended to be independent of machine and language, but some thought and experimentation may be required to make them work in a given environment. To aid the instructor in setting things up, the publisher is making available a diskette that contains (in complete form) many of the computer files described in the book, such as programs and databases, as well as solutions to some of the exercises, the author's programs for some of the figures, and various other utilities.

NECESSARY HARDWARE AND SOFTWARE

The only essential hardware in reading this book is a computer with a graphic output device (and a language to command that device). For example, a laser printer that accepts PostScript (or some other graphic language) will serve the needs of an entire class. The only essential software is an implementation of a programming language (C, Pascal, Lisp, and so on) for that computer. Chapter 2 discusses these requirements more thoroughly. These minimum requirements will suffice for doing all the exercises, but one can also make good use of more extensive software and hardware. For example, different students in a class may prefer to use different programming languages. One's software library begins with the diskette mentioned above and will obviously be extended through practicing on the exercises of the book, and possibly through sharing with other users. As for hardware, it is helpful to have as many options as possible: some students like to work on a (networked) minicomputer or mainframe, whereas others may prefer working on their own PCs, and so on. Any workstation or PC with a graphics screen can be programmed as a graphic output device. (Color, by the way, is not important for this work, although we mention a couple of color examples in §6.4.5.)

Advanced mathematical software (such as Mathematica) is not needed for the study of this book. Such software is capable of generating pictures like ours almost automatically. For example, in a few hours you can learn enough Mathematica to command a picture like our cover drawing (a rendition in color of a function of two variables). From this book's point of view, that drawing is the fruition of a semester's work in learning the necessary mathematical and programming skills (which have been incorporated into Mathematica and similar programs). So, one should maintain a sense of purpose in deciding when to use Mathematica and its relatives. An inner geometric understanding of graphics comes from working directly with the relevant concepts (especially languages and projections); later, one can make good use of all the features of Mathematica (which go beyond those of this book).

HOW TO USE THIS BOOK

This material can be learned at two levels. One can learn vector spaces, linear transformations and projective geometry, or one can learn vectors, matrices and homogeneous coordinates. At the level of computer applications, we recognize only the latter notions, but I believe the more abstract (or structuralist) notions of projective geometry provide a valuable conceptual foundation for the whole enterprise. Our principal theorem linking geometry with matrices (and hence with the applied methods of the book) is Theorem 4.13 of §4.4.5: *every collineation can be described by a matrix.* It assures us that no method beyond the matrix method will be required. Theorem 4.13 is a valuable reference point for those who wish to learn (or teach) this material at the pure or theoretical level: when you understand this theorem, all relevant definitions, and the full chain of reasoning leading to its proof, then you will have a basic theoretical understanding of the book.

On the other hand, one can study this material with a more direct path to the manipulative or computational aspects of the theory; they are summarized in §3.3 and §4.5. (The relevant formulas are extended to space in §5.3, which should be easy reading after one has mastered §4.5.) Even along this path, one needs to acquire a detailed understanding of matrices and a feeling for homogeneous coordinates. The first few sections of Chapter 6 should both test this understanding and make it firmer.

The book is designed so that it can be read sequentially from cover to cover. Nevertheless, sometimes more difficult material precedes less difficult material. For example, orthogonal matrices (§1.5.3) precede a much gentler approach to rotations of the plane (§3.3.2 and §3.3.3). Each chapter has a natural progression from easier to harder material. Therefore, on a first reading, or with any time limitations, it may be more profitable to read the early parts of each chapter,

with an idea of coming back later as time permits. The following plan may serve
as a guide.

I have evolved the following plan[1] for using the book in a one-semester
course at the University of Colorado. Six classes are devoted to a review of
linear algebra (Chapter 1), through §1.4. During this warm-up period I also
make sure that students know how to log in to the appropriate machines, how to
access printers, and so on. Then, three classes are devoted to learning the basics
of Chapter 2, through §2.3. Nine classes are devoted to the basics of Chapter
3, through §3.3. I assign a good number of the pictorial exercises in Chapter 3.
Even the more pedestrian ones are challenging at this stage; there is little point
in doing Chapter 6 until the exercises of Chapter 3 seem routine. Then, four
periods are devoted to Chapter 4 and two to Chapter 5. The objective at this
stage is to gain an understanding of homogeneous coordinates and a familiarity
with the matrices used for motions and projections of 3-space. Now, little more
than halfway into the semester, students are ready to tackle Chapter 6. At this
point I assign projects from Chapter 6, especially §6.1–§6.3, which can take a
student the rest of the semester to complete. I similarly urge other instructors to
give students several weeks to work some of the major exercises in Chapter 6. I
spend only four days on a formal presentation of Chapter 6, allowing the written
material to speak for itself. For the last thirteen classes, instructors have their
choice of material. Three options are a detailed study of §3.4, the important
proofs in §4.4, and the continuation of Chapter 6.

A second semester can easily be filled with undone projects from the first
semester, especially from the latter parts of Chapters 2, 3 and 6. I have had
this experience with selected students on an individual basis. Alternatively, a
full-year course could be organized by treating each section of the book in detail.

To aid the student, I have designated certain exercises or sets of exercises as
major pictorial exercises (see the index). Each of these exercises covers a major
theme of the book, and each of them represents a major accomplishment for
the student. The independent reader is also advised to do some of these major
exercises for a full understanding of this material. On the other hand, I have
designated some other exercises as *ambitious projects* (see the index). These are
important projects illustrating the material, interesting in their own right, but
somewhat more time-consuming and more peripheral to our central interests.
Therefore, one should embark upon them more selectively, knowing that they
may take one far afield and may be difficult to complete.

Although I have not made a formal bibliography for the book, I should
like to say that the notes contain references to some of my favorite books on
geometry, which I commend to the reader for further reading. With the exception
of two books on signal processing (which I haven't really read), every book to

---

[1]Here we assume a 44-class semester. The classes mentioned here number 41; two others were
used for exams and one as a general introduction.

which I refer—yes, even the PostScript *Language Reference Manual*—has my recommendation as a valuable and enjoyable work on geometry or computer graphics. One further book that deserves mention here is Thomas F. Banchoff's *Beyond the third dimension*.[2] Its lovely computer images represent the state of the art, and its mathematics overlaps with ours (although the presentation is nontechnical). I wish you good reading!

Developing this material—especially making the pictures shown here and many others—has been a tremendous joy for me. Like all mathematicians, for most of my life I experienced the perfection of these figures only in my mind. Only with recently available computer tools was I able to make pictures that both confirmed my inner knowledge of this perfection, and allowed me to share it with others. If there is any one benefit I wish to bestow on my readers, it is that they come to share this sense of beauty and perfection.

I leave the readers with two cautions concerning the beauty of the pictures that they can learn to make with the methods of the book. One is that besides the topics taught here, such as the mathematical precision of perspectivity and so on, there are other aspects to making good (realistic, beautiful, readable) mathematical drawings. See, e.g., *A Topological Picturebook*,[3] by George K. Francis, for another view on mathematical illustration. The other caution is to remember that there is a mathematical theory that underlies almost every one of our pictures. Even if the details of those theories are later forgotten, one can remember one's appreciation of the fact that there is a theory. As we said earlier, the ultimate perfection of these drawings lies in one's mind.

ACKNOWLEDGMENTS

This book could not have come into existence without the assistance of many people. I thank my many teachers, beginning with my parents, who helped me sharpen my mind in all the necessary ways, and especially those who taught me all the many bits of mathematics that I write about here. I myself learned much of the mathematics in this book during my undergraduate years at Swarthmore College, and so would like to thank both the professors there and the many people responsible for that unique learning environment.

I thank James Curry for bringing computer awareness to the Mathematics Department of the University of Colorado and encouraging professors—especially myself—to get involved. I thank Kirby Baker and Arlan Ramsay for continuing encouragement with this material, especially Kirby Baker for sharing many ideas with me about how he had pioneered such a course at UCLA. I thank the students at the University of Colorado for their support during periods of development of this material, especially John Carroll, Daniel Collins, Paul Hovda and Yvette Larue, who tested early versions of the material on ray tracing. I

---

[2]Scientific American Library, W. H. Freeman and Company, New York, 1990.
[3]Springer-Verlag, New York, Berlin, 1987.

thank Arlan Ramsay and Richard Holley for jumping in and teaching preliminary versions of this material. I should also like to thank the University of Colorado logicians: Richard Laver, Jerome Malitz, Donald Monk, Jan Mycielski and William Reinhardt. There is no doubt that my treatment of Chapter 2 was shaped by my long association with them. For help that is hard to classify, I thank Brent Browning, Peter Rasmussen, Randolph Back, Jennifer Hyndman, John Coleman, Ralph Freese; the Unixops support staff and the Mathematics Department secretarial staff at the University of Colorado; and the gentlemen from Bio-Crystal: Marc Pelletier, Steve Rogers and Paul Hildebrandt.

I thank my editor for this book, John Kimmel of Wadsworth and Brooks/Cole, who showed immediate and continuous confidence in this and all my work. I thank Marlene Thom of Brooks/Cole and Amy Hendrickson of TeXnology, Inc., for their excellent help in finalizing the manuscript. Drafts of the book were reviewed by: Kirby A. Baker, University of California, Los Angeles; Steve Cunningham, California State University, Stanislaus; Gerald A. Edgar, Ohio State University; Ralph S. Freese, University of Hawaii; and Jerry A. Johnson, Oklahoma State University. I thank them all for their efforts in improving the book, while taking responsibility myself for any failure to understand their suggestions and for any errors that may have gone undetected.

For their continued love, humor and support during the long writing of this work I thank my wife, Frances, and my sons, Alex and Matt.

Finally I thank my spiritual teacher, Chögyam Trungpa, who has taught me the great value of my own mind, and how I might use it to help illumine the world. May the lotus garden of his wisdom continue to bloom.

Walter Taylor
August, 1991

Contents

6   Applications of projective maps   315

The Geometry of Computer Graphics

1 Review of linear algebra

1.1 Vector spaces and linear maps

1.1.1 Definition of vector spaces

A *real vector space* **V** can be defined abstractly as a set V on which there are defined operations of *zero* (0), *addition* $(x + y)$, *subtraction* $(x - y)$ and *multiplication by any real number* α (denoted $\alpha \cdot x$, or simply αx). In other words, if α is a real number, and $x, y \in V$, then also $x + y \in V$, $x - y \in V$ and $\alpha \cdot x \in V$. The set V is called the *universe* or *underlying set* of **V**. Strictly speaking, V and **V** are not the same. The former is merely a set, and the latter is the same set together with the operations that make it a vector space. Nevertheless, in less formal presentations (homework, blackboard) it is generally permissible to ignore the distinction and write both in the same way. If the context permits, we may refer to a vector space simply as a *space*.

Such a set with operations $+$, $-$, $\alpha\cdot$ is defined to be a *real vector space* iff it satisfies the following axioms:

$$v_1 + v_2 = v_2 + v_1 \tag{1.1}$$
$$(v_1 + v_2) + v_3 = v_1 + (v_2 + v_3) \tag{1.2}$$
$$v + 0 = v \tag{1.3}$$
$$v - v = 0 \tag{1.4}$$
$$1 \cdot v = v \tag{1.5}$$
$$(\alpha + \beta) \cdot v = \alpha \cdot v + \beta \cdot v \tag{1.6}$$
$$\alpha \cdot (v + w) = \alpha \cdot v + \alpha \cdot w \tag{1.7}$$
$$\alpha \cdot (\beta \cdot v) = (\alpha\beta) \cdot v \tag{1.8}$$

Equation (1.1) is called the *commutative law*, (1.2) is called the *associative law*, (1.6) is called the *left distributive law*, and (1.7) is called the *right distributive law*. Equations (1.1–1.4) assert that $\langle V, +, -, 0 \rangle$ is an *Abelian group*. The juxtaposition of α and β in the right side of Equation (1.8) simply denotes their product in the real number system $\mathbb{R}$.

We say v *is a vector* to indicate that $v \in V$. If more than one vector space is under discussion, then we must be more careful and say $v \in V$, or $v \in W$, or whatever is appropriate. In the present context, a *scalar* is simply a real number, but we will use the term since it indicates a possible broader context. Actually, a vector space can have operations $\alpha \cdot v$ with α taken from any *field* of numbers, such as the field of *complex numbers*. The reader is referred elsewhere for the precise definition of *field*. For this course, it will be sufficient to know that the numbers α could be taken from either a more restricted set (such as the set of rational numbers) or over a more inclusive set (such as the set of complex numbers). In any given context, however, we should settle on one field of scalars. We generally settle on the field[1] of reals, although occasionally it will be useful to us to have complex scalars available when necessary (for example, in factoring Equation (1.45) to obtain eigenvectors and eigenvalues in §1.4, to which topic we return in §3.3.7, and in Exercise 3 of §1.5.3).

EXAMPLE

The foremost example of a vector space is the set of all n-tuples of real numbers, for some positive integer n. More precisely, we fix such an n and then define

$$\mathbb{R}^n = \{\langle x_1, \cdots, x_n \rangle : x_1, \ldots x_n \in \mathbb{R}\} \tag{1.9}$$

where $\mathbb{R}$ denotes the field of real numbers. Addition and scalar multiplication are defined in $\mathbb{R}^n$ as follows:

$$\langle x_1, \cdots, x_n \rangle + \langle y_1, \cdots, y_n \rangle = \langle x_1 + y_1, \cdots, x_n + y_n \rangle \tag{1.10}$$

$$\langle x_1, \cdots, x_n \rangle - \langle y_1, \cdots, y_n \rangle = \langle x_1 - y_1, \cdots, x_n - y_n \rangle \tag{1.11}$$

$$\alpha \cdot \langle x_1, \cdots, x_n \rangle = \langle \alpha x_1, \cdots, \alpha x_n \rangle \tag{1.12}$$

We leave it to the reader to check that with these operations[2] $\mathbb{R}^n$ is a vector space. It is an important fact that every finite dimensional vector space is isomorphic to $\mathbb{R}^n$ for some n (see Theorem 1.19).

In dealing with the $\mathbb{R}^n$, we often have occasion to write $\vec{x}$ as an abbreviation for $\langle x_1, \cdots, x_n \rangle$. Thus, for example, if we first introduce $\vec{x}$, then we may later refer to x_i, the ith component of $\vec{x}$. Likewise, we may use the notation $\vec{x} + \vec{y}$ for the vector

$$\langle x_1 + y_1, \cdots, x_n + y_n \rangle$$

---

[1] Of course, from the computational point of view, the real number system $\mathbb{R}$ is a fiction (and so is even the rational number system).

[2] $\mathbb{R}^n$ can be given other operations, notably the *inner product* operation, which we will introduce in §1.5.1. That operation is unnecessary—even extraneous—for making $\mathbb{R}^n$ into a vector space.

and similarly for the notations $\vec{x} - \vec{y}$ and $\alpha \cdot \vec{y}$.

1.1.2   Subspaces, spanning and linear independence

A *subuniverse* of a vector space $\mathbf{V}$ is a non-empty set $W \subseteq V$ (for V the universe of $\mathbf{V}$) such that W is *closed under the operations of* $\mathbf{V}$. This is to say that if $w_1, w_2 \in W$, then $w_1 + w_2 \in W$, $w_1 - w_2 \in W$ and $\alpha \cdot w_1 \in W$ for every $\alpha \in \mathbb{R}$. If these conditions hold, then, for example, the addition of vectors of the space $\mathbf{V}$, when restricted to vectors in W becomes an addition operation on W. In this way, the set W inherits vector space operations from those of V and becomes itself a vector space $\mathbf{W}$. Any vector space formed in this way from a subuniverse is called a *subspace of* $\mathbf{V}$. The notation $\mathbf{W} \subseteq \mathbf{V}$ may be used to indicate that $\mathbf{W}$ is a subspace of $\mathbf{V}$. Theorem 1.1 gives an example of subuniverses; in Corollary 1.28, we will see that this example is typical.

THEOREM 1.1   Let $\vec{\lambda} = \langle \lambda_1, \cdots, \lambda_n \rangle$ be any n-tuple of real numbers. The set

$$\{ \langle x_1, \cdots, x_n \rangle : \sum_{i=1}^{n} \lambda_i x_i = 0 \}$$

is a subuniverse of $\mathbb{R}^n$. $\square$

A finite sequence $\langle v_1, v_2, \cdots, v_m \rangle$ of vectors is called *linearly dependent* iff there exist scalars $\langle \alpha_1, \alpha_2, \cdots, \alpha_m \rangle$, **not all zero**, such that

$$\alpha_1 \cdot v_1 + \cdots + \alpha_m \cdot v_m = 0 \tag{1.13}$$

This equation may equally well be written as

$$\sum_{j=1}^{m} \alpha_i \cdot v_i = 0 \tag{1.14}$$

(We need to stipulate that not all α_i are zero, for the obvious reason that if they all were zero, then Equation (1.13) would follow directly from the axioms and hence would convey no information about the vectors $\langle v_1, v_2, \cdots, v_m \rangle$.)

Vectors $\langle v_1, v_2, \cdots, v_m \rangle$ are called *linearly independent* iff they are not linearly dependent; this means that Equation (1.13) cannot hold unless each α_i is zero.

A sequence $\langle v_1, v_2, \cdots, v_m \rangle$ of vectors is said to *span* or *generate* $\mathbf{V}$ iff the only subspace of $\mathbf{V}$ that contains all the v_i is $\mathbf{V}$ itself. It is not hard to check that $\langle v_1, \cdots, v_m \rangle$ spans $\mathbf{V}$ iff every vector $w \in \mathbf{V}$ is a *linear combination* of the vectors v_i, meaning that there exist scalars $\langle \alpha_1, \cdots, \alpha_m \rangle$ such that

$$\sum_{j=1}^{m} \alpha_i \cdot v_i = w \qquad (1.15)$$

THEOREM 1.2   For any vectors $\langle w_1, w_2, \cdots, w_m \rangle$ in $\mathbf{V}$, there exists a unique subspace $\mathbf{W}$ of $\mathbf{V}$ that contains each w_j and is spanned by $\langle w_1, \cdots, w_m \rangle$.

Proof $\mathbf{W}$ can be defined as the set of all vectors $\sum_{i=1}^{m} \alpha_i \cdot w_i$.   □

The subspace $\mathbf{W}$ of Theorem 1.2 is called the *linear span* of $\langle w_1, \cdots, w_m \rangle$ and is denoted $\overline{\langle w_1, \cdots, w_m \rangle}$.

A vector space $\mathbf{V}$ is called *finite dimensional* iff there exist finitely many vectors that span $\mathbf{V}$; in other words, iff there exists a finite integer m and a sequence $\langle v_1, \cdots, v_m \rangle$ such that $\langle v_1, \cdots, v_m \rangle$ spans $\mathbf{V}$. An *infinite dimensional* space is one that is not finite dimensional. (An example is formed by the set of all infinite sequences of real numbers, much like the spaces $\mathbb{R}^n$ of all sequences of a given finite length.) Although in other contexts infinite dimensional spaces are important, in this course we will consider only finite dimensional spaces. (Beginning in Chapter 5, we will work routinely with (abstract) four-dimensional spaces. By this we mean spaces that cannot be spanned by fewer than four vectors. Five-dimensional spaces make a brief appearance in §6.7. Also see §6.7 for a discussion of the physical meaning of dimension.)

LEMMA 1   If $v \in \overline{\langle w_1, \cdots, w_n \rangle}$, then $\overline{\langle w_1, \cdots, w_n, v \rangle} = \overline{\langle w_1, \cdots, w_n \rangle}$.   □

The following easy lemma establishes an important connection between linear independence and spanning sets and paves the way to our discussion of bases in §1.1.3.

LEMMA 2 (the Exchange Lemma)   If $v \in \overline{\langle w_1, \cdots, w_m \rangle}$ but $v \notin \overline{\langle w_1, \cdots, w_k \rangle}$ for some $k < m$, then

$$w_j \in \overline{\langle w_1, \cdots, w_{j-1}, v, w_{j+1}, \cdots, w_m \rangle}$$

for some j with $k < j \leq m$.   □

Proof   There exist scalars $\alpha_1 \ldots \alpha_m$

$$\sum_{j=1}^{m} \alpha_i \cdot w_i = v \qquad (1.16)$$

If all the coefficients $\alpha_{k+1} \ldots \alpha_m$ were 0, then we would have $\sum_{j=1}^{k} \alpha_j \cdot w_j = v$, which would imply that $v \in \overline{\langle w_1, \cdots, w_k \rangle}$. Since that would contradict our hypothesis, we know that $\alpha_j \neq 0$ for some j with $k < j \leq m$.

We rewrite Equation (1.16) as

$$\alpha_j \cdot w_j = v - \sum_{i \neq j} \alpha_i \cdot w_i$$

Since $\alpha_j \neq 0$, we may divide this equation by α_j to obtain

$$w_j = v - \sum_{i \neq j} \frac{\alpha_i}{\alpha_j} \cdot w_i$$

It is now apparent that w_j is in the span of v and all the w_i for $i \neq j$. $\qquad \square$

THEOREM 1.3   If $\langle v_1, \cdots, v_k \rangle$ is linearly independent and $\langle w_1, \cdots, w_n \rangle$ spans $\mathbf{V}$, then $k \leq n$, and the sequence $\langle w_1, \cdots, w_n \rangle$ may be renumbered so that $\langle v_1, \cdots, v_k, w_{k+1}, \cdots, w_n \rangle$ spans $\mathbf{V}$.

Proof   By induction on k. If $k = 0$, there is nothing to prove. Otherwise, by induction, we may assume that the sequence $\langle w_1, \cdots, w_n \rangle$ has been renumbered so that $\langle v_1, \cdots, v_{k-1}, w_k, \cdots, w_n \rangle$ spans $\mathbf{V}$. We know therefore that $v_k \in \overline{\langle v_1, \cdots, v_{k-1}, w_k, \cdots, w_n \rangle}$, but (by independence) that $v_k \notin \overline{\langle v_1, \cdots, v_{k-1} \rangle}$. Therefore, clearly w_k must exist (which says that $k \leq n$); and moreover, by the Exchange Lemma,

$$w_t \in \overline{\langle v_1, \cdots, v_k, w_k, \cdots, w_{t-1}, w_{t+1}, \cdots, w_n \rangle}$$

for some t with $k \leq t \leq n$. If we now renumber the vectors w_i by interchanging w_t and w_k, then we will have $w_k \in \overline{\langle v_1, \cdots, v_k, w_{k+1}, \cdots, w_n \rangle}$ It is now immediately clear that $\langle v_1, \cdots, v_k, w_{k+1}, \cdots, w_n \rangle$ spans $\mathbf{V}$. $\qquad \square$

THEOREM 1.4   Suppose that $\langle v_1, \cdots, v_k \rangle$ is linearly independent, that $\langle v_1, \cdots, v_k, w_{k+1}, \cdots, w_n \rangle$ spans $\mathbf{V}$, and that omission of any w_j from $\langle v_1, \cdots, v_k, w_{k+1}, \cdots, w_n \rangle$ yields a sequence of vectors that does not span $\mathbf{V}$. Then $\langle v_1, \cdots, v_k, w_{k+1}, \cdots, w_n \rangle$ is linearly independent.

Proof   We need to show that if

$$\sum_{i=1}^{k} \alpha_i \cdot v_i = \sum_{j=k+1}^{m} \beta_j \cdot w_j \tag{1.17}$$

then all α_i and all β_j are 0. First note that if we had $\beta_j \neq 0$, then we could divide the above equation by β_j to obtain w_j in the span of all the v_i and all the w_t for $t \neq j$. By Lemma 1, we would then have $\mathbf{V}$ spanned by the set of all the

v_i and all the w_t for $t \neq j$. This contradiction to our assumptions shows that each β_j must be 0. Since the b_j's are 0, Equation (1.17) reduces to

$$\sum_{i=1}^{k} \alpha_i \cdot v_i = 0$$

Now the fact that all α_i are 0 follows immediately from the assumption that $\langle v_1, \cdots, v_k \rangle$ is linearly independent.   □

COROLLARY 1.5   In a finite dimensional vector space **V**, **every minimal spanning set is linearly independent.** (In other words, if $\langle w_1, \cdots, w_n \rangle$ spans **V** and no proper subset of these vectors spans **V**, then $\langle w_1, \cdots, w_n \rangle$ is linearly independent.)

Proof   This is simply the special case of Theorem 1.4 with $k = 0$.   □

COROLLARY 1.6   If $\langle w_1, \cdots, w_n \rangle$ spans **V**, then every linearly independent subset of **V** has at most n elements. In particular, in a finite dimensional vector space, every linearly independent set is finite.   □

COROLLARY 1.7   In a finite dimensional vector space **V**, every linearly independent set can be extended to a finite set that is linearly independent and spans **V**.

Proof   By Corollary 1.6, every independent set is finite and hence has the form $\langle v_1, \cdots, v_k \rangle$ for some k. Since **V** is finite dimensional, it is spanned by $\langle w_1, \cdots, w_n \rangle$ for some finite n. By Theorem 1.3, extension of the sequence $\langle v_1, \cdots, v_k \rangle$ by some of the w_j's will yield a sequence that spans **V**. Now let us do this, while using the minimum possible number of w_j's. It follows from Theorem 1.4 that the resulting sequence is a linearly independent sequence spanning **V**.   □

COROLLARY 1.8   In a finite dimensional vector space **V**, **every maximal linearly independent set spans V.** (In other words, if $\langle v_1, \cdots, v_n \rangle$ is independent, but no larger set of vectors is independent, then $\langle v_1, \cdots, v_n \rangle$ spans **V**.)
                                                                                □

Exercise——

1. (Various parts.) Supply a proof for each theorem lemma or corollary of this section for which no proof has been included. (The instructor may assign one or more specific proofs.)

1.1.3   Bases and dimension

A sequence $\langle v_1, \cdots, v_m \rangle$ is called a *basis* (plural,[3] *bases*) of $\mathbf{V}$ iff it is linearly independent and spans $\mathbf{V}$.

LEMMA $\langle v_1, \cdots, v_m \rangle$ is a basis of $\mathbf{V}$ iff every element v of V can be written uniquely as a linear combination of the vectors v_i, i.e.,

$$v = \sum_{i=1}^{m} \alpha_i \cdot v_i$$

with the scalars α_i uniquely determined by v.   □

THEOREM 1.9   Every finite dimensional vector space $\mathbf{V}$ has a basis.

Proof   By definition of finite dimensionality, there exists some $\langle v_1, \cdots, v_m \rangle$ that spans $\mathbf{V}$. Choose such a $\langle v_1, \cdots, v_m \rangle$ that has m as small as possible. Then $\langle v_1, \cdots, v_m \rangle$ is a basis of $\mathbf{V}$, by Corollary 1.5.   □

To effectively carry out the proof of Theorem 1.9 would require one to be able to recognize whether a given vector w_j can be removed from the spanning set $\langle v_1, \cdots, v_m \rangle$. This requires one to determine whether w_j can be expressed as a linear combination of the other vectors. The procedure of column reduction defined in §1.2.4 gives us a systematic way to get a basis for any space defined as the image of a homomorphism. (Later, row reduction will do the same thing for kernels.) While bases exist, we will see that they are far from unique. In fact, the interplay between different bases of a vector space is an important underlying theme of the subject. Diverse as they may be, there is one thing that all bases of a given space $\mathbf{V}$ have in common: their number of elements.

COROLLARY 1.10   All bases of $\mathbf{V}$ have the same number of elements.

Proof   Immediate from Theorem 1.3.   □

This common number of elements is known as the *dimension* of $\mathbf{V}$. Thus, Corollary 1.10 may be thought of as saying that the dimension of $\mathbf{V}$ is well defined.

COROLLARY 1.11   Every linearly independent subset of $\mathbf{V}$ can be enlarged to form a basis of $\mathbf{V}$; every set of vectors that spans $\mathbf{V}$ contains a basis of $\mathbf{V}$.

---

[3]Thus *base* and *basis* are distinct words that have the same plural, at least when written. The only other case known to the author is that of *ax* and *axis*.

Proof   This is almost immediate from Corollaries 1.7 and 1.8.   □

COROLLARY 1.12   If **V** is a finite dimensional space and **W** is a subspace of **V**, then dim **W** $\leq$ dim **V**, with equality holding only if **W** = **V**. (In other words, if **W** is a proper subspace of **V**, then dim **W** < dim **V**.)   □

Exercises_____

1. Prove Corollary 1.12.

2. Prove that the n vectors

$$
\begin{aligned}
v_1 &= \langle 1, 0, 0, \cdots \rangle \\
v_2 &= \langle 0, 1, 0, \cdots \rangle \\
v_3 &= \langle 0, 0, 1, \cdots \rangle \\
&\ \ \vdots
\end{aligned}
$$

form a basis of $\mathbb{R}^n$. This basis is called the *standard basis* of $\mathbb{R}^n$.

3. Find a basis for the subspace **W** $= \{\vec{x}: x_1 + 2x_2 + 3x_3 = 0\}$ of $\mathbb{R}^3$. (Brute force will handle this exercise; later, we will see more systematic ways to go about it.)

1.1.4   Sums and direct sums of spaces

If **U** and **W** are any two subspaces of a space **V**, their *sum*, denoted **U** + **W**, is the smallest subspace of **V** that contains them both. The notation may be explained by the fact that

$$
\mathbf{U} + \mathbf{W} = \{u + w : u \in U, w \in W\}
$$

Of course, **U** ∩ **W** denotes the *intersection* of the two subspaces **U** and **W**. It also is a subspace, as the student may easily check.

Theorem 1.13 has an important application in analytic projective geometry, showing that, in a projective plane, any two lines have a point in common. (See Theorem 4.2 in §4.2.1.)

THEOREM 1.13 $\dim(\mathbf{U} + \mathbf{W}) + \dim(\mathbf{U} \cap \mathbf{W}) = \dim \mathbf{U} + \dim \mathbf{W}$.

Proof   Let $\langle v_1, \cdots, v_k \rangle$ be a basis of **U** ∩ **W**, so that the dimension of the intersection is k. We may extend this linearly independent set in two different ways: to form the basis $\langle v_1, \cdots, v_k, u_1, \cdots, u_{m-k} \rangle$ of **U**, and to form the basis $\langle v_1, \cdots, v_k, w_1, \cdots, w_{n-k} \rangle$ of **W**. (Thus, we have $m = \dim \mathbf{U}$ and $n = \dim \mathbf{W}$.) Now we claim that the vectors

$$\langle v_1, \cdots, v_k, u_1, \cdots, u_{m-k}, w_1, \cdots, w_{n-k}\rangle$$

form a basis of $\mathbf{U} + \mathbf{W}$. It is apparent that they span this space. For linear independence, let us assume that

$$\sum_{i=1}^{k} \alpha_i \cdot v_i + \sum_{i=1}^{m-k} \beta_i \cdot u_i + \sum_{i=1}^{n-k} \gamma_i \cdot w_i = 0$$

Denoting the three sums here by v, u and w, we have $v \in U \cap W$, $u \in U$, and $w \in W$. Since $w = -v - u$, we also have $w \in U$, and hence $w \in U \cap W$. Therefore, w is a linear combination of the vectors v_i, and so we have

$$\sum_{i=1}^{k} \alpha_i' \cdot v_i = w = \sum_{i=1}^{n-k} \gamma_i \cdot w_i$$

By the linear independence of $\langle v_1, \cdots, v_k, w_1, \cdots, w_{n-k}\rangle$, we know that each $\gamma_i = 0$, and hence that $w = 0$. A similar argument shows that each $\beta_i = 0$ and that $u = 0$. Therefore, $v = 0$; and so each $\alpha_i = 0$. This completes the proof that

$$\langle v_1, \cdots, v_k, u_1, \cdots, u_{m-k}, w_1, \cdots, w_{n-k}\rangle$$

is a basis of $\mathbf{U} + \mathbf{W}$. Now we can easily observe that the dimension of $\mathbf{U} + \mathbf{W}$ is $k + (m - k) + (n - k) = m + n - k$, to complete the proof of the theorem. □

A vector space $\mathbf{V}$ is said to be the *direct sum* of its subspaces $\mathbf{U}$ and $\mathbf{V}$ iff $U \cap W = \{0\}$ and $U \cup W$ spans $\mathbf{V}$; i.e.,

$$V = \{u + w : u \in U, w \in W\}$$

By the following theorem relating direct sums and bases, it is clear that if $\dim \mathbf{V} \geq 2$, then $\mathbf{V}$ can be written as a direct sum of subspaces in many different ways. The proof is left to the student.

THEOREM 1.14   If $\mathbf{V}$ is the direct sum of its subspaces $\mathbf{U}$ and $\mathbf{W}$, if $\langle u_1, \cdots, u_k \rangle$ is any basis of $\mathbf{U}$, and if $\langle w_1, \cdots, w_m \rangle$ is any basis of $\mathbf{W}$, then $\langle u_1, \cdots, u_k, w_1, \cdots, w_m \rangle$ is a basis $\mathbf{V}$. Conversely, if $\langle v_1, \cdots, v_n \rangle$ is any basis of $\mathbf{V}$ and $1 \leq k < n$, then $\mathbf{V}$ is the direct sum of its subspaces spanned by $\{v_1, \cdots, v_k\}$ and by $\{v_{k+1}, \cdots, v_n\}$. □

COROLLARY 1.15   If $\mathbf{V} = \mathbf{U} \oplus \mathbf{W}$, then $\dim \mathbf{V} = \dim \mathbf{U} + \dim \mathbf{W}$. □

COROLLARY 1.16 $\mathbf{V}$ is the direct sum of its subspaces $\mathbf{U}$ and $\mathbf{W}$ iff for every element v of $\mathbf{V}$ there exist unique elements u of $\mathbf{U}$ and w of $\mathbf{W}$ such that $v = u + w$. □

Of course, if we have $V = U \oplus W$ and $\dim U \geq 2$, then U itself is a direct sum of two subspaces, $U = U_1 \oplus U_2$. In this case, we can write $V = U_1 \oplus U_2 \oplus W$. We leave it to the reader to check that $\oplus$ is associative, so that parentheses are not needed in writing direct sums of three (or more) subspaces. In general, we can write

$$V = \bigoplus_{i=1}^{m} W_i$$

a decomposition of V as a direct sum of m subspaces. Direct sums will be useful to us in §§1.4 and 1.5. The proof of the following result is left to the reader; it is like that of Corollary 1.16.

THEOREM 1.17 $V = \bigoplus_{i=1}^{m} W_i$ iff each element of V can be expressed uniquely as a sum of elements of the subspaces W_i; i.e., for each $v \in V$ there exist $w_i \in W_i$ such that $v = \sum w_i$ and such that if $v = \sum w_i'$ with $w_i' \in W_i$, then $w_i' = w_i$ for $i = 1, \ldots, n$.   □

Exercises

1. Prove Theorem 1.14.

2. Prove Corollary 1.15.

3. Prove Corollary 1.16.

4. Prove Theorem 1.17.

5. Prove that $\mathbb{R}^4$ is the direct sum of its subspaces

$$\{ \langle x_1, x_2, x_3, x_4 \rangle : x_1 = x_3 = 0 \}$$

and

$$\{ \langle x_1, x_2, x_3, x_4 \rangle : x_2 = x_4 = 0 \}$$

1.1.5   Homomorphisms (linear transformations)

A *homomorphism* from vector space V to vector space W is a function $f : V \longrightarrow W$ that satisfies the following equations for all vectors $v, v' \in V$:

$$f(v + v') = f(v) + f(v') \tag{1.18}$$
$$f(\alpha \cdot v) = \alpha \cdot f(v) \tag{1.19}$$

(Equation (1.19) is really a family of equations, one for each scalar α.) The notations

$$f : \mathbf{V} \longrightarrow \mathbf{W} \quad \text{and} \quad \mathbf{V} \xrightarrow{f} \mathbf{W}$$

both mean that f is a homomorphism from $\mathbf{V}$ to $\mathbf{W}$. A homomorphism is also known as a *linear function* or a *linear map* or a *linear transformation*. A large part of this course will be concerned with linear maps. For instance, one may think of the formation of a visual image as brought about by a linear transformation from the *scene* (a three-dimensional space) to a two-dimensional (i.e., planar) viewing space (e.g., a film or a retina). This idea in fact pervades the book; we will encounter it in various forms in §4.1.1, §4.6, §4.7, §5.3.9, §6.1.7, §6.2.10, and elsewhere. In §1.2.1, we will see how to represent linear transformations with *matrices*. We close this section with a few general remarks about homomorphisms.

THEOREM 1.18   Let $\mathbf{V}$ and $\mathbf{W}$ be vector spaces, with $\langle v_1, \cdots, v_n \rangle$ a basis of $\mathbf{V}$. For an arbitrary sequence $\langle w_1, \cdots, w_n \rangle$ of vectors in $\mathbf{W}$, there exists a unique homomorphism $f : \mathbf{V} \longrightarrow \mathbf{W}$ such that $f(v_i) = w_i$ for each i. $\square$

An informal statement of this theorem is that a linear transformation f is determined by its values on the basis elements and that the values on basis elements are completely arbitrary. Thus, in dealing with finite dimensional spaces, a homomorphism is determined by a finite amount of information.[4] This information is usually packaged as a *matrix*; we will introduce matrices in §1.2.

Recall that a *bijection* or *one-one correspondence* between sets V and W is a map $: V \longrightarrow W$ such that, for each $w \in W$ there is a unique[5] $v \in V$ such that $f(v) = w$. In more detail, f is called *injective* or *one-to-one* iff $f(x) = f(y)$ implies $x = y$; and $f : V \longrightarrow W$ is called *surjective* (or is said to map V *onto* W) iff, for every $w \in W$ there exists $v \in V$ with $f(v) = w$. Thus, $f : V \longrightarrow W$ is a bijection iff it is an injection and a surjection. We may write $f : V \hookrightarrow W$, $f : V \longrightarrow\!\!\!\!\rightarrow W$, or $f : V \xrightarrow{\cong} W$ to denote that f is, respectively, injective, surjective, or bijective.

A homomorphism $f : \mathbf{V} \longrightarrow \mathbf{W}$ is called an *isomorphism* from $\mathbf{V}$ to $\mathbf{W}$ iff f is a one-one correspondence between V and W. We write $f : \mathbf{V} \xrightarrow{\cong} \mathbf{W}$ to indicate that f is an isomorphism from $\mathbf{V}$ to $\mathbf{W}$. We write $\mathbf{V} \cong \mathbf{W}$ and say that $\mathbf{V}$ *is isomorphic to* $\mathbf{W}$ iff there exists an f such that $f : \mathbf{V} \xrightarrow{\cong} \mathbf{W}$. Isomorphisms will be very important in our work, especially isomorphisms of the form $f : \mathbf{V} \xrightarrow{\cong} \mathbf{V}$, sometimes called *automorphisms* of $\mathbf{V}$. For instance, the changes of coordinates required for rotations of objects in 3-space may be expressed as automorphisms

---

[4]Well, that depends on whether a real number can be specified by a "finite amount of information."

[5]Be careful here. The existence of a unique such $w \in W$ for each $v \in V$ is simply the definition of f is a function.

of $\mathbb{R}^n$. From the abstract point of view, two spaces that are isomorphic may be regarded as almost the same.

LEMMA 3   A homomorphism $f: \mathbf{V} \longrightarrow \mathbf{W}$ is injective iff it has a *left inverse*; i.e., there exists a homomorphism $g: \mathbf{W} \longrightarrow \mathbf{V}$ such that $g \circ f$ is the identity function on V. Such an f is surjective iff it has a *right inverse*; i.e., there exists a homomorphism $g: \mathbf{W} \longrightarrow \mathbf{V}$ such that $f \circ g$ is the identity function on W. Such an f is an isomorphism iff it has a *two-sided inverse*; i.e., there exists a homomorphism $g: \mathbf{W} \longrightarrow \mathbf{V}$ that is both a left inverse and a right inverse to f.   □

LEMMA 4   If $f: \mathbf{V} \xrightarrow{\cong} \mathbf{W}$ and if $\langle v_1, \cdots, v_n \rangle$ is a basis of $\mathbf{V}$, then $\langle f(v_1), \cdots, f(v_n) \rangle$ is a basis of $\mathbf{W}$.   □

THEOREM 1.19   Two finite dimensional vector spaces are isomorphic iff they have the same dimension. Thus, every finite dimensional vector space is isomorphic to $\mathbb{R}^n$ for a unique value of n.

Proof   If $\mathbf{V}$ and $\mathbf{W}$ have the same dimension n, then we may let $\langle v_1, \cdots, v_n \rangle$ be a basis of $\mathbf{V}$ and $\langle w_1, \cdots, w_n \rangle$ be a basis of $\mathbf{W}$. By Theorem 1.18, there are homomorphisms $\mathbf{V} \xrightarrow{f} \mathbf{W}$ and $\mathbf{W} \xrightarrow{g} \mathbf{V}$ such that $f(v_i) = w_i$ and $g(w_i) = v_i$ for each i. It is not hard to check that g is a two-sided inverse of f and hence that $\mathbf{V} \cong \mathbf{W}$. Conversely, if $\mathbf{V} \cong \mathbf{W}$, then we may apply Lemma 4 to see that $\mathbf{V}$ and $\mathbf{W}$ have the same dimension.   □

For any homomorphism $f: \mathbf{V} \longrightarrow \mathbf{W}$, the set

$$\{v \in V : f(v) = 0\}$$

is known as the *kernel of f* and is denoted **KER** f. The set

$$\{f(v) : v \in V\}$$

is known as the *image of f* and is denoted **Im** f.

LEMMA 5   For any homomorphism $f: \mathbf{V} \longrightarrow \mathbf{W}$, the kernel of f is a subspace of $\mathbf{V}$, and the image of f is a subspace of $\mathbf{W}$.   □

For example, the subspace described in Theorem 1.1 is the kernel of a certain homomorphism. In fact, *every* subspace $\mathbf{W}$ of any space $\mathbf{V}$ is the kernel of a homomorphism.

THEOREM 1.20   Let $\mathbf{W}$ be a subspace of $\mathbf{V}$. Then there exists a space $\mathbf{U}$ and a homomorphism $f: \mathbf{V} \longrightarrow \mathbf{U}$ such that $\mathbf{W}$ is the kernel of f.

Proof   Let $\langle v_1, \cdots, v_k \rangle$ be a basis of **W**. By Corollary 1.11, this basis can be extended to a basis $\langle v_1, \cdots, v_n \rangle$ of **V**. Let **U** be any space of dimension $n - k$, with basis $\langle u_1, \cdots, u_{n-k} \rangle$. Then use Theorem 1.18 to define a homomorphism $\mathbf{V} \xrightarrow{f} \mathbf{U}$, by mapping v_i to 0 for $1 \le i \le k$ and by mapping v_{k+i} to u_i for $1 \le i \le n - k$. It is easy to check that the kernel of f is W.   □

When thought of as subspaces of **V** and **W**, the kernel and image of f will be denoted **KER** f and **IM** f, respectively. In dealing with an arbitrary homomorphism f, it is convenient to have a basis of **V** that is chosen with regard to the kernel and image of f, according to Theorem 1.21.

LEMMA   Let $f: \mathbf{V} \longrightarrow \mathbf{W}$ and let **U** be a subspace of **V**. Then f is injective on U iff $U \cap \mathbf{KER}\, f = \{0\}$. In particular, f is injective on all of V iff its kernel is $\{0\}$.   □

THEOREM 1.21   If $f: \mathbf{V} \longrightarrow \mathbf{W}$ is a homomorphism and **U** is any subspace such that $\mathbf{V} = \mathbf{U} \oplus \mathbf{KER}\, f$, then f maps **U** isomorphically to **IM** f.   □

The following corollary will be useful in showing us that the row rank of any matrix is the same as its column rank (see §1.2.7).

COROLLARY 1.22   For any homomorphism $f: \mathbf{V} \longrightarrow \mathbf{W}$,

$$\dim \mathbf{KER}\, f + \dim \mathbf{IM}\, f \;=\; \dim \mathbf{V}$$

Proof   Immediate from Theorem 1.21 and Corollary 1.15.   □

From Corollary 1.22, we get a considerable strengthening of Lemma 3 above, for the case that **V** and **W** have the same dimension.

COROLLARY 1.23   Let **V** and **W** be spaces of the same finite dimension n, and let $f: \mathbf{V} \longrightarrow \mathbf{W}$ be a homomorphism. Then f is an isomorphism if f has *either* a left inverse or a right inverse.   □

Exercises————————————————————————————————

1. Prove Lemma 3.

2. Prove Lemma 4.

3. Prove Theorem 1.21.

4. Prove Corollary 1.23.

5. Let **C** be the space of continuous functions on the interval $[0, 1]$, and define $I : \mathbf{C} \longrightarrow \mathbb{R}$ *via* $I(f) = \int_0^1 f(x)\, dx$. What does it mean to say that I is linear? Does this assertion represent some familiar facts about integration?

6. Let **D** be the space of real-valued functions f defined on $[-1, 1]$ such that the derivative $f'(x)$ exists for $x = 0$. Define $J : \mathbf{D} \longrightarrow \mathbb{R}$ *via* $J(f) = f'(0)$. What does it mean to say that J is linear? Does this assertion represent some familiar facts about differentiation?

1.2 Matrices

1.2.1 The matrix of a linear transformation

Given a homomorphism or linear transformation $f : \mathbf{V} \longrightarrow \mathbf{W}$, we can begin to obtain numerical information about f through the use of a basis $\langle v_1, \cdots, v_n \rangle$ of **V** and a basis $\langle w_1, \cdots, w_m \rangle$ of **W**. We know from Theorem 1.18 of §1.1 that f is completely determined by the vectors $f(v_j)$ for $1 \le j \le n$. Now each of these vectors is in W, and therefore is uniquely representable in the form

$$f(v_j) = \sum_{i=1}^m a_{ij} \cdot w_i \tag{1.20}$$

Therefore, each of the scalars a_{ij} is uniquely determined by f; and clearly, by Theorem 1.18 of §1.1, the converse holds as well: f is determined by the mn scalars a_{ij}.

By convention, the scalars a_{ij} are arranged into a rectangular array known as an $m \times n$ *matrix* (plural, *matrices*). From the strictly mathematical point of view, an $m \times n$ matrix is merely a function that takes values in the field of scalars,[6] and whose domain is the set $\{1, \cdots, m\} \times \{1, \cdots, n\}$. Nevertheless, an $m \times n$ matrix is always written more informatively, as an array

$$\begin{bmatrix} s_{11} & s_{12} & \cdots & s_{1n} \\ s_{21} & s_{22} & \cdots & s_{2n} \\ \vdots & \vdots & \ddots & \vdots \\ s_{m1} & s_{m2} & \cdots & s_{mn} \end{bmatrix}$$

of scalars s_{ij}, with m rows and n columns. This matrix may also be written $[s_{ij}]$ for short (if m and n are understood from the context). If $m = n$, then it is called a *square matrix*. At times we will denote matrices by capital letters $A, B, \ldots$, while retaining the possibility of writing A_{ij} for the scalar that appears

---

[6]In fact, the values might not be scalars, but only symbolic expressions for hypothetical scalars, as is the case for the following matrix.

in the ith row and j^{th} column of A. This scalar is sometimes called the i, j-entry of A.

Now, specifically, the *matrix associated to the linear transformation f, with respect to the bases* $\langle v_1, \cdots, v_n \rangle$ *and* $\langle w_1, \cdots, w_m \rangle$, is the matrix

$$\begin{bmatrix} a_{11} & a_{12} & \cdots & a_{1n} \\ a_{21} & a_{22} & \cdots & a_{2n} \\ \vdots & \vdots & \ddots & \vdots \\ a_{m1} & a_{m2} & \cdots & a_{mn} \end{bmatrix} \tag{1.21}$$

where the scalars are as defined by Equation (1.20). If the context is clear, it may be referred to simply as *the matrix of f*.

1.2.2 The product of two matrices

Let us suppose that

$$\mathbf{U} \xrightarrow{g} \mathbf{V} \xrightarrow{f} \mathbf{W}$$

that $\mathbf{V}$ and $\mathbf{W}$ have bases as described above, and that $\langle u_1, \cdots, u_p \rangle$ is a basis of $\mathbf{U}$. Further suppose that f is described as in Equation (1.20), and that g is described by the similar equation

$$g(u_k) = \sum_{j=0}^{n} b_{jk} \cdot v_j \tag{1.22}$$

(with one such equation holding for each value of j from 1 to n). Let us investigate the effect of the composite homomorphism $f \circ g$ on a basis element u_k:

$$\begin{aligned} f \circ g(u_k) \quad &= \quad f(g(u_k)) = f\left(\sum_{j=0}^{n} b_{jk} \cdot v_j\right) \\ &= \quad \sum_{j=0}^{n} b_{jk} \cdot f(v_j) \quad \text{(by linearity)} \\ &= \quad \sum_{j=0}^{n} b_{jk} \cdot \left(\sum_{i=1}^{m} a_{ij} \cdot w_i\right) \\ &= \quad \sum_{i=1}^{m} \left(\sum_{j=0}^{n} a_{ij} b_{jk}\right) \cdot w_i \\ &= \quad \sum_{i=1}^{m} c_{ik} \cdot w_i \tag{1.23} \end{aligned}$$

where

$$c_{ik} = \sum_{j=0}^{n} a_{ij} b_{jk} \tag{1.24}$$

for each i and k with $1 \le i \le m$ and $1 \le k \le p$.

Now it is obvious from our calculation of $f(u_k)$ that the matrix $[c_{ik}]$ defined in Equation (1.24) is the matrix of the composite homomorphism $f \circ g$. Therefore, for any matrices $[a_{ij}]$ and $[b_{jk}]$, we call $[c_{ik}]$ the *product* of the matrices $[a_{ij}]$ and $[b_{jk}]$. The product of matrices A and B may also be denoted AB or $A \times B$.

Let us be quite clear that the product AB of an $m \times n$ matrix A and an $s \times p$ matrix B exists iff $n = s$, and in that case AB is a $m \times p$ matrix. If $n \ne s$, *then the product AB does not even make sense.* From the practical point of view, the product

$$\begin{bmatrix} a_{11} & a_{12} & \cdots & a_{1n} \\ a_{21} & a_{22} & \cdots & a_{2n} \\ \vdots & \vdots & \ddots & \vdots \\ a_{m1} & a_{m2} & \cdots & a_{mn} \end{bmatrix} \times \begin{bmatrix} b_{11} & b_{12} & \cdots & b_{1p} \\ b_{21} & b_{22} & \cdots & b_{2p} \\ \vdots & \vdots & \ddots & \vdots \\ b_{n1} & b_{n2} & \cdots & b_{np} \end{bmatrix} \tag{1.25}$$

is formed very simply. To form the (i, k)-entry of the product $(1 \le i \le m, 1 \le k \le p)$, we simply multiply the elements of the ith row

$$\begin{bmatrix} a_{i1} & a_{i2} & \cdots & a_{in} \end{bmatrix}$$

by the elements of the kth column

$$\begin{bmatrix} b_{1k} \\ b_{2k} \\ \vdots \\ b_{nk} \end{bmatrix}$$

and then form the sum of these n products.

THEOREM 1.24   The multiplication of matrices is an *associative* operation, i.e., the equation

$$A(BC) = (AB)C \tag{1.26}$$

holds for all matrices A, B and C whenever all these products are defined.

Proof   By Theorem 1.18, we may assume that there are linear transformations

$$\mathbf{S} \xrightarrow{h} \mathbf{U} \xrightarrow{g} \mathbf{V} \xrightarrow{f} \mathbf{W}$$

such that A is the matrix of f, B is the matrix of g, and C is the matrix of h. It follows from the definition of products that AB is the matrix of $f \circ g$, $(AB)C$ is the matrix of $(f \circ g) \circ h$, BC is the matrix of $g \circ h$, and $A(BC)$ is the matrix of $f \circ (g \circ h)$. The theorem now follows from the associative law for functions: $f \circ (g \circ h) = (f \circ g) \circ h$. $\square$

The multiplication of matrices is *not commutative*, as can be seen from very simple examples such as

$$\begin{bmatrix} 0 & 1 \\ 0 & 0 \end{bmatrix} \times \begin{bmatrix} 0 & 0 \\ 1 & 0 \end{bmatrix} = \begin{bmatrix} 1 & 0 \\ 0 & 0 \end{bmatrix} \neq \begin{bmatrix} 0 & 0 \\ 0 & 1 \end{bmatrix} = \begin{bmatrix} 0 & 0 \\ 1 & 0 \end{bmatrix} \times \begin{bmatrix} 0 & 1 \\ 0 & 0 \end{bmatrix}$$

1.2.3   The identity matrix and inverse matrices

The *identity matrix* of rank n is the $n \times n$ matrix

$$I_n = \begin{bmatrix} 1 & 0 & \cdots & 0 \\ 0 & 1 & \cdots & 0 \\ \vdots & \vdots & \ddots & \vdots \\ 0 & 0 & \cdots & 1 \end{bmatrix}$$

It is not hard to check that this is the matrix of the identity homomorphism from $\mathbb{R}^n$ to itself. From this it follows in a straightforward way that if A is any $m \times n$ matrix, then $I_m A = A = A I_n$. When n is clear from the context, the identity matrix may be denoted I.

A matrix A is said to be *invertible* or *non-singular* iff there exist matrices B and C such that AB and CA are both identity matrices.

LEMMA   If they exist, the matrices B and C are unique and equal to each other.

Proof   We will show that any matrix B, as in the previous paragraph, is equal to any matrix C there. This will show that each is unique and that they are equal to each other. Here is the simple argument: $C = CI_n = C(AB) = (CA)B = I_n B = B$. $\square$

This unique B such that $AB = BA = I$ is called the *inverse* of A and is denoted A^{-1}. One must exercise caution in writing the expression A^{-1}, for whenever we write it we are implicitly asserting that A is invertible. If A is invertible, i.e., if $AB = BA = I$, then clearly there exists n such that A and B are both $n \times n$ matrices. Thus, A and B represent linear transformations $f : \mathbb{R}^n \longrightarrow \mathbb{R}^n$ and $g : \mathbb{R}^n \longrightarrow \mathbb{R}^n$ such that $f \circ g$ and $g \circ f$ are both the identity function on $\mathbb{R}^n$. Thus, by 1.2.2, the linear transformation f corresponding to A

is an isomorphism of $\mathbb{R}^n$ with itself. Conversely, if f is an isomorphism of $\mathbb{R}^n$ with itself, then its corresponding matrix A is invertible.

Exercise

1. If $B = A^{-1}$, then B is invertible, and $B^{-1} = A$.

In fact, if we already know that A is a square matrix, then the invertibility of A can be determined from the existence of a left *or* a right inverse.

LEMMA 6   If A is an $n \times n$ matrix and B is an $n \times n$ matrix such that either $AB = I_n$ or $BA = I_n$, then A is invertible and $B = A^{-1}$.

Proof   This follows immediately from Corollary 1.23 of §1.1.5.   □

For example, as the reader may check,

$$\begin{bmatrix} 2 & 3 & 2 \\ 2 & 1 & 1 \\ 1 & 5 & 3 \end{bmatrix} \begin{bmatrix} 2 & -1 & -1 \\ 5 & -4 & -2 \\ -9 & 7 & 4 \end{bmatrix}$$

$$= \begin{bmatrix} 2 & -1 & -1 \\ 5 & -4 & -2 \\ -9 & 7 & 4 \end{bmatrix} \begin{bmatrix} 2 & 3 & 2 \\ 2 & 1 & 1 \\ 1 & 5 & 3 \end{bmatrix} = \begin{bmatrix} 1 & 0 & 0 \\ 0 & 1 & 0 \\ 0 & 0 & 1 \end{bmatrix}$$

and so the inverse of $\begin{bmatrix} 2 & 3 & 2 \\ 2 & 1 & 1 \\ 1 & 5 & 3 \end{bmatrix}$ is $\begin{bmatrix} 2 & -1 & -1 \\ 5 & -4 & -2 \\ -9 & 7 & 4 \end{bmatrix}$. Finding the inverse to this 3×3 matrix—even determining *whether it exists*—is a non-trivial mathematical task that we will address in §1.2.6.

Not every matrix has an inverse, for instance

$$\begin{bmatrix} 0 & 1 \\ 0 & 0 \end{bmatrix}$$

has no inverse.

LEMMA 7   If A and B are invertible $n \times n$ matrices, then AB is an invertible $n \times n$ matrix.

Proof   We claim that $B^{-1}A^{-1}$ is the inverse to AB. To see this, we simply calculate

$$(AB)(B^{-1}A^{-1})$$
$$= ((AB)B^{-1})A^{-1} = (A(BB^{-1}))A^{-1} = (AI)A^{-1} = AA^{-1} = I$$

and a similar calculation shows that $(B^{-1}A^{-1})(AB) = I$.   □

1.2.4   Column operations on matrices

The Matrix (1.21) associated to f can be explained further if we assume that **W** is really $\mathbb{R}^m$ and that the basis $\langle w_1, \cdots, w_m \rangle$ consists[7] of the standard basis of $\mathbb{R}^m$. Let us moreover agree to write the standard basis elements of $\mathbb{R}^m$ as *column vectors*, i.e., as $m \times 1$ matrices, so that

$$w_1 = \begin{bmatrix} 1 \\ 0 \\ \vdots \\ 0 \end{bmatrix} \; ; \quad w_2 = \begin{bmatrix} 0 \\ 1 \\ \vdots \\ 0 \end{bmatrix} \; ; \quad \cdots \; , \quad w_m = \begin{bmatrix} 0 \\ 0 \\ \vdots \\ 1 \end{bmatrix} \tag{1.27}$$

Examining the jth column in Matrix (1.21), we compute from Equation (1.20) that

$$\begin{bmatrix} a_{1j} \\ a_{2j} \\ \vdots \\ a_{mj} \end{bmatrix} = a_{1j} \cdot \begin{bmatrix} 1 \\ 0 \\ \vdots \\ 0 \end{bmatrix} + a_{2j} \cdot \begin{bmatrix} 0 \\ 1 \\ \vdots \\ 0 \end{bmatrix} + \cdots + a_{mj} \cdot \begin{bmatrix} 0 \\ 0 \\ \vdots \\ 1 \end{bmatrix}$$

$$= \sum_{i=1}^{m} a_{ij} \cdot w_i = f(v_j) \tag{1.28}$$

In other words, we have proved the first sentence of Theorem 1.25.

THEOREM 1.25   The columns of the matrix associated to $f : \mathbf{V} \longrightarrow \mathbf{W}$ are the f-images of the basis vectors of **V**. The image of f is the subspace of **W** spanned by the columns of the matrix.   □

Thus for any matrix A, we will use the term *column space* for the subspace of **W** spanned by the columns of A. Theorem 1.25 can now be worded as follows:

COROLLARY 1.26   IMf is the column space of the matrix A associated to f.   □

Continuing with A the matrix of $f : \mathbf{V} \longrightarrow \mathbf{W}$, we wish to consider the effect of multiplying A on the right by various special $n \times n$ matrices that we will now define. First, for $1 \le j \le n$, and λ any **non-zero** scalar, let

---

[7]This assumption is in fact always satisfied if we replace f by $g \circ f$, where g is the isomorphism that maps each w_j to the jth standard basis element. Therefore, this assumption is really more of a convention than an assumption.

$$M_i(\lambda) \;=\; \begin{bmatrix} 1 & 0 & & \cdots & & 0 \\ 0 & 1 & & \cdots & & 0 \\ & & \ddots & & & \\ \vdots & & & \lambda & & \vdots \\ & & & & \ddots & \\ 0 & 0 & & \cdots & & 1 \end{bmatrix} \tag{1.29}$$

where λ occurs as the ith diagonal element, and all other diagonal elements are 1. For any i, j with $i \neq j$ and $1 \leq i, j \leq n$, and any scalar μ, let

$$A_{ij}(\mu) \;=\; \begin{bmatrix} 1 & 0 & & \cdots & & 0 \\ 0 & 1 & & \cdots & & 0 \\ & & \ddots & & \mu & \\ & & & & & \\ & & & & \ddots & \\ 0 & 0 & & \cdots & & 1 \end{bmatrix} \tag{1.30}$$

where the μ appears in the ith row and the jth column. (In other words, $A_{ij}(\mu)$ is like the identity matrix I_n except that it has μ in one off-diagonal position.) Finally, for any $i \neq j$, let

$$P_{ij} \;=\; \begin{bmatrix} 1 & & & \cdots & & & 0 \\ & \ddots & & & & & \\ & & 0 & & 1 & & \\ \vdots & & & \ddots & & & \vdots \\ & & 1 & & 0 & & \\ & & & & & \ddots & \\ 0 & & & \cdots & & & 1 \end{bmatrix} \tag{1.31}$$

In other words, P_{ij} is like the identity matrix I_n with its ith and j^{th} rows interchanged. Now the reader may check that each of the matrices we have defined is invertible, in fact:

$$M_i(\lambda)^{-1} = M_i(1/\lambda), \quad A_{ij}(\mu)^{-1} = A_{ij}(-\mu) \quad \text{and} \quad P_{ij}^{-1} = P_{ij} \tag{1.32}$$

Therefore, any product whatever of these special matrices is invertible.

Now, what happens if we multiply A on the right by a product S of these special matrices? Since S is invertible, it follows from the results of §1.2.2 that AS is the matrix associated to a composite map $f \circ g$ for some automorphism g of $\mathbf{V}$; in other words, AS is the matrix of some composite homomorphism

$$\mathbf{V} \xrightarrow{\;\cong\;} \mathbf{V} \xrightarrow{\;f\;} \mathbf{W}$$

This composite homomorphism has the same image space as does f; hence, it follows that *multiplying A on the right by S does not change the column space.*

We can therefore use multiplications of A on the right by the special matrices as a means of analyzing the column space (otherwise known as **IM** f). Let us call a matrix R *column-reduced* iff it has the following properties:

- The uppermost non-zero entry of each column is 1.

- (For each $j > 1$) the uppermost non-zero entry of column j lies at least one row below the uppermost non-zero entry of column $j - 1$.

- Any column consisting entirely of zeros lies to the right of any column that does not consist entirely of zeros.

- If the uppermost non-zero entry of some column occurs in row i, then every other entry of row i is zero.

For example,

$$\begin{bmatrix} 1 & 0 & 0 \\ 3 & 0 & 0 \\ 0 & 1 & 0 \\ 0 & 0 & 1 \end{bmatrix}$$

is column-reduced, but

$$\begin{bmatrix} 2 & 0 & 0 \\ 3 & 0 & 0 \\ 0 & 1 & 0 \\ 0 & 0 & 1 \end{bmatrix}, \quad \begin{bmatrix} 0 & 1 & 0 \\ 0 & 3 & 0 \\ 1 & 0 & 0 \\ 0 & 0 & 1 \end{bmatrix} \quad \text{and} \quad \begin{bmatrix} 1 & 0 & 0 \\ 3 & 0 & 0 \\ 4 & 1 & 0 \\ 0 & 0 & 1 \end{bmatrix}$$

are not, because they violate the first, second and fourth properties just stated.

Now it is possible to convert any matrix into a column-reduced matrix by multiplying A on the right by some of the special matrices mentioned earlier; in fact, there is an *algorithm* for doing so. Before explaining the algorithm, it is helpful to have a description of how the special matrices act on A when they multiply on the right.

- $AM_i(\lambda)$ is like A except that the ith column has been multiplied by λ. For example,

$$\begin{bmatrix} 1 & 2 & 3 \\ 4 & 5 & 6 \\ 7 & 8 & 9 \end{bmatrix} \begin{bmatrix} 1 & 0 & 0 \\ 0 & 2 & 0 \\ 0 & 0 & 1 \end{bmatrix} = \begin{bmatrix} 1 & 4 & 3 \\ 4 & 10 & 6 \\ 7 & 16 & 9 \end{bmatrix}$$

- $AA_{ij}(\mu)$ is like A except that the jth column has been augmented by μ times the ith column. For example,

$$\begin{bmatrix} 1 & 2 & 3 \\ 4 & 5 & 6 \\ 7 & 8 & 9 \end{bmatrix} \begin{bmatrix} 1 & -1 & 0 \\ 0 & 1 & 0 \\ 0 & 0 & 1 \end{bmatrix} = \begin{bmatrix} 1 & 1 & 3 \\ 4 & 1 & 6 \\ 7 & 1 & 9 \end{bmatrix}$$

- AP_{ij} is like A, except that the ith and j^{th} columns have been interchanged. For example,

$$\begin{bmatrix} 1 & 2 & 3 \\ 4 & 5 & 6 \\ 7 & 8 & 9 \end{bmatrix} \begin{bmatrix} 1 & 0 & 0 \\ 0 & 0 & 1 \\ 0 & 1 & 0 \end{bmatrix} = \begin{bmatrix} 1 & 3 & 2 \\ 4 & 6 & 5 \\ 7 & 9 & 8 \end{bmatrix}$$

Each of the three modifications of A described here is called an *elementary column operation on A*, or simply a *column operation*. Therefore, the right multiplication by S is equivalent to performing a sequence of column operations on A.

We now describe an algorithm to change a matrix A to a column-reduced matrix AS by a sequence of column operations. We imagine a pointer that allows us to keep track of a location in the matrix A; i.e., the pointer keeps track of a row i and a column j.

ALGORITHM (column reduction of a matrix)   Begin with the pointer at the upper-left entry of A (i.e., the pointer begins with $i = j = 1$).

- If the pointer has been moved out of the matrix (i.e., if i exceeds the number of rows, or if j exceeds the number of columns), terminate the algorithm. Otherwise, continue.

- If the portion of the pointer row, beginning at the pointer and looking right from there, consists entirely of zeros, move the pointer down one row (i.e., increase i by 1) and begin these instructions again.

- Otherwise, interchange the pointer column with one to its right (if necessary) so that the entry at the pointer is non-zero. (Only the numbers are interchanged; the pointer does not move.) This involves multiplying by P_{jk} for some $k > j$.

- Multiply the pointer column by a non-zero scalar so that the value at the pointer is 1. This involves multiplying by M_j for some λ.

- Subtract multiples of the pointer column from all the other columns (both right and left of the pointer) so that the pointer row is all zero (except for the pointer entry itself). This involves multiplying by various matrices A_{ij} with $i \neq j$.

- Move the pointer down one row and right one column (i.e., increase both i and j by 1), and begin these instructions again.

We leave it to the reader to verify that the algorithm does always terminate in a column-reduced matrix. In fact, there is only one column-reduced matrix that can be obtained by applying column operations to A (see Theorem 1.29 of §1.2.5), and so this algorithm must lead to that unique column-reduced matrix.

One virtue of column reduction is that it gives us a basis of the column space. The following lemma is immediate from the definition of being column-reduced.

LEMMA   If matrix A is column-reduced, then its non-zero columns are linearly independent vectors of **W**.

Clearly, then, the non-zero vectors in a column-reduced form of A form a basis of the column space, in other words a basis of the subspace **IM**f of **W**. The number of these non-zero columns is called the *column rank* of A, and clearly this is the dimension of the space **IM**f. We emphasize that, without going through column reduction (or some procedure tantamount to column reduction), it is usually *impossible* to tell the dimension of the image space.

By way of example, let us perform the column reduction of

$$\begin{bmatrix} 0 & 2 & 1 \\ 1 & 2 & 1 \\ 0 & 6 & 3 \\ 0 & 2 & 0 \end{bmatrix}$$

leaving the justifications to the reader. Successive steps in the reduction are

$$\begin{bmatrix} 2 & 0 & 1 \\ 2 & 1 & 1 \\ 6 & 0 & 3 \\ 2 & 0 & 0 \end{bmatrix} \quad \begin{bmatrix} 1 & 0 & 1 \\ 1 & 1 & 1 \\ 3 & 0 & 3 \\ 1 & 0 & 0 \end{bmatrix} \quad \begin{bmatrix} 1 & 0 & 0 \\ 1 & 1 & 0 \\ 3 & 0 & 0 \\ 1 & 0 & -1 \end{bmatrix}$$

$$\begin{bmatrix} 1 & 0 & 0 \\ 0 & 1 & 0 \\ 3 & 0 & 0 \\ 1 & 0 & -1 \end{bmatrix} \quad \begin{bmatrix} 1 & 0 & 0 \\ 0 & 1 & 0 \\ 3 & 0 & 0 \\ 1 & 0 & 1 \end{bmatrix} \quad \begin{bmatrix} 1 & 0 & 0 \\ 0 & 1 & 0 \\ 3 & 0 & 0 \\ 0 & 0 & 1 \end{bmatrix}$$

From all of this we deduce that, in this case, **IM**f is a 3-dimensional subspace of the 4-dimensional space **W** with a basis consisting of these column vectors:

$$\begin{bmatrix} 1 \\ 0 \\ 3 \\ 0 \end{bmatrix} \quad \begin{bmatrix} 0 \\ 1 \\ 0 \\ 0 \end{bmatrix} \quad \begin{bmatrix} 0 \\ 0 \\ 0 \\ 1 \end{bmatrix}$$

1.2.5   The rows of a column-reduced matrix

Let A be the matrix corresponding to a homomorphism $f : V \longrightarrow W$. As before, we will assume that W is the space $\mathbb{R}^m$, with the standard basis

$$
w_1 = \begin{bmatrix} 1 \\ 0 \\ \vdots \\ 0 \end{bmatrix} ; \quad w_2 = \begin{bmatrix} 0 \\ 1 \\ \vdots \\ 0 \end{bmatrix} ; \quad \cdots , \quad w_m = \begin{bmatrix} 0 \\ 0 \\ \vdots \\ 1 \end{bmatrix}
$$

as mentioned previously in Equation (1.27). A typical element of $W = \mathbb{R}^m$ will be denoted $w = \sum_{i=1}^{m} x_i w_i = \langle x_1, \cdots, x_m \rangle$. In Theorem 1.1, we saw that the set of vectors w that satisfy $\sum_{i=1}^{m} \lambda_i x_i = 0$ is a subspace of W. Here we will use the *rows* of a column-reduced form of A to represent $\mathbf{IM}f$ as a solution set of finitely many equations of this type.

It follows from the definition that if A is column-reduced, then the rows of A are of two types:

- A row that contains, for some j, the highest non-zero entry in the jth column. This entry is 1, and all other entries of the row are 0; in other words, the row is $\langle 0, \cdots, 0, 1, 0, \cdots, 0 \rangle$, with 1 in the jth position. We denote this row r_j and call it the jth *independent row of* A. The independent rows are $r_1 \ldots r_k$ for k the (column) rank of A. Clearly, r_{i+1} occurs below r_i in A, for each i.

- The other rows are called *dependent rows*; the number of dependent rows is $m - k$, where k is the rank of A. They may be denoted $s_1 \ldots s_{m-k}$. Each s_j has the property that any non-zero entry of s_j lies below the 1 of some independent row.

Notice that the dependent and independent rows can occur in any order whatever. It follows easily from our last remark about dependent rows that each dependent row s_j is a linear combination of the independent rows that lie above it. For example, in

$$
\begin{bmatrix} 1 & 0 & 0 \\ 0 & 1 & 0 \\ 5 & 7 & 0 \\ 0 & 0 & 1 \end{bmatrix}
$$

we have $s_1 = 5 \cdot r_1 + 7 \cdot r_2$. But, on the other hand, an independent row r_j is *not* a linear combination of the rows above it (since those rows all have 0 in the jth column).

We next observe that any linear dependence of the jth dependent row s_j on the previous rows implies that an equation of the form $\sum_{i=1}^{m} \lambda_i^j x_i = 0$ holds in the column space of A. For example, the above equation $s_1 = 5 \cdot r_1 + 7 \cdot r_2$ corresponds to the fact that the equation $x_3 = 5x_1 + 7x_2$ holds for each column of the displayed matrix, and hence holds in the space generated by its columns. Moreover, if K_j is defined so that s_j is the $K_j{}^{\text{th}}$ row of A, then the coefficients λ_i^j have the property that $\lambda_{K_j}^j = 1$ and $\lambda_i^j = 0$ for $i > K_j$. (Our example gives the equation for $j = 1$ and $K_j = 3$.)

THEOREM 1.27   If $\mathbf{W}$ is the column space of an $m \times n$ matrix A, then there exist an integer M with $0 \le M \le m$ and numbers $\lambda_i^j \in \mathbb{R}$, such that $\mathbf{W}$ is the set of vectors

$$\{\langle x_1, \cdots, x_m \rangle \ : \ \text{for } 0 \le j \le M \ \sum_{i=1}^{m} \lambda_i^j x_i = 0\}$$

(In other words, $\mathbf{W}$ is an intersection of M subspaces of the type described in Theorem 1.1.)

Proof   We continue to suppose that A is an $m \times n$ column-reduced matrix of rank k. We take M to be $m - k$, the number of dependent rows of A. For $1 \le j \le M$, we take the coefficients λ_i^j to be defined as they are just before this theorem. Finally, for each r with $1 \le r \le M$, we define $\mathbf{W}_r$ to be the subspace of $\mathbb{R}^m$ defined by the equations $\sum_{i=1}^{n} \lambda_i^j x_i = 0$ for $1 \le j \le r$. (In other terminology, $\mathbf{W}_r$ is the solution set of these equations.) As we remarked before the theorem, the column space $\mathbf{W}$ satisfies these equations, and so we have

$$\mathbf{W} \subseteq \mathbf{W}_M \subseteq \mathbf{W}_{M-1} \subseteq \ \cdots \ \subseteq \mathbf{W}_1 \subseteq \mathbb{R}^m$$

Now each equation $\sum_{i=1}^{n} \lambda_i^j x_i = 0$ involves a variable (the $K_j{}^{\text{th}}$) that does not appear in the equations with smaller j. Therefore, each subspace $\mathbf{W}_{r+1}$ is a proper subspace of $\mathbf{W}_r$ (and $\mathbf{W}_1$ is a proper subspace of $\mathbb{R}^m$). Therefore, as r increases, the dimensions of the spaces $\mathbf{W}_r$ must decrease, and so we easily see that $\mathbf{W}_M$ has dimension no more than $m - M = k$. But k is also the rank of A, i.e., the dimension of $\mathbf{W}$. Therefore, we have $\mathbf{W} \subseteq \mathbf{W}_M$, with both subspaces having the same dimension. Therefore, $\mathbf{W} = \mathbf{W}_M$ by Corollary 1.12, and the proof of the theorem is complete.   □

COROLLARY 1.28   For every subspace $\mathbf{W}$ of $\mathbb{R}^m$, there exist an integer M with $0 \le M \le m$ and numbers $\lambda_i^j \in \mathbb{R}$, such that $\mathbf{W}$ is the set of vectors

$$\{\langle x_1, \cdots, x_m \rangle \ : \ \text{for } 0 \le j \le M \ \sum_{i=1}^{m} \lambda_i^j x_i = 0\}$$

Proof   Since $\mathbf{W} \subseteq \mathbb{R}^m$, there is a basis $\langle w_1, \cdots, w_k \rangle$ of $\mathbf{W}$ with $k \le m$. Let A be an $m \times k$ matrix having the vectors w_i as its k columns. Clearly, $\mathbf{W}$ is the column space of A, and so the corollary is immediate from the theorem.   □

Our algorithm gave one way to start at an arbitrary matrix B and arrive at a column-reduced matrix A by applying column operations. Nevertheless, there are a number of ways one might proceed—sometimes one notices shortcuts, and so on. Theorem 1.29 assures us that it does not matter how we do our reduction (so long as we use legitimate column operations). Its proof is made possible by the row analysis of this section.

THEOREM 1.29   For any matrix B, there is a unique column-reduced matrix A that can be obtained from B by applying column operations.

Proof   Our algorithm shows that one such A exists. For uniqueness, let us suppose that both A and A' are column-reduced matrices obtained from B by applying column operations. Then both A and A' have the same column space as does B. Let us denote this common column space by $\mathbf{W}$.

We will next show that the independent and dependent rows of A (or A') are determined by the equations that hold in the column space $\mathbf{W}$. It follows directly from our analysis of the rows of A that the kth row of A is dependent iff each vector $\langle x_1, \cdots, x_m \rangle$ in $\mathbf{W}$ satisfies an equation

$$x_k = \sum_{i<k} \alpha_i \cdot x_i \tag{1.33}$$

that expresses x_k as a linear combination of components x_i for $i < k$. For each $i < k$ such that the ith row is dependent, $\alpha_i \cdot x_i$ can be eliminated from this equation, since x_i is itself a linear combination of earlier components. Thus, we see that if the kth row is dependent, then $\mathbf{W}$ satisfies Equation (1.33) with all coefficients $\alpha_i = 0$ except those α_i that correspond to independent rows of A.

We now see that the coefficients in Equation (1.33) are uniquely determined by this last condition. For suppose that $\mathbf{W}$ also satisfied

$$x_k = \sum_{i<k} \alpha_i' \cdot x_i$$

with all $\alpha_i' = 0$ except for those α_i' corresponding to independent rows. Subtracting this last equation from Equation (1.33) yields

$$\sum_{i<k} (\alpha_i' - \alpha_i) \cdot x_i = 0$$

We now have an equation that involves only x_i for independent rows; hence, it follows that all its coefficients $(\alpha_i' - \alpha_i)$ are zero. Hence, the uniqueness of the coefficients α_i is proved.

On the other hand, our row analysis of column-reduced matrices showed that the entries in the kth row of A could serve as coefficients α_i for Equation (1.33). Therefore, the only possibility for these entries is the unique family of coefficients α_i. Thus, we have seen that the dependent rows of A, and of A', are determined by the common space **W**. These rows are determined both in their locations and in their exact coefficients; hence, A and A' must be exactly the same matrix.   □

1.2.6   Calculating the inverse of a matrix

If A is a square matrix, then column reduction of A allows us to determine whether A is invertible. Moreover, in case A is invertible, the reduction algorithm can be extended to yield a calculation of the inverse matrix A^{-1}.

Let A be an $n \times n$ matrix. We know from Corollary 1.22 of §1.1.5 that A is invertible iff the associated linear transformation $f : \mathbb{R}^n \longrightarrow \mathbb{R}^n$ is surjective, and this happens iff the column space of A has dimension n. This in turn happens iff the column-reduced form of A has n linearly independent columns. Now the reader may easily check from the definition of being column-reduced that there is only one column-reduced $n \times n$ matrix that has n non-zero columns, namely, the identity matrix I_n.

Therefore, if we perform column reduction upon an $n \times n$ matrix A and the algorithm leads to the identity matrix, then A is invertible. Otherwise, A is not invertible.

Moreover, the precise steps used in the column reduction can be used to find A^{-1}, if this exists. For each step of the column-reduction algorithm consists in performing one column operation, which is equivalent as we have seen, to multiplying A on the right by one of the special matrices $M_i(\lambda)$, $A_{ij}(\mu)$ or P_{ij}. Combining all these right multipliers into one, the whole procedure is equivalent to multiplying A on the right by a single matrix S that is the product of all the special matrices that get used in implementing the algorithm for A. Well, this means that $AS = I$; in other words, the S here is the very inverse of A that we are looking for: $A^{-1} = S$.

By the way, if $A^{-1} = S$, then $A = S^{-1}$, and so Theorem 1.30 follows immediately.

THEOREM 1.30   Every non-singular matrix is a product of matrices $M_i(\lambda), A_{ij}(\mu)$ and P_{ij}.   □

In order to find A^{-1}, we need only keep track of the matrix S as it is formed. The easiest way to do this is to observe that $S = IS$, and so if all the special operations that we used above are right multiplied against I in the same order that we performed the multiplications in reducing A, then the resulting matrix will be S. Therefore, *the inverse matrix $S = A^{-1}$ can be calculated by subjecting I to the same column operations that were used to perform the column reduction of A.*

A systematic way to accomplish this is described in the following enhancement to the column-reduction algorithm.

ALGORITHM (the inversion of a non-singular $n \times n$ matrix)

- Enlarge the matrix A by adding n more rows that look like the identity matrix.

- Perform column reduction on the enlarged matrix.

- Examine the upper n rows. If they fail to form the identity matrix I_n, then A has no inverse, and the algorithm terminates by reporting this fact and outputting the reduced matrix.

- If the first n rows do form I_n, then A is invertible, and this fact can be reported by the algorithm. The last n rows form the inverse, which will be output by the algorithm.

By way of example, let us apply the algorithm to find the inverse of the matrix

$$\begin{bmatrix} 2 & 3 & 2 \\ 2 & 1 & 1 \\ 1 & 5 & 3 \end{bmatrix}$$

(In §1.2.3 we exhibited the inverse and calculated that it was correct. What is at stake now is to actually find the inverse from scratch.) So, we append three rows that form the identity matrix and then start performing column operations:

$$\begin{bmatrix} 2 & 3 & 2 \\ 2 & 1 & 1 \\ 1 & 5 & 3 \\ 1 & 0 & 0 \\ 0 & 1 & 0 \\ 0 & 0 & 1 \end{bmatrix} \begin{bmatrix} 1 & 3 & 2 \\ 1 & 1 & 1 \\ .5 & 5 & 3 \\ .5 & 0 & 0 \\ 0 & 1 & 0 \\ 0 & 0 & 1 \end{bmatrix} \begin{bmatrix} 1 & 0 & 0 \\ 1 & -2 & -1 \\ .5 & 3.5 & 2 \\ .5 & -1.5 & -1 \\ 0 & 1 & 0 \\ 0 & 0 & 1 \end{bmatrix} \begin{bmatrix} 1 & 0 & 0 \\ 1 & 1 & -1 \\ .50 & -1.75 & 2 \\ .50 & .75 & -1 \\ 0 & -.50 & 0 \\ 0 & 0 & 1 \end{bmatrix}$$

$$\begin{bmatrix} 1 & 0 & 0 \\ 0 & 1 & 0 \\ 2.25 & -1.75 & 0.25 \\ -0.25 & 0.75 & -0.25 \\ 0.5 & -0.5 & -0.5 \\ 0 & 0 & 1 \end{bmatrix} \begin{bmatrix} 1 & 0 & 0 \\ 0 & 1 & 0 \\ 2.25 & -1.75 & 1 \\ -0.25 & 0.75 & -1 \\ 0.5 & -0.5 & -2 \\ 0 & 0 & 4 \end{bmatrix} \begin{bmatrix} 1 & 0 & 0 \\ 0 & 1 & 0 \\ 0 & 0 & 1 \\ 2 & -1 & -1 \\ 5 & -4 & -2 \\ -9 & 7 & 4 \end{bmatrix}$$

The final matrix here shows that the inverse matrix is indeed

$$\begin{bmatrix} 2 & -1 & -1 \\ 5 & -4 & -2 \\ -9 & 7 & 4 \end{bmatrix}$$

This algorithm for finding the inverse of a matrix is eminently suitable for implementation[8] via any of the modern high-level computer languages such as Pascal, Lisp or C, as the reader may easily check.

We should point out that, in practice, it is often not necessary to carry out the entire algorithm to compute inverses of matrices. Many of our most useful matrices—introduced mainly in §§3.3, 4.5 and 5.3—have natural geometric definitions that can be understood in reverse to provide the inverse matrix. For instance, if the matrix R_θ corresponds to a clockwise rotation through angle θ, then the inverse matrix is simply the matrix $R_{-\theta}$ corresponding to a counter-clockwise rotation through angle θ. More formally, we can always get the inverse of a matrix A in this manner—by negating a parameter—if A lies in a *one-parameter subgroup*, a concept to be introduced in §3.3.

Another useful way to calculate inverses of certain matrices is to sum power series. The student may recall, say from a calculus class, that

$$(1 - A)^{-1} = 1 + A + A^2 + A^3 + \cdots + A^{n-1} + A^n(1 - A)^{-1}$$

for any real number $A \neq 1$ and any positive integer n. The same elementary algebra that establishes this equation for numbers remains valid if A is taken to be a matrix such that $1 - A$ is invertible. Thus, we know that if the powers A^n of A approach 0 (the zero-matrix) sufficiently fast as $n \to \infty$, then the infinite series

$$(1 - A)^{-1} = 1 + A + A^2 + A^3 + \cdots$$

converges to the inverse of $1 - A$. Hence, finite partial sums can be used as an an approximation to the inverse. In Equation (3.2.3) of §3.19, we describe a situation where this method has a practical application.

Exercises

1. Find the inverse of $\begin{bmatrix} 1 & 0 & .1 \\ 0 & 1 & 0 \\ .1 & 0 & 1 \end{bmatrix}$ and $\begin{bmatrix} 2 & 0 & .1 \\ 0 & 2 & 0 \\ .1 & 0 & 2 \end{bmatrix}$ using the power series method.

2. Find the inverse of $\begin{bmatrix} 1 & 3 & 1 \\ 0 & 1 & 17 \\ 0 & 0 & 1 \end{bmatrix}$ and $\begin{bmatrix} 2 & 3 & 1 \\ 0 & 2 & 17 \\ 0 & 0 & 2 \end{bmatrix}$ using the power series method.

---

[8]One tricky part is that in implementing the second step of the algorithm, whereby one interchanges columns to position a non-zero scalar a at the pointer, one must be sure that a is sufficiently far from zero to permit successful division by a.

1.2.7   Row operations on matrices

We continue to examine a homomorphism $\mathbf{V} \xrightarrow{f} \mathbf{W}$, with the spaces $\mathbf{V}$, $\mathbf{W}$ of dimension m and n, respectively, and the associated $m \times n$ matrix A.

Let us again examine the square matrices $M_i(\lambda)$, $A_{ij}(\mu)$ and P_{ij} of §1.2.4, only this time we will take them to be $m \times m$ matrices and consider what happens if A is multiplied on the *left* by one of these matrices or by a product of them.

We will not need to give the reader every detail, since most of what happens is just like what happened in §1.2.4, except that the notions of column and row are interchanged. Thus, multiplying on the left by $M_i(\lambda)$ multiplies all elements of the ith row by λ, multiplying on the left by $A_{ij}(\mu)$ augments the ith row by μ times the jth row, and multiplying on the left by P_{ij} interchanges the ith and j^{th} rows. These effects of multiplying on the left by $M_i(\lambda)$, $A_{ij}(\mu)$ and P_{ij} are called *elementary row operations* on the matrix A. There is a notion of *row-reduced matrix*, which, e.g., refers to the leftmost non-zero entry of a row where the previous definition referred to the uppermost non-zero entry of a column, and so on. There is an algorithm called *row reduction* that performs a sequence of elementary row operations on A to make it row-reduced.

As we saw in §1.2.4, the columns of A span $\mathbf{IM}f$, and after column reduction the non-zero columns form a basis of this space. There is no corresponding elementary conceptual description of the rows of A. Nevertheless, we can still observe that row reduction corresponds to multiplying A on the left by an invertible matrix S, and SA corresponds to the linear map

$$\mathbf{V} \xrightarrow{f} \mathbf{W} \xrightarrow{h} \mathbf{W}$$

for some automorphism h of $\mathbf{W}$. Since h is a bijection, if follows that, for any $v \in V$, $f(v) = 0$ iff $h \circ f(v) = 0$, and therefore $\mathbf{KER}\,h \circ f = \mathbf{KER}\,f$. Thus, *multiplying A on the left by S does not change the kernel of the associated linear map* $\mathbf{V} \longrightarrow \mathbf{W}$.

Let us carry out one example of row reduction to illustrate how our previous observation allows us to systematically find a basis for $\mathbf{KER}\,f$. Suppose that the matrix A is

$$\begin{bmatrix} 1 & 2 & 1 & 7 & 1 \\ 1 & 2 & 1 & 7 & 2 \\ 0 & 0 & 2 & 8 & 1 \end{bmatrix}$$

representing $\mathbb{R}^5 \xrightarrow{f} \mathbb{R}^3$. Then our row reduction of A proceeds as follows:

$$\begin{bmatrix} 1 & 2 & 1 & 7 & 1 \\ 0 & 0 & 0 & 0 & 1 \\ 0 & 0 & 2 & 8 & 1 \end{bmatrix} \quad \begin{bmatrix} 1 & 2 & 1 & 7 & 1 \\ 0 & 0 & 2 & 8 & 1 \\ 0 & 0 & 0 & 0 & 1 \end{bmatrix}$$

$$\begin{bmatrix} 1 & 2 & 1 & 7 & 1 \\ 0 & 0 & 1 & 4 & 0.5 \\ 0 & 0 & 0 & 0 & 1 \end{bmatrix} \qquad \begin{bmatrix} 1 & 2 & 0 & 3 & 0.5 \\ 0 & 0 & 1 & 4 & 0.5 \\ 0 & 0 & 0 & 0 & 1 \end{bmatrix}$$

$$\begin{bmatrix} 1 & 2 & 0 & 3 & 0 \\ 0 & 0 & 1 & 4 & 0 \\ 0 & 0 & 0 & 0 & 1 \end{bmatrix}$$

Now let us investigate the kernel of this last matrix. A typical vector in $\mathbb{R}^5$ may be denoted $\langle x_1, \cdots, x_5 \rangle$, and for this element to be in the kernel we need

$$\begin{bmatrix} 1 & 2 & 0 & 3 & 0 \\ 0 & 0 & 1 & 4 & 0 \\ 0 & 0 & 0 & 0 & 1 \end{bmatrix} \begin{bmatrix} x_1 \\ x_2 \\ x_3 \\ x_4 \\ x_5 \end{bmatrix} = \begin{bmatrix} 0 \\ 0 \\ 0 \\ 0 \\ 0 \end{bmatrix}$$

This matrix equation resolves into three ordinary linear equations for the five quantities $x_1, \cdots, x_5$:

$$\begin{aligned} x_1 + 2x_2 + 3x_4 &= 0 \\ x_3 + 4x_4 &= 0 \\ x_5 &= 0 \end{aligned}$$

These equations are trivial to solve if we regard the leading terms x_1, x_3 and x_5 as determined by them, while regarding the other variables x_2 and x_4 as not determined. Therefore, we solve them by taking x_2 to be an arbitrary scalar α and x_4 to be another arbitrary scalar β, and then we solve the three equations uniquely for x_1, x_3 and x_5:

$$\begin{aligned} x_1 &= -2\alpha - 3\beta \\ x_3 &= -4\beta \\ x_5 &= 0 \end{aligned}$$

Therefore, we may say that a general solution to the equation is

$$\begin{bmatrix} x_1 \\ x_2 \\ x_3 \\ x_4 \\ x_5 \end{bmatrix} = \alpha \cdot \begin{bmatrix} -2 \\ 1 \\ 0 \\ 0 \\ 0 \end{bmatrix} + \beta \cdot \begin{bmatrix} -3 \\ 0 \\ -4 \\ 1 \\ 0 \end{bmatrix}$$

or, equivalently, that the two vectors

$$\begin{bmatrix} -2 \\ 1 \\ 0 \\ 0 \\ 0 \end{bmatrix} \quad \text{and} \quad \begin{bmatrix} -3 \\ 0 \\ -4 \\ 1 \\ 0 \end{bmatrix}$$

form a basis of **KER** f.

It is, of course, no accident that the numbers $2, 3$ and 4 appearing in the row-reduced form of A reappear in the above basis for **KER** f; in fact, the procedure can be made completely systematic. By analogy with our treatment of column-reduced matrices in §1.2.5, let us divide the columns of a row-reduced matrix A into *independent* and *dependent* columns. (A column is independent if, for some i, it contains the leftmost non-zero entry of the ith row; this entry is 1, and all other entries of the column are 0.) Then **KER** f has one basis element v_j for each dependent column C_j. If the jth column C_j of A is dependent, the corresponding basis element v_k of **KER** f is determined as follows. Each non-zero entry λ in C_j lies in the same row as the one of exactly one independent column, C_k, for some $k < j$. We will designate this entry as λ_k. We now define v_k to be the $m \times 1$ matrix that has $-\lambda_k$ in column k (for the k values just mentioned) and has 1 in column j. It is not hard to check that these vectors form a basis of **KER** f.

Notice that in some sense column reduction and row reduction perform opposite or complementary tasks on subspaces of $\mathbb{R}^n$. If subspace **W** is specified by a basis (or even by a spanning set of k vectors), then column reduction leads (as in Corollary 1.28) to a set of $m - k$ (or more) equations whose solution set is **W**. On the other hand, if **W** is originally specified as the solution set of a set of k linear equations, then row reduction leads to a basis of **W** consisting of $m - k$ or more vectors.

The number r of non-zero rows in the row-reduced form of A is called the *row rank* of A. Clearly, r is the same as the number of rows that have a prominent 1 as described in the preceding paragraph. Since the columns are divided (as above) into those with a prominent 1 and those that correspond to basis elements of **KER** f, we see that

$$r + \dim \textbf{KER}\, f \;=\; n$$

the number of columns of A. Since in fact $n = \dim \textbf{V}$, we have

$$r \;=\; \dim \textbf{V} - \dim \textbf{KER}\, f$$

and so by Corollary 1.22 of §1.1.5, we have

$$r \;=\; \dim \textbf{IM} f$$

which is equal to the column rank of A by results in §1.2.4. In other words, *the row rank and the column rank of a matrix are the same number* (which is called the *rank* of A).

In §1.2.6, we saw how to calculate the inverse of an $n \times n$ matrix A by performing column operations on the $2n \times n$ matrix that is formed by placing the identity matrix I_n below A. Exactly the same thing works for row operations, and, *mutatis mutandis*, for the identical reasons. A has an inverse iff row reduction of A leads to the identity matrix I_n. Moreover, if A^{-1} exists, it can be calculated as follows. If the identity matrix is placed to the right of A so as to form an $n \times 2n$ matrix, row reduction of this matrix will lead to the identity matrix on the left and the inverse A^{-1} on the right. The sequence of intermediate steps will of course be very different; but the two methods, row reduction and column reduction, both lead to the same inverse matrix since inverses are unique.

1.2.8   Cosets

If $\mathbf{W}$ is a subspace of $\mathbf{V}$ and $v \in V$, then the $\mathbf{W}$-*coset of v* is the set

$$\mathbf{W} + v = \{w + v : w \in W\}$$

By a $\mathbf{W}$-*coset in* $\mathbf{V}$, we mean the $\mathbf{W}$-coset of v, for some $v \in V$. Our first lemma tells us that the space $\mathbf{W}$ is determined by any one of its cosets.

LEMMA 8   If C is a $\mathbf{W}$-coset, then, for any fixed $c_0 \in C$, $\mathbf{W} = \{c - c_0 : c \in C\}$.
    □

LEMMA 9 $\mathbf{W} + v = \mathbf{W} + v'$ iff $(v - v') \in W$.   □

LEMMA 10   If two $\mathbf{W}$-cosets $\mathbf{W} + v$ and $\mathbf{W} + v'$ have one vector in common, then $\mathbf{W} + v = \mathbf{W} + v'$.   □

THEOREM 1.31   For a fixed subspace $\mathbf{W}$ of a vector space $\mathbf{V}$, the family of all $\mathbf{W}$-cosets forms a partition of the set V. The associated equivalence relation $R_{\mathbf{W}}$ may be defined as follows:

$$v\, R_{\mathbf{W}}\, v' \quad \text{iff} \quad v - v' \in W$$

The $R_{\mathbf{V}}$-class of 0 is W.   □

For instance, if $\mathbf{V} = \mathbb{R}^2$ and $\mathbf{W}$ is a one-dimensional subspace, then geometrically $\mathbf{W}$ is a line L through $\langle 0, 0 \rangle$, and the cosets of $\mathbf{W}$ are the lines parallel to L. This is the formal interpretation of *line* that we will adopt at the beginning of Chapter 3.

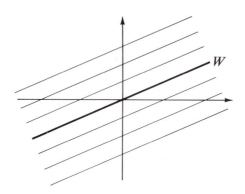

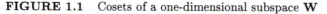

FIGURE 1.1   Cosets of a one-dimensional subspace **W**

Another use of cosets is for the construction of new vector spaces. If **W** is a subspace of **V**, let V/W denote the collection of *all* **W**-cosets in **V**. Elements of V/W (i.e., cosets) can be added by defining $(\mathbf{W}+v_1)+(\mathbf{W}+v_2)$ as $\mathbf{W}+(v_1+v_2)$. Similarly, elements of V/W can be multiplied by scalars by defining $\alpha(\mathbf{W}+v)$ as $\mathbf{W}+\alpha v$. We leave the proof of Theorem 1.32 to the interested student.

THEOREM 1.32   Under these definitions of addition and scalar multiplication, the set V/W acquires the structure of a vector space **V/W**. The dimension of this space is $\dim \mathbf{V} - \dim \mathbf{W}$.   □

The space **V/W** is called the *quotient space of* **V** *by* **W**. We will have a use for it in §1.4.

1.2.9   Systems of linear equations

The general system of linear equations

$$\begin{bmatrix} a_{11} & a_{12} & \cdots & a_{1n} \\ a_{21} & a_{22} & \cdots & a_{2n} \\ \vdots & \vdots & \ddots & \vdots \\ a_{m1} & a_{m2} & \cdots & a_{mn} \end{bmatrix} \begin{bmatrix} x_1 \\ x_2 \\ \vdots \\ x_n \end{bmatrix} = \begin{bmatrix} b_1 \\ b_2 \\ \vdots \\ b_m \end{bmatrix} \qquad (1.34)$$

may be more succinctly represented as $Ax = b$, where A is an $m \times n$ matrix, $b \in \mathbf{W}$ (a space of dimension m, which we may take to be $\mathbb{R}^m$), and x denotes an unknown (and perhaps non-existent) element of **V** (a space of dimension n, which we may take to be $\mathbb{R}^n$).

There are really two separate problems here:

- To find a single $a \in \mathbf{V}$, such that $x = a$ will solve the equation $Ax = b$, or to determine that no such solution exists

- Given such an a, to find the set of all solutions

A single $a \in \mathbf{V}$ that satisfies the equations is called a *particular solution* of the equation $Ax = b$. Let us retain our convention that A is the matrix of $f : \mathbf{V} \longrightarrow \mathbf{W}$.

THEOREM 1.33   If a is a particular solution of $Ax = b$, then

$$\{a + v : v \in \mathbf{KER}\, f\}$$

is the set of all solutions of $Ax = b$. $\square$

An equation is called *homogeneous* iff it has the form $Ax = 0$. For such equations, Theorem 1.33 simply says that the set of solutions is the kernel of f (which we knew already). Sometimes it is said that the equation $Ax = 0$ is *the homogeneous equation associated to* $Ax = b$. With this terminology, we can paraphrase the theorem as follows: *Let a be a particular solution to the equation $Ax = b$. The general solution is formed by adding a to any solution of the associated homogeneous solution.*

From the point of view of §1.2.8, our last assertion—or Theorem 1.33—can be restated as follows.

THEOREM 1.34   The solution set of the system of Equations (1.34) is a coset of the subspace $\mathbf{KER}\, f$ of $\mathbb{R}^n$. $\square$

As for the practicalities of solving Equation (1.34), we already saw in §1.2.7 how to solve the homogeneous equation $Ax = 0$, and so all that remains is to find a particular solution or to prove that none exists. For this there is a trick. What we wish to know, first of all, is whether b is in the vector space $\mathbf{IM}f$, which by §1.2.4 is the space generated by the columns of A. This will be true iff $\mathbf{IM}f$ is also equal to the space generated by b together with the columns of A. This, in turn, will be true iff $\mathbf{IM}f$ has the same dimension as the space generated by b together with all the columns of A. But this latter dimension is simply the rank of the so-called *augmented matrix*

$$\begin{bmatrix} a_{11} & a_{12} & \cdots & a_{1n} & b_1 \\ a_{21} & a_{22} & \cdots & a_{2n} & b_2 \\ \vdots & \vdots & \ddots & \vdots & \vdots \\ a_{m1} & a_{m2} & \cdots & a_{mn} & b_m \end{bmatrix} \tag{1.35}$$

Therefore, if the rank of the augmented matrix is larger than the rank of the matrix A, then the equation $Ax = b$ has no solution. On the other hand, if these two matrices have the same rank, then a solution does exist, and we may find one (particular) solution as follows. Consider the row-reduced matrix R that one forms by applying row reduction to the augmented matrix (1.35). Each of its non-zero rows contains a *prominent* 1, as explained in §1.2.7, namely a 1 that has nothing other than zeros to the left of it. We now form a particular solution a as follows. Whenever we have a prominent 1 as the (i, j)-entry of R, we take a_j to be $R_{i,n+1}$, i.e., the far right (or augmented) entry of the ith row of R. This determines k components of a, where k is the rank of A; the other $n - k$ components of a may be taken as zero.

THEOREM 1.35   The a determined in this way is a particular solution to the equation $Ax = b$.   □

Exercises_____

1. Prove Theorem 1.34.

2. Prove Theorem 1.35. (Hint: Use the methods discussed in §1.2.7. Notice that every row of R corresponds to an equation derived from the original Equations (1.34).)

1.3   Determinants

To every *square* matrix A there is associated a scalar denoted $\det A$ called the *determinant* of A. Understanding the definition of $\det A$ (and the associated calculations that are needed to evaluate it) demands a thorough understanding of the basic theory of vector spaces and linear maps; moreover, the theory of determinants extends and enriches this basic theory. On the other hand, none of the elementary drawing algorithms described in this book require one to calculate complicated determinants; in fact, every attempt has made to use matrices whose determinants can be seen at a glance. Determinants rather serve in a conceptual or explanatory capacity. For example, the theory of eigenvalues can hardly be explained without them—see §1.4 and §3.3.7. They also figure in discussions of area preservation (see §3.3.6) and discussions of the preservation or reversing of orientation (see the start of §3.3 and §5.3.5).

Therefore, it may be advisable for some students or groups of students to skip some of the more theoretical material that follows, especially the proofs in §1.3.2 and §1.3.3. A good practical understanding can be acquired by studying Equations (1.36), (1.37), (1.38), and (1.40) in §1.3.1 and the algorithms that are found in §1.3.4 and §1.3.5. We will base our first algorithm on Equation (1.42).

Before proceeding, we should say just a little about the idea of a permutation. A *permutation* of a set K is a function from K to itself that is one-to-one and onto. For K a finite set, every one-to-one function $A \longrightarrow A$ maps onto A; and, conversely, every function from A onto A is one-to-one. We limit our attention to permutations on finite sets, and in particular to the finite set $\{1, \cdots, n\}$. For us, then, a permutation is a bijection

$$\sigma : \{1, \cdots, n\} \xrightarrow{\cong} \{1, \cdots, n\}$$

For many considerations about permutations, what matters is that we have a set of n objects, not what the objects are. Therefore, we sometimes speak simply of "permutations on n objects" or "permutations on n letters."

The values of a permutation σ of $\{1, \cdots, n\}$ can be denoted in a number of ways, including the simple expedient of writing, e.g., $\sigma(1) = 2, \sigma(2) = 3, \sigma(3) = 1$ (as a permutation of $\{1, 2, 3\}$). However, it is more efficient to write $\sigma = (1, 2, 3)$ in what is known as cyclic notation. The notation simply means that 1 maps to 2, 2 to 3, and 3 to 1. A permutation may have more than one cycle, such as $\rho = (1, 3)(2, 4)$. Here the notation means that $\rho(1) = 3, \rho(3) = 1, \rho(2) = 4$, and $\rho(4) = 2$. Permutations may be multiplied via composition of functions: The product of ρ and σ is $\rho \circ \sigma$. For example, with the above examples of ρ and σ, we have $\rho \circ \sigma = (1, 4, 2)$. Under this operation of composition, the set of all permutations on n letters forms a *group*.

A permutation (i, j) that interchanges the numbers i and j and leaves all other numbers fixed is called a *transposition*. It is not hard to prove that *every permutation is a product of transpositions*. For example, the σ defined above is equal to $(1, 2) \circ (2, 3)$. Since we, so to speak, *factor* σ into a product of transpositions, one may think of this as a *factorization* result, like factoring a number into a product of prime factors. Unique factorization is far from true here, but at least the following important fact can be proved. A permutation σ can be factored either as a product of an even number of transpositions, or as a product of an odd number, but both cases cannot occur for a given σ. That is, the set of all permutation can be divided once and for all into two classes: the *even* permutations that can be factored as a product of an even number of transpositions and the *odd* permutations that can be factored as a product of an odd number of transpositions. The *identity function* on $\{1, \cdots, n\}$, by the way, is an even permutation, since it is the product of *no* transpositions (or, if you like, the square of any transposition whatever). The distinction between odd and even permutations will be important in our development of the theory of determinants.

For every permutation σ, we define $\varepsilon(\sigma)$ to be 1 if σ is an even permutation, and -1 if σ is an odd permutation. Therefore, $\varepsilon(\tau) = -1$ for every transposition τ; moreover,

$$\varepsilon(\sigma \circ \sigma') = \varepsilon(\sigma)\varepsilon(\sigma')$$

for any two permutations σ and σ'.

1.3.1   The defining properties of determinants

Here we present a postulational approach to determinants that is largely due to Karl Weierstrass (1815–1897). Let $\mathbf{V}$ be a vector space of dimension n, with $\langle v_1, \cdots, v_n \rangle$ a basis of $\mathbf{V}$. A *determinant for* $\mathbf{V}$ is a function

$$D_n : V^n \longrightarrow F$$

where F is the field[9] of scalars, that satisfies the following equations:

$$
\begin{align}
D_n(v_1 + v_1', v_2, \cdots, v_n) &= D_n(v_1, \cdots, v_n) + D_n(v_1', \cdots, v_n) \tag{1.36} \\
D_n(\alpha \cdot v_1, v_2, \cdots, v_n) &= \alpha \cdot D_n(v_1, \cdots, v_n) \tag{1.37} \\
D_n(v_{\sigma(1)}, \cdots, v_{\sigma(n)}) &= \varepsilon(\sigma) \cdot D_n(v_1, \cdots, v_n) \tag{1.38}
\end{align}
$$

(In Equation (1.37), α is an arbitrary scalar, and in Equation (1.38), σ is an arbitrary permutation of $\{1, \cdots, n\}$.) A function, such as D_n, that satisfies Equation (1.38) is called *antisymmetric*. (The *anti* comes from the fact that $\varepsilon(\sigma)$ may be -1.) Notice that it is in fact enough to assume only that

$$D_n(v_{\tau(1)}, \cdots, v_{\tau(n)}) = -D_n(v_1, \cdots, v_n) \tag{1.39}$$

for every transposition τ.

The reader may check that, in the presence of antisymmetry, Equations (1.36) and (1.37) imply all variants of themselves where the addition or scalar multiplication is performed in some coordinate other than the first, such as

$$D_n(v_1, v_2 + v_2', \cdots, v_n) = D_n(v_1, v_2, \cdots, v_n) + D_n(v_1, v_2', \cdots, v_n)$$

or

$$D_n(v_1, v_2, \cdots, \alpha \cdot v_n) = \alpha \cdot D_n(v_1, \cdots, v_n)$$

In other words, addition or scalar multiplication can be performed on any vector of the input to D_n, with the expected result. A function, such as D_n, that satisfies all of these equations is called *multilinear*. Thus, the definition of a determinant can be summed up by saying that a determinant on a space $\mathbf{V}$ of dimension n is an antisymmetric multilinear function from V^n to the field of scalars.

It is not hard to see that determinants are not determined by the conditions stated so far. If D_n is any determinant function and γ is any scalar, then $\gamma \cdot D_n$ is another determinant. (Even the case $\gamma = 0$—making D_n identically equal to zero—is a legitimate solution to Equations (1.36–1.38).) If we have no further information on the space $\mathbf{V}$, then very little more can be done to remove this

---

[9]Of course, this field of scalars will usually be the field $\mathbb{R}$ of real numbers; but, for instance, if $\mathbf{V}$ has complex scalars, then D_n will necessarily take complex values. On the other hand, if $\mathbf{V}$ has rational scalars, then we need only rational scalars to express the values of D_n.

uncertainty regarding the factor γ (except to postulate that D_n is not identically zero). Therefore, before stating our final postulate for determinants, we assume that *we are given a fixed basis* $\langle s_1, \cdots, s_n \rangle$ *of* $\mathbf{V}$, called the *standard basis*. This extra piece of data about $\mathbf{V}$ may be thought of as like something residing in the Bureau of Standards. For example, in the 3-dimensional case (which will concern us the most), the basis $\langle s_1, s_2, s_3 \rangle$ may be thought of as representing the three edges of a unit cube. With the standard basis now available, we can define a *normalized determinant* to be a determinant that satisfies the equation

$$D_n(s_1, \cdots, s_n) = 1 \tag{1.40}$$

1.3.2   The uniqueness of D_n

LEMMA 11   If $v_i = v_j$ for some $i \neq j$, then $D(v_1, \cdots, v_n) = 0$.

Proof   Let τ be the transposition that interchanges i with j. Since $v_{\tau(i)} = v_i$ and $v_{\tau(j)} = v_j$, Equation (1.39) yields

$$D(v_1, \cdots, v_n) = -D(v_1, \cdots, v_n)$$

which in turn yields the conclusion of the lemma. $\square$

COROLLARY 1.36 $D_n(v_1 + \mu \cdot v_k, v_2, \cdots, v_n) = D_n(v_1, \cdots, v_n)$ for any scalar μ and any k with $1 < k \leq n$. $\square$

LEMMA 12   If D_n is a normalized determinant on $\mathbf{V}$ and λ is an automorphism of $\mathbf{V}$, then $D_n^\star$ is also a normalized determinant on $\mathbf{V}$, where $D_n^\star$ is defined by

$$D_n^\star(v_1, \cdots, v_n) = D_n(\lambda(v_1), \cdots, \lambda(v_n))$$ $\square$

THEOREM 1.37   If D_n and D_n' are normalized determinants on a space $\mathbf{V}$ of dimension n, then $D_n = D_n'$.

Proof   We will prove by induction on k that

$$D_n(v_1, \cdots, v_k, s_{\theta(k+1)}, \cdots, s_{\theta(n)}) = D_n'(v_1, \cdots, v_k, s_{\theta(k+1)}, \cdots, s_{\theta(n)})$$ $\square$

for any two determinants D_n and D_n', for all $v_1, \cdots, v_k \in V$, for $\langle s_1, \cdots, s_n \rangle$ the standard basis, and for any injective map $\theta : \{k+1, \cdots, n\} \longrightarrow \{1, \cdots, n\}$. Clearly, this assertion (with $k = n$) implies the theorem.

We may first observe that it is enough to prove the simpler assertion that

$$D_n(v_1, \cdots, v_k, s_{k+1}, \cdots, s_n) = D_n'(v_1, \cdots, v_k, s_{k+1}, \cdots, s_n)$$ $\square$

(The more complicated assertion follows from the simpler one by an application of Lemma 12, with λ taken to be an automorphism that maps $s_{\theta(i)}$ to s_i for all $i > k$.) Now the assertion is obviously true for $k = 0$, since both sides are equal to 1 by normalization. Now, to prove the theorem for $k + 1$, we need to show that

$$D_n(v_1, \cdots, v_{k+1}, s_{k+2}, \cdots, s_n) = D'_n(v_1, \cdots, v_{k+1}, s_{k+2}, \cdots, s_n) \qquad \square$$

Now, by the multilinearity of D_n and of D'_n, it will be enough to prove that

$$D_n(v_1, \cdots, v_k, s_j, s_{k+2}, \cdots, s_n) = D'_n(v_1, \cdots, v_k, s_j, s_{k+2}, \cdots, s_n) \qquad \square$$

for all vectors $v_1 \cdots v_k \in V$ and for all elements s_j of the standard basis. This last equation is true for one of two reasons. If $j \geq k+2$, then both sides are 0, by Lemma 11. On the other hand, if $j < k + 2$, then the last equation is obviously true by induction.

Therefore, there is at most one normalized determinant. Generally speaking, from now on, *determinant* will mean *normalized determinant*. The uniqueness argument indicates in a general way how one might go about calculating determinants (although we recommend the more specific procedures given in §1.3.4 and §1.3.5). Even so, this does not assure that determinants really exist; i.e., that they can be defined in such a way that the defining Equations (1.36–1.38) hold in general. This question is answered in §1.3.3, which is rather technical.

1.3.3   The existence of a determinant function

Let V be a vector space of dimension n, with standard basis $\langle s_1, \cdots, s_n \rangle$. For $k = 1 \cdots n$, let V_k denote the subspace of V spanned by $\langle s_1, \cdots, s_k \rangle$ (and thus $V_n = V$). We recursively define determinants D_k on the spaces V_k, as follows:

$$D_1(\alpha \cdot s_1) = \alpha \qquad (1.41)$$

$$D_{k+1}(w_1 + \alpha_1 \cdot s_{k+1}, \cdots, w_{k+1} + \alpha_{k+1} \cdot s_{k+1})$$
$$= \sum_{i=1}^{k+1}(-1)^{i+k}\alpha_i \cdot D_k(w_1, \cdots, \widehat{w_i}, \cdots, w_{k+1}) \qquad (1.42)$$

Here $w_1, \cdots, w_{k+1} \in V_k$, $\alpha_1, \cdots, \alpha_{k+1}$ are scalars, and the notation $\widehat{w_i}$ means that the vector w_i is deleted from the argument for D_k. As the reader may easily check, every vector v_1 of V_{k+1} can be uniquely written in the form $w_1 + \alpha_1 \cdot s_{k+1}$; and so, in fact, the second equation does define D_{k+1} uniquely on V_{k+1}^{k+1}.

The reader should note carefully that Equation (1.42) is of a different character from Equations (1.36–1.38), which define the notion of determinant. Those defining equations concern D_n for a fixed value of n. Equation (1.42) involves both D_k and D_{k+1}, and hence can be used to define the D_k's by a recursive procedure. (D_1 is given an absolute definition by Equation (1.41); then, using (1.42), D_2 is defined in terms of D_1, D_3 in terms of D_2, and so on. This will be proclaimed as an algorithm in §1.3.4.) There is, therefore, no question of *proving* (1.42) from (1.36–1.38); since (1.42) is in fact a definition. To put it another way, §1.3.1 states axioms about determinants, while this section shows how to calculate them.

THEOREM 1.38   Each D_k is a normalized determinant on **V**.

Proof   Since the definition was recursive, the proof will be by induction on k. For $k = 1$ the theorem is almost obvious. Now let us suppose that the theorem holds for D_k, and consider the case of D_{k+1}. First, to check Equation (1.36) for D_{k+1}, we make the following calculation, which uses Equation (1.36) for D_k.

$$
\begin{aligned}
&D_{k+1}(w_1 + w_1' + \alpha_1 \cdot s_{k+1} + \alpha_1' \cdot s_{k+1}, \cdots, w_{k+1} + \alpha_{k+1} \cdot s_{k+1}) \\
&= \ \alpha_1 \cdot D_k(w_2, \cdots, w_{k+1}) + \alpha_1' \cdot D_k(w_2, \cdots, w_{k+1}) \\
&\quad + \sum_{i=2}^{k+1} (-1)^{i+k} \alpha_i \cdot D_k(w_1 + w_1', \cdots, \widehat{w_i}, \cdots, w_{k+1}) \\
&= \ \alpha_1 \cdot D_k(w_2, \cdots, w_{k+1}) + \alpha_1' \cdot D_k(w_2, \cdots, w_{k+1}) \\
&\quad + \sum_{i=2}^{k+1} (-1)^{i+k} \left(\alpha_i \cdot D_k(w_1, \cdots, \widehat{w_i}, \cdots, w_{k+1}) \right. \\
&\qquad\qquad\qquad\left. + \alpha_i \cdot D_k(w_1', \cdots, \widehat{w_i}, \cdots, w_{k+1}) \right) \\
&= \ D_{k+1}(w_1 + \alpha_1 \cdot s_{k+1}, w_2 + \alpha_2 \cdot s_{k+1}, \cdots, \alpha_{k+1} \cdot s_{k+1}) \\
&\quad + D_{k+1}(w_1' + \alpha_1' \cdot s_{k+1}, w_2 + \alpha_2 \cdot s_{k+1}, \cdots, \alpha_{k+1} \cdot s_{k+1})
\end{aligned}
$$

Then, to check Equation (1.37) for D_{k+1}, we make the following calculation, which uses (1.37) for D_{k+1}.

$$
\begin{aligned}
&D_{k+1}(\alpha \cdot w_1 + \alpha \cdot (\alpha_1 \cdot s_{k+1}), \cdots, w_{k+1} + \alpha_{k+1} \cdot s_{k+1}) \\
&= \ (\alpha\alpha_1) \cdot D_k(w_2, \cdots, w_{k+1}) \\
&\quad + \sum_{i=2}^{k+1} (-1)^{i+k} \alpha_i \cdot D_k(\alpha \cdot w_1, \cdots, \widehat{w_i}, \cdots, w_{k+1}) \\
&= \ \alpha \cdot \left(\sum_{i=1}^{k+1} (-1)^{i+k} \alpha_i \cdot D_k(w_1, \cdots, \widehat{w_i}, \cdots, w_{k+1}) \right) \\
&= \ \alpha \cdot (D_{k+1}(w_1 + \alpha_1 \cdot s_{k+1}, \cdots, w_{k+1} + \alpha_{k+1} \cdot s_{k+1}))
\end{aligned}
$$

Finally, we check Equation (1.38) only for the transposition $\tau = (r, s)$ with $r < s$.

$$
\begin{aligned}
&D_{k+1}(w_{\tau(1)} + \alpha_{\tau(1)} \cdot s_{k+1}, \cdots, w_{\tau(k+1)} + \alpha_{\tau(k+1)} \cdot s_{k+1}) \\
&= \ \sum_{i=1}^{k+1} (-1)^{i+k} \alpha_i \cdot D_k(w_{\tau(1)}, \cdots, \widehat{w_{\tau(i)}}, \cdots, w_{\tau(k+1)})
\end{aligned}
$$

$$= \sum_{i \neq r,s} (-1)^{i+k} \alpha_i \cdot D_k(w_{\tau(1)}, \cdots, \widehat{w_{\tau(i)}}, \cdots, w_{\tau(k+1)})$$

$$+ (-1)^{r+k} \alpha_s \cdot D_k(w_1, \cdots, w_r, \cdots, w_{k+1})$$

$$+ (-1)^{s+k} \alpha_r \cdot D_k(w_1, \cdots, w_s, \cdots, w_{k+1})$$

where in the last D_k-expression w_s appears where w_r would normally go, and w_r does not appear at all (and *vice versa* in the penultimate line). Now for each D_k that appears in the sum $\sum_{i \neq r,s}$, we may regard τ as a permutation of the variables appearing inside D_k, and induction gives us the required minus sign. In the other two terms, either w_r or w_s is $s - r$ places away from where it ought to be for the final formula, and so $s - r$ transpositions will put w_r or w_s where it ought to be. Therefore, induction yields that the expressions above are equal to

$$= -\sum_{i \neq r,s} (-1)^{i+k} \alpha_i \cdot D_k(w_1, \cdots, \widehat{w_i}, \cdots, w_{k+1})$$

$$+ (-1)^{r+k}(-1)^{s-r-1} \alpha_s \cdot D_k(w_1, \cdots, w_{k+1})$$

$$+ (-1)^{s+k}(-1)^{s-r-1} \alpha_r \cdot D_k(w_1, \cdots, w_{k+1})$$

$$= -\sum_{i=1}^{k+1}(-1)^{i+k} \alpha_i \cdot D_k(w_1, \cdots, \widehat{w_i}, \cdots, w_{k+1})$$

$$= -D_{k+1}(w_1 + \alpha_1 \cdot s_{k+1}, \cdots, w_{k+1} + \alpha_{k+1} \cdot s_{k+1}) \qquad \square$$

1.3.4   Calculation of determinants

It turns out that Equation (1.42), which was used for a recursive construction in §1.3.3, also yields an easy and systematic way to compute determinants. As one might expect, it is a recursive calculation. To see how this works, let us introduce a little notation and terminology. We are given a vector space with standard basis $\langle s_1, \cdots, s_n \rangle$. Since there is a unique normalized determinant on $\mathbf{V}$, we call it simply *the determinant* on $\mathbf{V}$. We then let

$$\begin{vmatrix} a_{11} & a_{12} & \cdots & a_{1n} \\ a_{21} & a_{22} & \cdots & a_{2n} \\ \vdots & \vdots & \ddots & \vdots \\ a_{n1} & a_{n2} & \cdots & a_{nn} \end{vmatrix} \qquad (1.43)$$

be another notation for the scalar value $D_n(v_1, \cdots, v_n)$, where $v_j = \sum_{i=1}^{n} a_{ij} \cdot s_i$ for each j. In other words, the expression (1.43) refers to the determinant of the column vectors

$$\begin{bmatrix} a_{1j} \\ a_{2j} \\ \vdots \\ a_{nj} \end{bmatrix}$$

$(j = 1 \ldots n)$. Since these n column vectors form an $n \times n$ matrix, we also allow ourselves to speak of *the determinant of a matrix*. Thus, one may denote the above determinant value as

$$\det \begin{bmatrix} a_{11} & a_{12} & \cdots & a_{1n} \\ a_{21} & a_{22} & \cdots & a_{2n} \\ \vdots & \vdots & \ddots & \vdots \\ a_{n1} & a_{n2} & \cdots & a_{nn} \end{bmatrix}$$

or even $\det A$, where A stands for the preceding matrix.

Equation (1.42) can be understood rather directly as an algorithm for calculating the determinant of the matrix (1.43). To apply that equation, we take k to be $n - 1$, w_j to be the column vector

$$\begin{bmatrix} a_{1j} \\ a_{2j} \\ \vdots \\ a_{n-1,j} \\ 0 \end{bmatrix}$$

and $\alpha_j \cdot s_{k+1}$ to be the column vector

$$\begin{bmatrix} 0 \\ 0 \\ \vdots \\ 0 \\ a_{nj} \end{bmatrix}$$

(for $j = 1 \ldots n$). The correctness of the following algorithm is then a direct translation of Theorem 1.38.

ALGORITHM (a provisional calculation of determinants by recursion)
Consider an $n \times n$ matrix:

$$A = \begin{bmatrix} a_{11} & a_{12} & \cdots & a_{1n} \\ a_{21} & a_{22} & \cdots & a_{2n} \\ \vdots & \vdots & \ddots & \vdots \\ a_{n1} & a_{n2} & \cdots & a_{nn} \end{bmatrix}$$

- If $n = 1$, calculate $\det A$ as a_{11} and terminate the algorithm. Otherwise continue.

- For $i = 1 \ldots n$, let A_i be the $(n-1) \times (n-1)$ matrix formed by deleting the ith column and the bottom row from the matrix A.

- For $i = 1 \ldots n$, obtain the determinant of A_i by the further application of this algorithm.

- Calculate the determinant of A as $\sum_{i=1}^{n}(-1)^{n+i} a_{ni} \det(A_i)$.

We call the algorithm provisional because a better algorithm will be presented in §1.3.5. It should be clear that following the above instructions leads to n calculations of an $(n-1) \times (n-1)$ determinant. Each of these calculations leads to $n-1$ calculations, and so on, for a total of $n!$ calculations; all these partial answers must in fact be retained almost until the calculation of $\det A$ is complete. The algorithm in §1.3.5 will avoid this problem.

The general procedure will be clear from the following example. In order to calculate the 3×3 determinant

$$\begin{vmatrix} 1 & 2 & 3 \\ 4 & 5 & 6 \\ 7 & 8 & 9 \end{vmatrix}$$

We first need to calculate three 2×2 determinants. Thus

$$\begin{vmatrix} 2 & 3 \\ 5 & 6 \end{vmatrix} \;=\; 2|6| - 3|5| \;=\; -3$$

$$\begin{vmatrix} 1 & 3 \\ 4 & 6 \end{vmatrix} \;=\; 1|6| - 3|4| \;=\; -6$$

$$\begin{vmatrix} 1 & 2 \\ 4 & 5 \end{vmatrix} \;=\; 1|5| - 2|4| \;=\; -3$$

Then we can compute

$$\begin{vmatrix} 1 & 2 & 3 \\ 4 & 5 & 6 \\ 7 & 8 & 9 \end{vmatrix}$$

$$= \; 7\begin{vmatrix} 2 & 3 \\ 5 & 6 \end{vmatrix} - 8\begin{vmatrix} 1 & 3 \\ 4 & 6 \end{vmatrix} + 9\begin{vmatrix} 1 & 2 \\ 4 & 5 \end{vmatrix}$$

$$= \; 7(-3) - 8(-6) + 9(-3) \;=\; 0$$

The procedure just described is known as *expansion by rows*, since, as we described it, the row $[a_{k+1,1}, \cdots, a_{k+1,n}]$ played a special role. Actually, any row can be used instead of the last row for an expansion of determinants. In fact, for any r with $1 \le r \le k+1$,

$$D_{k+1}(w_1 + \alpha_1 \cdot s_r, \cdots, w_{k+1} + \alpha_{k+1} \cdot s_r)$$

$$= \sum_{i=1}^{k+1}(-1)^{i+r+1}\alpha_i \cdot D_k(w_1,\cdots,\widehat{w_i},\cdots,w_{k+1})$$

where $w_1,\cdots,w_{k+1}$ are vectors in the span of $\langle s_1,\cdots,\widehat{w_r},\cdots,w_{k+1}\rangle$. (When we proved in §1.42 that any D_{k+1} satisfying Equation (1.42) is a determinant—i.e., satisfies Equations (1.36–1.38)—we could just have well used Equation (1.44) in place of Equation (1.42).) Therefore, Equation (1.44) *does* define D_{k+1} as a normalized determinant. By uniqueness, it is *the* determinant.)

Expansion by rows other than the last row can be useful if one row happens to contain a lot of zeros.

Obviously, exercises can be generated at will for those who need to confirm their ability to calculate determinants. In fact, the procedure is completely routine, and to do more than two or three exercises tests only whether you can slog through it without dropping a minus sign, rather than whether you really understand it. Even so, it's not a bad idea to do one exercise.

Exercises

1. Evaluate

$$\begin{vmatrix} 2 & 0 & 2 & 5 \\ 3 & 2 & 9 & 7 \\ 1 & 0 & 2 & 1 \\ 1 & 1 & 3 & 4 \end{vmatrix}$$

Since the procedure is so routine, what better way to show your understanding of it than to write a program that computes determinants?

2. Write a program to compute determinants using the preceding algorithm. To the extent possible, let your program exhibit the recursive nature of the algorithm. It would be best to have the heart of the program written as a subroutine. This subroutine can be called by whatever program happens to need determinants, or one can put it inside a small main program with I/O appropriate to giving a direct exhibit of the calculation of determinants. (The reader is warned that this is not the last word in the calculation of determinants. See §1.3.5.)

1.3.5   Determinants and column operations

There is another way to calculate determinants that is based on examining what happens to det A when A is multiplied on the right by one of the matrices $M_i(\lambda)$, $A_{ij}(\mu)$ or P_{ij} of §1.2.4. In this section, we will use the expression *special matrix* for a matrix of any one of these three types.

LEMMA 1 $\det AM_i(\lambda) = \lambda \det A$.

Proof   Immediate from Equation (1.37).   □

LEMMA 2 $\det AA_{ij}(\mu) = \det A$.

Proof   Immediate from Corollary 1.36 and antisymmetry.   □

LEMMA 3 $\det AP_{ij} = -\det A$.

Proof   This is just a restatement of Equation (1.39).   □

COROLLARY 1.39   If A is any $n \times n$ matrix and S is a special matrix, then $\det AS = \det A \det S$.   □

Recall from §1.2.4 that every matrix A is equal to a product $CS_1 \cdots S_t$, where C is column-reduced and each S_i is special. Now C is either the identity matrix or has a zero column, and, correspondingly, its determinant is either 1 or 0. This observation, together with Lemmas 1–3, immediately suggests an algorithm for computing determinants. This algorithm will be presented as another enhancement to the column-reduction algorithm. Notice that the following algorithm is obviously much less stack-intensive than our previous algorithm for determinants. There is no need to store anything besides a current matrix and a current value of the determinant.

ALGORITHM (computing determinants by column reduction)   While performing the column-reduction algorithm on a square matrix A, keep track of a current value D of the determinant.

- The initial value of D is 1.

- In performing an elementary column operation that consists of multiplying A by the special matrix $M_i(\lambda)$, revise D by multiplying it by $1/\lambda$.

- In performing an elementary column operation that consists of multiplying A by the special matrix P_{ij}, revise D by multiplying it by -1.

- In performing an elementary column operation that consists of multiplying A by the special matrix $A_{ij}(\mu)$, D is not changed.

- Upon completion of column reduction, if the reduced matrix is the identity, then $\det A = D$.

- Upon completion of column reduction, if the reduced matrix is not the identity, then $\det A = 0$.

The following corollary is theoretically interesting and moreover sometimes useful for calculations.

COROLLARY   If A and B are any two $n \times n$ matrices, then

$$\det AB \quad = \quad \det A \det B$$

Proof AB is the composite of linear maps that are represented by A and B, and so AB is invertible iff A and B are both invertible. Therefore, one side of the equation is zero iff the other side is zero. If neither side is zero, then A is a product of special matrices S_i and B is a product of special matrices T_j. The result now follows directly from Corollary 1.39.   □

Exercises

1. Develop a program that implements the algorithm. A general form of the algorithm would column-reduce any rectangular matrix and get the determinant in the case of a square matrix. While it's at it, the program should also evaluate the inverse of A (if A is square and its determinant is not zero). For all matrices, the output should include the column-reduced form of the matrix. This information will, of course, be redundant in the case of an invertible square matrix, but in some other cases it will be the most valuable part of the output.

2. One drawback to our algorithm for calculating determinants by column reduction is that it requires division, whereas determinants themselves make sense in contexts where division is not possible. (The first algorithm for determinants used only multiplication and addition; thus, for example, if the entries of A are integers, then $\det A$ must be an integer. This will be important when we consider the *characteristic polynomial* in §1.4; to see that it is a polynomial, we will need to know that it is calculated—as a determinant—without division.) The exercise here is to modify the column-reduction algorithm so that it calculates the determinant without performing any divisions. (Of course, if one is using column reduction to get the *inverse* of a matrix whose determinant is neither 0 nor ±1, then divisions are inevitable.)

1.3.6   Another formula for the determinant

The following is a general formula for the determinant of an $n \times n$ matrix $[a_{ij}]$, that is taken in some treatments as a definition:

$$\det[a_{ij}] \quad = \quad \sum_{\sigma} \varepsilon(\sigma) \prod_{j=1}^{n} a_{j\sigma(j)} \tag{1.44}$$

where the sum is taken over all permutations σ of $\{1, \cdots, n\}$. The validity of the formula can be seen by considering in a little more detail the line of reasoning of

§1.3.2, or by a direct grind[10] using multilinearity and the fact that, for $s_1 \ldots s_n$ the standard basis and for θ any function $\theta : \{1, \cdots, n\} \longrightarrow \{1, \cdots, n\}$, we have

$$
D_n\big(s_{\theta(1)}, \cdots, s_{\theta(n)}\big) = \begin{cases} \varepsilon(\theta) & \text{if } \theta \text{ is a permutation} \\ 0 & \text{otherwise} \end{cases}
$$

This formula does not seem to provide a very interesting way to calculate matrices. (For $n > 3$, its direct calculation by hand is error-prone, and a computer enumeration of permutations σ and their parities $\epsilon(\sigma)$ is far more complicated than the simple algorithm involving column reduction.) It does, however, have the advantage of showing us that *a matrix and its transpose have the same determinant.* For any matrix $A = [a_{ij}]$, the *transpose of A* is defined to be the matrix $B = [b_{ij}]$, where $b_{ij} = a_{ji}$ for each i and j. This in effect means that the rows of B are the columns of A and *vice versa.* Transposes will be taken up at greater length in §1.5.2.

THEOREM 1.40   If B is the transpose of A, then $\det A = \det B$.

Proof   From Equation (1.44) for determinants, we calculate

$$
\begin{aligned}
\det[b_{ij}] &= \sum_\sigma \varepsilon(\sigma) \prod_{j=1}^n b_{j\sigma(j)} \\
&= \sum_\sigma \varepsilon(\sigma) \prod_{i=1}^n b_{\sigma^{-1}(i),i} \\
&= \sum_\rho \varepsilon(\rho^{-1}) \prod_{i=1}^n b_{\rho(i),i} \\
&= \sum_\rho \varepsilon(\rho) \prod_{i=1}^n a_{i\rho(i)} \\
&= \det[a_{ij}]
\end{aligned}
$$
$\square$

Now we are able to see one more way to calculate the determinant of a matrix A. Let B be the transpose of A. Expanding B by columns is obviously equivalent to a new sort of expansion of A called *expansion by columns.* This really needs no explanation, except to say that it is like row expansion, but with the roles of the rows and columns interchanged. It follows immediately from the theorem that column expansion is one more valid way to calculate $\det A$.

---

[10]One more way to see it: Consider the tree generated by the recursive procedure for the exercise on page 45—the original problem of order $n \times n$ spawns n problems of order $(n-1) \times (n-1)$, each of these spawns $n-2$, and so on. There are $n!$ nodes to this tree, and these correspond to the $n!$ summands in the first formula of this section.

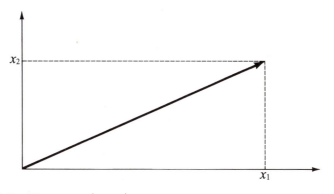

FIGURE 1.2 The vector $\langle x_1, x_2 \rangle$

Exercise_____

1. Give an alternate proof to Theorem 1.40, based on the fact that every non-singular square matrix is a product of special matrices $M_i(\lambda)$, $A_{ij}(\mu)$ and P_{ij}.

1.3.7 Determinants, area and volume

Let us think, in the usual way, of the *plane* as specified by the vector space $\mathbb{R}^2$, with standard basis $\langle s_1, s_2 \rangle$, where $s_1 = \langle 1, 0 \rangle$ and $s_2 = \langle 0, 1 \rangle$. A vector $\langle x_1, x_2 \rangle$ in $\mathbb{R}^2$ is represented in the plane as a directed line segment from the origin to a point with coordinates $\langle x_1, x_2 \rangle$. (See Figure 1.2.) (Thus, coordinates are really nothing more than the numerical specification of a vector.) In addition to the uses for them seen so far, we will use the standard basis vectors s_1 and s_2 to specify a unit of area. In other words, the square spanned by s_1 and s_2 is declared to have unit area.

Given two vectors v_1 and v_2, we say that the pair $\langle v_1, v_2 \rangle$ is *positively oriented* iff $\langle v_1, v_2 \rangle$ is linearly independent and v_1 is to the right of v_2 when viewed from the origin. (See Figure 1.3.) Such a pair is called *negatively oriented* iff $\langle -v_1, v_2 \rangle$ is positively oriented. If $\langle v_1, v_2 \rangle$ is linearly dependent, then the concept of orientation does not apply. For two vectors v_1 and v_2, define

$$\Delta_2(v_1, v_2)$$

to be the *area of the parallelogram spanned by v_1 and v_2*; i.e., the parallelogram that has v_1 and v_2 as two of its sides, signed according to the orientation of $\langle v_1, v_2 \rangle$. In other words, if $\langle v_1, v_2 \rangle$ is positively oriented, then $\Delta_2(v_1, v_2)$ is the numerical value of the area; and if $\langle v_1, v_2 \rangle$ is negatively oriented, then $\Delta_2(v_1, v_2)$

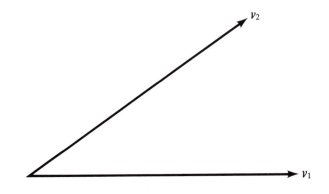

FIGURE 1.3 $\langle v_1, v_2 \rangle$ is positively oriented

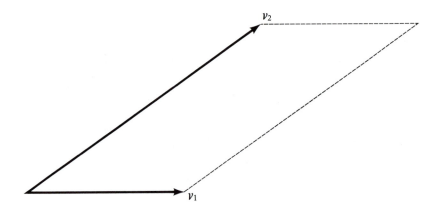

FIGURE 1.4   The area of this parallelogram is $\Delta_2(v_1, v_2)$

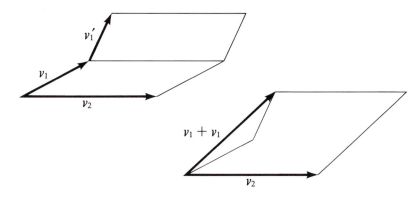

FIGURE 1.5   The addition axiom for areas

is the negative of the area. (When orientation is not defined, the area is zero, and so no sign is needed.) Thus, $\Delta_2(v_1, v_2)$ is known as the *signed area* of the parallelogram.

Now the connection between signed areas and determinants is very clear:

THEOREM 1.41 Δ_2 is a normalized determinant for $\mathbb{R}^2$.

Proof   Equation (1.38) is apparent from the definition of orientation. For Equation (1.37), it is clear that if one side of a parallelogram is enlarged by a factor of λ, then its area is also increased by a factor of λ. Finally, for Equation (1.36), Figure 1.5 has one drawing that shows the two parallelograms for $\Delta_2(v_1, v_2)$ and $\Delta_2(v_1', v_2)$, and a second drawing that shows the one parallelogram for $\Delta_2(v_1 + v_1', v_2)$. Then elementary Euclidean geometry yields the fact that the sum of the areas of the two smaller parallelograms is the area of the large parallelograms. (These figures have both $\langle x_1, x_2 \rangle$ and $\langle x_1', x_2 \rangle$ positively oriented. The reader is asked to supply the appropriate pictures for other orientations.)

Finally, the normalization Equation (1.40) amounts to our choice of unit area for the plane.   □

COROLLARY 1.42 $\Delta_2(v_1, v_2) \ = \ \det(v_1, v_2)$.   □

If one analyzed the preceding proof closely, one would see that we used not so much a definition of area as postulates about areas. An adequate set of postulates would be the following: congruent figures have equal areas, areas of figures that overlap only in line segments can be added to obtain the area of union, and the area of the unit square is 1. Thus, what we have here is really

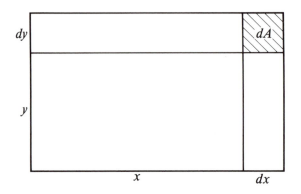

FIGURE 1.6   An area element formed by adding and subtracting parallelograms

a proof that area as defined by these postulates is forced to be equal to the determinant.

Let us look at how linear transformations affect areas. Let $f : \mathbb{R}^2 \longrightarrow \mathbb{R}^2$ be a linear transformation whose matrix (with respect to the basis $\langle s_1, s_2 \rangle$) is A. Take w_1 and w_2 to be any two vectors of $\mathbb{R}^2$, and let g be the linear transformation $\mathbb{R}^2 \longrightarrow \mathbb{R}^2$ that has $g(s_1) = w_1$ and $g(s_2) = w_2$. The matrix B of g obviously has w_1 and w_2 as its two columns. The reader may check that the parallelogram P spanned by $\langle w_1, w_2 \rangle$ is mapped by f onto the parallelogram $f(P)$ spanned by $f(w_1)$ and $f(w_2)$.

THEOREM 1.43   The area of the parallelogram $f(P)$ is $\det A$ times the area of P.

Proof

$$
\begin{aligned}
\text{Area}(P) &= \Delta(w_1, w_2) \\
&= D_2(w_1, w_2) \;=\; D_2(g(s_1), g(s_2)) \\
&= \det B \\
\text{Area}(f[P]) &= \Delta(f(w_1), f(w_2)) \\
&= D_2(f(w_1), f(w_2)) \;=\; D_2(f \circ g(w_1), f \circ g(w_2)) \\
&= \det AB \;=\; \det A \, \det B \qquad\qquad \square
\end{aligned}
$$

Thus, $\det A$ has been identified as a factor by which the areas of certain parallelograms (those with one vertex at $\langle 0, 0 \rangle$) are enlarged under the action of f. The real truth is that *all* measurable sets are increased in area by the same factor. For a naïve proof of this, let us consider a small rectangular area element dA with sides dx and dy, with its lower-left coordinate at point (x, y). A little easy geometry (see Figure 1.6) shows that

$$
\begin{aligned}
dA \;=\; & \text{Area}(P(x \cdot s_1, y \cdot s_2)) + \text{Area}(P((x + dx) \cdot s_1, (y + dy) \cdot s_2)) \\
& - \text{Area}(P((x + dx) \cdot s_1, y \cdot s_2)) - \text{Area}(P(x \cdot s_1, (y + dy) \cdot s_2))
\end{aligned}
$$

(where, e.g., $P(x \cdot s_1, y \cdot s_2)$ denotes the parallelogram spanned by $x \cdot s_1$ and $y \cdot s_2$). Now, under the action of f, all the parallelograms mentioned in this equation map to parallelograms that are det A times as big, and so—multiplying all the equations by det A—we see that the image of dA is an area element det A times as big as dA. This proves that if Γ is any figure that can be approximated with finite unions of rectangles—such as a circular disk—then the area of Γ is enlarged by a factor of det A when the figure is transformed under f. With Lebesgue integration, we can prove even a little more. Theorem 1.44 is included for the interest of those who have studied Lebesgue measure and the Jacobian. In intuitive terms, it says that any set Γ maps to a set $f(\Gamma)$ that has area (or measure) that is proportional by the factor $|\det A|$. Theorem 1.44 will not be needed for anything that follows.

THEOREM 1.44   If Γ is any measurable set in the plane, and $f : \mathbb{R}^2 \longrightarrow \mathbb{R}^2$ is a linear transformation with matrix A, then

$$
m(f[\Gamma]) \;=\; |\det A| \; m(\Gamma)
$$

where m denotes Lebesgue measure.

Proof   It is well known that the measure of $f[\Gamma]$ is found by integrating the absolute value of the *Jacobian* $J(x, y)$ of f over the region Γ. Now the Jacobian is defined to be the matrix

$$
J(x, y) \;=\; \det
\begin{bmatrix}
\dfrac{\partial f_1}{\partial x} & \dfrac{\partial f_1}{\partial y} \\[2mm]
\dfrac{\partial f_2}{\partial x} & \dfrac{\partial f_2}{\partial y}
\end{bmatrix}
$$

where f_1 and f_2 are the two components of f. But these partial derivatives are easily evaluated, yielding

$$
J(x, y) \;=\; \det A
$$

Therefore,

$$
m(\Gamma[A]) \;=\; \int_{\Gamma} |J| \, dx \, dy \;=\; |\det A| \int_{\Gamma} 1 \, dx \, dy \;=\; |\det A| \, m(\Gamma) \qquad \square
$$

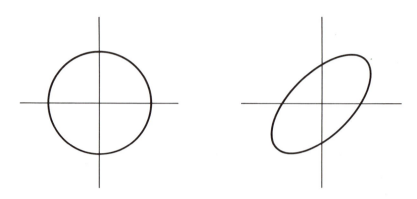

FIGURE 1.7   An ellipse and its image under f

For instance, if $\det A = 1$, then *all areas are preserved by f*; i.e., $m(f[\Gamma]) = m(\Gamma)$ for all measurable sets Γ. Nevertheless, we caution the reader that this does not mean that the image set $f[\Gamma]$ will look exactly like Γ. For instance, if Γ is an ellipse with axes a and b, then $f[\Gamma]$ will be an ellipse with axes a' and b'. We know from preservation of area that $a'b' = ab$, but most likely a will not be equal to a'. (Thus, $f[\Gamma]$ might be twice as long as Γ; but for the areas to work out right, it would have then to be twice as thin.)

Not surprisingly, for linear maps $f : \mathbb{R}^3 \longrightarrow \mathbb{R}^3$ there is a similar theory for the change undergone by *volume* under f. The only real difficulty here is to obtain a notion of *signed volume* of a parallelogram. The easiest way to do this is to forget about right, left and all that—this is not very sure ground mathematically—and simply define $\langle v_1, v_2, v_3 \rangle$ to be positively oriented iff $D_3(v_1, v_2, v_3) > 0$.

Although we will not prove them, we assure the reader that Theorems 1.45 and 1.46 have proofs that are identical except in detail to those that we gave for Theorems 1.41 and 1.44.

THEOREM 1.45   The signed volume of the parallelepiped spanned by $\langle v_1, v_2, v_3 \rangle$ is the determinant $D_3(v_1, v_2, v_3)$.   □

THEOREM 1.46   If Γ is any measurable set in space and $f : \mathbb{R}^3 \longrightarrow \mathbb{R}^3$ is a linear transformation with matrix A, then

$$m(f[\Gamma]) \;=\; |\det A|\; m(\Gamma),$$

where m denotes Lebesgue measure.   □

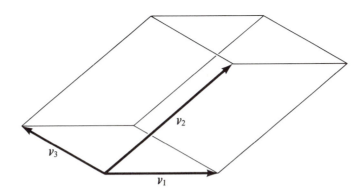

FIGURE 1.8   The parallelepiped spanned by v_1, v_2, v_3

In fact, Theorem 1.46 carries over to all higher dimensions $(n = 4, 5, \cdots)$, with essentially the same proof.

1.4   Eigenvalues and eigenvectors

This section, like the previous one on determinants, applies only to a linear transformation from a vector space $\mathbf{V}$ into *itself*.

Let $\mathbf{V}$ be a finite dimensional vector space and $f : \mathbf{V} \longrightarrow \mathbf{V}$ a homomorphism. A vector $v \in V$ is called an *eigenvector* of f if $v \neq 0$ and there is a scalar λ such that $f(v) = \lambda \cdot v$. If this holds, then obviously the scalar λ is uniquely determined by v and is called *the eigenvalue* of f associated to v. By *an eigenvalue of f*, we mean any scalar λ such that $f(v) = \lambda \cdot v$ for some non-zero v.

Likewise, if A is an $n \times n$ square matrix and $Aw = \lambda w$ for w a non-zero $n \times 1$ column vector, then we say that λ is an *eigenvalue of A* and that w is an *eigenvector of A associated to* λ. It is not hard to check that if A is the matrix of a linear transformation f with respect to some basis $e_1, \ldots, e_n$, then A and f have the same eigenvalues, and their eigenvectors are related as follows. If

$$A \begin{bmatrix} w_1 \\ \vdots \\ w_n \end{bmatrix} = \lambda \cdot \begin{bmatrix} w_1 \\ \vdots \\ w_n \end{bmatrix}$$

then $v = \sum_{i=1}^{n} w_i e_i$ satisfies $f(v) = \lambda v$; moreover, every eigenvalue of f arises in this way. Thus, in eigenvalue problems, we may pass back and forth between f and a representing matrix without further ado. In fact, Lemma 1 would be difficult to formulate without using a matrix for f.

In a number of areas of mathematics (such as linear differential equations), it is important to be able to find eigenvalues and eigenvectors. Once an eigenvalue λ is found, then an eigenvector can be found using the methods of §1.2.7 (solving the linear equations $Av = \lambda \cdot v$). Now to find the eigenvalues themselves, the next lemma is of some use.

LEMMA 1   Let A be the matrix of a linear transformation $f : \mathbf{V} \longrightarrow \mathbf{V}$. Then λ is an eigenvalue of f iff $\det(A - \lambda \cdot I) = 0$, where I denotes the identity matrix.

Proof   We know from §1.2.7 and §1.3.5 that $\det(A - \lambda I) = 0$ iff $A - \lambda I$ is the matrix of a transformation that is not one-to-one. Therefore, this equation holds iff there exists non-zero $v \in V$ such that $f(v) - \lambda \cdot v = 0$. Clearly, this last condition is equivalent to saying that v is an eigenvector with eigenvalue λ.   □

Let us refer to the equation

$$\det(\lambda I - A) = 0 \tag{1.45}$$

as the *eigenvalue equation of A* or the *characteristic equation of A*. By our preceding remarks, (the expanded form of) Equation (1.45) does not depend on the representation of f as a matrix, and so in fact it may be called the *characteristic equation of* the associated linear transformation f. Now Equation (1.45) may clearly be expanded by the methods of §1.3.4 or §1.3.6. For $\mathbf{V}$ a space of dimension n, it is clear that the left-hand side of Equation (1.45) expands into an nth degree polynomial in λ, which is known as the *characteristic polynomial of f*. It is in solving the nth degree Equation (1.45) that we first need to pay particular attention to the exact nature of the field F of scalars. In the rational field, there is generally no hope of solving n^{th} degree equations. In the real field $\mathbb{R}$, every equation of odd degree has a solution but some equations of even degree, such as $x^2 + 1 = 0$, have no solution. Therefore, we find it practical, at least for the moment, to admit scalars in the field $\mathbb{C}$ of complex numbers. It is well known that over this field, Equation (1.45) can be factored[11] as

$$(\lambda - \lambda_1) \cdots (\lambda - \lambda_n) = 0 \tag{1.46}$$

where the n *roots* $\lambda_1, \cdots, \lambda_n$ may or may not be distinct from one another. In the following easy result, the product includes each eigenvalue as often as it occurs in the above factorization. Theorem 1.47 gives us one more perspective on the determinant. The theorem is evident from Corollary 1.52, but it is simpler to prove it directly at the beginning.

---

[11]This is a pure existence result. There is no formula for the roots λ_i, and in general the equation must be solved by an approximation procedure.

THEOREM 1.47 $\det A = \prod_{i=1}^{n} \lambda_i$. Both are equal to the constant term of the characteristic polynomial (times a factor of -1 if n is odd).

Proof   The left-hand side of Equation (1.45) is a polynomial in λ, whose monomial of highest degree is λ^n. As is well known from the theory of polynomials and as can be seen from Equation (1.46), the constant term of this polynomial is $\prod_{i=1}^{n}(-\lambda_i)$. On the other hand, the constant term also results from substituting 0 for λ in this polynomial. Clearly, this substitution yields $(-1)^n \det A$.   □

So far we have identified two of the coefficients of the characteristic polynomial of A: The coefficient of λ^n is 1 and the coefficient of λ^0 (i.e., the constant term) is $\pm \det A$. Another coefficient is of particular importance: namely, the coefficient of λ^{n-1}. This coefficient, or rather its negative, is the *trace* of the matrix A, that is, the sum of its diagonal elements. Since the characteristic polynomial of a linear transformation f does not depend on the matrix used to represent f, we can define the *trace* of f to be the trace of any matrix representing f. Thus, every linear transformation from a space into itself has a well-defined trace.

Exercises

1. Find eigenvalues and eigenvectors for the following matrices:

$$\begin{bmatrix} -1 & -6 & -6 \\ 0 & -2 & 1 \\ 0 & -9 & 4 \end{bmatrix} \qquad \begin{bmatrix} 0 & 1 & 0 \\ 0 & 0 & 1 \\ 1 & 0 & 0 \end{bmatrix}$$

(Do not neglect the two complex roots to the characteristic equation of the second matrix.)

2. Looking ahead, find eigenvalues for some or all of the matrices described in §3.3, §4.5 and §5.3. (See also §3.3.7, where we give a brief discussion of the geometric significance of eigenvectors.)

3. Develop a computer algorithm to compute the characteristic polynomial of a matrix. This is basically a determinant calculation, and various approaches to these were considered in §1.3. One should make sure that one has a method of calculating determinants that does not require any division. Then the new ingredient is that we must work with polynomials in λ. The recommended way to proceed is to introduce a data type for polynomials and write subroutines for addition, subtraction and multiplication of polynomials. (A polynomial could, for example, be represented by the array of its coefficients. The computer doesn't contain anything called λ, so don't look for it; neither is it appropriate to take λ as a name for a storage location in memory.) Now the previous program could be applied to this problem by changing the appropriate floating point numbers into polynomials. (Ideally, the program would go

on to obtain approximate solutions to the characteristic polynomial—but to explain this would be beyond the scope of this book.) This will be a challenging problem, but one cannot really automate any of the material in §1.4 or §1.5 without beginning here. A useful middle course would be to limit the exercise to 3×3 matrices.

4. Define the *trace* of an $n \times n$ matrix $A = [a_{ij}]$ to be $\sum_{i=1}^{n} a_{ii}$, the sum of its diagonal elements. Prove that the coefficient of λ^{n-1} in $\det(\lambda I - A)$ is the negative of the trace of A. Explain the conclusion that was informally reached above; namely, that the trace is therefore well defined for any linear transformation from a finite dimensional vector space into itself.

If the n roots $\lambda_1, \cdots, \lambda_n$ are distinct, then we have a very simple situation indeed, as we can see from Theorem 1.48. This is a special case of Corollary 1.52.

THEOREM 1.48   Let $f : \mathbf{V} \longrightarrow \mathbf{V}$ be a linear transformation. Any set of eigenvectors of f with distinct eigenvalues is linearly independent. Thus, if $\dim \mathbf{V} = n$ and f has n distinct eigenvalues, then $\mathbf{V}$ has a basis consisting of eigenvectors of f.

Proof   Suppose that $\lambda_1, \lambda_2, \cdots \lambda_n$ are distinct scalars and that $f(v_i) = \lambda_i \cdot v_i$ for $1 \leq i \leq n$. We will prove by induction on k that $\langle v_1, \cdots, v_k \rangle$ is linearly independent. For $k = 0$, the assertion is trivial. Now assuming the truth of the assertion for $k - 1$, let us prove it for k. Thus, we are given $\sum_{i=1}^{k} \alpha_i \cdot v_i = 0$, and we need to see that each $\alpha_i = 0$. We calculate

$$
\begin{aligned}
0 &= \lambda_k \cdot \sum_{i=1}^{k} \alpha_i \cdot v_i - f\left(\sum_{i=1}^{k} \alpha_i \cdot v_i\right) \\
&= \sum_{i=1}^{k} (\lambda_k \alpha_i) \cdot v_i - \sum_{i=1}^{k} (\lambda_i \alpha_i) \cdot v_i \\
&= \sum_{i=1}^{k-1} (\lambda_k - \lambda_i) \alpha_i \cdot v_i
\end{aligned}
$$

By induction, $\langle v_1, \cdots, v_{k-1} \rangle$ is linearly independent, and hence $(\lambda_k - \lambda_i)\alpha_i = 0$ for each $i \leq k-1$. Since $\lambda_k \neq \lambda_i$ for $i \leq k-1$, we have $\alpha_i = 0$ for each $i \leq k-1$. It also follows immediately that $\alpha_k = 0$, and so linear independence has been proved.   □

COROLLARY 1.49   If $\dim \mathbf{V} = n$ and $f : \mathbf{V} \longrightarrow \mathbf{V}$ is a linear transformation whose determinant equation has n distinct roots $\lambda_1, \cdots, \lambda_n$, then there exists a basis of V under which the matrix of f is

$$\begin{bmatrix} \lambda_1 & 0 & & 0 \\ 0 & \lambda_2 & & 0 \\ & & \ddots & \\ 0 & 0 & & \lambda_n \end{bmatrix}$$

□

The matrix shown in the corollary is said to be *diagonal*; i.e., its only non-zero entries are the so-called diagonal entries a_{ii}. To *diagonalize* a linear transformation[12] $f : V \longrightarrow V$ is to find a basis of V for which the matrix of f is diagonal. Once we have specified a basis for a space V of dimension n, every $n \times n$ matrix A defines a linear transformation $f : V \longrightarrow V$. Then to diagonalize A is to diagonalize the corresponding f (this is independent of the choice of basis originally used for V). Clearly, a matrix A can be diagonalized if and only if V has a basis consisting entirely of eigenvectors of A. As the reader may check, it is equivalent to say that $A = SDS^{-1}$ where S is invertible and D is a diagonal matrix. (In fact, the diagonal entries of D are the eigenvalues of A and the columns of S are the eigenvectors; see also the proof of Corollary 1.63.)

Not every square matrix can be diagonalized. For instance, consider the $n \times n$ matrix

$$T_n = \begin{bmatrix} 0 & 1 & 0 & & 0 \\ 0 & 0 & 1 & & 0 \\ & & & \ddots & \\ 0 & 0 & 0 & & 1 \\ 0 & 0 & 0 & & 0 \end{bmatrix}$$

that has a diagonal stripe of 1's just above the main diagonal. One can easily check that T_n has characteristic polynomial $p_n(\lambda) = \lambda^n$, and hence all eigenvalues are 0. If T_n had a basis of eigenvectors, then T_n would be the zero matrix, which clearly it is not (if $n \geq 2$). Matrices like T_n play an important rôle in this theory, as we will see in Theorem 1.50.

THEOREM 1.50   Let $f : V \longrightarrow V$ be a linear transformation, where $\dim V = n$, and suppose that f satisfies $f^m = 0$ for some m. Then there exists a basis of V under which f has the matrix

---

[12]Notice that the *same* basis is here used for the domain and codomain of f, which happen to be the same space. It is a much easier problem to find (different) bases of V and W such that $h : V \longrightarrow W$ is diagonal. This is essentially the problem of row reducing a matrix for h, which we have already solved.

$$
T = \begin{bmatrix}
0 & a_1 & 0 & & 0 \\
0 & 0 & a_2 & & 0 \\
& & & \ddots & \\
0 & 0 & 0 & & a_{n-1} \\
0 & 0 & 0 & & 0
\end{bmatrix}
$$

where each a_i is either 0 or 1. Conversely, every such matrix T satisfies $T^n = 0$.

Proof   An easy calculation reveals that every matrix T of this type satisfies $T^n = 0$, and so the last sentence holds. We prove the main statement in the following equivalent form: *There is a basis*

$$\left\{ v_i^j : 0 \le j < N;\ \ 0 \le i < m(j) \right\} \tag{1.47}$$

of **V**, *such that*

$$f(v_{i+1}^j) = v_i^j \tag{1.48}$$
$$f(v_0^j) = 0 \tag{1.49}$$

for all $j < N$ and all $i < m(j) - 1$. (The integers $m(j)$ can be quite arbitrary, subject to $\sum m(j) = \dim \mathbf{V}$ and $m(j) \le n$ for each j. In fact, the largest of the $m(j)$ is the least m such that $f^m = 0$. Each block of r contiguous 1's among the entries a_i of T corresponds to $m(j) = r+1$ for some j. Clearly, $N = \dim \mathbf{KER}\, f$.)

Our proof of this assertion is by induction on the dimension of **V**. If $\dim \mathbf{V} = 0$, then there is nothing to prove, because the empty basis is of the required type (with $N = 0$). On the other hand, if $\dim \mathbf{V} > 0$, then we consider the subspace $\mathbf{V}_0 = f[\mathbf{V}]$ of **V**. Clearly, $\mathbf{V}_0$ has dimension less than that of **V**, and f maps $\mathbf{V}_0$ into itself. By induction, $\mathbf{V}_0$ has a basis (1.47) that satisfies Equations (1.48) and (1.49). We extend this to a basis of **V** as follows. Each $v_{m(j)-1}^j$ lies in $\mathbf{V}_0 = f[\mathbf{V}]$; we therefore choose $v_{m(j)}^j$ so that $f(v_{m(j)}^j) = v_{m(j)-1}^j$ for each j. (This involves increasing each $m(j)$ to $m(j) + 1$.) It is now obvious that Equation (1.48) holds for all appropriate values of i and j, and that Equation (1.49) continues to hold for $j < N$.

The vectors $\{v_0^j : j < N\}$ form a basis of $\mathbf{KER}\, f \cap \mathbf{V}_0$, and so vectors $\{v_0^j : N \le j < M\}$ can be found to make $\{v_0^j : j < M\}$ a basis of $\mathbf{KER}\, f$. Then it is evident that Equation (1.49) holds for all $j < M$. It now remains only to show that

$$\{ v_i^j : 0 \le j < M;\ \ 0 \le i < m(j)+1 \}$$

is a basis of **V**. But this follows directly from the facts that f maps

$$\{ v_i^j : 0 \le j < N;\ \ 1 \le i < m(j)+1 \}$$

one-to-one onto the basis (1.47) of $f[\mathbf{V}]$, and that

$$\{ v_0^j : 0 \le j < M \}$$

is a basis of **KER** f.   □

To continue our study of repeated eigenvalues, we first study how polynomials $p(x)$ can be applied to any square matrix A. For instance, if

$$p(x) \; = \; a_n x^n + a_{n-1} x^{n-1} + \cdots + a_1 x + a_0$$

then by $p(A)$ we mean the matrix

$$p(A) \; = \; a_n A^n + a_{n-1} A^{n-1} + \cdots + a_1 A + a_0$$

where powers of A are formed, of course, by matrix multiplication. One fact about polynomial operations on matrices is that if $p(x)$ and $q(x)$ are any polynomials, $p(A)$ commutes with $q(A)$; i.e., $p(A)q(A) = q(A)p(A)$. (We leave the proof to the student.) Recall that for any matrix B (or linear transformation f), **KER** B denotes the subspace consisting of vectors v such that $Bv = 0$. The direct sum $\mathbf{W}_1 \oplus \mathbf{W}_2$ was defined in §1.1.4.

LEMMA 2   Let A be any square matrix, and let $q(x)$, $r(x)$, $s(x)$ and $t(x)$ be polynomials such that $q(x)r(x) + s(x)t(x) = 1$. If $q(A)s(A) = 0$, then

$$\mathbf{V} = \mathbf{KER}\, q(A) \oplus \mathbf{KER}\, s(A)$$

Proof   Suppose that $v \in \mathbf{KER}\, q(A) \cap \mathbf{KER}\, s(A)$. By hypothesis, we know that $q(A)r(A) + s(A)t(A)$ is the identity matrix, and hence $v = q(A)r(A)v + s(A)t(A)v = r(A)0 + t(A)0 = 0$. Therefore, the intersection of the two kernels is $\{0\}$. On the other hand, if v is any element of $\mathbf{V}$, then $v = r(A)q(A)v + s(A)t(A)v$, where $q(A)r(A)v$ is in the kernel of $s(A)$ and $s(A)t(A)v$ is in the kernel of $q(A)$.   □

We will complete the eigenvalue analysis of an arbitrary linear transformation $f : \mathbf{V} \longrightarrow \mathbf{V}$ by considering polynomial equations satisfied by f. To begin, it is easier to consider the matrix A associated to f under some basis of $\mathbf{V}$. Consider the powers

$$A^0, \; A^1, \; A^2, \; \cdots, \; A^{n^2}$$

of A (formed under ordinary matrix multiplication—A^0 is the identity matrix). There are n^2+1 matrices shown here, each of which has only n^2 entries; therefore, they must satisfy some linear equation with non-zero coefficients. That is to say,

$$\sum_{i=0}^{n^2} \alpha_i A^i \; = \; 0$$

for some coefficients α_i, not all of which are zero. Another way to say this is that $q(A) = 0$, where $q(x)$ is the non-zero polynomial $\sum \alpha_i x^i$. Now there must be a smallest N such that $p(A) = 0$ for some non-zero polynomial p of degree N. We have already seen that $N \leq n^2$; we shall soon see that, in fact, $N \leq n$. Suppose that $p(x)$ and $p'(x)$ both have this smallest degree N and that $p(A) = p'(A) = 0$. The two polynomials $p(x)$ and $p'(x)$ can be different from each other, for one can be a non-zero constant multiple of the other. But we claim that if $p(x)$ and $p'(x)$ both have leading coefficient 1, i.e., $p(x) = x^N + \cdots$ and $p'(x) = x^N + \cdots$, then $p(x) = p'(x)$—if not, then $r(x) = p(x) - p'(x)$ would be a non-zero polynomial of degree $< N$ such that $r(A) = 0$, in contradiction to the minimality of N.

Thus, there exists a unique monic polynomial $p(x) = x^N + \cdots$ of smallest degree N such that $p(A) = 0$. This polynomial is called the *minimal polynomial of the matrix* A. Recalling that f is the linear transformation of $\mathbf{V}$ into itself defined by A, it is not hard to check that $p(x)$ is also the unique monic polynomial of smallest degree such that $p(f) = 0$. Therefore, we also call $p(x)$ the *minimal polynomial of* f. Like the characteristic polynomial, the minimal polynomial may not have any real roots; but if we allow ourselves to use complex numbers, then $p(x)$ will factor into linear factors, i.e.,

$$p(x) = \prod_{i=1}^{m} (x - \rho_i)^{n_i} \tag{1.50}$$

with each $\rho_i \in \mathbb{C}$ (and with all ρ_i distinct). Clearly, $N = \sum n_i$. It will be apparent from Theorem 1.51 that each ρ_i is an eigenvalue of A (or of f).

THEOREM 1.51   Let $f : \mathbf{V} \longrightarrow \mathbf{V}$ be a linear transformation of a finite dimensional vector space $\mathbf{V}$. Suppose that the minimal polynomial of f factors over $\mathbb{C}$ as in Equation (1.50). Then

$$\mathbf{V} = \bigoplus_{i=1}^{m} \mathbf{KER} \, (f - \rho_i)^{n_i}$$

Proof   By induction on the number m of distinct roots. If $m = 1$, the result is almost immediate. In this case, $p(x) = (x - \rho_1)^{n_1}$, and so $(f - \rho_1)^{n_1} = 0$ on the entire space $\mathbf{V}$, by definition of the minimal polynomial. In other words, $\mathbf{V} = \mathbf{KER} \, (f - \rho_1)^{n_1}$, and the theorem is proved.

For $m > 1$, we may factor $p(x)$ as $(x - \rho_1)^{n_1} q(x)$, where $(x - \rho_1)$ and $q(x)$ are relatively prime. By the theory of polynomials, there exist polynomials $r(x)$ and $t(x)$ such that

$$q(x)r(x) + (x - \rho_1)^{n_1} t(x) = 1$$

By Lemma 2 we therefore have

$$V = \mathbf{KER}\,(f - \rho_1)^{n_1} \oplus \mathbf{KER}\,q(f) \tag{1.51}$$

The student may check that if $v \in \mathbf{KER}\,q(f)$, then $f(v) \in \mathbf{KER}\,q(f)$, and so f may be regarded as a linear map $f : \mathbf{KER}\,q(f) \longrightarrow \mathbf{KER}\,q(f)$. On this subspace $q(f) = 0$ (by definition of $\mathbf{KER}$), and so the minimal polynomial of $f : \mathbf{KER}\,q(f) \longrightarrow \mathbf{KER}\,q(f)$ has at most $m - 1$ distinct roots. In fact, one can easily check its minimal polynomial is $\prod_{i=2}^{m}(x - \rho_i)^{n_1}$. Therefore, by induction, we have

$$\mathbf{KER}\,q(f) = \bigoplus_{i=2}^{m} \mathbf{KER}\,(f - \rho_i)^{n_i} \tag{1.52}$$

The theorem now follows by combining Equations (1.51) and (1.52).   □

COROLLARY 1.52   Let $f : V \longrightarrow V$ be a linear transformation of a finite dimensional vector space V. Suppose that the minimal polynomial of f factors over the field of scalars as in Equation (1.50). Then there is a basis of V under which the matrix A of f has the form

$$A = \begin{bmatrix} \mu_1 & a_1 & 0 & 0 & 0 \\ 0 & \mu_2 & a_2 & 0 & 0 \\ & & \ddots & \ddots & \\ 0 & 0 & 0 & \mu_{n-1} & a_{n-1} \\ 0 & 0 & 0 & 0 & \mu_n \end{bmatrix} \tag{1.53}$$

where the μ_i consist of $\rho_1, \rho_2, \cdots, \rho_m$, where each a_i is 0 or 1, and where $a_i = 1$ only if $\mu_i = \mu_{i+1}$.

Proof   Let us suppose that the minimal polynomial $p(x)$ of f factors as in Equation (1.50). For each $1 \le i \le m$, consider the linear transformation $g_i = f - \rho_i$ as acting on the subspace $\mathbf{KER}\,(f - \rho_i)^{n_i}$. Now g_i satisfies $g_i^{n_i} = 0$ on this subspace, and so, by Theorem 1.50, $\mathbf{KER}\,(f - \rho_i)^{n_i}$ has a basis $v_{i1}, v_{i2}, \cdots$ such that, for each j, $(f - \rho_i)(v_{ij}) = 0$ or $(f - \rho_i)(v_{ij}) = v_{i,j-1}$. (In particular, $(f - \rho)(v_{i1}) = 0$.) Thus, $f(v_{i1}) = \rho_i v_{i1}$, and $f(v_{ij}) = \rho_i v_{ij} + \epsilon_{ij} v_{i,j-1}$, where ϵ_{ij} is either 0 or 1.

Now to prove the theorem, we simply take the $\mu_1, \mu_2 \cdots$ to consist first of the vectors $v_{11}, v_{12} \cdots$, then $v_{21}, v_{22} \cdots$, and so on.   □

There is another way to describe the matrix of Equation (1.53). There are square blocks (submatrices) along the main diagonal of the form

$$
\begin{bmatrix}
\rho & 1 & 0 & & & 0 \\
0 & \rho & 1 & & & 0 \\
& & & \ddots & & \\
0 & 0 & 0 & & & 1 \\
0 & 0 & 0 & & & \rho
\end{bmatrix}
\tag{1.54}
$$

Outside of these on-diagonal blocks, all entries are zero. To each such block we associate the pair of numbers (n, ρ), where n is the number of rows and columns. The collection of all pairs (n, ρ) for the whole matrix (counted multiply if they occur more than once) is an *invariant* of the original linear transformation f, in that the same collection of pairs (n, ρ) occurs, regardless how we obtain the matrix (1.53) for f.

The form (1.53) is called the *Jordan normal form* of the linear transformation f. It is unique up to the order in which the blocks (1.54) occur. The blocks (1.54) are called the *elementary Jordan matrices associated to f*.

Exercises

1. Obtain the Jordan normal form for each of the two matrices that were given in Exercise 1 on page 57.

2. Prove that if $v \in \mathbf{KER}\, q(f)$ then $f(v) \in \mathbf{KER}\, q(f)$.

3. Prove that if $p(x)$ and $q(x)$ are any polynomials (with real or complex coefficients) and A is any square matrix, then the matrix $B = p(A)$ commutes with the matrix $C = q(A)$ (i.e., that $BC = CB$).

4. Working in the complex numbers $\mathbb{C}$, let A and B be any two $n \times n$ matrices. Prove that there exists a non-singular $n \times n$ matrix S such that $A = S^{-1}BS$ iff A and B have the same Jordan normal form; i.e., both generate the same collection of elementary Jordan matrices.

We now examine the relationship between the characteristic polynomial (1.46) of a matrix A, and its minimal polynomial (1.50).

LEMMA 3   For $1 \le i \le m$, A has an $n_i \times n_i$ elementary Jordan matrix

$$
\begin{bmatrix}
\rho_i & 1 & 0 & & & 0 \\
0 & \rho_i & 1 & & & 0 \\
& & & \ddots & & \\
0 & 0 & 0 & & & 1 \\
0 & 0 & 0 & & & \rho_i
\end{bmatrix}
$$

Proof   Let M be the size of the largest elementary Jordan matrix of this type. We will show that $M = n_i$. First, if M were larger than n_i, then $(A - \rho_i)^{n_i}$ would not have this submatrix 0; it would easily follow that (1.50) is not a polynomial that makes A zero. On the other hand, if M were less than n_i, then it would easily follow that $(A - \rho_i)^{n_i-1} \prod_{k\neq i}(A - \rho_k)^{n_k} = 0$, and hence the polynomial (1.50) is not minimal. These two contradictions complete the proof of the lemma.

$\square$

COROLLARY 1.53   The ρ_i are the same as the eigenvalues λ_j. More precisely, each ρ_i is equal to at least one of the eigenvalues λ_j; if $(x - \rho_i)^{n_i}$ is the highest power of $(x - \rho_i)$ dividing the minimal polynomial, then ρ_i is equal to λ_j for at least n_i values of j. Each eigenvalue λ_j is equal to ρ_i for exactly one value of i. $\square$

COROLLARY 1.54   The minimal polynomial of A divides the characteristic polynomial of A. $\square$

COROLLARY 1.55 A satisfies its own characteristic equation; i.e., $\prod(A - \lambda_i) = 0$.

$\square$

Exercise

1. Automate some or all of the methods of §1.4. Ideally, for a matrix A one's program would output all the information given in Corollary 1.52: the basis vectors, the μ_i (which are really eigenvalues), and the a_i. The first step would be to generate the characteristic equation (see Exercise 3 on page 57). Then one would have to solve this equation approximately—which entails a small theory in itself—to obtain the eigenvalues. Implementing Theorem 1.51 (which really involves implementing Lemma 2) will involve computing some polynomials of matrices so that the space **KER** $(f - \rho_i)^{n_i}$ can be concretely represented as the solution space of a specific matrix. Finally, one has to find specific bases as in Theorem 1.50. This may be the most challenging part conceptually. Along the way, tough decisions will be required concerning what to do when things are almost zero. All in all, this exercise is a tall order, which we present only because we think the student should realize that all of this material is in principle effective. The complete job would be worthy of a semester project in a computer algebra course. A middle course would be to do it for 2×2 or 3×3 matrices. Things are simpler in these cases. These simple cases could be used for drawing conics or quadric surfaces. (See Theorem 3.10 and remarks in §3.1.7.)

1.5   Inner products, transposes and symmetry

This section contains what may be thought of as an abstract version of geometry. Instead of dealing with the planes or space of Euclid, we deal with abstract vector spaces and inner products. This material can be taken as an algebraic foundation for coordinate geometry, especially for the theory of rotations that we will encounter in §3.3.2, §4.5.4 and §5.3.4. Nevertheless, we will generally take a more elementary approach in Chapters 3 and 4, developing our formulas and methods from elementary principles, and the student might be well advised to skip §1.5 on the first reading.

1.5.1   Inner products

A *symmetric bilinear form* on a real vector space $\mathbf{V}$ is a function

$$E : V^2 \longrightarrow \mathbb{R}$$

that satisfies the equations

$$
\begin{array}{rcll}
E(v_1, v_2) &=& E(v_2, v_1) & (1.55) \\
E(v_1 + v_1', v_2) &=& E(v_1, v_2) + E(v_1', v_2) & (1.56) \\
E(v_1, v_2 + v_2') &=& E(v_1, v_2) + E(v_1, v_2') & (1.57)
\end{array}
$$

(These are like Equations (1.36–1.38) for $n = 2$, only with antisymmetry (1.38) replaced by symmetry (1.55).) An *inner product* on $\mathbf{V}$ is a symmetric bilinear form such that $E(v, v) > 0$ for all non-zero vectors $v \in \mathbf{V}$. The next two lemmas show that, given a basis of $\mathbf{V}$, symmetric bilinear forms are in one-one correspondence with symmetric matrices. We return (in §1.5.4) to the question of symmetric matrices, from a somewhat different point of view. There we will see that the symmetric bilinear form E in Lemma 4 is an inner product iff the eigenvalues of $(E(v_i, v_j)$ are all positive.

LEMMA 4   Let $v_1, \cdots, v_n$ be a basis of $\mathbf{V}$. Every symmetric bilinear form E on $\mathbf{V}$ is determined by the $n \times n$ matrix of values $E(v_i, v_j)$. In other words, if E' is a symmetric bilinear form such that $E(v_i, v_j) = E'(v_i, v_j)$ for all i and j, then $E' = E$.

LEMMA 5   Let $v_1, \cdots, v_n$ be a basis of $\mathbf{V}$. If $[a_{ij}]$ is a symmetric $n \times n$ matrix of scalars; i.e., if $a_{ji} = a_{ij}$ for all i and j, then there exists a unique symmetric bilinear form E on $\mathbf{V}$ such that $E(v_i, v_j) = a_{ij}$ for all i and j.

Sketch of proof   Uniqueness comes from Lemma 5. To define $E(v, w)$, expand v and w as linear combinations of the basis vectors v_i, and then use bilinearity (Equations (1.56) and (1.57)).   □

Perhaps the simplest non-trivial symmetric bilinear form is the form E associated to the $n \times n$ identity matrix: $E(v_i, v_j) = 1$ if $i = j$ and 0 if $i \neq j$. Thus, E is given by the formula

$$E \left(\sum \alpha_i v_i, \sum \beta_j v_j \right) = \sum \alpha_i \beta_i$$

If our basis is the standard one on $\mathbb{R}^n$, then this is the standard inner product on $\mathbb{R}^n$, which is traditionally denoted

$$\langle \alpha_1, \cdots, \alpha_n \rangle \cdot \langle \beta_1, \cdots, \beta_n \rangle = \sum_{i=1}^{n} \alpha_i \beta_i$$

and which is often called the *dot product* because of this notation. It is not hard to check that this last formula does define an inner product on $\mathbb{R}^n$; i.e., if $v \neq 0$, then $v \cdot v > 0$. For all practical purposes, the student may think of the dot product as the *only* inner product.

In fact, for every inner product E on $\mathbf{V}$, there exists a basis of $\mathbf{V}$ such that the matrix associated to E under this basis is the identity matrix. In other words, up to isomorphism of vector spaces, there is only one inner product. Fixing an inner product E and regarding the basis as to be determined, we may observe that the crucial property of a basis, in defining the ordinary dot product, is that

$$E(v_i, v_j) = \begin{cases} 1 & \text{if } i = j \\ 0 & \text{if } i \neq j \end{cases} \tag{1.58}$$

Bases satisfying Equation (1.58) are called *orthonormal*[13] *bases for E.* (In fact, any set of vectors v_i satisfying Equation (1.58) is linearly independent, as the reader may easily check.) It is sometimes convenient to abbreviate the right-hand side of Equation (1.58) as δ_{ij}. In other words, δ_{ij} is by convention 0 unless $i = j$, in which case it is 1. Thus, orthonormality can be rephrased as $F(e_i, e_j) = \delta_{ij}$.

The construction appearing in the next proof is sometimes called the *Gram-Schmidt orthonormalization procedure.*

THEOREM 1.56   Let E be an inner product on a finite dimensional vector space $\mathbf{V}$. Then $\mathbf{V}$ has a basis that is orthonormal for E.

Proof   Start with an arbitrary basis $\langle w_1, \cdots, w_n \rangle$ of $\mathbf{V}$. We will replace the vectors w_i one at a time by orthonormal vectors v_i, so that after the kth replacement, $\langle v_1, \cdots, v_k, w_{k+1}, \cdots, w_n \rangle$ is a basis of $\mathbf{V}$. Suppose that we already have vectors $v_1, \cdots, v_{k-1}$ so that $E(v_i, v_j) = \delta_{ij}$ for $1 \leq i, j < k$. We will see how to get v_k. Define

$$v_k' = w_k - \sum_{j<k} E(v_j, w_k) \cdot v_j$$

---

[13] The word derives from *normal,* which is taken to mean $E(v_i, v_i) = 1$ for each i, and from *orthogonal,* which is a Greek-derived word meaning perpendicular (itself of Latin derivation). Two vectors are perpendicular in Euclidean space iff their dot product is zero.

Now for $i < k$, we may calculate

$$E(v'_k, v_i) = E(w_k, v_i) - \sum_{j<k} E(v_j, w_k)E(v_j, v_i)$$

$$= E(w_k, v_i) - E(v_i, w_k) = 0$$

Thus vectors $v_1, \cdots, v_k$ are all orthogonal to one another. For normality, we observe that v'_k is w_k minus a linear combination of the vectors w_j for $j < k$. Since the w_k are linearly independent, v'_k cannot be zero. Therefore, we let

$$v_k = \frac{v'_k}{\sqrt{E(v'_k, v'_k)}}$$

As the reader may check, this vector remains orthogonal to v_j $(j < k)$ and satisfies $E(v_k, v_k) = 1$. $\qquad\qquad\square$

Exercises

1. Prove that a real 2×2 symmetric matrix $[a_{ij}]$ defines an inner product on $\mathbb{R}^2$ if and only if $a_{11} > 0$, $a_{22} > 0$, and $a_{11}a_{22} - a_{12}^2 > 0$.

2. Find an orthonormal basis (under ordinary dot product) for the subspace

$$\{\, \langle x_1, x_2, x_3, x_4 \rangle \,:\, x_1 + x_2 + x_3 + x_4 = 0 \,\}$$

   of $\mathbb{R}^4$.

3. Let E be the inner product on $\mathbb{R}^3$ defined by the symmetric matrix

$$\begin{bmatrix} 2 & 0 & 1 \\ 0 & 1 & 0 \\ 1 & 0 & 2 \end{bmatrix}$$

   Find an orthonormal basis of $\mathbb{R}^3$ with respect to E.

4. Write a program to automate the Gram-Schmidt orthonormalization algorithm. Notice that the program automatically tests for linear independence of the vectors $w_1, \cdots, w_n$. If v_k should ever turn out to be 0, this would mean that, in fact, the vectors $w_1, \ldots, w_k$ are linearly dependent.

1.5.2   Transposes

For any matrix $A = [a_{ij}]$, the *transpose of A* is the matrix $A' = [a'_{ij}]$, where $a'_{ij} = a_{ji}$ for all i and j. In other words, the rows of A' are the columns of A, and the columns of A' are the rows of A.

LEMMA 6   If the product AB is defined, then so is the product $B'A'$, and $(AB)' = B'A'$. If A is invertible, then so is A', and $(A^{-1})' = (A')^{-1}$.   □

For the remainder of §1.5, we will assume that we are working in a real vector space $\mathbf{V}$ of finite dimension n and that we are given an inner product E, as in §1.5.1. For convenience, we will write $E(v, w)$ with the familiar dot product notation as $v \cdot w$. Moreover, we assume we have a fixed basis $\langle e_1, \cdots, e_n \rangle$ of $\mathbf{V}$ that is orthonormal for E. To simplify the notation, we will take $\mathbb{R}^n$ for $\mathbf{V}$, the ordinary dot product for E, and take e_j to be the vector $\langle 0, \cdots, 0, 1, 0, \cdots, 0 \rangle$. As in §1.2.9, we can identify a linear transformation f with its matrix A by writing vectors as $n \times 1$ matrices (i.e., columns). Under this convention, $f(v)$ *is* the matrix Av formed by matrix multiplication. Under this convention, we can also identify scalars with 1×1 matrices, so that we have, for example, the following two lemmas.

LEMMA 7   For any $v, w \in \mathbb{R}^n$, $v \cdot w = v'w$.   □

LEMMA 8   For any $n \times n$ matrix, and any $i, j \leq n$,

$$A_{ij} = e_i' A e_j$$

The next lemma characterizes the transpose of a matrix in a coordinate free way, in terms of the inner product.

LEMMA 9 A' satisfies

$$(A'v) \cdot w = v \cdot (Aw) \tag{1.59}$$

Conversely, if A' is any matrix that satisfies Equation (1.59) for all v and w, then A' must be the transpose of A.

Proof   The proof of Equation (1.59) may be left to the student. Conversely, if (1.59) holds, then we may apply it to $v = e_i$ and $w = v_j$, yielding $A_{ij}' = A_{ji}$, by Lemmas 7 and 8.   □

(Notice also that the inner product can also be recovered from the transpose operation. That is, suppose we have an abstract space upon which an inner product has been defined and that transposes are defined with respect to some (unknown) orthonormal basis. Then the inner product can be recovered via $v \cdot w = v'w$.)

1.5.3   Orthogonal matrices

A matrix A is defined to be *orthogonal* iff the product $A'A$ is the identity matrix I. It follows from the results about inverses of matrices in §1.2.3 that this is equivalent to $AA' = I$. Therefore, A is orthogonal iff A' is orthogonal. As we will see in §5.3.5, 3×3 orthogonal matrices correspond to rotations of space.

THEOREM 1.57 A is orthogonal iff the columns of A form an orthonormal basis of $\mathbb{R}^n$.

Proof   By Lemmas 7–9 of §1.5.2, we have

$$(Ae_i) \cdot (Ae_j) \; = \; (Ae_i)'(Ae_j) \; = \; e_i'A'Ae_j \; = \; (A'A)_{ij}$$

Therefore, the vectors Ae_i (i.e., the columns of A) are orthonormal iff $A'A$ is the identity matrix.   □

COROLLARY 1.58 A is orthogonal iff the rows of A (considered as elements of $\mathbb{R}^n$) form an orthonormal basis of $\mathbb{R}^n$.

Proof   The rows of A are the columns of A', and we already saw that A is orthogonal iff A' is orthogonal.   □

THEOREM 1.59 A is orthogonal iff $(Av) \cdot (Aw) = v \cdot w$ for all $v, w \in \mathbb{R}^n$.

Proof   If the condition holds, then

$$(A'A)_{ij} \; = \; e_i'A'Ae_j \; = \; (Ae_i) \cdot (Ae_j) \; = \; e_i \cdot e_j \; = \; \delta_{ij}$$

for all i and j. Therefore, $A'A$ is clearly the identity matrix. Conversely, for A orthogonal, take v to be $\sum_{i<n} \alpha_i e_i$ and w to be $\sum_{j<n} \beta_j e_j$. Then

$$
\begin{aligned}
(Av) \cdot (Aw) \; &= \; \sum_{i,j=1}^{n} \alpha_i \beta_j A(e_i) \cdot A(e_j) \\
&= \; \sum_{i,j=1}^{n} \alpha_i \beta_j \delta_{ij} \; = \; \sum_{i=1}^{n} \alpha_i \beta_i \; = \; v \cdot w
\end{aligned}
$$
□

Now in any vector space **V** with inner product, we can define the *length* or *norm* of a vector v by the formula

$$\|v\| \; = \; \sqrt{v \cdot v}$$

The *distance* between two vectors v and w is defined to be $\|v - w\|$; in other words,

$$d(v, w) = \sqrt{(v - w) \cdot (v - w)}$$

This distance accords with our understanding of distance in Euclidean space, as the student may check. (In other words, the Euclidean distance formula—the first formula of Chapter 3—easily follows from the formulas presented here.) By our hypothesis on inner products, if $v \neq w$, then $d(v, w) > 0$.

Notice that the inner product can be recovered from distances by the following easy formula:

$$v \cdot w = \frac{1}{2} \left[d(v, 0)^2 + d(w, 0)^2 - d(v, w)^2 \right] \tag{1.60}$$

COROLLARY 1.60   A matrix A is orthogonal iff A is distance-preserving, i.e., iff $d(Av, Aw) = d(v, w)$ for all vectors v and w.

Proof   Suppose first that A is orthogonal. Then

$$d(Av, Aw)^2 = (Av - Aw) \cdot (Av - Aw)$$
$$= (v - w) \cdot (v - w) = d(v, w)^2$$

(by Theorem 1.59). On the other hand, if A preserves distance, then it follows readily from Equation (1.60) that $(Av) \cdot (Aw) = v \cdot w$ for all v and w. Therefore, A is orthogonal, by Theorem 1.59.   □

THEOREM 1.61   The determinant of an orthogonal matrix is either 1 or -1.

Proof   By Theorem 1.40, $\det A' = \det A$, and so

$$(\det A)^2 = \det A' \det A = \det A' A$$
$$= \det I = 1 \qquad\qquad □$$

Therefore, $\det A = \pm 1$.

An orthogonal matrix A with $\det A = 1$ is called a *special orthogonal matrix*.

1.5.4   Symmetric matrices

A matrix A is *symmetric* iff it is equal to its transpose, i.e., iff $A' = A$.

LEMMA 10 A is symmetric iff it commutes with inner product, i.e., iff $(Av) \cdot w = v \cdot (Aw)$ for all vectors v and w.

Proof   If $A' = A$, then $(Av) \cdot w = (Av)'w = v'A'w = v'Aw = v \cdot (Aw)$. Conversely, if A satisfies the condition, then for all i and j we have

$$A'_{ij} = e'_i A' e_j = (Ae_i) \cdot e_j$$

$$= \; e_i \cdot (Ae_j) \; = \; e_i' A e_j \; = \; A_{ij} \qquad\qquad \square$$

LEMMA 11   If A is symmetric and $A^2 v = 0$, then $Av = 0$.

Proof

$$(Av) \cdot (Av) \; = \; (A^2 v) \cdot v \; = \; 0 \cdot v \; = \; 0$$

Thus, $Av = 0$. $\qquad\qquad \square$

LEMMA 12   If A is symmetric and $A^n v = 0$ for some $n > 0$, then $Av = 0$.

Proof   Iterating Lemma 11 yields the result for $n = 2, 4, 8, 16, \cdots$. These special cases obviously imply the general case. $\qquad \square$

With the aim in mind of diagonalizing symmetric matrices, we now return to the subject of eigenvalues that we began in §1.4. There, in order to factor the characteristic equation as $\prod(\lambda - \lambda_n)$ with each λ an eigenvalue, we had to admit complex numbers as our field of scalars. Here we will see that in the symmetric case this is not necessary. In what follows, $\overline{z}$ will denote the *complex conjugate* of a complex number z. That is, if $z = x + iy$ with $x, y \in \mathbb{R}$, then $\overline{z}$ is defined to be $x - iy$. If v is an n-tuple of complex numbers, $v = \langle z_1, \cdots, z_n \rangle$, then $\overline{v}$ denotes the n-tuple $v = \langle \overline{z_1}, \cdots, \overline{z_n} \rangle$.

LEMMA 13   If A is a real symmetric matrix and λ is an eigenvalue of A, then λ is real.

Proof   Suppose that $Av = \lambda v$ for some n-tuple v of complex numbers. Then
$$\begin{aligned} \lambda(v \cdot \overline{v}) \; &= \; (\lambda v)' \overline{v} \; = \; (Av)' \overline{v} \; = \; v' A' \overline{v} \\ &= \; v' A \overline{v} \; = \; v' \overline{(Av)} \; = \; v' \overline{(\lambda v)} \\ &= \; v' \overline{\lambda} \overline{v} \; = \; \overline{\lambda}(v \cdot \overline{v}) \end{aligned}$$
Now since $v \cdot \overline{v} \neq 0$, we have $\overline{\lambda} = \lambda$; in other words, λ is real. $\qquad \square$

LEMMA 14   Let A be a symmetric real matrix, with λ and μ eigenvalues of A with $\lambda \neq \mu$. Let v and w be eigenvectors associated to these eigenvalues; i.e., $Av = \lambda v$ and $Aw = \mu w$. Then $v \cdot w = 0$.

Proof

$$\lambda v \cdot w \; = \; (Av) \cdot w \; = \; v \cdot (Aw) \; = \; \mu v \cdot w$$

and so $(\lambda - \mu)(v \cdot w) = 0$. Since $\lambda \neq \mu$, we have $v \cdot w = 0$. $\qquad \square$

Finally, we diagonalize real symmetric matrices. This diagonalization will be used in discussing the general quadratic locus in §3.1.7.

THEOREM 1.62   For every real symmetric matrix A, there exists an orthonormal basis of $\mathbb{R}^n$ consisting entirely of eigenvectors of A.

Proof   By Lemma 13 and Corollary 1.54, the minimal polynomial of A factors completely over $\mathbb{R}$. By Theorem 1.51,

$$\mathbb{R}^n \;=\; \bigoplus_{i=1}^{m} \mathbf{KER}\,(A - \rho_i I)^{n_i}$$

for some integers n_i, where ρ_i are the distinct values of the (real) eigenvalues of A. Now each $A - \rho_i I$ is symmetric; hence, by Lemma 12, $\mathbf{KER}\,(A - \rho_i I)^{n_i} = \mathbf{KER}\,(A - \rho_i I)$. Thus,

$$\mathbb{R}^n \;=\; \bigoplus_{i=1}^{m} \mathbf{KER}\,(A - \rho_i I)$$

Using Theorem 1.56, choose an orthonormal basis of each direct summand $\mathbf{KER}\,(A - \rho_i I)$ and collect all these bases into one set. All vectors in this set are orthogonal to one another, by Lemma 14, and they form a basis of $\mathbb{R}^n$, by Theorem 1.14. Thus, we have an orthonormal basis of $\mathbb{R}^n$ consisting of eigenvectors.   □

The diagonalization can be expressly stated as a change of coordinates, as follows.

COROLLARY 1.63   A real matrix A is symmetric iff $A = ODO^{-1}$ for some real diagonal matrix D and some special orthogonal matrix O.

Proof   Suppose first that A is symmetric. Let $\langle v_1, \cdots, v_n \rangle$ be an orthogonal basis of eigenvectors, as given by Theorem 1.62. Define O to be the square matrix whose columns are $v_1, v_2, \cdots$; by Theorem 1.57, O is orthogonal. Thus, its determinant is $+1$ or -1. If it is -1, interchange two of the columns so that it becomes $+1$. Now $Oe_i = v_i$ for each i, and so $AOe_i = Av_i = \lambda_i v_i = O(\lambda_i e_i)$, where λ_i is the eigenvalue associated to v_i. Taking D to be the diagonal matrix

$$\begin{bmatrix} \lambda_1 & 0 & & 0 \\ 0 & \lambda_2 & & 0 \\ & & \ddots & \\ 0 & 0 & & \lambda_n \end{bmatrix}$$

we obviously have $AOe_i = ODe_i$ for each i. In other words, $AO = OD$, or $A = ODO^{-1}$.

Conversely, suppose that $A = ODO^{-1}$. Then

$$(Av) \cdot w = (ODO^{-1}v) \cdot w = (DO^{-1}v) \cdot (O^{-1}w)$$
$$= (O^{-1}v) \cdot (DO^{-1}w) = v \cdot (ODO^{-1}w)$$

$$= \ v \cdot (Aw)$$

and so A is symmetric by Lemma 10.   □

Exercises

1. Illustrate Corollary 1.63 for

$$A \ = \ \begin{bmatrix} 2 & 0 & 1 \\ 0 & 1 & 0 \\ 1 & 0 & 2 \end{bmatrix}$$

2. Prove that if A is an orthogonal matrix and λ is an eigenvalue of A, then $|\lambda| = 1$; i.e., $\lambda = e^{it}$ for some real t.

3. Let E be a symmetric bilinear form on a real vector space V of dimension n, and let the vectors $v_1, \ldots, v_n$ constitute a basis for V. Use Theorem 1.62 or Corollary 1.63 to prove that E is an inner product on V iff all eigenvalues of the matrix $[E(v_i, v_j)]$ are positive.

4. Prove that if A is an orthogonal matrix and $A^2 v = 0$ for some vector v, then $Av = 0$. (One needs a minor twist on the proof of Lemma 11.)

5. Discover and prove an analog of Corollary 1.63 for a special orthogonal matrix. (Using Exercise 4, one can find an analog to the proof of Corollary 1.63, but one will be left with a matrix that has diagonal blocks of the form $A = \begin{bmatrix} e^{it} & 0 \\ 0 & e^{-it} \end{bmatrix}$. These can be converted into the proper real form by observing that

$$\begin{bmatrix} e^{it} & 0 \\ 0 & e^{-it} \end{bmatrix} \begin{bmatrix} 1 & i \\ -1 & i \end{bmatrix} = \begin{bmatrix} 1 & i \\ -1 & i \end{bmatrix} \begin{bmatrix} \cos t & -\sin t \\ \sin t & \cos t \end{bmatrix}$$

Thus, if w_1 and w_2 are the two columns of the matrix just introduced, we have $Aw_1 = \cos t w_1 - \sin t w_2$ and $Aw_2 = \sin t w_1 + \cos t w_2$. Taking these as basis elements, we can force A to have (non-diagonal) real coefficients. Divide w_1 and w_2 by $\sqrt{2}$ to keep the basis orthonormal.)

6. Prove that if A is any 3×3 special orthogonal matrix, then there is an orthonormal basis under which A has the form

$$\begin{bmatrix} \cos \theta & -\sin \theta & 0 \\ \sin \theta & \cos \theta & 0 \\ 0 & 0 & 1 \end{bmatrix}$$

(In the terminology of §3.3 and §5.3, this result tells us that every orientation-preserving rigid motion of space that has a fixed point is a rotation about some axis. Note that the *trace* of this matrix is $1 + 2\cos\theta$, and therefore the trace of the original A must have been $1 + 2\cos\theta$, by the remarks about traces that follow Theorem 1.47 in §1.4.)

7. Analyze the matrix

$$A = \frac{1}{25} \begin{bmatrix} 15 & 12 & -16 \\ -20 & 9 & -12 \\ 0 & 20 & 15 \end{bmatrix}$$

according to the scheme of the preceding exercise. In other words, find an orthogonal matrix O and an angle θ such that $O^{-1}AO$ is the matrix of Exercise 6. (Notice that you can get $\cos\theta$ immediately from the trace of A, using the remarks of the preceding exercises.)

8. Write a program to automate the diagonalization of symmetric matrices by orthonormal bases. Most of the ingredients for such a program have already been made into previous exercises in §1.3, §1.4 and §1.5. (This is a hard exercise, but not as hard as the last exercise of §1.4.)

2 Languages for geometry

There are many things we might mean by the word *geometry*: ancient Greek geometry; high school geometry; any of a number of advanced mathematical disciplines such as algebraic geometry, differential geometry or projective geometry; the practical geometry of navigation, surveying, architecture and machinery; even any organized form of spatial coordinate data. Although there is a certain amount of overlap, each version of geometry has its own language:[1] Euclid will tell us to "produce" a line L containing point Q to meet another line L' at a point P; a theoretical mathematical treatise will contain a proof that P exists; and a blueprint will tell us a beam from Q to P should be 10 feet long. In order to make computer drawings of geometrically meaningful figures, one needs to learn how these various languages interact with one another, and how one can translate from one to another.

Languages for geometry can be roughly ordered according to their conceptual level. For example, we might give a number of different interpretations to the practical problem of designing and drawing a chair. Prior to any mundane concept like *chair*, mathematics provides an abstract conceptual framework: we have (among other things) an ambient 3-dimensional real vector space to contain the chair and give it coordinates, and projection maps to take the chair to a 2-dimensional picture. The task itself is stated in very human terms: design, draw, chair. A human designer might choose to model the problem in geometry (most likely in coordinate geometry). This mathematical model can then be translated into a computer program that calculates the desired parameters and finds the exact measure of all parts of the chair. (See §6.5.1.) A well-written program is still fairly conceptual. It retains a good degree of mathematical organization, but some of the human factors (aesthetics, economics, etc.) will no longer be apparent. At a much lower conceptual level, we have the output of

---

[1] Here we are using *language* in the technical sense of computer science and logic, as distinct from natural languages like French or Spanish. These languages are mostly very limited, and in some cases derive their expressive power from being embedded in a natural language. For this discussion, it does not matter which natural language is involved.

this program: It will probably consist largely of a long inventory (called a *file*) of requests to draw line segments in two dimensions (written, for example, in the device-independent language we will develop in §2.2). Here the concept of chair disappears, as does the concept of the third dimension. After that, another translation will be required to arrive at the native language of some output device, such as a screen or a printer. Sooner or later, even the concept of line disappears, and we are left with little more than fluctuating voltages, with no pattern that can be discerned (without viewing the picture).

These various linguistic or conceptual levels, along with the transitions between them, can be diagramed as follows. The ovals represent specifications of a picture at the various conceptual levels; the arrows give a general indication of what is required to translate between these specifications. We think of each oval as variable: it represents all graphics problems of a given large class; an arrow represents a fixed (but general) plan for changing the way that a graphics problem is specified.

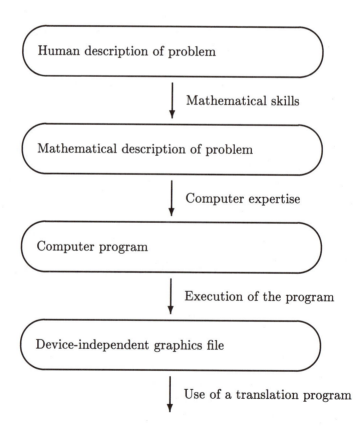

Picture on the chosen graphical output device

A major challenge implicit in the computer-related exercises of this book is to carry out some of the above-mentioned translations between conceptual levels. Problems can arise both in pure geometry (e.g., conic sections) or as somewhat applied problems (e.g., the problems in Chapter 6). One then needs to work on at least three levels: a mathematical statement of the problem and its solution, a computer implementation of that solution, and an output that describes the desired picture. (These are the middle three layers of the above chart.)

Since a large part of the book is already devoted to the language of mathematics, we won't particularly dwell on it in this chapter. We will instead make a few remarks about computer programs and device-independent graphics files.

The above flow chart is a recommendation, not an absolute necessity. Experience has shown that it represents a useful division of labor and of concepts, but there certainly exist other ways to organize the automation of geometric drawing. One thing we find useful is that the chart presupposes no commitment to any particular form of computation or of display. The computation could be done on widely varying hardware and operating systems, and the actual program could be written in almost any programming language. Likewise, the display could take place on any suitable and available device. In some classes, it may be that different students in the same class have different preferences or have different machines available to them. It is to be hoped that the above diagram is neutral to these various possibilities.

A class might work with a device configuration in which some features of the chart are merged. For example, in using a language like Mathematica, one can avoid explicit mention of commands to draw line segments. Nevertheless, such commands are there implicitly, and the student can get a good idea of what is happening by following the outlines of this book.

In some applications, the diagram may turn out to be too coarse. Sometimes it is useful to compute data twice—creating, for example, two different device-independent files. A good example is the calculation of Bézier curves: A first calculation can be used to determine the desired control points, yielding a device-independent file that contains commands to draw some Bézier curves with specified control points. This first device-independent file can then be taken as input for a second calculation, which will output a second device-independent file that contains commands for (a large number of) line segments that approximate those Bézier curves. (We will illustrate this in §3.2.6 and §6.5.) In general the reader should try to maintain an attitude of flexibility toward the possibilities inherent in these flow diagrams.

2.1   Computer languages

In keeping with our remarks in the introduction to the chapter, we do not advocate one computing system over another, or one computing language over another. We have endeavored to present our material in such a way that it is feasible to implement it in almost any environment. If one has access to a good programming language and can send output files to a graphic device, then one should be able to complete the exercises of this book. It helps, but is not essential, to have two kinds of graphic output devices. One should be a printer with some graphic capabilities, and the other should be a live graphic output device such as a terminal, a PC, or one window of a workstation. The former is useful for presenting classwork or other reports and for the decorative and artistic uses of this material that may occur to one; the latter is useful for getting immediate feedback.

Nevertheless, some computing systems offer more flexibility than others, and we urge readers of the book to study carefully their available options. We mention here a number of additional features that can make the student's job easier. The first two of these are probably the most important.

- A sophisticated programming environment, which may include debugging tools, automatic linking, and so on. Such an environment may also include an integrated editor.

- A good system for managing files, inputting them to other programs, sending them to the printer, and so on. It is very helpful to be able to send things to a print queue, instead of tying up a computer while things print.

- A system for the creating and editing files that goes beyond the bare minimum.

- A system for networking, remote access, and so on. Such a system may make it possible for some data (such as the continental outlines used in §6.1.1) and some programs (e.g., translators for device-independent commands) to be kept in one place and used by all students in a class.

- Electronic mail, or some other systematic way of sharing and distributing data, class requirements, program skeletons and so on, between students or between student and teacher.

- A program for typesetting or desktop publishing, for the preparation of final reports and documentation of one's work on this material.

None of these things is essential. Such things as multiple windows and pointing devices are useful if they aid in the implementation of one of the enhancements mentioned above, but otherwise they may be merely decorative. In any case, they likewise are not essential. Certain useful computer tools may even be counterproductive for learning the material of this course. The student needs to learn how to implement some theoretical notions (such as transformations) in computer programs, and some graphics packages have these ideas too tightly incorporated for the student to be able to work these things out for herself or himself. Thus it seems that the teacher will have to exercise some judgment over the choice of computing environment available to the student.

The heart of all the computer work implicit in our exercises is the programming language with which the exercises will be done. From this practical point of view, *computer* simply means an implementation of a programming language. It is far beyond the scope of this book to debate the relative merits of various programming languages. One's ultimate choice of language will probably arise out of a balance of practical and theoretical considerations, including availability, cost, speed, portability, old habits and so on. With so many considerations at stake, it is impossible for the author of the book to recommend any one language; in fact it is our general position that just about any modern programming language is adequate for the class. Nevertheless, we recommend a careful examination of the alternatives. Three useful features are defined data types, good program structure, and capability for programming in individual small modules. This last feature is particularly important when certain tasks, such as performing matrix multiplication, occur over and over in many contexts.

It is likewise beyond the scope of the book to teach computer programming per se. In our applied sections we strive for a clear mathematical exposition with formulas that can be worked out at the practical level, and we hope that such exposition can readily be implemented on a computer. No terribly sophisticated algorithms are essential to our work, although, of course, the instructor is free to impose higher standards of programming whenever it seems auspicious to do so. We do, however, provide occasional examples of programs, both to illustrate our material and to give the reader confidence in this arena.

LANGUAGES THAT PERFORM SYMBOLIC CALCULATIONS

Most of the general purpose programming languages allow you to define a function as a segment of code (called a *subroutine*, a *function*, or something similar). In most languages, however, the function definition must be hard coded into the program. Although you might write a program that gives the user a menu of functions, or invites the user to change some parameters, you nevertheless cannot set things up so that an arbitrary function is entered at runtime. Thus, for example, the code in §2.1.2 must have one or more lines rewritten if we wish, for example, to change $\sin 2x$ to $\sinh 2x$.

Although the minor editing and recompiling (or reinterpreting) involved are not a serious handicap to one's making pictures of many functions, we are speaking here of an inherent limitation of these programming languages: They are unable to treat a function as an object to be manipulated in the manner of strings and floating point numbers, etc. This limitation is felt more acutely in projects where we wish to make calculations about a function and its derivative. (Several such projects are to be found in §3.4.) In programs to carry out these projects we have to include separate code for the function and for its derivative. Every time we edit the code for that function, we have to make the corresponding changes to the code for its derivative.

There are a few sophisticated languages such as Mathematica, Maple, Macsyma and so on, that permit one to manipulate a function as an external object. These capabilities usually include, among many other things, the ability to calculate derivatives symbolically. It might therefore be of great interest to do the exercises of this book, especially those of §3.4, with such a language.

2.1.1   A language for sample programs

Although we do not advocate any one language, we do have a convention for writing illustrative programs. For the sake of having some standard, we will use the elementary parts of the C language as a lingua franca for describing programs. That is to say, each individual line of such a program will be a valid statement in C. In order to keep things simple, we deviate from real C in two ways. First, we omit a number of essential statements that are obvious or unnecessary to human readers, such as declarations of variables, inclusion of standard header files, and explicit proclamation of the main program. (We also do not include as many comments as we ordinarily would, since we are describing the programs in the text.) Second, we try to avoid any features of C that do not have direct counterparts in other languages. Therefore our examples will, we hope, be readable to all of our readers who have some experience with computing languages. (We do not require the reader to write any C code, and therefore only a passive understanding is needed. Nevertheless, the reader will of course need a thorough active understanding of *some* programming language.)

It may be valuable to review two points where C expresses itself a little differently from other programming languages, namely for loops, and formatted print (printf) statements. A for statement contains three clauses separated by two semicolons. In most cases these clauses tell one where to start the loop, how to end the loop, and how to go through the loop. In the example of §2.1.2, there is one loop. It begins with i = 0, it continues as long as i ≤ STEP (in other words, the indicated commands are executed for the last time when i = STEP), and after each pass through the loop, i is increased by 1 (as indicated by the C-shorthand i++). The scope of the loop is the material {...} enclosed in braces immediately after the for statement.

Equality is expressed in two ways. The single equality sign, as in A = ... , is an instruction to discard whatever value might be stored in A and to replace it with whatever appears on the right. The double equality sign (as in the if clause below) asks for a comparison between the values appearing on its two sides.

Printf has a large body of rules, of which we explain only what is needed to make our example comprehensible. A printf statement causes the first argument (the string enclosed by quotation marks (" ... ")) to be printed,[2] with the following changes. Any %f encountered in the string is not printed, but a floating point number is printed[3] instead, its value being taken from the storage location (variable) appearing as the next argument. Each %f appearing in the string requires its own argument to printf. In the following example, our first call to printf contains four %f's, and four arguments appear after the main argument (namely, LEFT, BOTTOM, RIGHT and TOP). These variables represent numbers that will be printed. Moreover, %d works exactly like %f, except that an integer (a *decimal*) is involved. Finally note that \n denotes *newline*. All of the printf commands in this example have a string that ends with \n, and hence each makes a separate line in the output file.

A program later in this chapter will read data from a file; this turns out to be a fussy business. Since there is no mathematical interest to this topic, we will not attempt to explain it, but hope it will be largely self-explanatory in the example. It is suggested that (in the context of a class) skeleton programs to do this sort of thing should be provided by the instructor as necessary.

2.1.2 A simple program to draw a curve

Computer expertise was our label for the second arrow in the diagram, i.e., the transition from a mathematical description of a problem to a computer program. Here we will give a brief illustration of this transition for a simple case, namely, a drawing of the curve $y = \sin 2x$ over the interval $[0, 2\pi]$. The program can be used as raw material for the solution of a large number of the exercises in Chapter 3. Moreover, this example will be illustrative of what has to be done to work out any of the graphical exercises of this book.

```
PI  =  3.1415926;

START_T  =  0.0 ;        STOP_T   =  (2*PI);

LEFT   =  -0.10;         BOTTOM  =  -1.10;
RIGHT  =   6.50;         TOP    =   1.10;

STEP  = 400;                       WIDTH = 6;

printf("w %f %f %f %f\n",LEFT,BOTTOM,RIGHT,TOP);
printf("W %d\n",WIDTH);
```

---

[2]On the author's system you can just say printf in your program, and the operating system allows you to specify a filename at runtime. In some other languages or operating systems, it may be necessary to name the output file in the program. Inquire locally.
[3]The number of decimal places can be controlled with a more detailed specification. For the simple specification %f, the number of decimal places is machine-dependent.

```
for (i=0; i<=STEP; i++)
{
    t =  START_T + (i/STEP)*(STOP_T - START_T);
    x = t;   y = sin(2*t);
    if (i == 0) printf("m %f %f\n",x,y);
    else        printf("l %f %f\n",x,y);
}
```

Exercises

1. Verify that the output of the preceding program is a file of 403 lines that begins as follows. (There are really two distinct things one could do here: make a working version of this program and run it, or follow the algorithm with pencil and paper. In the latter case, the precision indicated here is not important.)

```
w -0.100000 -1.100000 6.500000 1.100000
W 6
m 0.000000 0.000000
l 0.015708 0.031411
l 0.031416 0.062791
```

2. Write and use a version of this program in your own favorite language.

Our assumption linking pure mathematics and concrete drawings is that we can request a line segment to be drawn between two specified points. We do not concern ourselves with how an individual device might carry out such a request; we simply have to know a language for such requests. Our language for this purpose is described in detail in §2.2; for now it will suffice for us to know that w stands for *window*, W stands for the *Width* of the line being drawn, m stands for *move* (without drawing), and l stands for *line*. (As one can see, these are the kinds of requests that are output by our sample program.)

Now that we can read the sample program, and have some feeling for the kind of output it gives, let us see what it actually *does* at the mathematical level. As we said, our objective is to create a picture of the curve $y = \sin 2x$ over the interval $[0, 2\pi]$. Our first decision is that of a coordinate system for the picture. We assume, by convention, that the picture will ultimately be viewed in a rectangular window. To establish a coordinate system in that window, we need to give two values of the x-coordinate, namely, its values at the far left and far right of the window; and two values of the y-coordinate, namely, its values at the bottom and top of the window. In our program we have stored these values in LEFT, RIGHT, BOTTOM and TOP. Then the first printf statement in the program causes the first output line, which contains this window information.

Any values can be assigned to the variables LEFT, RIGHT, BOTTOM and TOP, but they should be selected so that the intended object appears in the window.

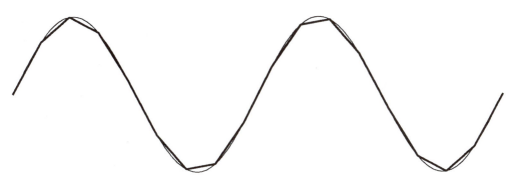

FIGURE 2.1   A jagged approximation to a sine curve; STEP = 17

For example, as the reader can observe, we have chosen the values -0.1, 6.5, -1.1 and 1.1, for the obvious reason that they make a window that is just a little bit larger than $[0, 2\pi] \times [-1, 1]$, which is the smallest rectangle containing the desired graph. Of course other considerations (including artistic considerations) might dictate a different choice. For example, a very small window will give one a blow-up of a small piece of the curve.

The next `printf` statement and its corresponding line in the output file have the effect of requesting a line of width 6. From the mathematical point of view, this request is purely decorative.

Finally, the `for` loop contains the actual calculation of the sin curve. As we said, our only expectation about output devices is that they can draw line segments upon request. Therefore, we communicate a curve to our device as a *piecewise linear approximation*, i.e., a collection of line segments. If points P and Q lie on a curve Γ, then the line segment joining P and Q can be regarded as an approximation to Γ, but it may be a very bad approximation if the curve Γ undergoes a lot of curvature between P and Q. Generally speaking, the quality of the approximation will be better if P and Q are chosen close together than if they are chosen far apart. Therefore, we will use points P_0, P_1, P_2, $\ldots$, P_N, arranged along Γ, with P_i rather close to P_{i+1} for each i. See Figure 2.1, in which we have also lightly sketched the sin curve itself.

Naturally, the quality of the approximation rises as the points P_i become closer together; therefore a better approximation requires more points. In our program, we have used STEP to denote the total number of segments (or *steps*) $P_i P_{i+1}$. In other words, STEP is the N that appears just above. Figure 2.2 shows an approximation to the sin curve that was made by increasing the number of steps. Besides choosing the total number of points, one needs to determine a scheme for distributing them somewhat evenly along the curve. The simplest

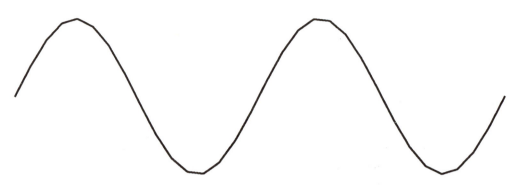

FIGURE 2.2   A jagged approximation to a sine curve; `STEP` = 31

plan, which we have adopted, is to space them evenly along the x-axis. (When we come to the more general *parametric representation* of curves in §3.1.1, it will be preferable (and more natural) to advance the parameter itself, rather than the x-coordinate, in equal small steps.) In this book we do not attempt to analyze how well these procedures approximate any given curve. Such questions belong more to advanced calculus (or numerical analysis) than to geometry, while our purpose here is to learn and apply geometric methods. Nevertheless, the student should always bear in mind that any picture (whether drawn by a computer or not) is only an approximation; it may convey much useful information, but no mathematical proof can be based on it. Therefore we leave it to the reader to strike a balance: `STEP` should be large enough to give the illusion of a smooth curve, while not so large as to waste either the user's time or computer resources. (The value 400 appearing in our program is on the large side.) Often it is wise to use small values of `STEP` during the development stage and then to make a presentation copy using a large value.

Now the `for` loop itself is easily described. Clearly the formula

```
t =  START_T + (i/STEP)*(STOP_T - START_T);
```

is linear in `i`, and hence causes `t` to take values that are evenly spaced. They begin with `i` = 0, which yields `t` = `START_T`, and end with `i` = `STEP`, which yields `t` = `STOP_T`. In other words, the parameter `t` is taken through `STEP` values that increase evenly from 0 to 2π. It is now immediate from the formulas

```
x = t;  y = sin(2*t);
```

that x and y are the coordinates of the point P_i mentioned above. The ith pass through the loop now ends with the outputting of a single line containing the letter l and the two coordinates of P_i. (When i = 0, l is replaced by m.) The first such output line, the one beginning with m, is a request to *move* to (i.e., begin a new drawing at) the point P_0. Each subsequent output line begins with l and is a request to draw a line from the previous point P_{i-1} to the current point P_i. Clearly the requested segments are exactly the segments appearing in the sin curve approximation that we already described. Therefore, the output of this program indeed gives a drawing of a sin curve.

One should remember that an algorithm or program for a picture is an important document, with its own niche in our scheme of things. As the reader can see from this example, it contains more detail, but less information, than a mathematical description of the problem. On the other hand, it contains less detail, but much more information, than its output (the device-independent file). As an important document, it should be accorded the respect of good writing. For a program, good writing generally means good documentation (comments) and good organization (dividing the program into easily understood units).

The following two exercises would of course be carried out with the methods of this section and the next.

Exercises

1. Experiment with changing the parameter STEP in our treatment of the sin curve.

2. Estimate the largest value of STEP that makes sense for your output device. (Assuming, for example, that the curve $y = f(x)$ goes once across the page with $|f'(x)| < 2$.)

3. Make a nice version of the sin curve. Desirable features might include labeled coordinate axes, some further grid lines, a caption to the figure, and your name. This exercise in a sense is a warm-up for Chapter 3, for all of these things will be useful there. All of these things are quite feasible with our device-independent language and should be automated where possible. (Here *automation* means that these features should be included in the program, preferably in subroutines that can be called by the curve-drawing program of §2.1.2. For example, the author has a subroutine called draw_axes() that calculates and outputs the correct device-independent commands for the co-ordinate axes (based on the values of LEFT, RIGHT, BOTTOM and TOP of §2.1.2).)

4. Students who have studied *Fourier series* (in a class on mathematics, physics or engineering) will recall that the infinite series

$$\frac{\sin x}{1} + \frac{\sin 3x}{3} + \frac{\sin 5x}{5} + \frac{\sin 7x}{7} + \cdots$$

converges pointwise on the interval $[-\pi, \pi]$ to the step function

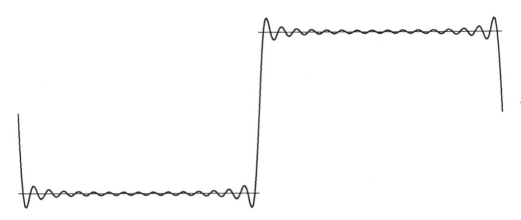

FIGURE 2.3   Fourier approximation of a step function

$$f(x) = \begin{cases} \pi/4 & \text{if } 0 < x < \pi \\ 0 & \text{if } x = -\pi,\, 0,\, \pi \\ -\pi/4 & \text{if } -\pi < x < 0 \end{cases}$$

The techniques that we now have available are adequate for exploring this convergence experimentally, and the interested reader is invited to do so. In Figure 2.3 we show the sum of the first sixteen terms. You might wish to make pictures of partial sums with more than sixteen terms. It would be well to compare your experimental work with the theory of this Fourier series, which is nicely expounded, for example, in M. A. Pinsky's *Introduction to Partial Differential Equations with Applications* (New York, McGraw-Hill, 1984), pp. 70–73. In particular, the theory predicts that the first maximum will always be greater than

$$\frac{1}{2} \int_0^\pi \frac{\sin x}{x}\, dx \;\approx\; 1.18\,\frac{\pi}{4}$$

In other words, the curve is overshot by some 9% of the height of the discontinuity occurring in $f(x)$. This 9% overshoot, which occurs whenever there is a step-function type discontinuity, is known as the *Gibbs phenomenon*, in honor of J. Willard Gibbs.

2.2   A device-independent language for line drawings

As we stated in the introduction to this chapter, we need a language in which to write device-independent files to describe our pictures. We mentioned a couple of features of our device-independent language in §2.1; here we describe it completely

This language lies—from our point of view—at a low level. It is utterly unconcerned with what the picture means or represents; its only concern is a set of commands for placing pen[4] to paper.

Each command is initiated by a single letter, which must be at the start of a line. Some commands must be followed by data; after all necessary data is included, comments may be appended to that line at will. The commands and their ideal interpretations are as follows:

% The null command. A comment may be written after the %. Ideally, the comment will be retained in those environments that permit comments. (For instance, translation to PostScript (where comments also begin with %), or to multiple windows on a screen, where the picture might appear in one window and comments in another.) A comment occurring in other sorts of commands will be lost upon interpretation.

w Window. This command is followed by four numbers which indicate the extreme values of the coordinates that will appear in the display. The first two numbers are the coordinates of the lower-left corner of the image, and the next two numbers are the coordinates of the upper-right corner.

r Clip region. This command is followed by four coordinates that are interpreted like the coordinates for w. Indicates a region of the paper where l coordinates can be drawn.

m Move pen (without writing) to the point with coordinates indicated.

l Engage pen and move in a straight line to the point with the two coordinates indicated. (Thus the first l command should be preceded by at least one m command.)

W The following integer indicates the width of the lines to be drawn by all subsequent l commands, until another W command is issued. Units are roughly in *pixels,* but these units may vary from device to device.

T Place text starting at the current position (i.e., at the place indicated by the most recent command that was either an m or an l). The entire line (after T) is read, and so no comments can be included on a line of this type.

t Same as T, only with a smaller font size.

x Same as T and t, with an intermediate font size.

---

[4]This language is simple for a human to read and so could be interpreted by a human using a pen and a piece of graph paper. Nevertheless, for real speed and accuracy, the role of *pen* should be played by a laser inside a printer or by an electron gun inside a cathode ray tube. Other possibilities include the pen of a plotter and a laser that can cut cloth (in an industrial setting).

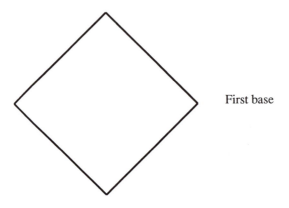

FIGURE 2.4   A baseball diamond

Except for the work in §2.5, §2.7, §6.4.4, §6.4.5 and §6.8, all the necessary drawings can be made, albeit crudely, using m, l and w alone. (Nevertheless, a number of enhancements to the language, to be introduced in due course, will make things easier and more meaningful.)

For example, the file

```
w 0.0 0.0 6.0 6
W 7
% Around the baseball diamond.
m 3 2 start at home plate
l 4 3 draw line to first base
l 3 4  "    "    " second base
l 2 3  "    "    " third base
l 3 2  "    "    " home plate
m 4.5 3
TFirst base
```

specifies the crude baseball diamond, with first base labeled as such, which is depicted in Figure 2.4. The various other descriptions are comments. Except for the one beginning with %, those comments will be discarded when the file is interpreted. The student should take the available implementations of this language and experiment with writing small picture files like this one.

Nevertheless, except possibly for occasional special effects, we are not really interested in hand-made files. Our practical interest is in computer programs that illustrate and apply the mathematical concepts described in these pages. For any given topic in this book, one could laboriously calculate by hand a few points of a picture, but it is almost always more satisfactory to ask a computer to make the calculations. Apart from the obvious practicality, there is the added advantage that a well-written modular program can parallel the theory and thereby provide a good mirror of one's understanding.

As we said in the chapter introduction, and illustrated in §2.1.2, the recommended technique is to write a program whose output is a file consisting of commands in the device-independent language This file can then be sent to any device, using an appropriate interpreter. Here are some of the advantages of this approach:

- This approach emphasizes the natural division of graphics work into two parts: the mathematical analysis of a geometrical situation to create a picture description and the creation of an actual image from that description. Graphics programs can be designed without any concern for the device on which their output will ultimately be displayed. In this way we can concentrate on the mathematics involved.

- In shared computing environments, one can do a large part of one's development work on a simple (non-graphics) terminal or monitor, thereby freeing scarce resources for other users.

- The primary output of a graphics program is a printable ASCII file that can be inspected for reasonableness before any real picture is made. This file may be useful for debugging.

- For similar reasons, a file in this language is easy to edit and to transport via modem. The language is simple enough that students can write their own implementations.

- For special artistic effects, the output of a graphics program can easily be modified or combined with other output files, without the necessity of redesigning the whole program.

- Pictures can be tested on any available graphics screen before sending to the printer.

- The implementation that translates this language to PostScript is designed to produce valid PostScript code that cannot stall the printer. (Similar remarks apply to other output devices.) This is particularly important when there is a shared device such as a printer.

- If a graphics program is making incorrect pictures, one can be reasonably sure that the problem is not related to the implementation of the picture language.

- In a shared environment, one compiled implementation of this language can be used by all students in one class. In this way there is a great savings of disk space.

Notice that among the advantages we do not include the possibility of sharing pictures with fellow students or others through the medium of files in our device-independent language. Although this is possible at the level of m, l and so on, human communication is better served at every one of the other linguistic levels. (Through human speech, mathematical description, well-commented programs, or by viewing actual pictures.)

This approach is intended as useful for a mathematics-oriented beginning class, but not as universal for all graphics work. Here are some circumstances under which it may become somewhat or even very inappropriate:

- In some institutional or industrial settings, one may need to follow an established pattern, which may involve following a commercial or canned graphics language such as IDL, the NCAR graphics package, Mathematica, and so on.

- There are in fact numerous different device-independent languages.[5] Some, like PostScript, are more sophisticated, and some, like CGM, are more compact. Sometimes files of commands in some of these languages are called *metafiles*. Some settings may call for the use of these other languages.

- Pixel-by-pixel descriptions will require a more sophisticated language, such as PostScript, GIF, etc. (see §2.7.1 below).

- For animations, or for graphics applications that involve getting images on the screen while a program is running, one will have to invoke other methods. Such methods may for instance require direct addressing of those parts of computer memory that control the appearance of the screen.

- For real graphics power and speed, one might want to design a chip that executes some of the tasks described in this book. For instance, a chip might be designed to compute pictures of the world and display them very fast, to give the illusion of continuous rotation. To utilize its power, one would want to pass the chip's output directly to screen hardware through dedicated wiring.

Nevertheless, in all of these advanced applications, the mathematical methods are those described here, and it is the author's hope that the general mathematical outlook gained here will carry over to any such advanced and specialized applications.

We include neither a precise declaration nor a precise semantics for this device-independent language. Thus we are thinking of a lingua franca that could be modified or enhanced to suit the circumstances. In particular it could be extended to include other features (colors, circular arcs, dots or other specialized icons, inclusion of other files, fresh pages, pausing, ...) that might be available on some output devices, or to include more sophisticated commands (such as the rotations, and so on, of §3.3). (For instance, note the introduction of I and V commands in our treatment of hidden line filtering in §6.4.1, and the introduction

---

[5]For a popular article mentioning a number of these languages, and discussing the ins and outs of translating between them, see Luisa Simone, "Vector file-conversion utilities." *PC Magazine*, 1991, *10* (2), 243–271. None of the hard and software mentioned there should be necessary for the mainstream use of this book.

of B, E and c commands when we discuss Bézier curves in §3.2.6.) Moreover, a 3-dimensional version of the device-independent language clearly makes sense, but we will not attempt to implement it until Chapter 6, where we apply our knowledge of projective maps to make three-dimensional pictures. On the other hand, we certainly allow for the possibility that on some output devices certain features might be rendered badly or not at all. Of course, as one adds features, the language becomes more unwieldy; we leave it to the individual user to strike his or her own balance.

THE DIRECT USE OF POSTSCRIPT

There may be a few readers for whom it makes sense to bypass our device-independent language and write output directly in PostScript. Technically speaking, this would not be difficult: one need only put the appropriate PostScript code into the `printf` statements of §2.1.2. Nevertheless, we recommend against this approach for a number of reasons. The foremost is that, as we mentioned, we plan a number of enhancements to our language (such as Logo commands, control points for spline curves, and 3-dimensional coordinates), and we would want all students to examine these enhancements to understand the general thrust of our methods. Second, full PostScript is such a sophisticated language that it would be difficult to interpret it for non-PostScript devices. Therefore the approach of directly writing PostScript should be used only when one is confident that one will not want to address non-PostScript devices.

2.3 Interpreting the device-independent language

An *interpretation* (or *implementation* or *translation*) of the device-independent language is a program that accepts a file in this language as input[6] and then yields the corresponding drawing as output on a given device. For example, if one applies the author's PostScript implementation of the picture language to the above example of a baseball diamond, the result is a file that looks like this:

```
%!
1.7 setlinewidth
    % Around the baseball diamond.
306.0 384.0 moveto
newpath
306.0 384.0 moveto
```

---

[6]The exact details of input will depend on the operating system, and the details of output will depend both on the operating system and on the device.

```
408.0 486.0 lineto
stroke
newpath
408.0 486.0 moveto
306.0 588.0 lineto
stroke
newpath
306.0 588.0 moveto
204.0 486.0 lineto
stroke
newpath
204.0 486.0 moveto
306.0 384.0 lineto
stroke
459.0 486.0 moveto
/Times-Roman findfont 14 scalefont setfont
(First base) show
showpage
```

which is pure PostScript code. (The unit of length is one *point*; there are 72 points to an inch.) This code could be sent directly to any device that interprets PostScript, such as many brands of laser printer.

One needs to have one interpretation for each of the available devices. (Ideally, these include one screen and one printer.) In the setting of a mathematics class, there are good reasons to have this basic need met by the instructor in advance: there is very little mathematical content to interpretation programs, one program can serve all students, and such a program is rather stable for a software object: one version can be used without change for an entire semester. Therefore the next section (§2.3.1) may be skipped, particularly on the first reading. On the other hand, readers may benefit from looking at a translation program, for a number of reasons. Someone studying this outside of any class, or even a class member who has access to some device not generally available to the class, will have to write his or her own translation program. Students that go deeply into this material will undoubtedly want to have some of the enhancements to the device-independent language that we mentioned near the end of §2.2. And finally, we mention that several of the basic projects described in Chapter 6—including drawing the stars and drawing the globe with continental boundaries—reduce, in outline, to translation programs. Therefore the program described in §2.3.1 can be used as a skeleton for those two projects. A somewhat similar situation holds also for our work involving Bézier curves. (See remarks in §3.2.6.)

2.3.1   A translation program

In this section we present a simple version of a program to translate device-independent files. The output here is PostScript code. For simplicity, we assume that we have an operating system capable of accepting files as *standard input* to a program. Therefore we do not expressly mention the input file. The program gives output (i.e., the PostScript file) as *standard output*; thus we also do not expressly name the output file. In an operating system that lacks the convention of standard input and standard output, these things would be handled differently. (The reading of files named in the program is covered briefly in §6.1.2.)

A program of this type, i.e., one that accepts input and modifies it systematically (frequently line by line), is often called a *filter* (since the simplest filters simply discard some lines and retain other lines). For some sorts of devices, instead of filtering the data, one needs to make direct calls to the graphics operations. For example, most graphics-equipped personal computers have a `line` command in one or more of their available languages. In general, one will have to consult a manual for the device. In any case, the mathematical calculations do not differ essentially from those described here.

We mention very briefly a few features of C that will appear in this program. The basic function for reading input is `scanf`. The first call to `scanf` does nothing but read and discard a newline (\n) character that remains unread from the previous line. The second call to `scanf` reads up to a newline and stores the result in a character array called `current_line`. The action taken is decided by the `switch` command, which simply takes an action depending on which `case` is valid, i.e., which character comes first in `current_line`. The `cases` are those in our description of the device-independent language, except that in this small example we include only those `cases` necessary to do the example of the baseball diamond. (The other `cases` are handled similarly.) A final `case` called `default` is invoked if none of the expressly mentioned `cases` holds. In this program, `default` is considered to be an error, for every line should begin with a character that is mentioned in one of the `cases`. Thus `default` prints an error message and causes the program to terminate early, in a manner described below.

Each `case` begins with a `sscanf` command; this is like the basic `scanf` command, except that it takes its input from a string (`current_line` in this program). The value Q returned by `sscanf` is a count of the number of successful conversions. An error is returned if this doesn't come out right; for instance, with a `w` (window) command, we need four coordinates. A number of error routines are available to print out what is wrong in various cases; we omit the details of those routines. After the `sscanf` command has been executed, all necessary data is available in the right places, and calculation (and possible output) can begin. This is mostly done in subroutines.

One should note also that `&` stands for a storage location, while `&&` means logical *and*. Logical *or* is `||`, and logical negation (*not*) is `!`. Finally, it is important to note that this file invokes a defined data type (*struct*) called point. Every point p has two coordinates, namely p.x_coord and p.y_coord. In the following code, p and q are points.

The overall structure of the program is a while loop. The variable no_input_errors is initialized to be non-zero, and the loop will continue as long as this remains non-zero. Various syntax errors (coded by the Q values returned by sscanf) will cause no_input_errors to become zero, thereby ending the loop. If the input file contains no syntax errors then ultimately, when the end of the input file is reached, there will be a failed call to scanf in the third line of the while loop. Then Q will be 0 in the fourth line, causing a break to end the while loop, thus ending the program.

The point p is used in the program as the storage for the two coordinates given in an l or m command. The previous value of p is stored (as q) for use in l only.

We hope we have described our program well enough that the reader who is not fluent in C can at least understand its structure in broad outline. The acid test of one's understanding is not whether one can analyze every detail, but rather whether one could write it in one's own favorite language. In fact it is not very complicated logically. Here then is the program.

```
no_input_errors = 1;        ok_to_draw_line = 0;

lower_left.x_coord = 0.0; lower_left.y_coord = 0.0;
upper_right.x_coord = 1.0; upper_right.y_coord = 1.0;

begin_drawing();
N=0;
while (no_input_errors)
{
  q = p;
  if (N>0) scanf("\n");
  Q = scanf("%[^\n]",current_line);
  if (Q <= 0) {error_1(); break;}
  switch(current_line[0])
  {
    case '%':
       Q = sscanf(current_line,"%*c%[^\n]",text);
       comment_print(text); break;
    case 'T':
       Q = sscanf(current_line,"T%[^\n]",text);
       textprint_large(text); break;
    case 'w':
       Q = sscanf(current_line,"w%lf%lf%lf%lf",
                   &lower_left.x_coord,&lower_left.y_coord,
                   &upper_right.x_coord,&upper_right.y_coord);
       if (Q <= 3) {error_w0(); no_input_errors=0;}
```

```
        if ( (lower_left.x_coord==upper_right.x_coord) ||
                  (lower_left.y_coord==upper_right.y_coord))
                                    {error_w1(); no_input_errors=0;}
        break;
    case 'W':
        Q = sscanf(current_line,"W%d",&width);
        if (Q <= 0) {error_W(); no_input_errors=0; break;}
        set_width(width); break;
    case 'm':
        ok_to_draw_line = 1;
        Q = sscanf(current_line,"m%lf%lf",&p.x_coord,&p.y_coord);
        if (Q <= 1) {error_m(); no_input_errors=0; break;}
        p.x_coord = (p.x_coord-lower_left.x_coord) /
                        (upper_right.x_coord-lower_left.x_coord);
        p.y_coord = (p.y_coord-lower_left.y_coord) /
                        (upper_right.y_coord-lower_left.y_coord);
        move_to(p); break;
    case 'l':
        if (!ok_to_draw_line){error_l1();
                                no_input_errors=0; break;}
        Q = sscanf(current_line,"l%lf%lf",&p.x_coord,&p.y_coord);
        if (Q <= 1) {error_l(); no_input_errors=0; break;}
        p.x_coord = (p.x_coord-lower_left.x_coord) /
                        (upper_right.x_coord-lower_left.x_coord);
        p.y_coord = (p.y_coord-lower_left.y_coord) /
                        (upper_right.y_coord-lower_left.y_coord);
        makeline(p,q); break;
    default:
        error_4(); no_input_errors = 0;
    }
    N++;
}
end_drawing();
```

The only calculation of any substance to appear in the program is the revision of the x and y coordinates of the point p that occurs in case m and case l. The formula for the x-coordinate is

```
p.x_coord = (p.x_coord - lower_left.x_coord) /
                  (upper_right.x_coord - lower_left.x_coord);
```

Three of the four numbers appearing on the right side are essentially constants, namely, the x-coordinates of the upper right corner and of the lower left corner (which appears twice). These are determined by a window (w) command, and would change only in the rare event that the window is changed. Thus the only real variable in the formula is the (original) value of p.x_coord. Clearly the formula is linear in this variable, and it is easily checked that the two extremes of the window are transformed into 0 and 1. That is, if the x-coordinate of p is the same as the x-coordinate at the lower left (or upper right) of the window, then the new value for the x-coordinate of p will be 0 (or 1). Thus, after this revision, the x-coordinates of points in the window range between 0 and 1, and the same is true for y-coordinates. These are the coordinates that are passed to the subroutines move_to and makeline. Thus these subroutines can be written once and for all, with an unvarying coordinate system: 0 at bottom and left of picture, 1 at top and right.

We now describe some of the subroutines called by the program. Some of the subroutines are merely error routines that give messages explaining what syntax error was encountered or how the program ended; we feel that these can safely be omitted. Notice, by the way, that the main body of our program is itself device independent. But sooner or later we have to relate to a specific device; this we do in listing the versions of our subroutines that give output suitable to a PostScript printer as follows:

```
begin_drawing()
{
    printf("%%!\n");
}

end_drawing()
{
    printf("showpage\n");
}

comment_print(text)
{
    printf("    %%%s\n",text);
}

textprint_large(text)
{
    printf("/Times-Roman findfont 14 scalefont setfont\n");
    printf("("); printf("%s",text); printf(") show\n");
}

set_width(width)
{
    x = width*(72.0/300.0);
    printf("%3.1f setlinewidth\n",x);
}

move_to(p)
{
```

```
    i = (p.x_coord * 72)*8.5;
    j = ((p.y_coord * 8.5) + 2.5) *72;
    if (i>0.0 && j>0.0 && i<612.0 && j<792.0)
    {
        printf("%4.1f %4.1f moveto\n",i,j);
    }
}

makeline(p,q)
{
    k = (p.x_coord * 72)*8.5;
    l = ((p.y_coord * 8.5) + 2.5) *72;
    i = (q.x_coord * 72)*8.5;
    j = ((q.y_coord * 8.5) + 2.5) *72;
    if (i>0.0 && j>0.0 && k>0.0 && l>0.0
          && i<612.0 && j<792.0 && k<612.0 && l<792.0)
    {
        printf("newpath\n");
        printf("%4.1f %4.1f moveto\n",i,j);
        printf("%4.1f %4.1f lineto\n",k,l);
        printf("stroke\n");
    }
}
```

Exercises

1. Step through the operation of this program on the example of the baseball diamond, to get a feeling for how it works.

2. Use your own favorite computer language to write a program that translates device-independent commands.

3. One could enhance the program by having it give an error message (on whatever channel is appropriate) saying how many segments were discarded for not being in the window.

4. Extend the program to implement the r (clip region) command. There are two ways to do this. The simple-minded way simply checks the location of both endpoints of a segment and refuses to print the segment unless both endpoints are in the clipping rectangle. A more sophisticated routine will actually calculate that portion of the segment that lies within the clipping rectangle and then will print exactly that visible portion. (Note that a segment may have a visible portion even if both its endpoints lie outside the clipping region.)

5. The following problem is mathematically similar to the previous one. In some applications one might want to be able specify a *line* (rather than a line

segment) and to have the program print whatever portion of it is visible in the window. For example,

```
w 2 2 4 4
m 2 1
L 5 4
```

would cause a line with slope 1 to appear in the lower right corner of the window. (Its visible portion would run between $\langle 3, 2 \rangle$ and $\langle 4, 3 \rangle$.) Experiment with implementing a feature like this.

6. Suppose you have a device that accepts commands for negative line segments; i.e., you can command the device to take away (erase, turn off, stop displaying) a given segment. (Various Tektronix devices have this feature; obviously the concept is not very meaningful for printers.) Add a command e, which works just like l, except that the corresponding line segment is erased. Assuming that you already have a device-independent interpreter on some device where erasing is possible, extend the interpreter to accept e commands. Experiment with the special effects that can be created in this way. For example one could draw a curve and then erase the entire curve.

7. Some (older) devices have no built in line-drawing capability and thus no line command of any kind. In this case one must calculate the image pixel by pixel, as in §2.7. That is, the routine makeline of our program above must be modified as follows. One should first set up (in the main program) an array that contains one integer for each pixel, with all values initially 1. Then makeline(p,q) calculates which pixels must be darkened to cause (the approximate appearance of) a segment joining p and q and changes the appropriate values to 0. After all input data has been read and acted upon, the main program will have a second phase which consists of outputting the raster image that has been created in memory. This is done almost exactly like the main program in §2.7.1, except that intensity values are read from the aforementioned array, rather than being calculated as $f(x, y)$. We don't really recommend this as an exercise unless you really have to do it, but it should be feasible with the tools at hand.[7]

8. Those readers in possession of an implementation of Awk might wish to check that the following Awk program will in fact translate device-independent code to PostScript. (Awk is a small programming language that specializes in reading files and acting on the data contained therein. (In other words, it is useful for the the design of line-based filters.) Its advantages for this application are that the main data reading loop is built in, and that it has a built-in

---

[7]For a thorough discussion of this issue, see e.g., §3.2 and §§19.3–4 of J. D. Foley, A. van Dam, S. K. Feiner and J. F. Hughes, *Computer Graphics*, second edition, Addison-Wesley Publishing Company, Reading, Massachusetts, 1990, or pp. 99–106 of *Graphics Gems* (edited by Andrew S. Glassner), Academic Press, Boston, 1990. (Articles by Paul S. Heckbert, Kelvin Thompson and Brian Wyvill.)

feature of pattern recognition. Thus, for example, /^t/ calls for an action to be taken for any input line that begins with t. Logical *or* is denoted | |, and so /^t/| |/^x/... calls for an action to be taken for any input line that begins with t or with x or ... . One major disadvantage of Awk is that it does not admit subroutines.) Anything following # is a comment. In Awk, $1 refers to the first *word* in an input line, $2 refers to the second word, and so on. $0 refers to the whole line.

```
BEGIN{
        ok_to_draw_line=0
                    # initialize window coordinates:
        LL_x = 0.0; LL_y = 0.0; UR_x = 1.0; UR_y = 1.0;
        printf("%%!\n") }


{q_x=p_x; q_y=p_y}    #save old p-values
/^%/                  #print any line beginning with %

/^t/{fontsize =  8}
/^x/{fontsize = 10}
/^T/{fontsize = 14}
/^t/||/^x/||/^T/ {
        printf "/Times-Roman findfont %d",fontsize
        printf "scalefont setfont\n("
        printf "%s", substr($0,2,length-1)
        printf ")  show\n" }
/^w/ {
        LL_x=$2; LL_y=$3; UR_x=$4; UR_y=$5 }
/^m/ {
        p_x=$2; p_y=$3 ;
        p_x = (p_x-LL_x) / (UR_x-LL_x);
        p_y = (p_y-LL_y) / (UR_y-LL_y);
        ok_to_draw_line = 1;
        i = (p_x * 72)*8.5; j = ((p_y * 8.5) + 2.5) *72;
        if (i>0.0 && j>0.0 && i<612.0 && j<792.0)
        {
            printf "%4.1f %4.1f moveto\n",i,j
        } }
/^l/ {
        p_x=$2 ; p_y=$3 ;
        p_x = (p_x-LL_x) / (UR_x-LL_x);
        p_y = (p_y-LL_y) / (UR_y-LL_y);
        i  = (p_x * 72)*8.5; j  = ((p_y * 8.5) + 2.5) *72;
        ii = (q_x * 72)*8.5; jj = ((q_y * 8.5) + 2.5) *72;
        if (i>0.0 && j>0.0 && i<612.0 && j<792.0)
        {
            printf "newpath\n"
            printf "%4.1f %4.1f moveto\n" ,ii,jj
```

```
                    printf "%4.1f %4.1f lineto\n" ,i,j
                    printf "stroke\n"
              } }
    /^W/ {
         x =   ($2)*(72.0/300.0);
         printf "%3.1f setlinewidth\n",x }
    END{
       printf "showpage\n" }
```

2.4 A Logo-like language

The computer language Logo is especially popular for elementary educational purposes, since it describes drawings in a very intuitive manner. (Many versions of Logo are in fact complete computer languages.) Here we will describe how one could make an extension of our device-independent language that has the basic geometric features of Logo.

Logo imagines a creature (animal, mineral or electronic, sometimes called a *turtle*) that walks about on a plane. The turtle follows a straight line until commanded to turn right or left through a given angle. It walks always straight ahead, through a distance specified by a command. Finally, the turtle carries a pen, which it can either engage or disengage on command. The engaged pen, usually thought of as *down*, leaves a track indicating the turtle's path. The disengaged (or *up*) pen leaves no track. For our purposes, it is appropriate to extend the device-independent language with the following five turtle commands:

U Pen up. Disengage pen.

D Pen down. Engage pen.

L Left. To be followed by the angular measure of one angle. Indicates that the heading of the turtle should be turned left by the indicated amount. This command neither changes the turtle's position nor generates any output.

R Similar, but a right turn.

F Forward. To be followed by a number. Turtle's position altered by moving the indicated distance in the direction of the turtle's heading (backwards, if the given number is negative). If pen is down, then a segment is drawn from the previous position of the turtle to its new position. If pen is up, no segment is drawn.

Generally speaking, it is simpler for the user to have the turtle measure angles in degrees, and that is the convention we will follow. For example, the file

```
    D
    F 1.3
```

```
L  72
F 1.3
L  72
F 1.3
L  72
F 1.3
L  72
F 1.3
```

will make a regular pentagon.

In interpreting this language, there is no reason not to mix Logo commands with commands already in use in our device-independent language. Probably there should be an m command before the first F command. One needs a convention as to the turtle's original heading. Nevertheless, it turns out to be easy to extend an existing interpretation of the device-independent language to include the turtle commands. (Cases can be added at will to a switch command.) The only extra features needed are some global variables for the turtle's current position and its heading. We trust that this can be left to the reader.

There are really two ways to proceed. One could upgrade the interpreters for one or two favorite devices to accept these five commands, and be done with it. Or one could write a program that translates the five new commands to ordinary device-independent code; then our basic device-independent translator can be coupled with this new translator according to the following diagram:

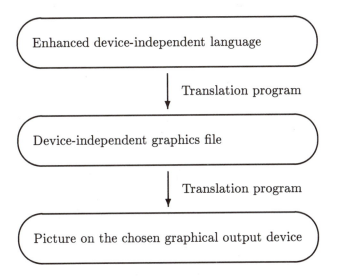

The latter approach typifies much of our work in this volume. We say just a few words about how it might be carried out. One can use the same overall structure of switching according to the first letter of a command line. The default action will be to output the line exactly as it was input. In other words, commands other than the five Logo commands will be passed unchanged. For the five Logo commands, one should simply output m and l commands that describe the lines that the turtle has to draw.

It is important to say a few words about the precision of data required for our algorithms. By the time one gets to a device-independent file, usually a part in 1000 (three or four significant figures) is adequate accuracy, since such an error would be invisible to the eye. (Nevertheless, greater accuracy may be required if one plans to blow up the figure by using tiny windows.) Even the B-splines that we will soon introduce can get by with this low level of precision, since their points are convex combinations of the control points. This Logo language is almost the only topic in the book where errors can readily accumulate. (If you begin facing north, turn right 1000 times, and each turn was really 89.99 degrees, what direction will you be facing?) Therefore, files of Logo commands should have all entries as accurate as possible, and the program should maintain its global variables (position and heading) with precision.

Full versions of Logo contain programming features such as loops and subroutines. For our purposes such sophisticated commands are not needed, since we have in mind that a progam in the user's native language will output (files of) Logo commands, for whatever figures are desired. In the author's experience, absolute positional commands (m and l) are generally easier to work with than are relative commands, except in a few special cases, such as tilings of the plane, where a few fixed lengths and simple angles recur often. We will look at one of these cases right now.

TILINGS OF THE PLANE

According to B. Grünbaum and G. C. Shephard, a *plane tiling* is a countable family of closed sets $T = \{T_1, T_2, \ldots\}$, which covers the plane without gaps or overlaps. This notion is explained at great length, with numerous examples, in their book *Tilings and Patterns*,[8] which contains far too much information to summarize here. We will mention only one example: the *Archimedean* or *uniform* tilings, composed of convex regular polyhedra, with all vertices equivalent. That is, there is a vector of integers $\langle m_1, m_2, \ldots \rangle$ such that at every vertex one sees, arranged cyclically, a regular m_1-gon, then a regular m_2-gon, and so on. This so-called *vertex figure* can be used to denote the tiling itself. Thus $\langle 4, 4, 4, 4 \rangle$ denotes the well-known checkerboard tiling. In Figures 2.5 and 2.6 we have illustrated $\langle 6, 6, 6 \rangle$ (the well-known honeycomb) and $\langle 3, 4, 6, 4 \rangle$. In the next exercise set, we will ask the reader to make drawings of some of the other Archimedean tilings. The complete list of vertex figures for Archimedean tilings (illustrated in Grünbaum and Shephard, p. 63, and in many other books) is as follows:

---

[8]W. H. Freeman and Company, New York, 1987.

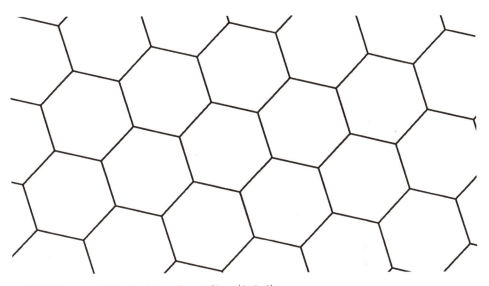

FIGURE 2.5   The Archimedean tiling $\langle 6, 6, 6 \rangle$

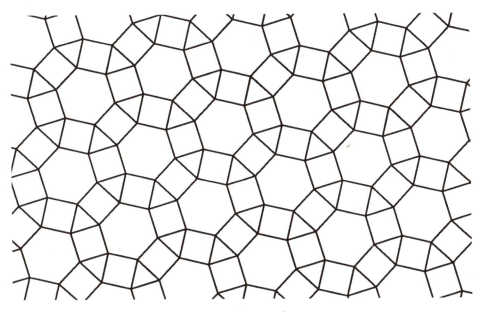

FIGURE 2.6   The Archimedean tiling $\langle 3, 4, 6, 4 \rangle$

```
3   3   3   3   3   3
3   3   3   3   6
3   3   3   4   4
3   3   4   3   4
3   4   6   4
3   6   3   6
4   4   4   4
3  12  12
4   6  12
4   8   8
6   6   6
```

Exercises

1. Extend a locally available interpreter of the device-independent language to an interpreter that will handle our list of five turtle commands. (Use either of the two approaches mentioned above.)

2. Make drawings of the uniform tilings that are illustrated in the text ($\langle 6, 6, 6 \rangle$ and $\langle 3, 4, 6, 4 \rangle$). For small patches of these tilings, one can make a file of Logo commands by hand, especially with the clever use of an editing program. The main idea is to snake through the figure in a systematic way. For large amounts of the tiling, a program can be taught to follow this systematic plan and output the needed file of Logo commands.

3. Re-do the previous exercise, after deliberately introducing small errors in the data. (For example, change all 60-degree angles to 59.9 degrees.) See what happens.

4. Actually *any* sequence of commands alternating F 1.0 with either R 60 or L 60 will take a walk through the edges of the tiling $\langle 6, 6, 6 \rangle$. If the choice between R and L is made at random, we have an example of a *random walk*. Make some pictures of random walks of this type. (In C, random numbers can be obtained with **rand()** or with **random()**. To make distinct pictures, one should use **srand()** or **srandom()** to introduce different starting points for the random sequence.) Experiment also with giving L and R unequal probabilities (e.g., 0.6 and 0.4).

5. Use your Logo commands to make pictures of some of the other Archimedean tilings.

6. For some more challenging paths that can be traced out with Logo, see Chapter 17, entitled "Worm paths," in Martin Gardner's *Knotted Doughnuts* (W. H. Freeman and Co., New York, 1986).

2.5   Painting regions of the plane

Until now our device-independent language and its various extensions have been concerned with the outputting of line segments. Another useful task that a graphic device may be asked to perform is to paint a region of the plane with some color. (On a black-and-white device, the color will be some shade of gray.) Usually the desired region is the interior of a polygon, and (for a monochrome device) the color is specified as a number. We propose the following device-independent commands for painting the interiors of polygons in the plane:

G Extreme gray values. This command is followed by two numbers which in-dicate the extreme values of the gray scale in the display. The first number indicates a numerical value for pure black, and the second number indicates a numerical value for pure white. (Default values are 0 for black and 1 for white.)

g Gray level. This command is followed by a single number indicating the gray level to be used until further notice.

P Begin polygon. This command should be followed by three or more L com-mands and then a q or a Q.

L Vertex of the desired polygon. This command is followed by two coordinates.

Q Draw and paint a polygon according to the current gray level. The vertices of the (plane) polygon are the points given by all L commands since the most recent P command, taken in the order listed. The last vertex is joined to the first to make a closed polygon. The interior is colored according to the current gray level, and moreover the outline of the polygon is drawn as a series of line segments (with line width given by the most recent W command).

q Paint polygon. This command is the same as Q, except that the outline is not drawn.

For example, the file

```
w 0 0 8.5 10
G 0 10
%  ----a solid black rectangle--------------
g 0
P
L 7.250 6.000
L 7.250 4.000
L 1.250 4.000
L 1.250 6.000
q
%  ----a solid gray rectangle--------------
g 5
P
L 4.884 8.098
```

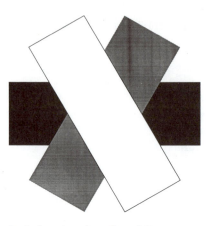

FIGURE 2.7   Three shaded rectangles; the white one was printed last

```
L 6.616 7.098
L 3.616 1.902
L 1.884 2.902
q
%  ---a white rectangle outlined in black---
g 10
P
L 1.884 7.098
L 3.616 8.098
L 6.616 2.902
L 4.884 1.902
Q
```

is expected to yield three rectangles like those shown in Figure 2.7. The main point to notice is that the last rectangle drawn, namely the white one, obliterates or covers all parts of the picture that were drawn before: in this case, parts of the gray and black rectangles. Likewise, the gray rectangle covers parts of the black one. It is as if the various polygons were cut out of opaque papers and then laid down on the page in the order listed or painted successively with opaque paint. In some of our work (§6.4.4 and §6.4.5) it is necessary to assume that the painting of polygons occurs in this opaque (or *later covers earlier*) manner; we refer to this condition as the *opaque painting condition* (OP). (The condition is satisfied for most devices.)

As usual, in order to go from device-independent code to the finished draw-ing, the user will need a program that interprets or translates device-independent code to an output device. It should not be too difficult to extend an existing interpreter by consulting the manual for the given device to see what is needed for the shading of polygons. An extension of the interpreter in §2.3.1 yielded the following PostScript code from the device-independent code just above. Printing this PostScript code yielded Figure 2.7.

```
%!
      %  ----a solid black rectangle--------------
0.000 setgray
newpath
522.0 547.2 moveto
522.0 424.8 lineto
90.0 424.8 lineto
90.0 547.2 lineto
closepath fill
      %  ----a solid gray rectangle--------------
0.500 setgray
newpath
351.6 675.6 moveto
476.4 614.4 lineto
260.4 296.4 lineto
135.6 357.6 lineto
closepath fill
      %  ---a white rectangle outlined in black---
1.000 setgray
newpath
135.6 614.4 moveto
260.4 675.6 lineto
476.4 357.6 lineto
351.6 296.4 lineto
closepath gsave fill grestore 0.00 setgray stroke
showpage
```

The reader should note that we have not specified exactly the semantics or intended meaning of Q and q. There is little or no ambiguity if all vertices are on the page and if they connect to form a *simple closed curve*, i.e., a curve that does not intersect itself. For curves that do cross themselves (such as the Lissajous figures of §3.1.4), the exact behavior may be device-dependent. (See e.g., page 71 of the PostScript Reference Manual[9] for two different shading schemes: the *even-odd rule* and the *non-zero winding number rule*.) We therefore advise the reader to proceed with a certain amount of caution when working with a new device. The most conservative approach is always to use polygons that are known to be simple closed curves. The algorithm described in §6.4.4 produces convex polygons except for a few cases that can be kept manageable. (See discussion of the algorithm in §6.4.4.)

[9]Copyright ©1985, Adobe Systems, Inc. Published by Addison-Wesley Publishing Company, Inc., Reading, MA.

Exercises

1. Extend a locally available interpreter of the device-independent language to an interpreter that will handle the new commands associated with the painting of polygonal regions. (Notice that this extension is qualitatively different from the extension that was requested for Logo in §2.4. That extension dealt with new commands, but not with new machine capabilities. This extension in fact deals with hitherto unmentioned capabilities. In principle, therefore, this exercise cannot be done without access to a manual for your device.)

2. Make drawings of some of the Archimedean tilings (§2.4) that have the tiles shaded to form an interesting pattern. For example, in coloring $\langle 3, 4, 6, 4 \rangle$, one might use one shade for the hexagons, a second shade for the squares, and a third for the triangles. $\langle 6, 6, 6 \rangle$ can be colored in three colors so that adjacent hexagons never have the same color. There are many interesting possibilities. (This exercise may be facilitated by making a single device-independent language that amalgamates the commands of Logo with the commands described here.)

3. Make an extension of the device-independent language that is appropriate for painting the interior of a region in color. One might for instance extend our device-independent language with a command C, which is used much like g, except that it is followed by three numbers that denote the intensities of red, green and blue light that must be mixed to form the desired color. Typically the intensities are to lie between 0 and 1. The corresponding command in PostScript is **setrgbcolor**. (Note that some devices restrict the number of colors[10] that can be present in any one picture.) Use this facility to make, e.g., some renditions of tilings in full color.

4. Prepare a file of device-independent commands for a flag or logo that has particular meaning for you.

5. Monochrome devices sometimes have the capability of painting polygonal regions with textures or patterns other than mere grays. You might inquire locally whether something like that is available to you. If so, you might want to make some pictures—say, of tilings—with some tiles that are filled with various patterns. The way of specifying a pattern is highly device dependent, and so one will have to enquire locally as to the correct method. (The relevant command in PostScript is **setscreen**; see pp. 190–195 of the *PostScript Tutorial and Cookbook* for a worked-out example. The reader is warned that dealing with **setscreen** is initially a little complicated.)

---

[10] If this number of colors is say 256, and a device-independent file calls for 257 or more colors, then obviously some coalescing of colors will have to take place upon implementation. Strategies have been developed to perform this coalescing while maintaining an effective picture. See e.g., pp. 287–293 of *Graphics Gems* [*op. cit.*] (article by Michael Gervautz and Werner Purgathofer) or §13.4 of Foley, van Dam, Feiner and Hughes [*op. cit.*].

6. In some applications, especially those of §6.4.5, we know that the shade is varying continuously, but we are forced to print each polygon P with a fixed shade. Some devices have a capability, called *intensity interpolation shading* or *Gouraud shading*, that can partly alleviate this problem. Let us suppose that we can independently calculate an intensity I_V for each vertex V of P. There are many ways that an intensity function $f(x, y)$ can be extended to the interior of P from the known values I_V. One simple method, the method usually associated to the name of Gouraud, defines $f(x, y)$ to be the unique function that is linear along each edge of the polygon and is linear along each horzontal line that intersects P. The first clause means that if

$$Q = \lambda V + (1 - \lambda)W$$

for vertices V and W and for some positive λ, then

$$f(Q) = \lambda f(V) + (1 - \lambda)f(W)$$

The second clause means that if

$$S = \lambda Q + (1 - \lambda)R$$

for edge points Q and R that have the same y-coordinate, and for some positive λ, then

$$f(S) = \lambda f(Q) + (1 - \lambda)f(R)$$

The exercise here is to prove that there is a unique $f(x, y)$ with these two properties, and that this unique $f(x, y)$ is continuous. Is $f(x, y)$ always a linear function of x and y? For example, what is $f(x, y)$ if P is the square with vertices $V_1 = \langle 0, 0 \rangle$, $V_2 = \langle 1, 0 \rangle$, $V_3 = \langle 1, 1 \rangle$ and $V_4 = \langle 0, 1 \rangle$, and $I_{V_1} = I_{V_2} = I_{V_4} = 0$, and $I_{V_3} = 1$?

7. If you have available a device that does Gouraud shading, make some drawings using this feature.

2.6 Recursion in geometry

Interesting effects can be achieved by making patterns repeat in a figure at differing scales. This is a large topic that occupies a good part of most books

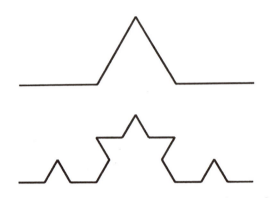

FIGURE 2.8   The basic replacement for making the Koch snowflake

on *fractals*.[11] Nevertheless, we include some simple examples in this chapter on languages for geometry, since the basic method is a form of recursion that is meaningful at several of the linguistic levels we have mentioned.

Our main example is a figure called the *snowflake*, which was invented by Helge von Koch in 1904. We begin with the arrangement K_1 of four segments that is shown at the left in Figure 2.8. All four segments have the same length, and all angles are multiples of 60 degrees. Now we introduce this same configuration at smaller scales by *regarding the configuration itself as a replacement for a segment*. That is, we now look at the basic configuration K_1 and see that each of its four segments can be replaced by a smaller version of K_1, thereby yielding the arrangement K_2 of sixteen segments that is shown at the right in Figure 2.8.

This replacement can be carried out over and over again. K_2 gives rise to K_3, which has 64 segments, and so on. It is almost intuitively clear that there is a limit curve K_∞, especially since the changes to go from K_i to K_{i+1} involve shifting some segments a distance no greater than $L/4^n$, where L is the length of the segment K_0. This idea can be made rigorous as follows. Let f_n map the unit interval $[0, 1]$ in a piecewise linear manner to K_n such that $f_n(i/4^n)$ is the ith vertex in K_n for $0 \le i \le 4^n$ (where the left-hand extremity of K_n is called its 0th vertex). One easily checks that $f_{n+m}(i/4^n) = f_n(i/4^n)$ for all $m \ge 0$. Thus a limit function f_∞ is defined for all rational numbers $i/4^n$, namely, $f_\infty(i/4^n) = f_n(i/4^n)$. It is not hard to see from the methods of advanced calculus that there is a unique continuous function $f_\infty(t)$ that has these values at $t = i/4^n$

---

[11] Fractals themselves are outside the scope of this book. See, for instance, Gerald A. Edgar, *Measure, Topology and Fractal Geometry*, Undergraduate Texts in Mathematics, Springer-Verlag, New York, 1990; B. Mandelbrot, *The Fractal Geometry of Nature*, W. H. Freeman and Company, New York, 1977, 1982, 1983; or Michael F. Barnsley, *Fractals Everywhere*, Academic Press, San Diego, 1988.

FIGURE 2.9   The snowflake of Koch

and that for each t the sequence $f_n(t)$ approaches f_∞. Now K_∞ can be defined as the range of the curve f_∞.

The *Koch snowflake* is an arrangement of three copies of K_∞ that correspond to three segments K_0 that are traversed clockwise around an equilateral triangle (see Figure 2.9). This curve has a number of properties interesting in analysis: It has no tangent vector anywhere, and it has infinite length but encloses a finite amount of area. It has *fractional dimension* equal to $\log 4/\log 3 = 1.2618\ldots$. (In other words, it is strictly speaking neither 1-dimensional nor 2-dimensional, but in between, in a sense that can be made precise. We give an informal argument for this value of the dimension at the end of this section.) These fascinating facts are a side issue for a book on pure geometry, and so the reader who wants to know more about them will have to look elsewhere (e. g., in the references of Footnote 11). Our main interest here will be in making a practical description of the Koch curve, and in understanding how it relates to the geometrical idea of similarity.

There is an *alternate definition* for K_n. It is the curve you get by starting with K_1 and replacing each of its four segments by one copy of K_{n-1} (reduced in size to fit where the segment fit before). We will ask the reader to prove this in Exercise 1 at the end of §2.6.

Our definition of K_n is somewhat akin to the often-heard definition of the *factorial*, $n!$ via

$$0! \;=\; 1$$
$$n! \;=\; n(n-1)!$$

We define $0!$ outright and then make the definition of $n!$ depend upon the value of $(n-1)!$; similarly we defined K_0 outright and made the definition of K_n depend on having a construction available for K_{n-1}. This nested form of definition is called *recursion*. It has a lot in common with (mathematical) *induction*, where a proof, rather than a mathematical object, is created in this nested way.

A literal understanding of recursion is that, for example, in order to calculate $3!$, we must set this problem aside until we know $2!$. We might for instance make ourselves a note saying, "When we know $2!$, multiply it by 3 to obtain $3!$." Then the calculation of $2!$ leads us to write another note (to ourselves), and we gradually build up a stack of notes. Finally we face the job of calculating $0!$, and this we can do immediately. This allows us to proceed to the calculation of $1!$, and so on. Finally we get back to the first calculation of $3!$ and the job is complete. (Note also the recursive treatment of the determinant that we described in §1.3.4.)

Geometric recursion is usually a little more complex than the simple recursion for $n!$, as is illustrated by the construction of the curve K_n. If, for instance, we want to calculate K_4, stretching between points P_0 and P_4 in the plane, we first have to determine the three intermediate points P_1, P_2 and P_3 required by the basic subdivision. The only thing we know is that (by the alternate definition given above) K_4 consists of four K_3 curves, one stretching from P_i to P_{i+1} for $i = 0, 1, 2, 3$. Since it may take us a little time to draw each of these, we write ourselves *four* notes. The first says to draw a K_3 from P_0 to P_1; the second says to draw one from P_1 to P_2; and so on. We put these notes on our stack. We continue by taking notes off the stack [12] and acting upon them. Usually one job, such as that of drawing a K_3 between a certain two points leads to four more jobs being put on the stack (e.g., four curves K_2). In this way the size of the stack grows and grows, until we finally reach some requests to draw K_0. This we can do immediately, since K_0 is a segment and we know how to draw segments. (In our scheme, this involves a `printf` statement commanding the computer to output an m or an l statement, etc.) Now the fourfold proliferation of tasks that we have described will ultimately lead to 4^n requests for segments K_0 (as we expected, since we know that K_n has 4^n segments).

This recursion scheme for K_n sounds a little complicated, but luckily many computing languages allow one to request a recursive calculation without any real

---

[12] All this discussion really ensures is that a correct picture will be made in the end. If one wants all elements of the curve to be drawn in some natural sequence, then one will have to make sure that jobs come off the stack in the right order. We leave it to the reader to investigate this for his local system.

concern for the details of how it is to be carried out. (In other words, the writer of the program need not be concerned with the stack.) This is accomplished by having one subroutine that calls itself one or more times (four times, in the example of the snowflake). In order for the program to terminate, that subroutine must contain some parameter that eventually causes the subroutine to terminate. This procedure is best illustrated in the following C code for K_n, which recapitulates the recursion described above. (Here p0, p1, etc., are *points*; that is, they are of a data type that has both an x-coordinate and a y-coordinate.)

```
KOCH(n,p0,p4)
{
if (n == 0)
{
   printf("m %f %f\n",p0.x_coord,p0.y_coord);
   printf("l %f %f\n",p4.x_coord,p4.y_coord);
}
else
{
   p1 = ... ;    p2 = ... ;    p3 = ... ;
   KOCH(n-1,p0,p1);    KOCH(n-1,p1,p2);
   KOCH(n-1,p2,p3);    KOCH(n-1,p3,p4);
}
}
```

The C compiler is capable of making sure that this code does all the tasks that we described. The termination of the algorithm (after doing the `printf` statements 4^n times) is fairly obvious from the fact that KOCH(n,...) calls KOCH(n-1,...) and that KOCH(0,...) makes no further calls to KOCH. In an exercise below we will ask the reader to supply the correct formulas for p1, p2 and p3 and then to carry out the program. Since the management of the stack is pretty complicated, we recommend against trying to extend our device-independent language to accommodate recursion. However, some devices are capable of carrying out recursion directly; in Exercise 21 we will give a reference to PostScript's capabilities along these lines.

We remark that if one works in the Logo-like language of §2.4, then almost no calculations are necessary. It is almost obvious that the following program correctly describes K_n.

```
koch(n,length)
{
if (n == 0)  printf("F %f\n",length);
else
{
   koch(n-1,length/3); printf("L  60\n");
```

```
        koch(n-1,length/3); printf("R 120\n");
        koch(n-1,length/3); printf("L  60\n");
        koch(n-1,length/3);
    }
}
```

In fact it may reasonably be argued that this small recursive program is the most succinct and elegant of the available definitions for K_n. All sorts of fractal curves can be drawn by changing the various parameters appearing in our Logo code for the snowflake. (See the books by Mandelbrot [*op. cit.*, especially pp. 42–73] and Edgar [*op. cit.*, especially pp. 19–36] for specific ideas.) Here we present only one more example.

In 1890, Giuseppe Peano—who is also known for his axiomatization of the natural number system—startled the mathematical world by defining a function that maps the unit interval $[0, 1]$ *continuously onto* the square $[0, 1] \times [0, 1]$. Thus we have the counterintuitive fact of a curve whose image is two-dimensional. In keeping with our remarks just above, we choose to define the nth Peano curve P_n by the following Logo-generating code:

```
peano(n,length)
{
if (n == 0)  printf("F %f\n",length);
else
{
    peano(n-1,length/3); printf("L  90\n");
    peano(n-1,length/3); printf("R  90\n");
    peano(n-1,length/3); printf("R  90\n");
    peano(n-1,length/3); printf("R  90\n");
    peano(n-1,length/3); printf("L  90\n");
    peano(n-1,length/3); printf("L  90\n");
    peano(n-1,length/3); printf("L  90\n");
    peano(n-1,length/3); printf("R  90\n");
    peano(n-1,length/3);
}
}
```

The resulting curves are depicted in Figures 2.10 and 2.11. In these figures we have modified the curves slightly so that the natural corners are avoided; in this way the eye can better trace out the path of P_n. Just as there were for K_n, there are piecewise linear functions $g_n : [0, 1] \longrightarrow P_n$ such that $g_n(i/9^n)$ is the ith vertex in P_n for $0 \leq i \leq 9^n$. Likewise a limit function $g_\infty(t)$ is defined for all $t \in [0, 1]$, and in fact $g_\infty(i/9^n) = g_n(i/9^n)$. This g_∞ is Peano's function mapping $[0, 1]$ continuously onto a square.

We began this section with the comment that geometric recursion can cause patterns to repeat at different scales. This repetition of patterns, sometimes

FIGURE 2.10   The basic replacement for making the Peano curve

FIGURE 2.11   The curve P_n of Peano for $n = 3$

called *self-similarity*, will be taken up again at the end of §3.3.5. Here it can be seen by direct visual observation of pictures of Koch curves K_n. To quantify this visual observation, we can proceed mathematically as follows. To simplify things, take a coordinate system with $f_n(0) = \langle 0, 0 \rangle$ for all n. Then it follows from the recursive definition of f_{n+1} that

$$f_{n+1}(t/4) \;=\; \frac{1}{3} f_n(t)$$

for $0 \le t \le 1$. From this it readily follows that

$$f_\infty(t/4) \;=\; \frac{1}{3} f_\infty(t)$$

for $0 \le t \le 1$. From this we see that *the first quarter of the Koch curve K_∞ looks exactly like the whole of K_∞, only with its size reduced by a factor of 3.*

We can use this last fact to give an informal argument that the dimension d of K_∞ has to be $\log 4 / \log 3$, as we mentioned above. Notice that if X is a 1-dimensional object, such as a segment, then magnifying X by a factor of 3 results in a segment $3X$ that can be dissected into three segments congruent to X. If X has dimension 2 (e.g., a square), then $3X$ can be dissected into $9 = 3^2$ squares congruent to X. For a cube, the number of pieces is $27 = 3^3$; and we may say in general that for a d-dimensional object X, if $3X$ can be dissected into M objects congruent to X, then $M = 3^d$. For $X = K_\infty$, we just saw that $3X$ can be dissected into four pieces congruent to X. Therefore the dimension (more properly, the *similarity dimension*) d of K_∞ satisfies

$$3^d \;=\; 4$$

From this one easily computes the required value of d.

Exercises

1. We gave two different recursive definitions of K_n. One involved the replacement of each segment of K_{n-1} by a smaller copy of K_1. The other involved the replacement of each segment of K_1 by a smaller copy of K_{n-1}. Prove that the two definitions yield the same set K_n. (The first definition is more useful for seeing that the limit curve K_∞ exists; the second definition is more useful for writing a simple recursive scheme to draw K_n.)

2. Prove that for every positive real L, there exists n such that the length of K_n is greater than L.

3. Prove that the area inside the Koch snowflake is $13/9$ the area of the original equilateral triangle.

4. Prove that the Koch snowflake can be decomposed in two different ways as a union of three curves K_∞. (Therefore the joints blend in and look like

naturally occurring parts of K_∞; thus the snowflake naturally has a seamless appearance.)

5. Prove that if $0 \le t_0 < t_3 \le 1$, then there exist t_1, t_2 with $t_0 \le t_1 < t_2 \le t_3$, such that the line L_{12} joining $f_\infty(t_1)$ and $f_\infty(t_2)$ is parallel to the original K_0. In the same way we can have L_{12} tilted at 60 degrees or 120 degrees to K_0. Thus conclude that K_∞ has no tangent lines.

6. Write a complete and correct version of the algorithm for KOCH. Execute it to make pictures of K_n for various values of n. Extend it so as to make also a picture of the snowflake. (If you have implemented the shading routines of §2.5, then you could shade the interior of the snowflake.)

7. Verify that our algorithm for koch is correct. If you have worked out an interpretation of the Logo commands (§2.4), execute the algorithm, thereby obtaining another way to draw the snowflake.

8. Let L denote the line that contains the original interval K_0 of the Koch curve. Describe the set $L \cap K_\infty$.

9. Investigate the set that is drawn by the following recursive Logo code. The limiting set here is what is usually called the *Cantor set*.

```
cantor(N,length)
{
if (N == 0)  printf("D\nF %f\nU\n",length);
else
{
    cantor(N-1,     length/3);
    printf("F %f\n",length/3);
    cantor(N-1,     length/3);
}
}
```

10. It is stated without proof in the text that the image of the continuous curve g_∞ is a square. To prove this you could show that there is a square S with the following two properties: (a) each P_n lies in S; (b) for each point P of S, and for arbitrary $\varepsilon > 0$, there exists an integer n and a point $Q = g_n(i/9^n) \in P_n$ such that $d(P, Q) < \varepsilon$. (Advanced calculus would give one an overview of what is going on in this exercise and the next, although the questions themselves have straightforward solutions that require only coordinate geometry and some appreciation of decimal expansions in base 9.)

11. (Notation continued from previous exercise.) Show that $g_\infty(13/36) = g_\infty(1)$. (This common value is one of the corners of the square S.) Let T be one of the corners of S besides the two corners $g_\infty(0)$ and $g_\infty(1)$. Find two different values of t so that, for each of them, $g_\infty(t) = T$. Find two values of t so that, for each of them, $g_\infty(t)$ is the center of the square S.

12. Implement an algorithm to draw P_n. (It is particularly nice to use a screen or other live output device, so that one can watch the curve slowly filling out a

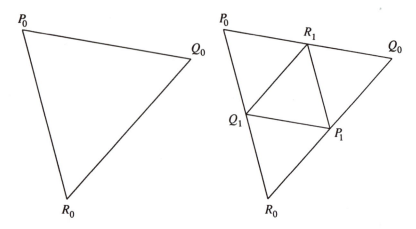

FIGURE 2.12   The subdivision of a triangle

square. For printing hard copy it is probably best to add some form of corner avoidance (as we did in Figure 2.11) so that one can see how intricately the curve is traced out. We trust that this can be left to the reader.)

13. Without making a drawing, estimate the largest value of n for which it makes sense to draw K_n or P_n on your output device. (The easiest analysis of this question comes from our routines for **koch** and **peano**.) Make some experiments to check your answer.

14. Verify our claim above that $f_{n+1}(t/4) = f_n(t)/3$.

15. Complete the calculation of the dimension d of K_∞, at the end of the section, as the ratio of two logarithms. Why do we not need to mention the base of the logarithms?

16. Make a calculation for P_∞ that is similar to our calculation of the similarity dimension K_∞. What value do you expect for d?

17. Suppose, for the sake of this exercise, that the languages available to you have no capability for recursion. (You of course can simulate this limitation by simply agreeing not to use the capability if you have it.) How then would you make a drawing of the snowflake (etc.)? (Hint. The first definition—with segments of K_{n-1} replaced by small replicas of K_1—is probably more relevant here than the alternate definition. One could use either absolute (m and l) commands or the relative (Logo) commands, but the Logo approach is probably more elegant, natural and succinct.)

18. Suppose that p0, q0, r0 denote three points in a plane. (In the program that follows, they will represent the data type **point**, i.e. storage for two real coordinates, as we have mentioned before.) Let us agree to let p1, q1, r1 denote, respectively, the midpoints of segments q0r0, r0p0, and p0q0 (see Figure 2.12). Describe the behavior of the following patch of code:

```
triangles(p0,q0,r0,n)
{
if (n==0)
{
        /* Draw the triangle: */
    printf("m %f %f\n",p0.x_coord,p0.y_coord);
    printf("l %f %f\n",q0.x_coord,q0.y_coord);
    printf("l %f %f\n",r0.x_coord,r0.y_coord);
    printf("l %f %f\n",p0.x_coord,p0.y_coord);
}
else
{
        /* Calculate  p1, q1, r1 as described above: */
                ...
        /* Make four triangles: */
    triangles(p0,q1,r1,n-1);
    triangles(p1,q0,r1,n-1);
    triangles(p1,q1,r0,n-1);
    triangles(p1,q1,r1,n-1);
}
}
```

You should be able to use this code for an alternate construction of one of the Archimedean tilings. Do at least two more of the Archimedean tilings in this recursive manner ($\langle 6, 6, 6 \rangle$ is a little tricky, but can be done in this way).

19. The tiling method in the preceding exercise is tantamount to the method that Grünbaum and Shephard (*op. cit.*, p. 534) call *inflation*: "...process of increasing the tiles by expansion, and then decomposing them into tiles of the original size." Study the method as described there, and use it to draw one of the Penrose tilings (described there). The relevant subdivision is given in Figure 10.3.14 on page 540. What is needed is a recursion relating eight kinds of figures: the L_A, S_A, L_B and S_B shown in that figure, and their mirror images. This project requires a precise understanding of that figure, but beyond that it is not terribly difficult.

20. If (full) Logo is your main language in working out the exercises of this book, then you can define the recursions necessary for snowflakes, Peano curves, etc., directly in Logo. (The necessary code differs only in minor details from the Logo-like code presented here. See, e.g., Chapter 1 of G. A. Edgar [*op. cit.*].)

21. The recursive description of a geometric figure can be expressed within the PostScript language. See pages 71–75 of the *PostScript Tutorial and Cookbook* (from Adobe Systems, Inc., published by Addison-Wesley, Reading, MA, 1985). If you have exclusive use of a PostScript device, you might make a com-

parative study to determine the relative advantages of lodging the recursion in the computing language and lodging the recursion in the device language. (Out of consideration for other users, we do not recommend sending untested PostScript code to the queue of a shared device.)

22. Even if you are planning to skip §3.4 (graphic topics in calculus), you can still use recursion to make a picture like that in Figure 3.62.

2.7 Pixeled images

We have discussed a number of ways that a graphics device can be commanded to display patterns of light and dark. These commands have all been based on our geometric conception of the plane displayed by the device, especially the geometric notions of *line segment*, *polygon* and *interior*. In other words, the commands organize the picture into recognizable geometric components. Moreover, this organization of pictorial data itself usually derives from a high-level conception of the picture that we are trying to draw, as we outlined in the diagram at the start of Chapter 2.

On the other hand, at a lower level, we can conceive of the output picture as an *intensity function* $f(x, y)$ defined over a region $A_1 \leq x \leq B_1$, $A_2 \leq y \leq B_2$. Here x and y are rectangular coordinates over the display, and $f(x, y)$ represents the shade (gray level) at point $\langle x, y \rangle$. For simplicity we will assume that the range of coordinates is $0 \leq x \leq 1$, $0 \leq y \leq 1$, and that $0 \leq f(x, y) \leq 1$, with 0 representing black and 1 representing white. In other words, $f(x, y)$ answers the question, "How dark is the picture at the point with coordinates x and y?" For most devices, answers to this question are essential: The machine needs to know whether to fire a pin that will print a dot, whether to shoot the laser, or how much voltage to apply to an electron gun. Thus the hardware (or its associated software) must effectively calculate $f(x, y)$, even if the calculation is inaccessible to the user. Here we explore ways that the mathematician or programmer could deal directly with the intensity function $f(x, y)$.

As the reader is aware, there is a natural one-to-one correspondence between subsets A of the unit square $[0, 1] \times [0, 1]$ and functions $f : [0, 1] \times [0, 1] \longrightarrow [0, 1]$, given by

$$f(x, y) = \begin{cases} 1 & \text{if } \langle x, y \rangle \in A \\ 0 & \text{otherwise} \end{cases}$$

This f is called the *characteristic function* of A. Thus the study of 0, 1-valued intensity functions is tantamount to the study of subsets of $[0, 1] \times [0, 1]$. (See the Exercises for various examples such as the interior of a circle and the notorious Mandelbrot set.) An intensity function that takes values other than 0 and 1 is not strictly speaking a characteristic function, nevertheless one sometimes thinks of $f(x, y)$ as defining a probabilistic or *fuzzy* set A (to use a term coined by L.

Zadeh). In other words, if $f(x,y) = 0.5$, then we think of $\langle x, y \rangle$ as halfway in A, and so on.

Many devices can accept an intensity function $f(x,y)$ directly from the user, and then produce a picture according to $f(x,y)$. In practice, this means that we have to tell the device the values of $f(x,y)$ for many closely spaced values of x and y. This way of delivering a picture involves handling data that is bulky and amorphous. Sometimes such data is forced upon one, for example, when dealing with photographs or video images. But what motivation would we have as mathematicians for favoring data of this type over the sort we mentioned above, namely data that is nicely organized by geometric concepts? The answer is that there are mathematical figures that defy any attempt at analysis into easily defined contours or shaded regions. Two topics in this book concern figures of this type, namely, elementary algebraic geometry (the study of loci of polynomial equations, §3.2.1), and ray tracing (§6.8). Nevertheless, those topics are not in the main stream of the book, and so this section could certainly be skipped on a first reading or until one decides to study §3.2.1 or §6.8.

Every real device ends up dealing *discretely* with intensity functions, and in almost all cases, as we said, an intensity function must be delivered discretely to the device.[13] This discreteness can cause a number of problems in the final image, especially if the data itself was gathered through the discrete sampling of some continuously varying quantity.[14] Here we merely issue the caution that things can go wrong, particularly if the image contains detail smaller than the distance between successive x and y values. With this warning, we will proceed to make pictures of this sort.

In order to make a discrete image of an intensity function $f(x,y)$, we divide the paper (or screen, etc.) into a rectangular array (sometimes called a *raster*) of small rectangles and obtain one value of $f(x,y)$ for each small rectangle. We then deliver to the output device the coordinates of the large rectangle, the number of smaller rectangles, and an orderly list of the various values of $f(x,y)$. We will refer to a file of data organized in this way as a *raster file*.

One problem is that a given device may not be able to display data as finely as we specify it. The paper or screen is divided into small (often rectangular) regions called *picture elements*, or *pixels* for short. Each pixel can be made darker or lighter according to the regulation of a voltage, the decision to fire a laser, or something similar. In some cases (such as the firing of a laser), an individual pixel may be able to register only two values: 0 (all black) and 1 (all

---

[13] An implementation of Mathematica can be programmed to accept a symbolic definition of an intensity function and then to display the corresponding picture. That however amounts to the bundling of various steps described in this section, including the ultimate delivery of discrete output to the screen or printer.

[14] For an analysis of these problems, see e.g., *Algorithms for graphics and image processing*, by Theodosios Pavlidis, Computer Science Press, Rockville, MD, 1982, or *The Mathematical Structure of Raster Graphics*, by Eugene L. Fiume, Academic Press, San Diego, 1989, or §14.10 of J. D. Foley, A. van Dam, S. K. Feiner and J. F. Hughes [*op. cit.*].

white). Generally speaking, we should try to respect these limitations and send the machine data that it can respect.[15] Thus, suppose for a moment that we are talking about a machine in which each pixel is either completely on or completely off (black or white). Then there is no point in commanding a very small rectangle (one or two pixels in each dimension) to take on an intermediate gray level. On the other hand, some machines have the capability of approximating a gray level on a somewhat larger rectangle by alternating white and black pixels in an appropriate manner. In requesting (say) Postscript to color small rectangles with different gray levels, one should of course be aware of these limitations and be prepared to experiment a little to get the most satisfactory approximation on paper of the real gray level $f(x, y)$. (See §2.7.2 for some related ideas.)

Due to the bulkiness of the data involved, we are not proposing an extension of our small device-independent language to raster files. PostScript is available as a device-independent standard (see §2.7.1), although the reader may need to make raster files for devices that do not operate under PostScript. (There are many other formats for rastered images, such as GIF and TIFF.) In general, a program to output a raster file requires two things: a subroutine to calculate $f(x, y)$ when needed, and a double loop structure to loop (horizontally and vertically) through all the small rectangles and to output (or to take some other action based upon) their $f(x, y)$ values in the correct sequence (along with auxiliary data required by the device at hand). The general idea is best conveyed by example, and so in §2.7.1 we present a program that goes through the necessary loops, and outputs appropriate PostScript code.

The reader probably should look briefly at that program to have some understanding, especially of the double loop structure involved. We recommend that appropriate programs be made available locally. (Many such programs are available at no cost through various computer networks.) If this is done, then the reader (or student) can certainly make pixeled images without any particular concern for the detailed operation of the device; all that is needed is a subroutine to compute $f(x, y)$. (Such a routine occurs at the end of our sample program, but ordinarily it might be kept in a separate file.)

Exercises

1. Draw the intensity function

$$f(x, y) = \begin{cases} 1 & \text{if } x^2 + y^2 \leq 1 \\ 0 & \text{otherwise} \end{cases}$$

---

[15] If a printer, for example, is running under the device-independent language PostScript, then you can tell it to print more finely than its pixel resolution. There is, however, no guarantee of what picture will be produced.

FIGURE 2.13   The conformal mapping $z \mapsto z^2$

The contour is a circle; we will have much simpler ways of drawing circles in Chapter 3.

2. Draw the intensity function

$$f(x,y) \;=\; \begin{cases} 1 & \text{if } 4x^2(1-x^2) \geq y^2 \\ 0 & \text{otherwise} \end{cases}$$

(The resulting contour is a Lissajous figure; see Exercise 4 at the end of §3.1.4.)

3. Using the polynomials $T_n(x)$ and $S_n(x,y)$ of §3.1.4, the algebraic method described there, and the general method of the previous exercise, plot some $0,1$-valued intensity functions whose contours are some more complex Lissajous figures.

4. Let z denote a complex number, $z = x+iy$. Suppose $x = m+r$ and $y = n+s$, where m and n are integers, and $0 \leq r, s < 1$. Define

$$g(z) \;=\; \begin{cases} 1 & \text{if } m+n \text{ is odd} \\ 0 & \text{otherwise} \end{cases}$$

Make drawings of the intensity functions $f(x,y) = g(z)$ and $f'(x,y) = g(z^2)$, where z^2 means the product zz of complex numbers. (Make a linear change of variable, if necessary, to allow x and y to range over a large interval, say $-5 \leq x, y \leq 5$.) The author's drawings are presented in Figure 2.13. Studying this pair of drawings can help increase one's understanding of the conformal mapping $f(z) = z^2$: it takes the distorted squares in the left-hand picture to the squares in the right-hand picture. (Notice that this correspondence is two-to-one: each square in the right-hand picture corresponds to two distorted squares on the left.) Such a pair of pictures can be made for any conformal mapping.

5. Define $g(x, y)$ to be the (characteristic function of) the well-known *Mandelbrot set*. It is well outside the scope of this book to discuss the Mandelbrot set[16] in detail; nevertheless we have all the tools at hand to make a drawing of it very easily. It is defined by considering iterations of the complex mapping $z \mapsto z^2 + c$ for complex z and c. Holding c fixed, we start with $z = 0$ and iterate this map many times (in principle, infinitely often). The Mandelbrot set is then defined to be the set of those complex c for which the iterated values of z remain bounded. The following patch of code yields an adequate approximation for the ideas of infinite iteration and remaining bounded. The range $0 \leq x, y \leq 1$ is not very appropriate for the Mandelbrot set; to view the whole set, use instead something like $-2 \leq x \leq 1$; $-1.5 \leq y \leq 1.5$. Then for a function $f(x, y)$ that is to be delivered to a program like the one in §2.7.1, we would introduce the appropriate linear change of variable. In other words, $f(x, y) = g(3x - 2, 3y - 1.5)$. The Mandelbrot set has notoriously fine detail, and one is encouraged to blow up the picture by working with different changes of variable that effectively give one smaller windows.[17]

```
g(x,y)   /* x  and  y  are the real and imaginary parts of  c* /
{
real = 0.0; imag = 0.0;   /* the real and imaginary parts of  z* /
for(k=0;k<100;k++)
{
    real0  =   real*real - imag*imag + x;
    imag0  =   2*real*imag + y;
    real   =   real0;
    imag   =   imag0;
    if (real*real + imag*imag > 2) return (0);
}
return (1);
}
```

6. It is an interesting exercise to try to express some or all of the Archimedean tilings (§2.4) as intensity functions on the plane. For example, a checkerboard can be drawn by the intensity function $f(x, y) = m + n \pmod 2$, where m and n are the integral parts of m and n, e.g. $x = m + r$, where m is an integer

---

[16]See for instance, B. Mandelbrot, *The Fractal Geometry of Nature*, W. H. Freeman and Company, New York, 1977, 1982, 1983, or H.-O. Peitgen and P. H. Richter, *The Beauty of Fractals*, Springer-Verlag, Berlin, 1986.

[17]The theory of the Mandelbrot set indicates that finer detail requires more iterations in the program (currently set to be 100). Moreover, we urge the reader to resist the temptation to linger over the mesmerizing effects of drawing the Mandelbrot set and to get on with the rest of the book.

and $0 \leq r < 1$. The tiling $\langle 6, 3, 6, 3 \rangle$ can be drawn with the intensity function $f(x, y) = m + n + r \pmod{2}$, where m, n and r are the integral parts of certain linear combinations of x and y. Can you do any others besides these?

2.7.1 A program to output a PostScript raster file

Here we display an illustrative program that calculates a PostScript description of the picture shown in Figure 3.20, namely, the locus of the cubic equation $x^3 - x = y^2$. More precisely, the intensity $f(x, y)$ is 0 (black) if the quantity $x^3 - x - y^2$ is positive, and 1 (white) if that quantity is negative. Thus the locus itself is the boundary between black and white.

The main command for PostScript raster output is `image`. For a full discussion of the `image` command we refer the reader to the Reference Manual for PostScript. In the sample program that follows, we will use a version of `image` that assigns 0 (black) or 1 (white) to each 4×4 array of pixels. As a slight complication to what we said previously, it turned out to be necessary to loop twice over the horizontal direction and twice over the vertical direction, for a total of four nested loops (over X, Y, m and k in the program that follows). All four of these variables are integers and essentially measure pixels.

There is no particular reason to color an array of 4×4 pixels all the same color, and a more useful version of the program allows one to choose the size of pixel array. (We have edited out this feature for printing here, since it is complicated for non-mathematical reasons.) A smaller pixel array, such as 2×2 or 1×1 yields a sharper picture, but at the cost of a larger data set (output of the program). (For 1×1, the output could be as much as sixteen times as big. Note that this can also imply a factor of sixteen for printing time, etc.) A useful middle path is to make coarse pictures for development work and then, when all the bugs are gone, to make a final copy at high resolution.

The program includes two other features for reducing output size: Certain long strings of PostScript are abbreviated (using the PostScript command `def`); and the program checks for larger regions that are all black or all white (see FF in the program).

This sample program assumes a device that accepts and displays an intensity function through the inputting of code (PostScript in this case); we therefore build an output file that is ready to send to the device. On the other hand, some devices require that certain machine-specific routines (say, to light up a specified pixel) be called within a program. In that sort of environment, one would use the appropriate routines in those places where we have things like `printf()` and `putchar()`. (A better solution would be to establish a raster file format; the master program would then just read such files and act on them.)

Since this is an advanced topic, we are presenting the program without too much explanation, either of the C code or of the meaning of the output. Nevertheless there are a few points in the program upon which we will comment; these are marked with double letters, AA, BB, etc.

```
#define MESH 300              /*  dots per inch; don't change  */
#define SIZE 6.4              /*  size of picture, in inches   */
#define DOTCOUNT (MESH*SIZE)  /*  size of picture, in dots     */
#define POINTS_PER_INCH 72

main()
{
char temp[300];
begin_picture();                                          /*AA*/
for (Y=0;Y < DOTCOUNT;Y+=32) for (X=0;X < DOTCOUNT;X+=32)  /*BB*/
{
   total=0;
   for (m=0;m <32;m+=4)                                   /*CC*/
   {
      CODE=0;
      for   (k=0;k<32;k+=4)                               /*CC*/
      {
         x  =  (X + k)/DOTCOUNT;
         y  =  (Y + m)/DOTCOUNT;
         ff =    f(x,y);  /* this must be  0  or  1 */
         CODE = (2*CODE) + ff;                            /*DD*/
         total += ff;
      }
      c = CODE/16;                                        /*EE*/
      if (c<10) temp[i]=c+'0'; else temp[i]=c-10+'A';
      c = CODE%16;
      if (c<10) temp[i]=c+'0'; else temp[i]=c-10+'A';
   }
   if (total==0)                                          /*FF*/
   {
      begin_small_bitmap(X,Y);
      printf("00");
      end_bitmap();
   }
   else if(total==64)
   {
      begin_small_bitmap(X,Y);
      printf("80");
      end_bitmap();
   }
   else
   {
      begin_bitmap(X,Y);                                  /*GG*/
      for (ii=0;ii<16;ii++) putchar(temp[ii]);
      end_bitmap();
   }
}
```

```
showpage();
}

begin_picture()
{
   double scaling_factor = (((double)POINTS_PER_INCH)/MESH);
   int size = 8;
   printf("%%!\n");
   printf("%3.2f %3.2f scale ",scaling_factor,scaling_factor);
   printf("%% This makes one unit = one pixel, at 300 DPI\n");
   printf("/x {image restore save} def\n");
   printf("/y {translate %d %d 1",size,size);
   printf(" [%4.5f 0 0 %4.5f 0 0]",(float)size/32,(float)size/32);
   printf("} def\n");
   printf("/z {translate 1 1 1 [0.03125 0 0");
   printf(" 0.03125 0 0]} def\n");
   printf("save\n");
}

begin_small_bitmap(X,Y)
{
   printf("%d %d ",X+200,Y+200);
   printf("z\n");
   printf("{<");
}

begin_bitmap(X,Y)
{
   printf("%d %d ",X+200,Y+200);
   printf("y\n");
   printf("{<");
}

end_bitmap()
{
   printf(">}\n");
   printf("x ");
}

showpage()
{
   printf("\nshowpage\n");
}

f(r,s)
{
z  =  g(r,s);
if  (z>0.0)  return (0);
```

```
return (1);
}

double g(x,y)                                                    /*HH*/
{
u  =  2*x - 1.0; v  =  2*y - 1.0;
return (u*u*u - u -v*v);
}
```

Comments on the program.

AA The subroutine `begin_picture()` lets PostScript know such things as the size of picture we want and the fact that we are going to deliver the intensity function as a single bit (0 or 1). It moreover tells PostScript to define x, y and z as new commands. The purpose here is to keep down the size of the file that is output by this program and given to PostScript.

BB This double loop involves increasing X and Y by 32; this amounts to a division of the picture into medium-sized blocks of 32×32 pixels.

CC The m and k loops keep us within one medium-sized block; each of these is divided into small (4×4) blocks. Thus m and k each take on eight values.

DD Here is where we actually call for an evaluation of the intensity function $f(x,y)$, which is defined at the end of the program. (The quantities x and y have been scaled to lie between 0 and 1.) The device of multiplying CODE by 2 and adding the binary digit `ff` has the effect of packing all the function values into a single integer CODE. From the size of the loop, we see that $0 \leq$ CODE < 256. At this point, we may simply think of CODE as containing eight bits that represent eight values of the intensity function. Meanwhile, we are keeping a running total (`total`) of all 64 function values in this medium-sized block.

EE Now PostScript will want the eight-bit integer CODE delivered in the form of two four-bit (hexadecimal) numbers. This is accomplished by the next four lines. The appearance of 10 relates only to the peculiarity of hexadecimal notation that the first ten digits are numerals, and the next six digits are letters. Notice that we don't release these digits right away, but rather hold them in the array `temp`.

FF Before releasing the array `temp`, we look at `total` to see if it is 0 or 64. These two extremes occur when this medium-sized block is all black or all white. In these cases it would be inefficient to output all of `temp`; instead we go to a subroutine that outputs information to tell postscript to make this medium block all black or all white.

GG Here we know that the medium-sized block is neither all black nor all white, and so we output the full list of 16 hexadecimal digits. Just before and after this task, we use the subroutines `begin_bitmap` and `end_bitmap` to output some PostScript code that is needed to let PostScript know where we are, and what we are doing. In particular, end_bitmap contains the string x, which was previously defined to be a string containing the basic command image.

HH Here is where we actually deal with the algebraic equation $x^3 - x = y^2$. We first change our variables (linearly) to u and v; this has an effect like a window command. We then calculate $g(u, v) = u^3 - u - v^2$. This value is ultimately passed to a subroutine—immediately above—that calculates $f(x, y)$. As promised, that subroutine yields either 0 (if $g(u, v) > 0$) or 1 (otherwise). To get a picture of a different algebraic locus, one would only need to use a different algebraic equation in this subroutine. In general to change to a different pattern of black and white (which might not be a locus at all) one would modify the definition of $f(x, y)$.

We will say just a few words about the PostScript output file. For a complete understanding, the reader will need to consult the Reference Manual for PostScript. The output is a file of 7,208 lines that looks like this, with the two occurrences of ... denoting omissions:

```
%!
0.24 0.24 scale % This makes one unit = one pixel, at 300 DPI
/x {image restore save} def
/y {translate 8 8 1 [0.25000 0 0 0.25000 0 0]} def
/z {translate 1 1 1 [0.03125 0 0 0.03125 0 0]} def
save
200 200 z
{<80>}
x 232 200 z
{<80>}
...
x 488 552 y
{<FFFFFFFFFFFFFFF8>}
x 520 552 y
{<FFFFFFFFFFFF00000>}
...
x 2088 2088 z
{<80>}
x
showpage
```

If we substituted for x, y and z, it would become

```
%!
0.24 0.24 scale % This makes one unit = one pixel, at 300 DPI
save
200 200 translate 1 1 1 [0.03125 0 0 0.03125 0 0]
```

```
{<80>}
image restore save 232 200 translate 1 1 1 [0.03125 0 0 0.03125 0 0]
{<80>}
image ...
   ...
image restore save 488 552 translate 8 8 1 [0.25000 0 0 0.25000 0 0]
{<FFFFFFFFFFFFFFF8>}
   ...
```

The pairs of numbers before `translate` indicate locations on the page; these regularly increase by 32 pixels, as expected. The material inside [...] is a PostScript matrix that is required with the `image` command. Each separate `image` command relates to what we previously called a medium-sized block (a 32×32 block of pixels). Note that `image` is postpositional, like all commands in PostScript; hence we describe an image completely before commanding it. The sequence 8 8 1 tells `image` that we are dividing that medium block into 8×8 smaller blocks, each of which will be given one bit of color (i.e., an intensity function of 0 or 1). The sequence 1 1 1 is analogous. The relevant data is enclosed in {< ... >}. The data takes two forms, according to the two ways of dividing the medium sized block. If it is divided 8×8, then there are sixteen hexadecimal digits, as we noted above. (The prevalence of F (four 1-bits) and 0 (four 0-bits) is easily explained by the fact that changes from black to white are very rare in this picture.) For the 1×1 division, we should see one bit (the whole medium block being black or white), but we actually see eight bits (as in 80). (PostScript simply throws away seven of them.) The `restore` and `save` commands allow us, among other things, to retain the scale that was established in the second line, to make all translations from the origin, and to save memory resources inside a PostScript device.

The program of this section contains no provision for rotation or other motion of the pixeled image; it is assumed here that, if necessary, such things will be done in the calculation of $f(x, y)$, the intensity function. To rotate or otherwise move discrete data, such as a pixeled image, is a little tricky, since a rotated pixel will not in general line up on top of one of the original pixels. Nevertheless there is a clever approximate solution to this problem, which we will describe in an exercise at the end of §3.3.6. Generally speaking, the manipulation of pixeled images as such belongs to the field of digital filtering and is beyond the scope of this book. For our purposes, it will be adequate to apply all desired manipulations to the intensity function $f(x, y)$, which is calculated *before* rasterization takes place.

Exercise

1. Design such a program in detail for a machine that is available to you. Make one program for gray scales as well as one for pure black and white. Ideally

such things as the number of pixels that are colored together will be kept as parameters so that the program may easily be revised.

2. If one is displaying an intensity function directly on a screen, one may wish to have the pixels light up in a scrambled order (i.e., here and there over the screen), rather than going systematically from top to bottom. Thus, one may be able to get a general impression of the picture long before the computation is complete. This is particularly useful for multiple revisions of a function F that takes a long time to compute. The following patch of code shows how this scrambling can be accomplished for a screen that is 200 pixels high and 320 pixels wide.

```
for (n=0; n<200; n+=1)
{
   for  (m=0; m<320; m+=1)
   {
      i  =  (13*m)%320;      j  =  (23*(m + n))%200;
      x  =  i/320;           y  =  j/200;
      ff  =   f(x,y);  /* this must be  0  or  1 */
      if (ff == 1)  pixel(i,j);
   }
}
```

(The operator %320 yields the remainder on division by 320, and so on. We assume the availability of a subroutine pixel() that turns on the designated pixel.)

The mathematical exercise here is to prove that this double loop cycles through all pixels exactly once. In other words, prove that the correspondence $\langle m, n \rangle \mapsto \langle i, j \rangle$ is one-one and onto. (Hint: $5 \cdot 320 - 123 \cdot 13 = 1$ and $87 \cdot 23 - 10 \cdot 200 = 1$.) The practical exercise is to incorporate code like this in a program for a device that is available to you.

2.7.2   A probabilistic filter

As we said, some devices can accept raster files that call for intensities strictly between 0 and 1, i.e., intermediate gray levels. This may be true even of machines whose individual pixels must be black or white; they achieve grays by the interspersal of black and white pixels. To achieve such grays, however, calls for grouping pixels (at least as many as the 4×4 of the last section), which contributes a certain coarseness to the picture.

Another approach can be used even for machines that have no gray-level facility, and it can be used to display an intensity function at the machine's highest level of resolution (i.e., with $f(x, y)$ computed separately for each pixel).

Of course we don't get something for nothing; in this probabilistic method,[18] our grays have a speckled or mottled appearance that is not as smooth as a large patch of smooth gray created by a good gray-level device.

The method is very simple. Suppose $g(x, y)$ is the true intensity function, with $0 \leq g(x, y) \leq 1$, and suppose that we need to use an intensity function $f(x, y)$ that only takes on the values 0 and 1. We ask for a random real number λ between 0 and 1, and then we define

$$f(x, y) = \begin{cases} 1 & \text{if } \lambda \leq g(x, y) \\ 0 & \text{otherwise} \end{cases}$$

One easily checks that—for fixed x, y and $g(x, y)$—the probability that $f(x, y) = 1$ is $g(x, y)$. Therefore $f(x, y)$ and $g(x, y)$ have the same expected values. In other words, over a small patch of the picture, the number of white pixels will be proportional to the gray level. For a drawing made this way, see Figure 6.51 in §6.8.

Here is a small patch of C code that accomplishes this purpose:

```
f(x,y)
{
y   =  rand()%1000;
w   =  y/1000;
if  (g(x,y) >= w) return (1);
return (0);
}
```

Here **rand()** yields a random integer in some (large but machine-dependent) range; the remainder operator % gives us a random integer in the range from 0 to 1000. Finally, dividing by 1000 gives a random number between 0 and 1.

---

[18]Probabilistic filtering is also known as *random dithering*. Other (non-random) methods of dithering are described in J. D. Foley, A. van Dam, S. K. Feiner and J. F. Hughes [*op. cit.*, §13.1], and in *Graphics Gems* [*op. cit.*, pp. 176–178] (article by Stephen Hawley).

3 Topics in plane analytic geometry

By the *plane* we may understand the 2-dimensional real vector space $\mathbb{R}^2$. Now a plane is usually thought of as having some additional structure, namely, the structure of distance and angles. The *distance* between $x = \langle x_1, x_2 \rangle$ and $y = \langle y_1, y_2 \rangle$ is

$$d(x, y) = \sqrt{(x_1 - y_1)^2 + (x_2 - y_2)^2}$$

as can be seen by applying the Theorem of Pythagoras to the diagram in Figure 3.1. For two non-zero vectors z and y, we define the *angle* $\angle x0z$ to be $\arctan(z) - \arctan(x)$. Then the angle $\angle xyz$ is defined in general to be $\angle(x - y)0(z - y)$.

The expression *plane analytic geometry* has come to mean the study of geometry (lines, distances, angles) through the algebraic representation $\mathbb{R}^2$ and the above interpretations of distance and angle. (A similar study of $\mathbb{R}^3$ is called the analytic geometry of space.)

The simplest object of study in plane analytic geometry is the *line*. It depends on one's point of view whether the equation of a line is something that can be proved or something that is taken as a definition. (One can introduce coordinates in an abstract plane and derive the equation from the axioms of geometry, or one can use linear equations to construct a *coordinate plane*. In the latter case, it is the axioms that have to be confirmed.) The derivations (involving similar triangles) are sufficiently familiar that we will omit them and simply state that in this book a line is a set of the form

$$\{x : \alpha_1 x_1 + \alpha_2 x_2 = \beta\}$$

for some $\alpha_1, \alpha_2, \beta \in \mathbb{R}$, with α_1, α_2 not both 0.

Thus in the terminology of §1.2.8, *a line is a coset of a 1-dimensional subspace of* $\mathbb{R}^2$. This statement of our interpretation of *line* has the conceptual advantage that it will work for any dimension: a line in $\mathbb{R}^n$ is a coset of a 1-dimensional subspace of $\mathbb{R}^n$.

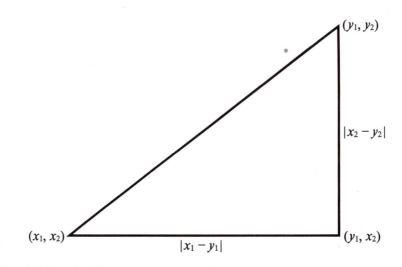
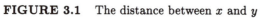

FIGURE 3.1   The distance between x and y

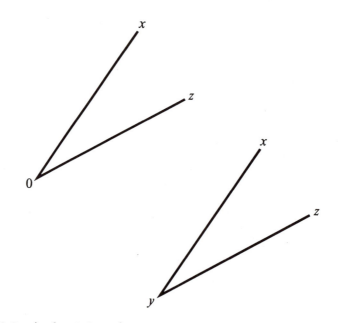

FIGURE 3.2   Angles $\angle x0z$ and $\angle xyz$

3.1 Conic sections

3.1.1 The circle

Let P be a point (i.e., vector), and let $R \in \mathbb{R}$ with $R > 0$. The *circle of radius R centered at P* is defined to be the set

$$\{x : d(x, P) = R\}$$

It is traditional in geometry to refer to sets defined in this way as *loci* (singular *locus*). This word has almost died out in view of the fact that the general set formation operation

$$\{x : \cdots \}$$

is now in widespread use in all branches of mathematics, but we will use it from time to time. By a *circle* we mean a circle of any radius centered at any point.

   The general problem for loci in analytic geometry is to take a geometric definition, like that of a circle, and then to find an equivalent, purely algebraic condition. In other words, we would like to be able to say that the circle of radius R centered at P is equal to

$$\{x : \phi(x_1, x_2)\}$$

where $\phi(x_1, x_2)$ is some algebraic condition on x_1 and x_2. Generally speaking, we do not repeatedly rewrite the set formation symbols $\{x : \cdots\}$, but write only the condition ϕ. For the circle, the problem is easily solved by going back to the definition of distance. The condition is easily seen to be

$$\sqrt{(x_1 - P_1)^2 + (x_2 - P_2)^2} = R$$

which is usually rewritten as

$$(x_1 - P_1)^2 + (x_2 - P_2)^2 = R^2$$

in order to avoid square roots. This last equation is called the *equation of the circle with radius R centered at P*. Things would be simpler if equations always stayed the way one wrote them, but they don't. For instance, the preceding equation can be expanded by the binomial theorem. Nevertheless the original form is easily recovered, as one may see by doing the next exercise.

Exercises

1. Find the center and radius of

$$x_1^2 + x_2^2 + x_1 = 0$$

2. What set is described by the equation

$$x_1^2 + x_2^2 - 2x_1 + 1 = 0?$$

3. Show that any equation of the form

$$x_1^2 + x_2^2 + Ax_1 + Bx_2 + C = 0$$

is the equation either of a circle or of a point or of the empty set. Find algebraic conditions on A, B and C that distinguish the three cases. In the case of a circle, give formulas in A, B and C for the radius and for the coordinates of the center.

From the point view of of *drawing* a circle, our work is not over. We could of course make a drawing by going over a drawing device (screen or paper) pixel by pixel and examining the equation with x_1 and x_2 taken to be coordinates of that pixel, and coloring the pixel black or white according to whether the equation comes out true for these values of x_1 and x_2. (See the first exercise of §2.7.) In complicated and unfamiliar cases this may be our only recourse (as in Figure 3.20 in §3.2.1), but when possible we like to be able to *parametrize* our curve so as to draw it quickly by using the segment drawing capabilities of our output devices.

By a *parametric plane curve* we mean a continuous function

$$\gamma : I \longrightarrow \mathbb{R}^2$$

where I is an interval of $\mathbb{R}$ (with the possibility of $I = \mathbb{R}$). Our convention is that we may express a parametrization by formulas for $\gamma(s)$ or $\gamma(t)$ or $\gamma(u)$; we do not always want to use the same letter for the parameter, since it is often of interest to compare two different parametrizations of the same curve.

A *parametric representation* of a locus L in the plane is a finite family $\{\gamma_i : 1 \leq i \leq M\}$ of parametric plane curves such that L is the union of the images of the γ_i. Most frequently we have $M = 1$; in other words we have a single curve γ such that L is the range of γ. We also say that L *is parametrized by* the curve γ, or by the curves γ_i. Our first parametrization follows immediately from the well-known fact that $\sin^2 t + \cos^2 t = 1$.

LEMMA 1   The circle of radius R centered at P is parametrized by the curve

$$\gamma(t) = P + R \cdot \langle \cos t, \sin t \rangle.$$

In fact the circle is parametrized by this curve for $0 \leq t \leq 2\pi$.   □

The following parametrization may not be so well known.

LEMMA 2   The circle of radius R centered at P is parametrized by the curve

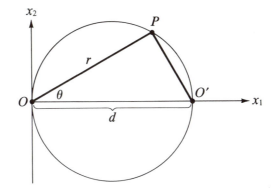

FIGURE 3.3   An eccentric equation for the circle

$$\gamma'(u) \;=\; P + R\cdot\langle\frac{1-u^2}{1+u^2}, \frac{2u}{1+u^2}\rangle$$

In fact the circle is parametrized by this curve for $u \in \mathbb{R}$. $\square$

(The lemma is proved by an easy calculation that we omit.) The reader may check that in fact the parameters u and t of these two parametrizations are related by the equation

$$u = \tan(t/2)$$

representing a change of variables that is familiar from calculus classes. Notice that it is slightly inaccurate to say that $\gamma'(u)$ parametrizes the circle, because the point $P + R\cdot\langle-1,0\rangle$ is not equal to $\gamma'(u)$ for any u. (It corresponds to $t = \pm\pi, \pm3\pi, \cdots$, in other words to $u = \tan(\pi/2)\cdots$.) Nevertheless, we admit this as a parametrization because this one point is the limit of other points that are given by the parametrization.

Before leaving circles, we mention one other form of equation for them. Let C be a circle of diameter d, situated to the right of the x_2-axis so that this axis is a tangent line to C at the origin O (see Figure 3.3). Taking P to be a general point on the circle C, we see that the triangle $\triangle OO'P$ has a right angle at P, since OO' is a diameter. Therefore, the length of the segment OP is $d\cos(\theta)$. Since (in this coordinate system) the length of OP is simply the polar coordinate r, we have the simple polar equation described in the next result.

LEMMA 3   The circle (as depicted in Figure 3.3) has the polar equation

$$r = \cos\theta$$

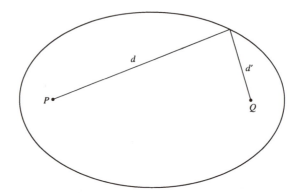

FIGURE 3.4   The ellipse: $d + d'$ is constant

The circle is thus parametrized by

$$\gamma''(\theta) = d \left\langle \cos^2 \theta, \sin \theta \cos \theta \right\rangle$$

for $0 \le \theta \le \pi$.

Proof   The polar equation is immediate from the previous discussion regarding the figure. The two coordinates of the parametric equation come from the known relation between rectangular and polar coordinates, namely $x_1 = r \cos \theta$ and $r_2 = r \sin \theta$. □

3.1.2   The ellipse

An *ellipse* is the locus E determined by two points P and Q, called the *foci* (singular *focus*) of E, with $d(P, Q) = 2c \ge 0$, and by a number $a > c$, as follows:

$$E = \{x : d(x, P) + d(x, Q) = 2a\}$$

(See Figure 3.4.) (Thus a circle is an ellipse with $P = Q$.) The following lemma may be proved by a long calculation; the secret is to keep moving a square root to stand alone on one side of the equation, so that squaring the sides of the equation will remove it.

LEMMA 4   If P and Q are points such that $P_2 = Q_2$, and $2a > d(P, Q) = 2c$, then the ellipse determined by P, Q and a has the equation

$$\frac{(x_1 - \frac{1}{2}(P_1 + Q_1))^2}{a^2} + \frac{(x_2 - P_2)^2}{b^2} = 1$$

where $b = \sqrt{a^2 - c^2}$. $\qquad\square$

The numbers a and b are called the *semi-major axis* and the *semi-minor axis* of the ellipse.

LEMMA 5 The ellipse with semi-major axis a and semi-minor axis b is parametrized by the curve

$$\gamma(t) = \langle \frac{1}{2}(P_1 + Q_1), P_2 \rangle + \langle a\cos t, b\sin t \rangle$$

In fact the ellipse is parametrized by this curve for $0 \le t \le 2\pi$. $\qquad\square$

LEMMA 6 The ellipse with semi-major axis a and semi-minor axis b is parametrized by the curve

$$\gamma'(u) = \langle \frac{1}{2}(P_1 + Q_1), P_2 \rangle + \langle a\frac{1 - u^2}{1 + u^2}, b\frac{2u}{1 + u^2} \rangle \qquad\square$$

Exercises

1. Prove the above three lemmas in detail.

2. Use the computer to prepare a picture illustrating the definition of *ellipse*. The picture could show a family of evenly spaced concentric circles centered at P and another family centered at Q. An appropriately drawn ellipse will pass exactly through intersection points of some circles from the two families.

3. What is the area of the ellipse with semi-axes a and b? (This exercise can be done now by any student with a year of calculus; it should be accessible to anyone after reading §3.3.5 and §3.3.6.)

4. What is the length of the ellipse with semi-axes a and b? It is in fact impossible to find an *elementary function* (i.e., a closed form expression) of a and b that expresses this length. The student could express it as an integral and verify informally that the usual (first and second year) techniques will not handle the problem. Those who have studied numerical analysis can try to approximate the length (make a table for various values of a and b). Others can try to find such a table in the mathematical literature. (Cf. also §3.4.9 and its footnote.)

3.1.3 The hyperbola

A *hyperbola* is the locus H determined by two points P and Q, called the *foci* of

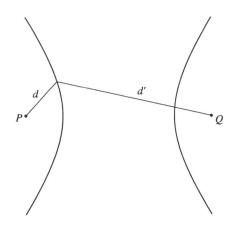

FIGURE 3.5   The hyperbola: $|d - d'|$ is constant

H, with $d(P, Q) = 2c$ and a number a with $0 < a < c$, as follows:

$$H = \{x : |d(x, P) - d(x, Q)| = 2a\}$$

(See Figure 3.5.) Notice that the hyperbola has two disconnected branches, one for which $d(x, P) - d(x, Q) = 2a$, and one for which $d(x, P) - d(x, Q) = -2a$.

LEMMA 7   If P and Q are points such that $P_2 = Q_2$, and $0 < 2a < d(P, Q) = 2c$, then the hyperbola determined by P, Q and a has the equation

$$\frac{(x_1 - \frac{1}{2}(P_1 + Q_1))^2}{a^2} - \frac{(x_2 - P_2)^2}{b^2} = 1$$

where $b = \sqrt{c^2 - a^2}$. □

The numbers a and b are called the *semi-major axis* and the *semi-minor axis* of the hyperbola.

Exercise

1. Prove the preceding lemma in detail. (In fact the calculation here is exactly like the calculation for an ellipse, except that minus signs are introduced here and there.)

   Before going on, the reader is asked to remember the *hyperbolic functions*

   $$\sinh x = \frac{e^x - e^{-x}}{2}$$

   $$\cosh x = \frac{e^x + e^{-x}}{2}$$

$$\tanh x \;=\; \frac{\sinh x}{\cosh x} \;=\; \frac{e^x - e^{-x}}{e^x + e^{-x}}$$

LEMMA 8   The right-hand branch of the hyperbola with semi-major axis a and semi-minor axis b is parametrized by the curve

$$\gamma(t) \;=\; \langle \tfrac{1}{2}(P_1 + Q_1), P_2 \rangle + \langle a \cosh t, b \sinh t \rangle$$

Its other branch is parametrized by

$$\gamma(t) \;=\; \langle \tfrac{1}{2}(P_1 + Q_1), P_2 \rangle + \langle a \cosh t, -b \sinh t \rangle \qquad\qquad \square$$

LEMMA 9   The right-hand branch of the hyperbola with semi-major axis a and semi-minor axis b is parametrized by the curve

$$\gamma'(u) \;=\; \langle \tfrac{1}{2}(P_1 + Q_1), P_2 \rangle + \langle a\frac{1 + u^2}{1 - u^2}, b\frac{2u}{1 - u^2} \rangle$$

Its other branch is parametrized by

$$\gamma'(u) \;=\; \langle \tfrac{1}{2}(P_1 + Q_1), P_2 \rangle + \langle a\frac{1 + u^2}{1 - u^2}, b\frac{-2u}{1 - u^2} \rangle \qquad\qquad \square$$

The reader may check that in fact the parameters u and t of our two parametrizations of the hyperbola are related by the equation

$$u = \tanh(t/2)$$

Exercises_____

1. Use the computer to prepare a picture illustrating the definition of *hyperbola*. The picture could show a family of evenly spaced concentric circles centered at P and another family centered at Q. An appropriately drawn hyperbola will pass exactly through intersection points of the two families. Warning: In the previous two lemmas and in the corresponding lemmas for ellipses, remember that b depends on a and that $2c = Q_1 - P_1$.

2. Use the computer to make a drawing that shows two points P and Q, several of the hyperbolas with foci P, Q, and several of the ellipses with foci P, Q. Observe that each ellipse meets each hyperbola at right angles, and then give an analytic proof of this fact. (Be careful; in order for right angles to look like right angles in the picture, the horizontal and vertical window coordinates must be chosen proportional to the horizontal and vertical dimensions of the actual device in use.)

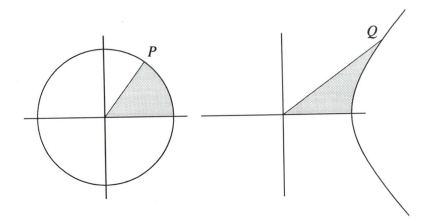

FIGURE 3.6   Geometric definitions of sin and sinh

The sine and cosine functions have an obviously geometric meaning, but at first glance the hyperbolic functions sinh and cosh do not. Exercise 1 provides a geometric meaning to sinh t and at the same time gives one more analogy between trigonometric and hyperbolic functions. (In fact, in view of the exercise, it seems reasonable to say *circular functions* instead of *trigonometric functions*.)

Exercises

1. Figure 3.6 has two drawings, one showing the unit circle defined by the equation $x^2 + y^2 = 1$, and the other showing one branch of what may be called the *unit hyperbola*, defined by the equation $x^2 - y^2 = 1$. In each drawing there is a shaded region, roughly triangular in shape, bounded by two segments and a connected piece of the curve (circle or hyperbola); the points P and Q are the upper right corners of these two regions. Prove that if $\frac{1}{2}t$ is the area of the left-hand region, then the vertical coordinate of P is $\sin t$, and analogously, if the area of the right-hand region is $\frac{1}{2}t$, then the vertical coordinate of Q is $\sinh t$. In other words, $\sin t$ can be defined as the vertical component of the point P, with P chosen to make the shaded area equal to $\frac{1}{2}t$, and $\sinh t$ has a completely analogous definition with P replaced by Q.

2. Using the definitions in the previous exercise, give elementary geometric proofs that $\sin t < t$ and $\sinh t > t$ for all $t > 0$.

3.1.4   The focus-directrix property; the parabola

Let C be any curve, D a line, and F a point. We say that C has the *focus-directrix property* with respect to F and D iff there exists a constant e such that

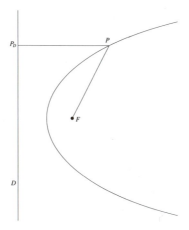

FIGURE 3.7   The definition of eccentricity; see Equation (3.1)

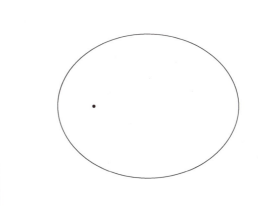

FIGURE 3.8   An ellipse with one possible focus and directrix

$$\frac{d(P,F)}{d(P,P_D)} = e \tag{3.1}$$

where P_D is the foot of the perpendicular from P to D, for all points P on C.
If Equation (3.1) holds for all points P on C, then e is called the *eccentricity* of
C (with respect to F and D).

THEOREM 3.1   Let E be the ellipse with foci P, Q, semi-major axis a and semi-
minor axis b. Then E has the focus-directrix property for eccentricity $e = c/a$,
with focus F taken as one focus, say Q of the ellipse E, and with directrix D
taken as the line perpendicular to $\overleftrightarrow{PQ}$ at X, where Q is between P and X, and
the distance from X to the center of the ellipse is a/e.   □

THEOREM 3.2   With F, D and e determined as in the previous theorem, the locus of all points satisfying Equation (3.1) is the ellipse E mentioned in that theorem.   □

Notice that the last two theorems are in a sense converse to each other. The first says that every point on the ellipse satisfies the focus-directrix property; the second says that every point satisfying the property lies on the ellipse. In other words, the focus-directrix property (with $0 < e < 1$) can be taken as an alternate definition of what we mean by an ellipse.

Proof of the two theorems   Let us assume as usual that the ellipse has semi-major axis a and semi-minor axis b and that $c^2 = a^2 - b^2$. We assume a coordinate system centered on the ellipse, so that the ellipse has equation $b^2x^2 + a^2y^2 = a^2b^2$. We take F to be the left-hand focus, which has coordinates $\langle -c, 0 \rangle$, and we take D to be the directrix at the left of the ellipse, i.e., the vertical line with equation $x = -a^2/c$. We let P denote an arbitrary point in the plane, and we give P the coordinates x and y. Thus P_D is the point with coordinates $\langle -a^2/c, y \rangle$. We now calculate

$$
\begin{aligned}
a^2\, d(P,F)^2 - c^2\, d(P,P_D)^2 &= a^2 \left((x+c)^2 + y^2 \right) - c^2 \left(x + \frac{a^2}{c} \right)^2 \\
&= a^2x^2 + 2a^2cx + a^2c^2 + a^2y^2 - c^2x^2 - 2a^2cx - a^4 \\
&= (a^2 - c^2)x^2 + a^2y^2 - a^2(a^2 - c^2) \\
&= b^2x^2 + a^2y^2 - a^2b^2
\end{aligned}
$$

Thus the coordinates of P satisfy the equation of the ellipse if and only if the quantity $a^2d(P,F)^2 - c^2d(P,P_D)^2$ is 0. But one easily checks that this last quantity is 0 if and only if Equation (3.1) holds for P. Thus every point on the ellipse satisfies the focus-directrix property, and conversely every point satisfying the property lies on the ellipse. In this way the two theorems are proved.   □

Theorems 3.3 and 3.4 have a proof that is so similar to the one we just did (with a few minus signs added) that we feel justified in omitting it.

THEOREM 3.3   Let H be the hyperbola with foci P, Q, semi-major axis a and semi-minor axis b. Then H has the focus-directrix property for eccentricity $e = c/a$, with focus F taken as one focus, say Q of the hyperbola H, and with directrix D taken as the line perpendicular to $\overleftrightarrow{PQ}$ at X, where X is between P and Q, and the distance from X to the center of the hyperbola is a/e.   □

THEOREM 3.4   With F, D and e determined as in the previous theorem, the locus of all points satisfying Equation (3.1) is the hyperbola H mentioned in that theorem.   □

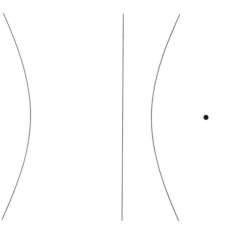

FIGURE 3.9   A hyperbola with one possible focus and directrix

From what has gone before, it can be easily seen that *every ellipse has eccentricity $e < 1$, and every hyperbola has eccentricity $e > 1$.* The remaining case of the focus-directrix property, therefore, is $e = 1$. The locus defined by Equation (3.1) with $e = 1$ is called a *parabola*. Its appearance is more or less as in Figure 3.7. In particular, there is no second focus. It is instructive to view the parabola as the limiting case of an ellipse with fixed focus F and directrix D, as $e \to 1$. The next theorem is very easy to prove.

THEOREM 3.5   Every parabola is defined by a quadratic equation. In particular, if the directrix is the horizontal line defined by $y = -d$ and the focus in $\langle 0, d \rangle$, then the parabola is the locus of the equation $y = x^2/4d$.   □

It is interesting to note that, like the ellipse and hyperbola, the parabola has a parametrization by trigonometric functions.

THEOREM 3.6   The parabola $y = x^2/4d$ is parametrized by

$$\langle x, y \rangle \;=\; \langle 2 \cos u, \frac{\cos 2u + 1}{2d} \rangle$$

and also by

$$\langle x, y \rangle \;=\; \langle \pm 2 \cosh t, \frac{\cosh 2t + 1}{2d} \rangle$$

(The trigonometric functions yield y-values between 0 and 2, and the hyperbolic functions yield y-values ≥ 2.)

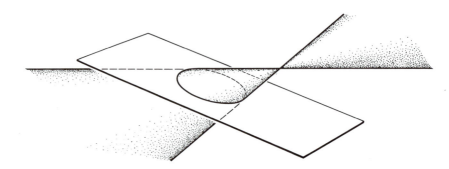

FIGURE 3.10   The intersection of a cone with a plane: elliptical cross section

Proof   In the trigonometric case, we compute that

$$4dy - x^2 \;=\; 2(\cos 2u + 1) - 4\cos^2 u$$
$$=\; 2(\cos 2u - (2\cos^2 u - 1))$$

and this last expression is zero by the laws of trigonometry. The hyperbolic case is handled by a similar calculation.   □

Exercise

1. Command the computer to make a picture showing several ellipses and several hyperbolas, all with the same focus and directrix, but, of course, with different eccentricities. In between these two families of curves, you could also show the parabola, with eccentricity 1. One striking feature of the picture is that one cannot identify the parabola by sight (if there are at least a dozen or so curves in the picture).

We close this section by pointing out that the family of all curves defined by the focus-directrix property is the same as the family of *conic sections*, that is to say the figures that result from intersecting a plane with a cone (see Figure 3.10 for one example). (The intersection can also be a point or an intersecting pair of lines—such figures are sometimes called degenerate conic sections.) The original beautiful geometric demonstration of this fact proceeds by defining the foci to be the points of contact of spheres that nestle inside the cone and meet the plane tangentially. We can however see it more directly—albeit more prosaically—by the algebraic methods of §3.1.7.

One reason that conic sections are important is that a circle anywhere in space will be seen as an ellipse when projected (unless, of course, it is seen edge-on, in which case it will project as a line segment).

LISSAJOUS FIGURES

According to the preceding trigonometric parametrization, the curve $\langle x, y \rangle = \langle \cos t, \cos 2t \rangle$ is a parabola. A modest generalization of these formulas yields a kind of curve that can be seen whenever there is harmonic motion with more than one natural frequency. The simplest case is perhaps that of an *oscilloscope*. This is a device for observing periodic fluctuations of voltages. An electron gun puts a bright dot on the screen; the deflection of the electron beam, and hence the position of the bright spot, are controlled by voltages, with separate voltages controlling the horizontal and vertical coordinates. Typically the voltages fluctuate rapidly, but periodically, so that the viewer perceives a fixed (or slowly evolving) pattern on the screen. The simplest periodic functions (both mathematically and electronically) are the trigonometric functions, and that is what we will consider.

Typically the x-coordinate is given a voltage fluctuation of some known standard frequency, while the vertical or z-coordinate is subjected to fluctuations of unknown frequency. (For reasons that will become apparent, it is useful to let z label the vertical coordinate.) A simple way to represent this situation mathematically is via the parametric equations

$$x = \cos(\beta t + \phi)$$
$$z = \cos(\alpha t + \psi)$$

With a suitable reparametrization we may assume that $\beta = 1$ and $\psi = 0$; hence a simpler version of the equations is

$$x = \cos(t + \phi)$$
$$z = \cos(\alpha t)$$

For general α, this curve is fairly wild, but for carefully chosen α has a very nice appearance. Suppose that α is a rational[1] number m/n, with m and n having no common divisor > 1. Reparametrizing the curve via $ns = t$, we have the equations

$$x = \cos(ns + \phi)$$
$$z = \cos(ms)$$

Now as s ranges from 0 to 2π, the x-coordinate will go through n periods (that is, it will go back and forth n times) and return to its original position. Likewise, the z-coordinate will go up and down m times and return to its original position. Thus the motion as a whole is periodic, and so we obtain a bounded closed plane

---

[1] Of course every number stored in a computer is rational, but the emphasis here is on $\alpha = m/n$ for small integers m and n.

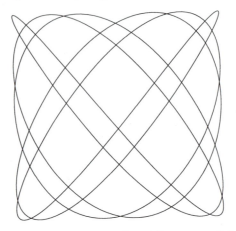

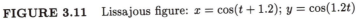

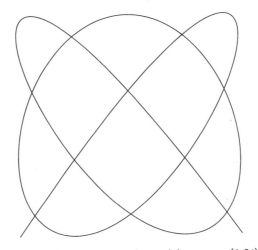

FIGURE 3.11   Lissajous figure: $x = \cos(t + 1.2)$; $y = \cos(1.2t)$

FIGURE 3.12   Lissajous figure: $x = \cos(t + \pi/2)$; $y = \cos(1.2t)$

curve. A typical example is shown in Figure 3.11. By appropriate change of the phase angle ϕ, the picture can be made more symmetric; see Figure 3.12.

Figures of this type are called *Lissajous figures.* There is a very simple way to visualize them, which has the advantage of accounting in a simple pictorial way for the changes that are seen as the phase angle ϕ is changed. Suppose we consider the space curve

$$
\begin{aligned}
x &= \cos(t + \phi) \\
y &= \sin(t + \phi) \\
z &= \cos(\alpha t)
\end{aligned}
$$

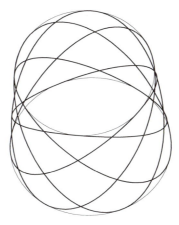

FIGURE 3.13   Cylindrical version of Lissajous figure

Clearly our (planar) Lissajous curve is the image of the space curve that one obtains by projecting to the x, z-plane, i.e., by discarding the y-coordinate. This motion in space is easy to describe, since the motion described by the x and y coordinates is simply motion around the circle $x^2 + y^2 = 1$, with $t + \phi$ representing the usual angular coordinate on this circle. Thus the x, y-motion has period 2π (under this parametrization). Meanwhile, motion in the z-coordinate is periodic with period $2\pi/\alpha$. If α is rational, then both periods have a common multiple, and so the full parametrization is itself periodic, and yields a curve that closes on itself to form a smooth closed curve Γ in space. This Γ lies in the cylindrical surface $x^2 + y^2 = 1$, and hence will be called a *cylindrical Lissajous figure* (see Figure 3.13). It should now be evident that changing the phase angle ϕ amounts merely to a rotation of the cylinder.

Interestingly, every Lissajous figure with rational α is like the parabola in being an algebraic curve, in the sense that it can be defined as the locus of roots of a polynomial equation in x and z. To see this, we first use the matrix equation

$$\begin{bmatrix} T_n(x) \\ S_n(x,y) \end{bmatrix} = \begin{bmatrix} 1 & 0 \\ 0 & y \end{bmatrix} \begin{bmatrix} x & x^2 - 1 \\ 1 & x \end{bmatrix}^{n-1} \begin{bmatrix} x \\ 1 \end{bmatrix}$$

to define polynomials[2] $T_n(x)$ and $S_n(x,y)$ for every $n \geq 1$. We then leave it to the reader to prove the following easy lemma by induction on n.

LEMMA   For any angle θ and any $n \geq 1$, $\cos n\theta = T_n(\cos \theta)$ and $\sin n\theta = S_n(\cos \theta, \sin \theta)$.   □

---

[2]T_n is called the nth Chebysheff polynomial, after P. L. Chebysheff (1821–1894). The polynomial S_n is included mostly for the purpose of facilitating the proof by induction.

We begin our algebraic analysis by considering the cylindrical Lissajous figure with $\alpha = m/n$, in the special case $\phi = 0$. In this case, by looking at the s-parametrization above, we have

$$\cos mns \;=\; T_m(\cos ns) \;=\; T_m(x)$$

and also

$$\cos mns \;=\; T_n(\cos ms) \;=\; T_n(z)$$

Thus we have two equations that are satisfied by points $\langle x, y, z \rangle$ lying on the cylindrical Lissajous figure:

$$x^2 + y^2 \;=\; 1 \tag{3.2}$$
$$T_m(x) \;=\; T_n(z) \tag{3.3}$$

In this special case (namely, the case of $\phi = 0$), Equation (3.3) does not contain y, and hence is already an equation for the planar Lissajous figure. The cylindrical Lissajous figure for arbitrary ϕ is obtained, as we said above, by rotating the cylindrical figure for $\phi = 0$ through an angle ϕ about the z-axis. Thus it is described by equations obtained by rotating Equations (3.2) and (3.3), as described in §3.1.6. (Actually, Equation (3.2) does not change under this rotation.) An equation for the corresponding planar Lissajous figure can then be obtained by eliminating y from these rotated equations. This can be accomplished by first replacing every occurrence of y by $\sqrt{1 - x^2}$ and then reorganizing the equation and squaring.

We illustrate this procedure in the simplest possible case, namely, $m = n = 1$. Since $T_1(x) = x$, Equations (3.2) and (3.3) become

$$x^2 + y^2 \;=\; 1$$

$$x \;=\; z$$

A rotation through angle ϕ yields the equations $x^2 + y^2 = 1$ and $x \cos \phi - y \sin \phi = z$. To eliminate y, we compute

$$(z - x \cos \phi)^2 \;=\; (y \sin \phi)^2 \;=\; (1 - x^2) \sin^2 \phi$$

which simplifies to

$$x^2 - 2xz \cos \phi + z^2 \;=\; \sin^2 \phi$$

which is the equation of an ellipse with semi-axes $\sqrt{1 + |\cos \phi|}$ and $\sqrt{1 - |\cos \phi|}$ that is tilted 45 degrees. In the special case of $\phi = \pi/2$, we have the circle $x^2 + z^2 = 1$.

Exercises 1–7 can be done by all students. The remaining exercises are for those students that want to enhance their understanding of algebraic curves (loci of polynomial equations).

Exercises

1. Make a number of computer pictures to illustrate the concepts of this section. Some of the pictures should have α a quotient of small integers. Some others should have α close to irrational, in the sense of not being m/n for small m and n. Experiment with changing the value of the phase angle ϕ.

2. A merry-go-round is operating at three revolutions per minute, and meanwhile its horses are going up and down five times per minute. A tiny light bulb on one horse's nose traces out a (space) curve that can be seen from across the park. What is this curve?

3. If $\alpha = m/n$, a fraction in lowest terms, then m and n cannot both be even. Thus three cases are possible: only m is odd, only n is odd, or both are odd. Determine how these three cases influence the general appearance of the picture, making computer pictures to justify your assertion. Also give a theoretical explanation.

4. An interesting thing happens when α is almost equal to a quotient m/n of small integers, i.e., $\alpha = m/n + \varepsilon$, with $n\varepsilon$ a small angle. We have

$$
\begin{aligned}
x(t + 2n\pi) &= \cos(t + 2n\pi + \phi) = x(t) \\
z(t + 2n\pi) &= \cos(\alpha t + 2m\pi + 2n\varepsilon) = \cos(\alpha t + 2n\varepsilon)
\end{aligned}
$$

Thus $\langle x(t + 2n\pi), z(t + 2n\pi) \rangle$ is almost like $\langle x(t), z(t) \rangle$, with a slight phase change after each period. (By the way, phase is relative; by a reparametrization a phase change in $x(t)$ is equivalent to a phase change in $z(t)$.) On an oscilloscope, one will perceive a gradual change of phase, which is to say one will actually perceive the cylinder as rotating. (One is helped by the fact that images on an oscilloscope decay, so that one is always looking at relatively recent images.) Make some computer pictures to illustrate this phenomenon. (For instance, try $\alpha = 1.202$.)

5. Make a picture of the figure with $\alpha = 2$ and $\phi = \pi/2$. Show that this figure is contained in the locus of the equation $4x^2(1 - x^2) = z^2$. Show that this locus contains no points outside the square $|x| \leq 1$, $|z| \leq 1$. (One can do this by rotating the equation $T_2(x) = T_1(z)$, as described above, or one can proceed directly.)

6. One can observe experimentally that near the origin the curves are nearly straight lines, all with the same slope (either positive or negative). Justify this observation theoretically, and determine what this common slope must be.

7. Write out the polynomial $T_5(x)$ in detail, and then show that $T_5(x) - 1$ has $4x^2 + 2x - 1$ as a factor. Use this knowledge to obtain simple expressions for the cosines of 72 degrees and 144 degrees (they are rational expressions in $\sqrt{5}$). (From our computer perspective, these expressions are not much use; after all, we routinely ask the computer to give us these—or any other—cosines as

real numbers. However, the student who has studied the idea of construction with ruler and compasses will recognize here a simple proof that the angle of 72 degrees, and hence the regular pentagon, are constructible in that ancient sense.)

8. Find the degree of the polynomial $T_n(x)$, and the degree of the (x part of) $S_n(x, y)$. We showed above that the Lissajous figure $\langle x, z \rangle = \langle \cos(m/n)t, \cos t \rangle$ satisfies the polynomial equation $T_m(x) = T_n(z)$. The exercise here is to show that these polynomials have the minimal possible degree in x and the minimal possible degree in z. (Hint: Count the number of times that a horizontal line meets the curve.)

9. Obtain the analogous result for Lissajous figures with non-trivial phase angle ϕ.

10. A Lissajous figure with irrational α cannot be described by any polynomial equation in x and z.

11. Prove the lemma about $\cos n\theta$ and $\sin n\theta$.

12. Find the correct polynomials to prove a version of the lemma with sin and cos replaced by sinh and cosh.

13. In the case of phase angle $\phi = 0$ and $\alpha = m/n$, the locus of $T_m(x) = T_n(z)$ contains points that are not parametrized by the Lissajous figure, in fact it contains points with $x > 1$ and $z > 1$. Show how to parametrize this part of the locus, and make a computer drawing that shows all parts. (Hint: Remember how we parametrized the parabola.)

3.1.5   A uniform parametrization of conic sections

Let us look again at Equation (3.1) that defines a conic section C in terms of a focus F, a directrix D, and an eccentricity e. Let r and θ denote coordinates from a polar coordinate system centered at F, with the coordinates positioned so that D is a vertical line at distance K to the left of F. Now, for a point P on C, let P_D be the foot of P on D, as in Equation (3.1) (see Figure 3.14). It is clear that the distance $d(F, P)$ is r, and the distance $d(P_D, P)$ is $K + r \cos \theta$. Therefore, Equation (3.1) yields

$$\frac{r}{K + r \cos \theta} = e$$

Simple algebra then leads to the *polar equation of the conic section C of eccentricity e*:

$$r = \frac{Ke}{1 - e \cos \theta} \tag{3.4}$$

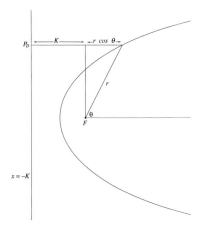

FIGURE 3.14   The polar equation of a conic

THEOREM 3.7   If C is a conic section of eccentricity e whose focus is at $\langle 0, 0 \rangle$, and whose directrix is a vertical line through $\langle -K, 0 \rangle$, then C is parametrized by the curve

$$\delta(s) \; = \; \frac{Ke}{1 - e \cos s} \langle \cos s, \sin s \rangle$$

Strictly speaking, if $e < 1$ then the ellipse C is parametrized by $\delta(s)$ for $0 \leq s \leq 2\pi$, if $e = 1$ then the parabola C is parametrized by $\delta(s)$ for $0 < s < 2\pi$, and if $e > 1$, then the hyperbola C is parametrized by two curves $\delta(s)$ (defined on intervals that are determined by the necessity of avoiding the zeros of the denominator $1 - e \cos(s)$).

Sketch of proof   Immediate from Equation (3.4) and the fact that $x_1 = r \cos \theta$ and $x_2 = r \sin \theta$. $\qquad\qquad\qquad\qquad\qquad\qquad\qquad\qquad\qquad\qquad\qquad\square$

Exercise_____

1. Repeat Exercise 1 of §3.1.4 (confocal conics). It will be much easier using this last theorem.

PLANETARY ORBITS

One of the great accomplishments of the seventeenth century was Isaac Newton's analysis of planetary motion.[3] Tycho Brahe, the court astronomer to Kaiser

_____

[3] Our historical source in discussing this topic was *An Introduction to the History of Mathematics*, Third Edition, by Howard Eves. Holt, Rinehart & Winston, 1969.

Rudolph II in Prague, died suddenly in 1601, leaving his successor, Johann Kepler, a mass of accurate observational data concerning the planets' apparent positions in the skies. By 1609, after eight years of intense analysis of this data, Kepler had formulated his first two laws, namely, that *each planet moves in an ellipse*[4] *with the sun at one focus,*[5] and that *the radius vector joining a planet to the sun sweeps out equal areas in equal intervals of time.*

In order to appreciate the magnitude of Kepler's accomplishment, one needs to appreciate that Brahe's observations did not really locate a planet in space. All they provided was right ascension and declination (see §6.2.1), relative to Earth, as functions of time. Distance from Earth was completely unknown. Kepler's accomplishment was therefore to make sense of this chaotic and incomplete data, in terms of beautiful and succinct laws. In other words, he presented laws that were beautiful both in their simplicity and in their unexpectedness and that had the power both to explain Brahe's observations and to allow further predictions[6] of planetary positions. Naturally enough, he made some contributions to the theory of conics; for example, he introduced the word *focus.* We could thus say that Kepler provided a remarkable hypothesis—the elliptical motion of planets— and proved that the available data fits this hypothesis very well. Nevertheless, at the time of Kepler's death in 1630, this hypothesis itself remained unexplained: why should planetary orbits be elliptical?

Newton's solution of this problem, some time before 1684, required advances both in mathematics and physics. The contributions to physics were the concept of gravitation attraction between heavenly bodies, a precise mathematical formula for this attraction, and his laws of motion, especially the third law, $F = ma$, *force = mass times acceleration.* The necessary mathematics was a great strengthening of the rudimentary calculus already known to Newton's predecessors. In the end, Newton showed that Kepler's laws follow[7] from universal gravitation and his laws of motion.

A modern derivation can be found in almost any book on mechanics. A number of steps are required to eliminate the time coordinate from the original equations based on Newton's laws. After time is eliminated, one obtains

---

[4]Each planet has its own eccentricity. For example the orbits of the first four planets (Mercury, Venus, Earth, and Mars) have eccentricities 0.206, 0.0068, 0.0167 and 0.0933, respectively. The Kepler-Newton theory says nothing about these values (which really arise as constants of integration in the theory that follows).

[5]The other focus is in outer space and has no special significance.

[6]One historian, William H. Donahue, has recently charged (in the *Journal of History of Astronomy*) that Kepler faked some data in working out a supposedly independent check of the theory for the planet Mars. Even if this charge withstands continued scrutiny, it goes more to the question of scientific methodology than to the question of mathematical brilliance.

[7]More properly, they follow for the case of a star with a single planet. In the case of a sun with more than one planet, the individual planets exert gravitational forces on one another, thereby causing deviations from the ideal of elliptical orbits. Luckily for Kepler, these effects are small in our solar system.

$$\frac{d^2}{d\theta^2}\left(\frac{1}{r}\right) + \frac{1}{r} = \frac{GMm^2}{p^2} \tag{3.5}$$

where M is the mass of the sun, m is the mass of the planet, p is the angular momentum of the planet, and G is a constant (equal to 6.67×10^{-8} in CGS units).

Exercises

1. From Equation (3.5), prove that every planetary orbit is a conic section with focus at the sun. In particular, note where the eccentricity enters your solution.

2. The solutions of the differential equation

$$\frac{d}{d\theta}\left(\frac{d^2}{d\theta^2}\left(\frac{1}{r}\right) + \frac{1}{r}\right) = 0$$

are the conics with focus at the origin.

3.1.6   Change of coordinates

Although we will go into this in more detail later in §3.3.2, we can state now that the linear map $f : \mathbb{R}^2 \longrightarrow \mathbb{R}^2$ given by the matrix

$$\begin{bmatrix} \cos\theta & -\sin\theta \\ \sin\theta & \cos\theta \end{bmatrix}$$

is a rotation of $\mathbb{R}^2$ through an angle θ. It is not hard to see that if Γ is the locus, say, of Equation (3.1) with eccentricity e, focus F and directrix D, then the f-image of Γ, which we will denote $f[\Gamma]$, is the locus of Equation (3.1) with eccentricity e, focus $f(F)$ and directrix $f[D]$. (This assertion is immediate from the fact that rotations preserve distances.)

Section 3.3 will be concerned with geometric descriptions of $f[\Gamma]$ for various sets Γ (including curves) and various linear transformations f. From the algebraic point of view, we might want to know the equation of $f[\Gamma]$—supposing that we already know in detail an equation for Γ.

THEOREM 3.8   An equation for $f[\Gamma]$ is found by taking an equation for Γ, replacing each occurrence of x_1 by $x_1\cos\theta + x_2\sin\theta$, and replacing each occurrence of x_2 by $-x_1\sin\theta + x_2\cos\theta$.

Proof   Clearly $x \in f[\Gamma]$ iff $f^{-1}(x) \in \Gamma$. Therefore to find out if x is in $f[\Gamma]$, we need to evaluate the function f^{-1} on $x = \langle x_1, x_2 \rangle$ and then test the equation on this $f(x)$. The result now follows from the fact that the matrix of f^{-1} is

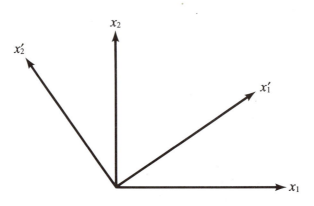

FIGURE 3.15   Rotated coordinates

$$\begin{bmatrix} \cos\theta & \sin\theta \\ -\sin\theta & \cos\theta \end{bmatrix}$$ □

Sometimes we follow a procedure a little more complicated than the one described in the statement of the theorem. We replace each occurrence of x_1 by $x_1' \cos\theta + x_2' \sin\theta$, and replacing each occurrence of x_2 by $-x_1' \sin\theta + x_2' \cos\theta$. Now of course, the equation of $f[\Gamma]$ has to be understood as relative to the new designation of the coordinates for a point. The reason it is sometimes done this way, is that we can think of the curve as not moving at all, only that the coordinate system has been moved, and in such a case, two coordinate systems can be placed in the same picture (see Figure 3.15).

COROLLARY 3.9   The equation of any conic section Γ in $\mathbb{R}^2$ has the form

$$Ax_1^2 + Bx_1x_2 + Cx_2^2 + Dx_1 + Ex_2 + F = 0 \tag{3.6}$$

If Γ is an ellipse, then the quantity

$$\Delta = B^2 - 4AC$$

is negative; if Γ is a hyperbola, then Δ is positive, and if Γ is a parabola, then Δ is zero.

Sketch of proof   We know that the standard equations described above have this form, and it is not hard to see from the theorem that the general form of equation is preserved by rotations. Now for the assertions about Δ, one needs to evaluate Δ for the standard equations of ellipse, hyperbola and parabola, and then to check that Δ is preserved by rotations (again using the theorem).   □

3.1.7   The general quadratic equation in two variables

Equation (3.6) is called the *general quadratic equation in two variables*, and the quantity $\Delta = B^2 - 4AC$ is called the *discriminant* of that equation. The converse to the last theorem is not completely true, since there exist quadratic equations that define curves other than conic sections. For instance, the equations

$$
\begin{aligned}
0 &= 0 \\
x_1^2 + 1 &= 0 \\
x_1^2 + x_2^2 &= 0 \\
(x_1 - x_2 - 3)^2 &= 0 \\
(x_1 - x_2 - 3)(x_1 - x_2 - 4) &= 0 \\
(x_1 - x_2 - 3)(x_1 + x_2 - 4) &= 0
\end{aligned}
$$

define, respectively, the whole plane, the empty set, a single point, a single line, a pair of parallel lines, and a pair of intersecting lines; but each of the equations is equivalent algebraically to a quadratic equation. If we agree to refer to these six geometric sets as *degenerate conics*, then we have the following result.

THEOREM 3.10   For any choice of the parameters $A, B, \cdots, F$, the set of solutions of Equation (3.6) is a (possibly degenerate) conic section.

Proof   Certainly the result holds if A, B and C are all 0, for then we have a linear equation. The case of $B = 0$, may be left to the reader. (It is like what follows, only simpler.) Therefore we will assume that $B \neq 0$.

We again consider the quantity $\Delta = B^2 - 4AC$, called the *discriminant* of Equation (3.6). We first consider the case when $\Delta = 0$. In this case, it is easily seen that $A \neq 0$ and that our equation reduces to

$$
A(x + \frac{B}{2A}y)^2 + \text{ linear terms } = 0
$$

From here it is not hard to see a rotation that will make this into a conic section in standard form. (It can be a parabola, the empty set, a single line or two parallel lines.)

Turning now to the case where $\Delta \neq 0$, we define

$$
\alpha = \frac{BE - 2CD}{\Delta}; \quad \beta = \frac{BD - 2AE}{\Delta}
$$

If we replace each occurrence of x_1 in Equation (3.6) by $x_1 - \alpha$, and each occurrence of x_2 by $x_2 - \beta$, and simplify, we obtain

$$
Ax_1^2 + Bx_1x_2 + Cx_2^2 + F' = 0 \tag{3.7}
$$

for some new scalar F'. (In other words, as the student may check by carrying out the calculation in detail, in this translated coordinate system the coefficients of x_1 and x_2 turn out to be zero.)

Now letting x denote the 2×1 matrix $\begin{bmatrix} x_1 \\ x_2 \end{bmatrix}$, we may rewrite Equation (3.7) in the notation of §1.5 as

$$x'Tx = -F' \tag{3.8}$$

where T is the symmetric matrix

$$\begin{bmatrix} A & \frac{B}{2} \\ \frac{B}{2} & C \end{bmatrix}$$

According to Corollary 1.63 of §1.5, there exists a 2×2 special orthogonal matrix O such that $T = ODO^{-1}$, where D is the diagonal matrix

$$\begin{bmatrix} A' & 0 \\ 0 & C' \end{bmatrix}$$

Thus Equation (3.8) translates into

$$x'ODO^{-1}x = -F'$$

From the orthogonality of O it follows readily that $x'O = (O^{-1}x)'$, and hence the equation of our conic reduces to

$$u'Du = -F'$$

where u is $O^{-1}x$. In two dimensions the change from x to $u = \begin{bmatrix} u_1 \\ u_2 \end{bmatrix}$ amounts merely to a rotation of the coordinate system. In this new coordinate system, the equation is simply

$$A'u_1^2 + C'u_2^2 + F' = 0 \tag{3.9}$$

where A' and C' are not both 0. Thus the curve is an ellipse, a hyperbola, the empty set, a point, a single line, a pair of intersecting lines or a pair of parallel lines.   □

There is an interesting point of comparison between the geometric material of this section and the diagonalization of matrices that we did in §1.5. There the orthonormal eigenvectors are uniquely determined (up to a multiple of ± 1) by the eigenvalues, unless the two eigenvalues are equal. In that case, the subspace consisting of eigenvectors has dimension 2, and any two eigenvectors can be chosen, so long as they form an orthonormal basis. Now at the end of the last

FIGURE 3.16 Hyperboloid of one sheet: $x_1^2 + x_2^2 - x_3^2 = 1$

proof, the eigenvalues are clearly A' and C' (i.e., the two diagonal entries of $O^{-1}TO$). If they are equal to each other, then Equation (3.9) defines a circle (or a degenerate conic). Clearly, by symmetry, the circle has the same equation no matter how we lay down a rectangular coordinate system at the origin. Thus the freedom in choice of eigenvectors corresponds to the symmetry of the circle.

One virtue of our abstract approach to the proof of Theorem 3.10 (i.e., our application of Corollary 1.63) is that the method extends immediately to three dimensions. We leave to the reader the job of examining the possible loci of quadratic equations in three variables. First one tries to remove the linear terms; if this is not possible, one has something analogous to a parabola (or a degenerate locus). If the linear terms can be removed, then we have a symmetric matrix that can be diagonalized. Non-degenerate loci of quadratic equations in three variables are sometimes called *quadric surfaces*. They are usually classified according to the signs of the real numbers that appear on the diagonal. For example, if three signs are positive, we have an *ellipsoid*, if two are positive and one negative, we have a *hyperboloid of one sheet*, if one is positive and two are negative, we have a *hyperboloid of two sheets*, and if 0 appears on the diagonal (i.e., if the determinant is 0), then we have a cylinder, a paraboloid, or any one of a number of degenerate loci, such as two parallel planes. It would seem that this topic is completely accessible at this point to the student who is interested and wishes to devote the necessary time to it. (The student should first have studied the orthogonal symmetric matrices in §1.5, or the treatment of three dimensional rotations in §4.5.4.)

FIGURE 3.17   Hyperboloid of two sheets: $-x_1^2 - x_2^2 + x_3^2 = 1$

FIGURE 3.18   Paraboloid: $x_3 = x_1^2 + x_2^2$

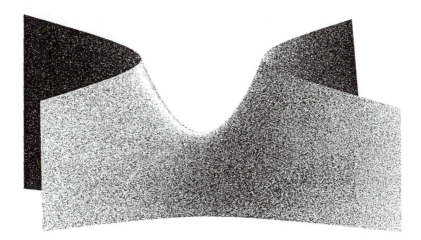

FIGURE 3.19   Hyperbolic paraboloid: $x_3 = x_1^2 - x_2^2$

We can now comment briefly[8] on why every non-degenerate conic section is a hyperbola, an ellipse, or a parabola. The equation $x_1^2 + x_2^2 = x_3^2$ defines a cone in space, with apex at $\langle 0, 0, 0 \rangle$ and extending straight up from the plane $x_3 = 0$. As we will see in §5.3.5, rigid motions of this cone in three space will still result in a quadratic equation. So let us move the cone anywhere in space and intersect it with the plane $x_3 = 0$. This simply means substituting 0 for x_3 everywhere in the transformed equation. Now by Theorem 3.10, the resulting curve of intersection, if not degenerate, is a hyperbola, an ellipse or a parabola.

Exercises

1. What sort of curve is $x_1 x_2 = 1$?

2. Carry out all the details of Theorem 3.10 for the following conics. This means that the coordinate system should be translated and rotated as necessary until the equation for the conic falls into one of the standard forms (or a degenerate form).

$$2x_1^2 + 72x_1x_2 + 23x_2^2 = 1250$$
$$34x_1^2 + 24x_1x_2 + 41x_2^2 = 625$$
$$x_1^2 + 2x_1x_2 + x_2^2 + 4x_2 = 16$$

---

[8]The ancient Greek proof involves no algebra, and is a beautiful example of reasoning in solid geometry. We urge the reader to take the time to look at that proof. See, e.g., page 9 of *Geometry and the Imagination*, by D. Hilbert and S. Cohn-Vossen, Chelsea Publishing Company, New York, 1952 and 1983.

3. Write a program to automate Theorem 3.10 completely. It could even end up drawing the conic. (There were previous exercises on automating the diagonalization of symmetric matrices, which could be applied here. Nevertheless, those were pretty massive exercises, since they referred to the case of $n \times n$ matrices. Here things are simpler since we are dealing only with 2×2 matrices.)

4. Analyze the following loci of quadratic equations in three variables. Diagonalize by an orthogonal matrix if necessary, and sketch as best you can. Sketching may not be easy, but in general, one can try to sketch the x_1, x_2-curve for various values of x_3, and hope to see the pattern. The material on shadows and horizons (§3.4.12) could be useful here. It may also be valuable to return to this material after studying either our section on graphing a function of two variables (§6.4) or our section on ray tracing (§6.8).

$$
\begin{aligned}
x_1^2 + x_2^2 - x_3^2 &= 1 \\
x_1^2 + x_2^2 - x_3^2 &= -1 \\
x_1^2 + x_2^2 - x_3 &= 1 \\
x_1 x_2 - x_3 &= 0 \\
x_1 x_2 + x_2 x_3 + x_3 x_1 &= 3
\end{aligned}
$$

5. Carry out the program of analyzing all possible loci of quadratic equations in three variables.

3.2   Cubic curves and splines

In §3.1 we considered curves that are defined—either explicitly or implicitly—by *quadratic* equations. Thus, for example, the quadratic parametric equations

$$ x_1 = a + t, \quad x_2 = b + kt^2 \tag{3.10} $$

explicitly define a parabola centered at $\langle a, b \rangle$. The reader may check that, in fact, except for some degenerate cases,[9] parabolas are the only curves that can be parametrized by quadratic functions of t. On the other hand, every conic section is defined by a quadratic equation like (3.6), and as we saw in Theorem 3.10, every such equation generates a (possibly degenerate) conic section.

As we move from quadratic to cubic polynomials (and possibly beyond), we have to pay attention to the distinction between curves that are defined implicitly (i.e., as loci) and those that are defined explicitly (i.e., parametrically). Section 3.2.1 immediately following contains a brief discussion of curves defined (implicitly) by cubic (and more general) polynomial equations, i.e., loci or solu-

---

[9]For example, the equations $x_1 = 0$, $x_2 = t^2$ yield the non-negative x_2-axis.

tion sets of equations like (3.6) but of higher degree. On the whole, loci are very complex, and hence less useful as a tool in graphics work. The remainder of §3.2 will be devoted to the study of curves that are (explicitly) parametrized by cubic polynomials, i.e., curves that can be parametrized as in Equation (3.10), only with cubic functions of t. Here the material takes a more practical turn than our discussion of conic sections in §3.1. We will see that cubic curves are sufficiently versatile to perform a number of practical tasks in computer-oriented geometry.

3.2.1 Algebraic geometry

Equation (3.6) has two variables (x_1 and x_2) and is *quadratic*, that is to say, each of its terms is a product of no more than two variables—x_1 times itself, or x_2 times itself, or the product of the two variables. Quadratic equations are also said to be of *degree* 2. One may obtain a more general kind of equation by augmenting either the number of variables or the degree. Clearly the number of variables corresponds naturally to the dimension in which we are working; e.g., in Equation (3.6), x_1 and x_2 are coordinates in a plane. Since this chapter is about plane geometry, we will keep this number of variables fixed at two. (See the end of §3.1.7 just above for some examples of loci of polynomial equations in three variables.)

For any polynomial equation of the form

$$F(x_1, x_2) = \sum_{i+j \leq N} a_{ij} x_1^i x_2^j = 0 \tag{3.11}$$

the corresponding *locus* is the subset of the plane consisting of points $\langle x_1, x_2 \rangle$ that satisfy (3.11). If $N = 2$, we have a quadratic locus; such loci were classified completely in Theorem 3.10. For $N \geq 3$, no simple[10] classification is possible. Nevertheless the study of such loci, known as *algebraic geometry*, is a very rich subject indeed. Many mathematicians specialize in this area for their entire career, and many feet of shelf space are given over to this subject in mathematics libraries. The subject is both ancient and modern: It goes back to the ancient Greeks, who studied conic sections, and some of the most powerful abstract algebra of the last hundred years was created for the purpose of analyzing algebraic loci. (Two rudimentary but important tools of algebraic geometry will be seen in this book: homogeneous coordinates (§4.1.3) and the use of complex numbers for coordinates (§4.4.1, §1.4).) From the perspective of this book we cannot say very much more about the subject in general, except to refer the student to the vast literature on the subject.

---

[10]Newton's work on *Opticks*, which appeared in 1704, contained an enumeration of 72 of the 78 possible forms that can be taken by a cubic curve. In this work he stated that any cubic curve can be taken by projective transformations to a curve defined by $x_1^2 = ax_2^3 + bx_2^2 + cx_2 + d$. (See footnote 3 for a reference.)

FIGURE 3.20   The locus of $x_2^3 - x_2 = x_1^2$

One way to plot the general algebraic locus (3.11) is to regard $F(x_1, x_2)$ as an intensity function, as in §2.7. More precisely, one could define

$$f(x_1, x_2) = \begin{cases} 1 & \text{if } F(x_1, x_2) > 0 \\ 0 & \text{otherwise} \end{cases}$$

Plotting $f(x_1, x_2)$ by the methods of §2.7 makes a picture that is black where F is negative and white where F is positive. In this way, the locus defined by (3.11) is seen[11] as the boundary between white and black. See Figure 3.20 where we have done this for the curve defined by $x_2^3 - x_2 = x_1^2$. (Also, all the exercises at the end of §2.7 are essentially of this type.)

We hasten to point out that it is in general impossible to find elementary functions parametrizing the locus (3.11) (as we were able to do in the special case of ellipses and hyperbolas). Therefore it is difficult to plot the locus as a curve. The locus (3.11) is obviously one of the level curves of F.

3.2.2   Cubic Bézier curves

In this section we explore what sorts of curves can be prescribed parametrically in two dimensions by cubic functions of t:

$$\begin{aligned} x_1 &= \gamma_1(t) = a_{13}t^3 + a_{12}t^2 + a_{11}t + a_{10}, \\ x_2 &= \gamma_2(t) = a_{23}t^3 + a_{22}t^2 + a_{21}t + a_{20}. \end{aligned} \tag{3.12}$$

---

[11]In some exceptional cases this won't really work. For instance, the equation $(x_1^2 - x_2)^2 = 0$ defines a parabola, but the left-hand side of this equation is never negative.

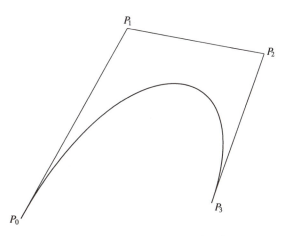

FIGURE 3.21   A cubic Bézier curve and its control polygon

To be very specific, let us suppose that we are interested in how this parametric curve looks for t restricted to the interval $0 \le t \le 1$. With the skills acquired so far, the student should have little trouble in making plots of some curves of this type for some randomly chosen values of the coefficients a_{ij}. These coefficients form a set of eight parameters that control the ultimate shape of the curve, but upon a little experimentation one will discover that this control is clumsy and unpredictable at best. One has pretty good control near $t = 0$; after all, $\gamma(0)$ is the starting point, $\gamma'(0)$ points in the tangent direction at the start, and so on. But near $t = 1$ it is very hard to see how the eight parameters determine the curve. Bézier's contribution was a different set of eight parameters (linearly related to the eight parameters of (3.12)) that gives us control over the shape of the curve in a much more pictorial and intuitive manner. In later parts of §3.2 we will see how to patch together curves of this type to yield good visual approximations of just about any smooth curve.

Bézier's eight parameters are the coordinates of four *control points* in the plane, P_0, P_1, P_2 and P_3. These four points form a (non-closed) polygon that is sometimes called the *control polygon* of the curve. The curve will start at end at P_0 and P_3, and will be tangent to the polygon at its starting and ending points (see Figure 3.21). The *cubic Bézier curve associated to this control polygon is* defined to be the curve parametrized by

$$\langle x_1, x_2 \rangle = B(t)$$
$$= (1-t)^3 P_0 + 3t(1-t)^2 P_1 + 3t^2(1-t)P_2 + t^3 P_3 \qquad (3.13)$$

for $0 \le t \le 1$.

LEMMA 10   The cubic Bézier curve (3.13) satisfies the following properties:

(1) $B(0) = P_0$ and $B(1) = P_3$.

(2) $B(t)$ is tangent to the control polygon at each end; more precisely, $B'(0) = 3(P_1 - P_0)$ and $B'(1) = 3(P_3 - P_2)$.

(3) $B(t)$ is a polynomial in t of degree at most 3.

(4) For each t, $B(t)$ is a convex combination of the points P_0, P_1, P_2 and P_3, i.e., a linear combination with non-negative coefficients that sum to 1.

(5) $B''(0) = 6(P_0 - 2P_1 + P_2)$ and $B''(1) = 6(P_1 - 2P_2 + P_3)$.   □

Exercises

1. For any real t and any points Q_0 and Q_1, define the *affine combination of Q_0 and Q_1* by t to be the point $A_t(Q_0, Q_1) = (1 - t)Q_0 + tQ_1$. Prove that the cubic Bézier curve associated to P_0, P_1, P_2 and P_3 can be presented using affine combinations in the following way:

$$
\begin{aligned}
R_0(t) &= A_t(P_0, P_1); \quad R_1(t) = A_t(P_1, P_2); \quad R_2(t) = A_t(P_2, P_3) \\
S_0(t) &= A_t(R_0, R_1); \quad S_1(t) = A_t(R_1, R_2) \\
B(t) &= A_t(S_0, S_1)
\end{aligned}
$$

2. Give a definition of a quartic (degree 4) curve that is defined by five control points. What properties does it have? Give the definition of a degree n curve that is defined in like manner by $n+1$ control points. (These are called Bézier curves of degree n.)

3. Command the computer to make cubic Bézier curves for the control polygons shown in Figure 3.22. It is an interesting exercise to see how closely one can approximate the Bézier curve by a freehand drawing, prior to looking at the precisely calculated picture. In doing this one gains an appreciation of the naturalness of the definition. (The computer program could be very simple, just invoking Equation (3.13) and making a curve as we did for conic sections. A more systematic approach will come later.)

4. What happens if the four control points are evenly spaced along a straight line (i.e., $P_1 = 2/3P_0 + 1/3P_3$ and $P_2 = 1/3P_0 + 2/3P_3$)?

5. What happens if $P_1 = P_0$ and $P_2 = P_3$?

6. What happens if $P_1 = P_3$ and $P_2 = P_0$?

7. Prove that the cubic Bézier curve with control points P_0, P_1, P_2 and P_3 is uniquely determined by parts (1), (2), (3) and (5) of Lemma 10.

8. Prove that the definition of the cubic Bézier curve is symmetric with respect to reversing the order of the control points. That is, if $B(t)$ is the cubic Bézier curve defined by P_0, P_1, P_2 and P_3, and $C(t)$ is the cubic Bézier curve defined

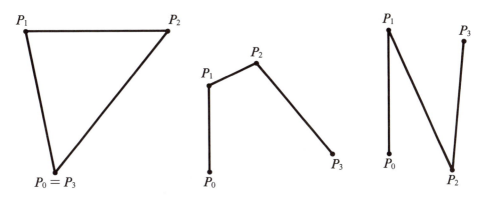

FIGURE 3.22 Make cubic Bézier curves for these polygons

by P_3, P_2, P_1 and P_0, then $C(t) = B(1-t)$. (In other words, they are the same curve traversed in opposite directions.)

9. Let the x_1-coordinate of the Bézier control point P_j be denoted P_{1j} (for $0 \leq j < 4$), and let a_{1j} $(0 \leq j < 4)$ be the coefficients of $\gamma_1(t)$ appearing in Equation (3.12). Assume that $\gamma(t)$ (of Equation (3.12)) and $B(t)$ (of Equation (3.13)) are really the same curve. Prove that the a_{1j} and P_{1j} are linearly related via

$$
\begin{bmatrix} a_{10} \\ a_{11} \\ a_{12} \\ a_{13} \end{bmatrix} = \begin{bmatrix} 1 & 0 & 0 & 0 \\ -3 & 3 & 0 & 0 \\ 3 & -6 & 3 & 0 \\ -1 & 3 & -3 & 1 \end{bmatrix} \begin{bmatrix} P_{10} \\ P_{11} \\ P_{12} \\ P_{13} \end{bmatrix}
$$

The inverse relationship is given by

$$
\begin{bmatrix} P_{10} \\ P_{11} \\ P_{12} \\ P_{13} \end{bmatrix} = \frac{1}{3} \begin{bmatrix} 3 & 0 & 0 & 0 \\ 3 & 1 & 0 & 0 \\ 3 & 2 & 1 & 0 \\ 3 & 3 & 3 & 3 \end{bmatrix} \begin{bmatrix} a_{10} \\ a_{11} \\ a_{12} \\ a_{13} \end{bmatrix}
$$

Of course, analogous linear relationships also hold between the other four coefficients of Equation (3.12) and the x_2-components of the Bézier control points.

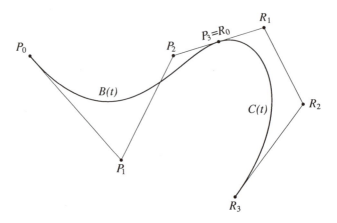

FIGURE 3.23   Cubic Bézier curves $B(t)$ and $C(t)$, meeting at $B(1) = C(0)$

3.2.3   Connecting two cubic Bézier curves

As we saw in Exercise 3 at the end of §3.2.2 (see also Figure 3.22), cubic Bézier curves[12] can take on a number of interesting forms, including loops and S-shaped bends. Nevertheless, if these curves are extended by using Equation (3.13) for values of t outside the interval $[0, 1]$, less versatility is encountered. For example, a cubic curve can make at most one loop or S-bend (why?). For close approximations to arbitrary curves, therefore, we need to patch together cubic Bézier curves. The objective is to patch things together as smoothly as possible, so that the joint is not detectable to the eye. This situation is depicted for two cubic Bézier curves in Figure 3.23. $B(t)$ is the cubic Bézier curve with control points P_i, and $C(t)$ is the cubic Bézier curve with control points R_i ($0 \leq i \leq 3$).

By part (1) of Lemma 10, we cannot make a continuous connection of the two curves unless

$$P_3 \ = \ R_0 \tag{3.14}$$

We also require that the curve formed by connecting $B(t)$ to $C(t)$ at $P_3 = R_0$ should be smooth at the junction. We in fact want no change in velocity as the curve is traversed according to the parametrization, and for this reason, we want $B'(1)$ to be the same as $C'(0)$. By part (2) of Lemma 10, this smoothness condition is equivalent to

$$3(P_3 - P_2) \ = \ 3(R_1 - R_0)$$

---

[12]Strictly speaking, there is no such thing as a *cubic Bézier curve*, as distinct from an arbitrary curve parametrized by cubic polynomials of t. Nevertheless, we use this expression to indicate our interest both in the curve and in its description via Bézier control points.

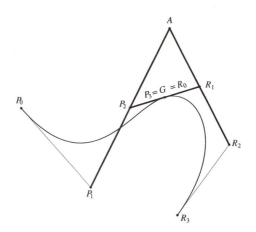

FIGURE 3.24   The **A**-frame condition

which in turn reduces easily to

$$G - P_2 = R_1 - G$$

where G is the common point, i.e. $G = P_3 = R_0$. This equation may be rewritten as

$$G = \frac{1}{2}(R_1 + P_2) \tag{3.15}$$

i.e., the common point is the midpoint between R_1 and P_2.

Finally, for a correct match between $B(t)$ and $C(t)$, we wish to have the second derivatives of $B(t)$ and $C(t)$ agree where they meet. This will assure that the same curvature occurs on both sides of the junction. By part (5) of Lemma 10, this condition is equivalent to

$$6(P_3 - 2P_2 + P_1) = 6(R_0 - 2R_1 + R_2)$$

which in turn reduces easily to

$$2P_2 - P_1 = 2R_1 - R_2 \tag{3.16}$$

When this condition holds, the common point denoted by both sides of Equation (3.16) will be denoted A (for *apex*).

Now the correct matching of two cubic Bézier curves is determined by Equations (3.14), (3.15) and (3.16). These three conditions are depicted in Figure 3.24; the point A is determined geometrically by the conditions that it should lie on lines $\overleftrightarrow{P_1P_2}$ and $\overleftrightarrow{R_1R_2}$, that P_2 should be the midpoint of the segment $\overline{P_1A}$, and that R_1 should be the midpoint of the segment $\overline{R_2A}$. If all of these conditions are satisfied, then we say that the **A**-*frame condition*[13] holds at the junction point G. The point A (determined by (3.16)) will be called the *apex* of this **A**-frame.

1. Prove Lemma 10.

2. Prove the assertion made above that a cubic Bézier curve contains at most one loop and at most one S-bend.

3. Command the computer to make some examples of joined cubic Bézier curves that illustrate the **A**-frame condition. Make some examples where the condition is satisfied and some where it is not. It would be especially interesting to see the appearance of curves that are joined with the correct slope but incorrect second derivatives.

4. Can one demand that the third derivatives also agree at the junction point?

3.2.4   Connecting several cubic Bézier curves

Of course, any number of cubic Bézier curves can be attached together by the methods of §3.2.3; one merely needs to make sure that the **A**-frame condition holds at each junction point. Nevertheless, to satisfy this condition is easier said than done, especially if one insists on treating all the Bézier control points as independent variables. Here we will describe a modified approach to piecewise cubic curves that is based on the cubic Bézier curves we have studied, but begins with different control points. (The Bézier control points are then treated as dependent variables; that is, they will be defined in terms of the control points we are about to introduce.)

Let us be given finitely many points A_0, A_1, A_2, $\cdots$, A_n in the plane. We regard these as control points for a piecewise cubic curve that we are going to draw in the plane. Except for A_0 and A_n, the points A_i will not lie on the curve; rather, they will serve as apices of **A**-frames that we will construct in order to ensure smooth joining of the cubic pieces. Therefore, we will call $A_0, \cdots, A_n$ *apical control points*.

As indicated in Figure 3.25, we begin by trisecting each segment $\overline{A_i A_{i+1}}$ (for $0 \leq i < n$). Each apex A_i (other than A_0 and A_n) lies on two of these trisected segments; each of these trisected segments has a trisection point that lies nearer to A_i. We then define G_i to be the point midway between these two nearby trisection points. (See Figure 3.25. A precise formula for G_i is given in Equation (3.17).) We can now define n cubic Bézier curves, as follows. The first

---

[13]The name **A**-*frame* is suggested by Figure 3.24. The terminology is that of Professor K. A. Baker of UCLA. The author is deeply grateful to Professor Baker for teaching him all the material of §3.2 and for his permission to present the material in this manner.

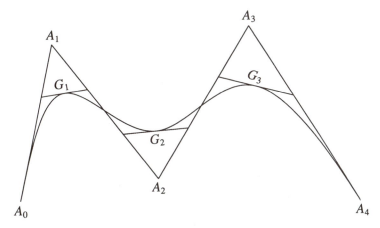

FIGURE 3.25   A piecewise cubic curve defined by apical control points

one has control points $P_0 = A_0$, $\underline{P_1}$, P_2, $P_3 = G_1$, where P_1 and P_2 the two trisection points of the segment $\overline{A_0 A_1}$ (and with P_1 the trisection point that is closer to A_0). The other cubic Bézier curves, except for the last one, have Bézier control points $P_0 = G_i$, $P_3 = G_{i+1}$, and P_1 and P_2 the two trisection points of the segment $\overline{A_i A_{i+1}}$ (with P_1 being the one closer to A_i). The final cubic Bézier curve is defined similarly, except that its fourth control point is of course A_n.

The definitions of all these points may sound complicated, but in fact they are all pretty obvious[14] in Figure 3.25. What should be obvious from the figure is that *the **A**-frame condition is satisfied at the junction points* $G_1, \cdots, G_{n-1}$. Therefore, if $B_i(t)$ denotes the ith cubic Bézier curve, it follows from §3.2.3 that $B_i(t)$ joins smoothly to $B_{i+1}(u)$ where $t = 1$ and $u = 0$. (As before, by a smooth join we mean that $B_i(1) = B_{i+1}(0)$, that $B_i'(1) = B_{i+1}'(0)$ and that $B_i''(1) = B_{i+1}''(0)$.)

The piecewise cubic curve defined in this manner is called the B-*spline*[15] *controlled by* points $A_0, \cdots, A_n$. (More technically, it is called the *relaxed B-spline determined by* $G_0, \cdots, G_n$. This means that the second derivatives are all zero at the two endpoints.)

The reader should experiment either with computer drawings or with free-hand drawings to get some feeling for how the appearance of a B-spline depends on the positions of the (apical) control points A_i. The situation is by and large pretty natural: beginning at the first control point, the curve is swept toward

---

[14]We leave it to the reader to see that the definition makes sense even if some of the A_i happen to be equal to one another.

[15]*Spline* originally meant—and still does mean—a drafting implement consisting of a rod or strip of some material that is flexible enough to pass through some desired points, but stiff enough that its curvature will vary continuously. What we are doing here is producing a mathematical analog of this kind of mechanical device.

each control point in turn, finally terminating at the last control point. One important point to notice is that each apical control point has only a local influence over the curve.

Exercise

1. Write a program that reads n and a sequence of apical control points $A_0 \cdots A_n$ and draws the associated B-spline. For the sake of learning about this material, it would be nice to have an option of including the A_i and all the auxiliary points mentioned above in the drawing. (The student now possesses all necessary tools to make this work. All that is really needed is the above definition of the auxiliary points (trisections and the G_i), and the basic Bézier formula (3.13). This exercise can later be incorporated into the interpolating curve that will be discussed in §3.2.5. A very detailed outline—for the three-dimensional case—appears in §6.5.2.)

3.2.5   Piecewise cubic interpolants

It is all very well to have a piecewise cubic curve defined by apical control points, as is the case for the B-splines defined in §3.2.4, but the difficulty remains that the apical control points do not lie on the resulting curve. A likely task we may face is to construct a curve that actually passes through some given sequence of points $G_0, \cdots, G_n$. Such a curve is called a *piecewise cubic interpolating curve*, or *piecewise cubic interpolant* through the points $G_0, \cdots, G_n$. Fortunately, we may obtain piecewise cubic interpolants by simply changing the point of view that we take toward the material in §3.2.4.

In §3.2.4, we defined some auxiliary points $G_1, \cdots, G_{n-1}$ in terms of the given control points $A_0, \cdots, A_n$, with the interesting property that the constructed curve passes through these new points G_i. It is convenient also to define G_0 and G_n to be A_0 and A_n, respectively; we still have all G_i on the constructed curve. We now observe that the $n+1$ points G_i depend linearly on the $n+1$ points A_i. As will be apparent, the associated determinant is not zero, and so we can invert this linear correspondence to determine $n+1$ points A_i from $n+1$ given points G_i. Having done this, we use the procedure of §3.2.4 to obtain a piecewise cubic curve passing smoothly through the points G_i. This curve is clearly a piecewise cubic interpolant.

Therefore, to obtain the desired interpolant through the G_i, all that remains is to make precise the linear relation between the A_i and the G_i. For this, we return to the A-frame condition as depicted in Figure 3.24. For $i \neq 0, n$ we observe first that the two trisection points that are near neighbors to A_i are

$$\frac{1}{3}\left(A_{i-1} + 2A_i\right) \quad \text{and} \quad \frac{1}{3}\left(2A_i + A_{i+1}\right)$$

Since G_i is the midpoint of the segment joining these two points, we may average the two expressions to obtain

$$G_i = \frac{1}{6}(A_{i-1} + 4A_i + A_{i+1}) \tag{3.17}$$

for $1 \le i \le n - 1$. Of course we also have the simpler equations

$$G_0 = A_0, \quad G_n = A_n \tag{3.18}$$

at the two endpoints. The construction of the desired interpolating curve now reduces to solving Equations (3.18) and (3.17) for A_i in terms of the given G_i. These equations can be recast into the somewhat more symmetric form

$$
\begin{bmatrix}
4 & 1 & & & & \\
1 & 4 & 1 & & & \\
 & 1 & 4 & 1 & & \\
 & & & & \ddots & \\
 & & & & 1 & 4
\end{bmatrix}
\begin{bmatrix}
A_1 \\ A_2 \\ A_3 \\ \vdots \\ A_{n-1}
\end{bmatrix}
=
\begin{bmatrix}
6G_1 - G_0 \\ 6G_2 \\ 6G_3 \\ \vdots \\ 6G_{n-1} - G_n
\end{bmatrix}
$$

Therefore, the interpolant can be constructed once we have an inverse to the $(n-1) \times (n-1)$ matrix

$$
M_{n-1} =
\begin{bmatrix}
4 & 1 & & & & \\
1 & 4 & 1 & & & \\
 & 1 & 4 & 1 & & \\
 & & & & \ddots & \\
 & & & & 1 & 4
\end{bmatrix}
$$

Of course, M_{n-1} can be inverted by any of the methods of §1.2, but it has a special form that makes it amenable to other treatments as well.

Letting I_{n-1} denote the $(n-1) \times (n-1)$ identity matrix, we clearly have

$$\frac{1}{4}M_{n-1} = I_{n-1} + E_{n-1}$$

where

$$E_{n-1} = \begin{bmatrix} 0 & 0.25 & & & & \\ 0.25 & 0 & 0.25 & & & \\ & 0.25 & 0 & 0.25 & & \\ & & & & \ddots & \\ & & & & 0.25 & 0 \end{bmatrix}$$

One can easily check that the powers of E_{n-1} converge rapidly to 0, and hence we can invert the last formula for M_{n-1} by using the well-known geometric series (see the end of §1.2.6), obtaining

$$4M_{n-1}^{-1} = I_{n-1} - E_{n-1} + E_{n-1}^2 - E_{n-1}^3 + \cdots \tag{3.19}$$

Exercises

1. Write a program capable of drawing piecewise cubic interpolants through a sequence of points $G_0, \cdots, G_n$. The program should be able to determine n and invert the matrix M_{n-1} (perhaps by summing the geometric series (3.19)). Thereupon the program can solve Equations (3.17) and (3.18) for the apical control points A_i. Following this, the program would follow the methods of §3.2.4 above (trisecting segments and so on) to draw the B-spline for the points A_i. (See, e.g., §6.1.2 for an outline of one program that reads in data.)

2. Prove that the determinant of M_{n-1} is

$$\frac{3 + 2\sqrt{3}}{6} \left(2 + \sqrt{3}\right)^{n-1} + \frac{3 - 2\sqrt{3}}{6} \left(2 - \sqrt{3}\right)^{n-1}$$

3. Investigate powers of the matrix E_{n-1}, with the aim of getting bounds on the size of the individual entries in E_{n-1}^k ($k = 1, 2, \cdots$). Use the information so obtained to determine the speed of convergence of the infinite series in Equation (3.19). Those students with a knowledge of the *spectral radius* ρ of a matrix could prove that $\rho(E_{n-1}) = 0.5 \cos(2\pi/n)$.

4. *A spurious inflection point.* Ask your program to draw the piecewise cubic curve through the four points $G_0 = \langle 7.4, 3.6 \rangle$, $G_1 = \langle 1.8, 4.0 \rangle$, $G_2 = \langle 1.0, 5.6 \rangle$ and $G_3 = \langle 0.8, 6.8 \rangle$ Also plot the piecewise linear curve (polygonal path) through these four points. Notice that the polygonal path is convex, but that the interpolating curve has an inflection point. Such an inflection point is called *spurious* in that its presence cannot be inferred visually from the raw data. If one is using splines and interpolants as drawing tools, as we describe in §3.2.6, we may not wish to have our drawing contain inflection points other

than those that we deliberately include in the data. A number of remedies have been proposed. We must refer the reader to more advanced works for the details. Spurious inflection points are less likely to crop up if one works with B-splines than if one works with interpolants.

3.2.6 Bézier curves as a language for geometry

The material here on (cubic) Bézier curves and B-splines was not included for reasons of any deep geometric significance, but rather for its practical utility in presenting curves. In almost every application of computer graphics, what we ultimately want is to output a picture. In the majority of cases, such pictures are composed of a number of curves. Having read §2.1.2, and having done the exercises of this chapter up to now, the student will appreciate that *curve* here does not mean the mathematical abstraction $\gamma(t)$ with t varying continuously, but rather a curve delivered *discretely* to the output device. In other words, small line segments are delivered to the device: small enough to trick the eye into believing in a smooth curve, but large enough to keep their total number manageably small.

This supply of small segments can be thought of as a form of data that we manipulate in graphics programs. The question then arises how best to store and manage this data. Earlier in this chapter we have focused on one way to manage the data: namely, if there is one explicit formula for the curve $\gamma(t)$ (such as for our parametrizations of conic sections), then one can simply calculate $\gamma(t)$ for a discrete sequence of t-values, deliver those coordinates to the output device, and then forget them. That is to say, you really don't have to store anything besides the formula for $\gamma(t)$. In §6.1 we will encounter the opposite extreme, of curves (continental boundaries) for which no formula is available at all. In that case all known information about the curves must be available as stored data.

With Bézier curves and B-splines we can come close to having the best of both worlds. Any desired shape can be created with such curves, and yet only a small amount of data has to be stored permanently. For example, a 10-piece B-spline is determined by 22 real numbers, but one might calculate (say) 40 or 50 points on each piece, thereby sending 500 points (1000 different numbers) to the output device. From this point of view, the B-spline approach represents a form of *data compression*.

Although B-splines, which are piecewise cubic, can only approximately render an arbitrary (non-cubic) curve, this is less of a limitation than it first appears. Piecewise cubic curves are certainly adequate for the design of everyday objects. If an object has some of its contours defined by such curves, then data about that object can be stored compactly, and can be easily manipulated by the methods described in this book. (One could for instance, obtain pictures showing how the object looks from near and from far, when rotated, when stretched in various directions, and so on.) We will take up this topic again in much greater detail in §6.5, for which the present section can be regarded as preliminary training.

At this point it should be clear that the B-spline method of describing piecewise cubic curves by their control points can be regarded as a refinement of the linguistic hierarchy in Chapter 2. A short inventory of control points is certainly more succinct and informative than the long list of device-independent commands that can be computed from them. On the other hand, one will often want to compute control points from some higher level specification of the problem. (We will give an example of such a computation in §6.5.1.) Thus the use of control points lies somewhere between computer programs and device-independent files in the classification of Chapter 2.

To make our ideas precise, let us define the B-*extension* of our device-independent language to have all the original commands together with five new commands:

B   The command to initiate B-spline data. No data occurs on the line with B. At least three lines immediately after a B command should be c commands.

A   The command to initiate data for a piecewise cubic interpolant. No data occurs on the line with A. At least three lines immediately after an A command should be c commands.

c   Control point, expressed as two real numbers. c commands may appear only in groups of three or more, and only sandwiched between a B command and an E command or between an A command and an F command. (More precisely, between B and E, c denotes an apical control point; between A and F, it denotes a point that the interpolating curve must pass through.)

E   End of data for one B-spline.

F   End of data for one piecewise cubic interpolant.

For example, when correctly interpreted, the file

```
w   0.0 2.0 8.0 8.0
A
c   7.4 3.6
c   1.8 4.0
c   1.0 5.6
c   0.8 6.8
F
```

gives a picture of the spurious inflection point described in an exercise just above, and the file

FIGURE 3.26   Heart-shaped B-spline

```
w 0 0 10 10
B  right side of heart
c 5 7.0
c 6 8.0
c 9 6.5
c 7 4.0
c 5 2.0
E
%
B  left side of heart
c 5 7.0
c 4 8.0
c 9 6.5
c 3 4.0
c 5 2.0
E
```

yields the heart-shaped figure. (The author made these files by hand, without much fuss. It is not terribly difficult, as the reader may determine by experimentation.)

The relationship between the B-extension of the device-independent language and our other languages can now be described by the following extension of (part of) the translation diagram in the introduction to Chapter 2:

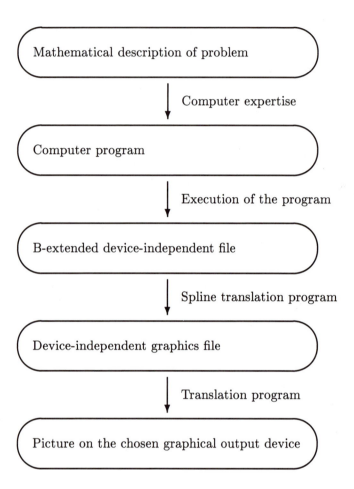

As we said in Chapter 2, this diagram is somewhat arbitrary, since it represents only one way to view the subject. We could, for instance, regard either of the two translation programs as a linguistic object in the foreground of our attention and hence place it in one of the ovals. Here we are regarding the arrows as representing somewhat permanent software objects, in the background of our attention, which have an existence that is independent of any one picture. Here, for instance, the calculation of B-splines can be set up as a stable software object that is used for many different pictures.

Generally speaking, it is advisable to separate the calculation of splines (i.e., the spline translation program) from the translation (or implementation) of the basic device-independent language. The simplest way to manage this is simply to let any command line (other than the five related to B-splines) pass through the spline translation program unaltered. On the other hand, some output devices have a feature of directly interpreting Bézier curves and B-splines. (For instance, PostScript has this capability for individual cubic Bézier curves.) If all one's output devices have this feature, then one might want to coalesce the two translations into one, and let all calculations of the cubic formulas be done by the output device. In studying this material for the first time, however, we generally recommend doing it the long way, to get the feel of it.

As indicated in the preceding diagram, what is now at stake is another translation. This is probably the easiest way to go about a systematic treatment of B-splines and piecewise cubic interpolants. One can take any interpreter for device-independent code—either the one from §2.3.1 or one supplied locally—as a skeleton or outline for a spline translation program. One simply needs to add five new cases and deal with them as appropriate. It is best to have the program store the control points in an array, and then process them after reaching an E command or an F command. Somewhere in the spline translation program, one will need to include the basic formulas of B-spline theory—the calculation of new control points, and of course the basic cubic formulas. Nevertheless it is pretty straightforward, and so we leave it as an important exercise. (A more complicated algorithm is described in detail in §6.5.2.) It is probably wise to include error messages for violations of the requirement that a B command is to be followed by c commands, and so on.

In building a B-spline translator, one will have to decide a value for the parameter STEP that occurs in all curve drawing programs. (An example was given in §2.1.2.) This is because a B-spline is ultimately composed of cubic curves, and each cubic curve will be described as STEP segments. A certain amount of experimentation is permissible here; certainly STEP = 50 is more than adequate in almost all cases. A minor advantage of giving B-splines directly to a device is that the device will make this decision, with, it is to be hoped, some regard for the parameters of the device itself. An enhanced version of the B-spline translator could be programmed to accept a command like

    B 40

that would initiate a B-spline with STEP taken to be 40. This refinement is probably not necessary in a first treatment of B-splines.

Exercises

1. Write a program to translate the B-extension of the device-independent language to pure device-independent language, and experiment using it on various data files that you make yourself. (This exercise overlaps wth the main exercises of §3.2.4 and §3.2.5, and could certainly be viewed as a complete replacement for those exercises.)

2. You may on occasion find it convenient to have an amalgamation of the B-spline language with the language for painting the interior of regions, as described in §2.5. In other words, the boundary of a painted region could be defined by one or more B-splines. This could be indicated by allowing a P-Q pair to sandwich the specification of one or more B-splines.

3. An interactive program (using a graphic input device such as a mouse) would allow the user to alter the positions of control points until the curve obtains the requisite shape. Ideally, such a program would save the data when the curve is as desired. This program may be technically complex, but the student who knows how to program a mouse would be rewarded with a program that is a very valuable adjunct to some of the other exercises in this book.

4. Write a program that translates directly from the B-extension of the device-independent language to PostScript. In other words, write a version of the program in §2.3.1 that is enhanced to accept directly the B, A, c, E and F commands. Calculate the individual Bézier control points as in previous exercises, but do not calculate the cubic curve itself. Instead, output its Bézier control points directly, with the syntax

```
x0 y0 moveto
x1 y1 x2 y2 x3 y3 curveto
```

for a cubic Bézier curve that has control points $\langle x_0, y_0 \rangle$, $\langle x_1, y_1 \rangle$, $\langle x_2, y_2 \rangle$, $\langle x_3, y_3 \rangle$. (Notice that $\langle x_0, y_0 \rangle$ is not mentioned in the curveto syntax; it is the *current point*, which can be specified with a moveto command, among many ways. In many contexts, the moveto command will not be needed. For example, here the point $\langle x_3, y_3 \rangle$ is the current point for a curveto command immediately following this one. For more information about these commands, consult the PostScript Reference Manual.) Determine experimentally whether it is more efficient to compute the cubics on your computer, or to let the PostScript device do it. (The STEP parameter mentioned above appears as the flatness parameter within PostScript, and can be reset with the setflat command, if you really wish to experiment.)

5. Determine B-spline parameters for the letters of the alphabet as you print them. (This will require a good bit of experimentation. Remember that at each corner you will have to start a new B-spline.) Then develop a translator that works as follows: It inputs a message and then makes a drawing showing the message printed in your hand. What extra difficulties would be present if one were to try this for cursive writing? Try to keep your personal data isolated in a small part of the program, or even have it read from a second input file, so that the program could easily be adapted to other users.

6. Experiment with the printing of music. Using B-splines, it is a straightforward task to draw individual notes, clefs, and so on. (For the distinction between

half-notes and quarter-notes, one would find it handy to have done Exercise 2 of this set.) The interesting part would be the development of an appropriate language for coding the music and making a translator that would take the musical code to the printed page. There are many things to consider; it may be easiest to begin with one voice and then later figure out how to include two or more voices. (Here again, the difficulty lies more in devising a good language than in drawing individual icons.) This would be an ambitious project, but it could be made even more ambitious as follows: Make a companion program that takes your musical language and interprets it directly as sound.

7. If you work in a technical area, with blueprints, flow charts, electronic diagrams, etc., work out some way to code such diagrams and to translate such code to actual pictures.

8. If you are interested in chemistry, do the same for molecular diagrams. (In some ways this exercise might better be postponed until we have worked with the third dimension.)

9. In a recent article in the *American Scientist*, the editors offered a chart that displayed some statistics by making various features of a cartoon character (curve of mouth, slant of eyebrows, etc.) correspond to some numbers extracted from those statistics. This seemed, to the author, an interesting new form of visual communication, with greater psychological impact than mere pie charts. They didn't state their exact methods for creating these diagrams, but certainly they might have used B-splines (and the other methods that we have had so far). The student now has all the tools to make such pictures. Again, one important part of the job would be to devise a simple language in which to express the features or statistics that we are interested in. The student is invited to try to make some similar charts. It doesn't have to be with faces; take some statistics that interest you, and use your imagination. (See "The pace of life," by Robert V. Levine, *American Scientist*, vol. 78, No. 5, September–October, 1990, pages 450–459. The diagram in question is on page 457. See also §4.7 of Clifford A. Pickover, *Computers, pattern, chaos and beauty: graphics from an unseen world*, St. Martin's Press, New York, 1990.)

10. Another application of B-splines involves thinking of the variable t (appearing in the root formula (3.13)) as explicitly representing *time*. Thus B-splines could be used for a crude form of animation. One could, for instance, consider a stick figure with a small number of designated points: knees, feet, head, hands, elbows, etc. These cannot be used as given, for they are not independent (e.g., the left hand must be a certain distance from the left elbow). So the first part of the exercise would be to determine some independent parameters (such as some angles). E.g., the angle between arm and torso at time t could be $B(t)$. One could then make a few drawings by hand and use these to determine control points for $B(t)$ (and the other parameters). Intermediate values of $B(t)$ would then be determined by (3.13) (or by its

extension to B-splines). The objective here is of course to keep the motion smooth, rather than jerky. In working out the **A**-frame condition, we applied geometric smoothness, but when t is changed to a time variable, that translates to smoothness in time. There are a lot of things to keep track of here, and it will be non-trivial to display the frames as animation, and so it would be a big project. (The author is indebted to Kirby Baker for mentioning this project.)

3.3   Some maps from $\mathbb{R}^2$ to $\mathbb{R}^2$

In the various parts of §3.3 we will be considering functions, or maps, from $\mathbb{R}^2$ to itself. Some possible properties of a function $f : \mathbb{R}^2 \longrightarrow \mathbb{R}^2$ that will interest us are as follows:

- f is a *collineation*. This means that f maps lines to lines (does not bend them). Most of the maps considered here will be collineations. The main theoretical conclusion of Chapter 4 will be that every collineation is definable by linear equations.

- f is a *rigid motion*. This means that $d(f(x), f(y)) = d(x, y)$ for any $x, y \in \mathbb{R}^2$. Informally, we say "distance is preserved by f."

- f is a *similarity map*. This means that $\angle f(A)f(B)f(C)$ is congruent to $\angle ABC$ for any three non-collinear points $A, B, C \in \mathbb{R}^2$. Informally, "angles are preserved by f." It follows from Euclid's Side-Side-Side Theorem that every rigid motion is a similarity, but the converse is false, as we will see.

- f is *area-preserving*. This property, already mentioned in §1.3.7, means that if A is any measurable set, then $\mu(f[A]) = \mu(A)$, where μ denotes Lebesgue measure (i.e., *area* for sets A that are not too complicated). Every rigid motion is area-preserving, but not conversely, as we will see.

- f is *orientation-preserving*. This means that the f-image of a picture of a right hand still looks like a right hand. More technically, for the sorts of maps we are talking about, we may use the determinant D_2 to say that f is orientation preserving iff $D_2(f(v_1) - f(0), f(v_2) - f(0))$ is positive whenever $D_2(v_1, v_2)$ is positive. (Compare earlier remarks about orientation in §1.3.7. If f is not a collineation then we have to talk instead about the sign of the Jacobian discussed there.)

- f has a *fixed point* P, i.e., $f(P) = P$.

- f *fixes every point along a line* L, i.e. $f(P) = P$ for every point P on the line L.

- f has a *fixed line* L, i.e., $f[L] = L$. This condition is weaker than the one just before, in that it requires only that f map L onto L, not that f should fix each point of L.

Under minor changes, such as substituting volume for area, all these concepts also make sense for maps $\mathbb{R}^3 \longrightarrow \mathbb{R}^3$, and we will later discuss some of them in that context (see §5.3).

A *group* of transformations of a set S is a collection $\mathcal{G}$ of maps $f : S \longrightarrow S$ with the following properties:

1. the identity function of S lies in $\mathcal{G}$;

2. if $f, g \in \mathcal{G}$, then $f \circ g \in \mathcal{G}$;

3. if $f \in \mathcal{G}$, then f is a bijection of S with itself, and the inverse mapping f^{-1} lies in $\mathcal{G}$.

If $\mathcal{G}$ is a group of transformations on S, then a *one-parameter group in $\mathcal{G}$* is a function

$$G : \mathbb{R} \longrightarrow \mathcal{G}$$
$$t \longmapsto G_t$$

such that

1. G_0 is the identity function on S;

2. $G_s \circ G_t = G_{s+t}$ for all $s, t \in \mathbb{R}$;

3. G_{-t} is the inverse of G_t for all $t \in \mathbb{R}$.

In fact, the group $\mathcal{G}$ does not really need to be mentioned here, since $\mathcal{G}$ can always be taken as equal to $\{G_t : t \in \mathbb{R}\}$. If we prefer not to mention a specific $\mathcal{G}$, then we may refer to G as a *one-parameter group of transformations of S*. The reader who has studied abstract algebra (not a prerequisite for this material) will recognize our $\mathcal{G}$ as an instance of the abstract idea of *group*, and will recognize G as a homomorphism $\langle \mathbb{R}, +, -, 0 \rangle \overset{G}{\longrightarrow} \mathcal{G}$. As we will see, the notion of one-parameter group will turn out to capture very nicely our intuitive idea that, e.g., rotations, can be done continuously through all angles, with for instance, a four-degree rotation being twice as much as a two-degree rotation.

In our applied work, the notion of one-parameter subgroup is particularly useful in making the inverse of a matrix G_t available with no further calculation (one simply needs to replace t by $-t$ in the formula for G_t).

Another useful application of one-parameter groups is the idea of orbits. For P a point and $\{G_t : t \in \mathbb{R}\}$ a one-parameter group of transformations, the *orbit of P under $\{G_t : t \in \mathbb{R}\}$* is the set $\{G_t(P) : t \in \mathbb{R}\}$. When we say *an orbit of $\{G_t : t \in \mathbb{R}\}$*, we mean the orbit of P under $\{G_t : t \in \mathbb{R}\}$ for some P. There is an analogy with planetary orbits: one can think of G_t as specifying a sort of law of motion, and of P as being forced to follow this law of motion. Thus in fact $P(t) = G_t(P)$ is a parametric description of a curve, and the orbit of P is the set of points $P(t)$ on this curve. The idea of orbits is useful in considering symmetry of a figure. Let us say that a geometrical figure F is *symmetric under the group $\mathcal{G}$* iff every motion in $\mathcal{G}$ maps F to itself. Thus, for example, any set of horizontal lines is symmetric under the group of translations parallel to the x-axis. (Translations are defined in §3.3.1.) Sometimes we use the alternate terminology that F is *invariant under* $\mathcal{G}$.

Now if $\mathcal{G}$ is a one-parameter group $\{G_t : t \in \mathbb{R}\}$, then the following simple calculation shows that every orbit of $\{G_t : t \in \mathbb{R}\}$ is invariant under $\{G_t : t \in \mathbb{R}\}$:

$$G_t(P(t')) \; = \; G_t(G_{t'}(P)) \; = \; G_{t+t'}(P) \; = \; P(t+t')$$

The same calculation also shows that if an invariant set F contains $P(t')$ for some t', then it must contain $P(t+t')$ for all t, which means that F contains the whole orbit. It follows that *orbits are the simplest invariant (symmetric) sets for a one-parameter group.* In many cases the orbits are old friends (lines, circles, etc.), but at least two new curves will arise for us as orbits (the logarithmic spiral and the helix).

Almost all of the maps discussed here will be composed from linear maps and one new kind of map, which we will now define.

Exercises

1. If Q lies on the orbit of P under $\{G_t : t \in \mathbb{R}\}$, i.e., if $Q = G_t(P)$ for some t, then the orbit of Q is the same as the orbit of P.

2. The set S on which $\{G_t : t \in \mathbb{R}\}$ acts (for the present S is the plane), is partitioned into orbits of $\{G_t : t \in \mathbb{R}\}$. This means that each point of S lies in exactly one orbit.

3. For any point $P \in S$, the singleton class $\{P\}$ is an orbit if and only if P is a fixed point of every G_t.

3.3.1   Translations

If $\mathbf{V}$ is any vector space, and $v \in V$, then *translation by v* is the function $T_v : V \longrightarrow V$ defined by

$$T_v(x) \; = \; x + v$$

for every $x \in V$.

LEMMA 11   Every translation is a rigid motion.

Proof   Follows from elementary facts about parallelograms.   □

LEMMA 12   The set of all translations is a group of transformations of $\mathbb{R}^2$. The assignment

$$t \longmapsto G_t \; = \; T_t \cdot v$$

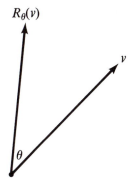

FIGURE 3.27 The geometric definition of R_θ

(for $t \in \mathbb{R}$) defines a one-parameter group of transformations of $\mathbb{R}^2$. If $v \neq 0$, its orbits are the lines parallel to the line joining v to the origin. □

LEMMA 13 If $v \neq 0$, the fixed lines of T_v are the line joining v to the origin and all lines parallel to this one, and moreover T_v has no fixed points. □

LEMMA 14 For any two points A and B in the plane, there exists a unique translation T such that $T(A) = B$. □

This translation T may be denoted T_{AB}. The formula for a translation is not given by a matrix, since translations are not linear[16] maps (why not?). Instead, we have:

LEMMA 15 For any $\alpha, \beta \in \mathbb{R}$, the map

$$\langle x_1, x_2 \rangle \;\longmapsto\; \langle x_1 + \alpha, \; x_2 + \beta \rangle$$

defines a translation of $\mathbb{R}^2$, and conversely every translation is given by a formula of this form. □

3.3.2 Rotations about the origin

We consider the map $R_\theta : \mathbb{R}^2 \longrightarrow \mathbb{R}^2$ that can be described geometrically as

---

[16]The concept that unifies linear maps with translations is that of *affine map*, which is introduced in §3.3.8. We will see in §4.5.1 that translations and linear maps together are adequate to describe all collineations of the plane.

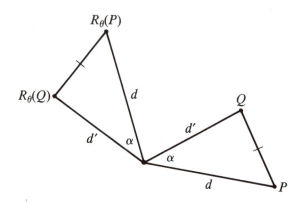

FIGURE 3.28 $d(P,Q)$ is determined by d, d' and α

follows. For any vector v, the vector $R_\theta(v)$ is formed by rotating v about the origin through the angle θ.

LEMMA 16 R_θ is a rigid motion of $\mathbb{R}^2$.

Proof   By Euclid's Side Angle Side Theorem, the distance between points P and Q in Figure 3.28 is determined by the distance from $\langle 0,0 \rangle$ to P and to Q and by the angle α. Clearly these are all preserved by R_θ.   □

LEMMA 17 R_θ is a linear transformation.

Proof   In Figure 3.29 we show the familiar parallelogram for the addition of vectors v and v'. By Lemma 17, this figure remains a parallelogram upon rotation, and therefore

$$R_\theta(v + v') \; = \; R_\theta(v) + R_\theta(v')$$

In other words, we have verified Equation (1.18) for linearity. The other linearity equation is easy to establish, and we leave that proof to the reader.   □

If $\vec{r}$ is the ray emanating from the origin and forming an angle θ with the positive x_1-axis (measured counterclockwise), then $R_\theta(1,0)$ is the intersection of $\vec{r}$ with the unit circle, and that point of intersection is obviously $\langle \cos\theta, \sin\theta \rangle$. Similar reasoning yields $R_\theta(1,0) \; = \; \langle -\sin\theta, \cos\theta \rangle$. In other words, we have proved

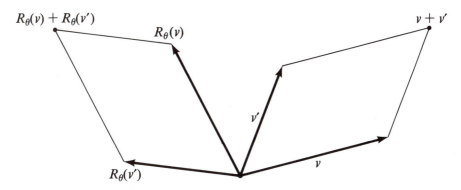

FIGURE 3.29   Rotating the diagram for vector addition

THEOREM 3.11   The matrix of R_θ is

$$\begin{bmatrix} \cos\theta & -\sin\theta \\ \sin\theta & \cos\theta \end{bmatrix}$$ □

LEMMA 18   The set of all rotations about the origin is a group of transformations of $\mathbb{R}^2$. The assignment

$$\theta \mapsto G_\theta = R_\theta$$

(for $\theta \in \mathbb{R}$) defines a one-parameter group of transformations of $\mathbb{R}^2$. Its orbits are the circles centered at the origin (including the circle of radius 0, which consists of a single point).

Proof   It is immediate from the geometric definition that $R_\theta \circ R_{\theta'} = R_{\theta+\theta'}$.
□

Here we will see that our geometric analysis has, as a side benefit, a proof of the addition formulas for sine and cosine.

COROLLARY 3.12   For any angles θ and θ',

$$\begin{aligned} \sin(\theta + \theta') &= \sin\theta\cos\theta' + \cos\theta\sin\theta' \\ \cos(\theta + \theta') &= \cos\theta\cos\theta' - \sin\theta\sin\theta' \end{aligned}$$

Proof   Multiply the matrices for R_θ and $R_{\theta'}$, and then apply the lemma.   □

3.3.3   Rotations about an arbitrary point

Actually, from the geometric point of view, there is nothing special about the origin, as far as rotations are concerned. Any point (i.e., vector) $v \in \mathbb{R}^2$ will serve just as well as a center of rotation. Thus we let R_θ^v denote a rotation of the plane about v through the angle θ. (Of course, R_θ is just equal to R_θ^0.)

LEMMA 19 $R_\theta^v = T_v \circ R_\theta \circ T_{-v}$.

Proof   The composite map effects a parallel translation of the entire picture bringing v to the origin. Then rotation through angle θ is performed at the origin, and then the picture is translated parallel, with the origin going back to v. Clearly this has the same effect as rotating the picture about v through angle θ.   □

COROLLARY 3.13   The set of all rotations about v is a group of transformations of $\mathbb{R}^2$. The assignment

$$\theta \mapsto G_\theta = R_\theta^v$$

(for $\theta \in \mathbb{R}$) defines a one-parameter group of transformations of $\mathbb{R}^2$. Its orbits are the circles centered at v (including $\{v\}$, the circle of radius 0).   □

LEMMA 20   If $\theta \neq 0, \pm 2\pi, \pm 4\pi \cdots$, then the unique fixed point of R_θ^v is v. Under this same condition, R_θ^v has no fixed line.   □

Exercise───

1. Suppose $v, w \in \mathbb{R}^2$, with $v \neq w$. What is $R_{-\theta}^v \circ R_\theta^w$? (Hint: It might be helpful to take v and w on the x_1-axis. One can gain a better intuitive understanding of composite motions by taking a piece of paper and applying the motions to it. Of course this approach does not supplant the calculations that are needed to verify the result.) Does this map belong to one of the categories already studied?

3.3.4   Reflections; the general rigid motion

Every map mentioned so far has been orientation preserving. For an example of an orientation-reversing map, we consider *reflection in a line L*. Having selected a line L, we define $R_L(P)$, for an arbitrary point P, as follows. Let F be the foot of the perpendicular from P to L. Then $R_L(P)$ is defined to be the unique point such that F is between P and $R_L(P)$ and $d(P, F) = d(F, R_L(P))$.

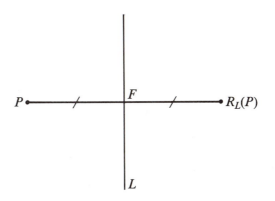

FIGURE 3.30 $R_L(P)$ is the reflection of P in L

THEOREM 3.14 R_L is a rigid motion of the plane that has L as a line of fixed points.

Sketch of proof   This can be proved by a number of applications of the theory of congruent triangles.   □

LEMMA 21   Reflection in the x_1-axis is a linear map given by the matrix

$$\begin{bmatrix} 1 & 0 \\ 0 & -1 \end{bmatrix}$$

Proof   Multiplication by this matrix maps $\langle x_1, x_2 \rangle$ to $\langle x_1, -x_2 \rangle$, and this indeed is a reflection in the x_1-axis.   □

LEMMA 22   If L is a line through the origin making an angle θ with the x_1-axis, then reflection in L is the linear map with matrix

$$\begin{bmatrix} \cos 2\theta & \sin 2\theta \\ \sin 2\theta & -\cos 2\theta \end{bmatrix}$$

Proof   It is not hard to see that $R_L = R_\theta \circ R \circ R_{-\theta}$, where R_θ and $R_{-\theta}$ are rotations about the origin, and R is reflection in the x_1-axis. Multiplying the matrices of these three maps gives the desired result.   □

Notice that, for $\theta = \pi/4$, this last matrix is $\begin{bmatrix} 0 & 1 \\ 1 & 0 \end{bmatrix}$, which is clearly the matrix P_{12} defined in (1.31) of §1.2.4. Thus, informally, the interchange of

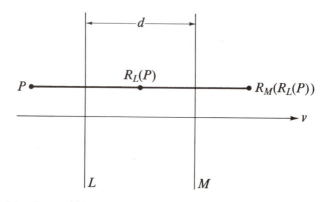

FIGURE 3.31   Lemma 23

coordinates x_1 and x_2 is the same as reflection in a line of slope 1 through the origin.

COROLLARY 3.15   Every reflection is orientation reversing.

Proof   One easily checks that the determinant of the matrix of Lemma 22 is -1, and hence reflection in any line through the origin is orientation reversing. The property of being orientation reversing does not, however, depend on the location of the origin, and therefore all reflections are orientation reversing.   □

Notice that no orientation-reversing map can be part of a one-parameter group of motions and so we do not include any results about one-parameter groups for reflections. We are now in a position to identify all rigid motions of the plane. In fact, they can all be formed from reflections, as we begin to see in Lemmas 23 and 24, which can be proved by elementary geometry.

LEMMA 23   Let L and M be parallel lines separated by a distance d. Define v to be a vector of length $2d$ and perpendicular to L such that, for any vector $w \in L$, the vectors v and $v + w$ lie on opposite sides of M (see Figure 3.31). Then $R_M \circ R_L$ is the translation T_v.   □

LEMMA 24   Let L and M be lines intersecting at point P and forming angle θ there (measured from L to M). Then $R_M \circ R_L$ is the rotation $R_{2\theta}^P$.   □

Lemmas 23 and 24 can be summed up by saying that the composition of any two reflections is either a translation or a rotation (or the identity map). We now begin our proof that in fact all rigid motions can be formed in like manner. We begin with a sort of converse to Theorem 3.14.

LEMMA 25   If R is a rigid motion and R has L as a line of fixed points, then either R is the identity function or R is reflection in L.   □

LEMMA 26   If R is a rigid motion and R has two distinct fixed points P and Q, then either R is the identity function or R is reflection in the line L joining P and Q.

Proof   It is not hard to check that $\overleftrightarrow{PQ}$ is a line of fixed points.   □

LEMMA 27   If R is a rigid motion with a fixed point P, then R is the composition of one or two reflections.

Proof   If R has a second fixed point, we may finish by appealing to Lemma 26. (The identity function is of course the product of two reflections.) Otherwise, we have $R(Q) \neq Q$ for some point Q. Now let L be the perpendicular bisector of the segment $\overline{QR(Q)}$. Elementary geometry shows that P lies on L, and so obviously $R_L \circ R$ fixes both P and Q. Therefore, by Lemma 26, $R_L \circ R$ is either a reflection or the identity motion:

$$R_L \circ R \ = \ R_1 \text{ or } 1$$

Multiplying these equations by R_L on the left, we obtain

$$R \ = \ R_L \circ R_L \circ R \ = \ R_L \circ R_1 \text{ or } R_L$$ □

THEOREM 3.16   Every orientation-preserving rigid motion of the plane is the composition of two reflections. Every orientation-reversing rigid motion of the plane is the product of three reflections.

Proof   The theorem certainly holds for the identity map, since it is equal to $R_L \circ R_L$ for any reflection R_L. On the other hand, if a rigid motion R is not the identity, then $f(P) \neq P$ for some point P. Taking L to be the perpendicular bisector of $\overline{Pf(P)}$, it is clear that the rigid motion $R_L \circ R$ has P as a fixed point. Therefore, by Lemma 27, $R_L \circ R$ is the product of one or two reflections. Now an argument like the preceding one shows easily that R is the product of either two or three reflections. Since reflections are orientation reversing and since the composition of two orientation reversing maps is orientation preserving, the division into the cases of two and three reflections follows immediately.   □

The two reflections may be the same as each other, in which case R is the identity map, or two of the three reflections may the same, resulting in a single reflection. In fact we have not yet seen a rigid motion that requires three

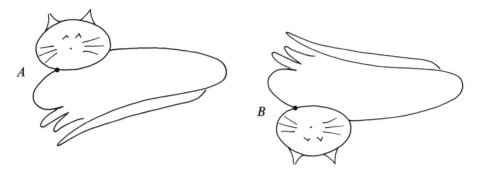

FIGURE 3.32   A cat and its image under the glide reflection G_{AB}

reflections to represent it. There do exist such rigid motions, namely, the *glide reflections*. For distinct points A and B, one may easily observe that

$$T_{AB} \circ R_L \; = \; R_L \circ T_{AB}$$

where T_{AB} is the translation defined just after Lemma 14, and R_L is reflection in the line $L = \overleftrightarrow{AB}$. We then define this composition of translation and reflection to be the *glide reflection from A to B*, and we denote it G_{AB}; see Figure 3.32.

LEMMA 28 G_{AB} is orientation reversing and has no fixed points.   □

Therefore, a glide reflection is not one of the earlier types that can be represented as a product of two or fewer reflections (for the earlier types either are orientation preserving or have a fixed point).

Actually the points A and B are not unique to the glide reflection G_{AB}.

LEMMA 29   If $\overleftrightarrow{CD} = \overleftrightarrow{AB}$, $d(C, D) = d(A, B)$ and the direction from C to D is the same as the direction[17] from A to B, then $G_{CD} = G_{AB}$.   □

On the other hand, the line $\overleftrightarrow{AB}$, the distance $d(A, B)$ and the direction from A to B are unique to G_{AB}.

---

[17] *Same direction* can be interpreted as meaning that the ray $\overrightarrow{AB}$ intersects the ray $\overrightarrow{CD}$ in a full ray.

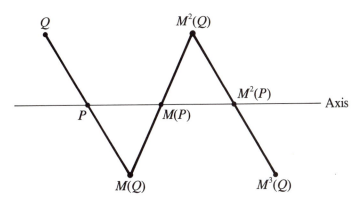

FIGURE 3.33   Finding the axis of a glide reflection

LEMMA 30   The line $\overleftrightarrow{AB}$ is the unique fixed line of G_{AB}, and the distance $d = d(A, B)$ is the constant value of $d(P, G_{AB}(P))$ for P on the line $\overleftrightarrow{AB}$. Moreover, if $G_{AB} = G_{CD}$, then $\overrightarrow{AB} \cap \overrightarrow{CD}$ is a ray.   □

Finally the last theorem of this section will show that we have now found every kind of rigid motion of the plane.

THEOREM 3.17   If M is a rigid motion that is orientation reversing and has no fixed points, then M is a glide reflection.

Sketch of proof   We need first to see that there is a point P such that $M(P)$ is between P and $M^2(P)$. We omit the details of this, referring the reader to Figure 3.33, in which Q is an arbitrary point and P is the midpoint of $\overline{QM(Q)}$. It is now not hard to check that $L = \overleftrightarrow{PM(P)}$ is a fixed line of M. Thus $R_L \circ M$ is an orientation-preserving rigid motion with L as a fixed line, and hence $R_L \circ M$ is the translation $T_{P,M(P)}$. It easily follows that $M = G_{P,M(P)}$.   □

COROLLARY 3.18   Every rigid motion of the plane is the identity, a reflection, a rotation, a translation or a glide reflection.   □

We could, therefore, at this point try to write a formula for the general rigid motion. This seems, however, to be less to the point than knowing how to analyze a rigid motion *via* translations, reflections and rotations. There is a very simple formula in §3.3.1 for translations, and the others are given by matrices. Instead of trying to combine these into one grand formula, it is probably better to use more than one set of variables in a program and transform the variables one step at a time, according to the manner in which one has analyzed the rigid motion in question. See the exercises in §3.3.9.

Exercise

1. Prove the assertion made above that an orientation-reversing rigid motion cannot belong to any one-parameter subgroup.

3.3.5 Magnifications

We are all familiar with the idea of a photographic reduction or enlargement, in which all figures are enlarged or reduced by the same scalar factor $\lambda > 0$. According to Theorem 3.19, maps that enlarge all distances by a constant factor are exactly the same as the *similarity maps* described at the start of §3.3.

THEOREM 3.19   A map $M : \mathbb{R}^2 \longrightarrow \mathbb{R}^2$ is a similarity map (i.e., it preserves angles) iff there exists a constant $\lambda > 0$ such that $d(M(v), M(w)) = \lambda d(v, w)$ for all vectors $v, w \in \mathbb{R}^2$.

Proof   If such a λ exists, then certainly M is angle-preserving by the Euclidean theory of similar triangles. Conversely, if M is angle preserving, pick any two vectors v_0 and w_0, and define λ to be

$$d(M(v_0), M(w_0))/d(v_0, w_0)$$

Now for u any vector not collinear with v_0 and w_0, it follows from angle preservation that $\triangle M(u)M(v_0)M(w_0)$ is similar to $\triangle uv_0w_0$ and hence that $d(M(u), M(w_0))/d(u, w_0) = \lambda$. Then if x is a vector not collinear with u and w_0, a similar argument shows that $d(M(u), M(x))/d(u, x) = \lambda$. Continuing in this way obviously leads to the equation $d(M(v), M(w))/d(v, w) = \lambda$ for any two points v and w of $\mathbb{R}^2$.   □

The constant λ is called the *scaling factor* of the similarity map M. It is not hard to see that, for each $\lambda > 0$, there is a unique similarity map that maps each ray through the origin to itself and has scaling factor λ. We call this similarity map *magnification by λ*, and denote it M_λ. It is not hard to see that the action of M_λ amounts to scalar multiplication by λ:

$$M_\lambda(v) = \lambda \cdot v$$

LEMMA 31   The set of all magnifications M_λ is a group of transformations of $\mathbb{R}^2$. The assignment

$$t \mapsto G_t = M_{e^t}$$

(for $t \in \mathbb{R}$) defines a one-parameter group of transformations of $\mathbb{R}^2$. Its orbits are the open rays emanating from 0 together with $\{0\}$.   □

LEMMA 32   The magnification M_λ is a linear map, whose matrix, in any co-ordinate system whatever, is

$$\begin{bmatrix} \lambda & 0 \\ 0 & \lambda \end{bmatrix}$$ □

Now that we have the magnification maps M_λ, we are actually in a position to describe the general similarity map.

THEOREM 3.20   If S is a similarity transformation, then $S = M_\lambda \circ R$ for some $\lambda > 0$ and some rigid motion R.

Proof   It is obvious that, if λ is scaling factor of S, then $M_{\lambda^{-1}} \circ S$ is a rigid motion.   □

It is surprising that, even if the R in the above theorem is a translation or a glide reflection, if $\lambda \neq 1$, then S has a fixed point, as we see in Theorem 3.21, whose proof is tantamount to that of the *Contraction Mapping Theorem* in the theory of complete metric spaces.

THEOREM 3.21   If S is a similarity map with scaling factor $\neq 1$, then S has a unique fixed point.

Proof   If S had two fixed points P and Q, then we would have

$$\lambda = \frac{\lambda d(P,Q)}{d(P,Q)} = \frac{d(S(P), S(Q))}{d(P,Q)}$$
$$= \frac{d(P,Q)}{d(P,Q)} = 1$$

This contradiction establishes the uniqueness of the fixed point. Now to establish the existence of the fixed point, we first consider the case $\lambda < 1$. We start with any point P and consider the infinite sequence

$$P_0 = P, \; P_1 = S(P), \; P_2 = S^2(P), \; \cdots, \; P_n = S^n(P), \; \cdots$$

We then observe that for any $m < n$,

$$d(P_m, P_n) \leq \sum_{i=m}^{n-1} d(P_i, P_{i+1})$$

$$\le \sum_{i=m}^{\infty} d(P_i, P_{i+1})$$

$$= \sum_{i=m}^{\infty} \lambda^i d(P_0, P_1)$$

$$= d(P_0, P_1)\frac{\lambda^m}{1-\lambda} = K\lambda^m$$

for some constant K independent of m and n. Since this last term approaches zero with m, P_i is by definition a Cauchy sequence, and therefore approaches a limit: $P_i \to P$ for some P. Since S is a continuous function, the sequence $S(P_i)$ approaches $S(P)$, but also, the sequence $S(P_i)$ differs from the sequence P_i only by not having the first term P_0. Therefore, in fact, $S(P_i)$ approaches P. Thus, by uniqueness of limits, $S(P) = P$, which is to say that P is the required fixed point of S.

Now if $\lambda > 1$, then the inverse map S^{-1} has scaling factor $1/\lambda < 1$, and hence has a fixed point P, i.e., $S^{-1}(P) = P$. It is easy to see that P is also a fixed point of S.   □

Exercises

1. Every similarity map has a fixed point, except for a translation or a glide reflection.

2. Suppose that elements of the plane $\mathbb{R}^2$ are represented as complex numbers. Recall that for $z = x + iy$ we let $\bar{z}$ denote the *complex conjugate* of z, namely $\bar{z} = x - iy$. Prove that in this framework, the similarity maps of $\mathbb{R}^2$ are precisely the maps $z \longmapsto aw + b$, for some complex numbers a and b, where w denotes either z or $\bar{z}$. (This follows easily from Corollary 3.18 and Theorem 3.20.) The orientation-reversing transformations have $w = \bar{z}$; the others have $w = z$. Identify conditions on a and b that separate rigid motions from similarity transformations with $|\lambda| \ne 1$, and that separate the various kinds of rigid motions from one another.

3. In the context of the previous exercise, give an alternate proof of Theorem 3.21. (For $z \longmapsto az + b$, this is easy linear algebra. For $z \longmapsto a\bar{z} + b = f(z)$, first get a fixed point for $z \longmapsto f(f(z))$, and then prove that this fixed point also works for f.)

4. The following riddle was popular in the author's family when he was a child and generated much heated debate. A piece of sheet metal has a circular hole in it, one inch in diameter. The metal is heated in an oven, causing the metal to expand by 5% in all directions, i.e., by a (linear) factor of 1.05. In the course of this expansion, does the hole get larger or smaller? By how much? Illustrate what happens with a computer drawing. (A somewhat larger factor may make a better drawing.)

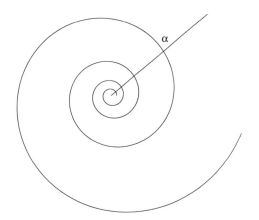

FIGURE 3.34   A logarithmic spiral: the angle α is constant

LOGARITHMIC SPIRALS (SEA SHELLS)

We can combine the effects of magnification and rotation into a single one-parameter group of similarity maps. Let us define

$$A_\theta \;=\; M_{e^{a\theta}} R_\theta \;=\; e^{a\theta} \begin{bmatrix} \cos\theta & -\sin\theta \\ \sin\theta & \cos\theta \end{bmatrix}$$

It is not hard to check that each A_θ is a similarity map and that together they form a one-parameter group. Now the orbit of $P = \langle A, 0 \rangle$ is the curve

$$P(\theta) \;=\; e^{a\theta} \begin{bmatrix} \cos\theta & -\sin\theta \\ \sin\theta & \cos\theta \end{bmatrix} \begin{bmatrix} A \\ 0 \end{bmatrix} \;=\; Ae^{a\theta} \begin{bmatrix} \cos\theta \\ \sin\theta \end{bmatrix}$$

Now it is clear that in polar coordinates, the angular coordinate of $P(\theta)$ is θ, and the radial coordinate is $Ae^{a\theta}$. Thus the orbit satisfies the polar equation

$$r \;=\; Ae^{a\theta}$$

or

$$\theta \;=\; \frac{\log r - \log A}{a}$$

It is not hard to check that every point that satisfies these equations is equal to $P(\theta)$ for some θ. Thus the orbit is the same as the curve defined by these equations, which is sometimes known as a *logarithmic spiral*. As the reader can observe by calculating, or by looking at Figure 3.34, the curve winds again and again around the origin, each time becoming larger by a factor of $e^{2\pi a}$.

FIGURE 3.35   The chambered nautilus

LEMMA   The angle α in Figure 3.34 is constant. In other words, the angle between the tangent vector and the radius vector from the origin is constant.

Proof   Immediate from the fact that each A_θ is a similarity map.   □

The logarithmic spiral can be found in nature in shells, notably the shell of the chambered nautilus (see Figure 3.35). Although we lack a complete theory of the mechanics of shell-building, we can theorize a little about how a natural process might lead to shells approximately like the logarithmic spiral. (We will reason in two dimensions rather than the naturally occurring three, without any loss of validity.) We postulate a creature that continues to grow uniformly in all its measurements: it is similar to itself at earlier times (but larger). The simplest model of this postulate is probably growth without moving: uniform expansion out from the center. But a shell won't expand once formed, and so the inhabitant of the shell has to move while expanding. Probably the simplest mathematical solution to this constrained problem is to let each element E_i on the creature's body follow a path

$$A_i e^{a\theta} \langle \cos(\theta - \phi_i), \sin(\theta - \phi_i) \rangle$$

for some amplitude A_i and phase angle ϕ_i. One of these body elements will be the part that lays down shell; thus the shell will take the shape of a logarithmic spiral.

Another plausibility argument can be based on the lemma. Assume as before, that the creature is expanding in all of its parts, so that it has no fixed unit of length to construct with. Therefore its constructions will be similar to one another over time. In particular, the angle α of outward flare (as in Figure 3.34) will remain constant, and thus the curve will follow a logarithmic spiral. Both of our arguments are unworkable for very small and very large θ: the development from a zygote must involve morphology very different from the adult form, and beyond a certain size limitations of available resources may cause growth patterns to modify. Notice also that the argument postulates no particular relationship between time t and the parameter θ. Some growth may occur fast, and other growth may occur very slowly (or growth may cease altogether). But as long as the geometric similarity conditions are met, i.e., as long as growth patterns remain constant, the angle α should remain unchanged.

Exercises

1. Prove the preceding lemma analytically, thereby obtaining a formula for α in terms of a.

2. Make pictures of logarithmic spirals.

SELF-SIMILAR FIGURES

We say that a subset F of the plane $\mathbb{R}^2$ is *self-similar* if there is a similarity map S with $\lambda \neq 1$ such that $S(F) = F$. Obviously, unless it is empty or consists only of the fixed point, such a figure F must be infinite, even unbounded. The most ready-made examples are the orbits of one-parameter groups of similarity maps. Thus for example any ray is self-similar and every logarithmic spiral is self-similar. Although there do exist non-trivial self-similar figures that do not look like logarithmic spirals, we will see an intimate connection between the two concepts.

It is helpful here to have a general notion of orbit for any group $\mathcal{G}$ of transformations (not just for a one-parameter group). If $\mathcal{G}$ is any group of transformations of X, and $P \in X$, the *orbit of P under $\mathcal{G}$* is the set $\{f(P) : f \in \mathcal{G}\}$. When we say *an orbit of P under $\mathcal{G}$*, we mean the orbit of P for some P. As before, the orbits of $\mathcal{G}$ are the simplest invariant sets for $\mathcal{G}$. Now the *orbit of P under a single transformation f* is simply the orbit of P under the group $\mathcal{G} = \{\ldots, f^{-2}, f^{-1}, f^0, f, f^2, \ldots\}$. It should be clear that a set F is self-similar iff F is a union of orbits of S for some similarity map S with $\lambda \neq 1$. In fact, these orbits, which we will call *similarity orbits*, are the smallest non-trivial self-similar figures. We will conclude the text here with a description of similarity orbits for an orientation-preserving similarity transformation, and then leave some related examples to the exercises.

Suppose that F is the similarity orbit of a point P under an orientation-preserving similarity transformation S. The reader will be asked to prove that

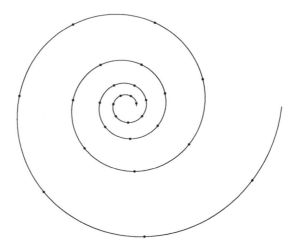

FIGURE 3.36   A similarity orbit

all the (positive and negative) powers of S are contained in a one-parameter group, either like that of Lemma 31 or like the group A_θ for the logarithmic spiral. Therefore the similarity orbit F lies in an orbit of the corresponding one-parameter group. As we have said, the two cases are that of a ray and of a logarithmic spiral. Therefore, unless F is linear (lies in a single line), it must be contained in a logarithmic spiral. In fact, as is almost evident, and as the reader may verify, *every non-linear similarity orbit consists of a set of points along a logarithmic spiral that are equally spaced with respect to their θ-coordinate* (see Figure 3.36).

Let us again consider the natural occurrence of (approximate) logarithmic spirals[18] in shells. This time we argue that they are inevitable as soon as we accept the hypothesis that the young of a species are similar to their adult forms. We observe the approximate correctness of this hypothesis all the time: baby horses look like adult horses, and so on. Thus we have similarity; *self-*similarity occurs only in those species that preserve a record of the creature's past morphology. The prime example of such a record is clearly the rigid, non-growing shell of a mollusk. This shell being approximately self-similar, it will contain (approximations of) similarity orbits. The existence of a hard shell obviously rules out rays as orbits; the only other possible orbits are those that lie on logarithmic spirals.

---

[18]For another discussion of the occurrence of shells in nature, see §12.3 of Clifford A. Pickover, *Computers, pattern, chaos and beauty: graphics from an unseen world*, St. Martin's Press, New York, 1990.

Exercises_____

1. Prove that every orientation-preserving similarity transformation S lies in one of the two types of one-parameter group. (In reality, we only defined those one-parameter subgroups for the case in which the fixed point is at the origin, and S might have its fixed point anywhere in the plane. Show how this discrepancy can be dealt with.)

2. Study the case of an orientation-reversing similarity transformation.

3. When the author was a child there was an ad in magazines that showed a Scotsman holding a bottle—not vertically, but at a slight angle. That bottle's label was a reduced version of the ad. In other words, it showed a Scotsman holding a bottle, and the label of that bottle showed a Scotsman holding a bottle, and so on ... . Assuming everything planar and assuming the label to be a precise photographic reduction of the ad, analyze the picture in terms of the concepts of this section. You might want to try making a sketch of this or a similar picture with the computer.

4. Consider the following fragmentary C program for Logo code:

```
printf("D\n");
length = 100;
reduction_factor = 0.9;
turning_angle = 10;
for (i=0; i<=100; i++)
{
    printf("F  %f\n",length);
    printf("L  %f\n",turning_angle);
    length = length * reduction_factor;
}
```

It puts out Logo code that looks something like the following:

```
D
F   100.0
L   10.0
F   90.0
L   10.0
F   81.0
    . . .
```

The exercise here is to analyze the resulting figure in terms of this section. In particular, prove that its vertices lie on a logarithmic spiral $r = Ae^{a\theta}$. (More precisely, it lies on a translate of such a spiral.) (The easy way to do this is to show that tracing out an arbitrary similarity orbit involves motions like those described here, namely, repeated turns through the same angle and forward motions that diminish in size by a constant factor. It is then a straightforward job to adjust the parameter a to match a given angular turn and reduction factor.) Make some pictures from this and similar Logo code. If the angle and the original step are made quite small, one can easily obtain some very nice renditions of logarithmic spirals in this way.

5. Analyze Figure 3.62 by the methods of this section.

6. There are four (orientation-preserving) similarity transformations S_1, S_2, S_3 and S_4, each with $\lambda = 1/3$, that map the Koch curve K_∞ (see §2.6) into itself. One of these is M_λ for $\lambda = 1/3$, as we saw at the end of §2.6, and the other three can easily be described.[19] Two of them (say S_2 and S_3) involve rotation by multiples of 60 degrees; the other two involve no rotation. Nevertheless, K_∞ is not a self-similar figure, since it is bounded and hence not closed under the action of S_i^{-1}. Obviously, for each i there is a smallest set K_∞^i containing K_∞ and self-similar with respect to S_i. Describe these sets as well as you can. (Locally K_∞^i looks just like K_∞, but it extends out to infinity.) Does there exist a rigid motion M taking K_∞^1 onto K_∞^2? If there does, what is M? If there does not, prove that it fails to exist. (The part about the existence of M could be fairly difficult.)

7. (Continuing the notation of Exercise 6.) Since K_∞ is closed under the transformations S_2 and S_3, it has similarity orbits all over the place (well, not really, but only the bounded portions of those orbits, as we remarked in Exercise 6). The first part of the exercise is to calculate the parameter a so that the S_2- or S_3-orbit of any point lies in a logarithmic spiral congruent to $r = Ae^{a\theta}$. Then identify various of these orbits in the picture. For example, one S_2-orbit consists of $f_\infty(0)$, $f_\infty(.1)$, $f_\infty(.11)$, $f_\infty(.111)$, ... (in base 4 notation). Therefore $f_\infty(1/3)$ is the fixed point of S_2. What are the coordinates of this point? There is also an S_2-orbit consisting entirely of points of the snowflake. Command the computer to make a picture that illustrates some of these facts; it could for instance show a logarithmic spiral that grazes smaller and smaller peaks of the snowflake.

CONFORMAL MAPPINGS

We remind those readers that have studied complex variables that the idea of angle-preserving transformation is not limited to collineations. If $f : \mathbb{R}^2 \longrightarrow \mathbb{R}^2$ is a differentiable map, then an angle (a pair of rays, emanating from one point P) will be mapped by f to a pair of smooth curves emanating from the point $f(P)$. If we replace the two curves by their tangent lines at $f(P)$, then we have an ordinary linear angle that we can measure in the traditional way. If this angle

---

[19]In fact, K_∞ can be described as the unique compact set that is the union of its images under S_1, S_2, S_3 and S_4. (See G. A. Edgar, op. cit., p. 107, or Michael F. Barnsley, op. cit., p. 82.)

always[20] turns out to be equal to the original angle at P, then we say that f is *angle preserving* or *conformal.*

In two dimensions, conformal mappings exist in abundance: they are the same as analytic functions of a complex variable. We may think of a vector $\langle x_1, x_2 \rangle$ as equivalent to a complex number $z = x_1 + ix_2$, thereby identifying $\mathbb{R}^2$ with the *complex plane* $\mathbb{C}$. Under this identification, a complex function $f : \mathbb{C} \longrightarrow \mathbb{C}$ is the same thing as a map $f : \mathbb{R}^2 \longrightarrow \mathbb{R}^2$. It is an elementary and basic result of complex analysis, that *if f is differentiable, then f is conformal at all points z where $f'(z) \neq 0$.* Here, by *differentiable*, we mean that df/dz exists; this is much stronger than saying that f is differentiable in the sense of functions $\mathbb{R}^2 \longrightarrow \mathbb{R}^2$. Functions $f(z)$ with the property that $f'(z)$ exists for all z are called *analytic* functions. (One also considers functions that are analytic only on subsets of $\mathbb{R}^2$.) Any polynomial or everywhere convergent power series in z defines an analytic function, and the latter class includes such functions as $\sin z$ and e^z. When we come to exercises on plane maps in §3.3.9, the reader with some experience in functions of a complex variable may add these to his or her portfolio. (See Exercise 4 of §2.7 for one way of drawing conformal mappings.)

3.3.6   Area-preserving transformations

We already saw in §1.3.7 that a *linear* transformation is area preserving iff the determinant of its matrix is either 1 or -1. It is also easily seen that a translation is area preserving, and therefore it is easy to see that every rigid motion is area preserving.

This last fact can also be seen from pure geometry: If f is a rigid motion and R is a rectangle measuring $a \times b$, then $f[R]$ is also a rectangle measuring $a \times b$. Since both rectangles have area ab, it follows that area is preserved for rectangles. It now follows that area is preserved for all figures, by an argument like the one already seen in §1.3.7.

Of course the magnification M_λ of §3.3.5 is *not* area preserving (unless $\lambda = 1$), since its determinant is λ^2.

In this section we will look at some examples of area-preserving transformations, both in the linear and non-linear case. In §3.3.7, we will present a more thorough analysis of the linear case.

In §1.2.4 we introduced the matrices

$$A_{12}(\mu) = \begin{bmatrix} 1 & \mu \\ 0 & 1 \end{bmatrix} \quad \text{and} \quad A_{21}(\mu) = \begin{bmatrix} 1 & 0 \\ \mu & 1 \end{bmatrix}$$

As we pointed out in §1.3.5, these matrices have determinant 1, and so the associated linear transformation, which we denote $S_{12}(\mu) : \mathbb{R}^2 \longrightarrow \mathbb{R}^2$, is area-

---

[20]Well, not *always* equal to the original angle at P; as noted in the following, exceptions necessarily occur when $f'(z) = 0$.

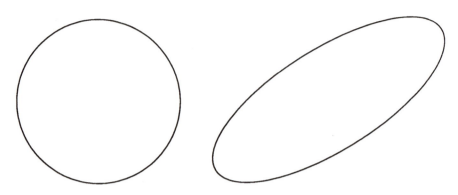

FIGURE 3.37 A 45-degree shear acting on the unit circle

preserving. In fact $S_{12}(\mu)$ has a very nice geometric description. For any line M parallel to the x_1-axis, given by the equation $x_2 = C$, a typical point $\langle x_1, C \rangle$ on M is moved by $S_{12}(\mu)$ as follows:

$$\begin{bmatrix} 1 & \mu \\ 0 & 1 \end{bmatrix} \begin{bmatrix} x_1 \\ C \end{bmatrix} = \begin{bmatrix} x_1 + \mu C \\ C \end{bmatrix} \tag{3.20}$$

In other words, the map $S_{12}(\mu)$ has the effect of sliding each line M parallel to the x_1-axis along itself, by an amount proportional to the distance of M from the x_1-axis. Such a map is called a *shear*. Of course shears can be defined relative to any line L in place of the x_1-axis. For any line L, we define $S_L(\mu)$ to be the map that slides each line M parallel to L along itself, through a distance μC, where C is the distance from M to L. (The direction convention is that if $\mu > 0$, then M should move to the right as seen from L.) According to Lemma 33, we in principle have a formula for every shear.

LEMMA 33 For any shear $S_L(\mu)$, there exists a rigid motion R such that the matrix of $R^{-1} \circ S_L(\mu) \circ R$ is $A_{12}(\mu)$.

Sketch of proof In fact R can be any rigid motion that maps L onto the x_1-axis. □

The parameter μ can be identified as follows: if N is any line perpendicular to L, then $\mu = \tan \theta$, where θ is the angle formed between $S_L(\mu)[N]$ and N (with θ considered positive if $S_L[N]$ has positive slope when viewed from L). We may then refer to $S_L(\mu)$ as a θ-*shear*, and we may refer to θ as *the angle of S_L*.

LEMMA 34 For a fixed line L, the set of all shears $S_L(\mu)$ is a group of transformations of $\mathbb{R}^2$. The assignment

FIGURE 3.38   A cat and its image under the λ-compression C_λ

$$\mu \mapsto G_\mu = S_L(\mu)$$

(for $\mu \in \mathbb{R}$) defines a one-parameter group of transformations of $\mathbb{R}^2$. Its orbits are the lines parallel to the x_2-axis.   □

Now the shears $S_{12}(\mu)$ can be used for an analysis of the arbitrary area-preserving linear map $f : \mathbb{R}^2 \longrightarrow \mathbb{R}^2$ that derives from the column reduction of §1.2.4. Starting with an arbitrary 2×2 matrix A with determinant ± 1, our first step in a column reduction of A may perhaps be an interchange of the first two columns (corresponding to a reflection in the 45-degree line through the origin). Our next step is a multiplication on the left by $M_1(\lambda)$, followed by $A_{12}(-\mu)$ for some μ, in order to get the first row equal to $\begin{bmatrix} 1 & 0 \end{bmatrix}$. There follows another left multiplication by $M_2(\kappa)$, followed by $A_{21}(-\nu)$, for some κ and ν. We finally observe that, by the remarks in §1.3.6, the determinant $D_2(A)$ is $\kappa\lambda$, and so $\kappa = \pm 1/\lambda$. We have therefore proved Theorem 3.22.

THEOREM 3.22   If A is the matrix of an area-preserving linear transformation, then, for some $\lambda, \mu, \nu \in \mathbb{R}$ with $\lambda > 0$,

$$A = R\, M_1(\pm\lambda^{-1})\, A_{12}(\mu)\, M_2(\lambda)\, A_{21}(\nu),$$

where R is either a reflection or the identity map.   □

An interesting special case occurs when R is the identity and $\mu = \nu = 0$. For $\lambda > 0$, the λ-*compression* is the matrix

$$C_\lambda = \begin{bmatrix} \lambda^{-1} & 0 \\ 0 & \lambda \end{bmatrix}$$

We may also let C_λ denote the linear transformation associated to this matrix. This is the effect that one can see in stretching out an elastic material (assuming its thickness does not change). For instance a section of rubber band might be pulled to twice its length, but then its width would have to be divided by two.

LEMMA 35   The set of all compressions C_λ is a group of transformations of $\mathbb{R}^2$. The assignment

$$t \mapsto G_t = S_{e^t} = \begin{bmatrix} e^{-t} & 0 \\ 0 & e^t \end{bmatrix}$$

(for $t \in \mathbb{R}$) defines a one-parameter group of transformations of $\mathbb{R}^2$. Each orbit is either $\{0\}$ or a branch of a hyperbola $x_1 x_2 = K$. $\square$

Of course stretching and compression can occur in directions other than along the x_1- and x_2-axes. We will see examples of this in §3.3.7.

We now look briefly at a non-linear analog of Equation (3.20). As we said above, this equation yields a parallel displacement of $\langle x_2, x_1 \rangle$—to the right or to the left—that depends only on x_2, not on x_1. One can imagine a thin strip at height x_2 sliding right or left—as a unit—by a fixed amount. The fact that locally this thin strip experiences a rigid motion can be advanced as another explanation, albeit an intuitive one, that area is preserved by shears. But from this intuitive point of view, there is no reason that the amount of horizontal motion has to be a linear function of x_2, or in fact any special sort of function. Therefore, by analogy with Equation (3.20), we define a *generalized horizontal shear* to be any map $f : \mathbb{R}^2 \longrightarrow \mathbb{R}^2$ that has the form

$$f(x_1, x_2) = \langle x_1 + g(x_2), x_2 \rangle,$$

for some differentiable function $g : \mathbb{R} \longrightarrow \mathbb{R}$.

THEOREM 3.23   A generalized horizontal shear is area preserving.

Proof   The Jacobian of f, introduced in §1.3.7, namely,

$$J(x, y) = \det \begin{bmatrix} \dfrac{\partial f_1}{\partial x_1} & \dfrac{\partial f_1}{\partial x_2} \\ \dfrac{\partial f_2}{\partial x_1} & \dfrac{\partial f_2}{\partial x_2} \end{bmatrix}$$

is easily calculated to be equal to

$$\det \begin{bmatrix} 1 & g'(x_2) \\ 0 & 1 \end{bmatrix}$$

which is seen to be equal to 1.   □

There is obviously a corresponding notion of generalized shear parallel to any line, and these can be composed to form all sorts of non-linear area-preserving transformations. For example, the map

$$f(x_1, x_2) = \langle x_1 + x_2^2, \ x_2 + x_1^2 + 2x_1 x_2^2 + x_2^4 \rangle$$

is composed of one generalized horizontal shear and one generalized vertical shear.

Exercises

1. Examine the matrices

$$H_t = \begin{bmatrix} e^t & 0 \\ 0 & 1 \end{bmatrix}$$

   from the point of view of this section. (H_t can be built from compressions and magnifications. The matrices H_t form a one-parameter group.) What effect do these matrices have on ellipses?

2. **Using shears to rotate pixeled images.** Shears (parallel to either axis) are very easy to carry out on pixeled images, for the following reason. Suppose, for definiteness, that we are speaking of $S_L(\mu)$, for L a horizontal line. Then $S_L(\mu)$ merely slides each row of pixels a certain distance, which is proportional to the distance of that row from L. (Clearly the distance through which they are slid must be rounded to the nearest pixel, but that is an easily computed approximation, with an easily managed error.) This observation is made more useful by the further observation that every rotation can be analyzed[21] as a product of horizontal and vertical shears. We will concentrate on the case of rotations about the origin, but our analysis is easily modified to handle the other cases as well. The first part of the exercise is to prove that the matrix product

$$\begin{bmatrix} 1 & 0 \\ \tan\theta & 1 \end{bmatrix} \begin{bmatrix} 1 & -\sin 2\theta \\ 0 & 1 \end{bmatrix} \begin{bmatrix} 1 & 0 \\ \tan\theta & 1 \end{bmatrix}$$

   is a rotation. The second part is to actually implement this on some pixeled data. (This should not be undertaken except by those who have gained some experience with pixeled images, through reading §2.7 or elsewhere.)

---

[21] Alan W. Paeth has informed the author that this analysis goes back to Gauss. For more information see Paeth's article, "A Fast Algorithm for General Raster Rotation," 179–195 in *Graphics Gems* [op. cit.].

3.3.7 Connections with eigenvalues and eigenvectors

Now let us see how the results of §1.4 help us analyze a linear map $f : \mathbb{R}^2 \longrightarrow \mathbb{R}^2$. Of course all four entries of a matrix A representing f are real numbers, and so the characteristic equation (1.45) has real coefficients. From the theory of equations we therefore know that the eigenvalues are either both real or both complex and not real, and that in the latter case one eigenvalue is the complex conjugate of the other. We will return to that case in a moment, looking first at the easier case of real eigenvalues λ_1 and λ_2. If $\lambda_2 = 0$, then we have the constant map 0 or we have

$$B^{-1}AB = \begin{bmatrix} \lambda_1 & 0 \\ 0 & 0 \end{bmatrix} \quad \text{or} \quad \begin{bmatrix} 0 & 1 \\ 0 & 0 \end{bmatrix} = \begin{bmatrix} 1 & 0 \\ 0 & 0 \end{bmatrix} \begin{bmatrix} 0 & 1 \\ 1 & 0 \end{bmatrix}$$

In all these cases the map is seen to be a combination of magnifications, projections, and possibly a reflection. The case of $\lambda_1 = 0$ is of course similar. Therefore we now consider the case $\lambda_1 \neq 0 \neq \lambda_2$.

If $\lambda_1 = \lambda_2$, then either f is the magnification M_{λ_1} of §3.3.5, or f can be represented by the matrix

$$\begin{bmatrix} \lambda_1 & 1 \\ 0 & \lambda_1 \end{bmatrix}$$

This, in turn, is a combination of a magnification with a shear. Finally, there is the possibility that λ_1 and λ_2 are distinct and non-zero.

Suppose therefore that $\lambda_1 \neq 0 \neq \lambda_2 \neq \lambda_1$ and that

$$B^{-1}AB = \begin{bmatrix} \lambda_1 & 0 \\ 0 & \lambda_2 \end{bmatrix}$$

Taking μ to be $\sqrt{|\lambda_1 \lambda_2|}$, we have

$$B^{-1}AB = \begin{bmatrix} \mu & 0 \\ 0 & \mu \end{bmatrix} \begin{bmatrix} \lambda_1' & 0 \\ 0 & \lambda_2' \end{bmatrix}$$

where $\lambda_1' \lambda_2' = \pm 1$. Of course the first matrix here is simply the magnification M_μ. The second matrix represents a transformation that is like the compressions of §3.3.6, except that the shrinking and magnifications do not necessarily occur along perpendicular axes. (If $\lambda_1 \lambda_2 = -1$, then the second matrix is a product of such a compression-like matrix with a reflection.)

___

Exercise_____

1. Show that the matrix

$$\begin{bmatrix} 24.5 & -30 \\ 18 & -22 \end{bmatrix}$$

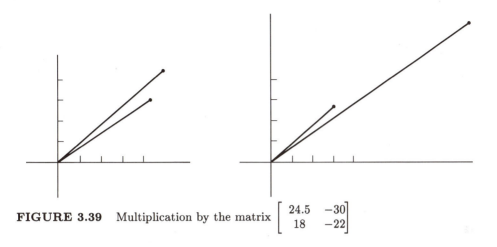

FIGURE 3.39 Multiplication by the matrix $\begin{bmatrix} 24.5 & -30 \\ 18 & -22 \end{bmatrix}$

(which has determinant $= 1$) doubles all vectors that are multiples of $\langle 4, 3 \rangle$, and divides by two all vectors that are multiples of $\langle 5, 4 \rangle$. Compare this analysis with an analysis of the matrix in the style of §3.3.6.

Finally, in the domain of real eigenvalues, there remains the case of

$$B^{-1}AB = \begin{bmatrix} \lambda & 1 \\ 0 & \lambda \end{bmatrix}$$

The reader is asked to show that this is composed of a magnification and a shear.

Finally, we come to the case of complex non-real eigenvalues.[22] What really happens here is this. We start with an ordinary real matrix A, while thinking of the entries as possibly complex numbers. Analyzing A by the methods of this section, we find eigenvectors v_1 and v_2 all right; the only problems are that the associated eigenvectors are complex numbers $\lambda_1 = r_1 e^{i\theta_1}$ and $\lambda_2 = r_2 e^{i\theta_2}$, and that the eigenvectors themselves have complex coordinates. Since the eigenvalues are the two solutions of a quadratic equation with real coefficients, they must be complex conjugate to each other: $\lambda_1 = r e^{i\theta}$ and $\lambda_2 = \overline{\lambda_1} = r e^{-i\theta}$. First let us notice that now we may write $A = M_r A'$, where M_r is magnification by r and A' has eigenvalues $e^{i\theta}$ and $e^{-i\theta}$

Now let v be an eigenvector of A' associated to the eigenvalue $e^{i\theta}$, in other words, $Av = e^{i\theta}v$. Applying complex conjugation, since all entries of A are real, we have

---

[22] The analysis here is much the same as the analysis alluded to in one of the exercises at the end of §1.5.4.

$$A\bar{v} = \overline{Av} = \overline{e^{i\theta}v} = e^{-i\theta}\bar{v}$$

and hence $\bar{v}$ is an eigenvector with eigenvalue $e^{-i\theta}$. We now consider a new basis of $\mathbb{C}^2$, consisting of $u_1 = i(v - \bar{v})$ and $u_2 = v + \bar{v}$. It is not hard to check that these two vectors are linearly independent, and moreover the elementary theory of complex numbers tells us that u_1 and u_2 have real entries and hence lie in $\mathbb{R}^2$. Therefore we may think of $\langle u_1, u_2 \rangle$ as *a basis of $\mathbb{R}^2$*. To see how A' acts on this basis, we calculate

$$\begin{aligned}
A'u_1 &= A'i(v - \bar{v}) = ie^{i\theta}v - ie^{-i\theta}\bar{v} \\
&= i\cos\theta(v - \bar{v}) - \sin\theta(v + \bar{v}) \\
&= \cos\theta u_1 - \sin\theta u_2
\end{aligned}$$

and

$$\begin{aligned}
A'u_2 &= A'v + \bar{v} = e^{i\theta}v + e^{-i\theta}\bar{v} \\
&= i\sin\theta(v - \bar{v}) + \cos\theta(v + \bar{v}) \\
&= i\cos\theta u_1 + \sin\theta u_2
\end{aligned}$$

Therefore, on the basis $\langle u_1, u_2 \rangle$, the matrix A' acts simply as a rotation. Therefore, since the vectors u_1 and u_2 may not be perpendicular to each other, nor even of the same length, we think of matrices of this type as *skew rotations*. In fact, we have proved Theorem 3.24.

THEOREM 3.24   For any non-zero 2×2 matrix A of real numbers, there exists an invertible 2×2 matrix B of real numbers such that either

$$B^{-1}AB = r\begin{bmatrix} 1 & 0 \\ 0 & 0 \end{bmatrix}$$

for some real r, or

$$B^{-1}AB = r\begin{bmatrix} \lambda_1 & 0 \\ 0 & \lambda_2 \end{bmatrix}$$

for some real λ_1, λ_2 with $\lambda_1\lambda_2 = \pm 1$, or

$$B^{-1}AB = \begin{bmatrix} \lambda & 1 \\ 0 & \lambda \end{bmatrix}$$

for some non-zero real λ, or

$$B^{-1}AB = r\begin{bmatrix} \cos\theta & -\sin\theta \\ \sin\theta & \cos\theta \end{bmatrix}.$$

for some real r and θ.   □

Exercise

1. Examine the matrices

$$\begin{bmatrix} 4 & 0 \\ 0 & .25 \end{bmatrix} \text{ and } \begin{bmatrix} \sqrt{2} & -\sqrt{2} \\ \sqrt{2}/2 & 0 \end{bmatrix}$$

from the point of view of the last theorem. Compare this analysis with an analysis of the two matrices in the style of §3.3.6.

We also could look at maps $\mathbb{R}^2 \longrightarrow \mathbb{R}^2$ that are defined by *symmetric* matrices as in §1.5. By Theorem 1.62, if A is any symmetric 2×2 matrix of real numbers, there is an orthonormal basis v_1, v_2 such that A is diagonal with respect to this basis. Supposing A to be non-singular, it has a non-zero determinant D. Therefore, in this coordinate system,

$$A = \begin{bmatrix} \mu & 0 \\ 0 & \mu \end{bmatrix} \begin{bmatrix} \lambda_1 & 0 \\ 0 & \lambda_2 \end{bmatrix}$$

where $\mu^2 = |\det A|$ and $\lambda_1 \lambda_2 = \pm 1$. The first of these two matrices is a magnification, and the second is either a compression or a compression combined with a reflection.

3.3.8   Affine maps and cubic Bézier curves

In any vector space $\mathbf{V}$, we say that a vector w is an *affine combination* of the vectors v_i iff there exist scalars $\langle \alpha_1, \cdots, \alpha_m \rangle$ such that

$$\sum_{j=1}^{m} \alpha_i \cdot v_i = w \tag{3.21}$$

and such that

$$\sum_{j=1}^{m} \alpha_i = 1 \tag{3.22}$$

In other words, an affine combination is a linear combination by scalars that satisfy (3.22).

Affine combinations are important because they are preserved both by linear maps and by translations. A linear map $f : \mathbf{V} \longrightarrow \mathbf{W}$ is of course a map that preserves every linear combination. I. e. f is linear iff

$$f\left(\sum_{j=1}^{m} \alpha_j \cdot v_j\right) = \sum_{j=1}^{m} \alpha_j \cdot f(v_j) \tag{3.23}$$

for all linear combinations $\sum_{j=1}^{m} \alpha_i \cdot v_i$. We now define an *affine transformation* $f : V \longrightarrow W$ to be a function $f : V \longrightarrow W$ that satisfies (3.23) for every *affine combination* $\sum_{j=1}^{m} \alpha_i \cdot v_i$, i.e. that satisfies (3.23) whenever $\sum_{j=1}^{m} \alpha_i = 1$. Every linear map is of course affine, but the converse is false.

LEMMA 36   Let V and W be vector spaces, and f an arbitrary function from V to W. Then f is an affine transformation iff there exists $a \in W$ and there exists a linear transformation $g : V \longrightarrow W$ such that $f(v) = g(v) + a$ for all $v \in V$.

Proof   It is not hard to check that if such a and g exist, then f is an affine transformation. Conversely, let us suppose that f is affine and prove the existence of the required g and a. To begin, we simply define $a = f(0)$, and then define $g(v)$ to be $f(v) - a$ for all $v \in V$. Clearly all that remains is to prove that this g is linear. So, we calculate

$$
\begin{aligned}
g\left(\sum_{j=1}^{m} \alpha_j \cdot v_j\right) &= f\left(\sum_{j=1}^{m} \alpha_j \cdot v_j\right) - a \\
&= f\left[\left(1 - \sum_{j=1}^{m} \alpha_j\right) \cdot 0 + \sum_{j=1}^{m} \alpha_j \cdot v_j\right] - a \\
&= \left[\left(1 - \sum_{j=1}^{m} \alpha_j\right) \cdot f(0) + \sum_{j=1}^{m} \alpha_j \cdot f(v_j)\right] - a \\
&= \sum_{j=1}^{m} \alpha_j \cdot f(v_j) - \left(\sum_{j=1}^{m} \alpha_j\right) \cdot a \\
&= \sum_{j=1}^{m} \alpha_j \cdot g(v_j)
\end{aligned}
$$

(At one stage in this calculation we used the linearity of f with respect to a certain affine combination.)   □

Now in case V and W are the same space, Lemma 36 can be interpreted as follows. A map $f : V \longrightarrow V$ given by $f(v) = g(v) + a$ for a linear map g is simply *the composition of the linear map g with the translation $v \mapsto v + a$.* Therefore, the lemma can be summed up by saying that *the maps from V to itself that preserve affine combinations are linear maps and translations and any composites of them.*

The above observation is important in the theory of Bézier curves for the following reason. Reading over §3.2, the student may observe that every linear combination in that section is in fact an affine combination. For the main cubic Bézier formula (3.13), this is expressly stated in part (4) of Lemma 10. The linear combinations appearing in the A-frame conditions (3.15) and (3.16) are clearly affine combinations. The construction of **A**-frames in §3.2.4 involves only affine combinations (e.g., the average of two points, or one of their trisection points). Finally, in the construction of a piecewise cubic interpolant in §3.2.5, the points G_i are affine combinations of the points A_i, as expressed by Equations (3.17) and (3.18). In fact, it is apparent from §3.2.5 that there is an invertible square matrix $[a_{ij}]$ such that each G_i is $\sum_j a_{ij} G_j$ and such that each row of a_{ij} sums to 1. In fact, the points A_i are also affine combinations of the points G_i, by Lemma 37.

LEMMA 37 Let B be an invertible square matrix such that each row of B sums to 1. Then the same is true of the inverse matrix B^{-1}.

Proof The condition on row sums is equivalent to the assertion that $Bv = v$, where $v = \langle 1, \cdots, 1 \rangle$. Clearly $Bv = v$ iff $B^{-1}v = v$. $\qquad\square$

Thus all the constructions of Bézier curves, B-splines and interpolants that involve linear combinations actually use only affine combinations. Therefore, these constructions are preserved by all affine transformations. Let us take a detailed look at what this means in the simplest case, namely, the case of a single cubic Bézier curve with control points P_0, P_1, P_2 and P_3. As in §3.2.2, the formula for $B(t)$ is

$$(1-t)^3 P_0 + 3t(1-t)^2 P_1 + 3t^2(1-t)P_2 + t^3 P_3$$

Now if f is any affine transformation, f moves $B(t)$ to

$$f\left((1-t)^3 P_0 + 3t(1-t)^2 P_1 + 3t^2(1-t)P_2 + t^3 P_3\right)$$

which is equal, since f is affine, to

$$(1-t)^3 f(P_0) + 3t(1-t)^2 f(P_1) + 3t^2(1-t)f(P_2) + t^3 f(P_3)$$

This last expression is the formula for the cubic Bézier curve with control points $f(P_0), \cdots, f(P_3)$. In other words, *the effect of an affine transformation f on a cubic Bézier curve can be achieved by simply applying f to the control points.*

It is now apparent that this line of reasoning applies equally well to all the related constructions, such as **A**-frames, B-splines and piecewise cubic interpolants. Thus, for example, piecewise cubic interpolants are preserved under all affine transformations. If $\gamma(t)$ is the piecewise cubic interpolant through $G_0, \cdots, G_n$, and f is any affine map—e.g., any rigid motion, shear, compression, etc.— then $f(\gamma(t))$ is the piecewise cubic interpolant through $f(G_0), \cdots, f(G_n)$.

Exercises

1. Let **V** and **W** be vector spaces, and let $f: V \longrightarrow W$ be an arbitrary function. Prove that f is an affine transformation iff f satisfies

$$f\left((1-\lambda)\cdot u + \lambda\cdot v\right) \;=\; (1-\lambda)\cdot f(u) + \lambda\cdot f(v)$$

for all $u, v \in V$ and all scalars λ.

2. The student who has already built a B-spline generator in §3.2.5 could easily obtain visual confirmation of the results of this section as follows. Make a list of six or eight points A_i, and draw the B-spline that they determine. Then rotate these points through some fixed angle and draw the B-spline determined by the rotated points. If the two curves are drawn on separate pieces of paper, it will be easy to determine experimentally that one is the rotational image of the other.

3.3.9 Exercises on maps $\mathbb{R}^2 \longrightarrow \mathbb{R}^2$

Each student should write programs to exhibit all of the kinds of maps $\mathbb{R}^2 \longrightarrow \mathbb{R}^2$ that we have seen in §3.3, and moreover to illustrate all the various forms of analysis of these maps that we have seen. Each student should begin with a test pattern. Some interesting test patterns were given as exercises in §3.1, such as patterns of ellipses and hyperbolas. A rectangular grid is less than ideal, because it doesn't have enough distinguishing features. A picture of something with a lot of detail is better. In any case, it is important that the pattern should contain only very small segments. (The student who has developed a computer program for piecewise cubic curves (§3.2.5 and §3.2.6) could make pictures in that way, but one can also do the exercises here without those tools.) Then the student should develop a portfolio of pictures indicating how this picture is transformed under all the types of maps that we discussed. Try to make the pictures as graphically effective as possible, experimenting with values of the parameters that best show the effects of the various kinds of maps. (One should plainly see the original pattern and also plainly see the distortion that it has undergone.) Exercises 1–4 indicate some (but not necessarily all) of the points that could be illustrated.

Exercises_____

1. For each of the one-parameter groups mentioned in §3.3, make several pictures showing the varying distortion of the picture for values of the parameter close to zero and values farther from zero. (Imagining that the parameter t represents time, ideally the one-parameter subgroup could be represented by a movie. One may have to settle for a few still pictures taken at various times.)

2. Experiment with expanding our device-independent language to include commands for some or all of the rigid motions. Write an interpreter for the expanded language and use it to build your portfolio of pictures of motions. In general, a command would contain a letter suggesting the motion and the

relevant parameters. One should have in mind a convention for the composition of two motions. (For example, one could stipulate that if a translation T_v is requested after a request for a rotation R_θ, then the motion currently in effect is $T_v \circ R_\theta$.) Some possible command types are

R Rotate through whatever angle is specified.

M Move (i.e., translate) by the vector whose coordinates are given.

I Reset transformation to the Identity Function.

{ A bracketing command; transformations after here to take effect only until matching } command. (This refinement will take an extra effort to program, and could certainly be omitted in one's first version of this language.)

} Bracketing command matching {.

3. Some pictures could show eigenvectors, or vectors u_1, u_2 introduced just before Theorem 3.24.

4. Show the effect of some non-linear area-preserving maps on your test pattern.

3.4   Some graphic topics in calculus

In this section we present some advanced geometric topics from calculus that are particularly amenable to illustration by computer drawings. Three semesters of university calculus would be an adequate preparation for study of this material. Chapters 4 through 6 do not depend on this material, and hence it could easily be skipped.

The theorems announced here must be proved independently of any drawings. Historically, the ideas are much older[23] than automatic computing. Nevertheless, the ideas are pictorial in nature, and the computer is particularly useful, since precise pictures are difficult to draw by hand.

In this treatise we are interested more in making effective drawings of mathematical phenomena than in rigorous proofs from analysis. Therefore, our presentation of this material is simple and direct, omitting a number of fine points. In particular, we assume differentiability without question, wherever needed. We also give no formal treatment of the *cusps* that arise naturally in the treatment of evolutes, allowing the pictures to speak for us on this topic.

The reader should note, however, that almost all the problems in §3.4 require functions that are known to be differentiable, in a very effective sense. There must be formulas for the derivatives. If one tries to apply these concepts to functions that arise from raw data, they are not well posed. For example, the

---

[23] Euclid's Book V contained all the ideas for computing evolutes of conic sections. The subject was taken up again by Huyghens, who wrote *Horologium oscillatorium* in Paris in 1673. In this work he got equations for the evolute of a parabola and of a cycloid. Information from H. Eves, *An Introduction to the History of Mathematics*, Holt Rinehart and Winston, New York, 1969.

continental boundaries that we will draw in a later chapter have no well-defined tangent lines.

3.4.1   The family of lines tangent to a curve

Suppose that a plane curve Γ is given locally by the parametric representation

$$\gamma : I \longrightarrow \mathbb{R}^2,$$

where I is an interval of $\mathbb{R}$. We will let γ_1 and γ_2 denote the two components of γ; in other words, $\gamma(t_0) = \langle \gamma_1(t_0), \gamma_2(t_0) \rangle$. The reader may recall from a calculus class that, for any fixed value of the parameter t_0, the vector $\gamma'(t_0) = \langle \gamma_1'(t_0), \gamma_2'(t_0) \rangle$ points in the direction of the curve Γ at the point $\langle \gamma_1(t_0), \gamma_2(t_0) \rangle$ of Γ. Now clearly the line parametrized by

$$\delta(t) = \langle x_0 + t\, \gamma_1'(t_0),\ y_0 + t\, \gamma_2'(t_0) \rangle$$

passes through $\langle x_0, y_0 \rangle$ in the same direction as Γ and hence is tangent to Γ at $\langle x_0, y_0 \rangle$. This equation may be rewritten as

$$x \quad = \quad x_0 + t\, \gamma_1'(t_0) \tag{3.24}$$

$$y \quad = \quad y_0 + t\, \gamma_2'(t_0) \tag{3.25}$$

and by eliminating the parameter t we obtain the single linear equation

$$(y - y_0)\gamma_1'(t_0) = (x - x_0)\gamma_2'(t_0). \tag{3.26}$$

Generally in §3.4 we will use t_0 for a parameter describing the curve Γ, with $\langle x_0, y_0 \rangle$ denoting a point on Γ. On the other hand, the unsubscripted pair $\langle x, y \rangle$ denotes a point on a tangent line (with parameter t, if one is needed).

3.4.2   Drawing the family of tangent lines

Section 3.4.1 makes it possible to draw the family of tangent lines to any curve Γ for which γ_1' and γ_2' can be evaluated. Probably the most practical course of action is to use Equations (3.24) and (3.25). The drawing of a single tangent line is a simple matter of fixing t_0, calculating the associated point $x_0 = \gamma_1(t_0)$, $y_0 = \gamma_2(t_0)$, calculating the derivatives $\gamma_0'(t_0)$, $\gamma_1'(t_0)$, and then plotting the lines determined by Equations (3.24) and (3.25).

One cannot, of course, plot the entire tangent line L, but only a segment $I \subseteq L$, which we will call the *displayed segment*. The exact choice of I cannot be dictated mathematically, but rather depends on the aesthetics of the picture being designed. One simple rule is to select in advance a rectangle R (possibly the whole piece of paper, possibly a smaller rectangle), and define I to be $R \cap L$. (Here is one place that one might find it handy to have done the fifth exercise at the end of §2.3.1.) Another simple rule—which we followed in drawing Figure

3.41—is to make all segments I the same length. In any case, one will usually want to take the two endpoints of I to have parameter values t of opposite signs, so as to show the point where L meets Γ as a tangent line. If one is making several pictures of this sort, it might be wise to write a subroutine that—given say x_0, y_0, $\gamma_1'(t_0)$ and $\gamma_2'(t_0)$—will output the two endpoints of $L \cap R$.

To depict the *family* of all tangent lines to Γ, we do not in fact draw them all (large regions of the picture would be solid black), but rather draw enough of them to suggest how they all look. Basically, this means that the parameter t_0 appearing in Equations (3.24) and (3.25) should be stepped through various values, and for each value of t_0 we draw the appropriate displayed segment of the tangent line L.

As an example, we may consider the ellipse

$$\gamma(t_0) = \langle a \cos t_0, b \sin t_0 \rangle$$

For this curve, we have $\gamma_1'(t_0) = -a \sin t_0$, and $\gamma_2'(t_0) = b \cos t_0$. Therefore, Equations (3.24) and (3.25) become

$$x = a \cos t_0 - at \sin t_0 \tag{3.27}$$

$$y = b \sin t_0 + bt \cos t_0 \tag{3.28}$$

Now if we wish our picture to be contained in the rectangle R defined by

$$|x| \leq A, \quad |y| \leq B,$$

then we use (3.27) to rewrite $x = \pm A$ as

$$a \cos t_0 - at \sin t_0 = \pm A$$

and solve for t, obtaining two solutions t_1 and t_2, with $t_1 < t_2$. Similarly we find t-values t_3 and t_4 with $t_3 \leq t_4$ that represent solutions of $y = \pm B$. Now define t_5 to be the larger of t_1 and t_3 and define t_6 to be the smaller of t_2 and t_4 (see Figure 3.40). Now the displayed interval will go from the t-value t_5 to the t-value t_6. (Warning: if $t_5 > t_6$, then the tangent line L does not meet the rectangle R, and so $I = R \cap L = \emptyset$. This can happen if A and B are small compared to a and b.) In Figure 3.41 we sketch a completed picture of tangent lines to an ellipse.

Exercises

1. Complete the job of making a picture of the family of all tangent lines to an ellipse. It may be interesting to make two pictures, one that contains the ellipse itself, and one that does not.

2. Do the same for parabolas and hyperbolas, or any other curves of your choosing.

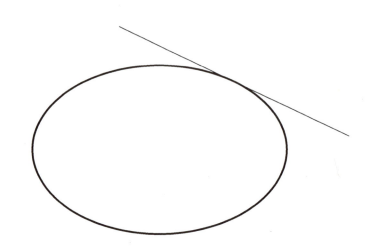

FIGURE 3.40   A tangent line to an ellipse

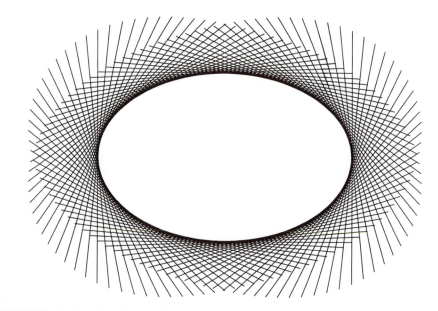

FIGURE 3.41   The family of tangent lines to an ellipse

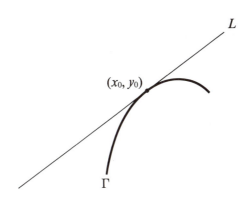

FIGURE 3.42 Γ lies all on one side of L

3.4.3   The enveloping curve of a family of lines

Thus for each curve Γ (parametrized by γ), there exists a family of lines L defined by Equations (3.24) and (3.25). We call this a *parametrized family of lines*, since there is one line $L(t_0)$ for each value of the parameter t_0. On the other hand, it is entirely possible to be given a parametrized family of lines $L(t_0)$ without reference to any curve Γ. For instance, if we are given the parametrized family described by Equations (3.27) and (3.28), we might not know that these lines are the tangent lines to an ellipse. In this section we consider how one might reconstruct the curve Γ from the lines given by Equations (3.24) and (3.25).

To begin with, we will represent a parametrized family of lines by an equation of the form

$$F(x, y, t_0) = 0 \tag{3.29}$$

that is linear in x and y. In other words, Equation (3.29) has the form

$$x\, A(t_0) + y\, B(t_0) + C(t_0) = 0 \tag{3.30}$$

For example, if t is eliminated from Equations (3.27) and (3.28), one obtains

$$xb \cos t_0 + ya \sin t_0 - (a^2 \cos^2 t_0 + b^2 \sin^2 t_0) = 0 \tag{3.31}$$

A curve Γ is called an *envelope* of the parametrized family (3.29) if each line of (3.29) is tangent to Γ. Recall that our objective here is to determine such a Γ from (3.29). Let us suppose that $\langle x_0, y_0 \rangle$ is a point on Γ that is not an inflection point of Γ, and that for the value t_0, Equation (3.29) determines a line L that is tangent to Γ at $\langle x_0, y_0 \rangle$. Since $\langle x_0, y_0 \rangle$ is not an inflection point, L lies

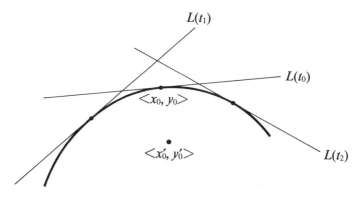

FIGURE 3.43   The tangent lines $L(t_1)$, $L(t_0)$ and $L(t_2)$, for $t_1 < t_0 < t_2$

locally all on one side of Γ. (See Figure 3.42.) Now let us examine the value of the function $F(x_0, y_0, t)$ for t near t_0. Clearly $F(x_0, y_0, t_0) = 0$.

THEOREM 3.25   If x_0 and y_0 are held fixed, then $F(x_0, y_0, t_0')$ has either a local maximum or a local minimum at $t_0' = t_0$ for t_0' close to t_0.

Proof   Let us consider $t_1 < t_0 < t_2$. The tangent lines for these three values of t_0 form a configuration like the one in Figure 3.43. Holding t_1 fixed, the function $F(x, y, t_1)$ is linear in x and y and hence must be always positive or always negative in the half-plane that lies to the south-east of the line $L(t_1)$, i.e., the half-plane determined by $L(t_1)$ that contains the points $\langle x_0, y_0 \rangle$ and $\langle x_0', y_0' \rangle$. A similar fact holds for $F(x, y, t_2)$. Now the value of $F(x_0', y_0', t)$ stays away from zero as t changes from t_1 to t_2, and so $F(x_0', y_0', t_1)$ and $F(x_0', y_0', t_2)$ are either both positive or both negative. By our preceding remarks, we must have $F(x_0, y_0, t_1)$ and $F(x_0, y_0, t_2)$ both positive or both negative. Since $F(x_0, y_0, t_0) = 0$, this value is a local maximum or a local minimum.   □

It follows immediately from the theorem that

$$F_3(x_0, y_0, t_0) = 0 \tag{3.32}$$

for $\langle x_0, y_0 \rangle$ the point where $L(t_0)$ makes tangential contact with Γ (where the subscript $_3$ refers to taking the partial derivative with respect to the third variable). From Equation (3.29) that defines $L(t_0)$, we also know that the point of tangency satisfies

$$F(x_0, y_0, t_0) = 0 \tag{3.33}$$

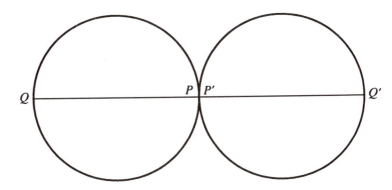

FIGURE 3.44   The coin on the right is to roll without slipping

In many cases, the curve Γ can be determined by eliminating t_0 from Equations (3.33) and (3.32). We will do this in one non-trivial case in Theorem 3.30.

Exercises

1. The author once saw a kit for embroidery art. One of the many suggested projects (when expressed in an appropriate coordinate system) was to stretch threads from $\langle 0, m \rangle$ to $\langle N - m, 0 \rangle$ (for integral values of m with $0 \leq m \leq N$). What curve is tangent to all these threads? (I.e., what would the envelope be if m were not restricted to integral values?)

2. Suppose $F(x, y, t_0)$ is $x + t_0 y + (1 - t_0)$. Sketch the parametrized family of lines. What curve is the envelope Γ? What happens to the method of this section?

3. Calculate the required partial derivative of Equation (3.31); then eliminate t_0 to rediscover the equation of an ellipse.

3.4.4   The cardioid

Let us imagine two coins, both of diameter d, placed on a table as in Figure 3.44. Point P of the left-hand coin just touches point P' of the right-hand coin. Q and Q' are the points diametrically opposed to P and P', respectively. Now suppose we keep the coin on the left fixed and roll the right-hand coin around

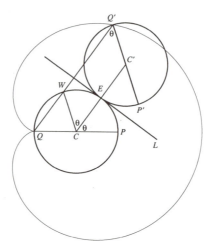

FIGURE 3.45 The right hand coin has moved into this new position

it. We define the *cardioid*[24] *of diameter* $2d$ to be the curve traced out by Q' as the right hand coin rolls. It turns out that this curve is somewhat heart-shaped, with a cusp forming at Q as the moving point Q' rolls eastward onto Q and then off again. (See the sketch in Figure 3.45.)

We begin our analysis of the cardioid by examining Figure 3.45. The points P, Q, P' and Q' are as described above (with P' and Q' moved into new positions). The centers of the coins are C and C', the new point of contact is E, and W is the point where the line $\overleftrightarrow{QQ'}$ meets the stationary coin. L is the line at E that is tangent to both circles.

Let us consider the reflection R_L in the line L. While we do not really have a mathematical definition of *rolling without slipping*, we can take it as meaning the arc from E to P is congruent to the arc from E to P', which means that $\angle PCE \cong \angle P'C'E$. It now readily follows that $R_L(C) = C'$, $R_L(P) = P'$, and $R_L(Q) = Q'$. Therefore, line $\overleftrightarrow{QQ'}$ is parallel to line $\overleftrightarrow{CC'}$ (since each is perpendicular to L). The segments CW and $C'Q'$, both being radii of the congruent coins, are congruent, and hence $CWQ'C'$ is a parallelogram. It now follows readily that angles $\angle CQW$, $\angle ECW$ and $\angle ECP$ are all congruent. We let θ be the measure of each of them, as indicated in Figure 3.45. With this preparation, we are ready to derive a parametric equation for the cardioid.

---

[24]The name means *heart-like*; compare with the English words *cardiac, cordial* and *accord*. In *The Geometry of Spatial Forms* (Ellis Horwood, Ltd., Chichester, 1983), Peter C. Gasson states that the cardioid was first studied by Roemer in 1674, and that the closely related *nephroid* (described below) was first studied by Huygens Gascharnhausen in the late fifteenth century.

THEOREM 3.26   Relative to a rectangular coordinate system with origin at the center C of the stationary coin, the cardioid of diameter $2d$ is parametrized by

$$\gamma(\theta) = d \left\langle (1 + \cos\theta) \cos\theta - \frac{1}{2}, \; (1 + \cos\theta) \sin\theta \right\rangle.$$

Proof   We recall that in Figure 3.45, $CWQ'C'$ is a parallelogram, and hence $\gamma(\theta)$ can be taken as the vector sum of the vectors $\overrightarrow{CW}$ and $\overrightarrow{CC'}$. Clearly then,

$$\gamma(\theta) = \frac{d}{2} \langle \cos 2\theta, \sin 2\theta \rangle + d \langle \cos\theta, \sin\theta \rangle$$

By using the well-known formula for $\cos 2\theta$, we arrive at the statement of the theorem. $\square$

Also from Figure 3.45 we may derive another geometrical definition of the cardioid. Choose a circle C of diameter d, and fix a point Q on C. Notice that every line L through Q that is not tangent to C meets C in a single point W besides Q. (For L vertical, we take W to be Q.)

THEOREM 3.27   The locus of points Q' such that $d(W, Q') = d$ is a cardioid.

Proof   Clearly $d(W, Q') = d$ for Q' on the cardioid, because $CWQ'C'$ is a parallelogram in Figure 3.45. Conversely, if we know the condition holds for Q' and W, then one can easily reconstruct Figure 3.45, thereby showing that Q' is on the cardioid. (Details of this reconstruction of the figure are left to the reader.) $\square$

In order to further comprehend this locus, it is helpful to look at Figure 3.46, which is essentially the same as Figure 3.45, with the moving coin removed, along with some of the auxiliary lines. We may imagine the line $\overleftrightarrow{WQ'}$ as a rigid rod that is constrained (by something like an eye bolt) to pass through Q. Moreover, the points W and Q' are permanently marked on this rod, at a distance d from each other. Now if we move the rod so that W follows the circle, then Q' will trace out a cardioid.

By moving our coordinate system to the cusp, we obtain a simpler polar equation for the cardioid.

THEOREM 3.28   The polar equation

$$r = d(1 + \cos\theta)$$

defines a cardioid of diameter $2d$ with cusp at the origin and with maximal extent along the polar axis.

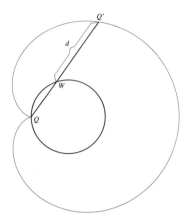

FIGURE 3.46   The cardioid is the locus of Q' as W remains on the circle

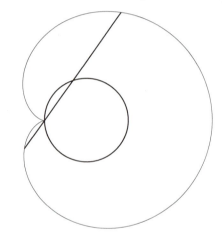

FIGURE 3.47   Corollary 3.29: all such segments have length $2d$

Proof   From the polar equation of Lemma 3 we know that in Figure 3.45, $d(Q, W) = d \cos \theta$. Then the result follows from the fact, established above, that $d(W, Q') = d$.

An alternate proof is available from the formula for $\gamma(\theta)$ that appears in Theorem 3.26; we leave the details of this calculation to the student.   □

We can now justify the use of the word *diameter* in our original definition of the cardioid. The corollary is illustrated in Figure 3.47.

COROLLARY 3.29   Every line through the cusp of a cardioid of diameter $2d$ meets the cardioid in a segment of length $2d$.

Proof   Since Theorem 3.28 refers to polar coordinates centered at the cusp Q, we know that the length of the segment cut off by the cardioid is $r(\theta)+r(\pi+\theta)$r. We then apply Theorem 3.28 to see that

$$r(\theta) + r(\pi + \theta) = d(1 + \cos\theta + 1 + \cos(\pi + \theta)) = 2d \qquad \square$$

Exercises

1. Draw the cardioid. Illustrate the definition by showing the stationary coin together with several positions of the moving coin.

2. Illustrate Theorem 3.27 by drawing the cardioid and the stationary coin, together with several positions of the rod that is constrained to pass through Q.

3. Prove that the cardioid of diameter d satisfies the equation

$$\left(x^2 + y^2 - 2dx\right)^2 = 4d^2\left(x^2 + y^2\right)$$

in rectangular coordinates. Plot this equation using the methods of §2.7.

4. Investigate what happens when the definition of a cardioid is modified to allow one coin to roll without slipping around a stationary coin, *where the two coins have unequal sizes*. Make computer drawings of the resulting curves. Note that in the general case we have a curve that does not close: after the moving coin has made one circuit around the stationary coin, the marked point Q' is not in its original position. (Exceptions to this statement occur when the stationary radius is an integral multiple of the moving radius.) Therefore one could make a picture that contains many revolutions of the moving coins. What is the limit of this picture as the number of revolutions approaches infinity? Make computer pictures to illustrate these phenomena.

5. **The nephroid.** Examine the situation of Exercise 4 more closely in the special case where the moving coin has diameter d and the stationary coin has diameter $2d$. This curve is called a *nephroid*, after its fancied resemblance to a kidney. Prove that the nephroid is parametrized by

$$\nu(\theta) = d\langle\cos 3\theta, \sin 3\theta\rangle + 3d\langle\cos\theta, \sin\theta\rangle$$

6. Investigate what happens when the characterization of a cardioid in Theorem 3.27 is modified so that the distance $d(W, Q')$ is still constant, but has a value other than the diameter d of the base circle. (Curves of this type were given the name *limaçon* by Pascal.) Ask the computer to draw some of these curves.

7. Prove that the area of a cardioid is six times the area of one of the coins that generate it.

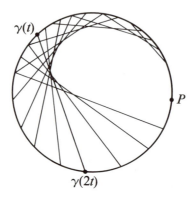

FIGURE 3.48   Light rays emanating from P and reflecting from a circle

8. Carry out the construction alluded to in the proof of Theorem 3.27, thereby completing that proof.

It turns out that the cardioid is the solution of an interesting problem of envelopes (in the sense of §3.4.3). In fact, as we shall see, this is perhaps the simplest envelope problem that occurs in nature. Let us begin with a unit circle C, which we take to be parametrized by

$$\gamma(t) = \langle \cos t, \sin t \rangle \tag{3.34}$$

for $0 \le t \le 2\pi$. We then consider the family of all lines that join $\gamma(t)$ to $\gamma(2t)$ for $0 \le t \le 2\pi$. See Figure 3.48.

THEOREM 3.30   The envelope of this family of lines is a cardioid of diameter 4/3, which is based on a circle (of radius 1/3) that is concentric with the original circle and has its cusp at the left.

Proof   We will use the method of §3.4.3, namely, the method of eliminating t_0 from Equations (3.29) and (3.32). As is well known, the line joining $\gamma(t)$ to $\gamma(2t)$ is represented by the equation

$$\frac{\sin 2t - \sin t}{\cos 2t - \cos t} = \frac{y_0 - \sin t}{x_0 - \cos t}$$

Clearing denominators and simplifying, we obtain

$$x_0(\sin 2t - \sin t) - y_0(\cos 2t - \cos t) - \sin t = 0 \tag{3.35}$$

We will therefore take the left-hand side of Equation (3.35) for $F(x_0, y_0, t)$. According to the methods of §3.4.3, we must also consider the equation $F_3(x_0, y_0, t)$

FIGURE 3.49   A cylindrical mug illuminated by a point source

$= 0$, which is obtained by differentiating with respect to t. In this case, our differentiated equation is

$$x_0(2\cos 2t - \cos t) + y_0(2\sin 2t - \sin t) - \cos t = 0 \tag{3.36}$$

The reader may check that Equations (3.35) and (3.36) have determinant $3(1 - \cos t)$, which is not zero except at $t = 0$. Therefore they have a unique solution, except possibly at $t = 0$, and hence they have at most one solution $\langle x_0 t, y_0 t \rangle$ that is continuous for all t. Therefore, to solve the equations, we will simply exhibit the continuous solution

$$\langle x_0, y_0 \rangle = \frac{2}{3} \left\langle (1 + \cos t)\cos t - \frac{1}{2},\ (1 + \cos t)\sin t \right\rangle \tag{3.37}$$

The student will need to check that in fact these values of x_0 and y_0 satisfy Equations (3.35) and (3.36). (This is a routine calculation requiring a few trigonometric identities.) By the methods of §3.4.3, we know that Equation (3.37) represents the envelope of the given family of lines. Comparing Equation (3.37) with Theorem 3.26, we see that in fact this envelope is a cardioid having the parameters described in the statement of the theorem.   □

A CARDIOID IN YOUR COFFEE CUP

We mentioned above that this envelope in the form of a cardioid occurs in nature. You can easily see it as the pattern formed by reflected light at the bottom of a coffee cup. For the most pronounced effect, the inner surface of the cup or mug should be close to cylindrical, and quite smooth and reflective, with a flat bottom, and there should be a point source of light overhead (see Figure 3.49). Not directly overhead, but slightly to one side. When these conditions are approximately fulfilled, one should see a bright pattern in the bottom of the cup that greatly resembles a cardioid, especially the part of the cardioid near the cusp.

For a mathematical understanding of this phenomenon, we begin with the following idealized situation. The bottom of the cup is the plane $x_3 = 0$, and the inner surface of the cup is formed by the half-cylinder

$$x_1^2 + x_2^2 = 1; \quad x_3 \geq 0$$

i.e., the points in space lying directly above the unit circle.

The exact pattern seen in the cup depends on the relative positioning of the cup and the light source S, as the reader can easily verify by experiment. We will not consider the general position of S, but rather two limiting positions of S for which exact calculations are possible. The first (indoor) case is that of a point source S rather close to the cup and directly above its rim. In this case, we can give S the coordinates $\langle 1, 0, h \rangle$, without any loss of generality. The second (outdoor) case is that of parallel rays of light arriving from a distant source such as the sun. (In the latter case, the pattern is seen by tilting the cup relative to the sun so that part of the cylindrical wall is illuminated.) We will treat the first case in detail, while relegating the second case to an exercise.

In the indoor case, the bottom surface of the cup will be illuminated by light rays that come directly from S and by rays that are reflected one or more times off the inner wall of the cup. We will disregard the direct illumination, since it is almost uniform and therefore makes only a negligible contribution to the pattern we see. As for multiply reflected rays, a small argument in solid geometry shows that if the height of the cup is less than half the height h of S above the bottom—the usual situation—then no ray can reflect more than once before striking the bottom. Therefore we are safe in assuming that the pattern we see is created by those light rays that are reflected once off the wall of the cup and then strike the bottom.

To analyze a single reflection of light from the cylindrical wall, let us consider a single point $\gamma(t) = \langle \cos(t), \sin(t), 0 \rangle$ on the unit circle (notation of Equation (3.34)). For future reference, we let $M(t)$ denote the line (in the base plane) joining $\gamma(t)$ and $\langle 1, 0, 0 \rangle$. All points lying above $\gamma(t)$, i.e., all points $\langle \cos(t), \sin(t), x_3 \rangle$ with $x_3 > 0$, form a vertical line $L(t)$. The source S and the line $L(t)$ together determine a (vertical) plane $\pi(t)$. Note that the intersection of $\pi(t)$ with the base plane $x_3 = 0$ is the line $M(t)$ (see Figure 3.50). All light rays coming from S to points in $L(t)$ must travel through the plane $\pi(t)$. Such rays are then reflected from the inner surface in the same manner that they would be reflected from the tangent plane. Therefore all reflected rays continue down to the bottom in a second vertical plane $\pi'(t)$, which is defined by the condition that $\pi(t)$ and $\pi'(t)$ make equal dihedral angles with the tangent plane to the cylinder along the line $L(t)$. These reflected rays therefore touch bottom along

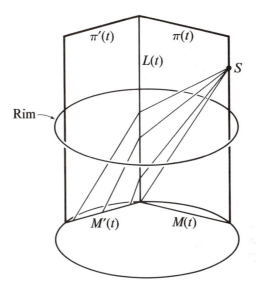

FIGURE 3.50 Analysis of light rays entering a cup

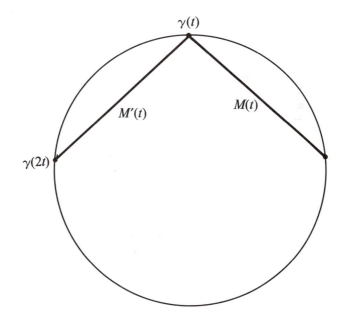

FIGURE 3.51 Figure 3.50, viewed from above

the intersection of two planes: the vertical plane $\pi'(t)$ and the horizontal plane $x_3 = 0$. This intersection of two lines is a line $M'(t)$ lying in the base plane.

Now the condition, stated above, about equal dihedral angles, translates in the base plane to the condition that lines $M(t)$ and $M'(t)$ meet the circle at equal angles. Therefore $M'(t)$ is the line joining $\gamma(t)$ with $\gamma(2t)$, i.e., one of the lines in Figure 3.48. (We captioned Figure 3.48 with this in mind.) By Theorem 3.30, these lines are the tangent lines to a cardioid of diameter 4/3, based on a circle centered at the origin. Therefore, the light reflected onto the bottom of the cup can be thought of as organized into this family of tangent lines.

So far, this proves nothing! In fact every point of the bottom is covered by some tangent lines, in accord with the fact that every point receives some illumination by reflected light. What we have neglected to discuss so far is the *intensity* of the light reaching the bottom. Now presumably this intensity is a complicated function of x_1 and x_2, whose precise calculation would be very difficult. Moreover, a precise calculation would put the role of the envelope (i.e., the cardioid) into the background. What we will do instead is have a general discussion of why we perceive the envelope as a light pattern.

What we need to do is imagine the cylinder as divided into small approximately planar vertical strips. Each of these will approximately function as a plane mirror, reflecting light rays from (a slight thickening of) plane $\pi(t)$ into light rays in (a slight thickening of) plane $\pi'(t)$. These rays will illuminate a (a slight thickening of) line $M'(t)$. We may refer to this illuminated zone as a *light strip*. A similar situation appears in Figure 3.48, where we showed lines $M'(t)$ with t more or less evenly stepped through values from 0 to 2π. Where these lines come very close to one another (especially just outside the cusp), the light strips just mentioned will pile up on another, causing intense illumination.

This phenomenon of increased light intensity is therefore a kind of partial focusing of the light rays reflected from the wall of the cup. Such a pattern of light intensification by partial or imperfect focusing is sometimes called a *caustic*, or sometimes a *catacaustic*. Caustic curves were studied by E. W. von Tschirnhausen in 1682, and by Jakob Bernoulli in 1692.

We should mention again that the above analysis required the source S of illumination to lie in a very special position, namely, directly above the rim of the cup. In Exercises 3–5, the student can examine what happens in another extreme case, namely that of parallel light rays arriving obliquely to the axis of the cup. The figure in that case is not a cardioid but a *nephroid*.

Exercises_____

1. Command the computer to prepare a picture illustrating Theorem 3.30. That is, draw a circle together with many of the lines connecting $\gamma(t)$ to $\gamma(2t)$. One version of this picture could also contain the cardioid as parametrized by Equation (3.37).

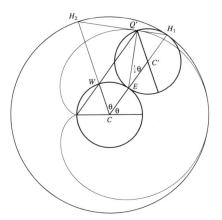

FIGURE 3.52   Geometric proof of Theorem 3.30

2. Give an alternate proof of Theorem 3.30 that is based on Figure 3.52 (which extends Figure 3.45). An outline of this proof is as follows: (a) A circle of radius $3d/2$ is drawn with center at C. (b) The lines $\overleftrightarrow{CC'}$ and $\overleftrightarrow{CW}$ meet that circle at H_1 and H_2, respectively. (c) The measure of $\angle Q'EC'$ is $\theta/2$. (d) $\overleftrightarrow{EQ'}$ meets $\overleftrightarrow{H_1H_2}$ at right angles. (e) Therefore $\overleftrightarrow{H_1H_2}$ is tangent to the cardioid.

3. For each θ in the interval $(0, 2\pi)$, let L_θ be the line joining $\langle \cos\theta, \sin\theta \rangle$ to $\langle \cos 3\theta, \sin 3\theta \rangle$. Sketch this family of lines and show analytically that the envelope has the equation of a nephroid. (See Exercise 5 on page 227.) In this connection, it might be interesting to perform some of the calculations with a symbol processing package. Possibilities are Macsyma, Mathematica, Maple and Derive. Command the computer to make a precise picture of this family of lines.

4. Give a geometric proof that the tangent lines to the nephroid form a family like the one described in Exercise 3.

5. Prove that the envelope described in Exercises 3 and 4 (i.e., the nephroid) is the light pattern seen in a coffee cup in the limiting case of parallel illumination. (By the way, the sun's angle of elevation will not influence the overall envelope that is perceived, although it will influence the relative intensities.)

6. Command the computer to make a picture of the caustic that appears in the bottom of the cup for a light source that is located somewhere between the two extremes that have been discussed so far. (One could calculate the effect of reflection from individual vertical surface elements of the cup, thereby numerically generating a family of lines. The envelope of this family will have an appearance that is similar to that of the nephroid and the cardioid.)

3.4.5   A differential equation

In this section we present an alternate solution to the problem of finding the enveloping curve of a parametrized family of lines. Here it is convenient to denote an arbitrary parametrized family of lines in the plane by

$$y = sx + f(s) \tag{3.38}$$

with the parameter now denoted by s. This parameter s represents the slope of a line of the family; to convert an arbitrary parametrized family into this form requires a change of variable $s = s(t_0)$, where $s(t_0)$ is a formula for the slope in terms of t_0. This can always be done if our family of lines has the property that for each $s \in \mathbb{R}$ (or for some smaller set of s), the family contains exactly one line of slope s; then $f(s)$ is simply the y-intercept of that line. (If a parametrized family contains a vertical line, it will be omitted in passing to this new parametrization.)

Exercise

1. Carry out this change of variable for Equation (3.31).

   Differentiating the last equation with respect to x yields $dy/dx = s$, which, when substituted into the original equation, yields

$$y = x\frac{dy}{dx} + f\left(\frac{dy}{dx}\right) \tag{3.39}$$

The differential equation (3.39) is known as *Clairaut's equation*, in honor of C. A. Clairaut (1713–1765). Its solutions include all the lines of the original parametrized family, but other—nonlinear—solutions are possible. If the curve Γ is tangent at each of its points to one line L of our parametrized family, then x, y and dy/dx are the same (at this point) for Γ and for L. Since Equation (3.39) holds for x and y varying along L, it must also hold for x and y varying along Γ. Therefore, solution of the differential equation (3.39) should yield an equation for Γ.

We may also use the algebraic properties of Equation (3.39) to see the division of solutions into a family of straight lines and one curve. For, differentiating (3.39), we obtain

$$\frac{dy}{dx} = \frac{dy}{dx} + x\frac{d^2y}{dx^2} + f'\left(\frac{dy}{dx}\right)\frac{d^2y}{dx^2}$$

which yields

$$0 = \left(x + f'\left(\frac{dy}{dx}\right)\right)\frac{d^2y}{dx^2}$$

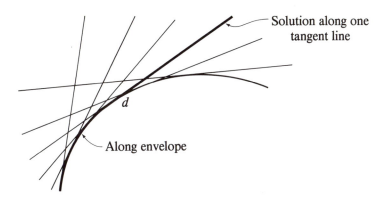

Solution along one
tangent line

Along envelope

FIGURE 3.53   A composite solution to Clairaut's equation

This equation has two types[25] of solutions. Those that arise from $d^2y/dx^2 = 0$ are the linear equations $y = sx + b$; comparison with the original equation of Clairaut shows that in fact $b = f(s)$, and thus these solutions are the ones we began with. If, however, we assume that $d^2y/dx^2 \neq 0$ then it may be canceled, yielding

$$0 = x + f'\left(\frac{dy}{dx}\right)$$

To solve this last equation, we make the substitution $x = -f'(u)$ for some new variable u, thereby obtaining

$$f'(u) = f'\left(\frac{dy}{dx}\right)$$

Assuming that f' is one-to-one, we may deduce

$$u = \frac{dy}{dx}$$

Using the fact that

$$\frac{dy}{dx} = \frac{dy}{du}\Big/\frac{dx}{du} = \frac{dy}{du}\Big/(-f''(u))$$

[25]There are also *composite* solutions: those that follow the curve Γ over some interval $c \leq x \leq d$ but follow the appropriate straight line for either $x \leq c$ or for $x \geq d$ (or both). This sort of solution is easily visualized from a picture; see Figure 3.53. As the reader may check, the composite solutions fail to have a second derivative.

we easily deduce

$$\frac{dy}{du} = -uf''(u)$$

whence one integration by parts yields

$$y = -uf'(u) + f(u) + C$$

From Exercise 1, we see that Clairaut's equation has a unique solution that is not linear over any segment of positive length, namely, the solution parametrized by

$$\langle x(u), y(u) \rangle = \langle -f'(u), -uf'(u) + f(u) \rangle \qquad (3.40)$$

Since this solution to Clairaut's equation is the unique one that is not linear (and since it is the unique solution not included in the original parametrized family (3.38)), it is sometimes called the *singular solution* to Clairaut's equation. As a solution to the problem of finding the envelope Γ to the lines defined by Equation (3.38), this solution is in fact more explicit than the one described in §3.4.3. Once the family of lines has been described in the special form of Equation (3.38), the application of this last formula is more or less automatic (assuming one knows how to evaluate the derivative of f).

Exercises

1. Prove that Clairaut's equation (3.39) is satisfied by $x = -f'(u)$ and $y = -uf'(u) + f(u) + C$, only for $C = 0$.

2. Use the methods of this section to analyze the family of lines

$$y = sx - x^3$$

and draw the associated envelope along with some of its tangent lines. (Notice that, although the curve has a cusp at the origin, one obtains a smooth parametrization of it.)

3. Redo the last two exercises of §3.4.3 using the methods of this section.

4. Work through all the details of this section for $f(s) = s$. You will see that in fact the envelope Γ does not exist, even though the method provides a putative solution.

3.4.6   The evolute of a curve

There is one very natural way that a parametrized family of lines may arise, namely, as the family F of lines perpendicular to a curve Γ'. Recall that line L is said to be *perpendicular* to curve Γ' at P' iff P' is a point on both Γ' and L,

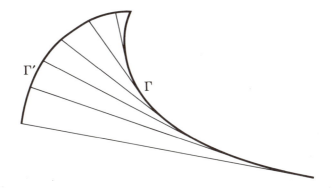

FIGURE 3.54   A curve Γ', its family of normals, and its evolute Γ

and the tangent to Γ' at P' is perpendicular to L. Thus, for every point P' on Γ' such that Γ' has a tangent at P', there is a uniquely defined perpendicular (or *normal*) line to Γ' at P'. The family F is defined to consist of all these lines.

It is not particularly difficult to write F as a parametrized family of lines. We use the familiar fact that two vectors are normal iff their dot product is zero. Therefore, the vector $\langle -\gamma_2'(t_0), \gamma_1'(t_0) \rangle$ is clearly perpendicular to the tangent vector $\langle \gamma_1'(t_0), \gamma_2'(t_0) \rangle$. Thus Equation (3.26) for the family of tangent lines is easily converted into the equation

$$(y - y_0)\gamma_2'(t_0) \;=\; -(x - x_0)\gamma_1'(t_0)$$

for the family F of normal lines.

Having defined the family F lines perpendicular to Γ', we define the *evolute* of Γ' to be the envelope Γ of F. Thus, to each point P' of Γ' there is a point P of the evolute Γ such that the line L joining P' and P is perpendicular to Γ' at P' and tangent to Γ at P. We say that point P' *corresponds to* point P (see Figure 3.54).

ALGORITHM (evolute of a curve)   The evolute Γ of a a curve Γ' can be obtained as follows:

- Parametrize the family of normals to Γ' according to method just described.

- Reparametrize into the form of Equation (3.38).

- Parametrize Γ with the solution given in Equation (3.40).

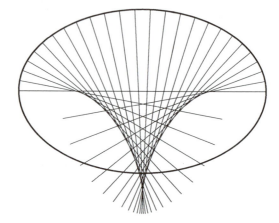

FIGURE 3.55   The evolute of an ellipse

Exercises_____

1. Using our earlier equations concerning the ellipse, write equations that parametrize the family F of lines perpendicular to an ellipse. Make a computer drawing that shows F together with the original ellipse. (It has the general shape sketched in Figure 3.55.)

2. Consider the curve Γ' that is parametrized by

$$\langle u, v \rangle \;=\; \alpha(t) \;=\; \langle -e^{-t}\sin t, e^{-t}\cos t \rangle$$

and the curve Γ that is parametrized by

$$\langle x, y \rangle \;=\; \gamma(t) \;=\; \langle e^{-t}\cos t, e^{-t}\sin t \rangle$$

Prove that, for each t, the line joining $\alpha(t)$ to $\gamma(t)$ is perpendicular to Γ' and tangent to Γ. Thus Γ is the evolute of Γ'. Command the computer to make an illustration of these facts. What sort of curves are these?

3.4.7   The evolute and centers of curvature

There is another kind of equation for evolutes, which we now examine, that involves *centers of curvature*. Let Γ' be parametrized by $\alpha(t)$. The line perpendicular to Γ' at $\alpha(t)$ is parametrized (with respect to u) by the equation

$$\langle x, y \rangle \;=\; \langle \alpha_1(t) - u\alpha_2'(t), \alpha_2(t) + u\alpha_1'(t) \rangle$$

This line meets the evolute Γ; denoting the corresponding u-value by $\mu(t)$, we obtain the following parametrization for Γ:

$$\gamma(t) = \langle \alpha_1(t) - \mu(t)\alpha_2', \alpha_2(t) + \mu(t)\alpha_1' \rangle$$

Differentiating the preceding equation with respect to t, we find that the tangent vector to Γ has coordinates

$$\gamma_1'(t) = \alpha_1'(t) - \mu'(t)\alpha_2'(t) - \mu(t)\alpha_2''(t)$$
$$\gamma_2'(t) = \alpha_2'(t) + \mu'(t)\alpha_1'(t) + \mu(t)\alpha_1''(t)$$

We now apply the condition that $\gamma'(t)$ should be perpendicular to $\alpha'(t)$, obtaining

$$0 = \alpha' \cdot \gamma' = \alpha_1'\gamma_1' + \alpha_2'\gamma_2'$$
$$= \cdots$$
$$= \alpha'(t) \cdot \alpha'(t) + \mu(t)\left[\alpha_2'(t)\alpha_1''(t) - \alpha_1'(t)\alpha_2''(t)\right]$$

from which we deduce that

$$\mu(t) = \frac{\alpha'(t) \cdot \alpha'(t)}{\alpha_1'\alpha_2'' - \alpha_2'\alpha_1''}$$

We now observe that

$$\alpha(t) - \gamma(t) = \mu(t)\beta(t)$$

for a vector $\beta(t)$ that has the same length as $\alpha'(t)$. Hence the distance between corresponding points $\alpha(t)$ and $\gamma(t)$ is

$$|\alpha(t) - \gamma(t)| = |\mu(t)\alpha'(t)| = \left| \frac{[\alpha'(t) \cdot \alpha'(t)]^{3/2}}{\alpha_1'\alpha_2'' - \alpha_2'\alpha_1''} \right|$$

As the reader may check in almost any calculus book, this last quantity is the *radius of curvature* of the curve Γ' at $\alpha(t)$. Thus $\gamma(t)$ is the *center of curvature* associated to the point $\alpha(t)$ on Γ'. In other words, among all circles C passing through $\alpha(t)$, the one that makes the closest contact with Γ' is the one centered at $\gamma(t)$. Thus the evolute of Γ' may be equivalently defined as *the locus of centers of curvature of Γ'*.

This fact may be informally seen by considering that the tangents to Γ at points near to $\gamma(t)$ are almost like concentric rays emanating from $\gamma(t)$. Hence, in a neighborhood of $\alpha(t)$, the curve Γ' is almost like a circle centered at $\gamma(t)$ (see Figure 3.56).

Exercise_____

1. Use the computer to make a picture that shows a curve Γ' and its evolute, together with one or two circles of curvature (along with the segment from $\gamma(t)$ to $\alpha(t)$).

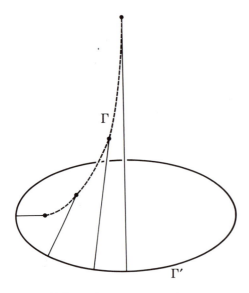

FIGURE 3.56
Centers of curvature

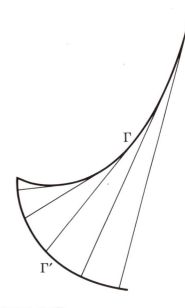

FIGURE 3.57
A curve Γ and an involute Γ'

3.4.8   Involutes of a curve

Given a curve Γ, an *involute* of Γ is a curve Γ' that results—informally speaking—from unwinding a string that is placed along Γ (see Figure 3.57). What we would like to do here is establish the reciprocal nature of the two procedures of forming the involute and forming the evolute. Before giving a formal proof, we first point out the intuitive nature of this assertion. As the string is unwound from Γ, with P the point of contact on Γ, very locally the curve Γ looks like a circle centered at P; therefore, Γ consists of the centers of curvature of Γ', and hence Γ is the evolute of Γ', by §3.4.7.

To study involutes more formally, let us be given a curve Γ—which for simplicity we assume to have no cusps or inflection points—and a point P on Γ.

Under reasonable conditions, the point P divides Γ into two connected subsets Γ_0 and Γ_1. We will assume that Γ is parametrized by $\langle x, y \rangle = \gamma(s)$ and that $P = \gamma(0)$. Under this parametrization, the sets Γ_0 and Γ_1 are the two sets $\{\gamma(s) : s \geq 0\}$ and $\{\gamma(s) : s \leq 0\}$; we will choose our notation so that

$$\Gamma_0 = \{\gamma(s) : s \geq 0\}$$

Furthermore, our equations here will be much simplified if we assume that the parameter s measures arc length. In other words, the arc length along Γ between $\gamma(s_0)$ and $\gamma(s_1)$ is $|s_1 - s_0|$. (We will return in §3.4.9 to the question of how such a parametrization may be found in practice.) For a useful computational consequence of this assumption about arc length, we begin with the usual formula for arc length, namely,

$$ds^2 = dx^2 + dy^2$$

from which we easily deduce

$$ds^2 = (\gamma_1'(s)\, ds)^2 + (\gamma_2'(s)\, ds)^2$$

and then

$$1 = (\gamma_1'(s))^2 + (\gamma_2'(s))^2$$

Differentiating this last equation with respect to s, we obtain

$$2\gamma_1'(s)\gamma_1''(s) + 2\gamma_2'(s)\gamma_2''(s) = 0$$

In vector notation, our equations are

$$|\gamma'(s)| = 1 \tag{3.41}$$
$$\gamma'(s) \cdot \gamma''(s) = 0 \tag{3.42}$$

(Informally, the first of these says that we travel along Γ with unit velocity, and the second says that acceleration is always perpendicular to the direction of travel.)

An important consequence of Equations (3.41) and (3.42) is that either $\gamma''(s) = 0$ or $\gamma'(s)$ and $\gamma''(s)$ are linearly independent. The former alternative is ruled out by our assumption that Γ has no cusps or inflection points. Therefore, $\gamma'(s)$ and $\gamma''(s)$ are linearly independent.

To represent the informal notion of unwinding a string, we imagine the string as placed along Γ_0, with its free end at P. After unwinding s units of string, we have exposed s units of arc length along Γ_0, and hence the point of contact between string and curve is $\gamma(s)$. The tip of the string is now s units back from $\gamma(s)$, i.e., in a direction opposite to the direction of travel along γ. (See notation in Figure 3.57.) In other words, $\gamma(s) - \alpha(s)$ is a vector of length s parallel to the unit vector $\gamma'(s)$. Hence it follows readily that

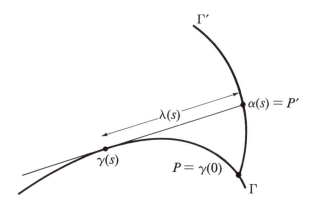

FIGURE 3.58   The proof of Theorem 3.32

$$\alpha(s) = \gamma(s) - s\,\gamma'(s) \tag{3.43}$$

Sometimes we refer to this Γ' as *the involute of Γ relative to P and Γ_0*.

THEOREM 3.31   Let Γ' be the involute of Γ relative to P and Γ_0. Then Γ_0 is contained in the evolute of Γ'.

Proof   What we need to show is that each tangent line to Γ_0 meets Γ' perpendicularly at some point. Specifically, we will show that the tangent line to Γ_0 at $\gamma(s)$ is perpendicular to Γ' at $\alpha(s)$. For this we need the tangent vector to Γ' at $\alpha(s)$. Differentiating Equation (3.43) with respect to s, we may express this tangent vector as

$$\alpha'(s) = \gamma'(s) - \gamma'(s) - s\,\gamma''(s) = -s\,\gamma''(s)$$

Now, for perpendicularity, we use Equation (3.42) to calculate

$$\alpha'(s) \cdot \gamma'(s) = -s\,\gamma''(s) \cdot \gamma'(s) = 0$$

which completes the proof.   □

Our second theorem shows that involutes are in fact determined by the property of the previous theorem. This theorem and its proof are diagramed in Figure 3.58.

THEOREM 3.32   Suppose that P divides curve Γ into Γ_0 and Γ_1, and that Γ' is another curve such that P lies on Γ' and Γ_0 is contained in the evolute of Γ'. Then Γ' is contained in the involute of Γ relative to P and Γ_0.

Proof   Let Γ be parametrized, as before, by $\gamma(s)$, where s represents arc length along Γ, with $P = \gamma(0)$ and $\Gamma_0 = \{\gamma(s) : s \geq 0\}$. For each $s \geq 0$, we know by hypothesis that the tangent line to Γ at s meets Γ' perpendicularly at some point P'. Let the coordinates of this P' be $\alpha(s)$; in other words, we may regard $\alpha(s)$ as a parametrization of Γ'.

Since $\alpha(s)$ lies on the tangent line to Γ, we know that

$$\alpha(s) = \gamma(s) - \lambda(s)\gamma'(s)$$

for some scalar $\lambda(s)$. Taking the derivative, we see that

$$\alpha'(s) = (1 - \lambda'(s))\gamma'(s) - \lambda(s)\gamma''(s)$$

On the other hand, since $\alpha'(s)$ is perpendicular to $\gamma'(s)$, we know from Equation (3.42) that $\alpha'(s)$ must be parallel to $\gamma''(s)$. As we observed after Equation (3.42), $\gamma'(s)$ and $\gamma''(s)$ are linearly independent, and so the coefficient of $\gamma'(s)$ in the last displayed equation must be zero. That is,

$$1 - \lambda'(s) = 0$$

and hence

$$\lambda(s) = s + C$$

It is not too hard to check that $\lambda(0) = 0$, and hence that $C = 0$. Thus $\lambda(s) = s$, and

$$\alpha(s) = \gamma(s) - s\,\gamma'(s)$$

Since this is the same as our original formula (Equation (3.43)) for the involute relative to P and Γ_0, the proof of the theorem is complete. $\square$

COROLLARY 3.33   Let Γ' and Γ_0 be as in the previous theorem. Arc length along Γ_0 corresponds to change in radius of curvature along Γ'. That is if P and Q are points on Γ_0 that correspond to points P' and Q' on Γ', then the arc length along Γ_0 between P and Q is equal to $|R_{P'} - R_{Q'}|$, where $R_{P'}$ (resp. $R_{Q'}$) is the radius of curvature of Γ' at the point P' (resp. Q').

Proof   Follows from Theorems 3.31 and 3.32 and §3.4.7. $\square$

Notice that the corollary shows the dependence of our work on the assumption (stated near the beginning of this section) that we are considering only a part of Γ that has no cusps or inflection points. The reader may observe in Figure 3.55 that if P and Q are symmetrically located on opposite sides of the evolute, then P' and Q' will have exactly the same radius of curvature, thus making $|R_{P'} - R_{Q'}| = 0$.

3.4.9   The drawing of involutes

The procedure implicit in §3.4.8 for drawing an involute of Γ is straightforward, except in one particular. Namely, that procedure relied on having Γ parametrized by $\gamma(s)$, where s is a parameter that measures arc length along Γ. The interesting fact is that for almost all familiar curves Γ—such as an ellipse[26]—the corresponding $\gamma(s)$ is not an elementary function of s, and therefore the formulas of §3.4.8 cannot be calculated by symbolic manipulation of formulas for $\gamma(s)$.

In practical terms, the problem is as follows. Suppose we are given parametric equations $\delta(t)$ for Γ (such as the parametric equations for an ellipse in Lemma 5 of §3.1.2). To reparametrize Γ as $\gamma(s)$ ($s =$ arc length along Γ), we first need to find an expression for s in terms of t. This means that we have to evaluate the integral

$$s = \int_{t_0}^{t_1} \sqrt{\delta_1'(t)^2 + \delta_2'(t)^2}\, dt$$

for arc length. Only in rare cases can this integral be evaluated in elementary terms.

We wish to point out that this necessity of calculating arc length along Γ is not just an accidental feature of the treatment we happen to have followed. Rather, it is inherent in the problem of calculating Γ'. This can be seen for instance from Corollary 3.33: as soon as we have a formula for Γ', we can compute radii of curvature for Γ' and hence obtain arc length along Γ.

Therefore, to make pictures of involutes in general, one will have to begin by first performing the above integration numerically and then using the formulas of §3.4.8. We leave the relatively straightforward details to the student who has some experience with numerical methods of integration.

Drawing the involutes to a curve Γ amounts to solving a certain system of differential equations: The tangent lines to Γ define a vector field $v(x, y)$ (which may be multiple-valued, but for which unique values can be selected locally). Then the solutions of

$$\alpha'(t) = \langle v_2(\alpha(t)), -v_1(\alpha(t)) \rangle$$

correspond to involutes of Γ.

Exercises

1. Give parametric equations for the involute of a circle. (Since arc length along a circle is easily given, these parametric equations can be given in closed form,

---

[26] In fact, the problem of measuring arc length along an ellipse gave rise to the *elliptic integrals* that were extensively tabulated at one time. Nevertheless the tabulation of answers for one problem does very little to aid the next problem that comes along.

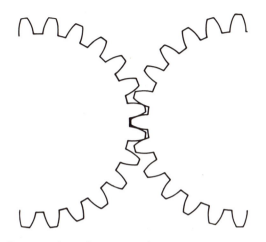

FIGURE 3.59   Cross section of two gears in contact

without any need for approximate calculation of arc length.) Make a drawing showing the involute with a number of lines perpendicular to it. The involute of a circle has practical application in §3.4.9. The interested student could consult some engineering books and extend this exercise to give some drawings of gears.

2. Develop a program that will draw a (parametrically given) curve Γ' and also its involute. (This would require amalgamating the methods of this section with some elementary form of numerical integration to get the needed arc length.)

THE DESIGN OF GEAR TEETH

The involute of a circle has a practical application in the design of gear teeth. We consider only the case of two gears that revolve about two stationary parallel axes L_1 and L_2, and which are cylindrical with respect to these axes, i.e., they have the same cross section in any plane perpendicular to these axes. (We therefore need only draw one cross section—see Figure 3.59.) Each gear consists in fact of a solid cylinder of *radius r*,[27] together with protuberances called *teeth*. Ideally, the axes of two gears are positioned so that that (most of the time) exactly two teeth are in contact (preferably tangentially). For a uniform notation, as in Figures 3.59 and 3.60, let us suppose that r is the radius of the left-hand gear, and r' is the radius of the right-hand gear.

---

[27]What we are calling the radius is a mathematical fiction that we use below to design the gear teeth and that allows us to determine ratios of rotational speeds. As long as the teeth are placed where the theory tells us, it is unimportant mathematically how much of the theoretical cylinder is filled with gear substance.

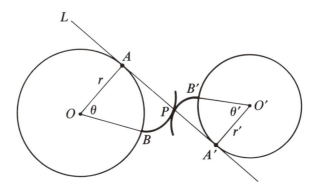

FIGURE 3.60 Involute gear teeth: $r\theta + r'\theta'$ remains constant

A prime requisite in the meshing of two gears is that their teeth should remain in perfect contact as both gears are rotated at angular velocities inversely proportional to their radii. (Equivalently, the two gears should have the same linear velocity at the surface of their cylinders.) One can easily see[28] that under these circumstances—if there is no friction—torque will be transmitted proportionally from one gear to the next. If this condition is not met, then—at best—transmitted motion will be jerky and the power source will experience a varying resistance, with which it may or may not be able to cope. If gears deviate too far from this ideal condition, or if too many bad gears are coupled together, machinery may become completely jammed and refuse to operate.

Happily, there is an almost immediate solution to this engineering problem via the involute of a circle. In Figure 3.60 we have drawn circles of radii r and r' centered at points O and O', which are separated by more than $r + r'$ so that there is some definite space between the two circles. Line L is tangent to the left-hand circle at A and to the right-hand circle at A'. Then we take P to be an arbitrary point on L between A and A'. Now B is taken to be the point on the left circle such that the length of arc $\overset{\frown}{AB}$ is the same as the length of segment $\overline{AP}$. B' is similarly constructed (with respect to A', on the right-hand circle). Involutes of circles drawn (as in Figure 3.60) from B and B' will meet at P; in fact they will each cross the line L at right angles, and thus they meet tangentially. We let θ be the measure of the angle $\angle AOB$ on the left-hand circle, and define θ' similarly with respect to the right-hand gear.

---

[28]This can be deduced from the conservation of energy. Imagine one string wound around each gear's cylinder, descending to weights, in such a manner that raising one weight lowers the other. Clearly this system is in equilibrium when the two weights are equal.

Let us think of A and A' as fixed reference marks for each of the two gears. Keeping them fixed, let us rotate the two gears while keeping the two involutes in contact. The resulting picture will continue to be as described above, and so we continue to preserve the relationship

$$\overset{\frown}{AB} + \overset{\frown}{A'B'} \;=\; d(A, A')$$

This is equivalent to

$$r\theta + r'\theta' \;=\; d(A, A')$$

If θ depends differentiably on the time t, we can differentiate to compare the angular velocities as

$$\frac{d}{dt}\theta' \;=\; -\frac{r}{r'}\frac{d}{dt}\theta$$

This clearly solves[29] the problem of rotating gears. It is nice that the solution for one gear is independent of the size of gear it is to be paired with and that the solution is in general independent of the intergear spacing.

A more pictorial way to say all this is that if we rotate the left-hand gear in Figure 3.60 with radial velocity v in the indicated direction, then the point P will move with velocity v along the segment $\overline{A'A}$ in the direction from A' toward A. Since the corresponding assertion also holds for the other gear, the two gears will remain in perfect contact as they turn at proportional speeds.

Exercises

1. Suppose that in Figure 3.60 we replace the line tangent to both circles by a *circle* tangent to both circles (see Figure 3.61). Revise the reasoning of this section to apply to this new diagram. (Instead of rolling the line off the circle, one must roll one circle off another circle. Curves produced in this way are called *cycloids*; a special case was the cardioid of §3.4.4.) Discuss the relative advantages and disadvantages of this new gear design. What happens if we try to make the circle exterior to both of the gears?

2. Develop a program that will show two real gears with involute teeth, and—in more than one frame—will show the gears slowly turning. Depending on available hardware, display this as a movie, or print a series of individual frames. (The computer work here is not difficult, especially if one has already

---

[29] We hasten to add that this is not the only solution. Notice also that we have not addressed the question of how to arrange teeth so that contact can be passed smoothly from one pair of teeth to another. In practice the ratio r/r' should be a rational number n'/n for relatively small n and n'. Then the left-hand gear will have n teeth, while the right-hand gear has n' teeth.

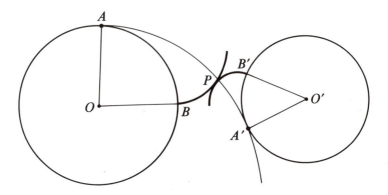

FIGURE 3.61 One circle tangent to two others

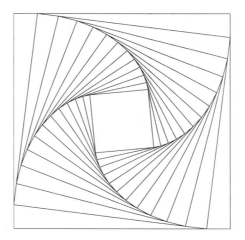

FIGURE 3.62 Nested squares

worked out the involute of a circle in §3.4.9, but one will need to look in some engineering book to see various other features of gear teeth: how are they spaced, how thick should they be, how far should the involute extend, and so on.)

3.4.10 Nested squares

Here we outline a kind of picture that is easily drawn by a recursive procedure that involves no calculus whatever, yet nevertheless illustrates evolutes and involutes. In Figure 3.62, we show a basic *tile* that can be placed repeatedly on the page to get interesting effects.

We begin with a square S_0. Inside S_0 we place a slightly smaller square S_1 so that the vertices of S_1 lie on the edges of S_0. We then continue to place squares $S_2, S_3, \cdots$ so as to form a nested sequence of squares. If the sizes do not change too rapidly, then the corners of the squares will appear to trace out four continuous curves. Since any edge of any of our squares is tangent to one curve and perpendicular to another, it is intuitively clear that, in the limit, each of these curves is the evolute of one of the others. Thus, here we have an example of *a curve Γ' congruent to its own evolute.*

In fact, the curves in this example already appeared (with analytic formulas) in the last exercise of §3.4.6. If we give the picture a coordinate system by taking $\langle 1, 0 \rangle$ $\langle 0, 1 \rangle$ $\langle -1, 0 \rangle$ and $\langle 0, -1 \rangle$ as coordinates of the four corners, then the two curves of that exercise are approximated by two of the curves here. Moreover it is clear from our discussion of self-similarity in §3.3.5 that this curve must be a logarithmic spiral.

Exercises

1. Make computer versions of the picture described here. Try making some interesting combinations of the given picture and its mirror image.

2. Prove geometrically that the limiting curve is the logarithmic spiral with $\alpha = \pi/4$. (The logarithmic spiral was defined in §3.3.5, and α is described there.)

3. Devise analogous recursive constructions that will—in the limit—create logarithmic spirals with some different values of the angle α.

3.4.11   Envelopes in general

The notion of envelope makes sense for any parametrized family of curves, not just for a family of lines. As in §3.4.3, we may consider an equation

$$F(x, y, \theta) = 0$$

which is like Equation (3.29), except that we no longer insist that F should be linear in x and y. For each fixed value of θ this equation defines a curve in the x, y-plane, and thus we have a parametrized family of curves. The *envelope* of this family is a curve that is tangent to all of them. Usually this means a curve that forms a boundary between points that lie on some curve in the family and points that do not.

To express the envelope analytically, we observe (as in §3.4.3) that for each point $\langle x, y \rangle$ on the envelope there is a value θ of the parameter satisfying both the above equation and

$$F_3(x, y, \theta) = 0$$

FIGURE 3.63   An exploding firework: trajectories and envelope

(which is analogous to Equation (3.32)). Therefore an equation in x and y may be obtained by eliminating θ from the two equations. (This may or may not be feasible in practice, depending on the complexity of the two equations. In fact, even if there is no easy way to eliminate θ, it may still be possible to use θ as a parameter to describe the envelope. See our following treatment of wakes.)

FIREWORKS

We illustrate this general idea of envelope by considering an aerial firework that ejects glowing sparks in every direction. Each spark follows a parabolic trajectory, which we can observe, especially if the sparks are chemically designed to leave a glowing trail. As well as observing the trails, we tend also to see their overall outline in the sky; this outline is an envelope. (See Figure 3.63; a similar phenomenon can also be observed from water spouting skyward from certain kinds of fountains, although the calculations here apply only when all the water jets are pumping out water at the same muzzle velocity.)

We will use a 2-dimensional coordinate system with y upward and x to the observer's right. A third coordinate z goes directly back from the observer. We will simplify the problem by considering only sparks that travel in the x, y-plane. Our justification is that, when viewed by a distant observer, these are the curves that define the visible outline. To calculate the trajectories and their envelope, we will first assume that the explosive center (or the base of the fountain) is at the origin of the x, y plane and that each spark (or water drop) is ejected at the same speed. (We ignore air resistance; the reader may observe that this simplification is less and less realistic as the original force of the explosion wears out.) Taking -1 for the acceleration of gravity, and 1 for the initial speed, and denoting the angle of originating velocity by θ, we have the following two equations for the x

and y coordinates of a spark:

$$x = t\cos\theta$$
$$y = -\frac{1}{2}t^2 + t\sin\theta$$

Eliminating the time variable, we obtain the equation

$$y\cos^2\theta + \frac{1}{2}x^2 - x\cos\theta\sin\theta = 0$$

which describes an individual trajectory. It turns out to be fairly complicated to approach this problem directly, by differentiating with respect to θ and then eliminating θ. Luckily there is a way to simplify the problem. Dividing the preceding equation by $\cos^2\theta$ yields

$$y + \frac{1}{2}(\sec^2\theta)x^2 - x\tan\theta = 0$$

or

$$y + \frac{1}{2}(1 + m^2)x^2 - mx = 0$$

where $m = \tan\theta$. Now the important thing here is that each of these two preceding equations describes exactly the same family of curves, namely, the family of all trajectories. Although we began with the θ parameter, the parameter m is just as valid and much more convenient. Therefore, the recommended procedure is now to take the derivative of this last equation with respect to m and then eliminate m to find the envelope. We leave the detailed calculations to the reader. We depict the envelope (which is itself a parabola) in Figure 3.63.

It should be fairly obvious that the envelope of the trajectories of an exploding firework has a direct physical significance: it is the outer limit of points that can be reached starting from the origin with the given initial velocity. Interestingly, this same limiting curve can be seen as the envelope of a family of circles. One way to think of the firework is as a spherical packet of sparks that expands outward in space. (Looking only in the x, y-plane, it is circular.) In the absence of gravity, the expansion would occur at the same constant rate in all directions, and so at time t the outer boundary of the packet would be a circle with radius proportional to t. Under gravity, we actually have the same circle, but it has fallen a distance $t^2/2$ due to the influence of gravity. In other words, at time t, the outer boundary is a circle of radius t centered at $\langle 0, -t^2/2 \rangle$:

$$x^2 + \left(y + \frac{t^2}{2}\right)^2 = t^2$$

This family of circles, and its envelope, are depicted in Figure 3.64.

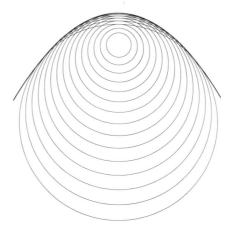

FIGURE 3.64   Exploding firework: expanding gasball and envelope

Exercise

1. Prove that the envelope of the trajectories and the envelope of the expanding circles have the same equation, namely $x^2 + 2y = 1$. Carry out the detailed calculation of this envelope, and make at least two computer drawings of the envelope. One could show the envelope with the parabolic trajectories (as in Figure 3.63); the other one could show the expanding circles (as in Figure 3.64). Experiment with simplifying the preceding equation by using $u = t^2/2$ as a parameter instead of t.

2. The *lemniscate of Bernoulli* is the curve given in polar coordinates by the equation

$$r^2 \; = \; 2a^2 \cos 2\theta$$

Draw the lemniscate using this equation directly (with θ as parameter), or by using the methods of §2.7. (Note that if $\cos 2\theta < 0$, then *no* r value satisfies the defining equation.) The lemniscate can be expressed as an envelope. Consider the hyperbola $xy = a^2$ and consider the family of all circles that have their center on this hyperbola and pass through the origin. Prove that the envelope of this family is a lemniscate.

THE WAKE OF A BOAT

A boat traveling on a large smooth body of water causes disturbances in the surface of the water that persist after the boat has passed. Under suitable conditions, the disturbances become organized and form a pattern called a *wake*, which trails behind the boat in its progress over the water. The aquatic disturbance caused by a large engine is hydrodynamically very complex, and well outside the scope of this book. Nevertheless, some features of the problem will yield to a geometric analysis if we make a few simplifying assumptions.

We will assume that every time the surface of the water is touched lightly, the outer boundary of the resulting disturbance is a circle centered at the point of contact, and whose radius is a fixed[30] function $R(t)$ of the time t elapsed since the water was touched. In other words, if you drop a pebble in the water at time t_0 and at point P, then at time $t_0 + t$ you will observe a circle of radius $R(t)$, centered at P. We of course have $R(0) = 0$ and $R(t)$ an increasing function of t. It seems physically reasonable to assume that $R(t)$ is differentiable and, in fact, a principal prediction[31] of wave mechanics is that in shallow water $R(t) = \lambda t$ for some constant *wave velocity* λ. Another assumption is that these effects are cumulative; therefore the overall disturbance can be described as the union of circles, one for each previous position of the boat, with the older circles of course being larger than the newer ones. In other words, we could imagine riding in a phantom boat that leaves no wake, meanwhile dropping pebbles in the water at regular intervals. Our pictures can only show finitely many such circles, but the actual wake is the envelope of the (infinite) family of all possible such circles.

Assume that the boat's position is given by a differentiable function

$$P(t) \; = \; \langle \gamma(t), \delta(t) \rangle$$

We will describe the family of circular ripples at a fixed time T. For each earlier time t (i.e., for $t < T$), we have a circle of radius $R(T - t)$ centered at $P(t)$ (which resulted from dropping a pebble in the water $T - t$ time units ago, at position $P(t)$). The equation of this circle is

$$(x - \gamma(t))^2 + (y - \delta(t))^2 \; = \; R(T - t)^2$$

and the desired wake is the envelope of all these circles. Therefore, we take the derivative with respect to the parameter t, thereby obtaining

$$-2\gamma'(t)(x - \gamma(t)) - 2\delta'(t)(y - \delta(t)) \; = \; -2R'(T - t)R(T - t)$$

Writing $\langle U, V \rangle$ for the vector $\langle x - \gamma(t), y - \delta(t) \rangle$ from $P(t)$ to a point $\langle x, y \rangle$ on the wake, we have the simplified equations

$$U^2 + V^2 \; = \; R(t)^2$$
$$\langle U, V \rangle \cdot \langle \gamma'(t), \delta'(t) \rangle \; = \; -R'(T - t)R(T - t)$$

---

[30] This is our most questionable assumption. In deep water, any disturbance causes waves with a spectrum of differing velocities. In shallow water of depth D, waves of small amplitude all have velocity approximately equal to $\sqrt{gD}$, where g is the gravitational constant. Therefore our geometric pictures here are only valid for shallow water.

[31] Let us underline the fact that we are not deriving anything in fluid dynamics or wave mechanics. We are merely making some geometric deductions from the existence of traveling waves.

In other words, the length of $\langle U, V \rangle$ is $R(T-t)$ and its dot product with the boat's velocity vector is $R'(T-t)R(T-t)$. It clearly follows that if $\alpha(t)$ is the angle between the velocity vector and $\langle U, V \rangle$, then

$$\cos \alpha(t) = \frac{R'(T-t)}{|\langle \gamma'(t), \delta'(t) \rangle|}$$

which is the ratio of the wave velocity to the boat speed.[32] Since the cosine function has no values greater than 1, it in now apparent that *when the boat is traveling slower than the wave velocity, there is no solution to the wake equations.*

Assuming now that the boat is traveling faster than the wave velocity, we will take the last equation to be a definition of $\alpha(t)$ (via the inverse cosine function). Now the expressions

$$\begin{bmatrix} \cos \alpha(t) & \mp \sin \alpha(t) \\ \pm \sin \alpha(t) & \cos \alpha(t) \end{bmatrix} \frac{\langle \gamma'(t), \delta'(t) \rangle}{|\langle \gamma'(t), \delta'(t) \rangle|}$$

clearly yield the two unit vectors that point in the direction of $\langle U, V \rangle$. (One for each of the two boundaries of the wake.) To obtain $\langle U, V \rangle$, we need only multiply by the known length $R(T-t)$ of the vector $\langle U, V \rangle$ to obtain

$$\langle U, V \rangle = R \begin{bmatrix} \cos \alpha & \mp \sin \alpha \\ \pm \sin \alpha & \cos \alpha \end{bmatrix} \frac{\langle \gamma', \delta' \rangle}{|\langle \gamma', \delta' \rangle|}$$

where of course all of these quantities depend on t. Then the wake itself is described by the curves $\langle U(t), V(t) \rangle + \langle \gamma(t), \delta(t) \rangle$.

The above equations are actually very simple to program. In programming them you have to tell the program $R(t)$, $R'(t)$, $\langle \gamma(t), \delta(t) \rangle$ and $\langle \gamma'(t), \delta'(t) \rangle$ (unless you are working in a language like Mathematica that can figure out derivatives). The program can calculate everything else. In many cases, this is obviously the best approach; there is little to be gained from attempting a closed analytical expression for $\langle U(t), V(t) \rangle$, for it would only be a messy and uninformative expression involving the inverse cosine function.

We continue the analytic approach in the special case of constant wave velocity λ and constant boat speed κ. Without loss of generality we might suppose that

$$P(t) = \langle \gamma(t), \delta(t) \rangle = \langle \kappa t, 0 \rangle$$

---

[32] These calculations are only valid for shallow water. In deep water the wave energy is spread over a spectrum of waves of different velocities. An analysis of this energy spectrum leads to the astonishing conclusion that, in deep water, $\sin \beta(t)$ is always equal to 1/3; in other words, the angle $\beta(t)$ is always 29° 28′. For a nice explanation of this fact, we recommend R. A. Tricker's *Bores, Breakers, Waves and Wakes*, Mills and Boon, Ltd., England, 1965, and American Elsevier, New York.

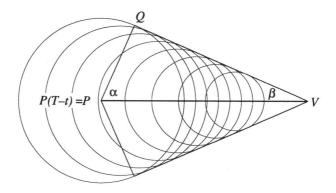

FIGURE 3.65   Wake from a boat with constant speed in shallow water

In this case, the boat's velocity vector $\langle \gamma'(t), \delta'(t) \rangle$ is $\langle \kappa, 0 \rangle$, and so $\alpha(t)$ reduces to the constant $\cos^{-1}(\lambda/\kappa)$. Now we obviously have

$$\langle U, V \rangle \;=\; R \begin{bmatrix} \cos\alpha & \mp \sin\alpha \\ \pm\sin\alpha & \cos\alpha \end{bmatrix} \langle \lambda(T-t), 0 \rangle$$

Thus the wake is a straight line, since these equations for U and V are linear in t. This situation is depicted in Figure 3.65, which we have labeled with all the relevant parameters. Notice that the angle α has a clear physical meaning in this picture; as we said above it is the angle between the boat's velocity vector and the vector $\langle U, V \rangle$ joining $P(T-t)$ to the point Q on the wake that touches the circle centered at $P = P(T-t)$. Since this circle is tangent to the wake at Q, we also see that the segment $\overline{PQ}$ meets the wake at right angles. Therefore PQV is a right angle, and so the angle β at $V = P(T)$ is complementary to α. Thus $\sin\beta = \lambda/\kappa$.

In fact, Figure 3.65 is approximately correct for any wake, as $t \to 0$, i.e., as we go to the limit of examining an infinitesimally small triangle PQV. The angle β does not change as we go to this limit, and so we observe that, for any wake whatever, the angle β satisfies $\sin\beta = \lambda/\kappa$.

Retaining our assumption that the boat moves along a straight line, let us watch what happens as the boat accelerates or decelerates. These two cases are illustrated in Figures 3.66 and 3.67. We have $\cos\alpha(t) = \lambda/v(t)$, where $v(t)$ is the boat's (time-dependent) velocity. Thus in the first of the figures (acceleration), $\alpha(t)$ is increasing with t, and so the wake is becoming more nearly parallel to the direction of travel. This gives a wake with a concave appearance as in Figure 3.66. On the other hand, a decelerating boat gives a wake with decreasing $\alpha(t)$ and a convex appearance as in Figure 3.67.

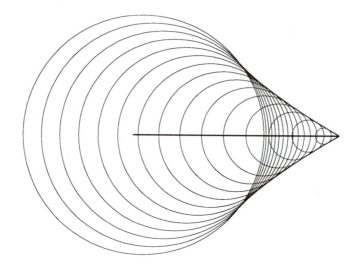

FIGURE 3.66   Accelerating from the wave velocity

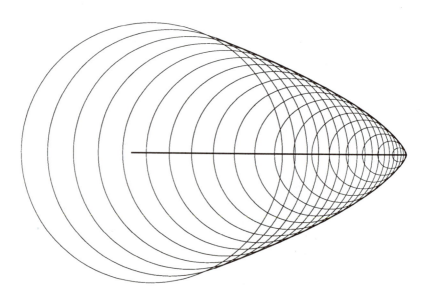

FIGURE 3.67   Decelerating to the wave velocity

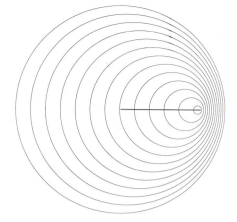

FIGURE 3.68   Subsonic flight

Exercises

1. Make some computer drawings of boats and their wakes in shallow water. The sample pictures given here should be good as examples to start with. Also make a picture of the wake behind a boat moving with constant speed in a circular arc.

2. Discuss the following problem. Suppose you have an accurate drawing that shows the path of a boat and an instantaneous picture of one side of the wake. Could one deduce the position of the boat at past times t? (Regard this as a purely mathematical problem.)

BREAKING THE SOUND BARRIER

It is interesting to repeat our analysis of wakes, with the boat replaced by an airplane. Of course, in this case, the disturbance occurs in the (3-dimensional) atmosphere, and its boundary is 2-dimensional instead of 1-dimensional. Nevertheless, our 2-dimensional pictures adequately represent a 2-dimensional view of the situation. The traveling disturbance in this case is generally known as sound. Our pictures are approximately correct for sound waves generated by an airplane, since in still air of one fixed temperature and pressure, sound has a fixed velocity λ. Figure 3.68 shows the flight of an airplane at subsonic speeds (i.e., speeds below the speed of sound). As we said above, the equation for $\alpha(t)$ has no solution, and there is no wake—as indeed is evident from the figure. Figure 3.65 can be regarded also as showing sound waves emanating from an airplane flying at supersonic speeds. In this context, $\beta(t)$ is called the *Mach angle*, and the cone of revolution of this angle (i.e. the full envelope) is called the *Mach cone*.

One significant difference between these two kinds of flight is that supersonic flight has a *zone of silence*, while subsonic flight does not. Regardless of

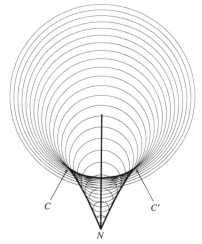

C C'

N

FIGURE 3.69   Breaking the sound barrier, ... or the bell of a Sousaphone?

how long the plane in Figure 3.65 has been in the air, a person standing out-side the Mach cone cannot hear it. When the cone reaches one, the plane will suddenly be audible.[33] On the other hand, a plane flying overhead at subsonic speeds will be heard with gradually increasing volume (and with a Doppler shift).

Figure 3.69 shows the gradual creation of the Mach cone as a plane accel-erates through the sound barrier. Notice that the resulting envelope (regarded as a plane curve) has two cusps, C and C'. From the cusps to the nose N of the plane, we have the two boundaries of the nascent Mach cone. The part of the envelope between the two cusps is something we have not seen before. It comes from the piling up of sound waves in front of the plane just as the plane reaches the speed of sound (which partly accounts for the energy needed to push through the sound barrier). Geometrically it can be explained as follows. Think of adding time t as a third dimension to Figure 3.69. Then think of the figure as depicting a surface with circular cross sections, with the circle created at time t being located in the plane with third coordinate t. This surface has roughly the shape of a tapering tube that bends near its wide end. In this way the shape of the surface is like that of a brass instrument, such as a Sousaphone. Thus the two parts of the envelope correspond to the two type of horizon that one can observe in looking at a Sousaphone. The (internal) horizon seen inside the bell corresponds to the part of the envelope between the cusps, and the (external) horizon seen below the bell corresponds to the part of the envelope between the

---

[33]This sudden audibility is not, however, the full cause of sonic boom. An airplane in supersonic flight also creates a *shock wave*, which we have not shown in Figure 3.65, and which is not predictable from purely geometric considerations. A shock wave occurs in air that is heated by friction of the motion. The heating increases the sound velocity and thus broadens the Mach angle.

FIGURE 3.70   A solid and its shadow

cusps and the nose. In §3.4.12, we take up the analogy between horizons and envelopes in earnest.

Exercises

1. Make a portfolio of computer drawings of mach cones, especially including one like Figure 3.69. Use the methods of this section to calculate the envelope and include the envelope in your drawing.

2. Another difference between subsonic travel and supersonic travel is this. In the subsonic case, an observer hears sounds in the order they were created. Thus, if a car drives by with the radio playing a song, one can make out the song, albeit a bit distorted by Doppler shift. This is far from true in the supersonic case. Illustrate this by using Figure 3.65, perhaps allowing the circles to grow (as they do with time).

3.4.12   Horizons and shadows

In viewing a surface, one often can see a boundary, or outline, between surface and non-surface. It is helpful to think of this in terms of ordinary objects, especially smoothly curved objects such as the curving surface of a car, a basketball, a cup or a smooth rock. This is the curve that we try to reproduce on paper when we make a sketch of the object. If we place a point source of light at the viewpoint and place a screen behind the object (as in Figure 3.70), the shadow will be a 2-dimensional figure that has the same outline as our original surface.

It is our general objective to give a mathematical description of this outline, or apparent contour, or shadow or *horizon* as it is sometimes called.[34]

In §5.6 below we will analyze this problem generally, but for the moment we will content ourselves with the limiting case where the object is very far from the viewer or, equivalently, that the shadow is formed by parallel rays of light. In this case the problem can be given a simple mathematical description as follows. We may assume that our surface is defined in space by an equation

$$F(x, y, z) = 0 \tag{3.44}$$

and that the light rays are parallel to the z-axis. Suppose that $\langle x, y, z \rangle$ is a point where these parallel light rays just graze the surface. Consider the vector

$$v = \langle F_1(x, y, z), F_2(x, y, z), F_3(x, y, z) \rangle$$

where F_i denotes the ith partial derivative of F. It is well know that v is either the zero vector or perpendicular to the surface. In the latter case, v is perpendicular to the vector $\langle 0, 0, 1 \rangle$ (since the latter is tangent to the surface), and so we have

$$F_3(x, y, z) = 0 \tag{3.45}$$

and in the fomer case ($v = 0$) we also have this equation, trivially. Therefore, if we can eliminate z from Equations (3.44) and (3.45), then we will have an equation defining a curve in x and y that represents the horizon or locus.

The reader is asked to notice that what we have done here is exactly what we did in §3.4.11, only from a slightly different point of view. For instance, we can disregard the third dimension and choose to regard the z appearing in Equation (3.44) as merely a *parameter*. (In other words, we think of Equation (3.44) as defining a family of x, y-curves, one for each fixed value of z.) From this point of view, Equation (3.44) is no different from the main equation of §3.4.11, since there is no effective difference in calling the parameter either z or θ. Moreover, the shadow described here obviously has a boundary, which is the envelope described in the previous section. Moreover, this interchange of concepts between the two section is also valid when applied in the reverse manner, for we may obviously take any F as might be given to us in §3.4.11 and then consider shadows of the figure given by Equation (3.44). Therefore, this section may be regarded as restating and confirming the previous one, from this different point of view.

There is one case where we can make a very practical application of Equations (3.44) and (3.45), namely, for $F(x, y, z)$ a quadratic function of x, y and z, i.e., a polynomial in these variables, all of whose terms are of degree ≤ 2. In this case, as is not hard to check, Equation (3.45) always turns out to be *linear*

---

[34]This usage is an extension of the original meaning of *horizon* as the boundary seen in looking at Earth (e.g., from a hill).

in x, y and z. Therefore, except in special cases, it is very easy to eliminate z from Equations (3.44) and (3.45). For example, for the surface

$$2xz + y^2 + z^2 = 1$$

taking the partial derivative with respect to z yields

$$2x + 2z = 0$$

and hence z can be eliminated by substituting $-x$ for z. Thus the shadow equation is

$$-x^2 + y^2 = 1$$

and hence the shadow is a hyperbola. In particular, it should be clear that in all cases the shadow is given by a quadratic equation.

Exercise

1. Find shadows of all the 3-variable quadratic equations mentioned in Exercise 4 on page 164 (in §3.1.7). One could find shadows in the direction of all three coordinate axes.

4 Plane projective geometry

All the collineations of $\mathbb{R}^2$ discussed in Chapter 3 mapped parallel lines to parallel lines, and this was in fact a necessary feature of collineations as we defined them there. Nevertheless, the reader must be familiar with drawings that depict parallel lines as if they intersected (at a so-called vanishing point). A drawing such as the one in Figure 4.1 can be thought of as a transformation from one copy of $\mathbb{R}^2$, the plane of the ground, to another copy of $\mathbb{R}^2$, the plane of the paper on which the picture was drawn. Such transformations are called *projective transformations*, and it is our objective in this chapter to study them. They share with collineations the property that lines map to lines, at least if we expand the class of lines to include *ideal lines*, which we will explain in §4.1.2. As part of the study of projective transformations, we will begin our study of a branch of geometry known as *projective geometry*.

4.1 Perspectivity and homogeneous coordinates

4.1.1 A simple perspective drawing

Let us return to the example of exactly how we see, draw[1] or photograph a scene such as the railroad tracks drawn in Figure 4.1. Let us specifically endeavor to understand mathematically what happens in making a photograph[2] of the scene. We begin by laying down a spatial coordinate system with horizontal axes labeled x_1 and x_2, and a vertical axis labeled x_3. It makes things a little easier if we

---

[1] Actually, techniques of drawing, as currently understood, are rather far from the ideas discussed here. The artist's eye does a splendid job of carrying out the perspectivity, so the artist needs no mathematics per se. The hard part is to get the hand to draw what the eye really sees. See, for example, *Drawing on the Right Side of the Brain*, by Betty Edwards, J. P. Tarcher, Inc., Los Angeles, 1979.

[2] It would take us too far afield to discuss the fine points of photography. Therefore, we imagine an ideal camera with infinite f-number, perfect focus, perfect lighting, distortionless lens, grainless film, no motion, and so on. Deviations from these conditions do in fact cause deviations from the theory we are describing.

FIGURE 4.1   Drawing of railroad tracks, with vanishing point at P

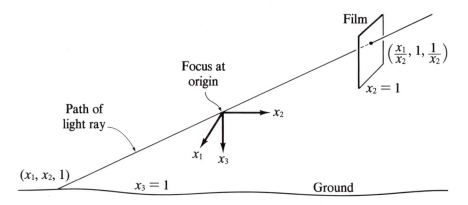

FIGURE 4.2   Coordinates of corresponding points on ground, lens and film

think of the positive x_3-axis as going down toward the ground from the origin. In fact, we take the origin one unit up from the ground, so that *the equation of the ground is*

$$x_3 = 1$$

We next position the camera with its lens at the origin, so that *the film lies in the plane with equation*

$$x_2 = 1$$

(see Figure 4.2).

Now let us investigate the transformation effected by the camera between a point $P_g = \langle x_1, x_2, 1 \rangle$ on the ground and the corresponding point $P_f = \langle x_1', 1, x_3' \rangle$ on the film. The operation of our ideal camera is very simple: it locates P_f on the film plane so as to be in a line with P_g and the lens point $\langle 0, 0, 0 \rangle$. Mathematically, the line through $\langle 0, 0, 0 \rangle$ and P_g consists of all scalar multiples $t \cdot P_g$. In other words, the line is parametrized by

$$P(t) \ = \ t \cdot \langle x_1, x_2, 1 \rangle$$

Therefore, to obtain the coordinates of P_f, we need only solve the equation

$$t \cdot \langle x_1, x_2, 1 \rangle \ = \ \langle x_1', 1, x_3' \rangle$$

From the second coordinates here, we obtain $tx_2 = 1$, i.e. $t = 1/x_2$, from which we easily obtain[3]

$$P_f \ = \ \langle x_1', 1, x_3' \rangle \ = \ \langle x_1/x_2, 1, 1/x_2 \rangle$$

Let us also write $P_f = \Pi(P_g)$, and say that Π is the *perspectivity between the ground plane and the film plane that is determined by lines through the origin.*

Let us see precisely what happened to the railroad track in this example. The two rails may be thought of as parallel lines in the plane $x_3 = 1$. More specifically, all we really know is that the track begins in the foreground (some small negative value of x_2) and continues for negative values of x_2 of larger and larger absolute value. Let us suppose therefore that we have the following parametrization of the two rails (with positive values of u approaching infinity):

first rail:
$$\begin{aligned} x_1(u) &= A + bu \\ x_2(u) &= -u \\ x_3(u) &= 1 \end{aligned}$$

second rail:
$$\begin{aligned} x_1(u) &= B + bu \\ x_2(u) &= -u \\ x_3(u) &= 1 \end{aligned}$$

Apply the perspectivity $\Pi : P_g \mapsto P_f$ to these points, we find the following parametrization for the lines in the film plane that image the two rails:

first line:
$$\begin{aligned} x_1(u) &= -\frac{A + bu}{u} \\ x_2(u) &= 1 \end{aligned}$$

---

[3]Many problems in computer graphics will yield to an analysis, like this one, of the path of light rays—which uses little more than the theory of similar triangles. Nevertheless, we feel that the approach to be outlined in this chapter can produce more informative and systematic methods of solution.

$$x_3(u) = -\frac{1}{u}$$

second line: $x_1(u) = -\frac{B + bu}{u}$

$$x_2(u) = 1$$

$$x_3(u) = -\frac{1}{u}$$

Reparametrizing these two lines via $s = 1/u$, we have

first line: $x_1(s) = -b - As$

$$x_2(s) = 1$$

$$x_3(s) = -s$$

second line: $x_1(s) = -b - Bs$

$$x_2(s) = 1$$

$$x_3(s) = -s$$

where now s is a positive variable approaching 0.

We see therefore that the lines that are Π-images of the two rails meet at the point $V = \langle -b, 1, 0 \rangle$. This of course is the *vanishing point* that we mentioned before. We can now resolve the apparent paradox that the rails do not meet on the ground, but appear to meet on the photographic image. *The point $V = \langle -b, 1, 0 \rangle$ has no corresponding point on the ground*, for there do not exist $x_1, x_2 \in \mathbb{R}$ such that $\langle x_1/x_2, 1, 1/x_2 \rangle = \langle -b, 1, 0 \rangle$. Thus the paradox of the vanishing point occurs because *perspectivity Π is not a bijection between the two planes* — some points, like $\langle -b, 1, 0 \rangle$, fail to be in the image of Π, and others, like $\langle 1, 0, 1 \rangle$, fail to be in the domain of Π.

Thus the perspectivity Π detects that certain points are missing from the ground plane, namely, for each b, a point P_b such that $\Pi(P_b) = \langle -b, 1, 0 \rangle$. Actually the absence of the point P_b can be seen from classical geometry. P_b ought to be a point that is collinear with the origin $\langle 0, 0, 0 \rangle$ and $\Pi(P_b) = \langle -b, 1, 0 \rangle$, but this is impossible, since the line determined by these two points obeys the equation $x_3 = 0$ and hence is *parallel* to the ground plane. Thus *the existence of parallel lines* can be seen as the source of major difficulties in the study of perspectivities. In the *projective geometry* that we are about to introduce, this difficulty is neatly overcome (at the expense of a little intuitiveness) by eliminating parallel lines altogether (see Theorem 4.2). Any two lines in a projective plane have a point in common, and in 3-dimensional projective space, any line meets any plane.

Exercise

1. Consider the parabola lying in the ground that is parametrized by $P(s) = \langle -1 - s^2, s, 1 \rangle$. What is the image of this curve on the film? (Identify it as a specific type of conic section.)

4.1.2   Ideal points and lines

Taking A in the equations for the first rail to be arbitrary, we see that the perspectivity Π maps the family of parallel lines

$$
\begin{aligned}
x_1(u) &= A + bu \\
x_2(u) &= -u \\
x_3(u) &= 1
\end{aligned}
$$

$(-\infty < A < \infty)$, to a family of lines

$$
\begin{aligned}
x_1(s) &= -b - As \\
x_2(s) &= 1 \\
x_3(s) &= -s
\end{aligned}
$$

$(-\infty < A < \infty)$ that has $V = \langle -b, 1, 0 \rangle$ as a common point. Thus there is a one-one correspondence between points in the film plane that have the form $\langle -b, 1, 0 \rangle$ and families of parallel lines on the ground (one family for each value of the parameter b)—except for the family of lines $\langle u + A, 0, 1 \rangle$ for $-\infty < A < \infty$.

The need for points like the points P_b mentioned in §4.1.1 gave rise to a tradition of assigning an *ideal point* (sometimes called a *point at infinity*) to each family of parallel lines. According to this tradition, the family of lines

$$
\begin{aligned}
x_1(u) &= A + bu \\
x_2(u) &= -u \\
x_3(u) &= 1
\end{aligned}
$$

$(-\infty < A < \infty)$ can be said to intersect in an ideal point P_b. Supposing that this idea can be carried out in a consistent manner, it follows that $\Pi(P_b) = \langle -b, 1, 0 \rangle$, and thus that P_b is the missing vanishing point.

Although the idea of ideal points may seem less intuitive than that of the ordinary points we are accustomed to, there is no real conceptual difficulty in adding them. After all, ordinary points were abstractions themselves in the first place. For a mathematical theory, however, it is not enough to voice our feeling that, ideally, there ought to be a point out at the end of every line. What is required is a consistent mathematical theory that includes the notions we seek—in this case, the ideal points. This is the theory of projective planes, which are the subject of §4.2. We will present this theory as a self-existing mathematical entity, having the ideas of this section as motivation but, strictly speaking, not requiring these ideas mathematically. First, however, we take one more look at our motivating example.

4.1.3   Homogeneous coordinates

Let us look some more at the ground plane, defined by the equation $x_3 = 1$. Recall that, to define the perspectivity Π on a point P_g of this plane, all we needed was to know the line L connecting P_g to the origin. This line consists of all scalar multiples $t \cdot P_g$ of the point P_g. Thus if $P_g = \langle x_1, x_2, x_3 \rangle$, then L is determined just as well by $\langle tx_1, tx_2, tx_3 \rangle$ as by $\langle x_1, x_2, x_3 \rangle$, as long as $t \neq 0$.

With this motivation, we introduce *homogeneous coordinates* in the ground plane as follows. Each point has coordinates $\langle x_1, x_2, x_3 \rangle$, with *not all three coordinates zero*. If $t \neq 0$, then the triple $\langle tx_1, tx_2, tx_3 \rangle$ is said to be *equivalent to* the triple $\langle x_1, x_2, x_3 \rangle$. The coordinates of a point with (ordinary, spatial) coordinates $\langle x_1, x_2, 1 \rangle$ are now taken to be these three numbers or any scalar multiple of them. Thus each point in that plane has three coordinates, but the coordinates are determined only up to a non-zero scalar multiple.

What is gained by this exotic way to coordinatize a plane? The main thing gained is the reappearance of the missing ideal points in a completely natural way. Notice that, if we assign homogeneous coordinates to an ordinary coordinate plane π by giving coordinates $\langle x_1, x_2, 1 \rangle$ to the point that has ordinary coordinates $\langle x_1, x_2 \rangle$, then there is no point of π with homogeneous coordinates $\langle y_1, y_2, 0 \rangle$. Points with these coordinates are precisely the ideal points that must be added to π to make a true projective plane, on which perspectivities can be defined as bijections.

Instead of trying to really make every line of the above precise, let us take what turns out to be an easier path. We will regard the discussion here as a necessary part of the motivation for the mathematically precise definition that we present in §4.2.

4.2   Analytic projective plane geometry

One often makes a distinction between the *synthetic* and *analytic* approaches to proving theorems in geometry. The synthetic approach proceeds from axioms, and the analytic approach proceeds from a model of geometry, usually a numerical model of some sort. (The prime example is the Descartes model of triples of real numbers for points and linear equations for lines and planes.) In projective geometry, both of these possibilities exist. We will concentrate on the analytic approach, although we will say a few words about synthetic projective geometry in §4.3.

4.2.1   Projective planes

As we saw in §4.1.3, the homogeneous coordinates of a point in an ordinary plane π are not uniquely determined, but form the set of scalar multiples of a point in $\mathbb{R}^3$, i.e., a 1-dimensional subspace of $\mathbb{R}^3$.

With this motivation, we define, for every 3-dimensional space $\mathbf{V}$, *the projective plane* $\boldsymbol{P}(\mathbf{V})$ *of* $\mathbf{V}$ to be the set of all 1-dimensional subspaces of $\mathbf{V}$, which we refer to as the *points* of $\boldsymbol{P}(\mathbf{V})$. For every 2-dimensional subspace $\mathbf{W}$ of $\mathbf{V}$, we define *the line* $L_{\mathbf{W}}$ *of* $\boldsymbol{P}(\mathbf{V})$ to be the set of points of $\boldsymbol{P}(\mathbf{V})$ that are subspaces of $\mathbf{W}$. By *a line* of $\boldsymbol{P}(\mathbf{V})$, we mean any $L_{\mathbf{W}}$. When we refer to *the projective plane* $\boldsymbol{P}(\mathbf{V})$, we generally mean the mathematical structure consisting of both the points and the lines of $\boldsymbol{P}(\mathbf{V})$. When we say "a projective plane," we mean $\boldsymbol{P}(\mathbf{V})$ for some $\mathbf{V}$; but the reader is advised that in the context of synthetic projective geometry (§4.3), there exist projective planes that cannot be coordinatized by any vector space.

We sometimes denote the plane $\boldsymbol{P}(\mathbb{R}^3)$ by the alternate notation $\boldsymbol{P}^2(\mathbb{R})$, or even $\boldsymbol{P}^2$, if context assures us that the field of scalars is $\mathbb{R}$. (The change of numbers from 3 to 2 is deliberate here. A projective plane is built from a 3-dimensional vector space!)

THEOREM 4.1   In any projective plane, for any two points P and Q, there exists a unique line $\overleftrightarrow{PQ}$ containing both P and Q.

Proof   Immediate from the fact that any two distinct 1-dimensional subspaces together generate a 2-dimensional subspace.   □

THEOREM 4.2   In any projective plane, any two distinct lines have a unique point in common.

Proof   Uniqueness is immediate from the previous theorem, for if lines L and M contain distinct points P and Q, then $L = \overleftrightarrow{PQ} = M$, and so L and M cannot be distinct lines. For the existence of a point of intersection of two lines, let L and M be distinct lines of the plane $\boldsymbol{P}(\mathbf{V})$, which is to say that L and M are distinct 2-dimensional subspaces of $\mathbf{V}$. Since they are distinct, the space $P + Q$ must be larger than either of them, and hence must have dimension larger than 2, and therefore has dimension 3. It now follows from Theorem 1.13 that $P \cap Q$ is a subspace of dimension 1; this is the required point that lies both on P and on Q.   □

4.2.2   Coordinatizing a projective plane

If we are given a basis $\langle v_1, v_2, v_3 \rangle$ of a 3-dimensional space $\mathbf{V}$, then we may assign coordinates $\langle \alpha_1, \alpha_2, \alpha_3 \rangle$ to an arbitrary point P of $\boldsymbol{P}(\mathbf{V})$, as follows. P is a 1-dimensional subspace of $\mathbf{V}$, and as such consists of all scalar multiples $t \cdot v$ of a non-zero vector $v \in \mathbf{V}$. Writing $v = \sum_{i=1}^{3} \alpha_i \cdot v_i$, we declare $\langle \alpha_1, \alpha_2, \alpha_3 \rangle$ to be *homogeneous coordinates of* the point P with respect to the basis $\langle v_1, v_2, v_3 \rangle$. It is clear that the triple $\langle \alpha_1, \alpha_2, \alpha_3 \rangle$ is determined only up to a non-zero scalar multiple, and so homogeneous coordinates themselves are determined only up to a non-zero scalar multiple. Notice that, since $v \neq 0$, *the homogeneous coordinates of P cannot all be zero.*

In particular, we coordinatize $P^2(\mathbb{R})$ according to the standard basis $v_1 = \langle 1, 0, 0 \rangle$, $v_2 = \langle 0, 1, 0 \rangle$ and $v_3 = \langle 0, 0, 1 \rangle$.

Throughout §4.2, let us fix a projective plane $P(V)$, and take coordinates with respect to a fixed basis $\langle v_1, v_2, v_3 \rangle$ of V.

4.2.3   The equation of a line in a plane

Just as in ordinary analytic geometry, each line has a linear equation.

THEOREM 4.3   Given any three scalars $\beta_1, \beta_2, \beta_3$, not all zero, the set of all points P with coordinates $\langle x_1, x_2, x_3 \rangle$ satisfying

$$\beta_1 x_1 + \beta_2 x_2 + \beta_3 x_3 = 0 \tag{4.1}$$

is a line of the projective plane $P(V)$. Conversely for every line L_W of this plane, there exist scalars $\beta_1, \beta_2, \beta_3$, not all zero, such that L_V is the set of points satisfying Equation (4.1).

Proof   It is not hard to check that Equation (4.1) defines a subspace of dimension 2. Conversely, given a 2-dimensional subspace W of V, we know from Theorem 1.20 and Corollary 1.22 of §1.1.5 that for some 1-dimensional space U there exists a homomorphism $f : V \longrightarrow U$ such that $W = \mathbf{KER}\, f$. Let u be a spanning vector of U, and let $\langle v_1, v_2, v_3 \rangle$ be the basis of V used to define homogeneous coordinates in $P(V)$. We then determine the required scalars $\beta_1, \beta_2, \beta_3$ by the condition that $f(v_i) = \beta_i \cdot u$ for $i = 1, 2, 3$. Now the point v with coordinates $\langle x_1, x_2, x_3 \rangle$ is in $W = \mathbf{KER}\, f$ iff

$$0 = f(v) = \left(\sum_{i=1}^{3} \beta_i x_i \right) \cdot u$$

Therefore clearly $v \in W$ iff Equation (4.1) holds.   □

4.2.4   Forming an ordinary plane by removing a line

In the plane $P^2 = P^2(\mathbb{R})$, let us consider the line L_0 that is defined by the equation $x_3 = 0$. We wish to see that if L_0 is removed from the plane P^2, then the remaining points and lines have the structure of the ordinary coordinate plane $\mathbb{R}^2$.[4]

To each point P of $\boldsymbol{P}^2 - L_0$, with homogeneous coordinates $\langle x_1, x_2, x_3 \rangle$, assign ordinary coordinates $\langle x_1', x_2' \rangle = \langle x_1/x_3, x_2/x_3 \rangle$. Notice that division by x_3 is allowed, because we have discarded those points for which $x_3 = 0$, and that the division process cancels out any multiplication by a scalar that might be applied to homogeneous coordinates. Therefore, we may conclude that the ordinary coordinates $\langle x_1', x_2' \rangle$ are well defined for all points of $\boldsymbol{P}^2 - L_0$.

THEOREM 4.4   Every line of $\boldsymbol{P}^2$ — except L_0 — intersects $\boldsymbol{P}^2 - L_0$ in an ordinary line of the coordinate plane $\mathbb{R}^2$ and, conversely, every line of $\mathbb{R}^2$ arises in this way.

Proof   By Theorem 4.3, a line L of $\boldsymbol{P}^2$ is given by an equation

$$\beta_1 x_1 + \beta_2 x_2 + \beta_3 x_3 = 0$$

Since $L \neq L_0$, we must have either $\beta_1 \neq 0$ or $\beta_2 \neq 0$. For points off the line L_0, we are allowed to divide by x_3, thereby obtaining the equation

$$\beta_1 x_1/x_3 + \beta_2 x_2/x_3 + \beta_3 = 0$$

or

$$\beta_1 x_1' + \beta_2 x_2' + \beta_3 = 0$$

Since $\beta_i \neq 0$ for $i = 1$ or $i = 2$, this is the equation of an ordinary line. On the other hand all these steps are reversible, so that from the equation of the ordinary line we may go back to the equation of a projective line.   □

This theorem is our precise mathematical replacement for the intuitive idea of ideal point that we had in §4.1.2. The plane $\boldsymbol{P}^2$ differs from $\mathbb{R}^2$ in having one extra line—which we may call *the ideal line*—and each point on that line is a point of the type that previously we called an ideal point.

4.3 Synthetic projective geometry

Theorem 4.1 is, as it stands, a familiar axiom of Euclidean plane geometry; and Theorem 4.2, although spectacularly false in Euclidean geometry, is at least of

---

[4]Actually there is nothing special about the line L_0; *any line L* may be removed to form an ordinary plane. To see this take a basis in which L has the equation $x_3 = 0$ and apply the arguments of this section.

the same style as Theorem 4.1. Thus is suggested the idea of looking for an axiomatic presentation of projective geometry.

To be useful, an axiomatic treatment of projective geometry ought to be relatively succinct, easily understood, easily seen to be true in analytic projective geometry, yet strong enough that the basic facts of geometry (say in P^2) can be deduced from it. In fact, the subject is vast, and many attempts have been made. At this point we mention only one possible system, an elegant one that we take from *Combinatorial Theory*, by Marshall Hall Jr., Blaisdell Publishing Company, Waltham, 1967. It is an axiom system that applies not only to planes, but to projective spaces of any dimension. (We will study only projective planes and projective 3-spaces.) Although Theorem 4.2 is often used as an axiom of projective geometry, this is not explicitly done here. (It is a fairly direct corollary of the second axiom.) Hall's axioms are

- There is one and only one line containing two distinct points.

- If A, B, C are three points not on a line, and if $D \neq A$ is a point on the line through A and B, and if $E \neq A$ is a point on the line through A and C, then there is a point F on a line with D and E and also on a line with B and C.

- Every line contains at least three distinct points.

These axioms hold in $P(\mathbf{V})$ for any vector space $\mathbf{V}$, with scalars from any field whatever, even possibly one of the *finite fields* (that we have not discussed). Therefore they are too general to adequately address questions of connectedness, continuity and ordering of the real number line $\mathbb{R}$ that are sometimes needed in dealing with $P^2(\mathbb{R})$. There are some very sophisticated—albeit more specialized—axiom systems, for instance the system of O. Veblen and J. W. Young[5] that address these questions. In this treatment, we omit any discussion of such axiom systems. An axiomatic system for real projective geometry ought to be strong enough to permit a synthetic proof of the result that we have derived analytically as Theorem 4.6 in §4.4.1. (In some treatments this is handled simply by taking Theorem 4.6 to be an axiom.)

4.4 Projective transformations of P^2

A *projective transformation* or *collineation* between two projective planes $P(\mathbf{V})$ and $P(\mathbf{W})$ is a one-to-one correspondence ϕ from the set of points of $P(\mathbf{V})$ to the set of points of $P(\mathbf{W})$ such that, for any three points P, Q and R of $P(\mathbf{V})$ P, Q and R are collinear iff $\phi(P), \phi(Q)$ and $\phi(R)$ are collinear. A collineation between $P(\mathbf{V})$ and itself is called simply a *collineation of $P(\mathbf{V})$*.

Collineations will be useful to us for the following reasons:

---

[5] *Projective Geometry*, Vol. I, Ginn and Company, Boston, 1910.

- They include—by disregarding the ideal line P_0 of §4.1.2—all the collineations that were studied in §3.3 (see §4.5).

- They include the perspectivities discussed earlier in this chapter (see §4.6). In fact, it should be clear that any arrangement of film and lens gives rise to a collineation.

- They are easily represented as 3×3 matrices.

- The idea generalizes easily to collineations of space (4×4 matrices) and perspective maps from space to a plane (3×4 matrices).

To examine the last two of these points, especially the next to the last one, let us consider an isomorphism $f : \mathbf{V} \longrightarrow \mathbf{W}$, between the 3-dimensional spaces $\mathbf{V}$ and $\mathbf{W}$. The associated plane map

$$f^{\bullet} : P(\mathbf{V}) \longrightarrow P(\mathbf{W})$$

is defined as follows. A point P of $P(\mathbf{V})$ is really a 1-dimensional subspace $\mathbf{U}$ of $\mathbf{V}$. Taking u as a generator of $\mathbf{U}$, we define $f^{\bullet}(\mathbf{U})$ to be the subspace of $\mathbf{W}$ that is generated by $f(u)$.

THEOREM 4.5 $f^{\bullet}$ is well defined and a collineation.

Proof   If another generator u' is taken, then $u' = \lambda \cdot u$ for some non-zero scalar λ. Clearly $f(u') = \lambda \cdot f(u)$, and so $f(u')$ and $f(u)$ generate the same subspace of $\mathbf{W}$; thus $f^{\bullet}$ is well defined. We know (say from Corollary 1.22) that an isomorphism of vector spaces maps 2-dimensional subspaces to 2-dimensional subspaces, and hence $f^{\bullet}$ respects collinearity. A similar argument applied to f^{-1} shows that $(f^{-1})^{\bullet} = (f^{\bullet})^{-1}$ also respects collinearity, and hence that $f^{\bullet}$ is a collineation. $\square$

The remainder of §4.4 is devoted to proving that there are no collineations of $P^2(\mathbb{R})$ besides those that arise in this manner; in other words, every collineation can be represented by a 3×3 matrix. (See Theorem 4.13 in §4.4.5, which is our main theoretical result about projective geometry.) A major tool in proving this linear representation result is Theorem 4.6, which we state in §4.4.1, but do not prove until §4.4.4. The reader who is interested only in the applications will lose no continuity in skipping from here to the beginning of §4.5.

4.4.1   Collineations that fix four points

The following theorem is one of the fundamental results of *real* projective geometry. It is however false for projective geometry over the field $\mathbb{C}$ of *complex* numbers, for the mapping that sends any vector v to its complex conjugate $\overline{v}$ is a non-identity collineation that fixes any point with real coordinates.

THEOREM 4.6   If f is a collineation of $\boldsymbol{P}^2(\mathbb{R})$ and f fixes four points, no three of which are collinear, then f is the identity function.

One cannot remove the requirement that no three of the four points are collinear. For instance, if f is the linear map with matrix

$$\begin{bmatrix} 1 & 0 & 0 \\ 0 & 2 & 0 \\ 0 & 0 & 1 \end{bmatrix}$$

then $f^{\bullet}$ fixes four non-collinear points (e.g., any three points on the x_1-axis and the ideal point with coordinates $\langle 0, 1, 0 \rangle$).

4.4.2   Defining arithmetic in a projective plane

The difficulty we face in proving a theorem like Theorem 4.6 of §4.4.1 is that collineations are defined in terms of the incidence relation of projective planes. In other words, incidence—the notion of a point's being on, or incident to, a line— is the only the mathematical notion appearing in the definition of collineation. Thus, a collineation may be defined, somewhat loosely, as a map that preserves the incidence relation. This notion seems at first glance to be a flabby and uninformative concept, incapable of providing any calculations that might serve us in our search for a proof. One of the prime discoveries of the projective geometers, however, was that *addition and multiplication of real numbers are definable in the plane* $\boldsymbol{P}(\mathbb{R}^2)$. (The full realization of this fact, which is itself a natural extension of the ideas of Descartes, is usually attributed to K. C. von Staudt around 1850.) After proving this fact, we may attack Theorem 4.6 with the theory of addition and multiplication of real numbers, which is to say we will have all of elementary algebra and calculus at our disposal. The reader will shortly see in detail how this comes to pass. After a preliminary lemma, we begin with the definition of addition, deferring the proof of Theorem 4.6 until we have proved a number of auxiliary results.

LEMMA 1   In a projective plane $\boldsymbol{P}^2(F)$, let L be any line, and let P and P' be any points not on L. Then there exists a collineation ϕ of this plane such that $\phi(P) = P'$ and such that $\phi(R) = R$ for every R on L.

Proof   Let us take our projective plane to be $\boldsymbol{P}(\mathbf{V})$, where $\mathbf{V}$ is a 3-dimensional space over the field F. Let $\langle v_1, v_2 \rangle$ be a basis for the 2-dimensional subspace of $\mathbf{V}$ corresponding to the line L, and then let $\langle v_3 \rangle$ be a basis of the 1-dimensional subspace corresponding to P. Since P is not on L, the vectors $\langle v_1, v_2, v_3 \rangle$ span a 3-dimensional subspace of $\mathbf{V}$, and so in fact they form a basis of $\mathbf{V}$. Let $\langle v_3' \rangle$ be a basis of the 1-dimensional space corresponding to P'. By Theorem 1.18, there exists a unique linear isomorphism $f : \mathbf{V} \longrightarrow \mathbf{V}$ such that $f(v_1) = v_1, f(v_2) = v_2$ and $f(v_3) = v_3'$. Thus we clearly have $f^{\bullet}(P) = P'$ and $f^{\bullet}(R) = R$ for each R on

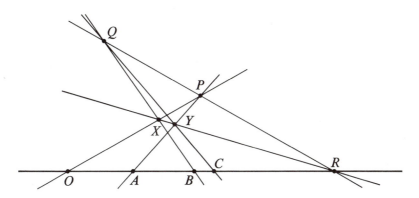

FIGURE 4.3 The configuration of addition in a projective plane

the line L. The fact that P' is not on L easily tells us that $f^{\bullet}$ is invertible and hence is a collineation. □

To begin our definition of arithmetic within projective geometry, we define an *addition configuration* in a projective plane $\boldsymbol{P}(\mathbf{V})$ to be a 9-tuple $\langle O, A, B, C, P, Q, R, X, Y \rangle$ of points, such that the following sets of points are collinear:

$$\{P, X, O\} \qquad \{Q, X, B\}$$
$$\{P, Y, A\} \qquad \{Q, Y, C\}$$
$$\{O, A, B, C, R\} \qquad \{P, Q, R\}$$
$$\{X, Y, R\}$$

but such that P, O and R are not collinear (see Figure 4.3).

Theorem 4.7 explains the terminology *addition configuration*.

THEOREM 4.7 Let us suppose that in the plane $\boldsymbol{P}(\mathbf{V})$, points O, A, B and C have (homogeneous) coordinates $\langle 0, 0, 1 \rangle, \langle a, 0, 1 \rangle, \langle b, 0, 1 \rangle, \langle c, 0, 1 \rangle$, respectively, and that R is the ideal point with coordinates $\langle 1, 0, 0 \rangle$. Then there exist points P, Q, X, Y such that $\langle O, A, B, C, P, Q, R, X, Y \rangle$ is an addition configuration, if and only if $a + b = c$.

Proof Let us first assume that $a + b = c$ and find the required four points to make an addition configuration. Let us define points P, Q, X and Y to be the points with (homogeneous) coordinates $\langle 0, 1, 0 \rangle, \langle -b, 1, 0 \rangle, \langle 0, 1, 1 \rangle, \langle a, 1, 1 \rangle$ (see Figure 4.4). Now to see that each of the seven sets of points (mentioned in the definition) is collinear, we simply write down—in the same order—seven linear equations in the variables x_1, x_2, x_3. The reader may easily check that, in each case, the linear equation defines a line that contains the points in question.

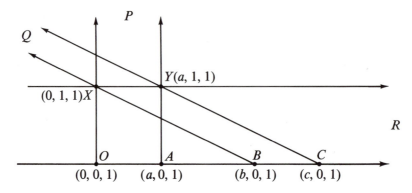

FIGURE 4.4   If $c = a + b$, this is an addition configuration

$$x_1 = 0 \qquad\qquad x_1 + bx_2 - bx_3 = 0$$
$$x_1 - ax_3 = 0 \qquad\qquad x_1 + bx_2 - (a+b)x_3 = 0$$
$$x_2 = 0 \qquad\qquad\qquad x_3 = 0$$
$$\qquad\qquad\qquad x_2 = x_3$$

Conversely, let us suppose that points P, Q, X, Y exist to form an addition configuration. The line joining O and R is clearly the line L with equation $x_2 = 0$. We know by the definition of *addition configuration* that P is not on L, and it is obvious that L also does not contain the point P' with homogeneous coordinates $\langle 0, 1, 0 \rangle$. It now follows from Lemma 1 that there exists a collineation ϕ fixing each point of L and such that $\phi(P) = P'$. Defining Q' to be $\phi(Q)$, X' to be $\phi(X)$ and X' to be $\phi(X)$, we immediately see that $\langle O, A, B, C, P', Q', R, X', Y' \rangle$ is also an addition configuration. To simplify notation, we will use the old notation P, Q, X, Y for the new points P', Q', X', Y'. Therefore, we may in fact assume that $\langle O, A, B, C, P, Q, R, X, Y \rangle$ is an addition configuration and that the coordinates of P are $\langle 0, 1, 0 \rangle$.

Now—assuming that this is a projective plane over the field $\mathbb{R}$ of real numbers—we may observe that the lines $\overleftrightarrow{OX}$ and $\overleftrightarrow{AY}$ are parallel (since they both contain the ideal point P), and that the lines $\overleftrightarrow{XB}$ and $\overleftrightarrow{YC}$ are parallel (since they both contain the ideal point Q). Therefore, it follows from the Euclidean theory of parallelograms that $OA \cong XY$ and $XY \cong BC$, which means that segments $\overline{OA}$ and $\overline{BC}$ have the same length. Thus

$$a - 0 = c - b$$

which means that $c = a + b$.

For a more formal proof, valid for any field of scalars, one can successively derive the following facts, starting from the coordinates and equations that are already known to us.

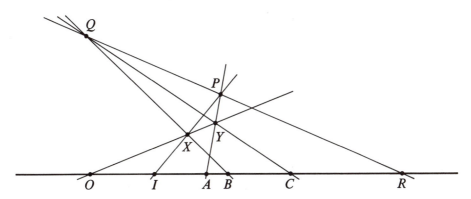

FIGURE 4.5   The configuration of multiplication in a projective plane

- The line $\overleftrightarrow{OP}$ has equation $x_1 = 0$.

- The line $\overleftrightarrow{AP}$ has equation $x_1 - ax_3 = 0$.

- For some k, the points X and Y have coordinates $\langle 0, k, 1 \rangle$ and $\langle a, k, 1 \rangle$.

- The line $\overleftrightarrow{BX}$ has equation $kx_1 + bx_2 - kbx_3 = 0$.

- The point Q has coordinates $\langle -b, k, 0 \rangle$.

- The line $\overleftrightarrow{QY}$ has equation $kx_1 + bx_2 - k(a+b)x_3 = 0$.

- The point C has coordinates $\langle a+b, 0, 1 \rangle$.

Since the coordinates of C are also known as $\langle c, 0, 1 \rangle$, we deduce that $c = a + b$.

□

Now we define a *multiplication configuration* in a projective plane $P(V)$ to be a 10-tuple $\langle O, I, A, B, C, P, Q, R, X, Y \rangle$ of points, such that the following sets of points are collinear:

$$\{P, X, I\} \qquad\qquad \{Q, X, B\}$$
$$\{P, Y, A\} \qquad\qquad \{Q, Y, C\}$$
$$\{O, I, A, B, C, R\} \qquad \{P, Q, R\}$$
$$\{X, Y, O\}$$

but such that P, O and R are not collinear (see Figure 4.5).
    Theorem 4.8 explains the terminology *multiplication configuration.*

THEOREM 4.8   Let us suppose that in the plane $P(V)$, points O, I, A, B and C have (homogeneous) coordinates $\langle 0, 0, 1 \rangle$, $\langle 1, 0, 1 \rangle$, $\langle a, 0, 1 \rangle$, $\langle b, 0, 1 \rangle$, $\langle c, 0, 1 \rangle$, respectively, and that R is the ideal point with coordinates $\langle 1, 0, 0 \rangle$. Then there

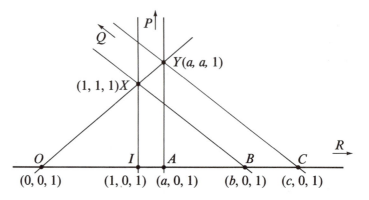

FIGURE 4.6   If $c = ab$, this is a multiplication configuration

exist points P, Q, X, Y such that $\langle O, I, A, B, C, P, Q, R, X, Y \rangle$ is a multiplication configuration, if and only if $ab = c$.

Proof   Let us first assume that $ab = c$ and find the required four points to make a multiplication configuration. Let us define points P, Q, X and Y to be the points with (homogeneous) coordinates $\langle 0, 1, 0 \rangle, \langle 1 - b, 1, 0 \rangle, \langle 1, 1, 1 \rangle, \langle a, a, 1 \rangle$ (see Figure 4.6). Now to see that each of the seven sets of points (mentioned in the definition) is collinear, we simply write down—in the same order—seven linear equations in the variables x_1, x_2, x_3. The reader may easily check that, in each case, the linear equation defines a line that contains the points in question.

$$x_1 = x_3 \qquad\qquad x_1 + (b-1)x_2 - bx_3 = 0$$
$$x_1 - ax_3 = 0 \qquad\quad x_1 + (b-1)x_2 - abx_3 = 0$$
$$x_2 = 0 \qquad\qquad\qquad\qquad x_3 = 0$$
$$x_1 = x_2$$

Conversely, let us suppose that points P, Q, X, Y exist to form a multiplication configuration. The line joining O and R is clearly the line L with equation $x_2 = 0$. We know by the definition of *multiplication configuration* that P is not on L, and it is obvious that L also does not contain the point P' with homogeneous coordinates $\langle 0, 1, 0 \rangle$. It now follows from Lemma 1 that there exists a collineation ϕ fixing each point of L and such that $\phi(P) = P'$. Defining Q' to be $\phi(Q)$, X' to be $\phi(X)$ and X' to be $\phi(X)$, we immediately see that $\langle O, I, A, B, C, P', Q', R, X', Y' \rangle$ is also a multiplication configuration. To simplify notation, we will use the old notation P, Q, X, Y for the new points P', Q', X', Y'. Therefore, we may in fact assume that $\langle O, I, A, B, C, P, Q, R, X, Y \rangle$ is a multiplication configuration and that the coordinates of P are $\langle 0, 1, 0 \rangle$.

Now—assuming that this is a projective plane over the field $\mathbb{R}$ of real numbers—we may observe that the lines $\overleftrightarrow{XI}$ and $\overleftrightarrow{YA}$ are parallel (since they both contain the ideal point P), and that the lines $\overleftrightarrow{XB}$ and $\overleftrightarrow{YC}$ are parallel (since they both contain the ideal point Q). Thus the Euclidean theory of similar triangles immediately yields

$$\frac{a}{1} = \frac{c}{b}$$

in other words, $c = ab$.

For a more formal proof, valid for any field of scalars, one can successively derive the following facts, starting from the coordinates and equations that are already known to us.

- The line $\overleftrightarrow{OR}$ has equation $x_2 = 0$.

- The line $\overleftrightarrow{IP}$ has equation $x_1 - x_3 = 0$.

- The line $\overleftrightarrow{AP}$ has equation $x_1 - ax_3 = 0$.

- For some k, the line $\overleftrightarrow{XY}$ has equation $x_2 - kx_1 = 0$.

- The point X has coordinates $\langle 1, k, 1 \rangle$.

- The point Y has coordinates $\langle a, ka, 1 \rangle$.

- The line $\overleftrightarrow{BX}$ has equation $kx_1 + (b-1)x_2 - kbx_3 = 0$.

- The point Q has coordinates $\langle (1-b), k, 0 \rangle$.

- The line $\overleftrightarrow{CY}$ has equation $kx_1 + (b-1)x - kabx_3 = 0$.

- The point C has coordinates $\langle ab, 0, 1 \rangle$.

Since the coordinates of C are also known to be $\langle c, 0, 1 \rangle$, we deduce that $c = ab$. $\qquad\square$

Notice that both the addition configuration and the multiplication configuration can be thought of as derived from the four points P, Q, X, Y and the six lines connecting all pairs of these four points. In fact, in both of these configurations, the points on $\overleftrightarrow{OA}$ are precisely the points of intersection of these six lines with $\overleftrightarrow{OA}$. Such a configuration—consisting of four points, no three of which are collinear, and the six lines determined by them—is called a *complete quadrangle*. A large part of synthetic projective geometry is concerned with complete quadrangles.

4.4.3   Automorphisms of the field $\mathbb{R}$ of real numbers

An *automorphism* of a field K is a bijection[6] $\alpha : K \longrightarrow K$ that satisfies the following two conditions for all x, y:

$$\alpha(x + y) = \alpha(x) + \alpha(y) \tag{4.2}$$
$$\alpha(x \cdot y) = \alpha(x) \cdot \alpha(y) \tag{4.3}$$

It follows readily from Equation (4.2) that we also have

$$\alpha(0) = 0$$
$$\alpha(x - y) = \alpha(x) - \alpha(y)$$

for all x and y, and it follows from Equation (4.3) that we also have

$$\alpha(1) = 1$$
$$\alpha(x/y) = \alpha(x)/\alpha(y)$$

for all x and for all $y \neq 0$.

For example, take K to be the field $\mathbb{C}$ of complex numbers, and define α to be the map

$$\alpha : z \mapsto \overline{z}$$

that maps each complex number z to its complex conjugate $\overline{z}$. Then, as is well known, α is an automorphism of $\mathbb{C}$. It is a *non-trivial* automorphism in the sense that there exist complex numbers z such that $\alpha(z) \neq z$. (In fact, this holds whenever z is a non-real complex number.) By contrast, the field $\mathbb{R}$ of real numbers has no non-trivial automorphisms, as we will see in Theorem 4.9. We begin with a lemma that asserts a special case of the theorem.

LEMMA 2   If α is any automorphism of the field $\mathbb{R}$ of real numbers, then

$$\alpha \left(\frac{m}{n} \right) = \frac{m}{n}$$

for all integers m and n with $n \neq 0$.

Proof   We already know that $\alpha(1) = 1$. Now by additivity (Equation (4.2)), we have

$$\alpha(2) = \alpha(1 + 1) = \alpha(1) + \alpha(1) = 1 + 1 = 2$$
$$\alpha(3) = \alpha(2 + 1) = \alpha(2) + \alpha(1) = 2 + 1 = 3$$
$$\vdots$$

---

[6]A *bijection* from K to K is a *one-to-one* function that maps K *onto* K.

and so on. Thus, in general, $\alpha(m) = m$ for any positive integer m. Now for any positive integer n, we have

$$
\begin{aligned}
n \cdot \alpha\left(\frac{m}{n}\right) &= \alpha(n) \cdot \alpha\left(\frac{m}{n}\right) \\
&= \alpha\left(n \cdot \frac{m}{n}\right) \\
&= \alpha(m) = m
\end{aligned}
$$

From this it follows immediately that $\alpha(m/n) = m/n$. We leave to the reader the extension of this result to negative values of m. $\square$

THEOREM 4.9   If α is any automorphism of the field $\mathbb{R}$ of real numbers, then α is the identity function.

Proof   Suppose that we knew α to be a *continuous* function. Then we could prove that $\alpha(x) = x$ for each $x \in \mathbb{R}$, as follows. For each $x \in \mathbb{R}$ there exists a sequence $x_1, x_2, x_3, \cdots$ of rational numbers such that $\lim_{n\to\infty} x_n = x$. By Lemma 2, $\alpha(x_n) = x_n$ for each n, and so

$$
\alpha(x) = \alpha\left(\lim_{n\to\infty} x_n\right) = \lim_{n\to\infty} \alpha(x_n) = \lim_{n\to\infty} x_n = x
$$

(with the second equality holding by continuity). Since these equations supply the desired result, it will be enough to establish the continuity of α.

If x is any positive real number, then $x = z^2$ for some real $z > 0$. By Equation (4.3), we have

$$
\alpha(x) = \alpha(zz) = \alpha(z)\alpha(z) = (\alpha(z))^2 \geq 0
$$

and so $\alpha(x)$ is also positive. We now claim that α is *order-preserving*, which is to say that if $u < v$, then $\alpha(u) < \alpha(v)$. To see this, note that the condition $u < v$ is equivalent to the condition that $v = x + u$ for some *positive* x. In this situation, we have

$$
\alpha(v) = \alpha(u + x) = \alpha(u) + \alpha(x)
$$

We already proved that $\alpha(x) > 0$, and hence we have $\alpha(u) < \alpha(v)$, which proves that α is order-preserving.

Finally, to complete the proof, we will show that *every order-preserving bijection of the set $\mathbb{R}$ of real numbers is continuous.*[7] Suppose that $f(x_0) = y_0$

---

[7]It is somewhat ironic that this one easy proof—with a slight modification needed at a local max or min—covers all cases of continuity proved so laboriously in freshman calculus courses.

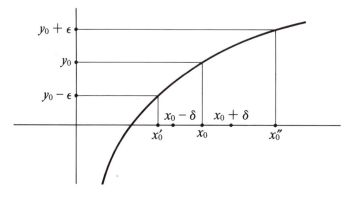

FIGURE 4.7   Proof that an order-increasing bijection is continuous

and that we are given a positive real number ε. We need to show the existence of a positive real δ such that

$$x_0 - \delta < x < x_0 + \delta \quad \text{implies} \quad y_0 - \varepsilon < \alpha(x) < y_0 + \varepsilon$$

To find such a δ, we let x_0' be $\alpha^{-1}(y_0 - \varepsilon)$ and let x_0'' be $\alpha^{-1}(y_0 + \varepsilon)$ and then take δ so that $x_0' < x_0 - \delta < x_0 + \delta < x_0''$. Then for any x with

$$x_0 - \delta < x < x_0 + \delta$$

we have

$$y_0 - \varepsilon \; = \; \alpha(x_0') < \alpha(x_0 - \delta) < \alpha(x) < \alpha(x_0 + \delta) < \alpha(x_0'') \; = \; y_0 + \varepsilon$$

(see Figure 4.7) thereby establishing continuity and thus completing the proof of the theorem.   □

4.4.4   The proof of Theorem 4.6

To prove Theorem 4.6 of §4.4.1, we will use our definitions to show that certain linear transformations ϕ must transform the coordinates along certain lines according to automorphisms of the field of scalars. Then, if $\mathbb{R}$ is the field of scalars, we may apply Theorem 4.9 of §4.4.3 to see that ϕ is trivial along one line.

THEOREM 4.10   Let $\mathbf{V}$ be a 3-dimensional vector space over a field K, and suppose that in the plane $\boldsymbol{P}(\mathbf{V})$, points O and I have (homogeneous) coordinates $\langle 0, 0, 1 \rangle, \langle 1, 0, 1 \rangle$, respectively, and that R is the ideal point with coordinates

$\langle 1, 0, 0 \rangle$. If ϕ is a collineation of $P(V)$ that fixes the points O, I and R, then there exists an automorphism α of K such that

$$\phi(\langle x, 0, 1 \rangle) = \langle \alpha(x), 0, 1 \rangle \tag{4.4}$$

for every point (with homogeneous coordinates $\langle x, 0, 1 \rangle$) of the line $\overleftrightarrow{OI}$.

Proof   Since ϕ is a collineation, and since ϕ fixes two distinct points (O and I) of the line L that is defined by the homogeneous equation $x_2 = 0$, ϕ must map each point of L to some point of L. Moreover, since ϕ is one-to-one, the only point that maps to R is R itself. Thus ϕ maps the set $L - \{R\}$ to itself; that is to say, each point P with coordinates $\langle x, 0, 1 \rangle$ is mapped to a point $\langle u_1, 0, u_3 \rangle$ with $u_3 \neq 0$. Therefore $\phi(P)$ can be assigned homogeneous coordinates $\langle y, 0, 1 \rangle$ for a unique $y \in K$. If we now define $\alpha(x)$ to be y, it is clear that α is a bijection of K satisfying Equation (4.4).

It remains for us to show that the α defined in this way is an automorphism of the field K of scalars, in other words, that α satisfies Equations (4.2) and (4.3) of §4.4.3. We prove these two equations by applying Theorems 4.7 and 4.8; since the two proofs are so similar, we will prove only the first of them (which concerns addition).

To prove that $\alpha(a+b) = \alpha(a) + \alpha(b)$, let A, B and C be the points on L with homogeneous coordinates $\langle a, 0, 1 \rangle$, $\langle b, 0, 1 \rangle$, $\langle a + b, 0, 1 \rangle$, respectively. According to Theorem 4.7, there exist points P, Q, X, Y such that the 9-tuple

$$\langle O, A, B, C, P, Q, R, X, Y \rangle$$

is an addition configuration. Since ϕ is a collineation, and since the definition of addition configuration mentions only certain collinearity relations, it is clear that the 9-tuple

$$\langle \phi(O), \phi(A), \phi(B), \phi(C), \phi(P), \phi(Q), \phi(R), \phi(X), \phi(Y) \rangle$$

is also an addition configuration. Now by Equation (4.4) the points $\phi(A), \phi(B)$ and $\phi(C)$ have homogeneous coordinates $\langle \alpha(a), 0, 1 \rangle, \langle \alpha(b), 0, 1 \rangle, \langle \alpha(a + b), 0, 1 \rangle$, respectively. Hence, $\alpha(a + b) = \alpha(a) + \alpha(b)$, by Theorem 4.7.   □

COROLLARY 4.11   Suppose that in the plane $P^2(\mathbb{R})$, points O and I have (homogeneous) coordinates $\langle 0, 0, 1 \rangle, \langle 1, 0, 1 \rangle$, respectively, and that R is the ideal point with coordinates $\langle 1, 0, 0 \rangle$. If ϕ is a collineation of $P^2(\mathbb{R})$ that fixes the points O, I and R, then ϕ fixes every point of the line L defined by the homogeneous linear equation $x_2 = 0$.

Proof   It is immediate from Theorem 4.9 that the automorphism α appearing in Equation (4.4) must be the identity function. Thus ϕ fixes every point of the line $\overleftrightarrow{OI}$, by Theorem 4.10.   □

COROLLARY 4.12   If ϕ is a collineation of $\boldsymbol{P}^2(\mathbb{R})$ that fixes three distinct points on a line L, then ϕ fixes every point of L.

Proof   Suppose that the three fixed points on L are S, T and U. Take a basis $\langle v_1, v_2, v_3 \rangle$ of $\mathbb{R}^3$ such that S is the subspace generated by v_1 and U is the subspace generated by v_3. Then T is the subspace generated by $\mu \cdot v_1 + \nu \cdot v_3$ for some μ and ν with $\mu \neq 0$ and $\nu \neq 0$. Let A be the matrix whose columns are $\mu \cdot v_1, v_2$ and $\nu \cdot v_3$, and let f be the corresponding linear transformation from $\mathbb{R}^3$ to itself. Clearly

$$f((1,0,0)) = \mu \cdot v_1$$
$$f((1,0,1)) = \mu \cdot v_1 + \nu \cdot v_3$$
$$f((0,0,1)) = \nu \cdot v_3$$

which is to say that $f^\bullet(R) = S, f^\bullet(I) = T$, and $f^\bullet(O) = U$, where the points R, I and O are as in the statement of Corollary 4.11. Thus the composite collineation

$$\psi = (f^\bullet)^{-1} \circ \phi \circ f^\bullet$$

has R, I and O as fixed points. It follows from Corollary 4.11 that ψ fixes every point of the line $\overleftrightarrow{OI}$.

To see that ϕ fixes every point of L, we first observe that if D is any point of L, then $(f^\bullet)^{-1}(D)$ lies on $\overleftrightarrow{OI}$. Therefore

$$
\begin{aligned}
\phi(D) &= f^\bullet \circ \psi \circ (f^\bullet)^{-1}(D) \\
&= f^\bullet \circ (f^\bullet)^{-1}(D) \\
&= D.
\end{aligned}
$$

This calculation completes the proof of the corollary.   □

We can now prove Theorem 4.6 of §4.4.1.

Proof of Theorem 4.6   Suppose the the collineation f fixes the four points P_1, P_2, P_3, P_4, no three of which are collinear. It is not hard to see that f fixes the six lines $L_{12} = \overleftrightarrow{P_1 P_2}$, L_{13} (similarly defined), and so on: L_{14}, L_{23}, L_{24} and L_{24}. Now clearly f fixes the unique point Q that lies on both lines L_{12} and L_{34}. Clearly $Q \neq P_1$, for otherwise P_1, P_3 and P_4 would be collinear and, similarly, $Q \neq P_2$. Therefore we see that f fixes three distinct points on L_{12} and hence, by Corollary 4.12, f fixes every point on L_{12}. Similar arguments show that each of the six lines $L_{12} \cdots L_{34}$ consists entirely of fixed points of f.

Now let us consider an arbitrary point P of $\boldsymbol{P}^2(\mathbb{R})$, and prove that $f(P) = P$. If P is one of the four points P_1, P_2, P_3, P_4, then $f(P) = P$ by hypothesis. Otherwise, it is not hard to check that P can lie on at most two of the six lines $L_{12} \cdots L_{34}$. Therefore, among the three pairs

$$\{L_{12}, L_{34}\}, \quad \{L_{13}, L_{24}\}, \quad \{L_{14}, L_{23}\}$$

there must be one pair of lines with neither containing the point P. Thus, without loss of generality, we may assume that P lies neither on L_{12} nor on L_{34}. Let A, A' be any two points on L_{12}, and define B, B' to be the unique points on L_{34} such that A, P and B are collinear and A', P and B' are collinear. Thus P is the unique point lying on lines $\overleftrightarrow{AB}$ and $\overleftrightarrow{A'B'}$. Since A, A', B and B' are all fixed by f, the lines $\overleftrightarrow{AB}$ and $\overleftrightarrow{A'B'}$ must also be fixed by f. Therefore their unique point of intersection, P, is also fixed by f. $\qquad\square$

4.4.5 Every collineation of $P^2(\mathbb{R})$ is given by a linear map

THEOREM 4.13   Every collineation of $P^2(\mathbb{R})$ has the form $f^\bullet$ for some isomorphism $f : \mathbb{R}^3 \longrightarrow \mathbb{R}^3$.

Proof   Let ϕ be a collineation of $P^2(\mathbb{R})$. Let $\langle v_1, v_2, v_3 \rangle$ be a basis of $\mathbb{R}^3$. Let P_i be the point (i.e., subspace) generated by v_i, and let Q_i be $\phi^{-1}(P_i)$ $(i = 1, 2, 3)$. Now define a linear transformation $g : \mathbb{R}^3 \longrightarrow \mathbb{R}^3$ by defining $g(v_i)$ to be some non-zero vector in the subspace Q_i $(i = 1, 2, 3)$. It is then easily seen that the composite collineation $\phi \circ g^\bullet$ fixes the three points P_1, P_2, P_3.

Now let R be the point (i.e., subspace) generated by $v_1 + v_2 + v_3$. Notice that (by algebra) this point is not collinear with any two of P_1, P_2, P_3, and therefore the same must be true of $\phi \circ g^\bullet(R)$. Therefore $\phi \circ g^\bullet(R)$ is the 1-dimensional space generated by $\alpha_1 \cdot v_1 + \alpha_2 \cdot v_2 + \alpha_3 \cdot v_3$ for some non-zero $\alpha_1, \alpha_2, \alpha_3$. Now define a linear transformation $h : \mathbb{R}^3 \longrightarrow \mathbb{R}^3$ by defining $h(v_i)$ to be $1/\alpha_i \cdot v_i$ $(i = 1, 2, 3)$. It is now not hard to calculate that the composite collineation $h^\bullet \circ \phi \circ g^\bullet$ fixes the four points P_1, P_2, P_3, and R. It therefore follows from Theorem 4.6 that $h^\bullet \circ \phi \circ g^\bullet$ is the identity map. Therefore, $\phi = (h^{-1} \circ g^{-1})^\bullet$. $\qquad\square$

Notice that this theorem, like Theorem 4.6, is false for $P^2(\mathbb{C})$ for similar reasons.

THEOREM 4.14   The linear map f of Theorem 4.13 is unique up to a non-zero scalar multiple. That is, for any linear isomorphisms $f, g : \mathbb{R}^3 \longrightarrow \mathbb{R}^3$ we have $f^\bullet = g^\bullet$ iff there exists a non-zero scalar λ such that

$$g(v) = \lambda \cdot f(v)$$

for all $v \in \mathbb{R}^3$.

Proof   It is not hard to see that if such a λ exists, then $f^\bullet = g^\bullet$. Conversely, let us suppose that $f^\bullet = g^\bullet$ and begin to prove that such a λ exists.

Concerning the linear transformation $h = g \circ f^{-1}$, we may observe that

$$h^\bullet = (g \circ f^{-1})^\bullet = g^\bullet \circ (f^\bullet)^{-1}$$

and hence that $h^\bullet$ is the identity function on $\boldsymbol{P}^2(\mathbb{R})$. Let $\langle s_1, s_2, s_3 \rangle$ be the standard basis of $\mathbb{R}^3$ (i.e., $s_1 = \langle 1, 0, 0 \rangle$, and so on), and let P_i be the point with s_i as homogeneous coordinates ($i = 1, 2, 3$). Since $h^\bullet(P_i) = P_i$ for each i, we have $h(s_i) = \lambda_i \cdot s_i$ for each i; in other words, the matrix of f is

$$A = \begin{bmatrix} \lambda_1 & 0 & 0 \\ 0 & \lambda_2 & 0 \\ 0 & 0 & \lambda_3 \end{bmatrix}$$

To show that $\lambda_1 = \lambda_2 = \lambda_3$—and thus complete the proof—we begin with the equation $h^\bullet(Q) = Q$ for Q the point with homogeneous coordinates $\langle 1, 1, 0 \rangle$. By definition, $h^\bullet(Q)$ has homogeneous coordinates $\langle \lambda_1, \lambda_2, 0 \rangle$, and hence from $h^\bullet(Q) = Q$ we deduce that $\lambda_1 = \lambda_2$. A similar argument applied to $R = \langle 0, 1, 1 \rangle$ yields $\lambda_2 = \lambda_3$. Therefore the matrix A of h has the form

$$\begin{bmatrix} \lambda & 0 & 0 \\ 0 & \lambda & 0 \\ 0 & 0 & \lambda \end{bmatrix}$$

which is the matrix for multiplication by λ. We have now shown that $g(f^{-1}(u)) = h(u) = \lambda \cdot u$ for any vector u. Taking u to denote $f(v)$, we have $f^{-1}(u) = v$, and hence $g(v) = \lambda \cdot f(v)$, as the theorem requires. $\qquad\square$

THE EFFECT OF COLLINEATIONS ON CONIC SECTIONS

With homogeneous coordinates, we can extend our understanding of conic sections to the projective plane $\boldsymbol{P}^2(\mathbb{R})$ as follows. Suppose $\langle x_1, x_2, x_3 \rangle$ are homogeneous coordinates of a point P in $\boldsymbol{P}^2(\mathbb{R})$. Consider the equation

$$Ax_1^2 + Bx_1x_2 + Cx_2^2 + Dx_1x_3 + Ex_2x_3 + Fx_3^2 = 0 \qquad (4.5)$$

The first thing to notice about Equation (4.5) is that it is *homogeneous of degree 2*, that is, each monomial in the equation contains exactly two variables (either the same variable twice, as in $Ax_1^2 = Ax_1x_1$, or two distinct variables, as in Bx_1x_2). This means that if $\langle x_1, x_2, x_3 \rangle$ is modified by a non-zero scalar multiplier λ then Equation (4.5) is modified only by being multiplied by λ^2 throughout, which has no effect on the validity of (4.5). Thus the truth or falsity of Equation (4.5) can be said to depend only on the point $P \in \boldsymbol{P}^2(\mathbb{R})$ and not on the choice of homogeneous coordinates used to describe P. In other words (4.5) has a well-defined *locus* in the projective plane $\boldsymbol{P}^2(\mathbb{R})$.

To determine the form of the locus for ordinary points, we simply examine the equation for points $\langle x_1, x_2, 1 \rangle$; in other words, we substitute 1 for x_3 in Equation (4.5), obtaining

$$Ax_1^2 + Bx_1x_2 + Cx_2^2 + Dx_1 + Ex_2 + F = 0$$

which is the familiar Equation (3.6) of §3.1.6. Thus, as far as ordinary points are concerned, this locus is a conic section. Therefore, we extend the terminology and say that the locus in $P^2(\mathbb{R})$ is a *conic section* in the projective plane.

The conic section defined in the projective plane by Equation (4.5) may also contain some ideal points. To examine this possibility, we substitute 0 for x_3 in Equation (4.5), obtaining

$$Ax_1^2 + Bx_1x_2 + Cx_2^2 = 0$$

Except for a few special cases like those in those occurring in the proof of Theorem 3.10, such as that of zero discriminant Δ, this equation is exactly like Equation (3.7) in that proof, but with $F' = 0$. Thus, as in that proof, the equation can be turned into $A'u_1^2 + C'u_2^2 = 0$, with new (real) variables linearly related to x_1 and x_2. The product AC is positive in the case of an ellipse and negative in the case of a hyperbola. Thus clearly our equation has two solutions (up to non-zero scalar multiples) in the case of a hyperbola, and no (non-zero) solutions in the case of an ellipse. Thus we have proved almost all of the following theorem; the parabolic case is left as an exercise.

THEOREM 4.15   Each non-degenerate conic meets the ideal line in at most two points: none for an ellipse, one for a parabola, and two for a hyperbola.   □

With this understanding of conic sections as loci defined with respect to $P^2(\mathbb{R})$, we can easily state and prove Theorem 4.16. The proof, which is left as an exercise, is based on the observation that the form of Equation (4.5) does not change if one replaces x_1, x_2 and x_3 by linear combinations of those variables.

THEOREM 4.16   The image of a conic section under a collineation is again a conic section.   □

Theorem 4.16 gives us a useful general overview for graphics; all circular elements will be represented as conics (often as ellipses). This overview is useful as a reality check, and occasionally computationally. But, as the reader will see in Chapter 6, we generally do not make an explicit effort to represent circles as ellipses; it just happens naturally.

Exercises

1. In our analysis of Equation (4.5), we set aside the case of discriminant $\Delta = 0$. Here the reader is asked to analyze that case, and thus complete the proof of Theorem 4.15.

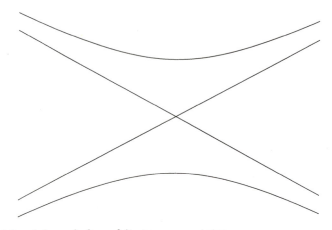

FIGURE 4.8   A hyperbola and its two asymptotes

2. **The asymptotes of a hyperbola.** Define the *center* of a hyperbola H to be the point midway between the two foci of H. The two ordinary lines that pass through the center and one or the other ideal point of H are called the *asymptotes* of H. These are the two intersecting lines seen in Figure 4.8. The exercise here is to begin with the hyperbola

$$\frac{x_1^2}{a^2} - \frac{x_2^2}{b^2} = 1$$

of §3.1.3, calculate its asymptotes, and make a picture of the situation. Then do the hyperbola $y = x + 1/x$.

3. Suppose that (one part of) a hyperbola is given functionally by $y = h(x)$, and that the corresponding asymptote has the linear formula $y = a(x)$. Prove that $h(x)$ and $a(x)$ are asymptotically related in the sense that $\lim_{x \to \infty} (a(x) - h(x))$ is 0.

4. One can also define the asymptotes of a hyperbola H to be *the lines that are tangent to H at its two ideal points P_1 and P_2.* The exercise here is to make sense of this alternative characterization of the asymptotes and to prove that it is correct. One approach would be to consider the limiting position of the tangent line at P, as P approaches either P_1 or P_2 along H. Another approach is to define a line L to be tangent to H at P_i if $f^\bullet(L)$ is tangent to $f^\bullet(H)$ at $f^\bullet(P_i)$ for a collineation $f^\bullet$ that moves P_i off the ideal line. One might for instance consider the action of the collineation $\langle x, y \rangle \mapsto \langle 1/x, y/x \rangle$ on the unit circle and on its two tangent lines $y = \pm 1$.

5. The first time the author computed Figure 3.9 of §3.1.4, he was surprised to see that it contained the asymptotes, which had not been intended as part

of the figure. Can you explain how this occurred? (Hint: The basic formula used for that figure was Equation (3.4) of §3.1.5.)

6. Prove Theorem 4.16.

7. Extend Theorem 4.16 by showing that the image of a *non-degenerate* conic section is always non-degenerate.

8. Prove that if C_1 and C_2 are *any two non-degenerate conics in* $P^2(\mathbb{R})$, then there exists a collineation $f^\bullet$ such that $f^\bullet(C_1) = C_2$. (Thus, up to moving around by collineations, there is exactly one non-degenerate conic section!) (Hint: Don't try to get a giant formula that covers all cases. First show that any ellipse can be moved to, say, the unit circle, e.g., by a similarity and a compression. Then prove a similar fact for hyperbolas and for parabolas. Finally, give one example of a collineation mapping a circle to a parabola, and one that maps a circle to a hyperbola.

9. Take another look, in the present context, at the exercise at the end of §4.1.1.

10. **The crescent moon.** Assume that the moon is a perfect sphere, and that the boundary of the illuminated part is a great circle. Likewise assume that the boundary of the visible portion is a great circle, and that a camera is positioned so that the visible outline makes a circular image on the film. (All these assumptions are very closely fulfilled in practice.) Here we wish to know the appearance of the moon (i.e., its image on film), when it is a crescent (or in any of its phases). Try to extract as much information as you can about this problem from elementary geometry. In §6.1 it will be very easy for us to make explicit drawings with a computer.

11. Consider a building with a perfectly circular driveway that meets the front plane of the building tangentially. From a window on the second floor just above the front door, you take a photo with your camera pointed toward the horizon. The image of the driveway on your film will of course be a conic. What sort of conic? What if, instead, the building is internal to the circular arc of the driveway? External? (One could draw this situation now, but it will be easier to do so after studying §6.3.)

12. Our extension of the theory of conic sections to the projective plane can be thought of purely algebraically. From that point of view, the main point was to add extra (homogeneous) variables to the original Equation (3.6) of §3.1.6 to yield the homogeneous Equation (4.5). The exercise here is to explore how this can be done for an arbitrary algebraic equation or locus. One could begin with the cubic in Figure 3.20. In homogeneous coordinates, its equation is

$$x_2^3 - x_2 x_3^2 = x_1^2 x_3$$

At what points does this curve meet the ideal line? (Can that be guessed from Figure 3.20?) Make sketches of, and answer similar questions for, the curves

$$x_1^3 - x_1 x_2^2 = x_3^2 x_2$$
$$x_3^3 - x_3 x_1^2 = x_2^2 x_1$$

that are formed from our original cubic by cyclically permuting the variables. (Hint: One could use the methods of §3.2.1 as a last resort for drawing these cubics. It is more interesting, however—and also simpler—to figure out a parametric representation.)

13. Prove the analog of Theorem 4.15, that the family of cubic curves is preserved under collineations. Find two non-degenerate cubic curves C_1 and C_2 such that no collineation maps C_1 onto C_2.

4.5   Representing plane motions as collineations

In §§4.5 and 4.6, we will back up our claim—made at the start of §4.4—that collineations of $P^2(\mathbb{R})$ include all the plane maps of §3.3 (except functions like $z \mapsto z^2$ and the non-linear functions described at the end of §3.3.6), and all the perspectivities of §4.1.1. In most cases we will simply present a 3×3 matrix A that represents a linear transformation $f : \mathbb{R}^3 \longrightarrow \mathbb{R}^3$ and leave it to the reader to check that $f^\bullet$ is the indicated sort of collineation. In this section, of course, we are talking about geometric transformations of the the (ordinary) plane that results from deleting the line $x_3 = 0$ from the projective plane $P^2(\mathbb{R})$.

4.5.1   Collineations of $P^2(\mathbb{R})$ that map the ordinary plane to itself

Let ϕ be a collineation of $P^2(\mathbb{R})$ that maps the ordinary plane (formed by deleting the line $x_3 = 0$ as described in §4.2.4) to itself. We of course know that ϕ is represented by a linear transformation $f : \mathbb{R}^3 \longrightarrow \mathbb{R}^3$ that has a matrix

$$\mathbf{A} = \begin{bmatrix} a_{11} & a_{12} & a_{13} \\ a_{21} & a_{22} & a_{23} \\ a_{31} & a_{32} & a_{33} \end{bmatrix}$$

Let P be the ideal point with homogeneous coordinates $\langle 1, 0, 0 \rangle$. Clearly $\phi(P)$ is not in the ordinary plane $x_3 \neq 0$; since the homogeneous coordinates of this point are $\langle a_{11}, a_{21}, a_{31} \rangle$, we see that $a_{31} = 0$. A similar argument shows that $a_{32} = 0$. Therefore every collineation of the points in the ordinary plane is given by a matrix

$$\mathbf{A} = \begin{bmatrix} a_{11} & a_{12} & a_{13} \\ a_{21} & a_{22} & a_{23} \\ 0 & 0 & a_{33} \end{bmatrix}$$

Since the matrix of a collineation is non-singular, we have $a_{33} \neq 0$, and then we may divide the entire matrix by a_{33} to obtain a matrix with $a_{33} = 1$. Finally the reader may check that

$$\begin{bmatrix} a_{11} & a_{12} & a_{13} \\ a_{21} & a_{22} & a_{23} \\ 0 & 0 & 1 \end{bmatrix} = \begin{bmatrix} 1 & 0 & a_{13} \\ 0 & 1 & a_{23} \\ 0 & 0 & 1 \end{bmatrix} \begin{bmatrix} a_{11} & a_{12} & 0 \\ a_{21} & a_{22} & 0 \\ 0 & 0 & 1 \end{bmatrix}$$

As we will see in §§4.5.2 and 4.5.3, this factorization amounts to a description of ϕ as a composition of a translation with a linear map. Thus linear maps and translations are adequate to describe all collineations that map the ordinary plane to itself. Combining this observation with the results of §3.3.8 we see that the collineations that map the ordinary plane to itself are precisely the affine maps $\mathbb{R}^2 \longrightarrow \mathbb{R}^2$.

4.5.2   Translations

For each vector $v = \langle v_1, v_2 \rangle$ in $\mathbb{R}^2$, consider the matrix

$$\mathbf{T}_v = \begin{bmatrix} 1 & 0 & v_1 \\ 0 & 1 & v_2 \\ 0 & 0 & 1 \end{bmatrix}$$

A point of $\mathbb{R}^2$ with coordinates $\langle a_1, a_2 \rangle$ corresponds to a point of $\boldsymbol{P}^2(\mathbb{R})$ with homogeneous coordinates $\langle a_1, a_2, 1 \rangle$, and $\mathbf{T}$ takes this point to the point of $\boldsymbol{P}^2(\mathbb{R})$ that has homogeneous coordinates $\langle a_1 + v_1, a_2 + v_2, 1 \rangle$. Clearly this is the same point that is obtained by applying the translation T_v of §3.3.1. Therefore $\mathbf{T}_v$ can be said to represent[8] the translation T_v.

4.5.3   Linear maps

Consider a linear map $f : \mathbb{R}^2 \longrightarrow \mathbb{R}^2$ with matrix

$$A = \begin{bmatrix} a_{11} & a_{12} \\ a_{21} & a_{22} \end{bmatrix}$$

It is not too hard to check that the enlarged matrix

$$\mathbf{A} = \begin{bmatrix} a_{11} & a_{12} & 0 \\ a_{21} & a_{22} & 0 \\ 0 & 0 & 1 \end{bmatrix}$$

---

[8]The reader may be interested to note that this representation is the one in force in the PostScript language. (See page 65 of the PostScript Reference Manual; that language does not explicitly mention the last row of the matrix (since it is always 001).

maps $b = \langle b_1, b_2, 1 \rangle$ to $\langle c_1, c_2, 1 \rangle$, where $\langle c_1, c_2 \rangle = f(b)$. Therefore every linear map of $\mathbb{R}^2$ to itself is described by a collineation of $\boldsymbol{P}(\mathbb{R}^2)$. Therefore we can describe all the linear maps of §3.3 by expanding their matrices in this manner; we proceed to do this in detail for a number of the more important cases.

4.5.4 Rotations

The matrix

$$\boldsymbol{R}_\theta = \begin{bmatrix} \cos\theta & -\sin\theta & 0 \\ \sin\theta & \cos\theta & 0 \\ 0 & 0 & 1 \end{bmatrix}$$

represents the collineation of $\boldsymbol{P}^2(\mathbb{R})$ that acts on the ordinary plane $(x_3 \neq 0)$ by rotation about the origin through angle θ.

4.5.5 Reflections

The matrix

$$\boldsymbol{R} = \begin{bmatrix} 1 & 0 & 0 \\ 0 & -1 & 0 \\ 0 & 0 & 1 \end{bmatrix}$$

represents the collineation of $\boldsymbol{P}^2(\mathbb{R})$ that acts on the ordinary plane $(x_3 \neq 0)$ by reflection in the line $x_2 = 0$.

4.5.6 Rigid motions

Every orientation-preserving rigid motion of the ordinary plane $(x_3 \neq 0)$ extends to a collineation with matrix

$$\begin{bmatrix} \cos\theta & -\sin\theta & v_1 \\ \sin\theta & \cos\theta & v_2 \\ 0 & 0 & 1 \end{bmatrix} = \begin{bmatrix} 1 & 0 & v_1 \\ 0 & 1 & v_2 \\ 0 & 0 & 1 \end{bmatrix} \begin{bmatrix} \cos\theta & -\sin\theta & 0 \\ \sin\theta & \cos\theta & 0 \\ 0 & 0 & 1 \end{bmatrix}$$

Every orientation-reversing rigid motion of the ordinary plane $(x_3 \neq 0)$ extends to a collineation with matrix

$$\begin{bmatrix} \cos\theta & \sin\theta & v_1 \\ \sin\theta & -\cos\theta & v_2 \\ 0 & 0 & 1 \end{bmatrix} = \begin{bmatrix} 1 & 0 & v_1 \\ 0 & 1 & v_2 \\ 0 & 0 & 1 \end{bmatrix} \begin{bmatrix} \cos\theta & \sin\theta & 0 \\ \sin\theta & -\cos\theta & 0 \\ 0 & 0 & 1 \end{bmatrix}$$

4.5.7 Magnifications

The matrix

$$\mathbf{M}_\lambda = \begin{bmatrix} \lambda & 0 & 0 \\ 0 & \lambda & 0 \\ 0 & 0 & 1 \end{bmatrix}$$

represents the collineation of $\mathbf{P}^2(\mathbb{R})$ that acts on the ordinary plane $(x_3 \neq 0)$ by magnification by a factor λ.

4.5.8 Shears

The matrix

$$\mathbf{A}_{12}(\mu) = \begin{bmatrix} 1 & \mu & 0 \\ 0 & 1 & 0 \\ 0 & 0 & 1 \end{bmatrix}$$

represents the collineation of $\mathbf{P}^2(\mathbb{R})$ that acts on the ordinary plane $(x_3 \neq 0)$ by the μ-shear $S_{12}(\mu)$.

4.5.9 λ-compressions

The matrix

$$\mathbf{C}_\lambda = \begin{bmatrix} \lambda^{-1} & 0 & 0 \\ 0 & \lambda & 0 \\ 0 & 0 & 1 \end{bmatrix}$$

represents the collineation of $\mathbf{P}^2(\mathbb{R})$ that acts on the ordinary plane $(x_3 \neq 0)$ by the λ-compression C_λ.

4.6 Representing perspectivities as collineations

Let us return to the perspectivity Π defined in §4.1.1. According to the equation derived there, Π maps a point P of $\mathbb{R}^3$ with coordinates $\langle x_1, x_2, 1 \rangle$ to a point Q of $\mathbb{R}^3$ with coordinates $\langle x_1/x_2, 1, 1/x_2 \rangle$. In fact, from the planar point of view, the third coordinate of P serves only to define the *ground plane* $x_3 = 1$, and the second coordinate of Q serves only to define the *film plane* $x_2 = 1$. Therefore, from the purely planar point of view we may discard these constant coordinates. If we do this, the equation for the perspectivity Π reduces to

$$\Pi(\langle x_1, x_2 \rangle) = \langle x_1/x_2, 1/x_2 \rangle$$

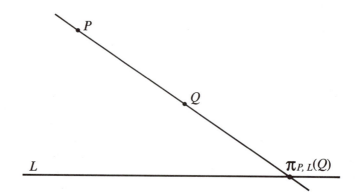

FIGURE 4.9   The projection $\Pi_{P,L}$ centered at P from P^2 to L

It is not hard to check that $\Pi = f^{\bullet}$, where f is the linear transformation of $\mathbb{R}^3$ with matrix

$$\mathbf{P} = \begin{bmatrix} 1 & 0 & 0 \\ 0 & 0 & 1 \\ 0 & 1 & 0 \end{bmatrix}$$

In fact a general argument can be made that every perspectivity is a collineation. If L is any line in the ground plane, L and the lens point determine a plane π. The intersection of π with the film plane is a line, which is the image of L. Therefore the image of every line is a line. (And now, of course, it follows from Theorem 4.6 that every perspectivity of a plane can be represented by a 3×3 matrix.) We will see more examples of perspectivities when we come to look at the 3-dimensional case.

4.7   Projection from a plane to a line

In a projective plane P^2, let L be a line and P a point not on L. We define a map $\Pi_{P,L} : P^2 \longrightarrow L$ by the stipulation that, for each point $Q \in P$, the points P, Q and $\Pi_{P,L}(Q)$ should be collinear, as shown in Figure 4.9. We have written the map $\Pi_{P,L}$ as if it were defined on all of P^2, but in truth it fails to be uniquely defined on the point P itself. (If $P = Q$, then the collinearity condition will hold for $\Pi_{P,L}(Q)$ taken to be any point on the line L.) Nevertheless, it is awkward to always write $\Pi_{P,L} : P^2 - \{P\} \longrightarrow L$, especially since the point P may change several times during a discussion. Therefore we adopt the convention that the point P need not be explicitly excluded from the domain: $\Pi_{P,L} : P^2 \longrightarrow L$ may

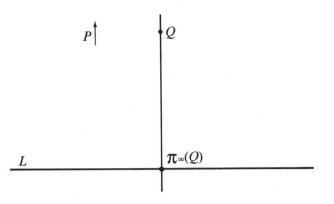

FIGURE 4.10   The projection Π_∞ from an ideal point

be taken as standing for the more precise formulation $\Pi_{P,L}: \boldsymbol{P}^2 - \{P\} \longrightarrow L$. If P and L are clear from the context, then we may write $\Pi_{P,L}$ simply as Π.

We will see that the map $\Pi_{P,L}$ is definable by a 2×3 matrix. For the moment, let us investigate the special case of P the ideal point with coordinates $\langle 0, 1, 0 \rangle$, and L the line $x_2 = 0$. Then we have the situation as depicted in Figure 4.10. This projection, called Π_∞ is defined for all non-ideal points Q, and in fact has a very simple description: a point with inhomogeneous coordinates $\langle x_1, x_2 \rangle$ is mapped parallel to the x_2-axis, to the point $\langle x_1, 0 \rangle$. Therefore, it is apparent that, in homogeneous coordinates, Π_∞ is given by the matrix

$$\boldsymbol{\Pi}_\infty = \begin{bmatrix} 1 & 0 & 0 \\ 0 & 0 & 0 \\ 0 & 0 & 1 \end{bmatrix}$$

Notice that $\boldsymbol{\Pi}_\infty$ is a singular matrix, i.e., it has zero determinant, and nontrivial kernel. In fact the kernel of Π_∞ consists of the one-dimensional subspace determined by $\langle 0, 1, 0 \rangle$, and this subspace is of course identical to the point P, by the way we defined homogeneous coordinates in §4.2.2.

Now let $\phi_{P,L}$ be a collineation that takes P to the point with coordinates $\langle 0, 1, 0 \rangle$ and takes L to the line with coordinates $x_2 = 0$. Consider the effect of applying $\phi_{P,L}$ to the configuration of Figure 4.9. We obviously obtain a configuration like that of Figure 4.10, only with Q replaced by $\phi_{P,L}(Q)$ and $\Pi_\infty(Q)$ replaced by $\Pi_\infty(\phi_{P,L}(Q))$. Therefore we have

$$\phi_{P,L}(\Pi_{P,L}(Q)) = \Pi_\infty(\phi_{P,L}(Q))$$

for every point Q in the domain of $\Pi_{P,L}$. It follows that

$$\Pi_{P,L} = \phi_{P,L}^{-1} \circ \Pi_\infty \circ \phi_{P,L}$$

An important special case occurs when L is taken to be the line with homogeneous equation $x_2 = 0$ itself, and P is an arbitrary point not on L. Then, by Lemma 1, we may assume that the collineation $\phi_{P,L}$ fixes every point of L. From this it easily follows that $\phi_{P,L}^{-1} \circ \Pi_\infty = \Pi_\infty$, and so the above equation for $\Pi_{P,L}$ simplifies to

$$\Pi_{P,L} = \Pi_\infty \circ \phi_{P,L}.$$

In other words, *projecting from P onto the line L with equation $x_2 = 0$ is equivalent to first moving the point P to infinity and then performing a parallel projection.*

In truth we do not really need Lemma 1 to prove the existence of $\phi_{P,L}$. We can see directly that if P has homogeneous coordinates $\langle P_1, P_2, P_3 \rangle$, then the matrix

$$\mathbf{E}_P = \begin{bmatrix} P_2 & -P_1 & 0 \\ 0 & P_2 & 0 \\ 0 & -P_3 & P_2 \end{bmatrix}$$

defines a linear map $f_{P,L}$ such that $f_{P,L}^\bullet = \phi_{P,L}$. Therefore the matrix associated to $\Pi_{P,L}$ is

$$\mathbf{P}_P = \mathbf{\Pi}_\infty \mathbf{E}_P = \begin{bmatrix} 1 & 0 & 0 \\ 0 & 0 & 0 \\ 0 & 0 & 1 \end{bmatrix} \begin{bmatrix} P_2 & -P_1 & 0 \\ 0 & P_2 & 0 \\ 0 & -P_3 & P_2 \end{bmatrix}$$

$$= \begin{bmatrix} P_2 & -P_1 & 0 \\ 0 & 0 & 0 \\ 0 & -P_3 & P_2 \end{bmatrix}$$

By the way, one can easily see from this matrix representation that the kernel of the linear map associated to $\Pi_{P,L}$ consists of all scalar multiples of $\langle P_1, P_2, P_3 \rangle$, in other words that $\Pi_{P,L}$ is defined on all points except P, in confirmation of what we already knew.

Earlier in this section we promised a representation of $\Pi_{P,L}$ as a 2×3 matrix. To do this, we simply delete the row of zeros in the last matrix above, obtaining

$$\mathbf{P}_P = \begin{bmatrix} P_2 & -P_1 & 0 \\ 0 & -P_3 & P_2 \end{bmatrix}$$

The meaning of representing the projection by this smaller matrix is simply that we really do not need the second coordinate, since the range of the projection is the line that satisfies $x_2 = 0$. If a point on this line with homogeneous coordinates $\langle x_1, 0, x_3 \rangle$ is represented by the simpler coordinates $\langle x_1, x_3 \rangle$, then these coordinates are provided by this matrix. Such coordinates may be called *homogeneous coordinates along a line.*

4.8 Fixed points and fixed lines

A *fixed point* of a collineation $\phi : P(V) \longrightarrow P(V)$ is a point P such that $\phi(P) = P$. If $f : V \longrightarrow V$ is a linear transformation such that $f^\bullet = \phi$, then a fixed point of ϕ is determined by a vector v such that v and $f(v)$ represent the same point of $P(V)$, i.e., a vector v such that $f(v) = \lambda \cdot v$ for some non-zero scalar λ. In other words, fixed points of ϕ correspond to eigenvectors of f.

Recall from §3.3.7 that the characteristic equation of an $n \times n$ matrix A is a polynomial equation of degree n (see Equations (1.45) and (1.46)). The eigenvalues are the roots of this equation. In the case at hand, $n = 3$, and so the characteristic equation is a cubic equation. Remembering the general fact that every cubic equation real coefficients has at least one real root, we know that every 3×3 matrix has at least one eigenvalue, and hence has at least one eigenvector. Therefore, *every collineation of $P^2(\mathbb{R})$ has at least one fixed point.* (Note, however, that some or all of the fixed points may be ideal points. For example, a translation moves every ordinary point but fixes every ideal point.)

A similar thing happens for fixed lines. Suppose that ϕ is the collineation determined by a linear transformation f, and that f has the matrix

$$
A = \begin{bmatrix} a_{11} & a_{12} & a_{13} \\ a_{21} & a_{22} & a_{23} \\ a_{31} & a_{32} & a_{33} \end{bmatrix}
$$

We first look for a description of the image line $f[L]$ for an arbitrary line L. Let us suppose that L has the equation $m_1 x_1 + m_2 x_2 + m_3 x_3 = 0$. Now a point P with coordinates $\langle x_1, x_2, x_3 \rangle$ lies on $f[L]$ iff

$$
f^{-1}(P) \in L \quad \text{iff} \quad \begin{bmatrix} m_1 & m_2 & m_3 \end{bmatrix} A^{-1} \begin{bmatrix} x_1 \\ x_2 \\ x_3 \end{bmatrix} = 0
$$

This condition is clearly equivalent to $P \in L$ iff the numbers m_1, m_2, m_3 are proportional to the three coordinates of

$$
\begin{bmatrix} m_1 & m_2 & m_3 \end{bmatrix} A^{-1}
$$

which is to say that

$$
\begin{bmatrix} m_1 & m_2 & m_3 \end{bmatrix} A^{-1} = \lambda^{-1} \cdot \begin{bmatrix} m_1 & m_2 & m_3 \end{bmatrix}
$$

for some non-zero scalar λ, in other words that

$$
\lambda \cdot \begin{bmatrix} m_1 & m_2 & m_3 \end{bmatrix} = \begin{bmatrix} m_1 & m_2 & m_3 \end{bmatrix} A
$$

This condition is easily seen to be equivalent to

$$
\begin{bmatrix} a_{11} & a_{21} & a_{31} \\ a_{12} & a_{22} & a_{32} \\ a_{13} & a_{23} & a_{33} \end{bmatrix} \begin{bmatrix} m_1 \\ m_2 \\ m_3 \end{bmatrix} = \lambda \cdot \begin{bmatrix} m_1 \\ m_2 \\ m_3 \end{bmatrix}
$$

The matrix

$$
\begin{bmatrix} a_{11} & a_{21} & a_{31} \\ a_{12} & a_{22} & a_{32} \\ a_{13} & a_{23} & a_{33} \end{bmatrix}
$$

is the *transpose* of the matrix **A**, which was defined in §1.5.2. What we have shown here is that *fixed lines of a collineation ϕ with matrix **A** correspond to eigenvectors of the transpose of **A**.*

Therefore (for reasons like those mentioned above), *every collineation of $P^2(\mathbb{R})$ has at least one fixed line.*

Exercises———————————————————————————————————

1. For each matrix **A** of §4.6 and §4.7, find the eigenvectors of **A** and identify them with the fixed points of the corresponding collineation.

2. For each matrix **A** of §4.6 and §4.7, find the eigenvectors of the transpose of **A** and identify them with the fixed lines of the corresponding collineation.

5 Projective geometry of space

In Chapter 4 (especially §4.2.1) we defined a projective plane to be the set of 1-dimensional subspaces of a 3-dimensional vector space. Here we will do the same thing in the next higher dimension. In this chapter we will state many things without proof, allowing the analogy with the lower-dimensional case to serve in lieu of proof. (Almost always the missing proofs are like the ones from Chapter 4.)

5.1 Projective spaces

5.1.1 Definitions

For any 4-dimensional vector space $\mathbf{V}$, we define *the projective space $\boldsymbol{P}(\mathbf{V})$ of $\mathbf{V}$* to be the set of all 1-dimensional subspaces of $\mathbf{V}$, which we call the *points* of $\mathbf{V}$. A projective space may also be called a *projective 3-space*. For every 2-dimensional subspace $\mathbf{W}$ of $\mathbf{V}$, we define *the line $L_{\mathbf{W}}$ of $\boldsymbol{P}(\mathbf{V})$* to be the set of points of $\boldsymbol{P}(\mathbf{V})$ that are subspaces of $\mathbf{W}$. For every 3-dimensional subspace $\mathbf{U}$ of $\mathbf{V}$, we define *the (projective) plane $\pi_{\mathbf{U}}$ of $\boldsymbol{P}(\mathbf{V})$* to be the set of points of $\boldsymbol{P}(\mathbf{V})$ that are subspaces of $\mathbf{U}$. By *a line* of $\boldsymbol{P}(\mathbf{V})$, we mean any $L_{\mathbf{W}}$, and by *a plane* of $\boldsymbol{P}(\mathbf{V})$, we mean any $\pi_{\mathbf{U}}$. When we refer to *the projective space $\boldsymbol{P}(\mathbf{V})$*, we generally mean the mathematical structure consisting of the points, the lines and the planes of $\boldsymbol{P}(\mathbf{V})$.

We sometimes denote the plane $\boldsymbol{P}(\mathbb{R}^4)$ by the alternate notation $\boldsymbol{P}^3(\mathbb{R})$, or even $\boldsymbol{P}^3$, if context assures us that the field of scalars is $\mathbb{R}$.

5.1.2 Elementary incidence theorems

THEOREM 5.1   In any projective space, for any two points P and Q, there exists a unique line $\overleftrightarrow{PQ}$ containing both P and Q.

THEOREM 5.2   In any projective space, for any three non-collinear points P, Q and R, there exists a unique plane π containing P, Q and R.   □

THEOREM 5.3   In any projective space, any two distinct coplanar lines have a point in common.   □

THEOREM 5.4   In any projective space, if π is a plane, and L is a line not contained in π, then π and L have a unique point in common.   □

THEOREM 5.5   In any projective space, if π and π' are distinct planes, then π and π' intersect in a line.   □

Exercise

1. Demonstrate the existence of two lines in $P^3(\mathbb{R})$ that have no points in common.

5.1.3   Homogeneous coordinates

Homogeneous coordinates in the present context are exactly like those coordinates in a projective plane, except that now there are four of them. More specifically, a point of $P^3(\mathbb{R})$ is a 1-dimensional subspace $\mathbf{W}$ of $\mathbb{R}^4$. Such a subspace $\mathbf{W}$ is determined by any vector $\langle x_1, x_2, x_3, x_4 \rangle \in \mathbf{W}$. Moreover, $\mathbf{W}$ is also determined by $\langle \lambda \cdot x_1, \lambda \cdot x_2, \lambda \cdot x_3, \lambda \cdot x_4 \rangle$, for any non-zero scalar λ. Therefore each point $\mathbf{W}$ may be given homogeneous coordinates that are determined only up to multiplication by a non-zero scalar.

5.1.4   The equations of lines and planes in $P^3(\mathbb{R})$

A single homogeneous equation

$$\beta_1 x_1 + \beta_2 x_2 + \beta_3 x_3 + \beta_4 x_4 = 0$$

defines a *plane* (i.e., 3-dimensional subspace) in $P^3(\mathbb{R})$. A family of two equations

$$\beta_1 x_1 + \beta_2 x_2 + \beta_3 x_3 + \beta_4 x_4 = 0$$
$$\gamma_1 x_1 + \gamma_2 x_2 + \gamma_3 x_3 + \gamma_4 x_4 = 0$$

defines the intersection of two planes. By Theorem 5.5 this intersection is a *line* unless the coefficients $\langle \beta_1, \beta_2, \beta_3, \beta_4 \rangle$ are proportional to the coefficients $\langle \gamma_1, \gamma_2, \gamma_3, \gamma_4 \rangle$.

5.1.5   Forming an ordinary 3-space by removing a plane

In the projective space $\boldsymbol{P}^3 = \boldsymbol{P}^3(\mathbb{R})$, let us consider the plane π_0 that is defined by the equation $x_4 = 0$. We wish to see that if π_0 is removed from $\boldsymbol{P}^3$, then the remaining points and lines have the structure of the ordinary coordinate space $\mathbb{R}^3$.

To each point P of $\boldsymbol{P}^3 - \pi_0$, with homogeneous coordinates $\langle x_1, x_2, x_3, x_4 \rangle$ assign ordinary coordinates $\langle x_1', x_2', x_3' \rangle = \langle x_1/x_4, x_2/x_4, x_3/x_4 \rangle$. Notice that division by x_4 is permissible because we have discarded those points for which $x_4 = 0$. Moreover, the division cancels any multiplication by a scalar that may have been performed upon our homogeneous coordinates. Therefore, we may conclude that the ordinary coordinates $\langle x_1', x_2', x_3' \rangle$ are well defined for all points of $\boldsymbol{P}^3 - \pi_0$.

THEOREM 5.6   Every plane of $\boldsymbol{P}^3$—except π_0—intersects $\boldsymbol{P}^3$ in an ordinary plane of the coordinate space $\mathbb{R}^3$, and conversely, every plane of $\mathbb{R}^3$ arises in this way. Every line of $\boldsymbol{P}^3$—unless it is contained in π_0—intersects $\boldsymbol{P}^3$ in an ordinary line of the coordinate space $\mathbb{R}^3$, and conversely, every line of $\mathbb{R}^3$ arises in this way. □

Thus projective space $\boldsymbol{P}^3$ differs from $\mathbb{R}^3$ in having one extra plane—which we may call the *ideal plane*.

5.2   Collineations of projective space

Collineations of projective space are exactly like collineations of a projective plane: They are defined as bijections that preserve the notion of collinearity. As before, for every bijective linear transformation $f : \mathbb{R}^4 \longrightarrow \mathbb{R}^4$, there is a corresponding $f^\bullet : \boldsymbol{P}^3(\mathbb{R}) \longrightarrow \boldsymbol{P}^3(\mathbb{R})$, defined as follows: $f^\bullet(\mathbf{V})$ is the space generated by $f(v)$ for any vector $v \in \mathbf{V}$.

THEOREM 5.7   Every collineation of $\boldsymbol{P}^3(\mathbb{R})$ has the form $f^\bullet$ for some isomorphism $f : \mathbb{R}^4 \longrightarrow \mathbb{R}^4$. The isomorphism f is unique up to a non-zero scalar multiple. □

5.3   A catalog of collineations of $P^3(\mathbb{R})$

5.3.1   The general collineation mapping $\mathbb{R}^3$ to itself

$$\begin{bmatrix} a_{11} & a_{12} & a_{13} & a_{14} \\ a_{21} & a_{22} & a_{23} & a_{24} \\ a_{31} & a_{32} & a_{33} & a_{34} \\ 0 & 0 & 0 & 1 \end{bmatrix}$$

As in §4.5.1, the preceding matrix can be factored as a product of a linear map and a translation:

$$\begin{bmatrix} 1 & 0 & 0 & a_{14} \\ 0 & 1 & 0 & a_{24} \\ 0 & 0 & 1 & a_{34} \\ 0 & 0 & 0 & 1 \end{bmatrix} \begin{bmatrix} a_{11} & a_{12} & a_{13} & 0 \\ a_{21} & a_{22} & a_{23} & 0 \\ a_{31} & a_{32} & a_{33} & 0 \\ 0 & 0 & 0 & 1 \end{bmatrix}$$

5.3.2   Translations

$$\begin{bmatrix} 1 & 0 & 0 & v_1 \\ 0 & 1 & 0 & v_2 \\ 0 & 0 & 1 & v_3 \\ 0 & 0 & 0 & 1 \end{bmatrix}$$

5.3.3   Reflections

For example, reflection in the x_1, x_2-plane is given by

$$\begin{bmatrix} 1 & 0 & 0 & 1 \\ 0 & 1 & 0 & 1 \\ 0 & 0 & -1 & 1 \\ 0 & 0 & 0 & 1 \end{bmatrix}$$

5.3.4   Rotations about one of the coordinate axes

Rotation about the x_3-axis is given by

$$\begin{bmatrix} \cos\theta & -\sin\theta & 0 & 0 \\ \sin\theta & \cos\theta & 0 & 0 \\ 0 & 0 & 1 & 0 \\ 0 & 0 & 0 & 1 \end{bmatrix}$$

Similarly, rotation about the x_2-axis is given by

$$\begin{bmatrix} \cos\theta & 0 & -\sin\theta & 0 \\ 0 & 1 & 0 & 0 \\ \sin\theta & 0 & \cos\theta & 0 \\ 0 & 0 & 0 & 1 \end{bmatrix}$$

We omit the obvious modification for the x_1-axis.

5.3.5 Rigid motions

Every rigid motion of ordinary space $(x_4 \neq 0)$ extends to a collineation with matrix

$$\begin{bmatrix} a_{11} & a_{12} & a_{13} & a_{14} \\ a_{21} & a_{22} & a_{23} & a_{24} \\ a_{31} & a_{32} & a_{33} & a_{34} \\ 0 & 0 & 0 & 1 \end{bmatrix}$$

with

$$\sum_{k=1}^{3} a_{ik}^2 = 1 \qquad (i = 1, 2, 3)$$

$$\sum_{k=1}^{3} a_{ik} a_{jk} = 0 \qquad (1 \le j < k \le 3)$$

and any matrix satisfying these equations is a rigid motion, by Theorem 1.59 and its corollary. All such matrices have determinant ± 1. The rigid motion is orientation-preserving iff the determinant is $+1$.

An interesting special case, with no counterpart in the plane, is given by the one-parameter group

$$G_\theta = \begin{bmatrix} \cos\theta & -\sin\theta & 0 & 0 \\ \sin\theta & \cos\theta & 0 & 0 \\ 0 & 0 & 1 & K\theta \\ 0 & 0 & 0 & 1 \end{bmatrix}$$

This motion corresponds to turning a screw through an angle θ; the parameter K corresponds to the pitch of the screw. (A screw with larger K travels farther for a given angular turn—and therefore has smaller mechanical advantage.)

5.3.6 Magnifications

The general magnification is

$$\begin{bmatrix} \lambda & 0 & 0 & 0 \\ 0 & \lambda & 0 & 0 \\ 0 & 0 & \lambda & 0 \\ 0 & 0 & 0 & 1 \end{bmatrix}$$

The matrix of the general similarity map is MR for M a magnification and R the matrix of a rigid motion. An interesting special case is seen in the following one-parameter group of similarities:

$$H_\theta = \begin{bmatrix} e^{a\theta}\cos\theta & -e^{a\theta}\sin\theta & 0 & 0 \\ e^{a\theta}\sin\theta & e^{a\theta}\cos\theta & 0 & 0 \\ 0 & 0 & e^{a\theta} & 0 \\ 0 & 0 & 0 & 1 \end{bmatrix}$$

Exercises

1. Describe the effect of the matrix

$$\begin{bmatrix} -1 & 0 & 0 & 1 \\ 0 & -1 & 0 & 1 \\ 0 & 0 & -1 & 1 \\ 0 & 0 & 0 & 1 \end{bmatrix}$$

2. **Euler's formula for a rotated vector.**[1] The reader who has studied the cross product of vectors in 3-dimensional space can do the following exercise. For any unit vector u, let R_θ^u denote the rotation about u through an angle θ. Prove Euler's formula that

$$R_\theta^u(v) \;=\; v \;+\; (1 - \cos\theta)(u \times (u \times v)) \;+\; \sin\theta(u \times v)$$

where $\times$ denotes the cross product of two vectors in 3-space. (Hint: Prove it first for $u = \langle 0,0,1\rangle$. In this case the calculation is easy. Then observe that the configuration representing the general case (including all the relevant cross product vectors) can be taken by a rigid motion into the configuration for the special case.) Applying this formula to the standard basis elements, i.e., to $v = \langle 1,0,0\rangle$ and so on, one could obtain a (messy) direct formula for the matrix of R_θ^u.

3. Prove that the motions G_θ of §5.3.5 form a one-parameter group of rigid motions.

4. Prove that the motions H_θ of §5.3.6 form a one-parameter group of similarities.

5. Describe the motion given by the matrix

[1]The author thanks N. Greenleaf for pointing out this formula to him.

$$\begin{bmatrix} 0 & 0 & 1 & 0 \\ 1 & 0 & 0 & 0 \\ 0 & 1 & 0 & 0 \\ 0 & 0 & 0 & 1 \end{bmatrix}$$

5.3.7 Shears

For example,

$$\begin{bmatrix} 1 & 0 & \mu & 0 \\ 0 & 1 & 0 & 0 \\ 0 & 0 & 1 & 0 \\ 0 & 0 & 0 & 1 \end{bmatrix}$$

5.3.8 Compressions

$$\begin{bmatrix} \lambda_1 & 0 & 0 & 0 \\ 0 & \lambda_2 & 0 & 0 \\ 0 & 0 & \lambda_3 & 0 \\ 0 & 0 & 0 & 1 \end{bmatrix}$$

where $\lambda_1 \lambda_2 \lambda_3 = 1$.

5.3.9 Projection from space to the plane $x_3 = 0$

Projection from the ideal point $\langle 0, 0, 1, 0 \rangle$—i.e., parallel projection—has the matrix

$$\begin{bmatrix} 1 & 0 & 0 & 0 \\ 0 & 1 & 0 & 0 \\ 0 & 0 & 0 & 0 \\ 0 & 0 & 0 & 1 \end{bmatrix}$$

Moving an arbitrary point P with coordinates $\langle P_1, P_2, P_3, P_4 \rangle$ to the ideal point $\langle 0, 0, 1, 0 \rangle$ is accomplished by the matrix

$$\begin{bmatrix} P_3 & 0 & -P_1 & 0 \\ 0 & P_3 & -P_2 & 0 \\ 0 & 0 & P_3 & 0 \\ 0 & 0 & -P_4 & P_3 \end{bmatrix}$$

As in §4.7, *projecting from P onto the plane π with equation $x_3 = 0$ is equivalent to first moving the point P to infinity and then performing a parallel projection.*

Thus the matrix for projecting directly from P is the product of these two matrices, which equals

$$\begin{bmatrix} P_3 & 0 & -P_1 & 0 \\ 0 & P_3 & -P_2 & 0 \\ 0 & 0 & 0 & 0 \\ 0 & 0 & -P_4 & P_3 \end{bmatrix}$$

To give a map directly from $\boldsymbol{P}^3(\mathbb{R})$ to $\boldsymbol{P}^2(\mathbb{R})$, we eliminate the third row, thereby obtaining

$$\begin{bmatrix} P_3 & 0 & -P_1 & 0 \\ 0 & P_3 & -P_2 & 0 \\ 0 & 0 & -P_4 & P_3 \end{bmatrix}$$

5.4   Applications to spherical trigonometry

In this section, we will briefly see how the theory of rotation matrices that we have developed so far will allow us to determine some of the relations of spherical trigonometry. (Spherical trigonometry is often applied to navigation problems, although the methods of §6.1 can be used instead.) In this section it will be convenient to use non-homogeneous coordinates; thus rotations of 3-space will be expressed by 3×3 matrices.

We will consider points on the surface S of a sphere; for convenience we take S to be centered at the origin O and to have radius 1. Points A and B on S are called *antipodal* iff they are distinct and the line joining them passes through the center O of S. A *great circle* of S is, by definition, the intersection of S with any plane that passes through O. If A and B are distinct non-antipodal points of S, then A and B lie on a unique plane containing O; hence they lie on a unique great circle.[2] A and B divide this circle into two arcs, one greater than a semicircle, the other smaller. The smaller arc is called the *(spherical) segment joining A and B*. Its arc length (on a sphere of radius 1) is called the (spherical) distance between A and B; it should be evident that this distance can also be defined as the measure a (in radians) of the angle $\angle AOB$. Notice that we always have $\sin a \geq 0$, since $a \leq \pi$. The segment from A to B is sometimes called the *geodesic* from A to B, since, as can be proved, it has the shortest arc length among all curves in S from A to B.

Now given three points A, B and C on S, the (spherical) angle $\angle ABC$ is measured by the angle (in the usual sense) (see Figure 5.1) between the tangent lines at B to the segments from B to A and to C. Equivalently, this angle can

---

[2] Notice on the other hand that if B is the antipode of A, then every great circle passing through A also passes through B.

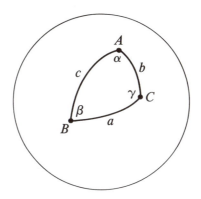

FIGURE 5.1   A spherical triangle

be measured as the dihedral angle between planes $\overline{OBA}$ and $\overline{OBC}$.

Now, given points A, B, C on S, no two of them either equal or antipodal, we have a *spherical triangle*. It determines six angles: α, β, γ, the spherical angles at A, B and C, and a, b, c, the (angular) lengths of spherical segments $\overline{BC}$, $\overline{CA}$ and $\overline{AB}$ (see Figure 5.1). Our objective here—just as in planar trigonometry—is to work out relationships between these six quantities.

Lemmas 1 and 2 can help us determine spherical angles and distances.

LEMMA 1   If A, B and C are points on the sphere with B the north pole ($\langle 0, 0, 1\rangle$), then $\angle ABC$ can be measured by projecting A, B and C to the plane $x_3 = 0$.

Proof   The planes $\overline{ABO}$ and $\overline{CBO}$ are both perpendicular to the plane $x_3 = 0$. Thus these two planes project to lines on the plane $x_3 = 0$, which meet at the dihedral angle.   □

LEMMA 2   The spherical distance between two points A, B on S is the angle θ with $0 \leq \theta \leq \pi$ such that $\cos\theta = A \cdot B$ (the dot product of A and B).

Proof   Since neither distance nor dot product is affected by rotation, we may rotate the sphere until both A and B are in the plane $x_3 = 0$. A further rotation (about the x_3-axis) will take A to $\langle 1, 0, 0\rangle$ and B to $\langle \cos\theta, \pm\sin\theta, 0\rangle$ for some positive θ. Since the plane $x_3 = 0$ intersects S in a great circle, it is clear that θ is the distance between A and B. An easy calculation shows that $A \cdot B = \cos\theta$.   □

THEOREM 5.8   Let $\triangle ABC$ be a spherical right triangle with right angle at C. Let its sides be denoted a, b, c, and its angles be denoted α, β and γ, as in Figure 5.1 (with $\gamma = \pi/2$). Then

$$\cos c = \cos a \cos b \tag{5.1}$$

and

$$\tan \alpha = \frac{\tan a}{\sin b} \tag{5.2}$$

and

$$\sin \alpha = \frac{\sin a}{\sin c} \tag{5.3}$$

Remark. Equation (5.1) is the *Pythagorean theorem* for right spherical triangles. Equations (5.2) and (5.3) are part of *Napier's rules* for spherical trigonometry. In particular, (5.3) is known as Napier's *law of sines*.

Proof   We begin with a rigid motion about the origin that takes C to the north pole. A further rotation will position A above the x_1-axis and B above the x_2-axis. Thus, without loss of generality, we may begin with the following coordinates for our points:

$$A = \langle \sin b, 0, \cos b \rangle$$
$$B = \langle 0, \sin a, \cos a \rangle$$
$$C = \langle 0, 0, 1 \rangle$$

We then apply the rotation

$$R = \begin{bmatrix} \cos b & 0 & -\sin b \\ 0 & 1 & 0 \\ \sin b & 0 & \cos b \end{bmatrix}$$

obtaining

$$A' = RA = \langle 0, 0, 1 \rangle$$
$$B' = RB = \langle -\cos a \sin b, \sin a, \cos a \cos b \rangle$$
$$C' = RC = \langle -\sin b, 0, \cos b \rangle$$

Now Equation (5.1) follows immediately from Lemma 2 (applied to A' and B'). For the other two equations we apply Lemma 1 to see that α is the angle between the plane vectors $\langle -\sin b, 0 \rangle$ and $\langle -\cos a \sin b, \sin a \rangle$. Equation (5.2) is immediate; for Equation (5.3) we calculate

$$\sin^2 \alpha = \frac{\sin^2 a}{\sin^2 a + \cos^2 a \sin^2 b}$$

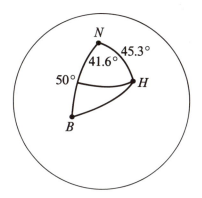

FIGURE 5.2   The distance between two cities

$$= \frac{\sin^2 a}{\sin^2 a + \cos^2 a - \cos^2 a \cos^2 b} = \frac{\sin^2 a}{1 - \cos^2 c}$$

$$= \frac{\sin^2 a}{\sin^2 c}$$

Since $\sin \alpha$, $\sin a$ and $\sin c$ are all ≥ 0, the desired equation follows.   □

Exercises_____

1. Boulder, Colorado, has longitude 105.3 degrees and latitude 40.0 degrees. Halifax, Nova Scotia, has longitude 63.7 degrees and latitude 44.7 degrees. What is the distance between these two cities? (Give the answer first in angular measure, and then an approximate answer based on the value of 4000 miles for Earth's radius.) (Hint: Begin with a spherical triangle whose vertices are the two cities and the North Pole. Drop a perpendicular from Halifax to the opposite segment, as indicated in Figure 5.2. Use Napier's formulas from there.)

2. Write a program that will get the spherical distance between any two cities.

3. Investigate the behavior of Equations (5.1–5.3) as the size of the triangle approaches zero. Equation (5.1) should approximately yield the ordinary Pythagorean theorem for small spherical triangles, and the other two equations should yield the usual (planar) definitions of $\tan \alpha$ and $\sin \alpha$. (This is hardly surprising, since everyday surveying involves triangles that are really spherical triangles of very small size compared with Earth's radius.)

5.5 Cubic Bézier curves and B-splines revisited

Since we looked at piecewise cubic curves in §3.2 and §3.3.8, we have introduced two important new features of geometry: the third dimension and projections (§5.3.9). Here we will briefly examine the rôle of cubic Bézier curves, B-splines and piecewise cubic interpolants in this wider context.

Our first observation is that the material in §3.2 carries over to ordinary 3-dimensional space with no changes. In effect, the third coordinate receives exactly the same treatment that is already given to the first two coordinates in §3.2. The reader who has written a program dealing with cubic Bézier curves in two dimensions should therefore be able to upgrade it to three dimensions with only minimal alterations. (In §6.3 we will solve the problem of actually printing pictures with 3-dimensional data.) Now it should also be apparent that the material in §3.3.8 carries over without change to three dimensions: If f is an affine transformation and C is a piecewise cubic curve (of any of the types studied) defined by control points $R_1, \cdots, R_n$, then f maps C to the piecewise cubic curve defined by $f(R_1), \cdots, f(R_n)$. As before, the affine maps are composites of translations with linear maps.

The situation for projective transformations is not so simple: *Projective transformations do not preserve cubic curves.* For a very simple example, let us consider the perspectivity that was constructed in §4.1.1. It mapped the plane $x_3 = 1$ to the plane $x_2 = 1$ via

$$\langle x_1, x_2, 1 \rangle \mapsto \langle x_1/x_2, 1, 1/x_2 \rangle$$

Now a cubic curve in the plane $x_3 = 1$ is parametrized by

$$\langle p(t), q(t), 1 \rangle$$

where $p(t)$ and $q(t)$ are cubic polynomials in t. But the image of this point under the mentioned perspectivity is

$$\left\langle \frac{p(t)}{q(t)}, 1, \frac{1}{q(t)} \right\rangle$$

Clearly the first and third coordinates here are not cubic polynomials. (They are quotients of cubic polynomials.) Nevertheless, this projected curve in fact has the properties generally demanded of splines: continuity, smoothness, and generally following the control points.

In dealing with this situation, one must be a little careful. If one insists on having a projection of a cubic curve, one must compute every point of the curve before projecting and then project each individual point according to the method of §5.3.9.

Exercises

1. Let $B(t)$ be the cubic Bézier curve with control points

$$P_0 = \langle -3, 0, 2 \rangle, \quad P_1 = \langle -3, -2/3, 2 \rangle$$
$$P_2 = \langle -3, -4/3, 7/3 \rangle, \quad P_3 = \langle -3, -2, 3 \rangle$$

Verify that the cubic Bézier curve defined by these three points is given by

$$B(t) = \langle -3, \ -2t, \ t^2 + 2 \rangle$$

Then verify that if P is the projection given (in homogeneous coordinates) by

$$\begin{bmatrix} 1 & 0 & 1 & 0 \\ 0 & 1 & 0 & 0 \\ 0 & 0 & -1 & 1 \end{bmatrix}$$

(i.e., projection through $\langle -1, 0, 1 \rangle$), then P maps this Bézier curve into a circle.

2. **A universal Bézier curve.** Let $B(t)$ be the cubic Bézier curve in $\mathbb{R}^3$ with control points

$$P_0 = \langle 0, 0, 0 \rangle, \quad P_1 = \langle 1, 0, 0 \rangle$$
$$P_2 = \langle 1, 1, 0 \rangle, \quad P_3 = \langle 1, 1, 1 \rangle$$

Prove that every cubic Bézier curve in space is derived from this one by an affine map. That is, if $B'(t)$ is any cubic Bézier curve in $\mathbb{R}^3$, then there exists an affine map $A : \mathbb{R}^3 \longrightarrow \mathbb{R}^3$ such that $B'(t) = A(B(t))$ for all t.

3. Let $B(t)$ be the cubic Bézier curve in $\mathbb{R}^3$ with control points

$$P_0 = \langle 0, 0, 0 \rangle, \quad P_1 = \langle a, 0, 0 \rangle$$
$$P_2 = \langle a, b, 0 \rangle, \quad P_3 = \langle a, b, c \rangle$$

(In other words, the segments of the control polygon can have arbitrary lengths but should be perpendicular to one another.) Prove that every cubic Bézier curve in the plane is a shadow —i.e., an image under parallel projection—of a suitable Bézier curve of this type, after a rigid motion. Sketch the curve and show intuitively why this is true. Also give a mathematical proof. (In Chapter 6 we will be able to make more precise pictures of these curves.)

4. Let $B(t)$ be any cubic Bézier curve in $\mathbb{R}^3$. Prove that if $B(t)$ intersects itself (i.e., if $B(t_0) = B(t_1)$ for some t_0, t_1 with $t_0 \neq t_1$, then $B(t)$ is a plane curve; i.e., there exists a plane P in $\mathbb{R}^3$ such that $B(t)$ lies in P for all t.

5.6 Horizons revisited

Here we can use the techniques of §5.3.9 to extend our earlier treatment of horizons (§3.4.12) to horizons (or shadows) of a figure K as seen from any viewpoint. To do this we use the matrix

$$
\mathbf{P} = \begin{bmatrix} P_3 & 0 & -P_1 & 0 \\ 0 & P_3 & -P_2 & 0 \\ 0 & 0 & P_3 & 0 \\ 0 & 0 & -P_4 & P_3 \end{bmatrix}
$$

of §5.3.9 that moves the point P with homogeneous coordinates $\langle P_1, P_2, P_3, P_4 \rangle$ to $\langle 0, 0, 1, 0 \rangle$ and fixes all points on the plane $x_3 = 0$. We first observe that the inverse of P is

$$
\mathbf{P}^{-1} = \frac{1}{P_3^2} \begin{bmatrix} P_3 & 0 & P_1 & 0 \\ 0 & P_3 & P_2 & 0 \\ 0 & 0 & P_3 & 0 \\ 0 & 0 & P_4 & P_3 \end{bmatrix}
$$

To be precise about shadows, let us always mean the shadow on the plane $x_3 = 0$. To find the shadow or horizon of K as seen from P, we need to find the lines through P that are tangent with K and intersect these lines with the plane $x_3 = 0$. The matrix $\mathbf{P}$ moves such lines to lines that are tangent to $P(K)$ and that pass through $\langle 0, 0, 1, 0 \rangle$. In other words, these lines are parallel to the x_3-axis, and so the problem has been reduced to parallel projection of the figure $P(K)$. Thus, in order to solve the problem, we need only determine an equation for the figure $P(K)$ and apply the methods of §3.4.12.

To begin, let us suppose that in ordinary coordinates the projection point is $\langle a_1, a_2, a_3 \rangle$ and the figure K is defined by the equation

$$
F(x_1, x_2, x_3) = 0 \tag{5.4}
$$

Now a point $\langle x_1, x_2, x_3 \rangle$ clearly lies in $P(K)$ iff its inverse image $\mathbf{P}^{-1}(\langle x_1, x_2, x_3 \rangle)$ lies in K, i.e., iff its coordinates satisfy (5.4).

Clearly the matrix $\mathbf{P}^{-1}$ takes the homogeneous coordinates $\langle x_1, x_2, x_3, 1 \rangle$ to

$$
\frac{1}{P_3^2} \langle P_3 x_1 + P_1 x_3, \; P_3 x_2 + P_2 x_3, \; P_3 x_3, \; P_3 + P_4 x_3 \rangle
$$

Returning to ordinary non-homogeneous coordinates, we have that $\mathbf{P}^{-1}$ takes $\langle x_1, x_2, x_3 \rangle$ to

$$
\left\langle \frac{P_3 x_1 + P_1 x_3}{P_3 + P_4 x_3}, \; \frac{P_3 x_2 + P_2 x_3}{P_3 + P_4 x_3}, \; \frac{P_3 x_3}{P_3 + P_4 x_3} \right\rangle \tag{5.5}
$$

Thus the equation needed for $\mathbf{P}(K)$ is found by substituting the three coordinates of Equation (5.5) in for x_1, x_2 and x_3 in Equation (5.4).

Let us work this out in more detail for one example; namely, let us find the horizon of the surface

$$2x_1x_3 + x_2^2 + x_3^2 = 1$$

of §3.4.12 as seen from a point $\langle 0, 0, s \rangle$ on the positive x_3-axis. Thus we may take $P_1 = P_2 = 0$, $P_3 = s$ and $P_4 = 1$, and Equation (5.4) in this special case becomes

$$2\left(\frac{sx_1}{x_3+s}\right)\left(\frac{sx_3}{x_3+s}\right) + \left(\frac{sx_3}{x_3+s}\right)^2 + \left(\frac{sx_2}{x_3+s}\right)^2 = 1$$

or

$$2x_1x_3 + x_2^2 + x_3^2 = \frac{(x_3+s)^2}{s^2}$$

Now to find the horizon in the manner of §3.4.12, we take the third partial derivative, obtaining

$$2x_1 + 2x_3 = \frac{2(x_3+s)}{s^2}$$

This yields a linear relation for x_3 in terms of x_1, which, when substituted into the surface equation, yields the equation

$$2\frac{s(1-sx_1)}{s^2-1} + x_2^2 + \frac{s^2(1-sx_1)^2}{(s^2-1)^2} = 1$$

that defines the horizon as a relation between x_1 and x_2. The coefficient of x_1^2 in this horizon curve is

$$\frac{2s^2 - s^4}{(s^2-1)^2}$$

which is negative for all $|s| > \sqrt{2}$. As the reader may check, the locus is actually empty for $|s| \leq \sqrt{2}$, and so in all cases of a visible horizon, the horizon is a hyperbola.

We can make similar calculations beginning with any quadric surface, i.e, using any F for which Equation (5.4) is quadratic in x_1, x_2 and x_3. Obviously the detailed calculations are complicated and depend very much on the surface and on the viewpoint. Nevertheless, one feature of the present calculation is clearly independent of the exact numbers, namely, the fact that the resulting horizon has a quadratic equation. Thus, *any horizon of any quadric surface is a (possibly degenerate) conic section.*

Exercises_____

1. Explain what it means to have an empty horizon.

2. Determine the horizon of Earth as seen from an altitude of 2000 feet as taken by a camera with a focal length of 2 inches. In other words, the film plane is $x_3 = 0$, the projection point is $\langle 0, 0, f \rangle$, and the earth is a sphere of radius R centered so as to be tangent to the x_3-axis, with its center $R + A$ from the origin (with $f = 2$ inches, $A = 2000$ feet, and $R = 4000$ miles). It would be enough to determine the radius of curvature of the image on the film.

3. Determine horizon curves as seen from $\langle 0, 0, s \rangle$ for the surfaces that are given in Exercise 4 at the end of §3.1.7.

4. (If one has automated the drawing of conic sections at the end of §3.1.7, then one could do this exercise.) Take some surface, such as the one described in the text or in Exercise 3, and automate the drawing of pictures of horizons of this surface from $\langle 0, 0, s \rangle$ as s is stepped through some range of values. If rapidly displayed, these pictures would constitute a movie of how the surface looks as one moves toward it or away from it.

6 Applications of projective maps

In this chapter we describe a number of applications of the techniques described earlier in the book. In one way or another the applications involve making pictures of 3- (or 4-) dimensional objects. The objects in question may be defined purely by a database (e.g., the continental outlines) or purely by some theoretical considerations (e.g., the graph of a function of two variables). Nevertheless all of these applications share the general methods for projecting onto a 2-dimensional viewing surface. Because of this similarity in method, we give the most complete details in §6.1, which therefore should be read carefully, even if the reader decides to concentrate on one of the other applications. We have not expressly stated many exercises in this chapter, since the implementation of each section is really a (large) exercise in itself. (The exception to this statement is §6.3, in which we present a large number of separate exercises. Elsewhere we have stated a few explicit exercises, but these generally relate to minor points; in most cases the main project is to carry out the algorithms under discussion.) For a full appreciation of this chapter, the student should carry out at least one of these applications from start to finish.

Generally speaking, the representation of 3-dimensional objects can be viewed as one more mathematical translation of the sort considered in Chapter 2. Regardless of the problem under consideration, working with three coordinates is not very different from working with two, and if we were content with numerical solutions there would be little more to be said. But our objective in the applied 3-dimensional problems of this chapter is always to output a 2-dimensional picture. The general method for doing this is to use a projection matrix, as described in §5.3.9. Thus, in broad outline, our task in this chapter is to implement the flow chart that appears on the next page.

A major difficulty with this flow chart is that it fails to discriminate between visible and invisible objects. (In general, some objects in the drawing will be opaque and hence will obscure other objects.) There is no practical algorithm that will distinguish the visible objects in all problems, although considerable success can be had in many particular well-defined classes of problems, as we shall see. We therefore do not begin with the general linguistic approach, but begin instead in our first two sections, with a method that works well for the problem of making charts of Earth and of the stars. This postponement of the translation method (until §6.3) should also make §6.1 and §6.2 more accessible to students who skipped our previous sections where translation methods were required. (In fact, the method outlined in §6.1 is tantamount to a translation program and hence could be a useful introduction to that method.)

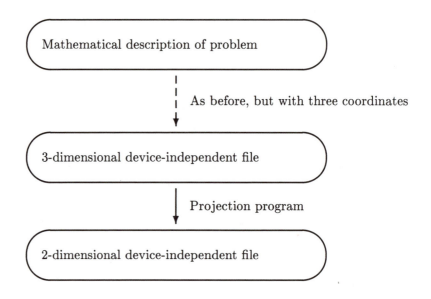

6.1   Projections of a globe

In this section we will apply the methods outlined earlier to the problem of projecting an image of Earth, with its continental boundaries, to a flat surface. In other words, we outline the writing of a program to make a picture of Earth, as it would be seen from space. Three important parameters are a *latitude* lat, a *longitude* long and an *altitude* alt. Our picture is to look as Earth would look from a spacecraft at distance alt above the point on Earth's surface with latitude lat and longitude long. (In other words the viewpoint is distant $R + $ alt from the center of Earth, where R is Earth's radius.)

6.1.1   The database

We suppose that we have a database containing the continental outlines in the form of a piecewise linear approximation. Specifically we will assume that we have a file called `continents.data`, divided into lines that have the form

FIGURE 6.1 A view of Earth from space

B θ ϕ

where B is a Boolean variable (i.e., B takes on the values 0 and 1), and θ and ϕ are readable as floating point numbers. For example, in the author's data file, the first five lines are

```
0 18.6 120.7
1 18.5 121.4
1 18.5 122.2
1 17.2 122.5
1 16.2 122.1
```

The second and third numbers represent latitudes and longitudes, respectively; i.e., θ is the latitude of a point on a continental boundary, and ϕ is its longitude.[1] The first number B serves to indicate whether we are going to actually draw a segment or whether we are merely moving our pen to begin a new segment. That is to say, if $B = 1$ we assume that the point on Earth's surface described by these coordinates is to be connected to the point described in the previous line. If $B = 0$, then we will simply record the values of these numbers and proceed to the next line of the file, without drawing anything. (Therefore, for these instructions to be meaningful, the very first line should always begin with 0. Moreover, two successive lines should not both begin with 0: While two such lines do not constitute an error, the first would never be used and would merely waste space in the database. In fact the 0 and 1 function just like the m and the 1 of our device-independent language.)

Exercise

1. Like Wyoming, the state of Colorado is roughly rectangular. It northern and southern borders are curves of constant latitude (41 degrees and 37 degrees), and its eastern and western borders are curves of constant longitude (102.1 degrees and 109.1 degrees). How accurate a picture of Colorado will we obtain if we simply add the following five lines of data to our database?

```
0 41.0 102.1
1 37.0 102.1
1 37.0 109.1
1 41.0 109.1
1 41.0 102.1
```

---

[1] In most databases, these are measured in degrees; for example, the five data lines shown here represent points on the island of Luzón in the Philippines.

6.1.2   Reading the database

So that the work in this course may concentrate on mathematics proper, we describe a shell program that gives all the necessary tools for the reading of the database, and for outputting the data as a file of device-independent commands (m, l, and so on). This of course accomplishes very little by itself, since continents.data differs in no significant way from such a file. Nevertheless the program should be useful for its input and output routines; between input and output the student should be able to interpose the calculations needed to get a true perspective view of Earth. (Some students may find it easier to base the work here on a translation program in the style of §2.3. Anyone who is really confident about this sort of thing can skip §6.1.2.) Most of the rest of §6.1 is about the details of such calculations.

One can of course run this program as it stands and make a plot of the output. In this way one will simply plot points as if latitude were a y-coordinate and longitude were an x-coordinate. Such a picture is called a *synoptic chart*; it gives a rough (topological) idea of geography, but not much more. The student will probably find it useful to do this anyway, as a warm-up exercise. Making a synoptic chart with a relatively small window will give one a pictorial idea of the spacing of the points in one's database.

We mention a few features of this program that have not appeared in our previous programs. The major new feature is that we allow input from a named file, whose name is abbreviated in the program as DATAFILE. Previously we took all input from unnamed files, presuming that the operating system is capable of selecting the actual input file. When one file is called repeatedly, it is often simpler to name that file in the program. In some operating systems the method described here is essential. The input file is actually accessed through a *file pointer*, here called fp_in, which can be thought of as a name that one can use to refer to a file inside a program. File pointers are created by the standard routine fopen(). (The "r" in our call to fopen() asks to have the file opened for reading. Consult a book on C for more information.) Input from the file is then done with fscanf, which works just like scanf, except that a file pointer must be indicated. Likewise this program makes occasional use of fprintf, which is like printf except that it requires a file pointer to receive the output. This is used in particular for the interactive part of the program, where a user is asked for the latitude and longitude. Here our named output file is stderr, which is a standard feature of UNIX systems. It allows an alternate output that does not mix with the main outputs (our printf commands in display( )). Alternatively, one could use fprintf with a named output file, while using printf for interactions with the user.

The while loop here is infinite; it ends when a call to fscanf fails (either for improperly formatted data or for lack of data), returning a negative value of Q. If the continents.data file contains no errors, the program will read all the data and then stop.

Notice that (as in previous programs) we tell `scanf` the address `&latitude` and not the value `latitude` (`scanf` needs to know the address where a new value of `latitude` will be stored). This will be handled differently in different languages. The author suggests that whenever possible the instructor supply sample programs that will give input and output functions that are correct on the local system.

```
#define DATAFILE "/faculty/yourprof/continents.data"

main()
{
FILE *fp_in, *fopen();
fp_in = fopen(DATAFILE,"r");

fprintf(stderr,"\nWhat latitude should we use?    ");
scanf("%lf",&latitude);
fprintf(stderr,"\n\nWhat longitude should we use?    ");
scanf("%lf",&longitude);

while (1)
{
        q = p;
        Q = fscanf(fp_in,"%d",&printing);
                if (Q <= 0) {error_1(); break;}
        Q = fscanf(fp_in,"%lf",&p.y_coord);
                if (Q <= 0) {error_2(); break;}
        Q = fscanf(fp_in,"%lf",&p.x_coord);
                if (Q <= 0) {error_3(); break;}
        if (printing==1) display(p,q,latitude,longitude);
}
label_picture();
fclose(fp_in);
}     /*END of MAIN*/

display(p,q,latitude,longitude)
{
printf("m %f %f",p.x_coord,p.y_coord);
printf("l %f %f",q.x_coord,q.y_coord);
}
```

We close this section with a few remarks about this program and what we will do with it.

1. `DATAFILE` can of course be changed to any other file from which you might want to take data. Sometimes for the purpose of testing and development it is handy to have a much smaller file.

2. The routines `error_1()`, `error_2()`, and so on, simply put various error message onto `stderr`. We have not included the detailed statements of these routines here, because it seems pretty clear what has to be said. If `DATAFILE` really exists, and if it does not deviate from the form specified above, then you should not obtain any of the error messages in running this program.

3. We get the values of lat and long interactively from the user; these quantities are mentioned at the start of §6.1. We didn't ask for alt because that is not used in this simple program. In modifying this program to view the world from altitude alt, you will also need to ask for alt right here.

4. The θ and ϕ mentioned above in §6.1.1 are read here simply as the y-coordinate and the x-coordinate of a point p. This accords with the fact that in this simple program ϕ and θ are treated as simply the coordinates of a point in the plane. Most likely in the final version the student will want to read this data into variables named `theta` and `phi`, and then use them to calculate the coordinates of a point (see §6.1.4).

5. The Boolean variable B mentioned above in §6.1.1 is read here as `printing`.

6. The routine `label_picture()` at present does nothing, but in the final version it would be nice to label your picture so that the various parameters (lat, long and alt) are not lost. It is best to automate such a procedure, i.e., to make it into a routine `label_picture(latitude, longitude, altitude)`.

7. The `display()` function presently does nothing more than plot coordinates as if the world were a Euclidean plane. (The main exercise can then be summed up by saying that the student is expected to write a correct program for `display()`.) We did not include any window coordinates in the main program. Some interesting views can be had with small windows. For example

   `W  8 38 20 44`

   will show some of the Mediterranean. Some other interesting views can be obtained with windows centered at these coordinates:

52	3	(Ireland, England and much of northern Europe)
8	79	(southern India and Sri Lanka)
16	122	(much of the Philippines, coast of China, island
		of Taiwan and one corner of Borneo).

8. The database can of course be expanded at will, to include rivers, political boundaries, the arctic circle, or any other feature of interest to the user. (But note the point made in the exercise at the end of §6.1.1.)

9. This simple program to read the database has no provision for comments. Nevertheless, one might find it helpful to allow them, especially if you modify or add to the database. It might be helpful to have words saying what part of the code is the Mississippi River, what part is the Ohio, and so on. The author is confident that the reader can supply this if and when it seems necessary.

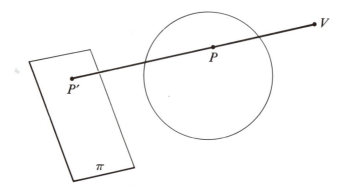

FIGURE 6.2 Projecting the globe to an oblique plane

6.1.3 A coordinate system for viewing the globe

To begin making a mathematical model of how we view Earth from space, we need to establish a system of coordinates in which to do our calculations. As we have noted before, the viewing operation really consists of a projection onto a plane from a point, such as we described with matrices back in §5.3.9. We have set ourselves the task of projecting from a viewpoint V located over (i.e., a distance alt radially outward from) an arbitrary point (given by lat and long) on Earth's surface. This requires us to project to a plane π that may be situated obliquely to our coordinate system (see Figure 6.2). While we could proceed directly in this manner, it is simpler to first rotate the sphere so that the point designated by lat and long is moved to the North Pole,[2] and then project from a point above the North Pole. (We will come to the specifics of this rotation in §6.1.5 below.) In view of the specific formulas that we have available, we ought to coordinatize space so that the plane π receiving the projection is the (x, y)-plane.[3] Things are further simplified by laying down coordinates in such a way that both the North Pole and the viewpoint V lie on the z-axis. We indicate in Figure 6.3 how this can be accomplished. One may imagine oneself seated at a table on which the x-axis goes off to the right, the y-axis goes straight back and from which the positive z-axis goes straight up. The globe is floating in space with its center a distance K above the origin. (For most of our work, the parameter K may just as well be 0.)

---

[2]I.e., the point on the sphere with largest z-coordinate, which is the point $\langle 0, 0, R \rangle$ for a sphere of radius R centered at the origin.

[3]Note that here and elsewhere, the x, y-plane could be replaced by any plane parallel to the x, y-plane (except the one parallel plane that contains the viewpoint). The only change would be a similarity transformation.

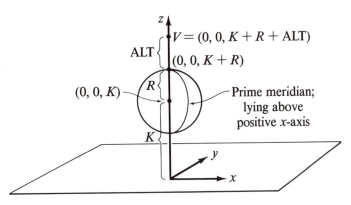

FIGURE 6.3   Projecting the globe to the (x, y)-plane

Thus the center of the sphere has coordinates $\langle 0, 0, K \rangle$, the North Pole has coordinates $\langle 0, 0, K + R \rangle$ (where R is the radius of the sphere), and the viewpoint V has coordinates $\langle 0, 0, K + R + \text{alt} \rangle$ (see Figure 6.3).

We will not, however, begin with the globe up in the air like this; we will begin simply by considering the case where the globe is centered on the origin $\langle 0, 0, 0 \rangle$, that is, the case where $K = 0$.

6.1.4   Coordinates for points on a sphere

We have almost completely specified how our globe is positioned in space, having nailed down the center and the North Pole. There remains, however, the possibility of rotating the sphere around the z-axis. To make a connection between the usual coordinates on a globe (latitude and longitude) and spatial coordinates (x, y and z), we need to specify this rotation. We do this by specifying that the prime meridian (semicircle of zero longitude) should lie above the positive x-axis. This feature may also be seen in Figure 6.3.

We can now make precise the connection between the spherical coordinates and the rectangular spatial coordinates. From Figure 6.4 it is apparent that the curve of constant latitude θ is a circle parallel to the x, y-plane, lying at height $R \sin \theta$ above (or below) that plane and centered on the z-axis. Clearly all points on this circle have z-coordinate $R \sin \theta$, and the radius of the circle is $R \cos \theta$, where R is the radius of the sphere. The point P with latitude θ and longitude

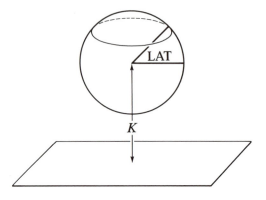

FIGURE 6.4   A circle of constant latitude

ϕ lies on this circle, at an angle of ϕ from the x-axis.[4] Since the radius of the circle is $R\cos\theta$, we see that the x- and y-coordinates of the point P are

$$
\begin{aligned}
x &= R \cdot \cos\theta \cdot \cos\phi \\
y &= R \cdot \cos\theta \cdot \sin\phi \\
z &= R \cdot \sin\theta
\end{aligned}
$$

Now, clearly, what is needed in revising the program of §6.1.2 is to calculate these values of x, y and z for every θ and ϕ that are read from the database. Since we are going to perform projective transformations on this point, it is in fact more useful to calculate *homogeneous coordinates* for the point P. For this, the equations are almost the same as before, namely,

$$
\begin{aligned}
x_1 &= R \cdot \cos\theta \cdot \cos\phi \\
x_2 &= R \cdot \cos\theta \cdot \sin\phi \\
x_3 &= R \cdot \sin\theta \\
x_4 &= 1
\end{aligned}
$$

6.1.5   Rotating the globe

Let P_0 be the point on the sphere that has latitude lat and longitude long; in other words, P_0 is the point that we wish to have in the center of our projected image of the globe. As we said in §6.1.3, we need to rotate the globe in such

---

[4]We thus have implicitly adopted the convention that positive values of longitude (in the range $0 < \text{long} < \pi$) represent what is often known as *longitude east of Greenwich* (e.g., most of Europe and Africa), and that negative values represent *longitude west of Greenwich* (e.g., North and South America). The author's database reflects this convention, and it should be used in entering lat and long into the program.

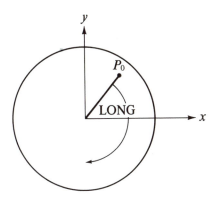

FIGURE 6.5   The point with latitude lat and longitude long, seen from above

a manner that P_0 is carried to the North Pole. We will carry out this rotation as a composition of two rotations. This first is a rotation about the z-axis that moves the points with longitude long until they are above the negative y-axis. Then a rotation about the x-axis will carry P_0 to the North Pole.

For the first rotation, about the z-axis, let us consult Figure 6.5, which shows our situation viewed from above. It is clear that a rotation through an angle[5] of $-(\text{long} + \pi/2)$—indicated by a curving arrow in Figure 6.5—will carry P_0 onto the negative y-axis. Consulting §5.3.4 we see that the matrix of this rotation (for homogeneous coordinates) is

$$\mathbf{D}_{\text{long}} = \begin{bmatrix} \cos(-(\text{long}+\pi/2)) & -\sin(-(\text{long}+\pi/2)) & 0 & 0 \\ \sin(-(\text{long}+\pi/2)) & \cos(-(\text{long}+\pi/2)) & 0 & 0 \\ 0 & 0 & 1 & 0 \\ 0 & 0 & 0 & 1 \end{bmatrix}$$

According to the laws of trigonometry, we also have

$$\mathbf{D}_{\text{long}} = \begin{bmatrix} -\sin(\text{long}) & \cos(\text{long}) & 0 & 0 \\ -\cos(\text{long}) & -\sin(\text{long}) & 0 & 0 \\ 0 & 0 & 1 & 0 \\ 0 & 0 & 0 & 1 \end{bmatrix}$$

In fact, the reader may easily check that $\mathbf{D}_{\text{long}}$ operates on the point P_0 as follows:

---

[5] Our database happens to be given in degrees, and lat and long may also be entered in degrees by the user, but we are using radians for a formal mathematical presentation. Notice that many compilers expect arguments to trigonometric functions to be given in radians, and so the student should be careful to convert all angles to radians (when appropriate).

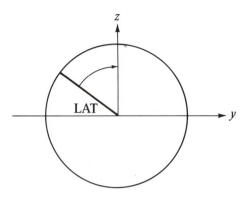

FIGURE 6.6   Side view after the first rotation (with x-axis toward the viewer)

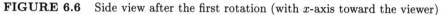

$$\mathbf{D}_{\text{long}} \cdot \begin{bmatrix} R \cdot \cos(\text{lat}) \cdot \cos(\text{long}) \\ R \cdot \cos(\text{lat}) \cdot \sin(\text{long}) \\ R \cdot \sin(\text{lat}) \\ 1 \end{bmatrix} = \begin{bmatrix} 0 \\ -R \cdot \cos(\text{lat}) \\ R \cdot \sin(\text{lat}) \\ 1 \end{bmatrix}$$

For the second rotation, about the x-axis, let us consult Figure 6.6, which shows a side view of our globe after it has undergone the first rotation $\mathbf{D}_{\text{long}}$. It is clear that a rotation through an angle of $-(\pi/2 - \text{lat})$—indicated by a curving arrow in Figure 6.6—will carry $\mathbf{D}_{\text{long}} \cdot P_0$ up to the North Pole. Consulting §5.3.4 we see that the matrix of this rotation (for homogeneous coordinates) is

$$\mathbf{C}_{\text{lat}} = \begin{bmatrix} 1 & 0 & 0 & 0 \\ 0 & \cos(-(\pi/2 - \text{lat})) & -\sin(-(\pi/2 - \text{lat})) & 0 \\ 0 & \sin(-(\pi/2 - \text{lat})) & \cos(-(\pi/2 - \text{lat})) & 0 \\ 0 & 0 & 0 & 1 \end{bmatrix}$$

According to the laws of trigonometry, we also have

$$\mathbf{C}_{\text{lat}} = \begin{bmatrix} 1 & 0 & 0 & 0 \\ 0 & \sin(\text{lat}) & \cos(\text{lat}) & 0 \\ 0 & -\cos(\text{lat}) & \sin(\text{lat}) & 0 \\ 0 & 0 & 0 & 1 \end{bmatrix}$$

Now to confirm the fact that the composite rotation $\mathbf{C}_{\text{lat}} \circ \mathbf{D}_{\text{long}}$ moves P_0 to the North Pole, we calculate that

$$\mathbf{C}_{\text{lat}} \circ \mathbf{D}_{\text{long}}(P_0) = \mathbf{C}_{\text{lat}} \left(\begin{bmatrix} 0 \\ -R \cdot \cos(\text{lat}) \\ R \cdot \sin(\text{lat}) \\ 1 \end{bmatrix} \right)$$

$$= \begin{bmatrix} 1 & 0 & 0 & 0 \\ 0 & \sin(\text{lat}) & \cos(\text{lat}) & 0 \\ 0 & -\cos(\text{lat}) & \sin(\text{lat}) & 0 \\ 0 & 0 & 0 & 1 \end{bmatrix} \cdot \begin{bmatrix} 0 \\ -R \cdot \cos(\text{lat}) \\ R \cdot \sin(\text{lat}) \\ 1 \end{bmatrix}$$

$$= \begin{bmatrix} 0 \\ 0 \\ R \\ 1 \end{bmatrix}$$

The preceding equation confirms that the point P_0 is mapped to the North Pole by these two rotations, so our only job now is to project the globe onto the plane.

Before projecting, let us observe that there remains one fine point, which was not included in our original specification of the problem, but which is traditional in drawing maps of the world. We speak of the expectation[6] that *north* should be *up* on a map. Now of course, this expectation cannot be met globally: Any representation that includes the North Pole (or the South Pole) will have north taking on all directions in the image, since *north* really means *toward the pole*. Nevertheless, if we relax the requirement to mean only that north should be generally upward near the center of the picture, then the requirement can be given the more precise mathematical formulation that the image of the North Pole under the composite rotation $\mathbf{C}_{\text{lat}} \circ \mathbf{D}_{\text{long}}$ should lie above the positive y-axis. To see that this actually holds,[7] we calculate

$$\mathbf{C}_{\text{lat}} \circ \mathbf{D}_{\text{long}} \left(\begin{bmatrix} 0 \\ 0 \\ R \\ 1 \end{bmatrix} \right) = \mathbf{C}_{\text{lat}} \left(\begin{bmatrix} 0 \\ 0 \\ R \\ 1 \end{bmatrix} \right)$$

$$= \begin{bmatrix} 0 \\ R \cdot \cos(\text{lat}) \\ R \cdot \sin(\text{lat}) \\ 1 \end{bmatrix}$$

The preceding equation clearly shows that the North Pole is rotated to a point above the positive y-axis.

6.1.6 Translating the globe

Now, after rotation, the globe may be translated upward by application of the matrix

[6]It was to meet this expectation that we went through the seemingly Byzantine procedure of rotating first to the *negative y-axis* (instead of, say, the positive *x-axis*). As we show in this paragraph, this procedure will cause north to be seen as *up* in the final picture.
[7]Actually, if it did not come out with north up, one could simply apply a rotation to the plane of the paper to orient north as one wishes.

$$
\mathbf{B}_K = \begin{bmatrix} 1 & 0 & 0 & 0 \\ 0 & 1 & 0 & 0 \\ 0 & 0 & 1 & K \\ 0 & 0 & 0 & 1 \end{bmatrix}
$$

6.1.7 Projecting the globe

We next follow the plan described in §5.3.9 of projecting from the viewpoint V by first moving V to the ideal point $\langle 0, 0, 1, 0 \rangle$ by application of the matrix

$$
\mathbf{A}_V = \begin{bmatrix} P_3 & 0 & -P_1 & 0 \\ 0 & P_3 & -P_2 & 0 \\ 0 & 0 & P_3 & 0 \\ 0 & 0 & -P_4 & P_3 \end{bmatrix}
$$

where P_1, P_2, P_3 and P_4 are the coordinates of V. As we can see from Figure 6.3, these coordinates are $P_1 = P_2 = 0$, $P_3 = K + R + \mathrm{alt}$, and $P_4 = 1$. Thus

$$
\mathbf{A}_V = \begin{bmatrix} K + R + \mathrm{alt} & 0 & 0 & 0 \\ 0 & K + R + \mathrm{alt} & 0 & 0 \\ 0 & 0 & K + R + \mathrm{alt} & 0 \\ 0 & 0 & -1 & K + R + \mathrm{alt} \end{bmatrix}
$$

As described in §5.3.9, the full operation of projecting a point P on our (translated) sphere to the x, y-plane consists in first multiplying by $\mathbf{A}_V$ and then discarding the third coordinate, thereby obtaining (homogeneous) coordinates of a point P' in the plane. This P' is a point that is possibly plotted in our program of viewing the globe. We say possibly, because we must still decide whether P is visible from V (see §6.1.10).

6.1.8 The main matrix for the world-viewing program

Consider the matrix

$$
\mathbf{G} = \mathbf{A}_V \mathbf{B}_K \mathbf{C}_{\mathrm{lat}} \mathbf{D}_{\mathrm{long}}
$$

This matrix $\mathbf{G}$ can play a significant role in our program to project the globe, inasmuch as it can be computed once and then used over and over, as we see in §6.1.9.

6.1.9 Summary of a plan for drawing the globe

If θ and ϕ are the latitude and longitude of any point in the database, then, as we saw in §6.1.4, the point

$$P_{\theta,\phi} = \begin{bmatrix} R \cdot \cos\theta \cdot \cos\phi \\ R \cdot \cos\theta \cdot \sin\phi \\ R \cdot \sin\theta \\ 1 \end{bmatrix} \tag{6.1}$$

lies on our sphere, and represents a point to be depicted in the picture we are making. Recall that we have replaced projection to an oblique plane by the simpler idea of rotating the sphere and then projecting from above the North Pole down to the x, y-plane. Therefore our steps are as follows.

ALGORITHM (a perspective drawing of Earth with its continents, first provisional form) Elements of the database are read one by one, and the following steps are performed for each element in turn.

- Calculate $P_{\theta,\phi}$.

- Multiply it on the left by the matrix $\mathbf{D}_{\mathrm{long}}$ and then by the matrix $\mathbf{C}_{\mathrm{lat}}$. This effects the desired rotation.

- Multiply the resulting element of $\mathbb{R}^4$ on the left by the matrix $\mathbf{B}_K$ to translate along the z-axis.

- Multiply the resulting element of $\mathbb{R}^4$ on the left by the matrix $\mathbf{A}_V$ to move the viewpoint V to infinity.

- From the resulting vector $\langle P_1, P_2, P_3, P_4 \rangle \in \mathbb{R}^4$, obtain ordinary spatial coordinates x, y and z in the usual way (i.e., $x = P_1/P_4$, and so on).

- Use the $\langle x, y \rangle$ as coordinates of a point P that may appear in the final picture.

- Decide whether to print P by determining whether the original point $P_{\theta,\phi}$ was visible from the original viewpoint V. (As we will see in §6.1.10, this determination can be made simply from the value of z just calculated.)

The second, third and fourth steps here amount to multiplying a vector of $\mathbb{R}^4$ on the left, first by $\mathbf{D}_{\mathrm{long}}$, then by $\mathbf{C}_{\mathrm{lat}}$, then by $\mathbf{B}_K$, and finally by $\mathbf{A}_V$. Clearly the effect is the same if we multiply all at once by the product of these four matrices, which is the matrix $\mathbf{G}$ calculated in §6.1.8. Therefore our plan may be simplified to consist of the following steps.

ALGORITHM (a perspective drawing of Earth with its continents, second provisional form) The matrix $\mathbf{G}$ defined above (combining rotations and projections) is calculated, and then elements of the database are read one by one, and the following steps are performed for each element in turn.

- Calculate $P_{\theta,\phi}$.

- Multiply it on the left by $\mathbf{G}$.

- From the resulting vector in $\mathbb{R}^4$, obtain ordinary spatial coordinates x, y and z in the usual way.

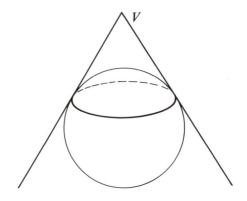

FIGURE 6.7   The circle of tangency

- Use the $\langle x, y \rangle$ as coordinates of a point P that may appear in the final picture.
- Use z to determine whether the original point $P_{\theta,\phi}$ was visible from the original viewpoint V.

6.1.10   The visibility of a point on the sphere from the viewpoint

We wish to draw only what can actually be seen from the viewpoint V (after the globe has been rotated). To make a simple determination of this visibility condition, we begin by considering the family of all tangent lines from V to the sphere. These form a cone C that intersects the sphere in a circle of constant height, called the *circle of tangency*, which we have depicted in Figure 6.7. (This circle of tangency is really the same as the *horizon* as discussed in §3.4.12 and in §5.6.) In Figure 6.8 we show a cross-sectional view from which one can calculate the latitude of this circle. In this figure, the points Q and Q' lie on the circle of tangency, and O is the center of the sphere. Segments $\overline{OQ}$ and $\overline{OQ'}$ are radii of the sphere. The angle λ is the latitude of the circle of tangency; it is seen again as half the apex angle. From the right triangle $\triangle VOQ$ (with right angle at Q), it can easily be seen that

$$\sin \lambda = \frac{R}{\text{alt} + R} \tag{6.2}$$

Having calculated λ from Equation (6.2), we then realize that (before translation) Q may be computed as

$$Q = \langle R \cdot \cos \lambda, 0, R \cdot \sin \lambda, 1 \rangle$$

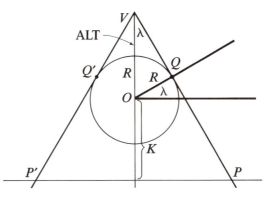

FIGURE 6.8   Calculating the angle of tangency

The point Q may now be used as a test point. Its z-coordinate (after application of the matrices $\mathbf{B}_K$ and $\mathbf{A}_V$) can be used as a test value for the z-value found in the last step of the algorithm presented in §6.1.9. Clearly points on the sphere higher than Q will be visible to V, and all other points on the sphere will be invisible to V. Since the transformations represented by the matrices $\mathbf{A}_V$ and $\mathbf{B}_K$ do not change the relative vertical positions of points between V and the x,y-plane, we may in fact perform the necessary height comparisons after applying $\mathbf{B}_K$ and $\mathbf{A}_V$.

Thus, in order to use Q as a test point, we first calculate

$$Q_{\text{test}} = \mathbf{A}_V \cdot \mathbf{B}_K \cdot Q$$

Then z_{test} is defined to be the z-coordinate of Q_{test} (after conversion from homogeneous to non-homogeneous coordinates). In other words

$$z_{\text{test}} = Q_3'' / Q_4''$$

where $\langle Q_1'', Q_2'', Q_3'', Q_4'' \rangle$ are homogeneous coordinates for Q_{test}.

Now we can restate the last step of the second version of the algorithm in §6.1.9 as follows.

- Decide whether to print P by testing for $z \geq z_{\text{test}}$.

6.1.11   The while loop revisited

Let us now examine how we should modify the shell program of §6.1.2 so that it will actually draw Earth as seen.

ALGORITHM (a perspective drawing of Earth with its continents)

Before entering the main while loop calculate once and for all the matrices $\mathbf{A}_V, \mathbf{B}_K, \mathbf{C}_{lat}$ and $\mathbf{D}_{lat}$—and from them the matrix $\mathbf{G}$. Then calculate the point Q_{test} and its z-coordinate z_{test}. Then enter the while loop and follow what has been stated already. To recapitulate, the main steps in one pass through the loop should be

- Store old value of p as q, as in the original program.
- Read `printing`, θ and ϕ from the database, if possible. (Don't forget to convert these values to radians, if appropriate.)
- Calculate homogeneous coordinates of $P_{\theta,\phi}$, using Equation (6.1).
- Multiply the corresponding 4-vector on the left by the matrix $\mathbf{G}$.
- From the resulting vector $\langle P_1, P_2, P_3, P_4 \rangle \in \mathbb{R}^4$, obtain ordinary spatial coordinates x, y and z in the usual way (i.e., $x = P_1/P_4$, and so on).
- Use the $\langle x, y \rangle$ as coordinates of a point p that might appear in the final picture.
- Consider p to be visible, hence printable, if $z \geq z_{test}$.
- If appropriate, display(p, q).

Refinements to the algorithm are made in §6.1.12 and §6.1.13.

6.1.12   Drawing the horizon circle

In drawing a picture of the features of the globe that are visible from a certain spot, it is nice to draw a circle that represents the horizon, i.e., the curve that divides our view of Earth from the empty space behind it. Clearly that curve can be determined from the material in §5.6, but it is easier to derive it directly from the diagrams that we already have.

It is not hard to see that the horizon is determined by the *circle of tangency* already described in §6.1.10. We see from Figure 6.7 that the horizon in the picture is the image of this curve under projection from V to the plane. Therefore to compute the horizon circle, we need only compute the values of a general point on the circle of tangency.

Actually, we already determined, in Equation (6.2) of §6.1.10, the latitude λ of the circle of tangency. Clearly a general point on the circle of tangency has homogeneous coordinates

$$
\begin{aligned}
x_1 &= R \cdot \cos \lambda \cdot \cos \psi \\
x_2 &= R \cdot \cos \lambda \cdot \sin \psi \\
x_3 &= R \cdot \sin \lambda \\
x_4 &= 1
\end{aligned}
$$

where ψ is a new parameter that ranges from 0 to 2π.

Therefore, the following steps will provide one with a drawing of the horizon:

- Discretize the parameter ψ (in a manner that should by now be familiar).
- For each discrete value of the parameter ψ, calculate $x_1, \cdots, x_4$ according to the formulas just above.
- Apply the matrix $\mathbf{A}_V \mathbf{B}_K$ to that 4-tuple.
- Calculate x and y as we did in the algorithm of §6.1.11 and carry on as in that algorithm.

6.1.13 Rescaling the picture

One thing we left out of the algorithm in §6.1.11 was an explicit statement of a window command, to get the picture nicely centered on the window of the device. We could of course leave this to trial and error, but a certain amount of analysis will make things easier. The main point of interest here is that the appropriate scaling factor depends on alt, as is easily seen from Figure 6.8. In fact the radius of the image circle is clearly

$$R_{\text{image}} = \tan \lambda \cdot (K + R + \text{alt})$$

From this equation it should be easy to have the computer generate an appropriate window command.

OTHER PROJECTIONS OF THE GLOBE

There is a general problem of depicting Earth's curved surface with a planar picture. Such pictures always involve distortion. The representations here are undistorted as drawings from outer space, but they do distort the curved surface, as one observes by looking near the periphery. A number of other drawing schemes have been invented that seek to minimize distortion in a number of ways. The *Mercator projection* is conformal, i.e., preserves angles, but distorts areas (with Greenland looking about as big as Africa). The *Sanson-Flamsteed sinusoidal mapping* and the *cylindric projection* preserve areas, but distort angles, and so on.

We regret having to omit a more detailed discussion of these topics, but we invite the reader to pursue them in other sources. The reader now has the necessary tools to make maps according to any of these mappings. For more information, the reader is referred, for example, to pages 307–326 of *Graphics Gems* [*op. cit.*] (articles by Andrew W. Paeth and Paul D. Barne).

Exercises

1. Learn something about other ways to map Earth's surface and make the associated drawings.

2. If you have available a database of lunar features, make some pictures of the moon's appearance. It would be interesting to show only the illuminated portion (the crescent). The boundaries of a crescent moon are easily added to the database, simply as longitude curves. (It would even be interesting to make pictures of the crescent moon's outline, without having any data about surface features.)

6.2   Projections of ideal points (stars)

In this section we shall describe an application of our ideas of linear transformations—especially rotations and projections—to another practical problem, that of depicting the positions of the stars in the sky as they are seen from a particular latitude at a given day and hour. The method is similar to that described in §6.1, and so we will present it more tersely, while describing those places where the method differs from the earlier one. Like §6.1, this section amounts to a practical problem for the student to solve using a computer, and the text that follows may be thought of as an explanation of how the theory that we have learned so far can be applied to a study of positions of stars. Figure 6.9 shows a typical example of the type of chart that one can make.

The objective of the exercise is as follows. Imagine yourself standing outdoors at an Earth location of latitude[8] λ, facing a compass direction γ and looking up toward the sky at an angle β from the horizon. On a clear night you will be rewarded with a view of stars, and if you continue to watch for a while, you will observe that these stars appear to move across the sky. Nevertheless, lengthy observation will show that, while moving, the stars maintain various characteristics, such as their brightness and color, and also maintain their positions relative to one another, so that many of the brighter ones can be recognized by their relations to their neighbors. Coming back the next night, one then observes that the same stars return to their original positions every day (more precisely, every 23 hours and 56 minutes). Therefore, the visible pattern of stars may be thought of as determined by the day and time, and so the exercise is (given suitable data about the stars) *to make a program that can predict the positions of the various stars in the sky*, based on λ and the time (both the day of the year and the hour). (In fact we will make a picture, not of the whole sky, but only of a small patch of sky centered on γ and β.)

---

[8]Longitude is not needed for this problem, since local time gives an adequate approximate compensation for differences in longitude. If local time were defined exactly—as it was, a century ago—then the compensation would be exact; as it is, our calculation of the local sidereal time will be inaccurate by up to 30 minutes, as one approaches the eastern or western boundaries of a time zone. Our level of accuracy certainly is adequate for making gross star charts; for serious telescope design, the time question would have to be addressed much more carefully.

FIGURE 6.9   A chart of the night sky

Continued observation of the stars inevitably leads to the idea that the stars look and behave like bright points attached to a distant spherical shell, sometimes called the *celestial sphere*, with Earth at its center. This point of view is strengthened by the observation of travelers that as one goes south (in the northern hemisphere), stars that were briefly visible over the southern horizon now move higher in the sky and become visible during more of the night,[9] and one even discovers some new stars. Therefore the Earth latitude λ of the observation point must be part of the essential data for solving our problem.

Our remarks so far were all known to the ancient world. It is of interest to note that even the elementary observation of unchanging star patterns very strongly suggests the use of *rigid* motions to solve the problem. Since Earth remains fixed, the motions must be reflections or rotations. Stars do not suddenly make large jumps across the sky, and so reflections are ruled out, leaving only rotations; and we surely will solve this problem using rotations. Therefore, our main advance—in this practical problem—over the ancient world seems to reside in our improved algebraic and numerical mastery of the theory of rotations (trigonometry, coordinates, matrices, etc.) rather than in any superior appreciation of pure geometry.

6.2.1   Celestial coordinates

To approach the problem of making star charts, we will need some rudimentary ideas of celestial coordinates. We emphasize that what we are presenting here is only a simplified version of a small fragment of the full astronomical theory of positions of the heavenly bodies. There is, for instance, no mention of the plane of the ecliptic (in which the sun and planets appear to move, and which passes near the familiar zodiac constellations), and stars are thought of as not moving relative to one another. We also ignore both the precession of Earth's axis of rotation (which slowly changes the position of *north* in the sky), and the small apparent annual change of position of nearby stars (parallax) that is caused by the motion of Earth in its orbit around the sun. Moreover, while assuming that the stars are distant enough to be considered as ideal points in calculations, we nevertheless assume that they are sufficiently close that any possible non-Euclidean or topological features[10] of the universe can be ignored. (In other words, we accept the simplifying hypothesis that our space is Euclidean.) Therefore, our simple model has Earth spinning at uniform angular velocity about a

---

[9]This motion of stars with latitude is probably the strongest evidence the ancients had for the round-Earth theory. In the third century B.C., Eratosthenes of Alexandria measured the angular change of one star (our sun) and thereby gave the first calculation of Earth's radius.

[10]Are there star triangles whose angle sum is less than 180 degrees? Could a light ray leave Earth and return? Such counterintuitive effects have never been observed, but they cannot be ruled out.

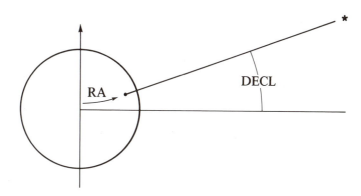

FIGURE 6.10   Celestial coordinates

fixed axis in a Euclidean space, with each star being a stationary bright point very far from Earth.

To lay down a coordinate system, we take the origin to be at Earth's center,[11] and then define the z-axis to be the axis of Earth's rotation, in such a manner that the North Pole has a positive z-coordinate. We thus have a natural definition for the z-axis. For the x- and y-axes, however, we will require an arbitrarily chosen reference point, which by convention is taken to be the apparent position of the sun at the time of the vernal equinox[12] (which occurs on or about March 21 of each year). Thus the x- and y-axes are defined in such a manner that on the vernal equinox the sun has positive x-coordinate and zero y-coordinate.

It is customary, however, to use the *spherical* coordinate system associated to the rectangular system that we just defined. *Declination* (DECL) refers to the angle of a point above or below Earth's equator (with positive angles referring to the northern hemisphere), and *right ascension* (RA) refers to the angle swept out in turning eastward from the x-axis to the star in question. The third spherical coordinate, r, is the distance from a point to the center of Earth. It does not appear in star charts, for two related reasons. First, a star's apparent position depends only on its DECL and RA, whereas changing its distance from Earth will not change its apparent position in the sky. Second, for the very reason that

[11]We hasten to add that we are not advocating a geocentric theory of the heavenly bodies. There is little doubt about the superiority of the heliocentric theory of Copernicus and Kepler. Nevertheless, for the purely geometric task of obtaining star coordinates, the geocentric theory is simpler.

[12]More formally: Twice a year the sun's apparent position lies on the plane $z = 0$, once moving upward, once moving downward. The moment when it crosses this plane in an upward (i.e., northerly) direction is called the vernal equinox.

r is not directly observed, r is hard (or impossible) to measure, and is therefore subject to much more uncertainty than is RA or DECL.

An alternate definition of RA and DECL is available through the following thought experiment. Imagine the situation—which recurs daily—in which the stars of RA zero lie directly over Earth's prime meridian. (A close approximation to this situation occurs at noon (GMT) on the day of the vernal equinox.) At such a moment, latitude corresponds exactly to DECL, and longitude corresponds exactly to RA. In other words, at this moment, if one stands at a point of latitude α and longitude β, then a star that is directly overhead will have DECL α and RA β.

The rectangular and spherical coordinates of a point in space are related by the usual equations

$$
\begin{aligned}
x &= r\cos(\text{DECL})\cos(\text{RA}) \\
y &= r\cos(\text{DECL})\sin(\text{RA}) \\
z &= r\sin(\text{DECL})
\end{aligned}
$$

6.2.2   Time

According to our simplifying assumptions, star positions do not depend on time, so long as we stick to the coordinate system laid down in the previous section. Nevertheless, bound as we are to the surface of rotating Earth, we perceive motion of stars. To analyze this motion, we need a time coordinate. Ordinary Earth time (of any time zone) is unsatisfactory for this purpose, since its basic unit (the day) refers to the periodic reappearance of the sun, and the sun is not one of the distant (fixed) stars. Therefore, astronomers customarily use another unit of time, namely the rotation period of Earth relative to the fixed stars. This unit of time is called the *sidereal day*.

The sidereal day is divided into 24 sidereal hours, and the hours into minutes and seconds, just as for ordinary solar time. Thus are defined intervals of *sidereal time*. For an absolute form of sidereal time, we need an origin for the time coordinate; this may be provided by right ascension. By definition, the *(local) sidereal time* at a point P on Earth's surface—other than P the North or South Pole—is defined to be the RA of the stars directly overhead.[13]

For the solution of our star-gazing problem, it is important to realize that one's view of the heavens from a location P on Earth depends on only two parameters, the latitude λ of P, and the sidereal time t at the moment of observation.

The use of the angle RA to measure sidereal time suggests that the sidereal day (likewise hour, and so on) should be thought of as a measure of angles: A sidereal day corresponds to 2π radians or 360 degrees (the angle of a full revolution), an hour to $2\pi/24$ radians, or 15 degrees, and so on. In fact, due to

---

[13]It is easy to see that the definition makes sense even if there are no stars directly above P.

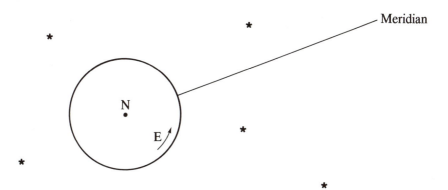

FIGURE 6.11   Equivalence of RA and sidereal time (view from the North Pole with arrow showing Earth's eastward rotation)

this close association of RA and sidereal time, star tables traditionally list RA in hours, minutes and seconds.

Again, this association of time with RA gives one more possible definition of RA. (Taking time units so that the fixed stars appear to rotate in one day, with 0 hours the time at noon on the vernal equinox), the RA of a celestial object O may be defined as the time when O crosses the meridian. (See Figure 6.11. The *meridian* is defined to be the plane that passes through the polar axis and through the point directly overhead.)

6.2.3   Calculating sidereal time

We give here an approximate calculation of sidereal time from solar[14] time and the calendar date. The calculation leaves out a lot of things that are important to serious astronomy, but nevertheless it will give an answer that is sufficiently close for purposes of general observation.

For the moment let us understand *time*, either sidereal or solar, to be a continuously increasing and unbounded real variable. That is, we do not reset our solar clock to zero at the end of a solar day, and we do not reset our sidereal clock to zero at the end of a sidereal day. We let t denote sidereal time and let s denote solar time. To give origins to these two time axes (i.e, to define $t = 0$ and $s = 0$), we arbitrarily choose a calendar year Y, such as $Y = 1991$. We take

---

[14]More specifically, *mean* solar time. This is the normal time on our clocks. The length of day is taken as the annual average, so that each day has the same length. This differs from true solar time—nowadays used only by sundials—in which the absolute length of a day varies slightly throughout the year.

t to be defined so that $t = 0$ at noon on the day of the vernal equinox of year Y, and we take s to be defined so that $s = 0$ at midnight of New Year's Day of year Y. (The convention for s is well known, and the convention for t was described in §6.2.1.)

There are good philosophical grounds[15] to believe that any two reasonable measures of time should be linearly related to one another. Therefore, using t to denote sidereal time and s to denote solar time, we know a priori that

$$t = A(s - s_0)$$

for some coefficient A and some solar time s_0. In fact, it is clear that s_0 is the solar time at noon on the day of the vernal equinox.

To determine the coefficient A, we return for a moment to our original naïve observations about stars. Suppose we mark the position of some favorite star S (say, by leaving a telescope firmly mounted on the ground) at exactly 8:00 one night, and then return the next night, waiting for S to return to its position of the night before. One ought to arrive a little early, because, one will observe, S comes back to its original position around 7:56, then at 7:52 the next night and so on. The advance per day is about 4 minutes, although one doesn't have to measure it precisely. What is important to this experiment is the observation that if one continues in this manner, S will return to its originally observed schedule (passing the telescope at 8 P.M.) after exactly a year has passed. Therefore we see that, during this period of 365 solar days,[16] there have occurred 366 sidereal days. From this, one easily deduces that $A = 366/365$, and hence that

$$t = \frac{366}{365}(s - s_0)$$

As we said—and as can be seen from the preceding equation—a year's change in solar time causes sidereal time to change by exactly 366 days. On the other hand, a sidereal day is the the rotational period for the apparent motion of the stars about Earth. Therefore, subtracting units of exactly one year from the time coordinate s causes no change in the star positions. Therefore, we do not in fact need to know the value of the year, and we never need consider s values of more than one year. Nevertheless, an exact number of sidereal days does not occur before the elapse of one year, and so—in practical terms—we must know both the both the day of the year and the clock time for s.

---

[15] Any reasonable measure of a time interval will be proportional to the number of times some experiment can be repeated in that interval, subject to possibly small round-off errors. If the experiment (either real or imagined) is taken to be of very short duration, then the round-off errors will be negligible, leading to true linearity in the limit.

[16] For simplicity, we are assuming a year of exactly 365 days. If you want to consider the effect of leap years, you may change the figures to 365.25 and 366.25. This would, however, still be an approximation.

The preceding equation may be applied exactly as it stands, but it can be simplified if we change our previously stated view about how we will measure time. The sidereal time t, when measured in days, can be changed by a whole number without changing the apparent star positions. Suppose that, in units of solar days,

$$s - s_0 = D + \frac{h}{24}$$

where D is an integer, and h is a (real) number of hours (< 24.0). (In other words, the solar time elapsed since equinoctial noon is D days and h hours.) Then

$$
\begin{aligned}
t &= \frac{366}{365}(s - s_0) = \frac{366}{365}\left(D + \frac{h}{24}\right) \\
&= D + \frac{1}{365}D + \frac{366}{365} \cdot \frac{h}{24}
\end{aligned}
$$

We may now reduce t by the integer D, yielding

$$t = \frac{1}{365}D + \frac{366}{365} \cdot \frac{h}{24} \tag{6.3}$$

From Equation (6.3), we obtain a practical scheme for calculating sidereal time t in hours:

- Determine the day D_C of the (calendar) year and the clock hour h_C.

- Subtract 80 from D_C and 12 from h_C, to determine D and h. (If h goes negative, borrow one day from D; if D goes negative, add 365 to D.) In this way, determine D and h, the solar days and hours elapsed since the vernal equinox.

- Calculate t from Equation (6.3).

- Note that we have calculated t in units of sidereal days. As calculated, t will satisfy $0 \le t < 2$. If $t \ge 1$, then one may subtract 1 from t to obtain t in the range $0 \le t < 1$.

- Multiply t by 24 to obtain sidereal time in hours, or multiply by 2π to obtain sidereal time in radians. (For our purposes, the latter is what is required.)

One side comment about Equation (6.3): Suppose we apply the equation to a time period over which the star positions do not change; this means $\Delta t = 0$ for the sidereal time t as described by Equation (6.3). Therefore

$$\Delta h = -\frac{24}{366}\Delta D$$

This means that each day the stars arrive earlier by about the 15th part of an hour; this is the "4 minutes" mentioned near the start of this section.

6.2.4   Two more necessary parameters

If we were making a picture of the entire sky, then we would need no parameters beyond the latitude λ and the sidereal time t. But the sky is notoriously hard to visualize in one piece, and instead we find it convenient to take a small snapshot of the sky. We direct our camera as follows.

First, we identify a north and a south direction at our location P. These follow the direction of a great circle through P and the two poles. Knowing north at P, we can determine all compass directions at P. These are determined by rotations R of the plane π_P that is tangent to Earth at P. For any angle γ, the compass direction γ is the direction to which north rotates when plane π is rotated through angle $-\gamma$.

The angle γ is known as *azimuth*, and the angle β is known as *altitude*. At a fixed point on the globe, every point in the sky is determined by the two coordinates azimuth and altitude. Each star in fact has an azimuth and an altitude, but these both depend on the location on Earth's surface space and on the time. In the main algorithm of §6.2 we will use azimuth γ and altitude β for one purpose only: They represent the direction in which we point our camera. In other words, facing the compass direction γ, we tilt our camera upward from the horizon by an angle β.

6.2.5   The database

The reader should have available a database containing, at the very least, DECL and RA of a number of the brighter stars. Ideally the database will contain the magnitude[17] of each star as well, so that the programmer may construct different icons for different magnitudes (say, large dots for bright stars and smaller dots for the dimmer ones). Without some such convention, the picture soon becomes cluttered, and familiar constellations become unrecognizable; if such information is not available, one will have to be very selective about which stars to include in the database. Further information might include the star's name and constellation name. If one has a color display, then one might be interested in information about the star's electromagnetic spectrum.

A commonly available database, the Yale Bright Star Catalog, has all stars listed in descending order of brightness, and begins as follows:

```
064509-1643-99SDA1a CMASirius
062357-5241-72SSF0a CARCanopus
141540+1911-11SSK2a BOOArcturus
183656+3847004SDA0a LYRVega
051641+4600006SDG8a AURCapella
```

---

[17] Many stars have magnitude that varies somewhat as a function of time. Thus a figure appearing in the table may be an average over known fluctuations of the brightness.

The first line can be analyzed as follows. The most easily readable information comes at the end of the line. The star's name is Sirius, and its constellation[18] is CMA (Canis Major). At the beginning of the line we have the six-character string 064509 followed by the five-character string -1643. The first of these strings connotes a RA of 6 hours, 45 minutes and 9 seconds. The second string connotes a DECL of −16 degrees and 43 minutes, in other words, the DECL is 16 degrees and 43 minutes below the celestial equator. On the other hand, the DECL of Arcturus, designated by the string +1911, is 19 degrees and 11 minutes north of the celestial equator. Thus the + and − signs immediately separate the northern and southern stars. For instance, our second star, Canopus, is sufficiently far south (52 degrees) that it cannot be seen in most of the continental United States.

In database parlance, by the way, one says that the first six characters form a *field,* as do the next five, and so on. The third field in this database, given by three characters, gives the star's magnitude. The main point to remember about magnitudes is that dimmer stars have larger magnitudes. Beginning with Vega, the three-character magnitude field is analyzed by putting a decimal point after the first character. Thus the magnitude of Vega is 0.04, and that of Capella is 0.06. The three first stars are special cases that have been written in special ways to preserve the three-character field width. Arcturus is really -0.11, and Canopus is really -0.72. The entry for Sirius can be read as -0.99, but Sirius is actually brighter than this.

The fourth and fifth fields are typified by the strings SD and A1a in the entry for Sirius. They have to do with various astronomical characteristics and need not concern us in a geometrical analysis of the situation. (In the following program, we read the fourth and fifth fields together into one array called type, in case someone should want to use them. If these features interest you, you can design different icons to represent them in your picture. The fifth field is the star's spectral type, from which one may infer a color to use on a color display.)

Our previous method of inputting data will not work here, since the formatted data input command scanf requires input fields to be separated by spaces. The method that works here is to read the fields, character by character, into special-purpose arrays (here called name, ra, decl, mag and type). Then values can be extracted from these arrays using sscanf (which reads arrays in a manner analogous to the manner in which scanf reads ordinary input.) We include the following program in case it might give the reader some ideas; nevertheless there are many ways to accomplish this task, which vary widely from language to language. We have not included the details of get_user_data(), since we have seen something similar before. Unlike our previous programs, this one illustrates the use of global variables (i.e., the variables ra_rads, etc., that are declared before main()). These variables can be accessed anywhere in the program, including

[18]One will have to consult an astronomical work for the other constellation names.

inside any subroutine. Notice also that comments may be inserted between /*
and */.

```
#define DATAFILE "/faculty/yourprof/stars.data"

/*Field widths in our database: */
#define RA_WIDTH      6
#define DECL_WIDTH    5
#define MAG_WIDTH     3
#define TYPE_WIDTH    6
#define CONSTELLATION_WIDTH  3

/* Data that will be taken from the database for each star: */

double ra_rads, decl_rads, magnitude;
char name[55];
char type[TYPE_WIDTH+1], constellation[CONSTELLATION_WIDTH+1];

main()
{
char dataline[100];

get_user_data();
fp_in = fopen(DATAFILE);

N=0;
while (1)
{
   for (i=0;i<100;i++) dataline[i]=0;
   Q = fscanf(fp_in,"%[^\n]\n",dataline);
                      if (Q <= 0) {error_1(); break;}
   Q = load(dataline); if (Q <= 0) {error_2(); break;}
   display();
   N++;
}
fclose(fp_in);
label_picture();
}    /* END of MAIN */

int load(dataline)
{
if (strlen(dataline)<RA_WIDTH+DECL_WIDTH+MAG_WIDTH) return (-2);
for (i=0;i<=50;i++)          name[i]=0;
for (i=0;i<=RA_WIDTH;i++)     ra[i]=0;
for (i=0;i<=DECL_WIDTH;i++) decl[i]=0;
for (i=0;i<=MAG_WIDTH;i++)    mag[i]=0;
for (i=0;i<=TYPE_WIDTH;i++) type[i]=0;
for (i=0;i<=CONSTELLATION_WIDTH;i++)  constellation[i]=0;
```

```
for (i=0;i< RA_WIDTH;i++)    (ra[i]=dataline[i]);
for (i=0;i<DECL_WIDTH;i++) (decl[i]=dataline[i+RA_WIDTH]);
for (i=0;i< MAG_WIDTH;i++)  (mag[i]=dataline[i+RA_WIDTH+DECL_WIDTH]);
for (i=0;i<TYPE_WIDTH;i++) (type[i]=dataline[i+RA_WIDTH+DECL_WIDTH
                                                    +MAG_WIDTH]);
for (i=0;i< CONSTELLATION_WIDTH;i++)  (constellation[i]=
            dataline[i+RA_WIDTH+DECL_WIDTH+MAG_WIDTH+TYPE_WIDTH]);
N = RA_WIDTH + DECL_WIDTH + MAG_WIDTH + TYPE_WIDTH
                                    + CONSTELLATION_WIDTH;
for(i=0;i<55;i++)           name[i]=dataline[i+N];
Q = sscanf(ra+0,"%2lf",&ra_hours);    if (Q<=0) return (-2);
Q = sscanf(ra+2,"%2lf",&ra_minutes);  if (Q<=0) return (-2);
Q = sscanf(ra+4,"%2lf",&ra_seconds);  if (Q<=0) return (-2);
switch(decl[0])
{
   case '+': decl_sign =  1.0; break;
   case '-': decl_sign = -1.0; break;
   default : return (-3);
}
Q = sscanf(decl+1,"%2lf",&decl_degrees);  if (Q<=0) return (-2);
Q = sscanf(decl+3,"%2lf",&decl_minutes);  if (Q<=0) return (-2);
/*calculate ra in radians: */
{
   u = ra_hours + (ra_minutes/60) + (ra_seconds/(60*60));
   ra_rads = (u/24)*2*PI;        /* 24hours = 2*PI radians */
}
/*calculate decl in radians: */
{
   u = decl_degrees + (decl_minutes/60);
   decl_rads = decl_sign*(u/360)*2*PI;
                                /* 360 degrees = 2*PI radians */
}
/*calculate magnitude: */
switch(mag[0])
{
   case '-':
   {
      Q = sscanf(mag+1,"%2lf",&magnitude); if (Q<=0) return (-2);
      magnitude = - magnitude/10;
      break;
   }
   default:
   {
      Q = sscanf(mag,"%3lf",&magnitude); if (Q<=0) return (-2);
      magnitude = magnitude/100;
   }
}
return (1);
```

```
}  /* END of LOAD() */

int display()
{
printf("\nThe name of the star is %s,",name);
printf("\n                 in the constellation %s",constellation);
printf("\n        Its ra in radians is %4.5f",ra_rads);
printf("\n        Its decl in radians is %4.5f",decl_rads);
printf("\n        Its magnitude is %4.5f",magnitude);
printf("\n        Its type is %s\n",type);
}
```

6.2.6   Rotating the globe and stars

We begin at sidereal time t at a location P on Earth's surface of latitude λ. We mount a camera at P, pointed toward compass direction γ, and elevated to angle β above the horizon.

Much as in §6.1.5, we will subject the stars and camera to four rotations. The first two rotations will bring P to the North Pole, and the next two rotations will change the orientation of the camera to point toward the North Pole in a standard orientation. In this rotated configuration, projection from the stars to the film will have a very simple form (see §6.2.10).

Since the sky's appearance depends only on t and λ, we may assume that our longitude is t. (If it is not, then we could simply relocate the prime meridian so as to make it true, without repositioning the camera or affecting any star positions.) Thus RA now corresponds with longitude, and t is the RA of stars overhead at P. Now, to rotate P to the North Pole, we may repeat the definitions of the two rotations $\mathbf{D}_{\text{long}}$ and $\mathbf{C}_{\text{lat}}$ of §6.1.5, with t for long and λ for lat. Thus we may define

$$\mathbf{D}_t = \begin{bmatrix} \cos(-(t+\pi/2)) & -\sin(-(t+\pi/2)) & 0 & 0 \\ \sin(-(t+\pi/2)) & \cos(-(t+\pi/2)) & 0 & 0 \\ 0 & 0 & 1 & 0 \\ 0 & 0 & 0 & 1 \end{bmatrix}$$

and

$$\mathbf{C}_\lambda = \begin{bmatrix} 1 & 0 & 0 & 0 \\ 0 & \cos(-(\pi/2-\lambda)) & -\sin(-(\pi/2-\lambda)) & 0 \\ 0 & \sin(-(\pi/2-\lambda)) & \cos(-(\pi/2-\lambda)) & 0 \\ 0 & 0 & 0 & 1 \end{bmatrix}$$

As in §6.1.5, it is clear that $\mathbf{C}_\lambda \circ \mathbf{D}_t(P)$ is the North Pole.

We next apply a translation to bring the North Pole down to the origin. Since the stars are essentially ideal points and ideal points are fixed by translations, we do not need a formula for this translation. (We will not bother to apply it to any star coordinates.)

Now our camera is mounted on the North Pole, which happens to be at the origin. There are not really any compass angles at the North Pole, but nevertheless, one may check that the camera's orientation, when viewed in the x, y-plane, is toward a point at angle γ to the right of the positive y-axis. Therefore, a rotation through angle γ about the z-axis will orient the camera so that it is pointing above the positive y-axis. This rotation is effected by the matrix

$$
\mathbf{B}_\gamma = \begin{bmatrix} \cos\gamma & -\sin\gamma & 0 & 0 \\ \sin\gamma & \cos\gamma & 0 & 0 \\ 0 & 0 & 1 & 0 \\ 0 & 0 & 0 & 1 \end{bmatrix}
$$

Exercise

1. Prove that, as claimed, $\mathbf{B}_\gamma$ will orient the camera so that it is pointing above the positive y-axis.

Finally, we need a rotation that will get the camera pointed straight upward. This is clearly the rotation about the x-axis that is given by the matrix

$$
\mathbf{A}_\beta = \begin{bmatrix} 1 & 0 & 0 & 0 \\ 0 & \cos(\pi/2 - \beta) & -\sin(\pi/2 - \beta) & 0 \\ 0 & \sin(\pi/2 - \beta) & \cos(\pi/2 - \beta) & 0 \\ 0 & 0 & 0 & 1 \end{bmatrix}
$$

6.2.7 The main matrix for the star-gazing program

It is clear that the matrix

$$\mathbf{A}_\beta \mathbf{B}_\gamma \mathbf{C}_\lambda \mathbf{D}_t$$

effects a rotation that brings the point P to the top of the globe and points the camera straight up at the sky. Since these four motions are collineations, the same stars remain in the camera's field of view that were there before rotating.

6.2.8 Pseudo-ideal points

Although we said that we would represent stars as ideal points, it is actually not practical to do so without a slight modification to the definition of ideal point. In brief, we introduced ideal points in §4.1.3 (and in the corresponding place in Chapter 5) as follows. To each ordinary point $\langle x, y, z \rangle$ we introduced homogeneous coordinates $(x, y, z, 1)$, and then we allowed multiplication by any non-zero scalar, so that $(x, y, z, 1)$ is equivalent to $(\lambda x, \lambda y, \lambda z, \lambda)$. Then ideal points were introduced as the only 4-tuples that cannot occur in this way, namely, 4-tuples of the form $(x, y, z, 0)$ (with x, y and z not all 0). The problem is that the ideal point with these coordinates is approached, as $\lambda \to 0$, both by $(x, y, z, 1/\lambda) = (\lambda x, \lambda y, \lambda z, 1)$ and by $(x, y, z, -1/\lambda) = (-\lambda x, -\lambda y, -\lambda z, 1)$. In other words, one ideal point is approached by rays going in opposite directions. Thus, given an ideal point, we do not know which of these rays represents a light ray from the corresponding star.

Another way to put the dilemma is as follows: $(x, y, z, 0)$ is equivalent to $(-x, -y, -z, 0)$. We definitely want these two 4-tuples to represent different stars, but—according to definitions presently in force—they represent the same (ideal) point in projective 3-space.

The way out of the dilemma is temporarily[19] to define a notion of pseudo-equivalence as follows. Two 4-tuples (x, y, z, w) and (x', y', z', w') are *pseudo-equivalent* iff there exists a *positive* λ such that $\lambda x = x'$, $\lambda y = y'$, $\lambda z = z'$ and $\lambda w = w'$. We may then consider the set of all 4-tuples (x, y, z, w) with $w \geq 0$ and with x, y, z and w not all 0. This set has one equivalence class of coordinates for every ordinary point (represented as $(x, y, z, 1)$), but *two* pseudo-ideal points $(x, y, z, 0)$ and $(-x, -y, -z, 0)$ on each line through the origin.

Let us consider the action of a rigid motion Φ (§5.3.5), or, more generally, any 4×4 matrix with $a_{41} = a_{42} = a_{43} = 0$ and $a_{44} = 1$, on our pseudo-projective space. Clearly, if P has non-negative fourth coordinate, then the same is true of $\Phi(P)$. Also, P is pseudo-equivalent to P' iff $\Phi(P)$ is pseudo-equivalent to $\Phi(P')$. Therefore the rigid motion Φ can be taken as a motion of pseudo-projective space. We therefore see that multiplication by the matrix $\mathbf{A}_\beta \mathbf{B}_\gamma \mathbf{C}_\lambda \mathbf{D}_t$ (described in §6.2.7) acts in a meaningful way in stars taken from our database.

Consider, on the other hand, a map f—such as a projection (§5.3.9)—that maps an ideal point Q to an ordinary point $f(Q)$. In our data structure, the ideal point Q splits into two pseudo-ideal points Q_0 and Q_1. (They lie at opposite ends of a line through the origin.) Clearly $f(Q_0) = f(Q_1)$, and so, as we have commented before, the projection will place both or neither of these two points onto the film plane. Therefore, we need to discriminate between them *before* projecting. This discrimination can easily be made on the basis of the third coordinate. Points visible, after rotation, from our location at the North Pole have positive third coordinate, and invisible points have negative third coordinate.

---

[19]This approach, by the way, is completely unworkable if one tries to do any serious projective geometry. The basic facts of §4.2 and §4.3 fail miserably in such a setting, as do all the later results. One must be very careful with this pseudo-projective geometry.

Exercises_____

1. We have coordinatized each star with an ideal point or even a pseudo-ideal point when it is necessary to discriminate one direction from its opposite direction. Here the exercise is to work out how ideal or pseudo-ideal points might be used to coordinatize rainbows. Although the mist creating the rainbow may be relatively close to the observer, if the source of light is at an ideal point (as we may take the sun to be), then the illusion is created of an infinitely distant rainbow. (The reader will have to consult an appropriate book on physics or meteorology for more information.) To give the problem a little more shape, one could coordinatize that part of the rainbow that has a fixed color. This has a circular appearance in the sky, and is in fact the intersection of a cone with the plane at infinity. Where should one point one's camera to make sure that the image is a perfect circle?

2. Let *point* mean either an ordinary point or a pseudo-ideal point. Extend each ordinary line to include the two pseudo-ideal points at its extremities, and extend the notion of *line* to include the set of all pseudo-ideal points. Prove that in this setting the basic facts of projective geometry do not hold. In other words, it is false that for any two points P and Q there exists a unique line containing P and Q (Theorem 4.1 of §4.2), and it is false that any two lines have a unique point in common (Theorem 4.2 of §4.2).

6.2.9   Discriminating the visible stars

Given one record of our database, there are two things we have to determine before actually printing an icon to represent the corresponding star. The first is whether the corresponding pseudo-ideal point S represents a star above the horizon; the second is whether S and the focal point lie on the same side of the film plane. Notice that these are separate questions. For instance, if β is small, then the camera's view-field will contain stars that are below Earth's horizon; we do not wish to show these in our picture. On the other hand, also when β is small, there will exist stars above the horizon (low and to the photographer's back) that will project to points on the film; these also must be excluded.

Fortunately, these two questions become very simple at certain well-chosen moments in the calculation. After the first two rotations ($\mathbf{D}_t$ and $\mathbf{C}_\lambda$), i.e., when our location P on Earth's surface has been rotated to the North Pole, the first question reduces to whether $x_3 \geq 0$. After the total rotation $\mathbf{A}_\beta \mathbf{B}_\gamma \mathbf{C}_\lambda \mathbf{D}_t$ is complete, the second question reduces to whether $x_3 \geq 0$.

6.2.10   Projecting the stars

We will use the same kind of projection that we used in §6.1.7. We will be projecting onto the x, y-plane from a *focal point* at distance F above the origin on the positive z-axis. According to §5.3.9, the matrix

$$\mathbf{P}_F = \begin{bmatrix} F & 0 & 0 & 0 \\ 0 & F & 0 & 0 \\ 0 & 0 & F & 0 \\ 0 & 0 & -1 & F \end{bmatrix}$$

defines a collineation that fixes the x, y-plane and moves $\langle 0, 0, F, 1 \rangle$ to the ideal point on the z-axis. Thus projection through the focal point is accomplished by first applying the matrix $\mathbf{P}_F$ and then discarding the third coordinate.

This simple operation therefore defines our camera; it is convenient to take F, which is known as the *focal length*,[20] in the actual units one wants to work with. For example, if F is taken as 8 inches, then the resulting picture will be accurate when viewed from 8 inches. Focal lengths much longer than 8 inches tend to show too few stars. Focal lengths much less than 8 inches will, of course, show more stars, but at the cost of more distortion. In fact, it is usually more comfortable to view a picture from a distance that exceeds its actual focal length; for example, the picture with focal length 8 inches might be viewed from 12 inches. This gives one the illusion of stepping back from the stars to see more of them together (which, of course, one cannot do with the real sky).

6.2.11   Reflecting the picture

If one follows the algorithm that is implicit in what has come so far (and will be made explicit in §6.2.12), then one will be surprised to see that one's pictures come out reversed. That is, the pictures will be mirror images of what one actually sees in looking at constellations in the sky. To explain this, consider that we habitually look at the stars outward: From Earth's viewpoint they look the same as if they were painted on a celestial sphere of some large radius. On the other hand, the globe is traditionally viewed from the outside, looking toward the center. This difference in traditional viewpoints accounts for exactly one reflection or reversal of orientation. Our theories for globe viewing and star viewing have not yet taken into account this difference in the ways the two things are viewed in real life, and hence we experience a discrepancy.

With this understanding, the situation is very easily rectified: We simply add a reflection $\mathbf{R}$ that changes the sign of the x-coordinate. Thus our final matrix should be

$$\mathbf{RP}_F = \begin{bmatrix} -F & 0 & 0 & 0 \\ 0 & F & 0 & 0 \\ 0 & 0 & F & 0 \\ 0 & 0 & -1 & F \end{bmatrix}$$

---

[20]Notice that, until we introduce $\mathbf{P}_F$, all quantities in this treatment are essentially dimensionless.

6.2.12   Summary of a plan for drawing the stars

Let us now examine how we could modify the shell program of §6.1.2 so that it will actually draw the stars as seen according to the parameters[21] t, λ, γ and β that we have already discussed.

ALGORITHM (making a star chart)   The program begins by getting from the user (either interactively or from a file) values of the parameters λ, γ and β, and the date and clock time (for the calculation of sidereal time). Then, before entering the main while loop one calculates once and for all the matrices $\mathbf{A}_\beta$, $\mathbf{B}_\gamma$, $\mathbf{C}_\lambda$ and $\mathbf{D}_t$, and opens the star database for reading.

The main steps in one pass through the while loop are

- Read `magnitude`, RA and DECL from the database, if possible. (Don't forget to convert these values to radians, if appropriate.)

- Calculate homogeneous coordinates of a pseudo-ideal point S as follows:

$$
\begin{aligned}
x &= \cos(\text{DECL})\cos(\text{RA}) \\
y &= \cos(\text{DECL})\sin(\text{RA}) \\
z &= \sin(\text{DECL}) \\
w &= 0
\end{aligned}
$$

- Multiply S on the left by the matrix $\mathbf{C}_\lambda \mathbf{D}_t$.

- If the third coordinate of S is negative, make no further analysis of this record, print nothing, and return to the first instruction to get a new record from the database.

- Multiply S on the left by the matrix $\mathbf{A}_\beta \mathbf{B}_\gamma$.

- If the third coordinate of S is negative, make no further analysis of this record, print nothing, and return to the first instruction to get a new record from the database.

- Multiply S on the left by the matrix $\mathbf{RP}_F$.

- Divide by the fourth coordinate to return S to ordinary coordinates, and then use x and y as the coordinates of a star to be printed (using an icon appropriate to `magnitude` that was read in the first instruction).

---

[21]The author has kept the focal length F as a parameter in the program, but of course this could be entered at runtime if you found that an interesting thing to do.

Exercises_____

1. Modify the algorithm so that instead of making pictures, it simply calculates the azimuth and altitude (see §6.2.4) for a given star at a given time. This information would be useful if one wanted one's picture (generated by the main algorithm) to be centered on a given star.

2. Using the methods of this section, make a picture of how the sun crosses the sky on a given day. A possible picture would be labeled with the latitude and the day of the year and would have a dozen or so sun icons, each labeled with an hour, showing where in the sky the sun appears at each hour. It would be helpful also to show the horizon. What do you predict if the picture is made for the southern hemisphere? Make some pictures to test your prediction. (Hint: Almost trivial modifications of the above program will do the job. The easiest way is probably to make a chart of fictitious stars, each one standing for the sun's position at a different hour of the day.)

6.3   3-dimensional device-independent files

As we said at the beginning of this chapter, a useful way to proceed is to develop a 3-dimensional version of our device-independent language. This way we achieve the usual division of labor and responsibility. One program has the responsibility of producing device-independent code representing a solution to a mathematical problem, and another program has the responsibility of making an actual picture out of that code. The latter program is called an *implementation* of device-independent code. In principle an implementation can be built once and used many times, although in practice one often revises it when new ideas come along. In §6.3 we will concern ourselves with a 3-dimensional language and implementations of it; beginning in §6.3.2 we will explore various ways to illustrate mathematical ideas by creating 3-dimensional files of device-independent commands.

6.3.1   The language itself

It is not hard to think up a basic set of commands. Probably anyone who has read Chapter 2 and has tried the language described there would suggest something like the following for use in three dimensions:

% As before.

w Window. This command is followed by six numbers, which serve to indicate the extreme values of the coordinates that will appear in the display.

r Clip region. This command is followed by six coordinates that are interpreted like the coordinates for w. Indicates a region of the space where l coordinates can be drawn.

m Move pen (without writing) to the point with the three coordinates indicated.

l Engage pen and move in a straight line to the point with the three coordinates indicated.

W As before, a width specification.

T,t,x As before, text.

For example, the six line segments produced by the following device-independent file are the six edges of a regular tetrahedron:

```
w -1 -1 -1 1 1 1
m  1.000  0.000  0.000
l -0.500  0.866  0.000
l -0.500 -0.866  0.000
l  1.000  0.000  0.000
l  0.000  0.000  1.414
l -0.500 -0.866  0.000
m  0.000  0.000  1.414
l -0.500  0.866  0.000
```

6.3.2   Implementations of the language

The implementation of a 3-dimensional device-independent language is never as concrete as implementations were for the 2-dimensional version. For that language, an output device such as a printer takes e.g., an l command and gives one an *actual line* on a piece of paper. In other words the *pen* mentioned in that command has an actual physical meaning. An architect or car designer may occasionally have the pleasure of seeing his or her plans executed in the 3-dimensional world, and one might dream about hiring a skywriter or sculptor. Nevertheless, there is no likelihood of obtaining real 3-dimensional models of our files of device-independent commands, except in unusual circumstances, and hence the pen mentioned in the 3-dimensional command is more a figure of speech. Although we can always leave open the possibility of genuine 3-dimensional interpretations (see e.g., §6.6), we usually content ourselves with the indirect approach of looking at 2-dimensional pictures of our 3-dimensional figures. Such pictures are readily made by applying the mathematical theory of projections that was described in §5.3.9 and has already been applied in §6.1 and §6.2.

In other words, we generally have the following understanding of how we will interpret commands in our 3-dimensional device-independent language. Essentially non-mathematical commands, such as %, T, t, x, and W, will simply be copied into the output file (for later processing[22] by whatever 2-dimensional device is used). The main graphic output commands will be understood as follows:

m Causes the output of another m command, which has two coordinates that are determined by projection.

l Causes the output of another l command, which has two coordinates that are determined by projection.

Before projecting, we must specify a plane to project onto and a viewpoint from which we project. It works well enough to keep the plane fixed as the x_1, x_2-plane, i.e., the plane defined by the equation $x_3 = 0$, and to allow the viewpoint to vary. One could ask the user interactively for the viewpoint, but it is easier (and more self-documenting) to add the viewpoint as one more instruction in the device-independent language. (In doing this we take the language one step away from the realm of pure 3-dimensional figures.) If we keep the film plane $x_3 = 0$ unchanging, then we may want to rotate the figure instead, and so this seems an appropriate time to introduce rigid motions into the device-independent language. Some commands of this sort that the author has used to extend the 3-dimensional device-independent language are

v Viewpoint. This command is followed by the three coordinates of the viewpoint.

V Viewpoint at infinity (corresponds to parallel projection). Requires three coordinates x_1, x_2 and x_3 to specify the ideal point $\langle x_1, x_2, x_3, 0 \rangle$.

R1 Rotation around some axis parallel to the x_1-axis. This command is followed by one real number to indicate number of degrees.

R2, R3 Similar for the other two axes.

R Arbitrary rotation. To be followed by coordinates designating the axis and one coordinate to designate the angle of rotation.

M Motion (translation). This command is followed by the three coordinates of a vector that is to be added to every point.

{ Begin group. Rigid motions mentioned between matching grouping symbols have effect only in that group.

} End group.

\ Escape. Does nothing but erase the \ and output the remainder of the line. This is useful if you wish to use an absolute 2-dimensional window command.

---

[22]Note in particular that the width command W will then refer only to the width of lines used to depict the object on paper or screen. A true 3-dimensional width or thickness of curves, which would transform properly under projections—looking thicker in the foreground—would be more difficult to set up. For a good example of the effectiveness of varying thickness, see the line drawings of K. H. Naumann and H. Bödeker that illustrate *Geometry and the Imagination*, by D. Hilbert and S. Cohn-Vossen, Chelsea Publishing Company, New York, 1952 and 1983.

It is unlikely that the reader will want to use all of these commands in a first implementation; one should incorporate them as they seem to be needed. By far the most useful commands are those for rotations. One problem with 3-dimensional computer drawings is that their appearance is a little unpredictable. Sometimes even a slight rotation can change an unreadable picture into a readable one.

We are more reluctant than ever to declare an exact semantics for this extended language, since there are a number of possibilities, with some tradeoffs and conflicting advantages. For instance, do rigid motions act only on the described object (the l and m commands), or do they act on the viewpoint as well? The former convention makes sense if one is modeling a fixed camera with an object rotating in its field of view, the latter if one is experimenting with different configurations of the camera. In any case, where does one put the centers of the rotations? Possibly at the center of the coordinate system, but it probably makes more sense to use the center of the window (i.e., the midpoint of the segment joining the two corners specified in a w command). The reader may have to make many of these decisions for herself or himself; in some circumstances it may be wise to set a standard for a whole class that is working together.

So, our objective is to build a translator (i.e., a program) that takes input from a file of 3-dimensional device-independent commands, and whose output is a file of 2-dimensional device-independent commands. This task should pose few additional problems[23] to the reader who has done some work on device-independent translation in Chapter 2 and the main project of either §6.1 or §6.2.

The interpretation of a 3-dimensional window command requires certain design decisions. A 3-dimensional window command like

```
w -1 -1 -1 1 1 1
```

defines a rectangular solid (in this case, a cube two units on a side). The projected image of this rectangular solid is a polygon in the plane; as illustrated in Figures 6.12 and 6.13, it may be a hexagon, or it may have fewer than six sides. What we need to do is to output a *2-dimensional* window command of an appropriate size to nicely contain this projected image. A simple way to do this is to obtain the x-coordinates of the images of *all eight corners of that solid*, and then to use the largest and smallest of these for x-coordinates of a 2-dimensional window; a similar procedure is used to obtain the y-coordinates. One drawback to this simple scheme is that if one is rotating the figure, then the image of the rectangular solid will change as the rotation is changed. As a result, differently rotated views of an object will appear in windows of different sizes

---

[23]To distinguish R, R1, R2 and R3 will take a slight new twist to the program, but it's nothing you can't handle by now.

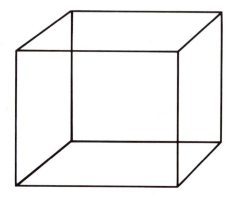

FIGURE 6.12   Hexagonal image of the 3-dimensional window

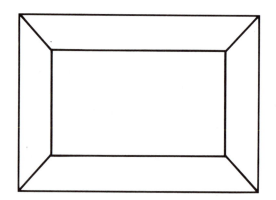

FIGURE 6.13   Another image of the 3-dimensional window

and hence will be hard to compare. In such circumstances, one wants a single 2-dimensional window that is independent of the rotation. There are two ways to handle this. One is to output a 2-dimensional window that is large enough to contain all rotated images of the solid window (we leave the calculations to the reader). Another solution is to write a 2-dimensional window command ad hoc. For this purpose we have suggested having an escape character (possibly \). Thus

```
\w  0 0 4 4
```

in a file of 3-dimensional device-independent commands would cause

```
w  0 0 4 4
```

to appear in the output file.

The main exercise of this section is of course to build a translator for 3-dimensional device-independent code. The student will have ample opportunity to try it on the mathematical material in the remainder of this chapter. Moreover the interested student of mathematics can doubtless find many things to draw in this way. Our exercises, and two special topics that follow, indicate some of the possibilities.

Exercises

1. Make a 3-dimensional drawing consisting of the edges of a cube. If you have implemented translations, then include a number of copies of the cube arranged to form a crystal lattice or jungle gym (see Figure 6.14).

2. Redo the seeworld program in the following manner. (Or do it this way for the first time.) One simple algorithm converts data of the form $\langle B, \theta, \phi \rangle$ into data suitable for reading by the translator for 3-dimensional device-independent code. (The mathematical details for doing this are found in §6.1.4. $B = 0$ corresponds to an m command, and $B = 1$ to an l command.) The resulting device-independent data is then processed like all other data in this section (after adding the desired rotations, etc., to the 3-dimensional device-independent code). The picture obtained in this way will be that of a transparent Earth, with continents on both sides visible at once. The reader may wish to think about how the visible elements could be distinguished in this context.

3. Using some picture file of device-independent data, embark on a study of the various motions of 3-dimensional space that were described in §5.3. This is a big project and could be taken up at various levels of thoroughness. Our suggestions in §3.3.9 for 2-dimensional space remain relevant here.

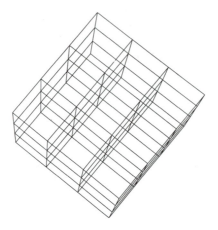

FIGURE 6.14   Cubes arranged to form a lattice (the crystal structure of sodium chloride)

4. If you are interested in architecture, make a database containing the linear elements of a building that interests you or that you would like to design. It is wise to include a lot of comments so that you can identify various members in the database. Make some pictures of your building from near and from far. Interior views are also a possibility.

RULED SURFACES (string figures)

In some special circumstances, it is possible to make drawings of curved surfaces using only straight lines. We illustrate this for the hyperboloid (of one sheet)

$$x^2 + y^2 = z^2 + 1$$

that was already mentioned and depicted in §3.1.7. Consider the line L defined parametrically by

$$\begin{aligned} x &= t \\ y &= 1 \\ z &= t \end{aligned}$$

(see Figure 6.15). It is immediately clear that these values of x, y and z satisfy the defining equation of the hyperboloid; in other words, the line lies entirely on that surface.

For our next step, we observe that the equation of the hyperboloid can be rewritten as

$$r^2 = z^2 + 1$$

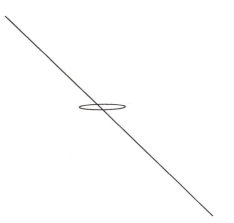

FIGURE 6.15   The unit circle and the line L

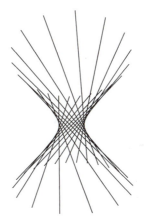

FIGURE 6.16   Hyperboloid (the family of lines L_θ)

where r is a polar coordinate, i.e., the distance from the z-axis. From this equation it is immediately apparent that the hyperboloid is invariant under rotations about the z-axis. In particular, rotating L through an angle θ about the z-axis yields a line L_θ that also lies on the hyperboloid. Doing this for all angles θ ($0 \leq \theta \leq 2\pi$), we obtain a family of lines L_θ in space that all lie on the hyperboloid (see Figure 6.16). Moreover, the following small argument shows that every point P on the hyperboloid lies on one of these lines. Since the z-coordinates of points on L take on all possible values, there exists a point Q on L such that P and Q have the same z-coordinate. Clearly the points on the hyperboloid with fixed z-coordinate form a circle, and hence a rotation about the z-axis through some angle θ will take Q onto P. Thus P lies on L_θ.

This situation is particularly simple to program. It can almost be done by hand. First note that, although we needed a parametrization of L for theoretical considerations, there is no need to use it in our file of device-independent commands. We simply use two convenient endpoints, say those with $z = -4$ and $z = 4$. Thus L can be represented by the commands

```
m  -4  1 -4
1   4  1  4
```

L_θ has endpoints that are easily obtained by rotating the x and y coordinates of the endpoints of L. Thus, for instance, the bottom endpoint of L_θ is $\langle -4\cos\theta + \sin\theta, 4\sin\theta + \cos\theta, -4 \rangle$. Thirty or forty evenly spaced lines L_θ will make a lovely picture of the hyperboloid.

It used to be popular to illustrate the rulings of the hyperboloid of one sheet by strings. Such *string figures* are on display in many mathematics departments, and rough versions can be made from scratch. One takes any sturdy box and removes two ends for visibility, leaving top and bottom and two sides. Then a circular ring of evenly spaced small holes is made both in the top and the bottom of the box. One string is stretched from top to bottom, not from a hole to its matching hole above, but to a hole partway around the circle. Say that these two holes correspond to each other, and then continue, by going clockwise around the two rings of holes, to make holes in the top ring correspond to holes in the bottom ring. Now one string is stretched between each hole in the bottom and the corresponding hole in the top. The resulting array of strings represents a family of lines like the L_θ that all lie on a hyperboloid of one sheet. You might also chance to see such an arrangement of lines in the kitchen, if spaghetti is stored in a tall glass jar or if straws are placed in a glass. The author prefers doing this sort of construction with a computer, but some readers may prefer the older methods.

For an interesting picture of gears based on these string figures, the reader is referred to page 287 of *Geometry and the Imagination*, by D. Hilbert and S. Cohn-Vossen, Chelsea Publishing Company, New York, 1952 and 1983.

Exercises

1. Make a picture that illustrates the family of lines L_θ.

2. Notice that the line M defined by the parametric equations

$$x = -t$$
$$y = 1$$
$$z = -t$$

lies on the hyperboloid. Prove that M is not the same as any L_θ. Define lines M_θ that are related to M as the lines L_θ are to L. Make a picture that shows both the lines L_θ and the lines M_θ.

3. Prove that the hyperboloid of two sheets, defined by

$$x^2 + y^2 = z^2 - 1$$

(see Figure 3.17) does not contain any line.

4. Calculate the exact equation of a string figure. Suppose that the equations of the top and bottom planes are $z = \pm C$ and that the two circular rings have radius R and are centered at $x = y = 0$. Rotating the figure if necessary, one can assume that one of the strings is stretched between $\langle A, B, C \rangle$ and $\langle -A, B, -C \rangle$, with $A^2 + B^2 = R^2$. (Thus our main example had $A = C = 4$ and $B = 1$.) The exercise here is to find the equation of the hyperboloid that contains these lines.

5. Prove that the *hyperbolic paraboloid*, defined by

$$z = y^2 - x^2$$

(see Figure 3.19) is a ruled surface. Illustrate this fact with an appropriate computer drawing. On the other hand, the paraboloid, defined by

$$z = y^2 + x^2$$

(see Figure 3.18) contains no lines.

THE PLATONIC SOLIDS (regular polyhedra)

A *polyhedron* (plural, *polyhedra*) is a figure in space composed of *vertices* (points), *edges* (line segments connecting some, but usually not all, pairs of vertices), and *facets* (convex polygons). It is generally assumed that each edge is the intersection of two of the facets; these two facets determine a *dihedral angle* (angle between two planes). If there exists $N \geq 3$ such that all the facets are congruent regular N-gons, and if all edges have the same dihedral angle, then the polyhedron is said to be *regular*. As the reader is probably aware, there are exactly five kinds of regular polyhedra, which we have depicted in Figure 6.17: the *tetrahedron* (with 4 vertices and 4 facets), the *cube* (with 8 vertices and 6 facets), the *octahedron* (with 6 vertices and 8 facets), the *dodecahedron* (with 20 vertices and 12 facets), and the *icosahedron* (with 12 vertices and 20 facets).

FIGURE 6.17   The platonic solids

We will consider briefly the construction of these five so-called Platonic[24] solids. One can make models of them out of cardboard,[25] but that method hardly suffices for present purposes, since it involves dihedral angles that are determined experimentally. What we need instead is a direct way to build a database containing coordinates of all the vertices. One can easily check that the numbers given in §6.3.1 for the tetrahedron are correct. (It helps to replace 0.866 by $\sqrt{3}/2$ and 1.414 by $\sqrt{2}$.) The cube is easy, and the octahedron is most easily obtained by taking as its vertices the centers of the facets of a cube. (Thus the octahedron is said to be the *dual* of the cube.) We now describe a way to select *two* vertices from each facet of a cube so as to obtain the twelve vertices of an icosahedron.

Imagine that a line segment of length 2α is symmetrically located in each facet of a cube, in the manner indicated in Figure 6.18, which means that a string wound tightly around the middle of the cube—any of its three possible equators—will alternately cross the segment in one facet and then lie along the segment in the next facet. (It is not hard to check that all six segments can be laid down in this manner.) Let us lay down a coordinate system so that the cube's six facets have equations $x = \pm1$, $y = \pm1$, $z = \pm1$. The segment in the front facet has endpoints $P' = \langle -\alpha, -1, 0 \rangle$ and $P = \langle \alpha, -1, 0 \rangle$. The segment in

---

[24]Naming the solids after Plato may be something of a misnomer. Euclid himself attributed them to the Pythagoreans and to Theaetetus (H. Eves, [*op. cit.*], p. 68).
[25]For some photographs of some absolutely astonishing cardboard models, see *Polyhedron Models*, by Father Magnus J. Wenninger, Cambridge University Press, 1970. Presumably all pictures in that book could be made by the methods of this book (together with a geometrical analysis of those figures).

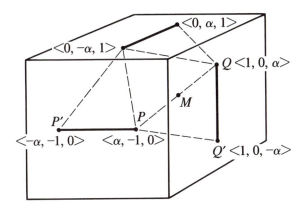

FIGURE 6.18   The construction of an icosahedron

the right facet has endpoints $Q' = \langle 1, 0, -\alpha \rangle$ and $Q = \langle 1, 0, \alpha \rangle$. The condition[26] that yields an icosahedron is that the segment $\overline{P'P}$ should be congruent to the segment $\overline{PQ}$. By equating the square of the distance $d(P', P)$ to the square of $d(P, Q)$, we obtain the quadratic equation

$$(2\alpha)^2 = (1 - \alpha)^2 + 1^2 + \alpha^2$$

that determines α. This equation has one positive solution, namely,

$$\alpha = \left(\sqrt{5} - 1\right)/2 = .61803\ldots$$

which is sometimes known as the *golden ratio*. With this information it is now easy to complete the list of vertices by hand. A list of edges can be found by completing the edge diagram that was begun in Figure 6.18. (The diagram is in fact very symmetric, and so it is not hard to prepare all this data by hand, with a small amount of clever editing.)

Finally, we remark that the dodecahedron can be found as the dual of the icosahedron. In other words, each of the twenty facets of the icosahedron has three vertices A, B, C. The affine combination $(A + B + C)/3$ is an algebraic representation of the midpoint of that facet. Doing this for all twenty of the facets of the icosahedron, we obtain the twenty vertices of a dodecahedron.

---

[26]This is really only a necessary condition for an icosahedron. In other words, all we are doing here is showing that *if* the figure is an icosahedron, *then* α must be the golden ratio (and this knowledge allows us to build the desired database). As to whether we really have an icosahedron, the argument here really shows that all the facets are congruent equilateral triangles. What is missing is a proof that all dihedral angles are equal.

Exercises

1. Make a 3-dimensional drawing consisting of the edges of an octahedron.

2. Complete the procedure for getting the data appropriate to an icosahedron. Use the translator for device-independent commands to get pictures of the icosahedron.

3. Complete the procedure for getting the data appropriate to a dodecahedron. Use the translator for device-independent commands to get pictures of the dodecahedron.

4. Show that eight of the twenty vertices of a dodecahedron are the vertices of a cube.

5. The following idea can be used to make a parallel projection of any convex polyhedron that shows only the visible facets. The idea is to have the edge data organized facet by facet and also have a normal vector to each facet. (This will cause many edges to be printed twice. For most output devices this causes no problem beyond that of keeping the device busy longer.) A facet is to be printed iff its normal vector points toward[27] the film plane $x_3 = 0$. The exercise here is to justify the above assertion and to implement the algorithm, thereby obtaining real pictures of some or all of the Platonic solids.

6. Make a series of pictures that show one or more of the Platonic solids slowly rotating. On the right sort of output device one could make a movie of this.

7. What is the dual of the tetrahedron? of the octahedron? of the dodecahedron?

8. Compute the dihedral angles in Figure 6.18 and thereby establish that the construction really yields an icosahedron. Every edge of the icosahedron is in fact symmetrically related either to $\overline{P'P}$ or to $\overline{PQ}$, and so in fact we really only have to compute these two dihedral angles or simply their cosines. In our figure, the dihedral angle at edge $\overline{PQ}$ is the same as the ordinary angle between the vectors $R - M$ and $Q' - M$, where M is the midpoint of $\overline{PQ}$. The cosine of this angle can be calculated in the usual manner with the dot product. A similar calculation works for the edge $\overline{P'P}$. To make sure the calculations are absolutely correct, they should be carried out symbolically with α. Show also that this common dihedral angle is about 138.19 degrees and that its sine is exactly 2/3.

6.3.3   Graphing a curve in space

Although we surveyed a few handmade examples in §6.3.2, we are mostly interested in the automatic creation of files for our 3-dimensional device-independent

---

[27] J. D. Foley, A. van Dam, S. K. Feiner and J. F. Hughes refer to this as "back-face culling." See §15.2.4 of their *Computer Graphics*, second edition, Addison-Wesley Publishing Company, Reading, Massachusetts, 1990.

language. One easy way to do this is via the parametric representation of curves in space. Our remarks in §3.1.1 are easily extended to space. By a *parametric space curve* we mean a continuous function

$$\gamma : I \longrightarrow \mathbb{R}^3,$$

where I is an interval of $\mathbb{R}$ (with the possibility of $I = \mathbb{R}$). In other words, a parametric space curve has three coordinate functions, $\gamma_1(t)$, $\gamma_2(t)$ and $\gamma_3(t)$.

As in the 2-dimensional case, we use piecewise linear approximations to make pictures of curves in space. Thus a computer program to draw a (parametrized) space curve is exactly like the program we described in §2.1.2 for plane curves, except that we need a third coordinate. The major changes would thus be as follows. A new variable z would be introduced, and the three lines

```
x = t;   y = sin(2*t);
if (i == 0) printf("m %f %f\n",x,y);
else        printf("l %f %f\n",x,y);
```

of our original program would change to

```
x = t;   y = sin(2*t);   z = cos(3*t);
if (i == 0) printf("m %f %f %f\n",x,y,z);
else        printf("l %f %f %f\n",x,y,z);
```

(or with whatever functions are desired for x, y and z). Somewhere along the line one will have to supply a viewpoint and a rotation, if desired. It should be simple enough for the reader to work out the details.

We are now back to the flow chart that was given at the beginning of this chapter; one program gives 3-dimensional device-independent output, and a second one converts it to 2-dimensional output by projection.

THE HELIX

Consider the curve $\gamma(\theta)$, where

$$\begin{aligned}
\gamma_1(\theta) &= \cos(\theta) \\
\gamma_2(\theta) &= \sin(\theta) \\
\gamma_3(\theta) &= K\theta
\end{aligned}$$

This curve, or any image of it under a rigid motion or similarity map, is known mathematically as a *helix*. It is the familiar curve of the threading of nuts and bolts or of a corkscrew. In fact the smooth operation of these everyday objects can be explained in terms of the one-parameter group of rigid motions G_θ that was introduced in §5.3.5. Let us revise our notation slightly so that, instead of standing for the 4×4 matrix in §5.3.5, G_θ stands for the rigid motion of $\mathbb{R}^3$

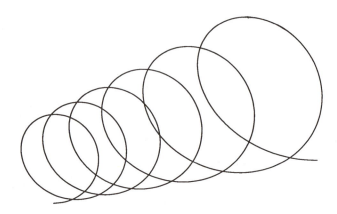

FIGURE 6.19   A helix

defined by that matrix. (It is a product of a rotation about the z-axis with a translation along that axis.) The significant fact is that

$$\gamma(\theta) \;=\; G_\theta\left(\langle 1,0,0\rangle\right)$$

as the reader may easily check. Thus the helix is the *orbit* of the point $\langle 1,0,0\rangle$ under the one-parameter group G_θ, and hence is invariant under these motions. This make perfect sense, since the G_θ were set up as being the motions of a screw. The G_θ continuously move the helix along itself, as we observe when we turn a screw.

SEA SHELLS AGAIN

Consider the orbit of the point $\langle 1,0,K\rangle$ under the one-parameter group H_θ defined in §5.3.6. Clearly this orbit has the parametric representation $\delta(\theta) = H_\theta(\langle 1,0,K\rangle)$. One easily calculates that

$$
\begin{aligned}
\delta_1(\theta) &= e^{a\theta}\cos\theta \\
\delta_2(\theta) &= e^{a\theta}\sin\theta \\
\delta_3(\theta) &= Ke^{a\theta}
\end{aligned}
$$

Since this curve combines some features of the helix and of the logarithmic spiral, we will call it the *logarithmic helix* (depicted in Figure 6.20). Notice that for $a\theta \to -\infty$, we have $\delta(\theta) \to \langle 0,0,0\rangle$ (which is the common fixed point of the similarities H_θ).

Clearly the x,y-projection of a logarithmic helix is a logarithmic spiral. As for that curve, there is a resemblance of the logarithmic helix to the shells of many marine (and some land) creatures, such as the many species of gastropods (snails, whelks, miters, conchs, etc.) (see Figure 6.21). As before, this resemblance to natural growth is partly explained by the self-similarity of the orbits of H_θ. We

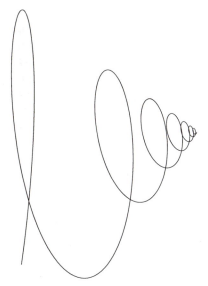

FIGURE 6.20   The logarithmic helix

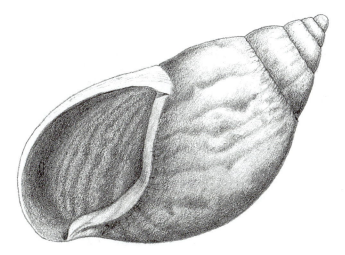

FIGURE 6.21   A sea shell

can think of $\Delta(T) = \{\delta(\theta) : \theta < T\}$ as representing a certain stage of growth. (There is no need to assume that T is proportional to time, although it might be approximately so. In any case we think of T as increasing with time.) At a later value of T, say T', it is clear that $\Delta(T')$ is similar to $\Delta(T)$ (with scaling factor $e^{a(T'-T)}$).

Exercises

1. Use the methods of this section to obtain 3-dimensional data for the helix. Experiment with different values of K. Show some pictures that illustrate the effect of the one-parameter group G_θ, for varying values of the parameter θ. Some interesting figures can be made putting more than one helix into the same picture (for instance, a helix together with one or more of its translates along the z-axis). What sort of motion will take the helix with one value of K onto a helix with a different value of K?

2. Use the methods of this section to obtain 3-dimensional data for the logarithmic helix. Experiment with different values of a and b. Show some pictures that illustrate the effect of the one-parameter group H_θ for varying values of the parameter θ.

3. Every logarithmic helix is contained in a cone. Conversely, any cone C with apex at the origin and symmetric about the z-axis is invariant under H_θ, and hence is a union of orbits. In other words, every such cone C is a union of logarithmic helices (and the apex). (Note that C contains a unique point $\langle 1, 0, K \rangle$; thus is the parameter K determined.) Make a drawing that shows many of these logarithmic helices fitting into one cone C.

4. Consider the drawing of the logarithmic helix in Figure 6.20. One can apparently place a slanted line just below the drawing that is tangent infinitely often to the curve in the drawing. Likewise, another slanted line is a sort of tangent boundary just above the drawing. The exercise here is to prove that this is no illusion: Such multiple tangent lines really do exist.

5. Prepare a file of 3-dimensional device-independent commands for the universal Bézier curve described in the exercises to §5.5, and make various pictures of the curve. (Rotate it and change the viewpoint.) Let your pictures illustrate the universality of the curve: get enough pictures to illustrate the fact that all shapes of cubic Bézier curves can be obtained.

6. The **Lissajous figure** was described in §3.1.4 as the projected image of the space curve

$$
\begin{aligned}
x &= \cos(t + \phi) \\
y &= \sin(t + \phi) \\
z &= \cos(\alpha t)
\end{aligned}
$$

which we are calling a cylindrical Lissajous figure. The exercise here is to make a file of device-independent commands and to prepare the associated drawings for this space curve. Make a number of projected images to try to get a good feel for this object. (Of course, some special projections will be Lissajous figures.) Do it of course for a number of different values of α (both rational and irrational). As we said before, changing the value of ϕ amounts to a rotation of this 3-dimensional figure and so does not need extensive exploration per se.

7. The cylindrical Lissajous figure is a special case of the space curve defined by

$$
\begin{aligned}
x &= \cos(Ls + \phi) \\
y &= \cos(Ms + \psi) \\
z &= \cos(Ns + \lambda)
\end{aligned}
$$

Its projections onto the coordinate planes are three distinct Lissajous figures, but the curve as a whole is something more. Two cases are especially interesting: (a) if L, M and N are small integers with no common factor, like 2, 3 and 5; (b) if each quotient L/M, L/N and M/N is irrational.

8. **Surfaces of revolution.** The reader may have studied surfaces of revolution in the second or third semester of a calculus course. Basically, a parametric curve $\langle \gamma_1(t), \gamma_3(t) \rangle$ in the x_1, x_3-plane (called the *generating curve*) is revolved about the x_3-axis to make a surface that is symmetric about that axis. We can easily make a drawing that shows a number of (discrete) positions of the generating curve as it is revolved about the axis. The curve revolved through angle ϕ is easily given by

$$
\begin{aligned}
\delta_1(t) &= \gamma_1(t) \cos \phi \\
\delta_2(t) &= \gamma_1(t) \sin \phi \\
\delta_3(t) &= \gamma_3(t)
\end{aligned}
$$

Make some pictures that show a surface of revolution from this point of view. (For example, step ϕ through 20 or 30 values from 0 to 2π.) Begin, for example, with the curve $\gamma_1(t) = t$, $\gamma_3(t) = 1/(1 + t^2)$, which peaks nicely at $t = 0$, but by all means experiment with a number of curves.

9. The surface of revolution of the previous exercises is (obviously) invariant under the action of rotations about the x_3-axis. Thus if P is any point on the generating curve, then the orbit of P (i.e., the circle it travels through during the revolution of the generating curve) lies on the surface of revolution. Therefore the surface of revolution can be suggested by drawing a number of these circles. Make some pictures of this type. (The two exercises can be combined: The circles and the copies of the generating curve will all meet at right angles. These curves are analogous to the parallels and meridians seen on a globe.)

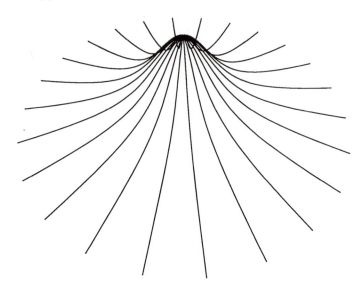

FIGURE 6.22   Surface of revolution: rotational images of the generating curve

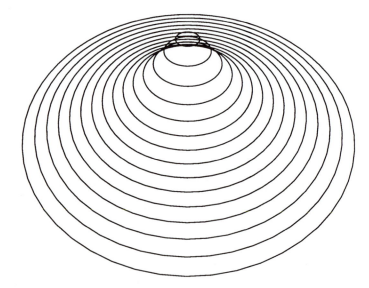

FIGURE 6.23   Surface of revolution: orbits of points on the generating curve

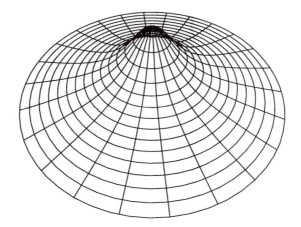

FIGURE 6.24   Surface of revolution: both kinds of curves

10. In a somewhat similar manner, one can make a curve that winds its way through a surface to reveal more of that surface. For instance, as we know, a typical point on a sphere of radius R is given by

$$
\begin{aligned}
x &= R\cos\theta\cos\phi \\
y &= R\cos\theta\sin\phi \\
z &= R\sin\theta
\end{aligned}
$$

for $-\pi/2 \le \theta \le \pi/2$ and $0 \le \phi \le \pi$. By making θ and ϕ depend on t, we get a parametric curve that traverses the surface of the sphere. The easiest way to do this is to take $\phi = Kt$ and $\theta = Lt$; thus,

$$
\begin{aligned}
x &= R\cos Lt\,\cos Kt \\
y &= R\cos Lt\,\sin Kt \\
z &= R\sin Lt
\end{aligned}
$$

The nicest effects come when K is either much larger than L or much smaller than L. The exercise here is to make pictures of these space curves and also of the similar space curves that lie in the *ellipsoid*

$$
\frac{x^2}{R_1^2} + \frac{y^2}{R_2^2} + \frac{z^2}{R_3^2} = 1
$$

(See §3.1.7 for a general discussion of quadric surfaces. In §6.8.1 we will learn how to depict ellipsoids with the method of *ray tracing*.)

11. Find simple equations for a space curve that winds its way through the paraboloid

$$
x^2 + y^2 = z
$$

Depict this situation.

12. Let us say that a *torus* is the surface formed by revolving the circle

$$(x_1 - A)^2 + x_3^2 = a^2$$

about the x_3-axis. (Usually we take $A \geq a$; the radius of the hole is $A - a$.) This surface clearly can be depicted by the means we already mentioned for surfaces of revolution; here is another interesting curve that winds its way around the torus:

$$
\begin{aligned}
x_1 &= (A + a \cos Kt) \cos Lt \\
x_2 &= (A + a \cos Kt) \sin Lt \\
x_3 &= a \sin Kt
\end{aligned}
$$

(This curve is depicted in Figure 6.47 of §6.6.) Make drawings of this curve both for $K \gg L$ and for $L \gg K$. An interesting special curve results when $A = a$ and $K = L$. Draw this curve and answer the following question about it: What is its image when projected to the x_1, x_2-plane?

13. Recall the exploding firework from §3.4.11; we can now make a drawing of how it really looks in space. For fixed θ and T, the equations

$$
\begin{aligned}
\gamma_1(t) &= t \cos \theta \\
\gamma_3(t) &= -\frac{1}{2}t^2 + t \sin \theta
\end{aligned}
$$

$(0 \leq t \leq T)$ give the trajectory of a spark emitted at angle θ in the x_1, x_3-plane. Rotating this curve through an angle ϕ about the x_3-axis will give the trajectory of a spark emitted at angle θ in an arbitrary compass direction. (This therefore involves the formulas for δ_i given just above.) For a realistic effect, one should keep T fixed and print a picture showing a number of values of ϕ and of θ.

THE SEA TURTLE

As was independently suggested by G. A. Edgar, on pages 195–196 of *Measure, Topology and Fractal Geometry* [*op. cit.*], one can describe a curve in space as the path of a creature or object that travels 3-dimensionally, such as a bird, fish, airplane or submarine. In keeping with the turtle metaphor begun by Logo (§2.4), we will ride a *sea turtle*.

To simplify the real motion of turtles in the sea, we postulate a turtle that moves in a straight line through a designated distance in the direction of his main body axis (a vector from tail to head). (Thus, for example, if his head is lower than his tail, the motion will take him downward in the water, and so on.) For curvilinear motion, we need to change this axial direction; for this purpose we allow the turtle to rotate his body about any of three axes. The three axes are taken relative to the turtle himself and pass through the center of his chest;

the first one is the main body axis that we already mentioned. A rotation about the main body axis is called a *roll*. (It does not change the direction of travel.) A second axis can be imagined as going skyward from the turtle's back when he is standing on dry land; a rotation about this axis is known as a *yaw*. A yaw does change the definition of travel; in fact the L and R commands of our land turtle obviously correspond to the special case of a sea turtle who is temporarily stuck on flat ground and whose only turns are yaws.

Finally, there is a third axis perpendicular to the other two—parallel to the line between the turtle's two front feet. A rotation about this axis is called a *pitch*. If a turtle starts in midwater, horizontal and facing east, and if he limits himself to forward motions and pitch commands, then his motion will stay in a vertical plane with east-west orientation. (He may well end up swimming upside down.)

The motions of the sea turtle are easily incorporated into a 3-dimensional Logo language. We will keep D, U and F as before, and add R, Y and P for roll, yaw and pitch (even though these letters may refer to other commands in other contexts).

Exercises

1. The three forms of sea-turtle rotation (R, P and Y) are redundant. Any one of them can be eliminated in favor of the other two. (On the other hand, at least two of them must be used in order to obtain true 3-dimensional motion, as may be inferred from remarks above.)

2. Consider a sea turtle that starts in midwater, oriented horizontally, and facing east, and accepts no directional commands besides P (pitch). As we mentioned, the turtle's path is planar. The exercise here is to prove that the path here is congruent to the path of a land turtle that is commanded in the following way. The forward (F) commands do not change; the pitch (P) commands are changed to L commands with the same angle. (Or, if you like, you can change pitch commands with negative angle to R commands with the corresponding positive angle.)

3. Write an implementation of the 3-dimensional turtle language. It is probably most practical to merely write a filter that translates the six commands U, D, F, R, Y and P to 3-dimensional m and l commands.

4. Show that the following (potentially infinite) file of sea turtle commands yields a piecewise linear approximation of a helix (§6.3.3). (In fact the numbers are immaterial; all that matters is to repeat the same three lines, comprising a forward motion, a roll and a yaw. One could also use a pitch and a yaw, or a pitch and a roll.)

```
D
F 100.0
```

```
R 30
Y 30
F 100.0
R 30
Y 30
F 100.0
R 30
Y 30
...
```

Make pictures of this situation for various values of the parameters.

5. Show that the following (potentially infinite) file of sea turtle commands yields a piecewise linear approximation of a logarithmic helix (§6.3.3). (All that really matters in this file is to have the turns repeat and to have the forward distances decrease with a constant factor.)

```
D
F 100.0
R 30
Y 30
F 90.0
R 30
Y 30
F 81.0
R 30
Y 30
F 72.9
...
```

6. The sea turtle is useful for drawing fractal images in three dimensions, in a manner analogous to that of §2.6. See G. A. Edgar [*loc. cit.*] for one example.

6.4 Graphing a function of two variables

A function $f(x, y)$ of two variables is often represented graphically in a 3-dimensional picture, as the surface defined by $z = f(x, y)$. Computers can be instructed to compute such pictures in much the same way that we produced a picture of Earth. The only difference is that instead of taking data from a database, one generates data to be plotted from the function $f(x, y)$ itself. Although our objective in §6.4.1 is to make a very realistic drawing with hidden parts removed, we begin with the simpler problem of making a drawing that shows all parts of the figure. The student should master this kind of drawing before going on to §6.4.1.

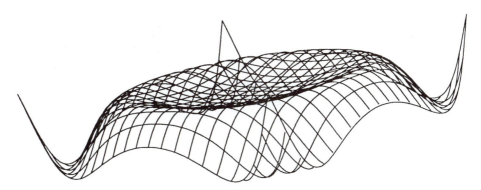

FIGURE 6.25   A wire grid representing $f(x, y) = (x^2 + y^2) \sin(x^2 + y^2)$

Generally speaking, the graph of a function of two variables is a featureless surface. The artistic rendering of such a surface can involve techniques of shading to mimic the visual effect of the play of light on a real surface. Nevertheless, our visual perception of shapes is often made easier by relying on surface features. If a sofa or a cushion is covered with a fabric that has a repetitive geometric pattern, we gain our impression of its shape partly by seeing how the pattern appears to bend. In the same way, we can add features to a mathematical surface to make its shape more apparent. A simple but effective way to do this is to inscribe some (more or less parallel) curves on the surface and then make a drawing of how those curves appear in space.

Thus we make a grid of evenly spaced lines parallel to the two coordinate axes in the x, y-plane, and then lift these lines to the surface $z = f(x, y)$. In other words for each line $L = \{\langle x, b \rangle : x \in \mathbb{R}\}$ or $L = \{\langle a, y \rangle : y \in \mathbb{R}\}$, we make a plot of $\{\langle x, y, z \rangle : \langle x, y \rangle \in L, z = f(x, y)\}$. In other words, we could imagine starting with a grid of somewhat elastic wires in the x, y-plane and then stretching them straight upward to meet the surface. If the surface is not too steep, then this illusion can be quite effective, as the reader will see in Figure 6.25. For obvious reasons, such representations of surfaces are often called *wire grid figures*.

The actual algorithm for making wire grid figures is relatively simple, in fact it amounts to nothing more than combining a number of space curves of the type we have already considered in §6.3. (Each wire is one space curve.)

To be very precise, we need first to pick a rectangular region $A_1 \leq x \leq A_2$, $B_1 \leq y \leq B_2$ in the x, y-plane. Then we need to plot the curves

$$\gamma_b(t) = \langle t, b, f(t, b) \rangle \qquad \text{and} \qquad \delta_a(t) = \langle a, t, f(a, t) \rangle$$

($A_1 \leq t \leq A_2$; $B_1 \leq t \leq B_2$) for selected values of a and b. Thus γ_b is a line parallel to the x-axis (lifted by f), and δ_a is a line parallel to the y-axis (lifted

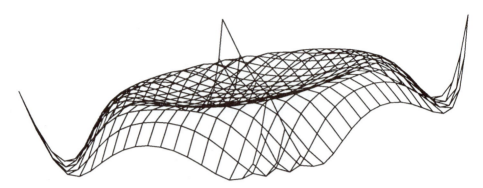

FIGURE 6.26   Piecewise linear wires

by f). It gives good visual results to let a take on twenty or so evenly spaced values between A_1 and A_2 (and similarly for b). As for plotting the curves γ_b and δ_a, there are two interesting alternatives. One may plot them with a STEP value exactly the same as the number of wires in either direction. This means that the function is evaluated on discrete grid points and strung tightly between those grid points (see Figure 6.26). Alternatively, one makes the STEP parameter much larger than the number of wires. In a picture of the latter type, the wires will have the advantage of following perfectly the contour of the surface. Pictures of the former type have several competing advantages: They are easier to shade, it is a little simpler to remove hidden lines from them, and they involve fewer function values and hence are faster to compute.

To make quick work of drawing functions of two variables, the reader should already have mastery over an interpreter for 3-dimensional device independent commands, as described in §6.3, and it is strongly recommended that this interpreter have a facility for rotations. Experience has also shown that very large values of $f(x, y)$ (i.e., steep surfaces) lead very quickly to pictures that are unreadable (even though correct). What is recommended is to begin the first time with $f(x, y) = 0$—which of course should show just the base grid. Then take $f(x, y)$ to be $Kg(x, y)$, where g is the function you're really interested in, and K is a parameter to scale the z-axis. Small values of K will put small ripples in the grid, and then one can quickly estimate a value of K that will make the clearest picture.

Exercise

1. You may wish to make a graph of a function of two variables that has already been computed by someone else (or by yourself on some other occasion, or on

some other computer system). That is to say, one may have available only a (finite) database that contains information about the function. The data might possibly take the form of individual lines like

```
1.2 1.3 7.9056
```

to mean that $f(1.2, 1.3) = 7.9056$. The exercise here is to modify the general plan of attack in this section so as to apply to functions defined in this way. (If this is your main interest, then do functions of two variables in this way[28] from the start.) The main thing one has to be careful with is the arrangement of the data. Even if all the function values are correct, there is no sensible way to plot them if the x and y values don't follow some sort of pattern. If the x and y values do follow a checkerboard pattern but are not in the right sequence, then the program will have to store the data in an array so that the curve-drawing routines can access them in the right order. Nevertheless, one can develop such a plotting routine, and moreover all the features of line removal that we are about to describe will carry over to such a plotting routine.

6.4.1 Removing hidden parts

The above approach portrays the surface as made of nothing but the wires. Thus we essentially see all the wires, including those wires that would normally be hidden if the surface were opaque. As the reader can see from Figure 6.25, parts of the picture may contain a confusing jumble of wires. A more readable and more realistic picture will result if we can find a way to treat the surface as opaque, and thereby not display those surface elements that would normally be hidden to the eye (see Figure 6.27).

Here we will outline one way to depict only those parts of the picture that would be seen with an opaque surface. Such algorithms are called *hidden-line removal algorithms*,[29] for the simple reason that they do not *add* anything to what we have done above. They act by examining the output of (or otherwise interacting with) a drawing program and deciding, for each element of output, whether that element is or is not visible. Then, obviously, only the visible elements are printed.

---

[28] In a sense this approach is preferable according to our philosophy of clear division of tasks. One really could separate the calculation of $f(\,,\,)$ from the plotting of the data. Nevertheless, we avoid this separation, since a full-scale version of it would require a complex extension of our language. Another problem is that this alternate approach encourages the storage of large files and the use of large arrays in programs.

[29] This is a class of algorithms rather than a single algorithm that is determined once and for all. Design of such algorithms is a detailed and technical topic in computer graphics.

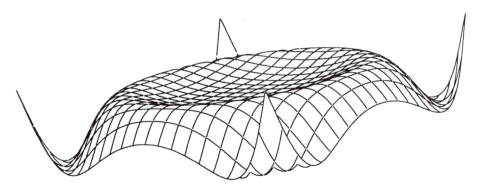

FIGURE 6.27   The same surface with hidden wires deleted

The algorithm we are going to present relies heavily on the fact that the surface is *connected* and *simply connected* (i.e., is made of a single piece with no holes) and that each vertical slice of the picture is connected. It is relatively crude from the standpoint of professional computer graphics, but will show the student how this sort of thing can be done, and moreover it does a reasonable job of depicting functions (see Figure 6.27).

This hidden-line algorithm is particularly simple in that it deals almost entirely with the image being created on the paper. In other words, it can be understood without any reference to how the image is being generated—calculation of $f(x, y)$, rotations, projections, and all that. The algorithm takes as input a sequence of requests to draw line segments (or possibly other graphic elements) on a piece of paper. In other words the algorithm described here fits into our flow charts in the following way:

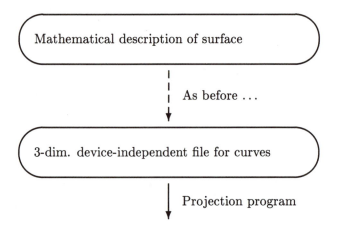

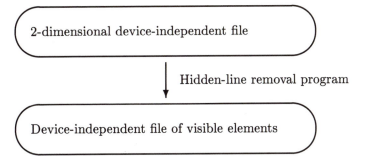

2-dimensional device-independent file

Hidden-line removal program

Device-independent file of visible elements

The only restrictions on the files of 2-dimensional device-independent commands input to the line removal algorithm are two conditions, which we call the *foreground condition* (**FG**) and the *continuity condition* (**CC**):

(**FG**) *If A and B are graphic elements such that B is hidden by A, then A should occur before B in the data stream.*

(**CC**) *At any given time, the picture delivered so far is connected and locally connected and meets each vertical line in a single interval.*

(In other words: foreground comes before background,[30] and at any time we can easily tell what part of the picture is visually blocked, just by knowing a simple *outline* of the picture so far.) Let us first see how we can ensure that our data stream satisfies conditions (**FG**) and (**CC**); then we can concentrate on the algorithm itself.

It is simplest first to discuss the picture made only with wires in the x-direction, i.e., the curves γ_b described above, and later to extend the method to the curves δ_a that run in the y-direction.

One needs to make sure that the y-coordinate of the viewpoint is smaller than the y-coordinate of all points in the picture, and then to enumerate the picture according to increasing y-coordinate. Quite specifically, suppose that the wires parallel to the x-axis have y-values[31] $y_0 < y_1 < \cdots$. We would organize our device-independent data so that the curve γ_{y_0} comes first, then γ_{y_1}, and so on. (The reader might naturally have done it this way anyway, but before now there was no reason to insist on this way of ordering the data.) In other words, the way we have described it here, the y-coordinate is receding in space, and we deliver closer y-coordinates before we deliver farther ones. It should be clear that if we follow this plan then conditions (**FG**) and (**CC**) will be satisfied.

---

[30] For a *background first* algorithm, see §6.4.4.

[31] Needless to say, these conditions have to be satisfied after any rotations take place. Thus one has to select the sequence $y_0, y_1 \ldots$ after one knows what rotation is in use. A small change of rotation won't move front to back, but a large one will. Just be a little careful and scrutinize your work. If the perspective makes it look as if background objects are covering foreground objects, then you probably have rotated the figure so far that you need to reverse the sequence $y_0, y_1 \ldots$.

To describe the algorithm for filtering out unseen elements from the data stream, we begin by laying down a coordinate system on the paper, with u measured horizontally and v vertically. (Due to rotations, it cannot be said that the u and v are related in any particular way to the coordinates x, y and z in use for the 3-dimensional surface.)

The central feature of the algorithm is that it maintains, and updates as necessary, two 'functions' $v_{high}(u)$ and $v_{low}(u)$ that indicate the largest and smallest v values that have so far been placed on the paper for a given u value. According to condition (**CC**), the region that is visually blocked is exactly the region outlined by the 'curves' $v_{high}(u)$ and $v_{low}(u)$. So, when a new graphic element arrives on the data stream, we first check to see if it is visible; and if so, we print it. We then also update the 'functions' $v_{high}(u)$ and $v_{low}(u)$ so that the space occupied by this new graphic element is now marked as visually blocked.

We have put the word *function* in quotes, because obviously a computer cannot store a function in the mathematical sense. What we have to do instead is to store an an array of values $v_{high}(u_n)$ for some closely spaced values $u_0, u_1, \ldots$. All of the calculations that follow turn out to be simpler if we modify the coordinate system so that these u-values are all integers, and accordingly we will do this. In particular it is simplest to assume that the incoming data stream (input file of 2-dimensional device-independent commands) satisfies the following *discreteness condition*:

(**DC**) *Every point mentioned in an* m *or an* l *command has horizontal (u) coordinate an integer. Moreover the u-coordinates of the governing window command are* 0 *and* N *for some large integer* N*.*

The incoming data can easily be put into this form[32] with an appropriate linear function and by rounding off as necessary; presumably the reader can take care of this. The first importance of the condition is that it allows us to treat the functions $v_{high}(u)$ and $v_{low}(u)$ as simple arrays[33] $v_{high}[N+1]$ and $v_{low}[N+1]$. We usually wish to delay the updating of these arrays until an auspicious point in the program, and so we introduce two more arrays $w_{high}[N+1]$ and $w_{low}[N+1]$, which will hold our changes to $v_{high}[N+1]$ and $v_{low}[N+1]$ until we wish to use them.

The choice of N requires some attention. If N is greater than the number of dots to the anticipated output device, measured horizontally, then the associated

---

[32]The reader should realize that of course the incoming data will have somewhat random u-coordinates; only in very exceptional situations will each i with $0 \leq i \leq N$ occur as a u-coordinate in the input. Therefore we will generally need to calculate values $v_{high}[i]$ and $v_{low}[i]$ by linear interpolation.

[33]In general $a[M]$ denotes an array whose values are $a[0], a[1], \ldots, a[M-1]$. In Pascal this would be denoted $a[1..M]$.

round-off error[34] is no worse than the kind of round off already being done by that device. On the other hand, the number of calculations is proportional to N, and obviously the machine has to store two (really four) arrays of size N. Therefore making N too large could lengthen performance time or push the computer past its limits. But notice that increasing N is safe from the point of view that it does not significantly affect the size of the output file. The author has found on his system, using a printer with 300 dots per inch, that $N = 3000$ gives very satisfactory results.

We generally think of the input data as organized wire by wire, which is to say one smooth curve γ_b at a time. It is generally advisable to update the arrays after each γ_b has been processed. This is harmless because the curve γ_b has been taken to go more or less sideways in the picture, and hence one part of γ_b does not visually block another part of γ_b in the picture. It is helpful, because if updated too soon, then the following undesirable situation could occur. If two successive commands were, say,

```
1  897 34.2
1  913 34.7
```

then the program might get confused into marking $\langle 897, 34.2 \rangle$ as covered before going on to draw the segment from there to $\langle 913, 34.7 \rangle$. Thus the hidden-line removal algorithm needs to be told when each γ_b has finished. Therefore a new command letter should be added to the device-independent language to indicate the end of a curve γ_b; for reasons that will be apparent later, the author has been using V for this purpose. In this way, we deviate very slightly from our announced plan of having a hidden-line removal algorithm that can be applied to the original device-independent language.

The algorithm can now be stated, in terms of steps that we will later define.

ALGORITHM (removal of hidden lines from a file of device-independent commands) The input is assumed to be in the 2-dimensional device-independent language, augmented with an end-of-curve designator V, and satisfying the discreteness condition (**DC**). It is further assumed that the input arises from a figure that satisfies the geometric conditions (**FG**) and (**CC**). We then proceed as follows:

- A w command is examined to make sure that its limiting u-coordinates are 0 and N for some large N. Then $N + 1$ is used as the size[35] of the arrays $v_{\text{high}}[N + 1]$ and $v_{\text{low}}[N + 1]$.

---

[34] The only danger of this sort of round off is if one later tried to make a blowup of the data by using a very small window. In this case one would see the jaggedness induced by the round-off errors.

[35] In practice, in some languages, it may be easier to decide N once and for all.

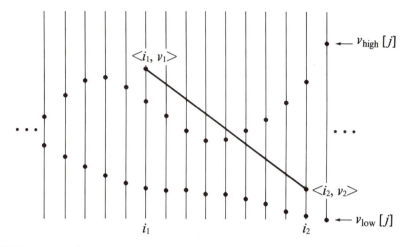

FIGURE 6.28   A partially hidden segment

- The arrays $v_{\mathrm{high}}[N+1]$ and $v_{\mathrm{low}}[N+1]$ are initialized with $v_{\mathrm{low}}[i]$ equal to the high coordinate given by the w command and with $v_{\mathrm{high}}[i]$ equal to the low coordinate given by the w command. (This means that nothing is visually blocked at the start.)

- Upon receiving a V command, we update the arrays $v_{\mathrm{high}}[N+1]$ and $v_{\mathrm{low}}[N+1]$.

- An m command is used in the obvious way to establish the first endpoint of a segment to be clipped to the visible region.

- An l command establishes the second endpoint of a segment to be clipped to the visible region (its first endpoint having been determined by a prior l or m command). The clipped (or visible) part of this segment is output as one or several segments, and the arrays $w_{\mathrm{high}}[N+1]$ and $w_{\mathrm{low}}[N+1]$ are modified as necessary to indicate what parts of the picture are blocked by this new curve.

- All commands except m, l and V are passed unchanged to the output file.

To update the arrays $v_{\mathrm{high}}[N+1]$ and $v_{\mathrm{low}}[N+1]$ means simply to replace their values by the values temporarily being stored in $w_{\mathrm{high}}[N+1]$ and $w_{\mathrm{low}}[N+1]$. The only other parts of the algorithm that need explanation are those of clipping a segment to the visible portion and modifying the arrays $w_{\mathrm{high}}[N+1]$ and $w_{\mathrm{low}}[N+1]$.

So let us suppose that the arrays $v_{\mathrm{high}}[N+1]$ and $v_{\mathrm{low}}[N+1]$ are given and that incoming data asks us to make a line segment from $\langle i_1, v_1 \rangle$ to $\langle i_2, v_2 \rangle$, where i_1 and i_2 are integers between 0 and N. In Figure 6.28 we have depicted this situation with $i_1 < i_2$ and with about half of the segment (the part near $\langle i_1, v_1 \rangle$)

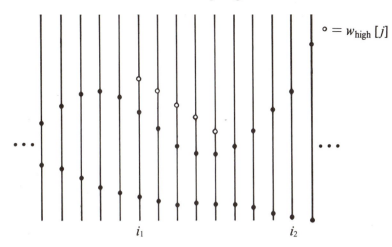

FIGURE 6.29   The revision made to $w_{\text{high}}[j]$

visible. With this picture, it is not hard to describe how the arrays $w_{\text{high}}[N+1]$
and $w_{\text{low}}[N+1]$ have to be modified. Wherever the new segment goes above
the array $v_{\text{high}}[N+1]$, the array $w_{\text{high}}[N+1]$ must be made as large as the
v-value on that segment. The corresponding new values $w_{\text{high}}[j]$ are indicated
by circles in Figure 6.29. And, correspondingly, wherever the new segment goes
below the array $v_{\text{low}}[N+1]$, the array $w_{\text{low}}[N+1]$ must be made as small as
the v-value on that segment. (This situation does not happen to arise in our
figures.) The actual calculation of the new values $w_{\text{high}}[j]$ and $w_{\text{low}}[j]$ involves
an obvious linear interpolation (Equation (6.4.1)). In terms of programming, it
will have to be expressed as a loop (in the variable j), since there is no telling
how many j values there may be between i_1 and i_2.

The determination of the visible segments to print is also very simple from
Figure 6.28. Any one of the tiny segments (determined by the given segment
and the vertical grid lines) is printable if both its endpoints are above the array
$v_{\text{high}}[N+1]$, which indicates the upper limit of the part that is known to be
visually blocked. We see this happening for some of the tiny segments near the
left in our drawing. Similarly, a tiny segment is printable if both its endpoints
are below the array $v_{\text{low}}[N+1]$, which indicates the lower limit of the part that
is known to be visually blocked. (This does not happen to occur in our picture.)
No other tiny segments will be considered printable. Certainly now an integer
variable j can be stepped from i_1 to i_2 while one determines and outputs all of
the tiny segments that are printable.

Following the path described so far would constitute a solution to our
problem, but not a very good solution. The first of two problems would be
the ensuing major increase in the size of the output file. The second would
be that the endpoints are so close together that rounding by a device could
cause a jagged appearance to the output. Therefore we modify the procedure by

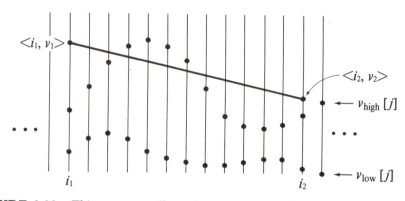

FIGURE 6.30   This segment will require two segments of output

demanding that *contiguous segments should be collected* prior to output. In most cases, this simply means delaying the issuing of an 1 command until a natural boundary is reached: until either $j = i_2$ or the interpolating linear function falls below $w_{high}[j]$ or above $w_{low}[j]$. Our picture is not completely typical; for example some of the tiny segments on the left might be hidden, in which case one would have to issue an m command when they emerge. Another situation is illustrated in Figure 6.30: One will have to terminate a segment with an 1 command and then begin a second segment with an m command when the given segment becomes visible again. In some cases we will even end up outputting the exact same segment that was input. (Clearly this happens until the first V command, and it tends to happen less often as one nears the end of the input file.) The opposite extreme is that one segment in the input file is completely blocked and causes no output whatever.

There are a number of little details to work out, but we feel the student should be able to make it work from here. Please note that there is absolutely nothing to compute (in the sense of evaluating a formula) besides the easy linear interpolation equation

$$v[j] \;=\; v_1 + (j - i_1)\frac{v_2 - v_1}{i_2 - i_1}$$

(Perhaps this equation could be kept in a subroutine.) All other computations are in the nature of logical decisions (branching by if clauses, and so on) based on comparisons (testing for $v[j] \leq v_{high}[j]$ and so on). It may be worthwhile to have a subroutine that can sort two values. One obvious pitfall is that if $i_1 = i_2$, then the denominator in the linear interpolation formula is 0. Therefore, the case $i_1 = i_2$ (which can occur) will have to be treated separately.

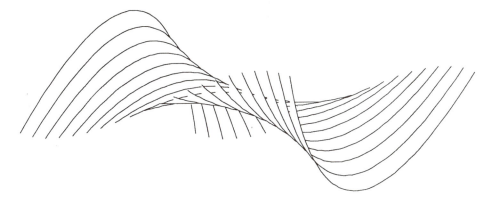

FIGURE 6.31 Each curve shows a little too much

This ends our discussion of the basic algorithm for removing hidden parts from a drawing of a function of two variables. Before going on, the reader should try to make it work at this level of complexity.

6.4.2 Refinements to our hidden-line algorithm

One thing will be noted immediately about our algorithm: It only uses the wires themselves to determine the region of the paper that is visually blocked. Particularly near the edges, and also near a curve in the surface, there may be regions of the paper that are visually blocked, and yet no wire has caused a record to be made of this in the arrays $v_{\text{high}}[N + 1]$ and $v_{\text{low}}[N + 1]$. If one has widely spaced wires (curves γ_b), then the resulting picture may be inaccurate to the extent that the eye will notice that something is wrong (see Figure 6.31).

One easy remedy is to compute more wires than one prints, say five or ten calculated for every one printed. In this way one increases processing time by a factor of five or ten, but in any case one does not increase the size of the output file. (One may even decrease its size by a little bit.) The algorithm in §6.4.1 can easily be modified to skip the printing step when a certain Boolean variable is zero. The author has found it simplest to divide the job as follows. In the program that computes our original 3-dimensional device-independent data, we make the decision about which curves γ_b will be visible and which will be invisible (i.e., included only for the eventual purpose of updating the arrays $v_{\text{high}}[N + 1]$ and $v_{\text{low}}[N + 1]$). We then split the V command (introduced above to indicate a new curve γ_b) into two commands, V and I, for *visible* and *invisible*. The line-removing program can then easily adjust its behavior (to keep silent or to output m and l commands) based on whether it has read I or V. Figure 6.32 shows the same surface as Figure 6.31, but with only one wire out of ten visible.

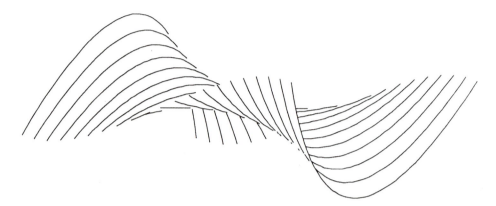
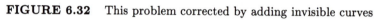

FIGURE 6.32   This problem corrected by adding invisible curves

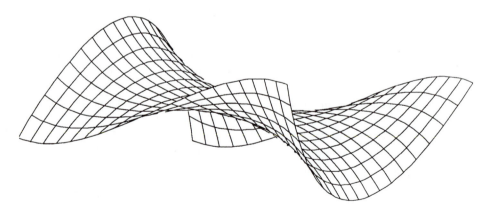

FIGURE 6.33   Curves γ_b and curves δ_a

Another obvious modification is that one might want to include the wires δ_a that run (roughly) in the perpendicular direction. The simplest way to do this is to imagine that one is starting a new picture (to fall on the same page). To manage this most simply, the author recommends the introduction of a new command R, to stand for *resetting* the arrays $v_{\text{high}}[N + 1]$ and $v_{\text{low}}[N + 1]$). In Figure 6.33 we superimpose the curves δ_a on the curves γ_b of Figure 6.32.

6.4.3 A polygonal method

We now discuss a slightly different approach that eliminates the necessity of calculating invisible wires. We are not referring to any change in the algorithm for removing hidden lines—which will remain unchanged—but to a way of organizing the 3-dimensional picture, and a particular way of organizing a file of 3-dimensional device-independent commands that describes it. This method is a little rough in its depiction of the surface as a sort of folded piece of paper with the linear approximation sometimes evident. It has the advantage, however, that hidden lines are perfectly removed from this approximate surface, without too much computing time.

Our point of view is now that the grid lines in the x, y-plane determine a checkerboard arrangement of squares. Our plan is to compute $f(x, y)$ *only at the vertices* of this checkerboard (corners of the small squares) and then deliver the line segments (lifted to the surface) four at a time,[36] *square by square.* Typically one sends the front row of squares, followed by a V command, then the second row, then a V, and so on. This completely explains what steps one has to take to make such pictures; the remainder of our discussion has to do with why it works so well.

Obviously this will make a wire mesh picture if one omits the algorithm for line removal. Let us see what happens when we run the resulting data through our line-removal program. Notice that each square of the checkerboard is lifted (by $f(x, y)$) to a quadrangular figure in space. (The actual lift by $f(x, y)$ is curvilinear, but we have simplified things by only calculating the corners.) This quadrangle will project to a quadrangular figure on the plane; and when updating is applied to all four sides of this quadrangle, we do not have any gaps. Therefore the line removal is perfect, and one will not see any gaps at all.

There is a slight problem in that the four corners of one small square will lift to a quadrangle in space that is generally not planar. (Recall that three points determine a plane—unless they are collinear—and so the fourth point would be on this plane only by accident.) Nevertheless the eye tries to see the individual quadrangles as planar, which gives pictures of this type a small amount of ambiguity and unreadability. (This is particularly evident in Figure

---

[36] Actually, the reader can see that it would be redundant to deliver all four edges from every rectangle. One can easily work out a scheme that sends out only those that have not been sent out before.

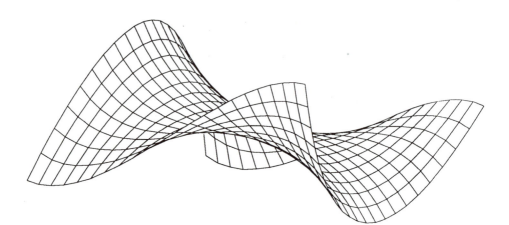

FIGURE 6.34 $z = x^3 - xy^2$ represented by small quadrangles

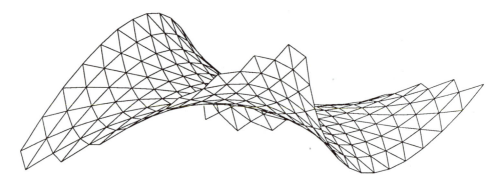

FIGURE 6.35   The same surface represented by small triangles

6.27.) One interesting remedy is to switch to a grid made of triangles, as depicted in Figure 6.35. The lifted vertices remain organized into a pattern of triangles, and of course each of these triangles (like all triangles) is planar. Therefore, in this case, the approximating surfaces is a union of triangles and hence easily visualized. For this reason the resulting pictures are less ambiguous and more readable. (They still are approximations, however.) The interested reader can work out the details.

6.4.4   The use of polygonal surface elements

In §6.4.1 (and subsequent sections) we presented one general plan for giving an opaque appearance to the wire grid representation of a function of two variables. Although that method requires a sophisticated algorithm for hidden-line removal, the output of the algorithm is a very simple device-independent file consisting essentially of m and l commands. Therefore, the most rudimentary output device can print pictures produced under that method. In this section we will describe a different opaque rendition of surfaces,[37] which requires no mathematical analysis of hidden elements, but relies instead on a greater sophistication of the graphic output device (described later in this section in Condition (**OP**)).

Mathematically, our method is that of §6.4.3. We calculate $\widehat{P} = \langle x, y, f(x, y) \rangle$ for each vertex $P = \langle x, y \rangle$ of a rectangular (checkerboard) grid in (some rectangular region of) the x, y-plane, saying that P is *lifted* to $\widehat{P}$. A small rectangle S of the checkerboard, with vertices $P_1, \ldots P_4$, is then lifted to a (curvilinear) quadrangle $\widehat{S}$ in space, with vertices $\widehat{P}_1, \ldots, \widehat{P}_4$. The quadrangle $\widehat{S}$ is then projected to a plane quadrangle S', by the usual methods. (The lifting and projecting are illustrated in Figures 6.36 and 6.37.) In §6.4.3 we printed the four edges of the projected quadrangle S'. (More precisely, we included requests for these edges in a device-independent file that was to be filtered through the hidden-line removal algorithm of §6.4.1.) Here we will instead print the projected quadrangle S' as a solid region of the plane of the output device.

By this we mean that we will ask our graphic output device to paint the interior of the plane quadrangle S' (in addition to possibly drawing its outline in the usual way with m and l commands). The quadrangle S' could be painted in any color (or shade of gray, for a monochrome device). In §6.4.5 we will return to the question of how best to determine the color; for the moment we will simply paint each quadrangle with the background color of the device. In other words, suppose for definiteness that our device puts black ink onto white paper; then we will outline each quadrangle in black (as in §6.4.3) and paint its interior white.

In doing this for a single quadrangle S' by itself, it is of course pointless to request that the interior of S' should be painted white, since that interior

---

[37]The algorithm described here falls into the general category of *list priority algorithms*. See §15.5 of J. D. Foley, A. van Dam, S. K. Feiner and J. F. Hughes, [*op. cit.*].

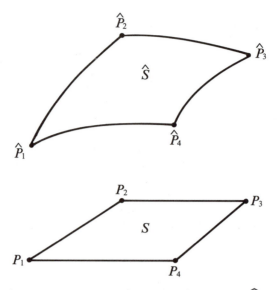

FIGURE 6.36   A rectangle S of the grid is lifted to a patch $\widehat{S}$ of surface

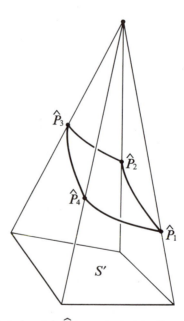

FIGURE 6.37   The rotated patch $\widehat{S}$ is projected to the plane of the paper

was white to begin with. The painting of interiors only becomes meaningful as we continue lifting all the retangles $S_1, S_2, \ldots$ in our basic grid to quadrilaterals $\widehat{S_1}, \widehat{S_2}, \ldots$ in space and then projecting these to painted quadrilaterals $S_1', S_2', \ldots$ on our piece of paper. If $\widehat{S_m}$ and $\widehat{S_n}$ are approximately collinear with the viewpoint, then they will be projected to the same spot on the paper, i.e., S_m' and S_n' will overlap. This overlapping corresponds to the fact that one of $\widehat{S_m}$ and $\widehat{S_n}$ is at least partly hidden by the other, say $\widehat{S_m}$ obscures $\widehat{S_n}$. In order to have a picture that correctly represents the surface as opaque, we need to include only those parts of S_n' that are not obscured by S_m'. The easy way to accomplish this is to print S_n' first and then later, when we come to S_m', to *erase* those parts of S_n' that are hidden by S_m'. Erasing is of course equivalent in this context to painting with an opaque white paint. Therefore our scheme will adequately represent the surface as opaque if the following two conditions are met:

(**BG**) *If A and B are graphic elements such that B is hidden by A, then B should occur before A in the data stream.*

(**OP**) *The output device can be commanded to paint a polygonal region so as to completely cover all graphic objects that previously existed in that region.*

The first condition, called the *background condition*, of course refers to the order in which one must loop through the small rectangles of the grid. It is the exact opposite of the foreground condition (**FG**) that appears in §6.4.1, and is very easy to implement in practice. The second condition, called the *opaque painting condition*, is obviously device dependent and has nothing to do with our mathematical analysis per se. Happily (**OP**) is true for many available graphic devices; in particular, it is a standard feature of the PostScript language. In §2.5 we discussed ways to add painting commands to our device-independent language. For the rest of this section, we will assume that the reader has worked out some way to implement (**OP**).

As we have described it so far, i.e., with all quadrangle interiors painted white, the method described here is about as powerful as the quadrangle method described in §6.4.3; it will in fact make pictures that are indistinguishable from Figure 6.34. It may be studied instead of the material in §§6.4.1 and 6.4.3, especially by classes or individuals who have less time to spend on this material, or may not have time for our hidden-line removal algorithm. For the benefit of such readers, we collect the various steps into a single algorithm. Our statement of the algorithm contains no explicit equations, since they are to be found in §6.1, which should be read and understood before working on this material.

ALGORITHM (hidden-element removal with an (OP)-device)   As elsewhere in §6.4, this algorithm yields device-independent code for a perspective drawing of a function $f(x, y)$, with x and y ranging over a rectangle $A \le x \le A_2$, $B_1 \le y \le B_2$ in the x, y-plane.

- Decide on a viewpoint, angles of rotation and so on. Set up the required (4×4) rotation and projection matrices, as we did, for example, in §6.1.

- Divide the intervals $[A_1, A_2]$ and $[B_1, B_2]$ into STEP subintervals, thereby subdividing the rectangle $[A_1, A_2] \times [B_1, B_2]$ into STEP^2 small rectangles.

- Construct a (double) loop to consider each of the small rectangles in turn. The rectangles can be dealt with in any order, so long as the background condition (**BG**) is satisfied. (The correct order depends of course on what rotations are in force.) For each small rectangle S in this loop, do the following:
  - Denote the four vertices of S by $P_1, \ldots, P_4$ and then do the following for $i = 1, 2, 3, 4$:
    * Calculate the planar coordinates x and y of P_i.
    * Calculate the point $\widehat{P}_i = \langle x, y, f(x, y) \rangle$ that actually lies on the surface we are drawing.
    * Append 1 as a fourth coordinate so that $\widehat{P}_i$ will have homogeneous coordinates.
    * Apply the appropriate 4×4 matrices, divide by the fourth coordinate to restore non-homogeneous coordinates, and project to the plane by discarding the third coordinate (see §6.1).
    * Call the resulting planar point P'_i.
  - Determine a gray level g (i.e., a shade) for the patch of surface in the region determined by $\widehat{P}_1, \ldots, \widehat{P}_4$.
  - Output device-independent commands to paint the interior of the quadrangle S', whose vertices are $P'_1 \ldots P'_4$, with gray level g. (See §2.5 for details of how this might be accomplished.)
  - Output device-independent commands to draw the four line segments that form the outline of S'.

The discussion so far has been concerned only with the single shade of white, i.e., $g = 1$ in the algorithm, but in §6.4.5 we will concern ourselves with more interesting ways to shade the figure. When $g = 1$, the last step of the algorithm is essential (unless we want a completely white picture), but for other values of g it may be preferable to leave out the last step and have no outlines (see §6.4.5).

This concludes our statement of the algorithm and how to use it. The remainder of §6.4.4 is concerned with some fine points about the algorithm and some problems one might experience with it. On the first reading of this material one is encouraged to skip to the beginning of §6.4.5.

Our analysis of this algorithm implicitly assumed (a) that the small curvilinear quadrangle $\widehat{S}$ is entirely visible (until such time as we discover that some or all of it is visually blocked by some closer parts of the picture) and (b) that the interior of the quadrangle S' is an adequate representation of the visual appearance of $\widehat{S}$. Although these assumptions usually hold, it can be seen that

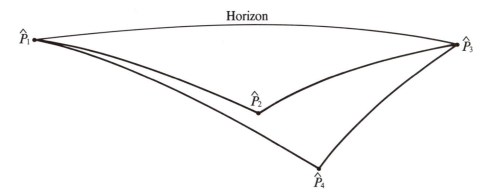

FIGURE 6.38   A curvilinear quadrangle straddling the horizon

they can fail for quadrangles $\widehat{S}$ that lie on a visual horizon of the picture. Figure 6.38 shows a somewhat exaggerated view of what can happen when $\widehat{S}$ just straddles the horizon. Clearly assumption (a) is false, since in fact $\widehat{S}$ is visually *self-blocking*, a possibility not hitherto taken into account. Moreover, S' is not even convex, and its interior fails miserably in providing a visual representation of $\widehat{S}$. The effect is very pronounced along the far ridge of Figure 6.27 (although that figure was made with the methods of §6.4.1).

A better pictorial representation of $\widehat{S}$ might be given instead by a triangle consisting of *two* sides of S' and the diagonal of S' that happens to run more or less along the horizon, but we do not really advocate adding such a complication to the program. Another approach might be to use a triangular grid all along, as in Figure 6.35. Then convexity ceases to be an issue, since all triangles are convex, but nevertheless the problem of self-obscuration remains. The triangular grid approach is interesting in its own right, but again we do not suggest it as a remedy to the basic problem that occurs along horizons. Instead, we suggest that the inaccuracies arising from a self-obscuring patch $\widehat{S}$ and its associated non-convex quadrangle S' can be kept harmless, by limiting the size of S.

As one learns in a class on advanced calculus, if the surface $z = f(x,y)$ is differentiable, then the vector $N(x,y) = \langle \partial f/\partial x, \partial f/\partial y, -1 \rangle$ is perpendicular to the surface. The visual horizon occurs where the line of sight meets the surface tangentially; in other words, where $N(x,y) \cdot M(x,y) = 0$, with $M(x,y)$ a vector from the center of projection (the eye) to $\langle x, y, f(x,y) \rangle$. If the above partial derivatives are continuous, then the scalar function $N(x,y) \cdot M(x,y)$ is also continuous. Suppose now that S is a small rectangle (e.g., one of those described in the algorithm), which happens to contain a point $\langle x_0, y_0 \rangle$ that lifts to a point $\langle x_0, y_0, f(x_0, y_0) \rangle$ on the horizon. In other words, $N(x_0, y_0) \cdot M(x_0, y_0) = 0$.

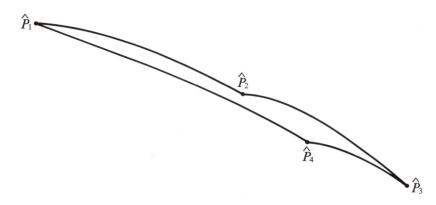

FIGURE 6.39   A sufficiently small quadrangle straddling the horizon

By continuity, *sufficiently small* rectangles S containing $\langle x_0, y_0 \rangle$ will have the property that the dot product $N(x, y) \cdot M(x, y)$ *is almost equal to* 0 for x and y ranging over S. This means that the curvilinear patch $\widehat{S}$ is viewed almost perpendicularly to the vector $N(x, y)$; in other words we are viewing $\widehat{S}$ almost edge-on. Therefore its image S' is a very elongated quadrangle, with any possible failure of convexity occurring as a very broad dent running the length of S' (see Figure 6.39). Thus, in this situation, while the quadrangle S' may still contain an inaccuracy, its general position—very close to the visible horizon—is quite correct, and it remains so close to convex that no error is noticed. This situation can be seen in Figure 6.34.

Thus, in order to keep inaccuracies within reasonable bounds, at least for surfaces with continuous partial derivatives, we only need to limit the size of small rectangles S in the partition of the rectangle $[A_1, A_2] \times [B_1, B_2]$. The exact size limits on S are probably best determined experimentally. Obviously, they have very much to do with how fast the normal vector $N(x, y)$ is changing. More technically, what we are trying to do is to keep the patches $\widehat{S}$ small relative to the *radii of curvature*[38] of the surface.

Our algorithm has the minor imperfection that it computes almost every function value $f(x, y)$ four times. Except on the edges of the big rectangle, every subdivision point $P = \langle x, y \rangle$ occurs as a vertex of each of four small rectangles $S_1 \ldots S_4$ that meet at P, and the algorithm would have us calculate $f(x, y)$ once while we are considering S_1, once while considering S_2, and so on. On

---

[38] Just as a smooth plane curve has a radius of curvature at each of its points—a fact to which we alluded in §3.4.7—at a point P on a smooth surface S in space, there are two radii of curvature. They are the radii of the largest and smallest circles that fit closely to S at P in planes perpendicular to S.

the author's system, a picture like Figure 6.34 (where $f(x, y)$ is merely a cubic polynomial) is computed so fast that there is no point to rework the algorithm. On the other hand, if one should wish to apply this algorithm to a function $f(x, y)$ that can only be computed very slowly, then one might begin to think of an algorithm that computes f as seldom as possible. One approach would be to compute and store, once and for all, a table of values of $f(x, y)$ for x and y ranging over an appropriate grid. We trust the details can be left to the reader.

Exercises_____

1. The method described here can be thought of as lifting the Archimedean tiling $\langle 4, 4, 4, 4 \rangle$ (i.e., an ordinary checkerboard pattern) to the surface $z = f(x, y)$. Likewise, the triangular method mentioned briefly at the end of §6.4.3—and depicted in Figure 6.35—can be thought of as lifting the Archimedean tiling $\langle 3, 3, 3, 3, 3, 3 \rangle$. Try lifting some of the other Archimedean tilings (see §2.4) to the surface $z = f(x, y)$. It may be possible to amalgamate one's implementations of the algorithm stated here and the Logo-like methods that were used in §2.4. An important thing to watch is that the turtle's path through the tiling (using Logo) is consistent with Condition (**BG**).

2. Do Exercise 1 of §6.4 in the present context.

6.4.5   The shading of polygonal surface elements

The method outlined in §6.4.4 utilized opaque painting (**OP**) only with white paint, for the express purpose of erasing hidden parts of the picture. Nevertheless, any colors whatever will serve the basic purpose of erasing unwanted parts of the picture, and here we will discuss some other schemes for coloring (or shading) the surface $z = f(x, y)$ that might be interesting either for representational accuracy or for some other reason. In other words, we are now addressing that step of the algorithm that says, "Determine a gray level g."

We first remark that almost any coloring scheme, defined according to some definite rule, has a good chance of lending some visual interest to the picture. For example, a simple checkerboard pattern will show the surface as covered by checkered cloth, and so on. Maps are sometimes colored with oceans blue, lowlands green, uplands brown, mountain tops white, and so on. It might add visual interest and readability to a surface $z = f(x, y)$ to use such colors (blue, green, etc.) according to the value of z. For example, the drawing on the cover of this book was prepared in this way. It shows the surface of Figure 6.34 ($z = x^3 - xy^2$), with each quadrangle colored according to its z-coordinate: greater z-coordinates are redder, and smaller z-coordinates are bluer. (The individual quadrangles in the cover drawing are much smaller than the individual quadrangles in Figure 6.34.)

On the other hand, for some purposes it might be most valuable to color the surface according to some dependent variable other than z; for example it might be that temperature varies over the surface and that one wants to display this temperature. (Cool spots could be blue and hot spots orange, for example.) The possibilities are limitless, and their incorporation into the algorithm is straightforward. If one has a clear formula for what value of g is wanted, then one need only have the algorithm compute that formula at the appropriate time. We trust that the details can be left to the reader.

One obvious way to color the elements of a surface is to emulate the appearance that the surface would have if it were a physical object illuminated in some natural way. In this way one hopes to make a realistic and readable picture of the surface, without introducing artificial features such as grid lines or climate zones (snowy peaks), etc. Any serious attempt at this emulation of nature leads inevitably to areas of physics that include the crystalline and molecular structure of surfaces and the nature of light itself. Thus the analysis of illumination goes beyond any considerations of pure geometry. Nevertheless, we can make a simple geometric study of one case, that of *diffuse reflection from a point source of light.*

More precisely, we will assume that our surface is illuminated by white light emanating from a single point source with coordinates $\langle L_1, L_2, L_3 \rangle$, and that the surface itself consists of an opaque gray material that reflects light only diffusely. This latter condition means that light falling on the surface is reflected uniformly in all directions. Some dull materials, like newspaper, unglazed pottery and plaster, tend to reflect light in this manner, although pure diffuse reflection occurs rarely if ever in nature. In any case, it turns out that a mathematical model based on these assumptions makes a good first approximation to the actual appearance of a dull surface.

To analyze the appearance of a surface emitting light by diffuse reflection, we begin with a simple thought experiment. Imagine a piece of paper lying on plane P, surrounded by a hemisphere of radius R that is centered in the paper and is cut off by plane P. (Assume that the paper is small relative to R, so that it effectively all lies at the center.) If the paper is emitting light by diffuse reflection, that light energy will fall uniformly over the hemisphere, which has area A proportional to R^2. Now the total light energy spread out over area A is independent of R, since it is simply the total light energy given off by the paper. Thus the light energy falling per unit of area on the hemisphere is proportional to R^{-2}. If we imagine locating our eye somewhere on this hemisphere, we find that the total amount of radiant energy reaching our eye will be proportional to R^{-2}. At the same time, however, the area of our retina occupied by the paper's image will also be proportional to R^{-2} (why?), and hence the radiant energy received per unit area of retina will be independent of R. Since diffuse reflection is, by definition, also independent of the direction of viewing, we can now see the fundamental fact about diffuse reflection: *The apparent intensity of a*

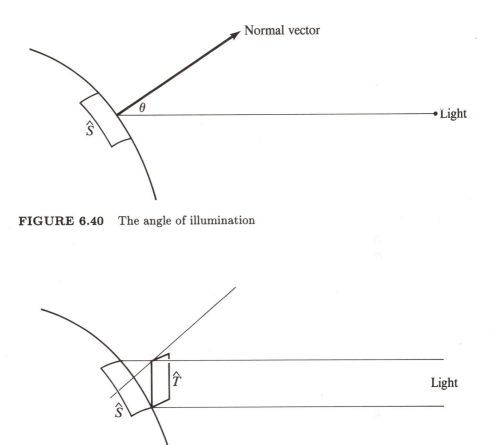

FIGURE 6.40   The angle of illumination

FIGURE 6.41   The density of light falling on $\widehat{S}$ is proportional to $\cos\theta$

surface element emitting light by diffuse reflection is independent of the position from which it is viewed.

So in order to determine a gray level g for a patch $\widehat{S}$ of surface under diffuse reflection, we need to know only how $\widehat{S}$ is being illuminated. The two geometric factors of importance are the angle θ of illumination (see Figure 6.40) and the distance R between $\widehat{S}$ and the point source of light. By an analysis like that of the previous paragraph, we see that *the intensity of light reaching $\widehat{S}$ is proportional to R^{-2}*. As we will see from Figure 6.41, this intensity is also proportional to $\cos\theta$. The figure shows parallel beams of light and edge-on views of two surface elements, the surface element $\widehat{S}$ that we are interested in, and an imaginary element $\widehat{T}$ that is in optimal position to catch the light rays. Moreover, $\widehat{T}$ is taken just large enough to shade $\widehat{S}$ so that both receive the same total radiant energy from the light source. The areas of $\widehat{S}$ and $\widehat{T}$ are obviously related by a factor of $\cos\theta$, and hence clearly the illumination on $\widehat{S}$ is proportional to $\cos\theta$.

Finally, we identify two non-geometric factors, namely, I, the total intensity of the light source, and K, a measure of the reflectivity, which in practice would depend on the actual materials used for the surface. These two factors together can be regarded as representing the constant of proportionality between the brightness and $R^{-2}\cos\theta$.

Thus we now have the equation

$$g = \frac{IK(\widehat{S})\cos\theta}{R^2} \tag{6.4}$$

for the gray level of a surface element $\widehat{S}$ that is exhibiting diffuse reflection. Here R is the distance from $\widehat{S}$ to the light source, and θ is its angle of illumination. We have expressed K as a function of the surface element $\widehat{S}$, since it may vary from point to point on the surface. The simplest model—with K constant—is quite adequate to make interesting pictures of surfaces. In that case, we have

$$g = \frac{IK\cos\theta}{R^2} \tag{6.5}$$

We have been discussing the case of a single color (gray) and a single light source. For color, one has to replace the scalar g by a vector $\langle R, G, B \rangle$, whose components are the intensities of red, green and blue light that are seen at the surface element $\widehat{S}$. Each of these colors is determined by an equation like (6.4), but with different coefficients for each color. For example if an object looks yellow, then it will have a high reflectivity for red and green light, but not for blue. Likewise if the light source is blue, then I will be high for the blue component and lower for the other two components. The values of R, G and B have to be computed separately and sent to a color device in whatever manner is appropriate. (For example, PostScript has the command `setrgbcolor` that directly sets R, G and B, and a related command `sethsbcolr` that sets these values indirectly.) For multiple light sources (whether monochrome or in colors) the final value of g (or of $\langle R, G, B \rangle$) is an obvious linear combination of the corresponding values for the individual light sources. An interested reader who has worked out the basic case of a single monochrome light can easily work out the details of all these enhancements

For the basic application of the methods of this section, the reader need only splice Equation (6.5) into the appropriate place in the algorithm of §6.4.4. Notice however that typically an output device is constrained to receiving gray scale values over a specific range. (PostScript, for example, has 0.0 for black, 1.0 for white, and no values are accepted outside the range $0.0 \le g \le 1.0$.) Therefore a linear change in variable may be required for g; we trust that details of this

FIGURE 6.42   Shading according to diffuse illumination

may be left to the reader. (The G command of §2.5 may be useful here.) Figure 6.42 shows an image that has been prepared in this way.

The calculation of Equation (6.5). We conclude §6.4.5 with a discussion of the values R and θ that are needed for the calculation of Equation (6.5). Using the notation of §6.4.4, the four corners of $\widehat{S}$ are $\widehat{P_1}, \ldots, \widehat{P_4}$. The affine combination

$$C = \frac{1}{4}\left(\widehat{P_1} + \cdots + \widehat{P_4}\right)$$

is an adequate approximation to the center of $\widehat{S}$. Denoting the three coordinates of C as $\langle C_1, C_2, C_3 \rangle$ and taking the light to be at $\langle L_1, L_2, L_3 \rangle$ as above, we obviously have

$$R = \sqrt{(L_1 - C_1)^2 + (L_2 - C_2)^2 + (L_3 - C_3)^2}$$

To calculate $\cos\theta$ we first need a vector that is perpendicular to the surface element $\widehat{S}$. We give an approximate method that is computationally easier than, say, calculating the partial derivatives. Figure 6.43 shows the four vertices $\widehat{P_1} \ldots \widehat{P_4}$ of $\widehat{S}$ and also the midpoints of the four segments they determine in order. In other words, H_1 is midway between $\widehat{P_1}$ and $\widehat{P_2}$, H_2 is midway between $\widehat{P_2}$ and $\widehat{P_3}$, and so on. Considering the triangle $\widehat{P_1P_2P_4}$, we see that the line H_1H_4 joins midpoints of two sides and hence is parallel to the third side $\widehat{P_2P_4}$. Likewise H_2H_3 is parallel to $\widehat{P_2P_4}$, and hence H_1H_4 and H_2H_3 are parallel to each other. Similar reasoning applies to the other two sides of the quadrangle $H_1H_2H_3H_4$, and hence this quadrangle is a parallelogram. In particular, $H_1H_2H_3H_4$ is *planar* and hence has a well-defined normal vector N. In fact, N can be defined as a vector that is perpendicular both to H_1H_2 and to H_2H_3. This is equivalent to

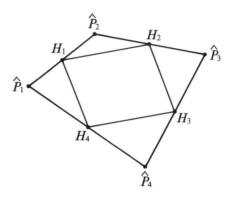

FIGURE 6.43   The search for a vector perpendicular to a non-planar quadrangle

saying that *the desired vector N is perpendicular to the two diagonals $\widehat{P_2P_4}$ and $\widehat{P_1P_3}$ of $\widehat{S}$.*

A good method for finding a vector in 3-dimensional space that is perpendicular to two other vectors r and s is to form the well-known cross product $r \times s$. While leaving it to the reader to look elsewhere for the theory of the cross product, we will make the particular calculations for the case at hand. Define

$$r = \langle r_1, r_2, r_3 \rangle = P_2 - P_3$$
$$s = \langle s_1, s_2, s_3 \rangle = P_1 - P_4$$

Then, for a normal vector, we may take

$$N = r \times s = \langle r_2 s_3 - r_3 s_2,\ r_3 s_1 - r_1 s_3,\ r_1 s_2 - r_2 s_1 \rangle$$

Finally, to get θ (or its cosine) from N, we simply calculate the angle between N and the vector

$$M = \langle L_1 - C_1,\ L_2 - C_2,\ L_3 - C_3 \rangle$$

which goes to the light from the center C of $\widehat{S}$. Thus $\cos\theta$ is given by

$$\cos\theta = \frac{N \cdot M}{|N|\,|M|}$$

Exercises

1. We have not really modeled our surface as completely opaque, but rather as translucent. The surface of Figure 6.42 appears to have light penetrating it; in other words, both sides appear to be radiating comparable amounts of

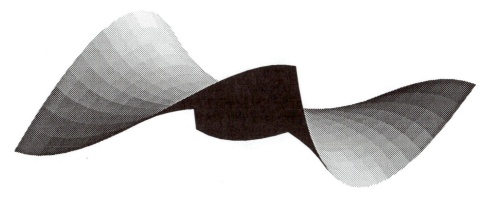

FIGURE 6.44   A surface illuminated on one side only

light. A slight modification of our calculation of g (Equation (6.4)) will cause the surface to look completely opaque. Namely, the value of g given by (6.4) should be changed to 0 whenever the viewpoint and the light source are on opposite sides of the surface. The g values for Figure 6.44 were calculated in this way. (Hint: One needs to compare the sign of $M \cdot N$ with the sign of $V \cdot N$, where V is a vector from the viewpoint to the center of $\widehat{S}$.) Partial translucence can be modeled by applying a factor K' to g on the dark side, with $0 < K' < 1$.

2. If our model of diffuse reflection from a point source makes a picture that looks too harsh to you, you can try adding a little *diffuse ambient illumination*. This simply means adding a constant amount of extra illumination to all surfaces. In other words a constant is added to g. Equivalently, one subjects g to a linear change of variables.

3. The effects we have talked about can be combined in various ways. For example, if you have available a color device, you can could draw a surface that is colored in some way and at the same time is illuminated by diffuse reflection. The significant equation is a vector version of (6.4). The surface color is determined by three (varying) reflectivities, $K_R(\widehat{S})$, $K_G(\widehat{S})$ and $K_B(\widehat{S})$, one for each of the three colors.

4. The reader is advised that the subject of illumination models contains a certain amount of magic. Equations are sometimes advocated for g because they look natural. (See e.g., §16.1 of J. D. Foley, A. van Dam, S. K. Feiner and J. F. Hughes, [*op. cit.*].) The reader might try replacing $\cos \theta$ in (6.4) by $\cos^n \theta$ for various positive integral values of n. (This equation is based on a physical theory developed by Phong Bui-Tuong in 1975.)

5. If you have available a device that gives Gouraud shading (see Exercises 6 and 7 of §2.5), you could try utilizing this feature for an improved drawing of a surface.

6.5   Bézier curves and engineering design

As we indicated in §3.2.6, one purpose of having cubic Bézier curves available is for the practical task of drawing pictures of real objects. Here we mention a project the student could undertake to exhibit the utility of this kind of work. Of course the project suggested here overlaps somewhat with the function of the many available CAD (computer-aided design) packages that are available. We hope that this discussion will give the reader some feeling about how such packages work.

Begin by selecting an object[39] that you would like to design, possibly a vehicle or piece of furniture. Make a rough sketch of the object, and do the best you can to get spatial coordinates for some of its more important features (corners, junctions, and so on). For curving members, add a few extra points as control points for a B-spline. One can thereby begin to assemble a 3-dimensional database for the object, using c for control points, and so on, as described for two dimensions in §3.2.6 and extended to three dimensions in §5.5. We will call such a database a *(3-dimensional) B-extended device-independent file.*

As we mentioned in §5.5, the reader can easily extend the Bézier translator of §3.2.6 to a translator that works in three dimensions. Therefore, by using all the tools at hand so far, the reader can arrange to make pictures—with arbitrary rotations, viewpoint, and so on—of any object that is represented by a 3-dimensional B-extended device-independent file. Thus one could make pictures of the object from all angles to really see what it looks like.

At this point, one could really begin to *design* the object in question. Every number in the database could be regarded as a design parameter, i.e., a knob one could turn to bring the picture closer to (or farther from) the desired design. At this point, all sorts of possibilities present themselves. For instance, there could be separate databases for various components of the picture, thereby allowing individual components to be resized or repositioned, using affine transformations. Certain points in the database could be regarded as depending on other points, and such dependencies could be programmed in. One could experiment with how the object looks when deformed by non-rigid motions such as compressions or shears.

---

[39]Bear in mind that our mathematical model is that of a line drawing rather than a shaded surface representation; choose an object that can be well represented this way. An object (such as a building) with all straight lines will not be suitable for illustrating the use of Bézier curves.

Therefore, in general, we are talking about organizing the job of designing and drawing real objects according to the following flow chart:

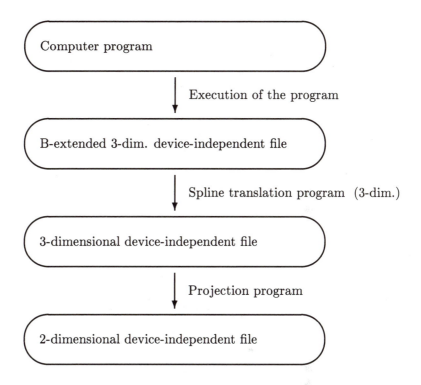

All aspects of this flow chart have been explained, except for the first oval, a program that can organize and output B-spline data. We illustrate this sort of thing in §6.5.1. For the benefit of students who did not do the B-spline exercises earlier in the book, we will give a detailed exposition of the B-spline algorithm in §6.5.2.

After the design stage is complete, one could of course use the final database to produce finished plans for the object. Plans could show projections from different angles. If the database is sufficiently well organized, one might find it possible and useful to make enlarged drawings of certain components, exploded views, views where hidden elements are removed, and so on. One could certainly make binocular images as described in §6.6.

6.5.1   A program to draw a chair

As we indicated above, it is sometimes helpful to have a program that generates B-spline data (here *data* refers to some lists of apical control points, each list describing a separate B-spline). Of course it is always possible to regard

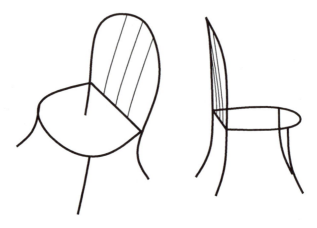

FIGURE 6.45   Two views of the chair

B-spline data as a kind of raw material that is not deduced from anything else. Nevertheless, there are many circumstances in which B-spline data itself naturally obeys some relationships and symmetries, and these relationships are most easily ensured by a having a program generate the data.

We illustrate this sort of thing by returning to an illustrative topic that we began in Chapter 2, namely, the designing of a chair. The chair we are designing is shown in Figure 6.45. It has a curving back that continues down the two back legs, a curving seat, two curving front legs, and three struts in the back. What we need is a list of apical control points to describe each of these curves. The control points depend largely on the inspiration of the designer, but we should notice one thing, namely, that a certain symmetry is desired (at least by this designer). We want the chair to be left-right symmetric, i.e., symmetric with respect to the vertical plane that runs from front to back through the middle of the seat. Thus for instance, the left half of the back curve depends on the right half, and so on. The purpose of the following program is simply to make explicit these dependencies. In other words, the program actually contains raw data for *half* the figure; these coefficients can be regarded as the *independent variables* of the problem. Coefficients for the other half of the figure, regarded here as *dependent variables*, are simply generated by reflection.

We hasten to point out that this program is only an illustration of the kinds of things that can be done. A figure can have other symmetry besides reflectional symmetry; for instance, Exercise 9 of §6.3.3 can be regarded as a way to introduce rotational symmetry into a figure. In addition to the question of symmetry, an important consideration is that of making sure that certain curves meet in the desired manner. For example, we might want one curve to start at the midpoint of another curve; this again can be programmed (although our example does not happen to contain this feature). From one point of view, the program that follows is very simple-minded: Its heaviest calculation is a reflection in the plane $x_1 = 0.5$ (via the formula $x_1' = 1.0 - x_1$). The program can nevertheless be justified on two grounds: First, trivial as these calculations may be, they are nonetheless repetitive, tedious and error-prone, and hence better left to a program. Second, the structure of the program strictly enforces the distinction between dependent and independent variables.

The astute reader will notice that we have not attempted a perfect isolation of the dependent from the independent variables. For example, the segment defined by **seat_back** is intended to be symmetric under the reflection defined above, but we have not bothered to program this symmetry. Moreover, we really want **half_seat_curve[0]** to be the same as **seat_back[0]** (why?). Sometimes the perfect programming of these things is governed by a law of diminishing returns. In any case, most programming of this type has a somewhat provisional character. We may after all decide that the back of the seat should be curved instead of straight, or that there should be five struts instead of three—to name only two of the vast number of design decisions that can be made. Most changes of that nature would require a redesign of the program. Nevertheless the program as it stands allows one to play around with the design parameters that have been included; if for instance you want the design to flare out more near the shoulders, it should not be too difficult to look over the data and see which parameter is a likely one to change.

This program illustrates the inclusion of data at the start of a program. We have (elsewhere) defined **point_3** as a data type with three coordinates, **coord_1** and so on. The overall effect of this is that if **ABC** is declared as a **point_3**, then **ABC.coord_1**, **ABC.coord_2** ...can be used as ordinary variables, while at the same time **ABC** can be referred to as an entity without need of mentioning the individual coordinates. The first declaration in the program declares **seat_back** as an array of two **points_3**, and moreover these two points are given values by directly stating all their coordinates (punctuated with commas and braces in an obvious way). These two points will serve as endpoints for the segment that runs straight across the back of the seat. The rest of the data is more or less self-explanatory. For example we include data for five of the ten control points for the main curve (back and rear legs), storing this data in the array called **half_back_curve**. The full data of **back_curve** is generated by symmetry inside the subroutine **set_up_data()**. In experimenting with the design parameters, one needs only to edit the start of the program to change some numbers.

Notice that, as indicated in the flow chart at the start of §6.5, this program takes no action on the data besides outputting commands m, 1, B, c, E, and so on, with the understanding that another program (a B-spline interpreter) will deal with those commands. This action mainly takes place within the subroutine **B_spline()**.

```
point_3 seat_back[2] = {{0.2,0.2,0.5}, {0.8,0.2,0.5}};
point_3 half_seat_curve[3] =
                { {0.2, 0.2, 0.5},
                  {0.1, 0.6, 0.5},
                  {0.3, 0.8, 0.5} };
point_3 half_back_curve[5] =
                { {0.1, 0.1, 0.1},
                  {0.2, 0.2, 0.2},
                  {0.2, 0.2, 0.5},
                  {0.2, 0.2, 0.8},
                  {0.4, 0.1, 1.1} };
point_3 right_backpiece[3] =
                { {0.358, 0.122, 1.256},
                  {0.358, 0.2,   0.7},
                  {0.358, 0.2,   0.5} };
point_3 center_backpiece[3] =
                { {0.500, 0.104, 1.292},
                  {0.500, 0.2,   0.7},
                  {0.500, 0.2,   0.5} };
point_3 right_front[3] =
                { {0.1,   0.771, 0.0},
                  {0.19,  0.671, 0.2},
                  {0.193, 0.671, 0.5} };
point_3 back_curve[10];
point_3 seat_curve[6];
point_3 left_backpiece[3];
point_3 left_front[3];

main()
{
set_up_data();

move_3(seat_back[0]); line_3(seat_back[1]);

B_spline(back_curve,10);
B_spline(seat_curve,6);
B_spline(left_front,3); B_spline(right_front,3);
B_spline(right_backpiece,3);
B_spline(center_backpiece,3);
B_spline(left_backpiece,3);
}

set_up_data()
{
for (i=0; i<5; i++)   back_curve[i] = half_back_curve[i];
for (i=5; i<10; i++)
{
```

```
            back_curve[i].coord_1 = 1.0 - back_curve[9-i].coord_1;
            back_curve[i].coord_2 =       back_curve[9-i].coord_2;
            back_curve[i].coord_3 =       back_curve[9-i].coord_3;
    }
    for (i=0; i<3; i++)    seat_curve[i] = half_seat_curve[i];
    for (i=3; i<6; i++)
    {
            seat_curve[i].coord_1 = 1.0 - seat_curve[5-i].coord_1;
            seat_curve[i].coord_2 =       seat_curve[5-i].coord_2;
            seat_curve[i].coord_3 =       seat_curve[5-i].coord_3;
    }
    for (i=0; i<3; i++)
    {
            left_front[i].coord_1 = 1.0 - right_front[i].coord_1;
            left_front[i].coord_2 =       right_front[i].coord_2;
            left_front[i].coord_3 =       right_front[i].coord_3;
    }
    for (i=0; i<3; i++)
    {
            left_backpiece[i].coord_1 = 1.0 - right_backpiece[i].coord_1;
            left_backpiece[i].coord_2 =       right_backpiece[i].coord_2;
            left_backpiece[i].coord_3 =       right_backpiece[i].coord_3;
    }
    }


B_spline(a,N)
{
printf("B\n");
for (i=0;i<N;i++)
{
   printf("c %7.3f %7.3f %7.3f\n",
                      a[i].coord_1,a[i].coord_2,a[i].coord_3);
}
printf("E\n");
}


move_3(P)
{
printf("m %7.3f %7.3f %7.3f\n",P.coord_1,P.coord_2,P.coord_3);
}


line_3(P)
{
printf("l %7.3f %7.3f %7.3f\n",P.coord_1,P.coord_2,P.coord_3);
}
```

6.5.2 An algorithm for B-splines

We outline an algorithm that could be used to translate 3-dimensional B-spline commands into 3-dimensional device-independent commands. Thus this algorithm is what is needed for the second arrow in the flow chart at the start of §6.5; the presumption is that its output will be processed by an interpreter for 3-dimensional device-independent commands. (An algorithm for 2-dimensional B-spline commands would work exactly like the one given here, with the third coordinate ignored.) We therefore assume that the input data has the form described in §3.2.6 (with three coordinates to each m, l and c command). We do not expressly mention piecewise cubic interpolants, but they could obviously be done in a similar manner.

In order to carry this out, the reader should have some experience with simpler translation programs, such as those mentioned in §2.3.1, §3.2.6 and §6.3.2. We therefore summarize some algorithmic steps that are familiar from those programs, in a manner such as "open the main data file" or "read one line of data and act on it." The main technical feature that one needs to add to those programs is an array of control points.

ALGORITHM (translation of B-spline data)

- Open the main data file (of B-spline data) for reading.

- If any data remains, read one line of data and act on it. If it is an ordinary device-independent command, output it unchanged. Otherwise, read a B command and act on it as follows:
  - Read and store lines of data beginning with c until an E command is encountered. The stored points will be used as apical control points A_i in what follows. The total number of lines read before E should be stored as the number N of apical control points.
  - According to the plan implicit in §3.2.4, loop through the $N - 1$ Bézier curves that constitute this one B-spline, as follows:
    * Compute four Bézier control points as described in §3.2.4.
    * Compute the coefficients for this individual cubic Bézier curve $B(t)$, according to Equation (3.13).
    * Divide the parameter t into M discrete steps t_i, where M is appropriately chosen to balance smoothness with reasonable computing and printing time. Enter a loop in which each t-step is treated as follows:
      · Calculate $P_i = B(t_i)$.
      · If $i = 1$ issue an m command with the coordinates of P_i.
      · If $i > 1$ issue an l command with the coordinates of P_i.
      · Go on to t_{i+1} if $i < M$; otherwise exit this loop.
    * Go to the next Bézier component of this B-spline if there is one; otherwise exit this loop.

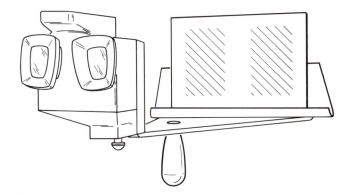

FIGURE 6.46   One model of stereoscope

 − Return to the second step of the algorithm.

• When the data is exhausted, end the algorithm.

Exercise_____

1. The object of a design program does not have to be 3-dimensional like our chair. In the 2-dimensional realm, one might design *patterns*—for an article of clothing, for a backpack, or even for a balsa model. In the case of clothing, it would be interesting to have the program able to generate the pattern in any size. (In dealing with patterns, there is another mathematical issue of great importance, namely, the optimal layout of the pieces. In other words, one wishes to minimize the scraps that occur when the cloth is cut. This optimization problem is beyond the scope of this book.)

6.6   Binocular vision

Most humans have the marvelous but subtle faculty of directly perceiving the third dimension through binocular vision. Two eyes at slightly different locations obtain slightly different pictures, and the brain is able to construct a sense of 3-dimensionality from these slight differences. The pair of pictures seen by the two eyes is called a *stereo pair*. In fact, a stereo pair is all that is needed to create a 3-dimensional impression. If each eye is presented, by whatever trick, with the scene it would have gotten from the original 3-dimensional scene, the brain will be given the illusion of that same 3-dimensional scene. It is straightforward to

FIGURE 6.47   Stereo pair for the torus

FIGURE 6.48   Stereo pair for the chair of §6.5.1

make a stereo pair with a camera or pair of cameras: One simply photographs the scene from two spots separated by the interocular distance (or with greater separation, for an enhanced effect). Interestingly, the binocular illusion can be experienced with stereo pairs consisting of relatively crude line drawings. It is our purpose here to see how this can be done with the tools at hand.

Devices called stereoscopes make it possible to look at stereo pairs in relative comfort and safety, thereby creating the illusion of a 3-dimensional image. Typically, a stereoscope has a lens for each eye; a paper containing the two images is placed behind the two lenses so that each eye can focus on its intended image from the stereo pair. Some general parameters can be determined by examining a given stereoscope: the approximate size used for each image and the separation between images. These parameters should be determined for any available

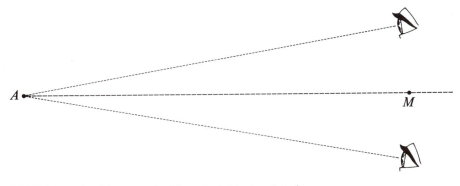

FIGURE 6.49   Two eyes looking straight at point A

stereoscope and should be followed pretty closely for images to be viewed on that scope.

For human eyes the interocular distance is about three inches, and that distance will work well enough if the objects viewed have dimensions about like those of chairs, tables and normal rooms. For some other objects, a different interocular distance may be appropriate. Our moon, for example, appears flat because the interocular separation of three inches is negligible compared to the moon's distance, and so both eyes receive virtually identical images. By the same token, Earth will appear flat when viewed by a human from a motionless vantage point in space. However, in running the seeworld problem we have the option of setting the interocular distance at any value we like. Changing it to something much larger (i.e., a distance commensurate with Earth's diameter) will result in the possibility of a genuine binocular view.

The general configuration of binocular vision is diagramed in Figure 6.49, which is best interpreted as seen from above. Each eye has turned slightly, so as to center the point A in its field of vision. From our point of view, this means that the two eyes are forming images by projecting onto two different planes from two different points. This could pose a problem for us until we realize that the diagram contains a certain rotational symmetry. More precisely, there is an obvious rotation about a vertical axis through point A that carries one eye onto the other. Therefore, the scenes seen by the two eyes are exactly the same except for this rotation about a vertical axis.

Using this observation, we can in fact make a stereo pair for any object for which we have a file of 3-dimensional device-independent commands. In this way, the stereo pair takes on the role of an interpretation of the 3-dimensional device-independent language. The method requires that we have a program (as mentioned in §6.3.2) that can project 3-dimensional device-independent commands to the plane and that incorporates rotations about a vertical line. Having such an interpreter, we take our 3-dimensional device-independent file and do something like the following.

ALGORITHM (stereo pairs from 3-dimensional device-independent data)

- Make two copies of the device-independent file. Let us agree that the first copy has to do with the right eye and that the second has to do with the left eye.

- Precede each copy by a rotation about a vertical line through A. The rotation for the first copy should map the right eye to the midpoint M, and the second rotation should map the left eye to M.

- Precede the two copies by 2-dimensional window commands (\w) that will cause the two images to be of the right sizes and relative positions for a stereo pair (the first image to the right of the second by about three inches and each image about two or three inches in size).

- Add appropriate commands to project each image along the line $\overleftrightarrow{AM}$. (In each case, this will involve rotating the figure so that the line $\overleftrightarrow{AM}$ is vertical and then projecting to the x_1, x_2-plane.)

- Apply the projection program to obtain 2-dimensional code.

The reader is urged to experiment making stereo pairs. In some cases, one can modify an existing program in a manner suggested by the algorithm, rather than using the algorithm directly (for example, this applies to the Earth-viewing program of §6.1). Stereo pairs can be made for just about any 3-dimensional object (including the ray-traced objects that will be described in §6.8). If you did the molecule exercise at the end of §3.2.6, that could be repeated here to make stereo pairs. For some interesting stereo pairs in the mathematical literature, see G. A. Edgar [*op. cit.*, p. 197] (fractals), or G. K. Francis, *A topological picturebook*, Springer-Verlag, New York, 1987, pp 32–33 (pinch points).

By the way, it doesn't really make sense to make stereo pictures of the stars, at least not with the database that was described in §6.2. The stars are of course distributed throughout space (the celestial sphere is a fiction), and so pictures of stars could make interesting stereo pairs (with interocular distance taken to be at least as large as the diameter of Earth's orbit). The problem is that the data available to us does not really contain spatial positions.

6.7   4-dimensional space

At least once in any college geometry course the author is asked to explain *the fourth dimension*. At this point, having laid a foundation both in the theoretical notion of dimension (Chapter 1) and in the practical representation of objects of ordinary 3-space (Chapter 3), we can profitably look into this question.

We somewhat unexpectedly place this discussion in a chapter on applications, since we believe that the student may be able to make some pictures that help reveal things about 4-dimensional geometry (see §6.7.3). The great geometer H. S. M. Coxeter wrote in 1947:[40]

> As for . . . figures in four or more dimensions, we can never fully comprehend them by direct observations. In attempting to do so, however, we seem to peep through a chink in the wall of our physical limitations, into a new world of dazzling beauty. Such an escape from the turbulence of ordinary life will perhaps help to keep us sane. On the other hand, a reader whose standpoint is more severely practical may take comfort in Lobatschewsky's assertion that "there is no branch of mathematics, however abstract, which may not some day be applied to phenomena of the real world".

6.7.1 Is there a physical meaning to 4-dimensional space?

Before addressing the question as stated, let us examine our basis for believing that our ambient space is 3-dimensional. If our space were really a vector space in some absolute sense, then we could construct a basis, determine that it contains three vectors, and that would be that! We must concede, however, that vector algebra is a structure imposed on space by our minds and only experienced indirectly. There is, however, ample direct confirmation of the 3-dimensionality of our world. It is, for example, hard to argue with the experience that points are unambiguously located in space by three coordinates, but that two coordinates will not suffice.[41]

There are also indirect consequences of the theory of 3-dimensional space, such as the simple fact that one can construct three lines mutually perpendicular to one another, but not four such lines. A subtler consequence arises from measure theory: If an object is made twice as big in all its dimensions, then its mass increases by a factor of 2^3. This simple property can be verified with simple equipment and with a minimal requirement of theoretical superstructure. It is by such simple indirect inferences that we are, in fact, quite confident in asserting that this space is 3-dimensional.

---

[40] Coxeter, H. S. M., *Regular polytopes*, Pitman, New York, 1947.

[41] Georg Cantor startled the mathematical world by showing in 1878 that points can be located in 3-space with *two* or even *one* real coordinate. As Cantor recognized, the catch is that these counterintuitive coordinate functions are not continuous (nor do they have any simple geometric meaning).

Our ambient space is not only 3-dimensional in the sense of having three coordinates, it is completely homogeneous, or symmetric, with respect to these three coordinates. The coordinate system can be rotated (by any rotation matrix), and the resulting coordinates will measure space just as before. No one 3-dimensional coordinate system is more spacelike than any other, or distinguished[42] in any way that we know of.

In considering 4-dimensional space, we also face two possibilities. Such a space could be either abstract or concrete, and we could turn our attention toward either of these possibilities. For the abstract spaces, little problem remains for us. We have already seen n-dimensional spaces, and they are really not much more difficult for $n = 4$ than they are for $n = 3$. (In either case one has to absorb the concepts of linear independence, and so on.) We have seen 4-dimensional spaces applied mathematically (for homogeneous coordinates), and we know how to model them in terms of 4-tuples of real numbers. If this abstraction were the sole requisite for a 4-dimensional space, then things would be simple indeed.

The more problematic question is that of some physical manifestation of 4-dimensional space. Human imagination has long been awake to the possibility of another dimension that we do not perceive or have not yet learned to perceive. Let us look first at the most straightforward kind of fourth dimension, namely, another dimension that is completely homogeneous with the three we already know, in the sense mentioned above. A homogeneous 4-dimensional space would require the existence of four mutually perpendicular lines, which no one has ever seen. Moreover, in such a space, if the size of an object is doubled, its mass should increase by a factor of 2^4, and this is in direct contradiction to commonplace observations in everyday life. Therefore, it seems possible to rule out completely any homogeneous fourth dimension.

Passing to non-homogeneous worlds, there is the intriguing possibility that true space has four (or more) dimensions and that we are confined to a subspace of three dimensions. While there is no real evidence for this theory, it is at least consistent—we can imagine 2-dimensional creatures living out their lives, sort of as our pets, on a plane[43] that we can look at from a comfortable armchair in 3-space. So, why could there not be 4-dimensional beings watching us? Better yet, consider the following. We could help the Flatlanders travel from point A to point B by bending their plane so that A touches B; by analogy, maybe we could induce our own 3-space to bend in its 4-space, so as to provide us with instantaneous travel. Thus we have the "space warp" of science fiction. Nevertheless these speculations still have the obvious drawback of dealing with

---

[42]This statement refers to the hypothetical condition of space before objects are introduced. Once objects are introduced—such as a solid earth—we of course do have reference points for distinguishing one coordinate system from another.

[43]Of course, the fundamental inspiration for this analogy was the book *Flatland*, by Edwin A. Abbott.

things that have never been observed, and so it can hardly be said that we have found the fourth dimension here.

Time is a fourth coordinate that can be assigned to any point in space, and hence can be regarded as a possible fourth dimension. It certainly has the advantage of being observable. Nevertheless the time coordinate differs so radically from spatial coordinates that its inclusion as a fourth coordinate may seem somewhat artificial. (Why not include the temperature as a fifth coordinate, and so on?) This is really an extreme form of non-homogeneity: We measure time differently, we cannot move about in time, we cannot rotate ourselves so that our head is earlier than our feet, and so on. From this naïve point of view, it is clear that time cannot be admitted as a very natural sort of fourth dimension.

Nevertheless, a more sophisticated view of the world can make the 4-dimensional *space-time* seem a little more natural. The underlying geometric model of Einstein's theory of special relativity is a 4-dimensional vector space initially coordinatized by three spatial coordinates x_1, x_2 and x_3 and one time coordinate t. In this model, the former weakness of inhomogeneity is incorporated in the theory as one of its strengths. The distance d between two *time-points* $\langle x_1, x_2, x_3, t \rangle$ and $\langle x_1', x_2', x_3', t' \rangle$ is a complex number defined by

$$d^2 = \sum_{i=1}^{3}(x_i - x_i')^2 - (t - t')^2$$

with the minus sign expressing the (very real) difference between time and space. (This sum is a symmetric bilinear form in the sense of §1.5.1; it is not an inner product as defined there.) Homogeneity reappears here in modified form: Coordinates can be changed so long as this distance is preserved. In fact, according to the theory, the true nature of the universe cannot be seen without allowing such changes of coordinates. The vector $\langle 1, 1, 1, 0 \rangle$ is no more purely spatial than is $\langle 1, 1, 1, 1 \rangle$ (since both have positive real norm). From this vantage point it is less clear whether we have found the fourth dimension. It would seem reasonable to call time the fourth dimension as an affirmation of special relativity, but one should be very careful not to read in any more than this. Time is *still* not a spatial dimension.

Returning to the question heading this section, we certainly see that there is a physical meaning to 4-dimensional space, at least under the right interpretation. For example, the four coordinates of the Einstein-Lorentz space-time have a very real meaning. Nevertheless, a really strict interpretation of fourth dimension, as being completely like the three known spatial dimensions, has to be rejected for lack of evidence.

6.7.2   Can one perceive 4-dimensional space?

Actually we might even ask, "Can we perceive 3-dimensional space, and if so, how?" The answer to this question is very complex, and we won't attempt it here, except to say that our perception of 3-dimensional space seems highly indirect. We assemble and integrate all sorts of sensory data to form a coherent picture of a 3-dimensional whole. One mathematical purpose of this chapter has been to understand data of one kind, namely, the 2-dimensional representation of 3-dimensional objects. The mathematical tool here has been the *projection* mapping defined in §5.3.9 and applied in §6.1 and §6.2.

We can also use projection mappings from 4-space to 2-space as a small window on the world of 4-dimensional geometry. We will only give a few hints about how this may be accomplished, leaving most of the details to the reader. For representing projections, etc., as collineations, it is convenient to turn to projective 4-space $P^4(\mathbb{R})$, and thus to use five homogeneous coordinates. By analogy with §5.3.9, we can see that the 5×5 matrix

$$\begin{bmatrix} P_4 & 0 & 0 & -P_1 & 0 \\ 0 & P_4 & 0 & -P_2 & 0 \\ 0 & 0 & P_4 & -P_3 & 0 \\ 0 & 0 & 0 & P_4 & 0 \\ 0 & 0 & 0 & -P_5 & P_4 \end{bmatrix} \tag{6.6}$$

moves a point with homogeneous coordinates $\langle P_1, P_2, P_3, P_4, P_5 \rangle$ to the ideal point $\langle 0, 0, 0, 1, 0 \rangle$, and that

$$\begin{bmatrix} 1 & 0 & 0 & 0 & 0 \\ 0 & 1 & 0 & 0 & 0 \\ 0 & 0 & 0 & 0 & 0 \\ 0 & 0 & 0 & 0 & 0 \\ 0 & 0 & 0 & 0 & 1 \end{bmatrix} \tag{6.7}$$

projects $P^4(\mathbb{R})$ onto the 2-dimensional subspace defined by $x_3 = x_4 = 0$. Combining these two matrices with rotations will give projection from any view point, as before.

Another basis for our perception of 3-dimensional space is motion. Watching things move helps us form our concept of space. Likewise, it would seem that one's concept of 4-dimensional space can grow if one watches[44] enough pictures of moving objects. Therefore it will be of interest to us to apply rotations to objects in 4-space before projecting them. By analogy with §5.3.4, we can see that the 5×5 matrix

[44] Actually, this is a somewhat untried area. As more people develop programs of the type described here, and as these programs are developed on more and more sophisticated hardware, we will see what kind of 4-dimensional consciousness can arise.

$$\begin{bmatrix} \cos\theta & 0 & -\sin\theta & 0 & 0 \\ 0 & 1 & 0 & 0 & 0 \\ \sin\theta & 0 & \cos\theta & 0 & 0 \\ 0 & 0 & 0 & 1 & 0 \\ 0 & 0 & 0 & 0 & 1 \end{bmatrix} \tag{6.8}$$

effects a rotation (at least when considered with respect to the subspace generated by x_1 and x_3). Therefore we will call this transformation a rotation. (It is certainly orthogonal in the sense of §1.5.3.) Notice that there are six possibilities depending on which which two of the first four coordinates are rotated; we do not list them all.

The orthogonal transformations of 4-space contain a one-parameter subgroup of a type we have not seen before. For $\alpha, \beta \in \mathbb{R}$ with $\alpha, \beta \neq 0$ and for a parameter $t \in \mathbb{R}$, consider the matrix

$$G_t = \begin{bmatrix} \cos\alpha t & -\sin\alpha t & 0 & 0 & 0 \\ \sin\alpha t & \cos\alpha t & 0 & 0 & 0 \\ 0 & 0 & \cos\beta t & -\sin\beta t & 0 \\ 0 & 0 & \sin\beta t & \cos\beta t & 0 \\ 0 & 0 & 0 & 0 & 1 \end{bmatrix} \tag{6.9}$$

The student may verify that the G_t are orthogonal and that they form a one-parameter group. If α and β have a common integral divisor, say $\alpha = m\gamma$ and $\beta = n\gamma$ for some $\gamma \in \mathbb{R}$ and some positive integers m and n, then $G_t = I$ for $t = 2\pi/\gamma$. On the other hand, if α/β is an irrational number, then G_t is never I (except when $t = 0$). What the matrices G_t do is to rotate two perpendicular planes at different angular velocities α and β. If these angular velocities are not comparable, then the combined rotation will never come back where it started. For obvious reasons, we call these motions *bi-rotations*.

6.7.3   Some objects of $P^4(\mathbb{R})$

THE 4-DIMENSIONAL LISSAJOUS FIGURE

The orbit of the point $\langle \cos\phi, -\sin\phi, 1, 0\rangle$ under the one-parameter group G_t of bi-rotations is the set

$$_\phi L^4_{\alpha\beta} = \{\langle\cos(\alpha t - \phi), \sin(\alpha t - \phi), \cos\beta t, \sin\beta t\rangle : t \in \mathbb{R}\}$$

as the reader may easily verify. If this set is projected to $\mathbb{R}^3$ by forgetting the fourth coordinate, we clearly obtain the cylindrical Lissajous figure that was discussed in §3.1.4 and again in Exercise 7 of §6.3.3. In fact one really doesn't need ϕ, since $_\phi L^4_{\alpha\beta}$ can be obtained from $L^4_{\alpha\beta} = {_0}L^4_{\alpha\beta}$ by a rotation through the angle ϕ. Therefore the one figure $L^4_{\alpha\beta}$ contains all the necessary information about Lissajous figures with angle ratio α/β. It is clearly the most symmetric form of this Lissajous figure.

THE TESSARACT

The student who wants to look at some 4-dimensional objects should begin with the 4-dimension hypercube, or *tessaract*. Its vertices (in non-homogeneous coordinates) are the sixteen 4-tuples of 0's and 1's: $\langle 0,0,0,0\rangle$, $\langle 0,0,0,1\rangle$, and so on. It has an edge between two vertices iff they differ in exactly one coordinate,[45] such as $\langle 0,0,0,0\rangle$ and $\langle 0,0,0,1\rangle$. If we snip each edge in two, we will have four half-edges attached to each vertex, making 64 half-edges or 32 edges in all.

THE CROSS POLYTOPE IN 4-SPACE

Another interesting 4-dimensional object is the analog of the octahedron. It has eight vertices, which in non-homogeneous coordinates are

$$\langle \pm 1,0,0,0\rangle, \quad \langle 0,\pm 1,0,0\rangle, \quad \langle 0,0,\pm 1,0\rangle, \quad \langle 0,0,0,\pm 1\rangle$$

Each vertex V is connected to six others: all those that have 0 in the coordinate where V has ± 1. (Thus the total number of edges is 24.) Obviously an analogous figure with $2n$ vertices occurs in n-dimensional space. Coxeter has suggested calling these figures *cross polytopes* because their vertices lie at the extremities of the cross-like figure consisting of those portions of the coordinate axes that have coordinate values between -1 and 1.

Exercises

1. Make various views of $L^4_{\alpha\beta}$ for some interesting values of α and β.

2. Make a picture of various projections of the tessaract. See how the picture changes as various rotations are applied. Also observe the effect of matrices like G_t in Equation (6.9).

3. Make a similar investigation of the cross polytope.

6.8 Elementary ray tracing

Our mathematical model for drawing (or vision, if you like, or photography) is that of projective transformations, as worked out in Chapters 4 and 5. The camera of Figure 4.2 is modeled by a transformation $T: \mathbb{R}^3 \longrightarrow F$, where F is the plane of the film; T is itself given by a 3×4 matrix in a manner that is by now familiar. The diverse applications in Chapter 6 have all had a common plan: we begin with an inventory of geometric objects (usually line segments) in $\mathbb{R}^3$; we apply T to these objects one by one, and thus we determine an inventory

---

[45]This is a definition, not something that we could prove. Our only basis for the definition is that it seems to incorporate some significant ideas about ordinary cubes, and hence that it makes a reasonable analogy.

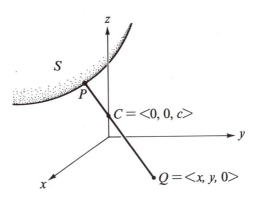

FIGURE 6.50   The basic configuration of ray tracing

of objects (again usually line segments) to be drawn on F. These objects of F are collected as a file of m and l commands (etc.), which can be sent to a device for display. This approach to the problem is in fact inherent in the flow chart appearing at the beginning of Chapter 2.

The method of *ray tracing* focuses instead on the *intensity function* $f(x, y)$, with x and y ranging over the film plane F. Let us recall from §2.7 that in general, an intensity function $f(x, y)$ is the shade (gray level) at point $\langle x, y \rangle \in F$. Here we specifically mean the gray level that appears at $\langle x, y \rangle$ in a photograph of the scene we are interested in. As we saw in §2.7, all we need in order to make a computer simulation of that photograph is a knowledge of the intensity function. Thus ray tracing can be defined as the use of a mathematical model to determine $f(x, y)$ as a function of x and y.

The basic model (or simulation) still involves the transformation $T : \mathbb{R}^3 \longrightarrow F$ that we mentioned above, although we will not need to use T in our calculations. Figure 6.50 shows the general model and establishes notation for the calculations that follow. (Figure 6.50 is not very different from Figure 4.2 or Figure 4.9, although the three figures differ in notation.) The film plane F is taken to be the x, y-plane; a typical point Q of F is coordinatized as $\langle x, y, 0 \rangle$. The focal point, also known as the center of the projection, is denoted C and is assumed, without loss of generality, to lie on the z-axis: $C = \langle 0, 0, c \rangle$. The transformation T is defined for all $P \neq C$ by the condition that $T(P)$ is the unique point Q on F such that C, P and Q are collinear.

Another important difference from previous models lies in our point of view about the objects being drawn. Formerly (except in §6.4.5) we had an inventory of lifeless black line segments, which we drew as plain black segments. We now think of the drawn objects as emitting their own light, which, falling on our film through the focus C, creates the intensity pattern $f(x, y)$. Thus the transformation T represents the focusing of light on the film plane F through C. In other words, a light source at a point $P \in \mathbb{R}^3$ contributes to the intensity at the point $Q = T(P)$ but not to the intensity at any other point of F. Thus the intensity $f(x, y)$ at a point $Q = \langle x, y, 0 \rangle$ is determined by the set of all points $P \in \mathbb{R}^3$ that satisfy $T(P) = Q$. This set is called the *inverse image* of Q under T and is denoted $T^{-1}(Q)$. It is evident from the above discussion (and from Figure 6.50) that this inverse image is the line that joins C and Q. Moreover, we usually limit our attention to the the part of this line that lies above the film plane (or, in a strict camera model, above the focal point C). In other words, to determine $f(x, y)$, we have to examine the *ray* $\overrightarrow{QC}$ that starts at $Q = \langle x, y, 0 \rangle$ and heads toward the focal point C. From the physical point of view, we are imagining a ray of light reaching Q through C; in tracing this light ray backward, i.e., from Q back toward C and beyond, we are looking for the first light source that we might encounter. Although it may not be true in all applications, we will begin by making the simplifying assumption that this closest light source is the only significant contribution to $f(x, y)$.

The reader should always remember that when we speak of tracing a ray from a point $Q = \langle x, y, 0 \rangle$ in the film plane through the focus C toward the scene, we are implicitly speaking of doing this for a large collection of x and y values. For a sharp picture, the points $\langle x, y, 0 \rangle$ have to be spread out somewhat densely over a region of the film plane. We need not deal explicitly in this section with the task of constructing a double loop of x and y values, since we already did that job in §2.7. Nevertheless we should bear in mind that making a ray-traced image will require more computing resources than the other techniques described in this book—both in storage and in CPU time. On many systems, high-resolution pictures will also waste user time, both by requiring more time for computing and by delaying the print queue. (A useful technique is to begin a ray-tracing project with coarse images. When it looks like the mathematics is reasonably correct, the various parameters such as light location and intensity can be adjusted at a finer resolution. Finally, when the picture is really right, a presentation copy can be run off at the highest available resolution.)

The major weakness of ray tracing is this rather mindless quality of continually redoing the same calculations, with almost no change between one ray and the next one. On the other hand, it has a number of strengths, among which we may note the following. It can handle scenes that are hard to analyze any other way, such as interpenetrating solids. It handles shadows very easily. Hidden surface removal happens almost automatically, since there is really nothing to remove; one simply has to find the source of illumination that is closest to the film, as we remarked above. Perhaps most interesting of all, one can continue to trace a ray after it bounces off a reflective surface, thereby getting good renditions of scenes containing (not necessarily planar) mirrors (see §6.8.3). For all these reasons, ray tracing has become a complete field of endeavor, about

FIGURE 6.51 A ray-traced image of an ellipsoid

which many whole books have been written; like so many topics in this book, we present only the basics.

Relying on a sampling procedure, ray tracing is better suited to solid objects than to points and lines. (A true mathematical line is so thin that all rays could miss it, even though it lies in the field of vision.) Thus in this simple treatment we will suppose that the only possible sources of light along the ray $\overrightarrow{QC}$ are background illumination (a constant) and diffuse reflection from a surface S (or from surfaces $S_1, S_2, \ldots$), which is itself being illuminated by a point source of light. We have shown S in Figure 6.50 as a somewhat spherical surface. Thus the situation is much like that of §6.4.5, and we will in fact use the formula given there for the intensity of diffuse reflection. The basic mathematical problem is now clear: We have to find the point or points in S that lie in $T^{-1}(Q)$, which is to say that we have to find the points where the ray $\overrightarrow{QC}$ meets S. In particular, we want to find the first such point along the ray.

6.8.1 The main calculation of intensity

For this section we fix a point $Q = \langle x, y, 0 \rangle$ on the film plane F; our objective will be to calculate $f(x, y)$, the intensity of light focused on Q. Arbitrary points in the ambient space $\mathbb{R}^3$ will be denoted $\langle x_1, x_2, x_3 \rangle$. The ray $\overrightarrow{QC}$ is parametrized by the affine combination

$$\Gamma(t) = Q + t(C - Q) = (1 - t)Q + tC$$

for $(t \geq 0)$, or in coordinates,

$$\Gamma(t) = \langle (1-t)x, (1-t)y, tc \rangle \tag{6.10}$$

The validity of these equations can be confirmed by observing first that they are linear in t, and then that $\Gamma(0) = Q$ and $\Gamma(1) = C$. We now need to see where $\Gamma(t)$ hits the surface S; in other words, we need to find the smallest positive value of t such that the three coordinates of $\Gamma(t)$ satisfy the equations that define the surface S.

At this point, we need to have a specific equation for S; the difficulty of the next step depends greatly on the nature of this equation. Things are relatively easy for S a quadric surface, i.e., a surface defined by a quadratic equation in x_1, x_2 and x_3 (see the end of §3.1.7), for in this case the unknown t will be defined by a quadratic equation. We will discuss in detail the case of an *ellipsoid*, i.e., the surface defined by the equation

$$\frac{(x_1 - a_1)^2}{r_1^2} + \frac{(x_2 - a_2)^2}{r_2^2} + \frac{(x_3 - a_3)^2}{r_3^2} = 1 \tag{6.11}$$

To find points where the ray intersects S, we substitute the three coordinates of $\Gamma(t)$ into Equation (6.11), thereby obtaining

$$\frac{((1 - t)x - a_1)^2}{r_1^2} + \frac{((1 - t)y - a_2)^2}{r_2^2} + \frac{(tc - a_3)^2}{r_3^2} = 1 \tag{6.12}$$

Obviously, if t_0 is a root of this equation, then $\Gamma(t_0)$ is a point that lies both on the ray $\overrightarrow{QC}$ and on the surface S. The point of interest to us is $\Gamma(t_0)$ for t_0 the least positive root of (6.12).

Collecting the coefficients of the various powers of t, we transform Equation (6.12) into

$$At^2 + Bt + C = 0 \tag{6.13}$$

where

$$A = \frac{x^2}{r_1^2} + \frac{y^2}{r_2^2} + \frac{c^2}{r_3^2} \tag{6.14}$$

$$B = \frac{2x(a_1 - x)}{r_1^2} + \frac{2y(a_2 - y)}{r_2^2} - \frac{2a_3c}{r_3^2} \tag{6.15}$$

$$C = \frac{(a_1 - x)^2}{r_1^2} + \frac{(a_2 - y)^2}{r_2^2} + \frac{a_3^2}{r_3^2} \tag{6.16}$$

As the reader well knows, the solutions of the Quadratic Equation (6.13) are

$$t_0, t_1 = \frac{-B \pm \sqrt{B^2 - 4AC}}{2A} \tag{6.17}$$

The exact character of these roots is determined by the discriminant $D = B^2 - 4AC$. If D is negative, then t_0 and t_1 are complex, and (6.13) has no real roots. This corresponds to the the very real possibility of a ray that does not touch

S at all; in this case the only light reaching $\langle x, y \rangle$ is that of the background illumination. Thus in this case $f(x, y)$ is defined to be the constant background value.[46]

If D is positive, then the equation has two real roots. If both of them are negative, then some of the ellipsoid lies below the film plane; and if exactly one of them is negative, then the point $\langle x, y \rangle$ of the film plane lies inside the ellipsoid. Thus we would usually regard a negative root as indicating an error in the setup; upon discovering one we would abort the program and revise the parameters (such as the a_i and the r_i) so as to correct this error.

Thus we now look at the case of two positive roots t_0 and t_1. The line of sight from $\langle x, y \rangle$ through C intersects S in two points, $\Gamma(t_0)$ and $\Gamma(t_1)$. We choose notation so that $P = \Gamma(t_0)$ is the closer of these points; therefore, we now know that $f(x, y)$ is the apparent brightness of the surface S at point P. We now make use of the equation for apparent brightness that we developed in §6.4.5. To paraphrase Equation (6.4),

$$f(x, y) \;=\; \frac{IK(P)\cos\theta}{R^2}$$

where I is the total intensity of the light source, $K(P)$ measures the reflectivity of the surface at P, R is the distance from P to the light source, and θ is the angle of illumination at P. As before, the simple model that has K constant is quite adequate to make interesting pictures of surfaces; thus we have

$$f(x, y) \;=\; \frac{IK\cos\theta}{R^2} \tag{6.18}$$

Leaving the straightforward calculation of R^2 to the reader, we will briefly discuss the calculation of $\cos\theta$, for θ the angle of illumination. As we stated in §6.4.5, θ is the angle between the vector M that goes from P to the point source of light and a vector N that is perpendicular to the surface S at P (sometimes called a *normal* vector to S at P). Thus

$$\cos\theta \;=\; \frac{N \cdot M}{|N|\,|M|} \tag{6.19}$$

The calculation of M is an easy subtraction. As for N, it is well known (and the proof can be found in any advanced calculus book) that if S is the surface defined by

$$F(x_1, x_2, x_3) \;=\; 0$$

and if P lies on S, then the vector

---

[46]The most effective background value seems to depend on the device. For paper, it is 1.0; on a dark screen with glowing pixels, it is 0.0.

$$N = \langle F_1(P), F_2(P), F_3(P) \rangle$$

is perpendicular to S at P (where $F_1(x_1, x_2, x_3)$ denotes the first partial derivative $\partial F / \partial x_1$, and so on). Computing partial derivatives for the case at hand, we have

$$N = 2 \left\langle \frac{(1-t_0)x - a_1}{r_1^2}, \frac{(1-t_0)y - a_2}{r_2^2}, \frac{t_0 c - a_3}{r_3^2} \right\rangle \qquad (6.20)$$

We now summarize all these calculations.

ALGORITHM (intensity function for ray tracing)   We assume fixed coordinates x and y on the film plane. We also assume fixed values of the intensity I, the reflectivity K, the position $\langle L_1, L_2, L_3 \rangle$ of the point source of light, the position $\langle 0, 0, c \rangle$ of the focus, the parameters $a_1 \ldots r_3$ that define an ellipsoid, and a constant value for background illumination.

- Use Equations (6.14–6.16) to calculate the coefficients A, B, C of the quadratic Equation (6.13).

- Calculate the discriminant $D = B^2 - 4AC$.

- If $D \le 0$, the desired value of the intensity function is the background value, and the algorithm is complete.

- Otherwise, calculate the real roots t_0 and t_1 by Equation (6.17).

- If either of these roots is negative or zero, abort the algorithm with a warning that something is wrong with the parameter set.

- Sort t_0 and t_1 so that t_0 is the smaller positive value.

- Evaluate $P = \Gamma(t_0)$ using Equation (6.10).

- Evaluate the normal vector N, by substituting t_0 into Equation (6.20).

- Evaluate M and R^2 in the obvious way from P and $\langle L_1, L_2, L_3 \rangle$.

- Evaluate $\cos \theta$ from Equation (6.19).

- Evaluate the intensity $f(x, y)$ from Equation (6.18).

Figure 6.51 shows a ray-traced image of an ellipsoid. In making such pictures, as with all pixeled images, one will have to decide how to handle gray values. We have handled grays by running them through the probabilistic filter described in §2.7.2; thus the printer was told only to paint individual pixels black and white. Those students with access to gray scales (as in the PostScript language) can handle this question differently.

We have not dwelt upon the obvious fact that various linear changes of variable may be necessary. For instance, the rasterization program in §2.7.1 evaluates $f(x, y)$ only for $0 \le x, y \le 1$. Usually one will want x and y to range over a different rectangle, and hence a linear change of variable will be needed. On the other hand, the preceding algorithm has generated its output on a somewhat arbitrary scale, which is not necessarily the scale of values between 0 and 1 that makes sense for gray values. We trust that in any application the reader can work out the required linear changes of scale.

In some of the exercises that follow we indicate some further directions that a student could pursue. We strongly advise, however, that one should have obtained a working version of the algorithm for the ellipsoid, with good readable pictures, before going on to the more sophisticated exercises. Many of these exercises could be deferred until after the inclusion of rotations in §6.8.2.

Ray-tracing algorithms can be discouraging for beginners, since there is little if any immediate feedback: You more or less have to have the algorithm complete and correct before you get any picture at all. Nevertheless, there are some precautions that one can take to minimize this problem. Before beginning the exercises here, one should have some confidence in working with the material on rasterized images in §2.7. One should practice that material using simple intensity functions that have nothing to do with ray tracing. Then one should implement the algorithm given here for the intensity function as a separate routine that can be checked for reasonableness. Finally the two can be put together for a ray-traced picture.

Exercises

1. What happens when the discriminant $D = B^2 - 4AC$ is zero? What does this correspond to geometrically?

2. Implement the preceding algorithm to make a ray-traced image of an ellipsoid. Experiment with changing the parameters, especially the location of the light $\langle L_1, L_2, L_3 \rangle$.

3. Actually, the preceding algorithm is not much more difficult to work out than is an algorithm for the general quadric surface

$$\sum_{i,j=1}^{3} a_{ij} x_i x_j + \sum_{i=1}^{3} b_i x_i + c = 0$$

(One has to change the equations for A, B and C and the equation for the normal vector N.) Make such an algorithm and apply it to make pictures of the hyperboloids depicted in Figures 3.16 and 3.17.

4. Perform a symbolic calculation of the discriminant $D = B^2 - 4AC$ from the relevant formulas for A, B and C. (Use either Equations (6.14–6.16) or the corresponding formulas that were developed in working Exercise 3.) Show that the resulting expression for D is *quadratic* in x and y. Thus we see that any horizon of a quadric surface is a conic section (as we saw once before in §5.6).

5. Make a ray-traced image that shows several ellipsoids, perhaps interpenetrating or partially eclipsing one another.

6. Make a ray-traced image of two ellipsoids, one casting a shadow on the other. (To find out if P on S is in the shadow of the other ellipsoid S', one has to find out if the segment from P to the light source intersects S'. This involves parametrizing that segment (say as $\Delta(t)$), substituting $\Delta(t)$ into the equation of S', and checking the determinant of the resulting quadratic equation. Obviously points in the shadow are given a very low intensity—0.0 in the simplest model.)

7. The surface S can be decorated by assuming that the reflectivity is a function $K(P)$ of the location of a point P on S. (It is easy to splice a definition of $K(P)$ into a working program for ray tracing; the only difficulty will be in finding interesting functions $K(P)$. Supposing S to be a sphere, one could easily color it black and white according to longitude or latitude or both. A much greater challenge would be to color it like the black and white patches on a soccer ball.) Exercises 6 and 7 can be simplified by omitting the light of diffuse reflection.

8. Readers with some experience in the solution of algebraic equations (in this case, an equation of fourth degree) might wish to make a ray-traced image of a *torus* T. This was defined in the exercises at the end of §6.3.3 as the surface formed by revolving about the z-axis a circle that lies off that axis. (See Figure 6.47 for a picture of the torus.) Here we modify the equation given there by a shift in the z-direction, so as to move T away from the film plane. In other words, T is now taken to be the surface formed by revolving the following curve in the x, z-plane about the z-axis:

$$(x - A)^2 + (z - B)^2 = a^2$$

As is well known, a revolved point satisfies the same equation with x changed to $\pm\sqrt{x^2 + y^2}$:

$$\left(\pm\sqrt{x^2 + y^2} - A\right)^2 + (z - B)^2 = a^2$$

By formally expanding the first squared term and isolating the square root term, one arrives at

$$\pm 2A\sqrt{x^2 + y^2} = -x^2 - y^2 - z^2 + 2Bz - A^2 - B^2 + a^2$$

Squaring both sides of this equation leads to an equation of the fourth degree in x, y and z. Now the three components of (6.10) can be substituted for x, y and z, yielding an equation of the fourth degree in t. This equation must be solved for t before continuing with the algorithm. (The solution of fourth-degree equations is well known since the work of Ferrari in 1540. For a useful modern account, see e.g., *Graphics Gems* [*op. cit.*, pp. 404–407] (article by Jochen Schwarze).)

9. A plane surface G can be an interesting subject for ray tracing if it is decorated in some way. (Of course, G should not be parallel to the film plane—that isn't wrong, but tracing rays would be a waste of time.) The relevant equations are like those in this section, only easier. All *lines* from $\langle x, y, 0 \rangle$ through the focus (except those parallel to G) will intersect G exactly once. Remember that we are only interested in those intersection points $\Gamma(t)$ that have $t > 0$. The simplest decoration to try is a checkerboard pattern (alternating squares of black and white). In fact, one can give G any intensity function $f_G(x, y)$; the intensity function $f(x, y)$ computed for the film plane F can then be thought of as a perspective version of f_G. Thus, once one has a working version for, say, a checkerboard pattern, one can change f_G to any of the intensity functions that were examined in the exercises of §2.7, such as Lissajous figures, the Mandelbrot set, and Archimedean tilings. Thus, in effect, one can now do all those exercises in perspective. The checkerboard is seen in perspective in Figure 6.52.

10. One could combine some of the effects described so far by placing some ellipsoids behind an (obliquely placed) screen (plane) that is partially opaque and partially transparent. The design could be controlled by any 0, 1-valued intensity function, such as those mentioned in Exercise 9. Thus, for example, we could look at a cluster of ellipsoids through a window in the shape of the Mandelbrot set. The screen and the ellipsoids could each be illuminated with a point source of light.

6.8.2   The effect of affine transformations

As with other ways of imaging 3-dimensional objects, one often wants the ability to rotate or otherwise move a picture for the most effective view. The algorithm of §6.8.1 contained no provision for performing geometric motions (rotations, translations, etc.) on the objects that appear in a ray-traced image. To simplify the discussion, we will assume as before that we are making an image of the ellipsoid S defined by Equation (6.11) and that M is an affine transformation that we wish to apply to S. (In other words, we wish to obtain an image, not of S, but of $M(S)$.) In §3.1.6 we outlined a way to write an equation for $M(S)$; the basic method was to substitute the three components of the formal expression $M^{-1}(\langle x_1, x_2, x_3 \rangle)$ for x_1, x_2 and x_3 in the equation for S. That method will work here, but it is probably simpler to proceed according to another plan, which we now describe.

Before implementing rotations (or other rigid motions), we need to decide what is and what is not rotating. Specifically, supposing that a motion M is applied to S, do we apply M also to the position $\langle L_1, L_2, L_3 \rangle$ of the light source? If S moves alone, that is like a photographic situation in which we keep our camera and lighting fixed, but move the subject. If both the subject and its light source move, relative to film and focus, that is like a photographic situation in which we keep the lighting unchanged, but move the camera around. In this section we will treat the latter case, that of moving both S and $\langle L_1, L_2, L_3 \rangle$. (The other case is similar and has been left to the reader as an exercise.)

For $Q = \langle x, y, 0 \rangle \in F$, we need to find the point P' where the ray $\overrightarrow{QC}$ contacts $M(S)$ and then to find the apparent brightness of the surface $M(S)$ at P' (with light source $M(\langle L_1, L_2, L_3 \rangle)$). Since this brightness depends only on various surface parameters and various relative distances and angles (but not on absolute positions), we get the same value if we subject all geometric elements to the same rigid motion M^{-1}. In other words, we could instead say that we need to find the point $P = M^{-1}(P')$ where the ray $\overrightarrow{M^{-1}(Q)M^{-1}(C)}$ contacts S and then to find the apparent brightness of the surface S at P (with the lamp in its original position). But this turns out to be the problem we already solved in the algorithm of §6.8.1, except that the ray $\overrightarrow{QC}$ must be replaced by the ray $\overrightarrow{M^{-1}(Q)M^{-1}(C)}$. We outline the changes that have to be made, while leaving the details to the reader.

The ray $\overrightarrow{QC}$ has already been given the linear parametrization $\Gamma(t)$. Obviously $\overrightarrow{M^{-1}(Q)M^{-1}(C)}$ has the parametrization $M^{-1}(\Gamma(t))$, and obviously this parametrization is linear in t as well. In other words, we have

$$M^{-1}(\Gamma(t)) = \langle \alpha_1 + \beta_1 t, \alpha_2 + \beta_2 t, \alpha_3 + \beta_3 t \rangle \tag{6.21}$$

The first job of any program would be to determine the coefficients α_i and β_i appearing in (6.21). For this purpose, it would be wise to take M as a product of rigid motions from well-known one-parameter groups of motions (rotations about coordinate axes, and so on), as we did for the world-viewing project in §§6.1.5 and 6.1.6. Then one can easily work out M^{-1} as a product of simple factors and work out the coefficients α_i and β_i. We leave to the reader the job of implementing this in an algorithm.

Substituting (6.21) into the defining Equation (6.11) of the ellipsoid, we obtain the quadratic equation

$$\sum_{i=1}^{3} \frac{(\alpha_i + \beta_i t - a_i)^2}{r_i^2} = 1 \tag{6.22}$$

which is a necessary and sufficient condition for $M^{-1}(\Gamma(t))$ to lie on S. As before, this quadratic equation simplifies to the form (6.13), although now the coefficients are

$$A = \sum_{i=1}^{3} \frac{\beta_i^2}{r_i^2}$$

$$B = \sum_{i=1}^{3} \frac{2\beta_i(\alpha_i - a_i)}{r_i^2}$$

$$C = \sum_{i=1}^{3} \frac{(\alpha_i - a_i)^2}{r_i^2}$$

Having already calculated α_i and β_i ($1 \leq i \leq 3$), the algorithm can now calculate A, B and C according to these equations. At this point, the algorithm continues exactly as in §6.8.1; there is no need for any further mention of the rigid motion M.

Exercises

1. Implement the algorithm described here.

2. Implement the algorithm with the alternative notion of rigid motion: The surface S undergoes the motion M, but the light source does not. (Hint: Proceed as above, but apply M^{-1} to $\langle L_1, L_2, L_3 \rangle$ before calculating the θ and R needed for apparent brightness.)

3. Enhance any of the exercises in §6.8.1 with the inclusion of rigid motions.

4. Now that rotations are available, one can apply the methods of §6.6 to make stereo pairs where each image in the pair is made by tracing rays. Such pictures tend to be more effective if they contain some landmarks, such as a sphere or plane decorated with some patterns. The pictures of §§6.8.3 and 6.8.4 are also suitable for making stereo pairs.

6.8.3 Reflections

In this section we describe some elementary techniques for ray-traced images that include reflections from a curved mirror. Before beginning, one should have done the simple case of an ellipsoid S alone and the case of a plane G alone. Our basic setup could then be that of a plane G and an ellipsoid S, neither blocking the other, and positioned so that some of G can be seen reflected in S. (The desired effect is illustrated in Figure 6.52, which was made by the author's student Paul R. Hovda.) Some intensity function should be ascribed to G so that it will have an interesting pattern (checkerboard or whatever). Then rays are traced as follows. If a ray misses the ellipsoid (i.e., if $D \leq 0$), then we treat the picture exactly as in the case of G alone; in other words, we return the intensity of a point on G. On the other hand, if a ray $\overrightarrow{QC}$ hits the ellipsoid S, we stop the ray $\overrightarrow{QC}$ at its contact point P on S and then follow the ray $\overrightarrow{PR}$ that represents the course of reflected light at P (see Figure 6.53). The next step in the calculation is therefore to determine a point R that defines the path of reflected light.

To facilitate the calculation we let n be an outward unit normal vector to S at P and q and r be unit vectors from P toward Q and R, respectively.

FIGURE 6.52 9×9 checkerboard reflected in floating mirror ball

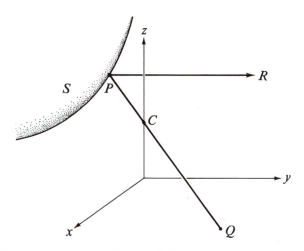

FIGURE 6.53   Tracing a ray reflected off S

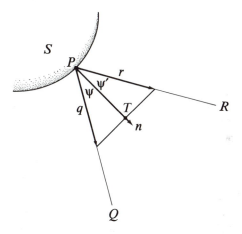

FIGURE 6.54   The three unit vectors for reflection

The unit vectors n and q can easily be calculated from our previous work. To calculate r, we observe that the mathematical condition for reflection is that q, n and r should be coplanar, and that n should bisect the angle between q and r. In other words, in Figure 6.54, the angles ψ and ψ' should be equal, and the segment joining the tips of q and r should meet n at a point T. Obviously the two triangles in Figure 6.54 are congruent, and so that segment meets n at right angles, and T is its midpoint. Therefore the distance from P to the midpoint T is $\cos\psi$; in other words

$$\frac{q+r}{2} = (\cos\psi)n$$

which yields

$$r = 2(\cos\psi)\,n - q = 2(n\cdot q)n - q$$

At this point we are in a position to parametrize the reflected ray; and the algorithm proceeds as before, by finding the point of intersection (if any) of this ray with the plane G. The rest of the job can thus be left to the reader.

We should point out that our argument in §6.4.5, showing that apparent brightness under diffuse reflection is independent of the viewpoint, is not consistent with the inclusion of curved mirrors. Therefore, one should be wary of attributing any realism to intensity calculations of that type. (We omit any attempt to make valid calculations in this realm.) Decorative features, however, like the squares of a checkerboard, are rendered accurately.

Exercises

1. Implement the algorithm implicit in this section for tracing rays that reflect off a shiny surface. Make a picture like that in Figure 6.52 or modify it to follow your imagination.

2. Prove that the curves seen in the mirror in Figure 6.52 are describable by an algebraic equation in x and y. Estimate the minimal degree of such an equation.

3. Although it is a little more complicated, ray tracing through a *lens* is possible by a method like the one described here. (The main extra complication is that in traveling through a lens, a ray changes direction twice—once when entering the lens and once when exiting.) The reader who has studied elementary geometric optics is invited to make an image that includes a simple lens. It is suggested that again one could use a checkerboard both as a background and as the object that appears in the lens.)

4. As a plane drawing, Figure 6.52 has the following property. If P is any point on the 9×9 checkerboard, and P' is the corresponding image point as seen reflected in the mirror ball, then P and P' are collinear with the center of the ball. Observe this fact experimentally, and show geometrically why it is true. (Hint: One can determine corresponding points most easily by counting squares. For the geometric argument, show that there is a plane through the focal point that contains P, P' and the center of the ball.) This property can be used as an external check on the correctness of calculation used in making figures of this type. Extend the result to surfaces of revolution. What goes wrong for ellipsoids that are not surfaces of revolution?

6.8.4   Convex polyhedra

A *convex polyhedron* is a solid figure bounded by finitely many planes $G_1, G_2, \ldots$, such that, for each i, the figure lies only on one side of G_i. If you pass a knife through a brick of cheese as often as you like, making sure that each cut is planar and cuts all the way across, then each piece will be a convex polyhedron. For a more precise mathematical definition, a *halfspace* is the set of points that lie on one fixed side of a given plane G, or on G itself, and a *convex polyhedron* is the intersection of a finite collection of halfspaces.

There are a number of ways to define a halfspace H. One is by a plane G (in $\mathbb{R}^3$) and a point U not on G. Then H can be defined as the set of points P such that the segment PU does not meet G. The plane G is (obviously) uniquely determined by H and is called the *bounding plane* of H. On the other hand, U can be taken as any point in $H - G$ and hence is not uniquely determined.

A halfspace H can also be defined by a point V *on* G and a unit vector N that is normal to G and moreover points *out from* the halfspace H. Here N is uniquely determined, but V is not (it could be any point on G). From this latter description, we easily get an algebraic formulation of halfspaces. For an arbitrary point $X = \langle x_1, x_2, x_3 \rangle \neq V$ of $\mathbb{R}^3$, let us consider the angle between N and the non-zero vector $X - V$. If X lies on G, then this is a right angle (since V also lies in G and N is a normal vector). If we move X into H from G, the angle becomes larger, i.e., obtuse; and if we move to the other side of H, the angle becomes acute. Thus $X \in H$ if and only if the angle between N and $X - V$ is obtuse or a right angle, which is to say if and only if the cosine of that angle is negative or zero. Expressing the cosine by the dot product, we see that X to belong to H if and only if

$$\frac{N \cdot (X - V)}{|N||X - V|} \leq 0$$

The factor $|N||X - V|$ is always positive and hence has no influence on the positivity of the remainder of the expression on the left. Thus we may discard it to obtain the simpler condition

$$N \cdot (X - V) \leq 0$$

or

$$a_1 x_1 + a_2 x_2 + a_3 x_3 \leq b \tag{6.23}$$

where $N = \langle a_1, a_2, a_3 \rangle$ and $b = N \cdot V$. Such a condition is called a *linear inequality*; clearly the corresponding linear equation (with $\leq$ replaced by $=$) is the equation of the bounding plane G.

We have proved that every halfspace can be expressed by an inequality (6.23), for appropriately chosen a_j and b. The converse result, that (6.23) always defines a halfspace, is left to the reader. All the coefficients in (6.23) can be multiplied by a positive scalar without changing its meaning, and we usually permit this. (In other words we do not require the vector of coefficients to be a unit vector.) Now a convex polyhedron C, being a finite intersection of halfspaces H_i ($1 \leq i \leq N$), is defined by a finite set of inequalities of type (6.23). In other words, for some linear functions

$$L_i(x_1, x_2, x_3) \; = \; a_{i1}x_1 + a_{i2}x_2 + a_{i3}x_3$$

$(1 \leq i \leq N)$, C is the set of $\langle x_1, x_2, x_3 \rangle$ that satisfy

$$L_i(x_1, x_2, x_3) \; \leq \; b_i \qquad\qquad\qquad\qquad (6.24)$$

for $1 \leq i \leq N$. To complete the notation, we let G_i denote the bounding plane of the ith halfspace H_i. It is determined by (6.24), with $\leq$ replaced by $=$.

There are a number of different degenerate convex polyhedra (see Exercise 2 following this section), which we wouldn't want to draw, because they are either too large (such as a halfspace itself) or too small (lines, points, etc.). For drawing purposes we are interested in convex polyhedra that are *bounded* (i.e., the entire figure lies within a fixed radius of the origin) and are truly 3-dimensional (i.e., a solid sphere—perhaps small, but solid—can be placed inside the figure). In fact, given a set of inequalities (6.24), it is a non-trivial undertaking to determine whether the set is bounded, 3-dimensional, or even non-empty (especially if the number of variables is much greater than three). Questions of that sort belong to the theory of *linear programming*, about which much has been written. In this area, however, we generally work with sets of inequalities that represent known convex polyhedra.

The subject of convex polyhedra underlines the fundamental difference, which we described at the start of §6.8, between ray tracing and our other methods. In §6.3.2 we drew convex polyhedra (Platonic solids) by projecting their edges one by one. Here the edges play no role in the definition of *convex polyhedron*. The edges are visible in a ray-traced image only by contrast between zones (facets) of different color or illumination.

Since the surface of a convex polyhedron C is composed of various planar surfaces G_i, it makes a very suitable subject for ray tracing. The method here is a simple generalization of our previous work in tracing rays to a single (decorated) plane; therefore we continue to work with the notation established in §§6.8.1 and 6.8.2. We will therefore suppose a ray $\Delta(t) = M^{-1}(\Gamma(t))$, which is parametrized as in (6.21). This ray will meet some or all of the planes G_i; our first job is to find values t_i of the parameter t such that $\Delta(t_i)$ lies on G_i. (This is simple linear algebra, using the equation version of (6.24).) Our job is to determine the first place where the ray enters the polyhedron C.

The general situation is sketched (2-dimensionally) in Figure 6.55, which shows the ray $\Delta(t)$ encountering first G_2, but not entering C at that time, but later entering C as it crosses G_1.

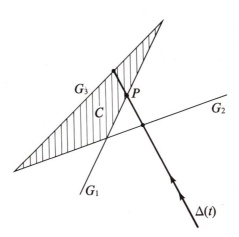

FIGURE 6.55   Ray $\Delta(t)$ meets G_2 before entering C at P

To facilitate the task, we define a vector, or array, $\langle B_1(P), \ldots, B_N(P)\rangle$ of 0's and 1's, for all $P \in \mathbb{R}^3$, as follows:

$$B_i(P) = \begin{cases} 1 & \text{if } P \in H_i \\ 0 & \text{otherwise} \end{cases}$$

Equivalently, we have

$$B_i(P) = \begin{cases} 1 & \text{if } L_i(P) \le b_i \\ 0 & \text{otherwise} \end{cases}$$

Clearly, P lies in the polyhedron C if and only if

$$\langle B_1(P), \ldots, B_N(P)\rangle = \langle 1, \ldots, 1\rangle \tag{6.25}$$

Our task will now be centered on keeping track of the array $\langle \ldots B_i(P) \ldots \rangle$ as the point P moves along the ray $\Delta(t) = M^{-1}(\Gamma(t))$.

We begin, obviously enough, by evaluating $L_i(\Delta(0))$ for each i and then using those values to evaluate $B_i(\Delta(0))$. If

$$\langle B_1(\Delta(0)), \ldots, B_N(\Delta(0))\rangle = \langle 1, \ldots, 1\rangle$$

then the point $\langle x, y, 0 \rangle$ of the film plane lies inside the polyhedron C. Usually we would consider this a faulty setup; the algorithm should be aborted accordingly if this happens. Thus we will assume that at least one $L_i(\Delta(0))$ is 0. Before continuing, our algorithm must sort the values t_i (where $\Delta(t)$ meets G_i) that we determined above. Then, considering the positive values of t_i in increasing order, we repeatedly revise $\langle B_1(P), \ldots, B_N(P)\rangle$ until we find a t_i with

$$\langle B_1(\Delta(t_i)), \ldots, B_N(\Delta(t_i)) \rangle = \langle 1, \ldots, 1 \rangle$$

This is clearly the value of t_i at which $\Delta(t)$ enters the polyhedron C, and the corresponding G_i is the plane we see along this ray. If, on the other hand, the array $\langle 1, \ldots, 1 \rangle$ is never realized, then we know that this ray does not strike C, and we use the background color for $\langle x, y, 0 \rangle$.

By *revising* $\langle B_1(P), \ldots, B_N(P) \rangle$, we mean the following. If $L_i(\Delta(0)) > 0$, then at $t = t_i$, $L_i(\Delta(t))$ must change from positive to negative; in other words, the ray is leaving the halfspace H_i at this point. Therefore we change 1 to 0 in the ith component. Similarly, if $L_i(\Delta(0)) < 0$, then the ray is entering H_i at $t = t_i$, and so we must change 0 to 1 in the ith component. A minor modification to these rules is necessary in the rare case that some $L_j(\Delta(0)) = 0$. In this case, the ray could be either leaving H_j or entering H_j at $\Delta(0)$; this is easily determined by checking $L_j(t_i)$ at the first non-zero t_i. (If $L_j(t_i) = 0$, then in fact the whole ray lies in the plane G_j. In this very rare case, we just take $B_j(\Delta(t))$ to be 1 for all t.)

At this point either we have decided to use the background color or we have determined i and t_i such that the ray enters C by crossing plane G_i at point $P = \Delta(t_i)$. Now apparent brightness under diffuse reflection, $f(x, y)$, can again be calculated with Equation (6.18)—with R calculated as before and with the normal vector N given by the vector $\langle a_1, a_2, a_3 \rangle$ of coefficients for the plane G_i. As usual, diffuse ambient light can be included by adding a constant to $f(x, y)$, if this is desired. Now a rasterized image (§2.7) with $f(x, y)$ determined in this way will yield a picture of the convex polyhedron C with diffuse reflection.

Exercises

1. Prove that Inequality (6.23) describes a halfspace as long as $\langle a_1, a_2, a_3 \rangle \neq \langle 0, 0, 0 \rangle$.

2. According to the definition, the following are all convex polyhedra: $\mathbb{R}^3$, the empty set, any halfspace, any plane, any line, any ray, any line segment, any single point, and any convex polygon in any plane. The exercise is to prove this fact by illustrating how a given figure of each type can be represented as an intersection of halfspaces. Also give sets of linear inequalities to determine one figure of each type.

3. Prove that the collection of all halfspaces is exactly the collection of sets $M(H)$, where M is any rigid motion of $\mathbb{R}^3$ and H is the special halfspace

$$\{ \langle x_1, x_2, x_3 \rangle \in \mathbb{R}^3 : x_3 \leq 0 \}$$

4. Suppose that all the b_i in (6.24) are multiplied by a fixed positive real scalar K. What geometric effect does this have on C? What if K is negative?

5. Prove that if every b_i in (6.24) is non-negative, then the corresponding convex polyhedron C is non-empty. If each b_i is positive, then C contains a sphere.

DATABASES FOR CONVEX POLYHEDRA

Obviously, in order to make an image of a convex polyhedron C by the methods described here, one needs data representing C as an intersection of halfspaces. The simplest form for such data is simply an organized collection of the coefficients a_{ij} and b_i ($1 \leq i \leq N$, $1 \leq j \leq 3$) appearing (implicitly) in (6.24). Here we will describe the data as an $N \times 4$ matrix that is written in the form of a computer file. (In other words, the first line of the file contains a_{11}, a_{12}, a_{13} and b_1, and so on.)

In writing an implementation of the algorithm described here, one can either enter the halfspace data into the program itself or set up the program to read the data from a file. The latter approach, while requiring a greater initial investment of labor, is obviously more flexible in the long run. As the data is read in, it should be collected in the proper sort of 2-dimensional array. (It would be wise to check for $\langle a_{i1}, a_{i2}, a_{i3} \rangle = \langle 0, 0, 0 \rangle$ as the data is read in, and if this occurs to abort the program with a warning.) We leave the details to the reader—but see §6.1.2 for one example of reading data from a file.

Of course, almost any set of data is a valid representation of *some* convex polyhedron, but if data is taken at random, the results will be disappointing. (Who wants a drawing of the empty set, or of only one wall?) Therefore it is wise to use data that is known in advance to represent a figure of interest.

A good place to start is with the Platonic solids that were introduced (and drawn differently) in §6.3.2. The regular tetrahedron and the cube may be left to the reader (for the tetrahedron, which requires four halfspaces, see the description given in §6.3.1). The regular octahedron has a description that is very easy because of the obvious symmetry involved, namely,

1.00000	1.00000	1.00000	1.00000
1.00000	1.00000	-1.00000	1.00000
1.00000	-1.00000	1.00000	1.00000
1.00000	-1.00000	-1.00000	1.00000
-1.00000	1.00000	1.00000	1.00000
-1.00000	1.00000	-1.00000	1.00000
-1.00000	-1.00000	1.00000	1.00000
-1.00000	-1.00000	-1.00000	1.00000

Data for the icosahedron is not without symmetry, but nevertheless is a good deal more complicated. In the following exercises the reader will be asked to check that the following twenty halfspaces enclose the icosahedron that is depicted in Figure 6.18.

0.00000	1.61803	0.61803	1.61803
-1.61803	-0.61803	0.00000	1.61803
1.00000	-1.00000	1.00000	1.61803
0.61803	0.00000	-1.61803	1.61803
0.00000	1.61803	-0.61803	1.61803
1.61803	-0.61803	0.00000	1.61803
-0.61803	0.00000	1.61803	1.61803
-1.00000	-1.00000	-1.00000	1.61803
0.00000	-1.61803	0.61803	1.61803
1.61803	0.61803	0.00000	1.61803
-0.61803	0.00000	-1.61803	1.61803
-1.00000	1.00000	1.00000	1.61803
0.00000	-1.61803	-0.61803	1.61803
0.61803	0.00000	1.61803	1.61803
1.00000	1.00000	-1.00000	1.61803
-1.61803	0.61803	0.00000	1.61803
-1.00000	1.00000	-1.00000	1.61803
-1.00000	-1.00000	1.00000	1.61803
1.00000	1.00000	1.00000	1.61803
1.00000	-1.00000	-1.00000	1.61803

Exercises

1. Carry out an implementation of the algorithm that was informally described in this section. A number of the following exercises suggest data for convex polyhedra to which the algorithm can be applied.

2. Write out the data set for a regular tetrahedron. (Hint: use the tetrahedral vertices from §6.3.1 and use the fact that the tetrahedron is self-dual.)

3. Write out the data set for an Egyptian pyramid—square base with four iso-morphic isosceles triangles meeting at an apex that lies directly above the center of the base.

4. Write out the data set for a cube with edges parallel to the coordinate axes.

5. Verify the claim in the text that a certain set of eight halfspaces encloses a regular octahedron.

6. Verify the claim in the text that a certain set of twenty halfspaces encloses the icosahedron described in Figure 6.18. (Hint: Direct calculations will show that PQQ' is the plane associated to the sixth line of data and that the adjacent plane (across segment PQ) is the plane associated to the third line of data. Each of the remaining planes is symmetric to one of these two, in one way or another.)

7. Here we illustrate the fact that one or more of the halfspaces defining C may be redundant. (In other words, one of the linear inequalities (6.24) may be

redundant.) Show that if we augment the database for the icosahedron with the line

    1.00000   0.00000   0.00000   1.00000

then we still have the icosahedron.

8. Among the twenty facets of the regular icosahedron one can find a set of eight, which, when extended, form a regular octahedron. Prove this fact and work out some way to illustrate it. (Hint: Examine closely the given databases.)

9. Write out the data set for a regular dodecahedron. (Hint: The coefficients a_{ij} of the twelve planes enclosing a regular dodecahedron can be taken to be numerically the same as the coordinates of the twelve vertices of a regular icosahedron. Explain why this should be so and carry out the details.)

10. One interesting way to draw a convex polyhedron is to paint each of its facets a different color or to alternate colors between the the different facets in such a way that adjacent facets have different colors. (This is particularly useful as a means to keep track of the different plane surfaces when the figure is rotated.) The simple way to do this is of course to use a different reflectivity K for each plane G_i. In working with a color device, each of the three reflectivities (for red, green and blue) could vary from plane to plane. This version can be simplified by omitting the light of diffuse reflection.

11. **Non-convex polyhedra.** The method that we have outlined is not in fact limited to convex polyhedra. As we mentioned before, the planes G_i carve space into small pieces like so much cheese. In fact, any combination C of these pieces is a valid subject for imaging by the methods of this section. The only modification necessary is to the criterion (Equation (6.25)) for membership in C. That criterion can be described as the *logical conjunction* (i.e., the *and*) of the individual criteria that $P \in H_i$ $(1 \le i \le N)$. In fact (6.25) can be replaced by *any* Boolean combination of the individual criteria. A very nice result is obtained by fixing a small positive integer M and changing (6.25) to

$$B_i(P) = 1 \quad \text{for all } i, \text{ with } M \text{ or fewer exceptions}$$

(So our main treatment was for $M = 0$.) One nice thing about the non-convex polyhedron constructed in this way is that it has all the symmetry that was possessed by the original convex polyhedron. Figure 6.56 shows the figure that results from the hyperplanes of the icosahedron, with $M = 5$. Figures of this type are called *stellations*, after the Latin word for *star*. Some stellations

FIGURE 6.56   Fifth stellation of the icosahedron

require Boolean combinations that are much more complex than the one we have given here.[47]

[47]See, for instance, *The Fifty-nine Icosahedra*, by H. S. M. Coxeter, P. Du Val, H. T. Flather, and J. F. Petrie, University of Toronto Press, 1938; reprinted by Springer-Verlag, Berlin, 1982. See also *Polyhedron Models*, by Father Magnus J. Wenninger, Cambridge University Press, 1970.

Index